ADVANCE PRAISE

"Locher's chapter on Beirut reveals for the first time a true account of the circumstances of this tragedy and the crippling consequences of organizational defects. Every joint officer must know and every American will want to understand this pivotal history."—Gen. Bernard W. Rogers, former Supreme Allied Commander in Europe

"For twenty years as a Marine and nine more in the White House . . . I watched with growing anguish the pointless loss of life caused by dysfunctional Pentagon decision making. The best tribute to Jim Locher's role in passage of the Goldwater-Nichols Act—so well recorded in *Victory on the Potomac*—lies in the lives saved throughout future generations."—Robert C. "Bud" McFarlane, National Security Adviser to President Ronald Reagan

"Locher had a ringside seat at the most important change in the U.S. military establishment since the 1947 creation of the secretary of defense and Joint Chiefs of Staff. His insights into the Goldwater-Nichols Act provide an unparalleled view of a critical instance in history—one which contributed significantly to success in the Gulf War!"—Gen. Edward C. "Shy" Meyer, former Army Chief of Staff

". . . the first comprehensive account of the how and why of the historic Goldwater-Nichols legislation. Uniquely, this important book offers the insight of an individual who was there at the creation and served to bring it to life. This is a classic work not to be missed."—Sean O'Keefe, former Secretary of the Navy

"This volume is of immense historical interest; but it also has everything the most demanding mystery reader could hope for: a plot with many twists; diverse, interesting, well defined characters; intrigue at the highest (and sometimes the lowest) levels; and a satisfying ending (though as the book suggests, there is still much to do)."—William K. Brehm, former Assistant Secretary of Defense

"Locher weaves contemporary events into a rich tapestry of insights on the constitutional separation of powers, military history, legislative politics, and civil-military relations. This authoritative account of how a good idea became public law must be read by every military officer and student of government."—Michael B. Donley, former Assistant Secretary of the Air Force

"... a masterful and exciting story, the stunning denouement of which was passage of the long overdue 1986 Goldwater-Nichols legislation—to the dismay of those who had long opposed such measures and to the benefit of the United States and the armed forces that serve it."—Lt. Gen. John H. Cushman, Sr., former Commander of I Corps Group in Korea

"Jim Locher gives us his thoroughly researched, well-thought-out, insider's view of the hard-fought struggle in Congress and the Pentagon to shift power from the military departments to a Joint Chiefs chairman and a reinvigorated Joint Staff under his control."—Gen. W. Y. Smith, former Deputy Commander in Chief, U.S. European Command

"Generations of historians will consider Jim Locher's book the authoritative record of one of the most important defense laws in the nation's history. But this important book speaks to a much broader audience of scholars, students, and citizens. The book, showing Congress in one of its finest hours, provides a much-needed counterpoise to the negative perspective of Capitol Hill held by many citizens."—Archie D. Barrett, senior House of Representatives staffer for the Goldwater-Nichols Act

VICTORY ON THE POTOMAC

Texas A&M University Military History Series
Joseph G. Dawson III, General Editor

Victory on the Potomac

The Goldwater-Nichols Act Unifies the Pentagon

James R. Locher III

Foreword by Sen. Sam Nunn

Texas A&M University Press   •   College Station

Library of Congress Cataloging-in -Publication Data

Locher, James R., 1946–
    Victory on the Potomac : the Goldwater-Nichols act unifies the
Pentagon / James R. Locher, III ; foreword by Sen. Sam Nunn.—
1st ed.
        p. cm.—(Texas A&M University military history series ; 79)
    Includes bibliographical references and index.
    ISBN 1-58544-187-2 (cloth: alk. paper)
    ISBN 1-58544-398-0 (pbk.)
    1. United States. Goldwater-Nichols Department of Defense
Reorganization Act of 1986—Legislative history.   2. United
States. Dept. of Defense—Reorganization—Legislative history.
3. United States—Armed Forces—Reorganization—Legislative
history.   I. Title.   II. Series.
KF7252.L63   2002
355.6'8'0973—dc21   2001006545
ISBN 13: 978—1-58544-398-7 (pbk.)

CONTENTS

Part 1: The Fog of Defense Organization

Part 2: Drawing Battle Lines

Part 3: Marshaling Forces

Part 4: March to Victory

ILLUSTRATIONS

For Norma

FOREWORD

Passing the Goldwater-Nichols Defense Reorganization Act was one of Congress' finest hours in recent memory. The campaign to reform the Department of Defense began on February 3, 1982, when Gen. David Jones, USAF, the chairman of the Joint Chiefs of Staff, appealed to the House Armed Services Committee for reform of the joint system. The long struggle to make defense reorganization a reality—it took four years and 241 days, a period longer than America's involvement in World War II—involved many heroes: Gen. Edward "Shy" Meyer, USA, later echoed General Jones's reform call; Sen. Barry Goldwater and Cong. Bill Nichols provided critical bipartisan leadership for reform in Congress; and several congressional staffers, particularly Jim Locher from the Senate Armed Services Committee and Arch Barrett from the House Armed Services Committee, helped build the intellectual capital necessary for Congress to overcome enormous opposition from the Pentagon and the executive branch in passing this landmark legislation.

Victory on the Potomac masterfully tells this fascinating and historically important story. Jim Locher's vivid account will make readers feel like their elbows are on the conference table watching the clash of giant personalities and power politics. Jim's involvement at every step enables him to accurately recreate this legendary legislative story, which has made a deep imprint on America's military capability. Locher's meticulous research and numerous interviews permit him to relate events from all perspectives: Senate, House, White House, National Security Council staff, five Pentagon components, presidential commission, think tanks and universities, media, and the retired military community. Locher's portrayal of the passage of Goldwater-Nichols will fascinate anyone interested in how the machinery of American government works.

In formulating the Goldwater-Nichols Act, Congress thoroughly studied defense reorganization. When work started, members knew little about the arcane but critical issues of the structure and processes of the Free World's largest and most complex bureaucracy. When Barry Goldwater became chairman of the Senate Armed Services Committee in January, 1985, he gave defense reorganization his highest priority and adopted a genuinely bipartisan approach, making me, the committee's ranking Democrat, an equal partner. Barry and I agreed to appoint Jim Locher as the senior reorganization staffer to represent us both, and he led the team that helped Congress "get smart" on this complex but critically important subject. Our committee studied military operations as far back as the Spanish-American War for their organizational lessons. We examined forty years of debate on defense organization in search of the best ideas. Our committee and its House counterpart also developed new concepts, especially concerning unified warfighting commanders. A 645-page study directed by Jim Locher for the Senate Armed Services Committee had a tremendous impact on congressional thinking, as we passed Goldwater-Nichols with the threat of a presidential veto.

The National Archives ranked the Goldwater-Nichols Act as the Senate Armed Services Committee's most important legislative achievement during its first fifty years. The act addressed a huge problem—the inability of the military services to operate effectively together as a joint team—and solved it. By establishing a clear chain of command and focusing operational responsibility in the warfighting commanders, Goldwater-Nichols made possible the remarkable military successes of the 1990s. I still take great satisfaction in my role in helping pass the Goldwater-Nichols Act and believe it was one of my most significant contributions to our national security.

The status quo in military matters is not acceptable, and at the beginning of the twenty-first century, the need for a new look at defense organization is increasingly apparent. Although the services now fight jointly, greater jointness may now be required in how the department "organizes, trains, and equips"— the title 10, U.S. Code, functions assigned to the separate services. The increased power of the chairman of the Joint Chiefs of Staff enabled by Goldwater-Nichols may need recalibrating to assure the ability of the secretary of defense and his staff to effectively exercise civilian control of the military. Despite many efforts, some of which I personally led, to address the fundamental roles and missions of the services, the Department of Defense still looks much the same as it did at the end of the Cold War. For those who believe that it is time for another Goldwater-Nichols, Jim Locher's fascinating account is must reading. *Victory on the Potomac* reminds us that reorganizing defense is hard, but that it can be done, that Congress must lead, and that the payoff is high.

Sen. Sam Nunn
Atlanta, Georgia

ACKNOWLEDGMENTS

After each major event of the long campaign to produce the Goldwater-Nichols Act, Sens. Barry Goldwater and Sam Nunn would implore me, "You must write a book to record this important history. Keep great notes." Such was the genesis of *Victory on the Potomac*. I did keep great notes, which Chris Cowart, chief clerk of the Senate Armed Services Committee, painstakingly organized before the committee sent them to the National Archives.

In November, 1993, as I began to consider this book, journalist and author Doug Waller encouraged me, insisting that the act's history was fascinating as well as important. Doug's valuable comments on initial drafts helped to point me in the right direction. Bill Mogan advised me to attend Barnaby and Mary Conrad's Santa Barbara Writers Conference, which I did twice. Like a sponge, I soaked up a tremendous amount of knowledge at those conferences, especially during workshops led by Cork Millner.

Grants from the Smith Richardson Foundation and David and Lucile Packard Foundation funded important research and interviews, enabling the comprehensive telling of the Goldwater-Nichols story. General Shy Meyer, a Smith Richardson board member, was instrumental in gaining approval of my grant. The National Defense University Foundation, under Pres. Jim Dugar and Executive Directors Tom Gallagher and Frank Eversole, administered both grants and provided outstanding support. These grants permitted me to hire Bridget Grimes as a research assistant. Bridget's untiring efforts helped to ensure that this book was thorough, accurate, and filled with colorful detail. Lieutenant General Dick Chilcoat, president of the National Defense University, also supported my research and designated me a distinguished visiting fellow.

Ben Schemmer assisted me as my literary agent, mentor, teacher, editor, counselor, critic, supporter, and friend. In each capacity, he gave generously and contributed enormously to the book. Working with Ben, I learned about the art of writing and much more. Ben also introduced me to Bill Kloman, a first-rate copy editor. Bill copyedited the entire manuscript and showed me the craft of word economy.

Members of the staff at Texas A&M University Press made all of the hurdles of preparing the manuscript for publication less trying and provided sound advice at every step. Dale Wilson, a freelancer who copyedited the manuscript for the Press, meticulously reviewed the manuscript and helped to make it as good as it could be.

Many colleagues and friends took a genuine interest in this book. They allowed me to interview them repeatedly, reviewed draft chapters, and provided access to their personal papers. This list is headed by Arch Barrett, Dave Jones, Bill Brehm, Bill Crowe, Mike Donley, Gerry Smith, Jeff Smith, Rick Finn, Arnold Punaro, Chris Mellon, Kim Wincup, David Berteau, Barry Blechman, Ted Crackel, Shy Meyer, Bud McFarlane, and Bernie Rogers. Their recollections brought the story to life and provided important perspectives. I am indebted to them for their contributions and generous support.

I also appreciated the friendship of Peggy and Bill Stelpflug, whom I met during a research trip to Auburn University. Their son, Billy, died in the terrorist bombing of the marine barracks in Beirut in October, 1983. Peggy and Bill provided new insights on that tragedy, assisted my efforts to accurately tell the Beirut story, and encouraged my work on this book.

Three prominent defense historians reviewed the book: Al Goldberg, historian for the Office of the Secretary of Defense, Walter Poole of the Joint History Office, and Mark Sherry of the U.S. Army Center of Military History. Their advice and comments were invaluable. The review of the book's narrative of the Grenada invasion by Ronald Cole of the Joint History Office was also helpful. Al Goldberg and the Joint History Office also granted access to their interviews of former officials and officers.

I benefited from extensive access to government archives. Senators Nunn and Strom Thurmond granted me permission to conduct research in the Senate Armed Services Committee files on the Goldwater-Nichols Act maintained by the National Archives. Marie Dickinson, Chris Cowart, and Jay Thompson of the committee staff aided my research, and Chuck Alsup provided summaries from the committee's executive sessions. Doc Cooke, director of administration and management at the Pentagon, approved my access to files of the secretary and deputy secretary of defense. Sandy Meagher and Brian Kenney provided first-rate assistance in facilitating my examination of these archives. Bernard Cavalcante and Judy Short of the Operational Archives Branch, Naval Historical Center, assisted my research in Navy Department files. Leo Daugherty provided special help in the personal papers collections at the Marine Corps Historical Center, as did David Keough in the Manuscript Archives of the U.S. Army Military History Institute.

Gaining information from the files of the Joint Chiefs of Staff was more challenging. Admiral Denny Blair, then Joint Staff director, and Brig. Gen. David Armstrong, USA (Ret.), director of joint history, helped start the process. Ed McBride and his Joint Staff office and Cdr. Jeff Morris in the Office of the Secretary of Defense worked hard to respond to my Freedom of Information Act request.

Mike Donley and John Douglass, former National Security Council staff members, facilitated early access to their files at the Ronald Reagan Library.

Eventually, the Defense Department sponsored my research there, helped gain White House support, and obtained the required approvals from the State Department, Central Intelligence Agency, and National Security Council. Doc Cooke played the instrumental role at the Pentagon. Donna Dillon—aided by Rod Soubers, Sherrie Fletcher, and Cate Sewell—superbly assisted me during my four visits to the Reagan Library.

I also conducted extensive research in the Barry M. Goldwater Collection at the Arizona Historical Foundation, and I am indebted to Patricia Etter, James Allen, Paula Liken, and Sheila Brushes for their assistance. Dwayne Cox and Bev Powers facilitated my research in the William F. Nichols Papers at the Auburn University Archives. Naomi Nelson directed research and provided materials from the Sam Nunn Archives at Emory University, and Kathryn Stollard, Sheran Johle, Norma Hart, and Susan Eason did the same for the John G. Tower Papers at Southwestern University. Arch Barrett, a true friend, conducted research for me in the Tower Papers during a visit to Georgetown, Texas.

Public affairs offices in the Pentagon provided many of the book's photographs. I especially appreciated the help of Ken Carter of the Office of the Secretary of Defense, Joan Asboth and Lt. Col. Doug Wisnioski of the Joint Staff, Ron Hall of the air force, Robert Melhorn of the army, and CPO Richard Toppings of the navy. Steve Branch provided photographs from the Ronald Reagan Library, and Kathy Vinson and Gene Tillson assisted with photographs from the Defense Visual Information Center.

I performed much of my library research at the National Defense University Library, where the entire staff—Jean-Marie Faison, Mary Friedline, Alta Linthicum, Rosemary Marlow-Dziuk, Bruce Thornlow, Carolyn Turner, and Cheryl Weidner—worked hard to meet my needs. I also benefited from the professional assistance of Debbie Reed and Christine Baldwin at the Pentagon Library.

My uncle, Jack Locher, a retired college English professor, marked up each of my drafts with red pencil, helping me to fix errors, both large and small. My son, Jay, the family's youngest English scholar, teacher, and writer, also examined every page, offering creative ideas for more vivid storytelling. I also need to acknowledge the contributions of the family cat, Marshmallow. Every morning, she joined me at my writing desk, serving as a steady, consoling companion on this long journey.

All of this generous support combined, however, does not equal the contributions of my wife, Norma. Without her love, encouragement, understanding, and counsel, this book would not have been possible.

ACRONYMS

ANGLICO	Air-Naval Gunfire Liaison Company
BLT	battalion landing team
CIA	Central Intelligence Agency
CINC	commander in chief
CINCPAC	commander in chief, Pacific Command
CINCPACFLT	commander in chief, Pacific Fleet
CJCS	chairman, Joint Chiefs of Staff
CMRC	Congressional Military Reform Caucus
CNA	Center for Naval Analyses
CNO	chief of naval operations
CSIS	Center for Strategic and International Studies
CSSG	Chairman's Special Study Group
DoD	Department of Defense
EUCOM	European Command
FECOM	Far East Command
FY	Fiscal Year
FBI	Federal Bureau of Investigation
HASC	House Armed Services Committee
JCS	Joint Chiefs of Staff
JROC	Joint Requirements Oversight Council
JSOC	Joint Special Operations Command
JWCA	Joint Warfighting Capabilities Assessments
LANTCOM	Atlantic Command
MFO	Multinational Force Organization
MAU	marine amphibious unit
NATO	North Atlantic Treaty Organization
NDU	National Defense University
NME	National Military Establishment
NSA	National Security Agency
NSC	National Security Council
NSDD	National Security Decision Directive
OJCS	Organization of the Joint Chiefs of Staff
OMB	Office of Management and Budget
OMC	Office of Military Cooperation
ONI	Office of Naval Intelligence
OSD	Office of the Secretary of Defense

PACOM	Pacific Command
PACAF	Pacific Air Forces
PPBS	Planning, Programming, and Budgeting System
PLO	Palestine Liberation Organization
RDJTF	Rapid Deployment Joint Task Force
SACEUR	Supreme Allied Commander, Europe
SASC	Senate Armed Services Committee
SECDEF	secretary of defense
SECNAV	secretary of the navy
SFRC	Senate Foreign Relations Committee
SIOP	Single Integrated Operational Plan
SOF	special operations forces
SOUTHCOM	Southern Command
SWPA	Southwest Pacific Area
UNAAF	Unified Action Armed Forces
USA	U.S. Army
USAF	U.S. Air Force
USARPAC	U.S. Army, Pacific
USC	United States Code
USFJ	U.S. Forces, Japan
USMC	U.S. Marine Corps
USN	U.S. Navy

VICTORY ON THE POTOMAC

Prologue

Turf, Power, Service

If the Navy's welfare is one of the prerequisites to the

nation's welfare—and I sincerely believe that to be

the case—any step that is not good for the Navy is

not good for the nation.

—Fleet Adm. Ernest J. King, 1945

"This legislation would cripple the Joint Chiefs of Staff [JCS]," snapped Gen. John A. Wickham Jr. as he glared at Sen. Barry Goldwater and Sen. Sam Nunn, "with serious consequences for the nation's security." Continuing his attack on their draft bill to reorganize the Department of Defense (DoD), the army chief angrily charged, "This bill would rob the service chiefs of their proper authority, denigrate their role, and complicate their administration of the services."[1]

Goldwater's and Nunn's pained expressions and rigid posture signaled that the emotion and hostility of Wickham's outburst had rocked them. I was equally shocked. The top Republican and Democrat on the Senate Armed Services Committee (SASC), accompanied by me and two other committee staff members, were meeting in early February, 1986, with the five-member JCS. Convened on the chiefs' turf in their hallowed conference room in the Pentagon, known as the "Tank," the meeting focused solely on Goldwater's and Nunn's reorganization legislation. Designed to end military disunity and infighting, the senators' bill would mandate the most sweeping reforms in nearly forty years.

The Pentagon badly needed reform. The military bureaucracy had tied itself in knots since World War II and lost outright the Vietnam conflict and three lesser engagements: the USS *Pueblo* seizure, the Desert One raid, and the peacekeeping operation in Beirut. The Korean War, *Mayaguez* rescue, and Grenada incursion were hardly resounding victories. Decision making had become so convoluted, fiefdoms so powerful and inbred, lines of authority so confused, and chains of command so entangled that the military hierarchy had repeatedly failed the nation. Third-rate powers and terrorists had humiliated America. Tens of thousands of troops had died needlessly. Unprecedented levels of defense spending were not making the nation more secure. Goldwater and Nunn were resolved to fix this dysfunctional system. The fiefdoms were equally determined to preserve their power and independence.

"As the bill is drafted," Wickham thundered, "it would leave uncertain who within the Army would be responsible for giving advice on operational matters. Would it be the chief or would it now be the secretary? The upshot of this confusion would be an erosion of the chief's authority to provide military advice."[2] Now in full stride and with righteous indignation powering his words, Wickham signaled the coming of a lengthy harangue.

The senators had known this would be a tough meeting. The Pentagon had vigorously opposed reorganization efforts since their beginning four years earlier, and the current service leaders were ranked as the most strident antagonists. Yet Goldwater and Nunn were not prepared for the rage and level of animosity they were facing. They never expected the top brass—whose rise to four-star rank requires cool, professional demeanor—to be explosive hotheads. Moreover, as powerful legislators, Goldwater and Nunn were accustomed to respectful treatment by generals and admirals—not the rough-and-tumble of this encounter.

The meeting's high-decibel start troubled me. The chiefs had firmly criticized reorganization in testimony and interviews. But behind closed doors, they were mounting an all-out assault. In an unusual arrangement, I served as the senior reorganization staff member for both Chairman Goldwater and ranking Democrat Nunn. Wickham had stunned my two bosses and put them on the defensive. His success with shock tactics would embolden two other chiefs—Adm. James D. Watkins and the Marine Corps's Gen. P. X. Kelley—whose views were even stronger. I realized that this session was going to be brutal.

As Wickham attacked, Kelley grumbled disparaging comments under his breath—loud enough for the tone if not always the words to be heard.[3] At age seventy-six, Goldwater was hard of hearing, so the commandant's mutterings were not audible to him. The feisty Arizonan would not have tolerated such disrespectful behavior.

"The proposed strengthening of the service secretaries is ill-considered,"

Wickham declared. "It would come at the expense of the service chiefs. The most damaging aspect is making each chief's performance as a Joint Chief subject to the direction and control of his service secretary. The chiefs would no longer be able to provide independent military advice."[4]

By the majority of accounts, the service chiefs—with rare exceptions—dominated their supposed civilian bosses. But the dictatorial rule of Navy Secretary John F. Lehman Jr. drove Wickham's worries. The army chief had watched Lehman accumulate power, ruthlessly impose his will, and humiliate top sailors and marines. Wickham feared that Goldwater and Nunn had modeled their legislation on the seemingly popular Lehman. He did not know that the two senators held an unfavorable view of the navy secretary. Wickham saw a threat, and his alarm was genuine.[5]

This confrontational meeting occurred on the eve of the SASC's first session to consider Goldwater and Nunn's bill. More than a year earlier, the two leaders had formed a partnership to tackle this controversial topic. Despite their best efforts, their committee remained bitterly divided on reorganization. Ironically, Goldwater's Republican colleagues were his strongest opponents. Goldwater and Nunn were not certain that they could muster enough votes to make progress. Thus, they stood on shaky ground on Capitol Hill when they came to the Pentagon for their stormy meeting.

The aging Republican luminary and rising Democratic star made an attractive political combination, and they rarely faced such long odds on a defense issue. Seldom were their allies so few and their adversaries so numerous and powerful. Not only were Goldwater and Nunn confronting the Pentagon, they also were fighting off Capitol Hill colleagues, military associations, defense contractors, veterans groups, retired officer and noncommissioned officer associations, and others who sat in the military's corner for one reason or another. Goldwater and Nunn's fight against DoD antireformers and their horde of allies made for a David-and-Goliath battle on the Potomac.

The senators and staff members Richard D. Finn Jr., Jeffrey H. Smith, and I assembled in the JCS chairman's office shortly before six o'clock in the evening on Monday, February 3. William J. Crowe Jr. was the eleventh chairman and the third admiral to hold the military's most prestigious post. With a Princeton doctorate in politics, he was a true warrior-statesman. Balding and stocky, Crowe looked like an affable granddad. With his heavyset build—Annapolis classmates called him "the Neck"—Crowe could also be mistaken for a Soviet admiral. I admired his keen intellect, common sense, and ability to rise above the service parochialism that dominated Pentagon politics. Goldwater and Nunn also respected Crowe.

The admiral's demeanor telegraphed the ordeal ahead. A friendly Oklahoman with a big smile and a bigger heart, Crowe typically offered a warm welcome and a story or two. On this day, he was cordial, but he was troubled and distracted. Our host spun no stories.

1. Senators Barry Goldwater and Sam Nunn. (©1986, *The Washington Post.* Reprinted with permission. Photo by James K. W. Atherton.)

The admiral led our small delegation to the Tank, where the four service chiefs waited. I had expected to find a space-age room equipped with high-technology gadgets—a setting fit for the weighty issues debated there—but the Tank looked like dozens of other nondescript Pentagon meeting rooms.

Although the setting was ordinary, the atmospherics were extraordinary. The tight-jawed, brooding faces of the nation's top warriors generated a powerful tension. The stars on their shoulders, braid on their sleeves, and ribbons on their chests testified to their experience, accomplishments, and skills. These were hardened veterans, equally adept on the battlefield and in the bureaucracy.

Crowe placed Goldwater and Nunn across from him at the big table in the center of the room. The chiefs' places were set by tradition. Wickham and Watkins flanked the two senators. The air force chief, Gen. Charles A. Gabriel, sat next to Crowe, and Kelley occupied a seat around the corner from Watkins. We staffers sat behind Goldwater and Nunn. Two Joint Staff officers—Brig. Gen. Arnold Schlossberg Jr., USA, and Capt. Richard D. DeBobes, USN—sat next to me. Schlossberg handled reorganization for the joint chiefs. DeBobes was their legal adviser and legislative assistant. Vice Admiral Powell Carter, Joint Staff director, sat at Crowe's left. The chairman's assistant, Lt. Gen. John Moellering, USA, sat behind his boss.

Crowe opened by stating his reservations about the bill in tough but constructive language. From my lengthy, private discussions with Crowe, Goldwater and Nunn knew that the admiral supported the goals of the draft bill. But if Crowe strayed far from the party line in this meeting with his fellow chiefs, he

2. Members of the Joint Chiefs of Staff in December, 1985 *(left to right):* Gen. John A. Wickham, Jr., army chief of staff; Gen. Charles A. Gabriel, air force chief of staff; Adm. James D. Watkins, chief of naval operations; Adm. William J. Crowe Jr., chairman (seated); and Gen. P. X. Kelley, commandant of the Marine Corps. (DoD photo.)

would become an outcast. His comments were not comforting, but they were expected.[6]

Wickham spoke next. He epitomized an army general: distinguished, all-American looks, intellectual, spiritual, professional. A brilliant career had earned him high regard in the Pentagon and on Capitol Hill. His reputation for courtesy and graciousness made the intemperate harshness of his attack more startling. Oddly, much of Wickham's wrath was focused on an imagined issue in the draft bill. For twenty-five minutes he accused Goldwater and Nunn of trying to place each chief under his service secretary's control in the performance of his separate responsibilities as a joint chief. The senators had no intention of making this change. It had never been raised as an issue during four years of reorganization debate. Seizing on a technical error in the draft bill, Wickham had leaped to a fictive conclusion. To berate Goldwater and Nunn on this alleged problem wasted the chiefs' limited time with the senators. Goldwater and Nunn listened in silent disbelief. Wickham's comments were so far off the mark that they did not have the slightest idea what he was talking about.

I worried about what my two bosses were thinking. For more than a year, opponents had criticized their every step. It had been a long struggle already, and greater challenges lay ahead. I wondered if this explosive session would demoralize them. Facing an all-out fight from the Pentagon, would they press ahead? Did they still think this battle could be won? Would Goldwater continue to risk alienating his Republican colleagues, undermining his ability to lead the committee? Would Nunn be prepared to see his impeccable defense record tarnished by a crushing defeat? How much faith did the two senators have in each other? Given my critical role, how much confidence did they have in me?

Twenty minutes into Wickham's diatribe, Goldwater slammed his cane on the table and returned fire. "I am offended by your accusations that the bill would cripple the chiefs," Goldwater said. "I've always been one of the strongest defense supporters in Congress. I resent your attack on my genuine efforts in this bill to strengthen the military. After all that I've done for the armed services, I can't believe that you are accusing me of taking actions that would harm the military." The senator paused and glowered at the chiefs before issuing this warning: "If you think you can bully Sam and me, you are mistaken. You might be able to bully others, but I think you're taking big risks with your confrontational tactics."[7]

The chiefs' unmoving faces conveyed that Goldwater's arguments had not changed any minds or cooled any passions. Undaunted by the SASC chairman's tough response, Kelley renewed the offensive. "It is clear that the testimony of the chiefs before your committee was completely ignored in the drafting of this bill. I am troubled that the views of others on security matters carry more weight than the views of the service chiefs who are the nation's principal military advisers."[8]

Goldwater rebuffed Kelley's complaint, then asked me to respond to Wickham's assertions. I knew every word in the draft bill and recognized the error that had seized the army chief's attention. Given the acrimony, I responded as respectfully as possible. "General Wickham has, indeed, found a technical error in the draft bill," I began. "I see how it could lead to misinterpretations of the provision's intent. The needed editorial fix is simple. The provision in question needs to be moved to a separate paragraph. When that's done, it will be clear that the chiefs are independent of the service secretaries in performing their duties as joint chiefs."[9]

My statement made Wickham even angrier. He had spent twenty-five minutes huffing and puffing to construct an argument that had been undone in twenty-five seconds. The general appeared unconvinced. Under his breath, Kelley sent barbs in my direction.

Given their vast power and influence, service officials—military and civilian—liked things the way they were. The services controlled the JCS. They also dominated the unified commands—the major warfighting commands consisting of forces from two or more military departments—by limiting the authority of unified commanders and keeping their service component commanders independent. The services gained the upper hand with the defense secretary by offering self-serving advice, locking arms whenever the secretary threatened core interests, and circumventing him with appeals to Congress.

The services and congressional allies had defeated efforts by Pres. Harry S. Truman and Pres. Dwight D. Eisenhower to curtail their power and create a more unified DoD. These defeats—particularly of Eisenhower—had intimidated others who thought of challenging the services. Twenty-eight years after Eisenhower's last reorganization effort, Goldwater and Nunn were finding that many on their committee still supported the services on organizational matters.

Even if Wickham and the other chiefs thought that reforms were needed, they did not want them taking place on their watch. The services had dominated military affairs since the JCS first met in February, 1942. The current chiefs did not want service histories to say that they had been incapable of defending the services' powerful place in Pentagon decision making.

The two chiefs who spoke after Wickham, Watkins and Kelley, also sharply attacked the bill. Tall, cool, and aloof, Watkins was called "the Cardinal" in navy circles. The moniker signified the navy chief's haughty personality as much as his Catholic devoutness.[10] The admiral labeled the bill "terribly flawed and certainly not in the best interests of national security."[11]

Escalating the rhetoric, the barrel-chested Kelley boomed in his Boston-accented command voice: "If this bill were enacted, I would have deep concerns about the future security of the United States. I know of no other document which has concerned me more in my thirty-six years of uniformed service to my country."[12]

The chiefs seemed to attack in a pack. Exaggerations and oversimplifications flew across the table: "The bill would give the chairman too much authority."[13] The unified commanders would end up becoming "warlords." "Our combat commanders would become bureaucrats instead of warfighters."[14] "The bill would create chaos." "It provides a complex, unworkable solution to an ill-defined problem."[15] "The commanders would become mired in contracting."

Nunn rebutted the chiefs: "In our three years of studying reorganization, no deficiency has been as clearly or painfully demonstrated as the weaknesses of the unified commanders. Every time we've failed or performed poorly—such as Vietnam, *Mayaguez*, *Pueblo*, Beirut, Grenada—it can be traced to the lack of unity of command." He paused, then continued in a more determined tone: "Unity of command gets a lot of lip service here in the Pentagon. But it is woefully implemented. We will continue to be plagued by operational problems until we strengthen field commanders. We must give them the authority they need to meld units from all services into an effective fighting force."[16]

Although I knew that the chiefs' sharp rhetoric and hot-tempered behavior had jolted Goldwater and Nunn, my disbelief was greater and more painful. As a West Pointer with ten years of Pentagon experience, I was devastated by the unsightly spectacle of America's top officers emotionally and closed-mindedly arguing narrow, outmoded service perspectives. West Point's motto, "Duty, Honor, Country," had been instilled in me as a cadet. But now I was hearing something different. It sounded like "Turf, Power, Service." These dedicated patriots and most of their predecessors over four decades honestly believed in the canard "What's good for my service is good for the country."

Gabriel spoke last. The air force chief was subdued and deliberate. The slow cadence of his North Carolina drawl matched his personality. Gabriel rarely showed emotion and seldom turned an issue into a crusade—and reorganization was not one of Gabriel's crusades. The air force chief ended the meeting in the same constructive tone that Crowe had begun it. Yet, although neither Gabriel nor Crowe had participated in the tirade, they never disagreed with their boisterous colleagues. Throughout the meeting, the chiefs presented a united front.[17]

As the senators rose to depart, Crowe, Gabriel, and Wickham gathered to shake their hands. Watkins and Kelley made no effort to do so. They looked like two old salts spoiling for a bar fight.[18]

As we walked back to Crowe's office, I again worried about the senators' thinking. Would the beating they had taken in the Tank cause them to change course? Would the vehement opposition of three chiefs and cautions sounded by Crowe and Gabriel convince Goldwater and Nunn to delay their planned legislative work or set less ambitious goals?

When we entered Crowe's office, his executive assistant handed me a thick package of papers, including a long letter from Secretary of Defense Caspar W. Weinberger. A handwritten note on top read: "Jim Locher, Attached is the department's response to the staff bill. Please deliver to Senator Goldwater. Thanks, Colin Powell."[19] Then a major general, Powell was Weinberger's senior military assistant.

Looking at the half-inch-thick stack of papers in my hand, Goldwater asked, "What's that?"

When I responded, "The department's official comments on the draft bill," Goldwater exclaimed, "Jesus!"

Crowe made his office available for Goldwater and Nunn to privately compare notes with Finn, Smith, and me. The senators were still dazed. Neither said a word.

"Well, what do you think?" I inquired.

"Christ, could you believe all of that crap?" Goldwater blurted. "I've never seen the chiefs that worked up."

"I knew they felt strongly," Nunn interrupted, "but I never expected to see them that emotional."

"Their turf is the most important thing to them," Goldwater continued. "When it's threatened, there's no reasoning with them. The chiefs' message to us was clear. They don't believe in reorganization, and they're telling us to go to hell."[20]

"I also couldn't believe how ill-informed many of their arguments were," Nunn added. "They can't get past the emotion to see the real issues."[21]

"Where in the hell did Wickham get the idea that we wanted to subordinate the work of the joint chiefs to the service secretaries?" Goldwater wanted to know. "They seemed to take the worst possible interpretation of every provision."[22]

"Wickham privately told me he agreed with some parts of the bill," Nunn interjected. "So, I didn't expect him to be the most hostile chief. But he went ballistic."[23]

"If the Pentagon is ever going to be straightened out, the only hope is for Congress to do it," Goldwater concluded. "The services are so parochial and powerful, there's no way the executive branch will ever get it done."

"You're right," Nunn responded. "And Barry, I hate to say this, but for more than a year we've bent over backwards trying to work with the Pentagon. After tonight, I don't think there is any way to cooperate with the chiefs on reorganization. There may not be anyone in the Pentagon that we can openly work with."[24]

Struggling to reconcile his respect for the joint chiefs, individually and collectively, and disappointment over the outcome of the meeting, Goldwater said: "I hate to see it happen this way, but we don't have any choice. The system is flawed, and we've got to fix it."

"You know," I interjected, "tomorrow morning we're going to get another dose of these arguments from the chiefs' allies on the committee. Do you still want to hold the session in the morning?"[25]

"I didn't hear anything that changed my mind," Goldwater answered. "I think we ought to proceed as planned. What do you think, Sam?"

"We're headed for a bitter and divisive battle in our committee, but I don't see any reason to delay," Nunn replied.[26]

The chiefs had had their showdown with the SASC leaders. If the meeting had been intended to alter Goldwater's and Nunn's thinking, the chiefs had fired blank rounds. If the meeting had been designed to intimidate the senators by emotional saber rattling, it had backfired. What the senators saw and heard shocked and temporarily unnerved them, but they were not about to back down. Goldwater and Nunn emerged from the skirmish in the Tank with the understanding that the coming battle would be bloody. Even more important, they knew it was a fight they had to win.

But could they?

PART
1

The Fog of
Defense
Organization

CHAPTER 1

The Rise of
Service Supremacists

Although most history books glorify our military

accomplishments, a closer examination reveals a

disconcerting pattern: unpreparedness at the start of

a war; initial failures; reorganizing while fighting;

cranking up our industrial base; and ultimately

prevailing by wearing down the enemy—by being

bigger, not smarter.

—Gen. David C. Jones, USAF, 1982

In the early 1980s, powerful army, navy, air force, and Marine Corps officials and organizations dominated the Pentagon. "The overwhelming influence of the four services" was judged to be "completely out of proportion to their legally assigned and limited formal responsibilities."[1] The services wielded their influence more to protect their independence and prerogatives than to develop multiservice commands capable of waging modern warfare. They also blunted efforts to make their separate forces, weapons, and systems interoperable.

The services achieved this preeminent position and accumulated unprecedented political muscle during World War II. In the postwar period, the navy and Marine Corps flexed this muscle and, with the help of congressional allies, repeatedly weakened the plans of Presidents Truman and Eisenhower to unify the military. Although the war had amply demonstrated the need for tighter integration, the navy and Marine Corps were determined to preserve their autonomy. After Eisenhower's attempt to overhaul the military in 1958, no serious reorganization effort occurred for nearly a quarter of a century, despite a succession of operational setbacks and administrative fiascos.[2]

In contrast to the power, prestige, and public approval of the twenty-first-century military, strong antimilitary sentiments dominated public attitudes from the time of independence until Pearl Harbor. Americans generally rejected and neglected their armed forces.[3] The nation's historic antipathy toward the military conflicts with popular notions. History books abound with military heroes like George Washington, Andrew Jackson, Robert E. Lee, John J. "Black Jack" Pershing, and Sergeant York. But the public's esteem and affection for uniformed heroes did not carry over to the military profession.

Americans rejected the concept of a military profession, convinced that "amateur" citizen soldiers could and should provide security.[4] Instead, America focused on the military's technical skills, producing an overemphasis on engineering and science that would plague the army and navy into the twentieth century. Prior to the Civil War, "much of the energy of the Army and the Navy was devoted to the essentially civilian pursuits of exploration, scientific research, and internal development."[5] This technical orientation hindered development of competence in planning, operations, and command. In the early 1900s, Rear Adm. Alfred Thayer Mahan, the navy's premier strategist, "repudiated the tendency of professional naval officers to stake out their profession by emphasizing highly technical skills," leaving the essential planning and operations functions "to the nonprofessionals."[6]

The nineteenth century passed without major organizational changes. Before 1903, Congress enacted only two significant statutes: creation of the positions of secretary of war in 1789 and secretary of the navy in 1798. Army officers "displayed little interest" in organization before the Spanish-American War. An essay contest on army organization in 1900 did not produce a winner because "none of the articles submitted was judged worthy of the award."[7]

Soon after America emerged as a world power, the Spanish-American War revealed organizational weaknesses. Notwithstanding the victory over Spain, the army performed poorly, and the army and navy failed to cooperate. Relations were so strained at the end of fighting in Cuba that the army commander refused to turn captured Spanish ships over to the navy or allow a navy representative to sign the surrender document.

Reacting to the army's dismal performance, Pres. William McKinley sacked his secretary of war. It was, however, unrealistic to expect the War Department to manage a war with "which it had never been organized or equipped to deal."[8]

The lack of sufficient authority in the hands of civilian and military leaders in the War and Navy Departments was the most severe deficiency. No one—not even the secretaries—had enough power to be in charge. The army technical services (Corps of Engineers, Quartermaster Corps, Ordnance Department, and Signal Corps) and navy bureaus (Yards and Docks, Ordnance, Supplies and Accounts, Construction and Repair, and Steam Engineering) remained virtually independent fiefdoms, their autonomy guaranteed by Congress.[9]

Neither department had designated a senior officer to represent professional military interests and provide operational advice. Ironically, officers represented civilian-like technical interests while the civilian secretaries handled professional military and operational matters.[10]

A third major problem: Except for the president, no one coordinated activities of the War and Navy Departments. During the nineteenth century, the president's role as sole coordinator did not overburden him. In the twentieth century, domestic affairs increasingly demanded the president's attention. The expanded scope and complexity of military activities further taxed the chief executive. His inability to coordinate army and navy activities was not understood until the Pearl Harbor disaster provided compelling evidence.[11]

Nevertheless, the first four decades of the twentieth century had witnessed a continuous—albeit largely unsuccessful—search for organizational improvements. The two most significant reforms occurred in the aftermath of the Spanish-American War. In 1903, Elihu Root, a New York corporate lawyer who knew nothing about war or the army, reluctantly accepted McKinley's request that he head the War Department. The new secretary "made vigorous efforts to inform himself." Root focused on correcting ineffective central control and poor performance of professional military functions. The General Staff Act of 1903 authorized his solution: an army general staff, headed by a chief of staff.[12] Drawing ideas from the German military, Root envisioned the General Staff serving as "the directing brain which every army must have, to work successfully." To gain control of the autonomous technical services, Root prescribed that the chief of staff's duties include "immediate direction of the supply departments."[13] Also in 1903, Root and his navy counterpart signed an order establishing the Joint Army-Navy Board, which they charged with addressing "all matters calling for cooperation of the two services." The board was the precursor of the Joint Chiefs of Staff.[14]

The Root reforms had profound consequences: the Army and Air Force Departments still operate on the foundation they laid. Yet opposition to them from War Department elements remained strong until the magnitude and complexity of World War I mobilization and management proved to them the need for a general staff. Congress continued to be skeptical of the General Staff's "interference" in the bureaus' work.[15]

Lacking the pressures of the army's wartime demands and failures, navy organizational reforms lagged far behind, despite determined efforts by reformers. In 1900, responding to naval officers' pressures for a naval general staff to provide "central direction and control," the navy secretary created instead the General Board, tasked merely with developing plans and furnishing advice. Navy Secretary Josephus Daniels "regarded a general staff not simply as unwise but as undemocratic and 'un-American.'"[16]

Beyond the navy's General Board, the only other significant pre–World War II reform in naval organization occurred in 1915 when Congress created the position of chief of naval operations (CNO). Naval officers had pressed for a "powerful commanding" admiral, but Secretary Daniels succeeded in limiting the CNO's authority. After 1920, the navy undertook "no important changes of any kind" until 1940.[17]

These early army and navy reorganizations achieved vastly different results. The army centralized authority under the secretary and chief of staff. The navy remained decentralized with autonomous bureau chiefs. The army emphasized control; the navy relied on cooperation and coordination. The two services "developed entirely different management systems, as two duchies might," contributing significantly to army-navy organizational disputes during and after World War II.[18]

The revered concept of independent command at sea also shaped naval attitudes on organization. "Independent command of ships at sea is a unique, godlike responsibility unlike that afforded to commanding officers in other services," explained Carl H. Builder. "Until the advent of telecommunications, a ship 'over the horizon' was a world unto itself, with its captain absolutely responsible for every soul and consequence that fell under his command." The navy gloried in this independence and resisted organizational arrangements that encroached "into the details of its command and control."[19]

The Joint Army-Navy Board's early work focused on minor matters. Its "virtual disappearance" during World War I attested to its limited role. Although the secretaries of war and the navy strengthened the board after the war, the two departments did not view it "as a means of drawing the two armed forces into ever closer integration." The army and navy limited the board to "providing sufficient coordination to allow the two services to continue to operate autonomously in all major essentials."[20]

The board prescribed "mutual cooperation" as the favored method of interservice interaction, disregarding centuries-old lessons on the need for unity of command. In December, 1941, army and navy commands relied on mutual cooperation to coordinate the defense of Hawaii.[21]

During the forty years before Pearl Harbor, antimilitary attitudes of the public and Congress remained a principal obstacle to restructuring. Congress also had other objectives in slowing or denying reform. Seeking to check the power of the executive branch in military affairs, Congress frustrated many reforms that would have strengthened central authority. Such reforms, Congress reasoned, would invigorate the executive branch to Capitol Hill's disadvantage.

Local politics also played a role. The technical services and bureaus generated jobs and contracts in congressional districts. Preserving their independence enhanced continued congressional control of resources. Alliances between Congress and the technical services and bureaus stymied reorganization.[22]

The lack of a consensus on principles for organizing the military exacerbated the obstacles to reform. Experts debated issues for decades without resolution. Beyond arguments over the relative importance of technical and operational skills, unsettled issues included centralization versus decentralization, the absence of a national military strategy, the division of civilian and military responsibilities, and the merits of the general staff concept.[23]

The advent of military aviation blurred the distinction between land and sea warfare—the basic organizing principle since the republic's beginning—and signaled the need for adjustments in organization and warfighting concepts. The demonstration of airpower's potential in World War 1 raised expectations for creation of a separate military department. In 1919, Brig. Gen. William "Billy" Mitchell, looking beyond the immediate goal of a separate air force, predicted: "If we look forward, there will be a ministry of defense, combining army, navy, and air force under one direction." Few shared Mitchell's vision.[24]

In 1941, with war again looming, military groups focused on the need for more effective interservice coordination. In June, the navy's General Board offered a plan that envisioned "the superimposition of a joint general staff with a single chief of staff serving the president directly and the establishment of unified commands in all theaters and coastal defense areas." With isolationists accusing the Roosevelt administration of "leading the country down the road to war," senior officers concluded that consideration of the board's sweeping proposal was "impossible because of the political repercussions."[25]

In early December, the War and Navy Departments were still in the early stages of addressing their organizational problems. The two "virtually autonomous" departments remained incapable of harmonizing internal business activities and coordinating land, sea, and air operations.[26] The humiliating Japanese surprise attack on Pearl Harbor on December 7 painfully exposed the woeful command structure and limitations of mutual cooperation. The public outcry dictated a unified effort by American fighting forces. President Franklin D. Roosevelt designated theater commanders, such as Gen. Dwight D. Eisenhower, Gen. Douglas MacArthur, and Adm. Chester W. Nimitz, to provide unified command.[27] Wartime logistics requirements doomed the independence of the technical services and bureaus, although the navy bureaus continued to resist control by central authority.[28]

Another invention of necessity reached farther. To ensure an effective Anglo-American military relationship, Roosevelt formed the JCS to deal with a British counterpart. Initially, this body consisted of the army chief of staff, Gen. George C. Marshall Jr.; the commanding general of the Army Air Forces, Gen. Henry H. "Hap" Arnold; and the CNO, Adm. Ernest J. King. At Marshall's urging, Roosevelt added his chief of staff, Adm. William D. Leahy, as a fourth member.

Creation of the JCS represented Roosevelt's principal organizational response to wartime policy and planning requirements. Notably, the president did not create complementary organizations and officials to provide a robust civilian perspective in planning and directing the war. The chiefs filled every inch of this vacuum. They became the president's military, diplomatic, political, and intelligence officers.[29]

American inexperience in multiservice coordination stunned Field Marshal Sir John Dill, the senior British officer assigned to Washington for liaison. Of the JCS's early work, he wrote to London, "The whole organization belongs to the days of George Washington."[30]

Despite inauspicious beginnings, the JCS filled a crucial need. In providing the president integrated, multiservice advice, the JCS attained "a degree of unified purpose and accomplishment without precedent." But it had one fatal weakness. Consisting of four equals—two generals and two admirals—the JCS was unable to reach a decision except by unanimous agreement. On many occasions, "decision by the Joint Chiefs proved to be impossible." One early issue exemplified this defect.[31]

The British had recommended the diversion of steel from battleship and heavy-cruiser construction to build more landing craft and convoy escort ships. Only King opposed the diversion. "When Leahy remarked that it looked to him as though 'the vote is three to one,' King replied coldly that so far as he was concerned, the Joint Chiefs was not a voting organization on any matter in which the interests of the Navy were involved."[32] He demanded a veto, not simply a vote.

The requirement for unanimity allowed the chiefs to successfully address "the larger problems of strategy and operations . . . only briefly and with respect to a limited range of issues." The chiefs' record did "not justify the conclusion that World War II was a test of the JCS which established its value beyond substantial doubt."[33]

Institutional weaknesses in Washington also undermined efforts to establish unity of command in the field. In 1945, a JCS special committee reported that in all theaters of operation "complete integration of effort has not yet been achieved because we are still struggling with inconsistencies, lack of understanding, jealousies and duplications." Of the intense army-navy competition and mistrust, Britain's Air Marshal Sir John Slessor wrote, "The violence of

3. Admiral William D. Leahy (*seated at head of table*) presides at a meeting of the Joint Chiefs of Staff in 1944. Generals George C. Marshall and Henry H. Arnold are to Leahy's right and Adm. Ernest J. King is to his left.

interservice rivalry in the United States had to be seen to be believed and was an appreciable handicap to their war effort."[34]

The enormous wartime role given to the JCS and the vast power and influence it accumulated proved troubling after the war. Determined to maintain civilian control of the military, civilian leaders, especially Congress, had kept the military weak and isolated, often too much so for the nation's good. Roosevelt had placed the sacred principle of civilian control at risk. He did not limit the chiefs to military affairs. They had significant political roles. Next to the president, they were the most powerful force in the war effort. Two generations of leaders would struggle to reestablish control over these military heavyweights.[35]

The JCS's operating style magnified its power and influence. Its closed staff approach permitted it to make decisions "relatively unfettered and unobserved." It also had complete freedom in determining "what it would and would not consider, with whom it would and would not deal, and the extent to which it would expose its internal workings." Throughout the war, the JCS used a model that resembled the Supreme Court. Given the chiefs' administrative duties, this approach—with its poor communications, uncertain corporate attitudes, and lack of expeditiousness—created major wartime problems and proved equally troubling in peacetime.[36]

Roosevelt was comfortable with the military juggernaut he had created, but controlling it depended on the president's personality and bureaucratic skills. Even before Roosevelt's death, the chiefs had determined to avoid a return to their services' previous isolation and neglect. Marshall remembered all too well "how the Army was dismantled and virtually destroyed during the years between the world wars." In one instance, an army regiment transferred from Philadelphia to St. Louis had to walk because no money was available to transport the men by train. The chiefs wanted to preserve their strong position. When Roosevelt died on April 12, 1945, the balance of power in civil-military relations shifted in favor of the newly influential chiefs.[37]

The JCS's wartime pattern of behavior was both well established and accepted. The chiefs also emerged from the war as larger-than-life heroes—the victors of the greatest war ever fought. No longer "the cowed and submissive men of the 1930s," the individual chiefs and the JCS as an institution "were viewed as the military equivalent of the Oracle of Delphi."[38]

The combination of precedent and JCS stature obstructed postwar reorganization. The wartime weakening of civilian control—the cardinal principle that had governed civil-military relations since the American Revolution—presented the greatest challenge. In 1945, Admiral Leahy unashamedly observed that except for the president himself, "the Joint Chiefs of Staff at the present time are under no civilian control whatever." Abandoning their favorable prewar attitudes toward civilian control, the chiefs wanted their new exalted status institutionalized. Not only did they want to become a permanent body with vast duties, they wanted to report only to the president.[39]

The Allied victory over Germany and Japan gave birth to the myth that the joint chiefs had effectively executed their wartime responsibilities. As Pres. John F. Kennedy said, "The greatest enemy of the truth is very often not the lie—deliberate, contrived, and dishonest—but the myth—persistent, persuasive, and unrealistic."[40] The JCS myth endured for two generations and contributed to the prolonged battle to rein in the excessive power of the chiefs and correct resulting organizational distortions.

The first skirmishes over unification were fought during the war. Shortly after its creation, the JCS considered the navy General Board's idea of a joint general staff and single chief of staff. Marshall supported the plan, but "opposition in Navy quarters was inveterate and sincere." The navy's objection centered on the absence of "a corps of officers thoroughly cognizant of the capabilities, limitations, and tested doctrines of all branches of the two services."[41]

In early 1943, army officers expressed dissatisfaction with the JCS system. They saw the War and Navy Departments as "competing, often hostile, bureaucracies" and judged the result to be "duplication of effort and considerable unnecessary confusion . . . ultimately retarding the war effort with an incalculable increase in casualties and destruction."[42]

Later that year, Marshall forwarded for JCS consideration an army plan for a single Department of National Defense, with a secretary, four under secretaries, and a single chief of staff. The Army Air Forces favored this approach because it offered the greatest potential for an independent and equal status for aviation. The navy—fearful of domination by the army and a newly independent air force—continued to oppose unification and defend the status quo, finding "positive virtue in its continued independence and separateness."[43]

At King's request, the Joint Strategic Survey Committee, a strategy advisory group, evaluated the army plan. The committee, composed of two generals and two admirals, favored a single department. Its March, 1944, report observed that "the outstanding lesson of this war is that modern warfare is made up of . . . 'unified' operations." The members concluded that "all military elements should be so closely interlocked and interrelated that the concept of one whole is preferable to articulated units."[44] The committee recommended that the JCS accept the principle of "three services [army, navy, air force] within one military organization" and appoint a special committee to study the issue. Leahy and King disagreed with the committee's report, but agreed to appoint a special committee consisting of two army and two navy officers and chaired by Adm. James O. Richardson.[45]

In April, 1945, the Richardson Committee reported that its members—except for Richardson—were "unanimously in favor of a single department system." The report claimed, "This view is supported by Generals of the Army MacArthur and Eisenhower, Fleet Admiral Nimitz, Admiral Halsey" and the "great majority of the Army officers and almost exactly half of the Navy officers whose views were heard." The committee recommended a secretary of the armed forces to preside over the single department and a commander of the armed forces supported by a general staff. The JCS would continue, but only as an advisory body, and would include the new secretary and commander as well as the service chiefs.[46]

The day after the Richardson Committee submitted its report, Roosevelt died of a cerebral hemorrhage. He had served as assistant navy secretary during World War I and had such a "notorious partiality" for the navy that Marshall once asked, "At least, Mr. President, stop speaking of the Army as 'they' and the Navy as 'us.'" Roosevelt never took a public position on unification, but Leahy reported that the president was never "in favor either of a unification of the armed forces, or of an independent air force." The navy believed that Roosevelt would never force unification on them.[47]

Roosevelt's successor, Harry Truman, had a different attitude. His thirty-five-year army affiliation began in 1905 when he joined the National Guard. Truman served as an artillery captain in France during World War I, and after the war remained in the organized reserves. He attained the rank of colonel and attended annual summer training through 1940. Within days of Truman's swearing in, a close friend told a Missouri audience, "During the Roosevelt administration the White House was a Navy wardroom; we're going to fix that."[48]

Truman was interested in military organization and "had studied every plan that had been suggested through the years for its improvement." Pearl Harbor strengthened his conviction of the need for unified command in Washington and the field. During World War II, as chairman of the Senate Special Committee to Investigate the National Defense Program, he was appalled by "the waste and inefficiency existing as a result of the operation of two separate and uncoordinated military departments." In 1944 he published a magazine article in which he argued the case for a single department: "Proof that a divine Providence watches over the United States is furnished by the fact that we have managed to escape disaster even though our scrambled professional military setup has been an open invitation to catastrophe. . . . An obvious first step is a consolidation of the Army and the Navy that will put all of our defensive and offensive strength under one tent and one authoritative, responsible command—a complete integration that will consider the national security as a whole."[49]

Marshall and Arnold supported the Richardson Committee's call for a single department, while Leahy and King remained opposed "on the grounds that a single military department would be inefficient, would weaken civilian control of the military, and was contrary to wartime experience that showed the superiority of a joint over a unitary system." With this final disagreement, the JCS as an institution lost its opportunity to influence reorganization.[50]

The reorganization conflict escalated into "a wrenching, bitter struggle." The prospect of an independent air force "engendered fear and dismay in the Navy and Marine Corps." Senior Army Air Forces officers questioned the need for navy and Marine Corps aviation. The army and Marine Corps also had differing views on land warfare missions. The army argued that the marines "should be restricted to duties with the fleet, and have only lightly armed units for shore operations." The navy and Marine Corps opposed unification as a way of "protecting their functions and the composition of their forces." The Marine Corps saw the struggle as a fight for survival.[51]

Secretary of War Henry L. Stimson ridiculed "the peculiar psychology of the Navy Department, which seemed to retire from the realm of logic into a dim religious world in which Neptune was God, Mahan his prophet, and the United States Navy the only true Church. The high priests of this Church were a group of men to whom Stimson always referred as 'the admirals.'"[52]

In 1940 and afterward, Stimson found "the admirals" were "still active and still uncontrolled by either their secretary or the president. This was not [Navy Secretary William F.] Knox's fault, or the president's, as Stimson saw it. It was simply that the Navy Department had never had an Elihu Root. 'The admirals' had never been given their comeuppance."[53]

Not surprisingly, Truman advocated the War Department's point of view. In December, 1945, the president told Congress, "There is enough evidence now at hand to demonstrate beyond question the need for a unified department." Truman proposed a single Department of National Defense headed by a secretary of national defense, assistant secretaries for land, naval, and air forces, and a single chief of staff.[54]

Navy Secretary James V. Forrestal led the naval service's opposition. He informed the White House "that the proposals in the message were 'completely unworkable' and that it would be impossible for him and senior naval officers to testify in support of them."[55]

Truman resisted the initial reaction of his staff to "screw the Navy," aware "that Forrestal represented a serious political problem. He was a large, immensely respected public figure; he was the acknowledged Navy spokesman, and the Navy position had formidable support in the Congress and in the body politic." The president understood that his efforts to unify the services would escalate into a major political battle.[56]

Truman's proposals renewed congressional fears of a loss of power to an executive branch with a centralized military structure. Capitol Hill's interest in diffusion of military power had local political dimensions as well. With the formerly independent technical services and bureaus now under firmer control, close relationships with the military departments would work to Congress' advantage on money and job issues, especially if higher authority was less able to constrain the departments. Congress would give priority to preserving service independence, as it had done earlier for the technical services and bureaus.[57]

Conceding the strength of the navy and its congressional supporters, Truman abandoned the idea of a single chief of staff and accepted statutory creation of the JCS. Heavy navy and Marine Corps lobbying on Capitol Hill watered down the president's final compromise. The National Security Act of 1947—which codified the final agreement—created a unified structure, the "National Military Establishment," with three subordinate departments: army, navy, and an independent air force. The act created the position of secretary of defense to head this new organization, but limited his powers and staff, forcing him to rely on cooperation among the services.

The National Security Act did not diminish the service chiefs' power, which they used to erect a service-dominated system. Although the unified commands had shown their utility in wartime, the chiefs restricted the authorities of the unified commanders and empowered their service component commanders. When the chiefs were done, these commands were unified in name only.[58]

Eisenhower later said of the 1947 debate and compromise: "In that battle the lessons were lost, tradition won. The three service departments were but loosely joined. The entire structure . . . was little more than a weak confederation of sovereign military units. Few powers were vested in the new secretary of defense. All others were reserved to three separated executive departments."[59]

The 1947 act provided a weaker organization than the wartime arrangement. It assigned to an impotent defense secretary the job of harmonizing the work of three powerful military departments. The act permitted the services to solidify their positions, including emasculation of the unified commands, which the law barely recognized. It also left the defense secretary's relationships with the service secretaries undefined. Most significant, the act focused almost exclusively on the civilian side. It left the military side unreformed and gave statutory legitimacy to a dysfunctional, service-dominated JCS. At the time, few understood the extent of the National Security Act's shortcomings and how service supremacists would resist each attempt to fix them.

Truman offered the defense secretary post to Secretary of War Robert P. Patterson. When he declined, the president turned to Forrestal, the legislation's principal architect. Shortly before assuming his new position on September 17, 1947, Forrestal wrote to a friend: "this office will probably be the greatest cemetery for dead cats in history."[60]

Within nine frustrating months, Forrestal came to view his concept as unworkable. He had been unable "to exercise effective control over the feuding military services and to resolve the disputes over budgets, weapons, strategic plans, and roles and missions." The secretary concluded that the National Security Act needed to be amended.[61]

In meetings held in mid-1948, Forrestal found support from the army and air force for placing "more central authority in the hands of the secretary of defense." The navy, on the other hand, "reacted with open bitterness." Forrestal's campaign to strengthen the position of defense secretary "cost him the remaining support and loyalty" of the navy, "and the loss was a heavy emotional blow to him."[62]

In early October, 1948, Forrestal "acknowledged to the president that the 1947 act was inadequate, [and] that he couldn't make it work." Forrestal had veered close to outright insubordination while the act was being formulated, but the president graciously accepted his admission. He made "no 'I-told-you-so' attempt to demonstrate his own prior wisdom on the subject."[63]

In an effort to bring about needed changes, Forrestal lobbied Congress to create a commission on executive branch organization. Headed by former president Herbert Hoover, the commission established a task force that analyzed the 1947 act and issued "a devastating indictment of Forrestal's original conception."[64] Its report declared that "centralized civilian control scarcely exists [and] the Joint Chiefs of Staff are virtually a law unto themselves."[65]

In response to the Hoover Commission recommendations, Truman proposed statutory changes in March, 1949. In August, Congress redesignated the

4. President Harry S. Truman and General of the Army Dwight D.
Eisenhower meet in December, 1950.

National Military Establishment as the Department of Defense, established the new position of JCS chairman, and expanded the defense secretary's powers and staff. Congress rejected other proposals, including designating the new JCS chairman as the principal military adviser.

The war in Korea preempted further action on organizational problems for the remainder of Truman's administration. During the 1952 presidential campaign, Eisenhower criticized DoD's faction-ridden organization. Following his election, the five-star general appointed a committee headed by Nelson A. Rockefeller to conduct a thorough review of the department's organization.[66] The committee's recommendations focused on the defense secretary's authority, bypassing the thorny issue of JCS reform altogether. Eisenhower incorporated the committee's recommendations into Reorganization Plan No. 6, which he submitted to Congress.

Although numerous representatives opposed the plan, it went into effect on June 30, 1953, when neither house took disapproving action within sixty days. The plan increased the number of assistant secretaries of defense from three to nine and abolished various boards and assigned their functions to the defense secretary. It gave the JCS chairman authority to manage the Joint Staff and approve its members and placed the service secretaries in the operational chain of command—a change designed by Eisenhower to strengthen civilian control.

Eisenhower continued to press unsuccessfully for improved control over the services and a more unified perspective by the JCS. In October, 1957, the Soviet launch of the *Sputnik* satellite thrust DoD's performance into the spotlight. The president seized this opportunity to direct another review of defense organization.

In January, 1958, Eisenhower listed defense reorganization as his first priority in his State of the Union address. Defense Secretary Neil H. McElroy established a panel—headed by his assistant, Charles A. Coolidge—that proposed to increase the defense secretary's power, strengthen the JCS chairman, remove the service secretaries and chiefs from the chain of command, and place an enlarged Joint Staff more under the chairman's control.

In transmitting his recommendations in a message to Congress in April, Eisenhower expressed his vision for DoD: "Separate ground, sea, and air warfare is gone forever. If ever again we should be involved in war, we will fight it in all elements, with all services, as one single concentrated effort. Peacetime preparatory and organizational activity must conform to this fact. Strategic and tactical planning must be completely unified, combat forces organized into unified commands, each equipped with the most efficient weapons systems that science can develop, singly led and prepared to fight as one, regardless of service."[67]

Much of Congress reacted negatively. Representative Carl Vinson, pronavy chairman of the House Armed Services Committee (HASC), accused the bill of tending toward a "Prussian-type supreme command." He called it an "open invitation" for a powerful military man to seize control of the government. The HASC deleted or watered down numerous provisions, but the Senate convinced the House to accommodate some of Eisenhower's objections to the House bill.[68]

The resulting Defense Reorganization Act of 1958 strengthened the defense secretary's authority, especially over the military departments. It elevated the status of the JCS chairman and nearly doubled the Joint Staff's size, but deleted the chairman's authority to manage the Joint Staff, granted in 1953. Although the act gave the unified commanders full operational command of assigned forces and removed the military departments from the operational chain of command, the services never complied with these provisions.

The 1949, 1953, and 1958 reorganizations thus took steps toward a unified establishment, but none addressed the inherent weakness of the JCS: its control by the services. Defense organization continued to favor the interests of the services too much and the broader interests of national defense too little.

For almost thirty years after 1958, administrations did not request and Congress did not enact significant statutory changes to defense organization. The inability of war hero Dwight Eisenhower—with his great prestige and influence in military affairs—to overcome opposition to reform convinced others not to challenge the unyielding alliance between the services and Congress. Although the service-dominated structure repeatedly demonstrated its flaws over the next three decades, administrations studied, but did not propose, reforms.

During his campaign for president, Kennedy commissioned an advisory committee on defense organization chaired by Sen. Stuart Symington (D-Missouri), the first air force secretary. Like previous reports, Symington's found that the services' excessive role "must be corrected. At present, defense planning represents at best a series of compromised positions among the military services."[69] The report's radical solutions—centralize power in the defense secretary and a chairman of a joint military staff, consolidate combat forces in four unified commands, eliminate the JCS and military departments—generated widespread criticism. Moreover, the incoming administration never seriously considered them because Defense Secretary Robert S. McNamara believed his own management reforms would fix Pentagon problems.[70]

Within three months of his inauguration, Kennedy experienced firsthand the dismal quality of military advice when the JCS botched its review of Central Intelligence Agency (CIA) plans for an American-sponsored landing by anti-Castro Cuban exiles at the Bay of Pigs. Kennedy was especially disillusioned with the advice from "his own branch of the service, the Navy, and its chief." The president recalled asking Adm. Arleigh Burke, "Will this plan work?" and the CNO had said, "As far as we've been able to check it out, the plan is good." The invasion ended in disaster. Concerned by the poor quality of the JCS's advice, Kennedy "inserted [retired general] Maxwell Taylor between himself and the Joint Chiefs of Staff" as his military and intelligence adviser.[71]

The Vietnam War magnified DoD's institutional shortcomings, especially the JCS's inability to formulate quality advice and the absence of unified command in the field. Emotional controversies, such as charges of undue civilian interference, obscured organizational lessons. General David C. Jones, a subsequent JCS chairman, called the conflict "perhaps our worst example of confused objectives and unclear responsibilities, both in Washington and in the field." Unity of effort did not exist in the theater; each service "considered Vietnam its own war and sought to carve out a large mission for itself." Even during the 1975 evacuation of Saigon, "responsibility was split between two separate commands, one on land and one at sea; each of these set a different 'H-hour,' which caused confusion and delays."[72]

On January 23, 1968, North Korean naval vessels seized the USS *Pueblo*, an intelligence-gathering ship, approximately fifteen miles off the North Korean coast. American forces were unable to respond during the four hours available for decisive action. Inadequate command arrangements were cited as the principal reason: "There was no effective unity of command below CINCPAC [commander in chief, Pacific Command], and those links in the chain of command, CINCPAC and above, who possessed sufficient authority were too far away to influence the situation."[73]

In the midst of Vietnam, Pres. Richard M. Nixon appointed a Blue Ribbon Defense Panel to evaluate DoD's organization. The panel's report, issued in July, 1970, highlighted many problems described ten years earlier in Senator Symington's report and recommended changes "almost as radical." The Nixon administration adopted only three lesser recommendations of the panel's fifteen proposals on organization. This inaction "resulted from political obstacles in Congress and the military services at a time of Vietnam exigencies and declining budgets."[74]

An act of piracy on the high seas on May 12, 1975, two weeks after the evacuation of Saigon, again drew American attention to Asia. "Have been fired upon and boarded by Cambodian armed forces," announced a Mayday message from the American merchant ship SS *Mayaguez*. "Ship is being towed to unknown Cambodian port." Once the thirty-nine-man crew anchored the ship near Koh Tang Island, the Cambodians moved them to the mainland. After a slow response, the American military recaptured the crewless *Mayaguez*, and the Cambodians released the seamen. American forces needlessly attacked Koh Tang Island and suffered eighteen dead and fifty wounded without achieving a single military objective. A critique concluded: "The Mayaguez incident, while it may have been some sort of political success, was a military failure."[75]

In 1977, Pres. Jimmy Carter directed DoD to reexamine its organization. Five reports resulted. Despite their quality and persuasiveness, the administration did not act on the recommendations. The best-known report, *National Military Command Structure Study* authored by Richard C. Steadman, reinforced earlier observations that the JCS organization "virtually precludes effective addressal of those issues involving allocation of resources among the services . . . except to agree that they should be increased without consideration of resource constraints."[76]

Although reorganization studies focused on operational problems, disunity of effort was also glaring in administrative and support areas. Carter's defense secretary, Harold Brown, cited examples of wasteful practices that seriously weakened war readiness during his tenure: "U.S. Army and Air Force units in

Europe have difficulty communicating because their systems were developed separately and are not interoperable. Because the Navy and Air Force use different refueling equipment, tanker aircraft of one cannot refuel fighters of the other without an equipment change. Until recently, even that option was not available."[77]

The Carter administration's weak political standing on military matters contributed to inaction on reorganization. The president's prestige took another blow on April 24, 1980, when the military raid to rescue fifty-three Americans held hostage in Tehran failed. After the mission was aborted, eight servicemen died when a marine-piloted helicopter and air force transport plane collided on a desert landing strip.

The failed Iranian rescue mission "clearly marked the decline of American military prestige and confidence."[78] National defense became a key issue in the 1980 presidential election. Ronald Reagan's platform, responding to the public's mood, called for revitalizing the military. It promised "an immediate increase in defense spending."[79]

But the Republican platform devoted only five sentences to defense management and organization. It criticized "the ill-informed, capricious intrusions" of the Office of Management and Budget (OMB) and program analysts in the Office of the Secretary of Defense (OSD) on planning and budget issues. "Orderly planning by the military services has become impossible," the platform declared. By attacking central authority and promoting service prerogatives, the platform positioned Reagan and his party on the side of those who opposed a more integrated DoD.

Following his landslide victory, Reagan kept his campaign promise to pour money into defense hardware and operations. But correcting the Pentagon's problems required more than additional funds. Former Secretary of Defense Melvin R. Laird soon would argue that "neglect of organizational issues . . . is self defeating. Without an effective command structure, no level of defense spending will be sufficient to meet the needs of the nation's security."[80]

Reagan and Defense Secretary Caspar Weinberger did not understand that the excessive power of the four services was undermining the unity required to defend the nation's interests. They did not perceive how service separatism contributed to operational failures, most notably and costly in Vietnam, but also in the tragic *Pueblo* and *Mayaguez* incidents and failed Iranian hostage rescue mission. They ignored the penetrating critiques of the Hoover Commission, Rockefeller Committee, Coolidge panel, Symington report, Blue Ribbon Defense Panel, and Steadman report.

Since World War II, efforts to integrate the military progressed only when a president and defense secretary provided forceful and visionary leadership. Not only were Reagan and Weinberger not prepared to play this role, their policy sympathized with service aspirations. Without presidential leadership, improvements in defense organization appeared impossible. Service supremacists had erected nearly impenetrable barriers to change. Congress—guardian of the law—liked the role ceded to it by the diffusion of Pentagon power. A reform campaign mounted against such opposition seemed hopeless.

Despite the odds, one general was prepared to try.

CHAPTER 2

Jones
Breaks Ranks

Everyone admires courage and the greenest garlands

are for those who possess it.

—John F. Kennedy, *Profiles in Courage*

General David Jones, chairman of the Joint Chiefs of Staff, anxiously awaited his chance to testify to the House Armed Services Committee. His boss, Defense Secretary Cap Weinberger, seated to his right, was finishing a long opening statement. Jones knew his testimony would annoy Weinberger, infuriate Pentagon colleagues, and spark intense criticism. Cognizant that he was about to start a holy war over the military's most sacred turf, Jones just hoped that his testimony would compel Congress to act.[1]

Weinberger and Jones were appearing during a closed session on February 3, 1982—four years to the day before Goldwater's and Nunn's pivotal meeting in the Tank. Seated in the HASC's large, ornate main hearing room, the secretary and the general were presenting their initial budget statements. This hearing was normally open to the public, but the committee had agreed to close it because the president had not yet submitted his budget to Congress.[2] A closed hearing provided a favorable environment for Jones to "drop his bombshell."[3] Without making headlines, he could describe the poor functioning of the JCS and urge the enactment of legislation to reform the nation's senior military body.[4]

Jones had decided that he could not delay this message any longer. This might be his last appearance before the HASC. In less than five months he would complete his second two-year term as chairman and retire. By then he would have a total of eight years of service as a JCS member, longer than anyone in the body's forty-year history. Jones would have another opportunity to urge reform when he testified before the Senate Armed Services Committee several days later, but he expected most SASC members to be hostile to his proposals. He believed the HASC would provide a more favorable audience.

The general had told Weinberger and the service chiefs that he planned to express "concerns about how the system operated," but only a few close advisers knew what Jones was about to say.[5] Even Jones did not know how he would proceed until the last minute. "Driving to the hearing, I was collecting my thoughts on how to do it."[6]

Jones figured his testimony might chill his "cool, never close relationship" with Weinberger, but he did not think the secretary would fire him.[7] Although strong-willed, Weinberger lacked forcefulness on personnel matters.

A Harvard-educated lawyer and courteous gentleman, Weinberger was a longtime friend and confidant of President Reagan. His vast government experience did not include assignments in defense, where he acknowledged his novice status. Despite Weinberger's pleasant demeanor, stubbornness ranked as his most prominent trait. Once he made up his mind, he seldom changed it.

Jones anticipated criticism and even personal attacks from active and retired officers. The bitter defense debates during the Carter administration had hardened him to adverse commentary. "I had enough criticism when I was chairman that I enjoyed stirring up the pot a little bit," Jones confided.[8]

When Weinberger reached the end of his statement, Jones's H-hour arrived. Peering down from the massive, three-tiered wooden rostrum that seated all forty-five HASC members, Chairman Mel Price inquired, "Before we ask any questions of the secretary, General Jones, do you have a statement you would like to make to the committee?" Jones—tall, fit, polished, and more youthful appearing than his age of sixty—looked like a modern aviator general.[9]

The committee members sat there unaware of the historic stand Jones was about to take. The nation's top officer would break ranks with Pentagon colleagues and ask Congress to reform his organization. Not since Lt. Gen. J. Lawton Collins introduced War Department proposals in 1945 had a serving officer initiated an effort to reform the JCS.[10]

"I look forward to testifying on the budget issues," Jones began, "however, there is one subject I would like to mention briefly here."[11] The general took a deep breath. "It is not sufficient to have just resources, dollars and weapon systems; we must also have an organization which will allow us to develop the proper strategy, necessary planning, and the full warfighting capability."

Then, in nine words, Jones started a war over defense organization that would last for five years: "We do not have an adequate organizational structure today." He quickly added, "at least in my judgment."

"We have made improvements," Jones said, but those "improvements have

5. General David C. Jones during his service as air force chief of staff.
(U.S. Air Force photo.)

only been made at the margin; we need to do much more. . . . To be able to fight in today's environment . . . will require the concerted efforts of all four services. The services can't operate alone."

Of the JCS, Jones said: "We are basically a committee system. . . . Committees are very good in a deliberative process, but they are notoriously poor in trying to run things, particularly the committee that I head, because of some unique characteristics." The general, using the word *characteristics* as a euphemism for problems, cited five "characteristics."

"Starting in World War II, the Joint Chiefs of Staff began to operate on the basis of unanimity. For an action to be taken, there had to be unanimous consent to that action." He noted that in the National Security Act of 1947, "if the chiefs cannot come to an agreement, a unanimous agreement among the five of us, we then inform the secretary of defense and, as appropriate, the president." These pressures for unanimity resulted in "the least common denominator in order to get some sort of agreement."

The second characteristic Jones cited was the five staff levels through which JCS papers passed. He explained that the services exercise "almost a de facto veto at each level in that each service knows that ultimately unanimity is the goal."

He next discussed the "great institutional pressures on people within the services," and indirectly raised the service chiefs' conflict of interest: "It is very difficult for a chief as head of a service to say more resources ought to go to another service rather than his own." He described the "great personnel turnover" on the Joint Staff, where officers served for an average of only two years. He also expressed concern about the "few rewards for joint service."

The general told the committee that in the time he had left in office, he would "work with my colleagues first because many of these things can be solved by the chiefs unanimously agreeing to change. I will then work with the administration—the secretary of defense, and the president—which may include submitting legislative proposals."

Jones closed by offering five recommendations. Although he described them as "specific," he provided only broad directions. The general proposed strengthening "the role of the chairman." In preparing joint papers, Jones said "service staff involvement . . . should be limited to inputs rather than debates." He recommended that "the Joint Chiefs should receive their advice on joint issues from the joint system rather than from their own service staff." Jones said he would "give the commanders in chief in the field, those whom we hold responsible for fighting the forces, an increasing role." Finally, he proposed to "enhance the preparations and rewards for joint duty."

Jones concluded his eight-minute statement by saying, "I look forward to working with the committee, Mr. Chairman, on this important subject in the months ahead."

America's top officer settled back in his chair. He had done it. These problems needed to be aired. The military brotherhood would not like it, but the Pentagon had to overcome crippling service parochialism. The general thought his statement might intrigue members, but he did not expect them to ask many questions. Congressmen come to such hearings with prepared questions in their areas of interest. Few pose questions pertaining to issues about which they know and care little. That was fine with Jones. He feared that an overwhelming response would create a firestorm, alarm Weinberger, and cause him to become an overt opponent. The general just wanted his ideas to catch hold with someone on the committee.[12]

Member after member posed questions without a single reference to his testimony. Finally, Cong. Donald J. Mitchell (R–New York) asked, "Do the mechanics of instituting the changes that you recommended to the Joint Chiefs structure have to be legislative?"[13]

"The chiefs could agree to many of them themselves," replied Jones, "some would be addressed within the administration; and there would be some legislative changes which I would propose to the Congress, particularly pertaining to limitations on the Joint Staff."

After nearly four hours of testimony, that brief exchange marked the only time a member raised the issue. Jones worried that the hearing would end without anyone really following up on his testimony.[14] At last, near the end of the afternoon session, Cong. Ike Skelton (D-Missouri), a military history buff, zeroed in on Jones's remarks. "When . . . did you become concerned about the operation of the Joint Chiefs of Staff?" the junior HASC member asked.[15]

"I have had ever since I was a colonel, when I first came to Washington, some fundamental concerns about the organization of the Joint Chiefs," the general revealed. "It was about a year ago that I decided to take on the task of making major changes."

In response to another question from Skelton, Jones disclosed that he had commissioned a study of the JCS's organization. He also announced that he was "going to go public in the next couple of weeks with a fairly extensive article that will outline the problems and my views on the problems."

Skelton asked if it would be possible for the committee to be briefed on the study and Jones's recommendations. "I would be available in the days ahead to brief you," the general replied. "I would even expect or recommend committee hearings."

Skelton understood the dynamic at work: "This seems to me to be a rather courageous thing for you to do. I think it is something that should get the utmost attention from this committee and from Congress."

Jones planned for his article, "Why the Joint Chiefs of Staff Must Change," to appear in the February, 1982, issue of *Directors & Boards*, a business journal.[16] Like his closed-session testimony, he selected this obscure forum in order to avoid generating too much attention. "Right at that point, I didn't want to ignite too great a fire, but I wanted to get started."[17] Jones forwarded drafts of his article to higher authority. Deputy Defense Secretary Frank C. Carlucci wrote across the front of his copy, "Dave, I skimmed this, since I had read original. Looks good to me."[18]

In the article, Jones skillfully elaborated on the five problems he had cited in his congressional testimony, but much of his message was implied, not direct. Knowing that Pentagon colleagues would blast him, Jones attempted to minimize the effects of their explosion by avoiding blunt criticisms.

The article chronicled the two-hundred-year history of "enforced diffusion of military authority" and resulting deficiencies. Jones initially discussed de facto service vetoes during the staffing of JCS papers, and pressures for unanimity. He revealed that harmonizing disparate service positions often produced papers that are "watered down or well waffled." He also lamented that the JCS, "understandably reluctant to forward disagreements . . . invest much time and effort to accommodate differing views of the chiefs." Jones decried the "inadequate cross-service and joint experience in our military, from the top down."[19]

Jones called the service chiefs' conflict of interest a "spokesman-statesman" dilemma. He said he did not see how the existing arrangement could work given the resource and mission issues that heightened this conflict. He called it "unreasonable to expect the service chiefs to take one position as service advocate . . . and a totally different position in the joint arena."

Although Jones's article provided more information on his recommendations, the outlines of his proposals were just beginning to take shape. To strengthen the chairman, Jones envisioned removing service chiefs from making recommendations on resources and missions. To further empower the chairman, he added a new recommendation: "The chairman should be authorized a deputy." The general cited continuity during the chairman's absence and his need for assistance as reasons. To limit service staff involvement in the joint system, he advised: "We should abolish the current system. The role of service staffs can and should be reduced to providing information inputs." Jones proposed switching each service chief's reliance for advice on joint matters away from his own staff to the Joint Staff, but did not explain how that change would be engineered.

Jones discussed two changes to increase the role of unified commanders. He envisioned the chairman "in consultation with the combatant commanders" providing the interservice perspective on resources and missions. He also foresaw "strengthening of the unified commander's role with respect to his service component commanders" whose "attention is often drawn more to service issues than to interservice coordination problems."

Regarding the need to "broaden the training, experience, and rewards for joint duty," Jones recommended interservice exchanges of junior officers, upgraded preparation, improved education, and making joint assignments career enhancing. Recognizing the services' total control of personnel matters, he observed, "It is difficult to see how present patterns can be changed, however, without some influence by the chairman on the selection and promotion of officers."

Despite Jones's indirect problem descriptions and vague proposals, the article presented a clear message: Jones advocated strengthening the position of joint officers—especially the chairman, unified commanders, and members of the Joint Staff. Service chiefs and their staffs would be assigned lesser roles.

Shortly after testifying on Capitol Hill, Jones abandoned his low-profile approach. He decided to release his article earlier and more visibly by agreeing to its mid-February publication in a prominent defense magazine, *Armed Forces Journal*.

Jones also discussed his proposals with reporters on February 17. The media jumped on the story. John Chancellor provided the first coverage that evening on the *NBC Nightly News*, observing that Jones "thinks the organization of the Joint Chiefs is cumbersome [and] in urgent need of modernization—too much interservice rivalry."[20]

The next morning, all major newspapers carried articles on Jones's views. The *Washington Post*, under the headline "Chairman Asks Major Changes in Joint Chiefs," characterized Jones's action as "an unprecedented call for major reform of his own organization." "Fierce opposition to the plan is likely," the *Wall Street Journal* predicted. "The individual military services aren't likely to want to give up any of their influence." The *Journal* also saw prospects for resistance on Capitol Hill: "Some members of Congress may oppose the plan, arguing that investing such authority in one individual could lead to a single, all-powerful military command."[21]

Over the next two weeks, newspapers continued reporting on Jones's proposals, and a dozen or so favorable editorials appeared. The *New York Times* covered the issue most frequently and extensively. On February 25, it noted the unusual nature of the chairman's effort: "Rarely have military officers, bred in the tradition of keeping their own counsel except when asked by properly constituted civilian authority, undertaken so public a campaign for change." A *Times* article on March 1 commented prophetically: "In the Pentagon and in civilian circles studying the military establishment it is assumed that General Jones has opened a controversy that will continue for years before something is done."[22]

Believing that media attention to Jones's criticisms might erode the public consensus for the defense buildup, Weinberger alerted Reagan. In his February 26 weekly report, the secretary summarized Jones's criticisms and proposals and offered his assessment: "While little is new in the proposal, it is receiving emphasis at a much higher level than before. Past blue ribbon panels have made similar recommendations, and while most agree that change is overdue, it has been slow in coming. Many of these changes could be made without new legislation. A few, including strengthening the role of the chairman, require legislative change and the specifics are still being discussed."[23]

In closing, Weinberger concluded: "General Jones has not yet submitted to me a formal recommendation for change. When he does, I will provide you with an assessment of its value and a recommendation regarding the administration's stance." This closing seemed disingenuous. Jones could not submit a formal proposal without unanimous JCS support. In addition, Jones's plea to Congress meant that he had given up working the issue with Weinberger.[24]

Although his report had a favorable tone, Weinberger remained noncommittal. To avoid connection with Jones's ideas, he struck from a draft of his memorandum a phrase that said Jones's article had been "previously reviewed by me and White House staff members."[25] Weinberger did not hint that he had misgivings about Jones's campaign and feared its consequences for the administration's defense agenda.

Significantly increasing the defense budget dominated the administration's defense efforts. Weinberger had made that task a personal crusade. In fulfilling the mandate from the 1980 election, Reagan initially asked Congress to add $6.8 billion to Carter's fiscal year (FY) 1981 budget. The new president then proposed a $26.5 billion increase for the following fiscal year. Congress complied with both requests, reducing them by less than 1 percent. The budget proposal for FY 1983—the one that Weinberger and Jones had just presented to the HASC— would jump spending by another $37.6 billion to $259.8 billion.

Determined to continue this growth rate, Weinberger feared that Jones's reform agenda would slow momentum.[26] However, before the secretary openly opposed reform, he apparently wanted to see if the president expressed an interest.

When Jones's recommendations became public, I was a senior SASC staff member. Having spent ten years as a "whiz kid" systems analyst in OSD, I was acquainted with the problems Jones had identified. My four years on the SASC staff convinced me that the majority of members would reject the general's recommendations. Many members had strong ties to the services—especially the navy and Marine Corps—and were certain to support the predominantly antireform views of their uniformed friends.

Although I had to project how most senators would react to the message, I knew how they felt about the messenger. The committee was not enamored with Jones. Many members associated him with what they viewed as the failed defense policies of the Carter administration. Fifteen months earlier, in the weeks following Reagan's election in November, 1980, Republican SASC members discussed with the new administration whether the president should replace Jones. The rationale for removing the chairman centered on his support for ratification of the Strategic Arms Limitation Talks (SALT) II agreement and Panama Canal treaty and his failure while air force chief of staff to lead a fight against Carter's cancellation of the B-1 bomber.

Reagan's Pentagon transition team leaked word of Jones's impending ouster to the *Washington Star,* which declared, "REAGAN TO DISMISS GEN. JONES" in a two-inch headline across its front page on December 19. The subtitle read, "Wants Own Chairman of the Joint Chiefs." The article reported the conservatives' claim that Jones "was little more than a rubber stamp for President Carter's defense policies." In response to charges that firing the chairman would politicize the position, Reagan aides "contend that Jones himself 'politicized' the office by being a willing lobbyist for and defender of the Carter White House."[27]

At the time, Jones was visiting Israel on an official trip. The general's Pentagon office called his room in the King David Hotel, overlooking the old walled city of Jerusalem. "Chairman, we hate to tell you the bad news," said a staff officer, "but the *Washington Star* headline right across the top of the front page— the whole headline—says President-elect Reagan is going to dismiss you."[28]

"Where better to be when you're crucified than in Jerusalem," Jones responded.

The general told his spokesman to say, "While General Jones serves at the pleasure of the president, he intends to finish his term and will not resign voluntarily." If Reagan wanted the general out, he would have to take the unprecedented step of firing him.

The incumbent defense secretary, Democrat Harold Brown, and a predecessor, Republican James R. Schlesinger, blasted the idea of firing Jones. Contrary to views expressed by Reagan aides, both were convinced that such a move would politicize the top military post. "What concerns me here is that what may be at issue is a discharge for loyalty to civilian authority, for living by the rules," Brown said. "If that's done, it would be sending the wrong message to all military officers . . . that they have to anticipate the future political point of view and be loyal to that rather than subordinate to civilian superiors."[29]

In an article appearing on the *Washington Post*'s editorial page, Schlesinger observed: "The charge against General David Jones was rather novel—not dereliction of duty but fulfillment of duty to his civilian superiors. Jones apparently had been *insufficiently insubordinate* to his commander in chief." The commentary put the incoming administration on the defensive and forced it to reconsider the plan to fire Jones.[30] Finally, on February 10, Secretary Weinberger announced that President Reagan had decided to keep Jones until his term ended sixteen months later. If the president and secretary could have, they would have selected someone else. Years later, Weinberger continued to refer to Jones as the "holdover" chairman.[31]

Knowing that others were uneasy with him was not a new feeling for Jones. Throughout his career he had made the military bureaucracy anxious with his penchant for fixing problems. Not only were colleagues annoyed by Jones's rock-the-boat style, they also had trouble anticipating his next move. He perplexed Gen. Edward C. "Shy" Meyer, the army chief of staff when Jones was JCS chairman: "He's a very complex individual. It's hard to figure out sometime just what he has in mind."[32] Jones's private nature, independence, and nontraditional attitudes complicated efforts to decipher him.

Despite the lack of a college degree, Jones was well educated and well read. He also exhibited superb analytical skills. The first time I heard Jones's name was in connection with his bent for first-rate analysis. In the summer of 1974, after Jones's appointment as air force chief of staff, my boss, the assistant secretary of defense for program analysis and evaluation, met with the general. Afterward, the assistant secretary reported to his staff: "Jones is a breath of fresh air. He takes an analytical approach to issues. He's really a forward thinker." Jones earned "a reputation as one of the new breed in the military hierarchy" as "an administrator, a planner, a shrewd bureaucratic manager more intent on planning budgets than manning weapons."[33]

Jones's quiet, humble, even-keeled personality and wry sense of humor belied his drive to make improvements. In contrast to the military's conservative tradition, Jones welcomed change. His insights into the ills of complex systems and organizations enabled him to develop a vision for change. Some believed Jones was selected to serve as chairman mainly for "the problem-solving managerial talent that he had demonstrated . . . as head of the Air Force and prior to that as commander in chief of the U.S. Air Forces in Europe."[34] As air force chief of staff, he substantially reduced headquarters staffs by reorganizing commands. In Europe, Jones created a small operational and planning headquarters that integrated allied air forces into a cohesive organization.

Jones pressed his staff to match his commitment to making improvements. An air force general said, "I've never seen him slam a desk or shout at anybody. But at the same time, he is exasperated with people about half the time. It's hard to work for him if you're mediocre. He demands that everybody be as good as he is—and that's pretty tough."

When Jones encountered roadblocks in the JCS arena, he worked outside normal channels or convened informal groups. The marine commandant, Gen. Robert H. Barrow, complained that Jones "tends to be secretive and ad hoc."[35] Jones's improvisations evoked stronger feelings from other senior officers. One labeled him "a two-faced son-of-a-bitch." Another described Jones as "the most manipulative bastard, cynical, self-aggrandizing man I've ever met."[36]

Given the frequent criticism, Jones needed a sense of humor, and he reportedly had a good one. *Time* reported a well-known story during Jones's service as air force chief: "When a USAF airperson won a nude beauty contest in Florida last year, some officials nervously brought the matter to Jones' attention during a staff conference. After a report on the incident was read, there was a moment of silence. Jones settled the question by observing, 'Well, at least she wasn't in uniform.'"[37]

The Carter administration was not an easy one in which to serve as JCS chairman. Defense experts, including many officers, repeatedly disagreed with the president's policies. Jones battled within the administration, but much to the consternation of colleagues, he did not disagree with the president in public. Carter's decision to cancel the B-1 bomber exemplified Jones's approach. "There was absolutely no ambiguity about where Jones stood," an official said about the general's support for the B-1. "But when the decision was made, he decided to fully support the commander-in-chief and not be party to a civilian-military effort to overturn the decision in Congress."[38]

Time titled its article on Jones's selection to serve as chairman "Team Player for the Joint Chiefs."[39] Jones agreed with that description, adding, "That is the best way to get things done and to have influence within the administration."[40] Jones adhered to his team-player philosophy throughout the troubled years under Carter and during his initial reform efforts. But Jones's inability to fix joint system defects caused him to do something he had never done before. He broke ranks. The general had always saluted when superiors made decisions he did not favor. But not this time. This cause was too important to the nation's security and the military's professionalization. The general, who had been a maverick inside and a team player outside, now became a maverick outside.

Although Jones's call for reform came during his last year as chairman, he was convinced of the need much earlier. For years, he had believed the joint chiefs would reform themselves. Eventually, he concurred with Rear Adm. Alfred Thayer Mahan's conviction that no service could agree to give up sovereignty, but would have to have reorganization forced upon it from outside.[41]

Jones's concerns about the JCS dated back to 1955 and his assignment as an aide to Gen. Curtis E. LeMay, then four-star commander of the Strategic Air Command (SAC).[42] By that tour's beginning, Jones had served in uniform for thirteen years. After graduating from high school in 1939, he attended the University of North Dakota and Minot State College until his enlistment in the Army Air Forces in 1942. Jones never formally completed his college education.

LeMay—the model for Gen. "Buck" Turgidson in the 1964 movie *Dr. Strangelove*—provided Jones a different, but valuable education. At a young age, Jones learned about the Byzantine workings of the military bureaucracy. LeMay, whom Jones refers to as "my mentor,"[43] told his lieutenant colonel aide, "Your first job is to learn, and second is to serve, and don't mix up your priorities." The general ensured that Jones attended all high-level meetings and reviewed key Washington correspondence.[44]

Two years after leaving SAC, Jones attended the National War College, where classmates, whose Pentagon tours had made them cynics and skeptics, told tales about the convoluted JCS processes. After the war college, Jones became part of the Pentagon bureaucracy. His Air Staff job included being "the huckster for the B-70 bomber," the program that eventually produced the B-1. When Defense Secretary McNamara opposed the program, Air Force Chief of Staff General LeMay, Jones's old boss, sought the support of the other chiefs.

Lieutenant General David A. Burchinal, air force deputy chief of staff for operations, told Jones, "We need a thick study on the need for the B-70."

"How thick?" Jones asked.

"The Washington phone book."

Jones understood that LeMay and Burchinal wanted a big study that they could wave around. He and a colleague spent all night just putting papers together. "In case somebody asked for the study, it had to say something about the B-70, but really it was nothing but a collection of papers that we put circular binders on."

Jones attended the Tank session "when LeMay and Burchinal waved the books." Watching them claim without challenge that those books proved the need for the B-70, Jones thought, This is a charade. He was further dismayed when the other joint chiefs, caught between LeMay and McNamara, "waffled their way out of that fight."

In 1969, during a seven-month tour in Vietnam, where Jones served initially as the Seventh Air Force's deputy chief of staff for operations and later as its vice commander, he observed rampant service parochialism in action. It produced "at least six different air wars: Navy in the north, Air Force in the north, strategic one, Air Force in the south, Vietnamese, and Army helicopters."

While commanding the Second Air Force in Louisiana in 1970, Jones saw why the joint system remained unreformed. When President Nixon's Blue Ribbon Defense Panel submitted its report, the air force asked Jones to come to Washington to rebut the joint system part of the report and argue that it should not be strengthened. Jones told Air Force Chief of Staff Gen. John D. Ryan "that I felt the joint system ought to be strengthened, and he said, 'You may be right, but this is not the way to do it.'" Jones followed orders. Given the emotion surrounding this subject, he knew that he couldn't change the chief's mind.

In 1971, Jones assumed command of U.S. Air Forces Europe, a component of the U.S. European Command. During that three-year tour, he observed the power of the services and the weakness of the unified command. "I had three bosses: American unified commander, NATO regional commander, and Air Force chief. The chief had the greatest influence on me because he assigned my people, gave them jobs, and had the money."

In 1974, Secretary Schlesinger selected Jones to serve as air force chief of staff. Post-Vietnam problems beset his service, and Jones focused his attention on correcting them. Of his JCS responsibilities, he confessed: "It bored me a great deal to go down there to the Tank, to sit there. I was a good soldier, and I would go when I was in town. So, I attended as well as anybody and participated as well as others, but my heart wasn't in it."

In 1978, President Carter nominated Jones to serve as JCS chairman. He had already acted as chairman for four months because his predecessor, Gen. George S. Brown, also an air force officer, was dying of cancer. However, before the president could appoint Jones to the top job, the Senate had to advise and consent to his appointment. During Jones's nomination hearing in May, 1978, Sen. Sam Nunn, a bright, young Democrat from Georgia, questioned him on JCS performance. The senator's perceptiveness impressed the general.[45]

Nunn told the nominee, "Since I have been here I have never felt that the Joint Chiefs function very well . . . Basically they are service heads who come together to ratify the decisions of the individual services and that very seldom do the Joint Chiefs take positions that would differ with one of the individual services. I will admit my view is not shared by all and probably not by you."[46]

Nunn asked Jones if he had "any plans for the operation of the Joint Chiefs of Staff which would differ from the current operations."

Jones sympathized with Nunn's statement, but he responded carefully on this explosive subject: "First, I recognize there is a conflict of interest being a service chief and a member of the Joint Chiefs of Staff. However, I have found it invaluable to have the members of the Joint Chiefs, except for the chairman, to be service chiefs, because you really stay up to date on what is going on . . . on balance there are more pluses than minuses."

The general added, "I plan to work with my colleagues to do what we can to improve the functions of the Joint Chiefs of Staff," although he believed "on many of these issues affecting national security, that the chiefs rise above their own service interests."

Nunn replied skeptically to the general's "theoretical concept" that the JCS "rise above service rivalry . . . I don't think it has ever been that way. I am not saying it is worse now. I don't think it is. I don't think it ever will be that way."

Nunn urged Jones "to address those issues and to the extent that it needs any kind of legislative change I would hope you would keep us informed of it, because I have a great deal of faith in you. Yet as an institution, I must frankly say I don't have a whole lot of faith in the Joint Chiefs, I do as individuals, but not as an institution."

Although Jones intended to alter the way the JCS operated, he underestimated the resistance he would encounter. The new chairman found that the chiefs wanted more influence, especially with the president on budget issues, but they were not prepared to lessen their own independence as the price for greater corporate influence. He proposed ideas to get each chief away from his single-service perspective. "What about having an operations deputy from another service and a half dozen officers from the joint system work joint issues for you and prepare you for joint meetings?" Unwilling to diminish their roles as service spokesmen, the chiefs were not interested. After repeated rejection of his proposals, Jones began to think that outside authority would have to mandate meaningful change.[47]

On April 25, 1980, a military raid to rescue fifty-three Americans held captive in Iran failed. Code-named Operation Eagle Claw,[48] the mission was aborted when only six of eight helicopters arrived at the rendezvous point in Iran, labeled "Desert One," and one of those was broken. In departing, a helicopter collided with a C-130 transport plane. Five airmen and three marines died in the explosion, which destroyed both aircraft. The other five helicopters were abandoned with valuable secret documents, weapons, and communications gear on board.

The Pentagon commissioned two reports on the shocking failure: one by the Joint Staff and the other by a Special Operations Review Group formed expressly for the inquiry. Admiral James L. Holloway, a former CNO, headed the review group of six senior officers. The group's charter—directing it to make no

6. The remains of a burned-out U.S. helicopeter lie in front of an
abandoned chopper at Desert One in Iran.
(Associated Press photo.)

mention of the president, White House, defense secretary, or JCS—limited it to
"tactical and technical matters."[49] The Joint Staff similarly focused on operational
and material deficiencies, such as "insufficient tactical and airborne satellite radio capability."[50] Although both reports provided insightful analyses, neither
addressed the overarching organizational problems that doomed the operation.

The complexity of the Iranian rescue mission would have challenged a well-
organized military proficient in both joint and special operations.[51] The
Pentagon's unpreparedness was so immense that even six months of organizing, planning, and training could not overcome institutional deficiencies. Ten
years after a similar raid into North Vietnam had failed to rescue American
prisoners of war from a prison on the outskirts of Hanoi—a raid that also took
six months to organize—DoD still did not have a joint organization capable of
carrying out the mission.[52]

The JCS and the mission commander, Maj. Gen. James B. Vaught, USA,
"had to start, literally, from the beginning to establish a joint task force, create
an organization, provide a staff, develop a plan, select the units, and train the
force before the first mission capability could be attained."[53] Absence of joint
doctrine and procedures and lack of cross-service experience by task force
officers and units compounded the difficulty of these ad hoc tasks. Even Vaught,
a top-flight, combat-tested Ranger, had no exposure to multiservice missions.[54]
Failure to train task force elements together further undermined unity of effort.

Each element trained under its own commander using its parent service's procedures.[55]

The Joint Staff did not have a "staff planning element with expertise on missions of this type,"[56] and all five joint chiefs lacked special operations experience.[57] A planning staff was created, but it was an ad hoc, inexperienced group with unclear lines of authority and responsibility. The resulting structure was "so confused and bureaucratic as to make communications among its members difficult, and, in some cases, almost impossible."[58]

An existing JCS contingency plan was rejected "as not being useful."[59] In developing a new plan, the inexperienced Joint Staff planning element became "totally preoccupied with the fear that the operation might be compromised before the raid."[60] According to Jones, the staff knew that "if the Iranians had fifteen-minutes of warning, they could disperse the hostages."[61] Obsessed by operational security, the staff overcompensated: excessive compartmentalization of the plan—restricting each participant's knowledge to his or her part—and bypassing normal reviews fragmented preparation and allowed conceptual flaws to go undiscovered.[62]

In the post-Vietnam drawdown, the air force neglected its responsibility to provide long-range infiltration helicopters for special operations like the planned raid. By 1980, such air force helicopters were too few or unproven, forcing the selection of eight navy RH-53D mine countermeasures helicopters. Because the helicopters would launch for the raid from an aircraft carrier, navy pilots and marine copilots were initially designated to fly them even though they had no training and experience for the low-level, terrain-hugging flights that a clandestine, nighttime insertion would require.[63] The air force had ninety-six pilots who were qualified and experienced in such operations. The decision not to use the most capable of these pilots proved costly.

After the first rehearsal exposed serious pilot deficiencies, marines were assigned to thirteen of the pilot and copilot seats. Two navy aviators and one air force pilot filled the remaining seats. The choice was a great mistake. The marine pilots "became lost, had difficulty in navigating, and failed to reach Desert One on time and with the required number of helicopters."[64]

The chaos and confusion at Desert One epitomized the Pentagon's lack of proficiency in joint operations. The joint task force had not established command and control procedures or clear lines of authority at Desert One. In the darkness and haze of blowing sand and with the deafening roar of aircraft engines, no way existed to determine "who was in charge."[65] The on-the-scene commander, Col. James H. Kyle, USAF, spoke of "there being four commanders at the scene without visible identification, incompatible radios, and no agreed-upon plan, not even a designated location for the commander."[66] Helicopter pilots later said they "did not know or recognize the authority of those giving orders."[67]

"The whole operation deserves considerable criticism," said Jones. Years later, he identified service separateness as the principal cause for the failed raid. "I saw terrible problems in the services' efforts to work with each other. My director of operations on the Joint Staff, an army officer, knew little about the army outside his branch and nothing about the other services. No existing organization could run the operation. Everybody gave it their best, but the fact that we hadn't been ingrained in working and training together proved insurmountable."[68]

This debacle convinced Jones to seek outside help to reform the JCS. But the failed raid had gravely wounded the administration. The president and defense secretary could not muster sufficient support to take on a controversial issue. Jones determined that he would have to wait until after the presidential election. If the election produced a new administration, he would approach the incoming secretary. Alternatively, "If Carter had been reelected, Harold Brown would have been willing to take on this battle." In Brown's view, a voter mandate for a second term might create a favorable climate for a reform initiative.

On June 16, 1980, two months after the failure in the desert, Jones appeared at a SASC hearing on his nomination for a second two-year term as chairman. This time, Sen. Strom Thurmond (R–South Carolina) questioned Jones about the joint system. The general's thinking on reform tactics was evolving. Jones still envisioned the executive branch playing the central role. He did not see a major role for Capitol Hill.

When Thurmond gave Jones the chance to talk about required improvements, Jones stressed, "We need to be more joint. . . . We need to do much more in being an integrated fighting force in the days ahead." Although Jones had considerable evidence of the services' inability to operate together, he had the failed Iranian rescue mission most in mind.[69]

Referring to reports of "so much jealousy between the different services," Thurmond wanted to know if Jones was satisfied with the situation.[70]

"No; I am not satisfied," Jones responded. The general vaguely explained that DoD's organization resulted from a compromise, which "brings with it some disadvantages." He did not elaborate.

Jones was careful in articulating recommendations. Initially, he cited only one noncontroversial idea: the need "to have even greater incentives for the best people to go into joint jobs."

Thurmond wanted to know more. He wanted Jones's views on the role the services should have in operations vis-à-vis the joint system.

Noting the impact of their control of the budget, Jones replied, "The services have great influence on operations." He diplomatically suggested, "I would move toward an increased role for joint operations."

Thurmond pressed Jones for specific recommendations. The senator would not permit him to evade his questions.

"I would strengthen the role of the chairman," Jones said. Concerned that he would be accused of trying to build an empire, Jones noted that such a change would require considerable time, so this strengthened role would apply to his successor. Jones also said he thought the Joint Staff was too small. He cited the potential for an enlarged staff to help the chairman play a greater budget role. He also advocated "some increased independence for the Joint Staff from the services." Fearing that he had been too outspoken, Jones added that he was "not suggesting major surgery now. I think that in an evolutionary way we can make some improvements."

Five months later, after Ronald Reagan's election, Jones approached the secretary of defense designate about reorganizing the JCS. "Weinberger initially indicated he'd be interested in looking at my proposal," the general recalled, but "it was clear that he didn't want to be involved in a fight that, in his judgment, might sidetrack the budget buildup."[71]

When Jones pressed Weinberger, the secretary said, "If we take on this issue, they'll think we're all screwed up over here."[72]

"We *are* all screwed up," Jones answered.

Weinberger responded with "courteous silence."[73]

Jones was determined to try to reform the JCS before he retired. Without the secretary's support, the general could not see a way to gain the president's endorsement. Jones decided to look to Congress for help.[74]

Near the end of January, 1981, Jones met with and then wrote to Senator Goldwater. His letter complained that tradition "requires a 5-0 vote on every recommendation" of the JCS. "I would like for us to strengthen the role of the military and, very frankly, the role of the chairman, in order for the system to react more quickly and effectively, and for there to be less of a need for debate and compromise on every issue." Goldwater listened sympathetically but did not respond to Jones's letter.[75]

Jones's inability to gain the support of Weinberger, Reagan, or Goldwater forced him to reconsider internal means for fixing the JCS system. He decided that he needed an in-depth, objective study that could attract support across the services. The chairman's authority to hire consultants offered a promising mechanism. Normally, the top officer's only source of independent analysis was the Chairman's Staff Group—five officers who worked solely for him. He could not task the Joint Staff with a study. Only the JCS could. Even if Jones succeeded in convincing his colleagues to commission a study, institutional weaknesses would dilute the product's candor. In contrast, a group of experienced consultants could rigorously examine problems and recommend solutions. Jones also had another reason: "I didn't want Joint Chiefs reform to be a Jones crusade. The consultants broadened the reform effort."[76]

Jones knew what consultants to use. In 1978 and 1980, DoD had conducted two large mobilization exercises, Nifty Nugget and Proud Spirit. Both the JCS and OSD had used consultants to evaluate these exercises. Jones's close friend, William K. Brehm, had contributed significantly to the evaluation team's work. Jones wanted Brehm to head the JCS study.

The chairman planned that four retired officers—one from each service—who had also served as exercise evaluators, would join Brehm. This group represented a 1981 version of the Richardson Committee, which had examined postwar organizational requirements for the JCS in 1944 and 1945. The study team's officers were Gen. Walter T. "Dutch" Kerwin, a former army vice chief of staff; Gen. William V. McBride, a former air force vice chief; Gen. Samuel Jaskilka, a former marine assistant commandant; and Adm. Frederick H. "Mike" Michaelis, a former commander of the Naval Materiel Command. All four had retired in 1978, and the JCS had selected them as evaluators because of their recent active duty, respect by service leaders, and reputation for being among the most nonparochial officers.[77]

Brehm had earned the respect and admiration of many during his ten years in senior Pentagon positions. He had served in three assistant secretary positions: one in the army and two in OSD. Brehm was an expert on defense organization and understood the inherent weaknesses of the joint system. Jones also selected him because of his leadership style and reputation for honesty, selflessness, and consideration. Knowing that service parochialism, emotion, and controversy would challenge the group's unity, Jones felt that Brehm could foster trust and openness among the members of the study team.[78]

In a meeting on February 23, 1981, Jones asked Brehm—then chairman of the board of Systems Research and Applications Corporation, a consulting firm—to develop a plan for evaluating JCS organization. He had envisioned a two- to four-month study, but the group took eleven months—meeting only once or twice per month—to complete its report. When Jones received the final report in April, 1982, only two months remained until his retirement.

Close relationships among the incumbent joint chiefs seemed to favor an objective examination. Each service chief participated in a small Christian group, called the JCS Fellowship Breakfast, with Jones, Brehm, and other senior officials and officers. This group, formed by Jones and Brehm in 1974, had led to "deepened relationships, trust, and understanding." Brehm believed that the frank discussions on explosive JCS reform issues would not have been possible without these relationships.[79]

Knowing that the chairman had a right to consult with others, Jones asked for the chiefs' reactions to his study plans, but not their concurrence. According to Jones, "None objected to the study. One said it could be done in-house."[80] Reflecting Jones's position that this was his study, the team was named the Chairman's Special Study Group (CSSG). Jones and Brehm soon decided to add another army officer, Lt. Gen. Charles A. Corcoran, to the group. Corcoran had retired in 1973 after a tour as chief of staff of the Pacific Command.

Brehm said his group "realized that change—were it to mean anything—would have to be substantial and would be seen by many as painful. We all knew that previous attempts at change had been largely futile. Perhaps we had different degrees of passion about the need for change but we definitely shared General Jones' assessment: The joint system was broken, and it had to be fixed."[81]

"It was important that the whole team feel authorship of the report," Brehm concluded. "We needed all five of the military guys to sign up."[82] Each member would "have a major role in persuading the chiefs of the wisdom of our recommendations, once we have formulated them."[83] Brehm recalled that he and his colleagues "wanted to deliver the chiefs' support for reform."[84]

In July, the group began interviewing senior officers on the nonattribution basis needed to assure candor. Brehm scheduled sessions with the air force chief of staff, Gen. Lew Allen Jr., and the CNO, Adm. Thomas B. Hayward. The tall, bald, even-tempered Allen had earned a doctorate in physics and was highly respected as a scientist and advanced weapons specialist. The freckled, sandy-haired Hayward came from the naval aviation community. He commanded the Pacific Fleet before being selected to serve as CNO in 1978.

Both chiefs were unhappy about the JCS's role and status. Allen supported some of Jones's themes. He thought that the chiefs "must restore confidence in the [JCS] system to get the secretary of defense's and president's ear." Allen recommended that the "chairman should act as 'senior military adviser'" and be "properly supported" in that role. Noting the inherent conflict of interest, Allen argued, "The service chiefs should not try to provide joint advice on resource allocation issues."[85]

Hayward sailed off in a different direction. He was "very concerned about the lack of direct input to the president." He argued that the "members of the JCS *should* be able to meet with the president, say, quarterly." If this could be arranged, "Then word would get around and others in the system would pay attention to the JCS views. Joint Staff papers would then be listened to, and undoubtedly would improve since there would be an interested audience." He added that another result would be "better people" being assigned to the Joint Staff.[86]

A skeptic would have thought the admiral had confused form with substance. If the JCS continued to provide only watered-down advice, what difference would it make how often they went to the White House?

Unknown to the study group, six months earlier, Hayward had circulated to the other joint chiefs a sixteen-page "SECRET–EYES ONLY" memorandum expressing "fairly frank" views on "improving the effectiveness of the Joint Chiefs of Staff."[87] Early navy staff work had also addressed JCS credibility. One paper was titled "How to Reestablish the JCS as a Creditable Agency."[88]

Hayward lamented the "steady erosion of JCS authority . . . since the days of World War II when the chiefs dealt directly with the president on matters of grand strategy and military policy." "In recent years," Hayward's memorandum noted, the JCS "frequently have lagged events; waited for advice to be solicited, or for others to formulate the key issues." The military advisers also diminished their influence by "reluctance to challenge the president's premises, to disagree with his policies, or to bring him bad news." The process of advising the president, Hayward added, was "complicated by strong secretaries of defense" who "have impeded a free flow of communication between the chiefs and the president."[89]

The admiral also criticized staff support, but devoted only one sentence to this problem: "The JCS's effectiveness is diluted by an overgrown staff and cumbersome staff process which, on policy issues, is often incapable of timely action, and tends toward verbose, lowest-common-denominator products which lack imagination and impact."

Hayward suggested that three factors would determine JCS effectiveness: access to the president and Congress, assertiveness in presenting views, and the quality and timeliness of those views. He assigned the lowest priority to the third factor, the one that reformers viewed as the principal source of the JCS's diminished influence.

In the CSSG's early interviews, nearly all senior officers characterized the joint system as flawed. Admiral Thomas H. Moorer, JCS chairman in the early 1970s registered one notable contrary view: "The chiefs function very well. . . . There is nothing wrong with the system. . . . No drastic changes are necessary. . . . Problems are not caused by poor organization. They are with us and always will be. . . . You will never solve the problem of getting topnotch people on the Joint Staff."[90]

Despite Moorer's position, evidence of the need for reform began to mount. On July 21, Brehm wrote to Jones: "It is clear that frustration levels are high among the principals. It's a sad commentary indeed. You are absolutely right about the need for change, and the urgency."[91]

The next day, the group interviewed Marine Commandant Barrow, a tall, soft-spoken Louisianan. Labeling JCS duties as his "most frustrating" ones, Barrow reported, "I don't look forward to Joint Chiefs meetings. . . . The agenda is often trivial."[92]

Barrow told the group that the organization's "basic concept is flawed." The commandant criticized the tendency toward the "lowest common denominator." He revealed, "Two members of the Joint Chiefs of Staff are violently opposed to split papers" and "constantly seek agreement to avoid" split votes. Of the top post, Barrow said, "I wouldn't have the chairman's job."

On October 7, the group saw General Meyer. The army chief was convinced that the joint system needed dramatic changes. The JCS, he exclaimed, "can't carry out our constitutional responsibilities. Even with a congruence of views now [in the new administration], we can't get military advice to have an impact." Years earlier, while serving as deputy chief of staff for operations, Meyer was convinced that "the system falls apart as soon as a crisis occurs."[93] Meyer wanted to focus each service chief on running his service, not providing military advice. He proposed an advisory group "made up of the chairman and four 'retiring' four-star officers." By retiring, Meyer meant that they would not be competing for a follow-on job, such as chief or chairman, increasing the likelihood of obtaining more independent, better advice. "I think the president and defense secretary would use [such] advice if they could get it," he concluded.

Brehm's group also gathered testimony on JCS ills from the often powerless four-star warfighting commanders. General Donn A. Starry, the army officer heading the U.S. Readiness Command, expressed the strongest views: "It is regrettable but true that a rational and relevant military voice has not spoken, and but infrequently been sought, in Washington since the Bay of Pigs. For understandable reasons, no one trusts advice provided by military folk. Military strategy in today's operational world is bankrupt."[94]

Starry also blasted the JCS: "So long as the Joint Chiefs and their organization continue to split along service lines and exhibit gross service parochialism, their service to the nation is of limited value. In fact, for what the organization costs us, and for what it produces, it probably should be done away with."

By early December, the CSSG had hammered out preliminary findings and alternatives. These indicted the existing system and hinted at dramatic changes. As the group's views became known, service politics would threaten, but not break, this consensus.

The group confirmed what Jones already knew: the JCS had little credibility or effect. "Military advice is seldom sought and seldom heeded." Causes included the service chiefs' "conflict of interest" and an institutionally weak chairman. Moreover, Joint Staff "procedures inhibit independence and substance of joint papers." The group also cited poor management of joint officers as a major problem.[95]

The group concluded that the department "should retain the JCS concept," but modernize its organization, policies, and procedures. Its preliminary recommendations began to outline four powerful ideas. The first proposed a strengthened chairman serving as senior military adviser and possibly given authority to make decisions when service interests pervaded an issue.

The second idea hinted at establishing a deputy chairman. Although the CSSG did not explicitly include this proposal, it did argue for eliminating the practice of having service chiefs serve as acting chairman. The group also suggested that lack of a deputy weakened the chairman and created continuity problems.

The third idea envisioned a joint officer management system. The group proposed a joint duty specialty for officers, improved preparation for joint assignments, continuity in joint positions, and rewards for joint duty.

The CSSG's last idea proposed increasing Joint Staff independence by reducing or eliminating the need for unanimous agreement and lessening service involvement in the joint process. Joint Staff officers would author joint papers, with the services providing only information and advice. The practice of each service staff analyzing every joint issue would end as well.

Armed with these findings and recommendations, Brehm and the group's appropriate service member met with each service chief. Generals Allen and Barrow were supportive, but Allen indicated that he "tends to oppose the deputy chairman idea."[96] Barrow "was not sure about establishing four Service Chief Support Groups" in the Joint Staff to prepare each chief on joint issues.[97] Brehm reported to Jones, "I wouldn't want to predict at this point where they will come down on individual propositions, but there is certainly a willingness to make change of some kind." Brehm added, "On one specific, Bob Barrow said emphatically that he would endorse the concept of a deputy chairman."[98]

On December 23, Brehm and General Kerwin met with Gen. Shy Meyer and his vice chief, Gen. John W. Vessey Jr. Although agreeing that the recommendations were "a move in the right direction," Meyer complained that the proposals were "not a bold enough step." He advised the study group to "say what is needed, not deal with the art of the possible." Brehm hoped that Meyer would eventually back the group's proposals as a start toward his more ambitious scheme.[99]

The CNO torpedoed prospects for consensus among the chiefs in a meeting with Brehm and Michaelis on December 28. Hayward questioned the utility of the group's work. He found problems with the idea of a deputy chairman and expressed navy opposition to a career path for joint officers, citing a shortage of naval personnel.[100] Challenging a fundamental conclusion, Hayward did not agree that JCS papers represented the lowest level of concurrence, or if they did, he was not aware of papers being faulted because of it. The admiral's earlier memorandum had described Joint Staff papers as tending "toward verbose, lowest-common-denominator products which lack imagination and impact," but none of Brehm's team knew of that opinion.[101]

Despite their conflicting reactions, Brehm believed he "could somehow convince the chiefs to rally around our basic proposals." Brehm later explained: "I knew the men well; I knew them to be thoughtful; I knew them to be interested in good government; and I knew them to be frustrated with the traditional ways of doing things in the joint arena. Naturally, I felt that the logic of what we were suggesting was compelling, if not overwhelming." But in hindsight, Brehm "failed to take into account the influence others would have upon them—others who did not share our convictions."[102]

Powerful Navy Secretary John Lehman disagreed vehemently with Jones and the CSSG. Behind the scenes, unknown to Hayward and Barrow, Lehman had been tracking the group's work. His watchdog was a retired marine: Brig. Gen. J. D. "Don" Hittle, who had opposed unification in the 1940s and 1950s and had helped convince key congressmen to weaken the unifying provisions of the National Security Act of 1947. Hittle later served as assistant to the secretary of defense for legislative affairs, SASC special counsel, and navy assistant secretary for manpower and reserve affairs. Defense experts knew Hittle as a shrewd practitioner of power politics on Capitol Hill and in the Pentagon.

On September 10, 1981, Hittle warned Lehman "that the pressure for defense reorganization is building up *and* that it is coordinated." A *Washington Post* article on the defense budget by retired army general Maxwell D. Taylor alarmed Hittle. He claimed that Taylor's "real targets, of course, are naval aviation and the Marine Corps. This is, in essence, the old Army-Air Force attack on our balanced seapower." In Hittle's view, the fact that Tom Wicker's *New York Times* column "applauded Taylor's views" should dispel "any doubts that the Taylor article was an isolated unorchestrated opinion."[103]

A subsequent Hittle memorandum to Lehman, marked "VERY PERSONAL," focused on the CSSG, warning: "This whole operation is loaded with potential trouble for the Navy and Marine Corps, yet it is being handled, and viewed by some, in a too casual manner." Without naming names, Hittle's comments targeted Hayward and Barrow. Hittle "strongly recommended at the earliest opportunity" that Lehman tell Hayward and Barrow to ensure that they saw the report before any action was taken, request that any reform affecting Lehman's authority be referred to him, and object to proposals that would be contrary to the National Security Act of 1947.[104]

Another Hittle "PERSONAL FOR" memorandum advised Lehman that the "CNO should be fully apprised of your concern over the Jones-Brehm project." The retired general also noted the Marine Corps had "a *small* high-powered group taking preliminary steps . . . in the event the Jones-Brehm caper comes to a boil."[105]

On December 17, Hittle again urged Lehman to instruct Hayward and Barrow on reorganization. Notes on the memorandum indicated a decision to put this issue on the agenda of Lehman's next weekly sessions with the CNO and commandant. A note reading "done during commandant/secretary of the Navy meeting" dated January 4 indicated that Barrow had received his instructions.[106]

"Secretary Lehman and I had compatible views on Joint Chiefs reform," Hayward later recalled. "We spoke a number of times on this issue. Secretary Lehman did not give me any instructions regarding the matter, for to do so would have been highly improper and he knew that." Hayward viewed the secretary's authority as limited: "The secretary can give the service chief instructions on a few matters, but not across the board and certainly not of this kind."[107]

The Brehm group's meetings with the service chiefs in December, 1981, represented the high-water mark for JCS support of reform. The CSSG had almost succeeded in convincing the service chiefs to support reorganization. Three chiefs joined Jones in favoring reform, although Meyer's insistence on more far-reaching reforms fractured this solidarity. Only Hayward remained outside the reform camp. Soon, however, Barrow—possibly under pressure from Lehman and marine antireformers—would abruptly abandon his proreform stance.

Having spent eight years as a member of the JCS, Jones saw more easily than Brehm the lurking gridlock. After the CSSG briefed him on December 30 on the chiefs' adverse reactions, the chairman began considering a change in course: most likely, he would have to abandon his hopes for internal agreement.[108]

7. Members of the JCS meet in the Pentagon, November, 1979. *Left to right:* Gen. Edward "Shy" Meyer, army chief of staff; Gen. Lew Allen, air force chief of staff; Adm. Tom Hayward, chief of naval operations; Gen. Bob Barrow, marine commandant; and Gen. David Jones, chairman. (DoD photo.)

Despite the chiefs' comments, the CSSG did not yield on any recommendation. Its final report retained each preliminary proposal and added others. Explicitly addressing a previously hinted idea, the group recommended a four-star vice or deputy chairman. It also added a new recommendation to increase unified command involvement in Joint Staff activities.[109]

Reaching agreement, Brehm said, "was not a problem for anybody except Mike Michaelis. He was getting the same kind of abuse, I suspect, at night on the telephone that the CNO was getting."[110]

Hayward denied being pressured by anybody, especially former naval officers. "I received *no pressure* from any of the retired community." He didn't need to be: "I was strongly opposed to the concept of the reform package."[111]

By late January, Jones was "convinced that if we were going to make fundamental change, there would have to be outside pressure. It would have to come from Congress."[112] Armed with a near-final CSSG report, Jones set his sights on taking these ideas to Congress at an early opportunity. Being close to retirement made him more comfortable with this approach because it would not "look like empire building and self-aggrandizement."[113]

The chairman announced his plans to the CSSG at a meeting on January 27: "On the broader issues, I am going to the Hill next week." There, he said, he would "drop hints about the work going on." Jones further informed the group, "An article will be published soon also, to help build external support."[114]

The CSSG report formed the basis of Jones's testimony to the HASC on February 3 and his magazine article. His testimony addressed five recommendations, omitting only the proposal for a vice chairman—an idea he endorsed in his article.

On April 9, Brehm submitted the group's seventy-three-page report, *The Organization and Functions of the JCS*, which became known simply as the "Brehm Report." Jones decided not to ask the JCS to address it. "The opposition was such that an effort to gain approval through the formal staffing process would have been counterproductive."[115]

Like all initial efforts on complex subjects, the CSSG's work would be improved upon over the next five years. Nevertheless, the Brehm Report became the intellectual wellspring for key concepts: chairman as principal military adviser, vice chairman, joint specialty officer, and independent Joint Staff.

Rarely did the military brotherhood criticize a senior officer on Capitol Hill. But Jones's critics abandoned this tradition in their determination to crush his reform campaign. Following Jones's testimony on February 3, Pentagon reform opponents reacted fiercely to what they viewed as turncoat behavior. They made efforts to discredit him, claiming, "General Jones—not organization defects—is to blame for the flawed policies and failed operations of recent years." As a Senate staff member, I heard a constant drumbeat of such attacks.

Jones had given priority to the national interest and knowingly paid an enormous price for breaking ranks. Although his critics showed their delight at his approaching retirement, their denunciations had no impact on him. Having drawn attention to crippling deficiencies and offered powerful fixes, Jones saw his forty-year career ending on a high note. He viewed his call for JCS reform as his most significant contribution to the nation's security.[116]

Jones had done his duty. Now, it was up to Congress.

CHAPTER 3

The House Fires the First Shot

A journey of a thousand miles

must begin with a single step.

—Lao-tzu, *The Way of Lao-Tzu*

W hen General Jones delivered his "bolt out of the blue" call for JCS reform, one House Armed Services Committee staffer in the audience,
Archie D. Barrett, knew exactly what the general was talking about. Barrett
had joined the HASC staff nine months earlier following his retirement as an
air force colonel. Although he was still learning the ropes on Capitol Hill, Barrett
knew defense organization: He had devoted the last four years of his twenty-
four-year career to that complex subject.[1]

Jones's bold call for reform, especially with Weinberger seated beside him,
stunned Barrett. The retired colonel knew the Pentagon's aversion to reorganization. He wondered how much Jones had told Weinberger about his plans.
Barrett watched the secretary for a clue to his attitude. As usual, Weinberger's
face remained inscrutable. Looking around the dais at the committee members, Barrett wondered if any of them truly comprehended what General Jones
was saying. Most of them, he knew, were unfamiliar with the inner workings
of the Department of Defense, especially its arcane organization issues. Such
matters seldom involved Capitol Hill. Sensing that no one else had grasped the
significance of Jones's remarks, Barrett let out a sigh: Well, I do.

As the hearing moved into the question period, Barrett waited anxiously
to see the reaction by his boss, Cong. Richard C. White (D-Texas), Investigations Subcommittee chairman. He would be key to any legislative response.

To Barrett's dismay, White's questions indicated he had no interest in Jones's testimony.

Back in his office mulling over the hearing, Barrett concluded: This is big stuff. Our subcommittee has to do something. We have jurisdiction here. White would have little incentive to take on this emotional, complex issue. The nine-term congressman had already announced he would retire when the session ended in eleven months. The subcommittee's agenda was full. Adding another major issue would tax members and staff. Moreover, the members' noticeable disinterest in Jones's testimony would add to White's reluctance.

Jones had hoped his ideas would catch hold with someone on the HASC, but he was thinking of a congressman, not a staffer. Nevertheless, his ideas would not have caught hold at all had it not been for Barrett. With his background in organization and his staff position on the subcommittee having jurisdiction, Barrett was ideally placed to respond to Jones's call for reform.

Arch Barrett graduated from West Point in 1957 and spent the first twenty years of his career in purely air force assignments. The Texas native copiloted B-47 bombers in the Strategic Air Command. His high class standing at the Point—seventh out of 546 classmates—led to a teaching assignment in the Air Force Academy's Political Science Department. To prepare, he entered the doctoral program in political economy and government at Harvard University, where he wrote his dissertation on House voting. Years earlier, knowing Barrett's interest in politics, fellow cadets wrote in the West Point yearbook that he "would make a capable senator from Texas."[2]

Before completing his teaching tour, Barrett reported for F-4 fighter training en route to Southeast Asia. He flew the F-4 in Vietnam in 1968 and 1969, earning the Distinguished Flying Cross. After completing his academy tour, Barrett served back-to-back assignments in Europe. His next stop was the Pentagon, where his work for the deputy chief of staff for plans and operations on the Air Staff exposed him to the inner workings of bureaucracies and taught him how poor organization hinders good leaders.

In response to President Carter's campaign promise to reorganize the federal government, the Pentagon initiated the Defense Organization Study. When OSD needed an officer to serve on the small secretariat overseeing the study, the air force nominated Barrett. Led by prominent outsiders, the study group examined the Pentagon's structural deficiencies and proposed far-reaching reforms. When the comprehensive study appeared headed for the dustbin, Barrett decided to write a book to preserve the research and further develop promising proposals.

Barrett next secured an assignment as a senior research fellow at the National Defense University (NDU), the Pentagon's premier academic institution, where he wrote *Reappraising Defense Organization*, a 325-page examination of problems, including ones later raised in Jones's testimony. Upon its release in

8. Major Arch Barrett next to his F-4 aircraft in Vietnam, July, 1969.
(U.S. Air Force photo.)

1983, *Armed Forces Journal* commented, "Barrett's study is not only far better written, but is much more succinct and better organized than most of the 1977–80 DoD-funded reorganization studies."[3]

After completing his book, Barrett retired from the air force and looked for work on Capitol Hill. He described as "purely coincidence" his arrival on the HASC Investigations Subcommittee staff shortly before JCS reorganization became an issue. Barrett's West Point classmate, William H. L. "Moon" Mullins, then General Dynamics's director of legislative affairs, had arranged an interview for Barrett with Congressman White. The Investigations Subcommittee chairman told Barrett, "You're the guy I want."

Barrett did not expect to work on Pentagon reorganization. The subcommittee had not examined organization issues for years and had no plans to raise the subject. Jones's testimony changed his expectations, however. Smart, dedicated, and ambitious, Barrett began the task of persuading White to respond to Jones's call for reform. The subcommittee's senior staff member, John Lally, supported Barrett's efforts.

"Mr. Chairman," Barrett told White, "when the top military officer says that the JCS system is fatally flawed, Congress can't sit idly by. And your subcommittee is the one that has jurisdiction. You, sir, must lead this effort."

Based solely on this argument and in the absence of any interest, expertise, or commitment, White decided to launch an inquiry. In a press release announcing the subcommittee hearings, White said, "If there is any way to improve the efficiency of the current Joint Chiefs of Staff organization, it should be instituted immediately." He also intended to complete the subcommittee's work "so that any necessary legislation may be acted upon before the adjournment of the 97th Congress."[4]

Even though White ranked as the HASC's fourth most senior Democrat, he was not the ideal member to lead this charge. "White was not highly regarded by his colleagues on the committee," said a staffer. "[I]n his general demeanor and the issues he took on that he didn't know a lot about, he could well go astray and fulfill their low estimation of him." Few members, if any, were likely to join White's assault on the powerful JCS and their numerous allies.[5]

Barrett's newness did not permit him to reassure members about White's effort. Congressmen and senators are wary of advice from new staffers. They want to see a record of proven performance before taking a public position based upon a staff member's work. Barrett had earned his impressive credentials in a different world. On Capitol Hill, the former colonel would have to gain the members' confidence the old-fashioned way: he'd have to earn it.

Lally assigned Barrett, who was well prepared intellectually to support the inquiry, the lead role. The former pilot had his book and supporting documentation to help structure the hearings. Barrett knew who had expertise on the JCS and was acquainted with many of these current and former officials. In addition to his work and academic preparations, Barrett possessed the skills, discipline, and drive to tackle the enormous challenge of Pentagon reform. Of his time at West Point, Barrett said, "I was very much a hive. I studied all the time." Cadets use the slang term "hive" to characterize a person who studies hard and excels as a result. Barrett was "well known for his academic achievements" and "always working, even after taps."[6]

In his book, Barrett reaffirmed deficiencies repeatedly cited by study groups for twenty-five years. He identified four significant problems: inability of the service-dominated joint organizations to perform their primary functions of providing advice and employing forces, weaknesses of the service secretaries, overwhelming influence of the four services, and OSD's flawed management approach, particularly neglect of its policy-making role.[7]

In considering solutions, Barrett advanced two premises. He argued that far-reaching proposals eventually attain the realm of political unreality, regardless of how logically appealing and theoretically satisfying they might be. He further postulated that affected organizations impose bounds that make some alternatives unrealistic. Convinced that opposition from the Pentagon and its allies would doom anything more than limited reorganization, he recommended only a few modest changes.[8]

Barrett explained his book's guiding precept in a letter to General Jones: "I tried to remain within the bounds of what might be politically feasible (within the Pentagon and on Capitol Hill). . . . applying that constraint caused me to rule out National Military Advisers, for example."[9]

"[Y]our politically constrained proposals do not go far enough," replied Jones. "What is needed is a preponderance of influence by the CJCS [chairman, JCS]–CINC [commander in chief of a combatant command] axis on joint issues, rather than merely some institutional influence which allows that voice to be heard among those of the services."[10]

Later, when Barrett asked Jones to write the book's introduction, the general expressed the same view: "Arch Barrett's analysis supports the need for far-reaching actions, but because he is greatly concerned with political practicality, his recommendations are very modest. Politics, after all, is the art of the possible. Nevertheless, I dare to hope that our actions may yet match our rhetoric when we proclaim that national security must be above politics—partisan, bureaucratic, sectional, or any other kind."[11]

Barrett "thought that the political boundaries for doing anything were very, very narrow—only a slight congressional window" and also felt "the secretary of defense had the authority to take care of these problems internally, and that was the only way to handle them." He "was not pushing for a great amount of change."

White accepted Barrett's assessment of reform politics and agreed that any legislation should be modest to reflect reality. Despite evidence of problems elsewhere in the Pentagon, neither White nor Barrett nor Lally considered expanding the inquiry beyond the narrow range of JCS issues raised by Jones.

On March 4, 1982, the administration grabbed back defense headlines from Jones's reform proposals. President Reagan announced his selection of Gen. Jack Vessey, the army vice chief, to replace Jones in mid-June. This decision surprised both Pentagon insiders and the media. After the announcement, one well-connected officer said of rumors about the next JCS chairman, "The first time I heard Vessey's name was today."[12]

A month earlier, a *New York Times* piece on leading candidates for the job placed the CNO, Adm. Tom Hayward, in front. Next on its list were three army generals: Bernard W. Rogers, Donn A. Starry, and John Wickham. The article also indicated that two other admirals, Harry D. Train II and Robert L. J. Long, might be selected if Hayward failed to get the job. The article did not even mention Vessey.[13]

Announcing his selection, the president called Vessey "a soldier's soldier." White House officials said Reagan wanted to stress "traditional qualities of military leadership" over bureaucratic skills. The president wanted "a proven combat officer" for a job often held by a manager. Vessey's "nonpolitical" reputation impressed the president. One Reagan aide said: "We have for about twenty years placed in the military a very high importance on a knowledge of cost-benefit analysis, on decision processes for the allocation of resources and on scientific management techniques. All that is very worthwhile for the management of a peacetime or a wartime army, but it came at the expense of lessened importance on such traditional areas of focus as history, strategic concepts . . . and somewhat at the expense of a concern for the leadership of men and women."[14]

Although the criticism was indirect, experts read the aide's comments as a slap at the outgoing chairman. They also demonstrated how poorly Reagan and Weinberger understood the skills that they would need in their senior military adviser. Their next selection of a JCS chairman—more than three years later—would disregard the superficial ideas they had expressed in March, 1982.

When choosing a new army chief of staff in 1979, Carter reportedly had passed over Vessey because he opposed the president's plan to withdraw U.S. troops from Korea. By choosing Vessey, Reagan also meant to contrast his judgment with Carter's on military issues.

Reagan and Weinberger selected the new chairman by going to central casting. They wanted the top officer's image to match the one they were creating for the administration. A week after the announcement, Weinberger gushed in his weekly report to Reagan that Vessey "is regarded as a 'soldiers' general,' much like Omar Bradley was, and has been branded a 'mud soldier' by the press."[15] Those were exactly the kind of popular characterizations they desired. Nor did the fact that the seventy-one-year-old Reagan had selected the oldest candidate—Vessey was fifty-nine—go unnoticed. One army officer quipped, "Age is a little more 'in' nowadays."[16]

The military highly regarded Vessey for his long record of service, command assignments, and rise through the ranks from private to general. Colleagues described him as "the best of the four stars," "wise old man," "cautious and conservative," and "quiet, thoughtful." Vessey preferred to gain consensus before moving ahead. His early efforts as chairman would magnify this tendency as he sought to overcome the divisions in the JCS that occurred during Jones's tenure. Thus, at a time when the nation needed a military leader who would challenge the joint chiefs' consensual approach, it received a chairman who was comfortable with it.

Two weeks after announcing Vessey's selection, Reagan named his choices for the top navy and air force jobs, replacing Admiral Hayward and General Allen, whose four-year terms would conclude at the end of June. The president tapped Adm. James Watkins to serve as CNO and Gen. Charles Gabriel as air force chief of staff. Watkins, the first nuclear submariner chosen for the top navy billet, was described as "a tough cookie" and was compared with the demanding head of the nuclear navy, Adm. Hyman G. Rickover. Gabriel was just the opposite. Colleagues described him as "very laid back" and "easygoing."[17]

As the hoopla over the selection of Vessey, Watkins, and Gabriel was quieting down, the army chief, Gen. Shy Meyer, publicly presented his own bold ideas on joint system reform. The military viewed Meyer, an infantry combat veteran of Korea and Vietnam, as a brilliant leader. Admiral Bill Crowe described Meyer as "a very young Army chief of staff with some rather innovative ideas and the courage to challenge ingrown beliefs." The admiral added that Meyer was "an articulate intellectual individual with a reputation for knowing what he was talking about."[18] Meyer's endorsement increased interest in JCS reform and fit the historic pattern of army chiefs. Marshall, Eisenhower, Bradley, "Lightning Joe" Collins, and Maxwell Taylor had all pushed for a more unified military.

Like Jones, Meyer selected the *Armed Forces Journal* as the medium for presenting his views. In an April article titled "The JCS—How Much Reform Is Needed?" Meyer pressed his case for even more radical reforms: "The changes urged by General Jones, while headed in the right direction, do not go far enough." Meyer was most concerned about the "divided loyalty"—to their service and the JCS—"demanded of service chiefs."[19]

Meyer recommended "major surgery" to end the practice of "dual-hatting." He suggested that a body of full-time advisers—a National Military Advisory Council—be created, drawing on "distinguished four-star rank officers, not charged with any service responsibilities, who would never return to their respective services." Others—notably General Bradley in 1952, General Taylor in 1959, and Senator Symington in 1960—had previously proposed this concept. Meyer endorsed Jones's proposal for an alter ego for the chairman: "One of the council members could be appointed vice chairman for continuity purposes." Meyer envisioned that "this body of military advisers would examine military alternatives and recommend strategic scenarios to govern how the military departments are to organize, equip, and prepare their forces for war."

9. General Edward "Shy" Meyer, army chief of staff.
(U.S. Army photo.)

Although the National Military Advisory Council distinguished Meyer's approach from Jones's, his other recommendations were consistent with and further advanced Jones's ideas. Meyer explained the chairman's "greatly enhanced role and increased influence" by saying "he would direct planning and operations and be able to speak his own mind as well as disagree with the opinion of the council." Meyer also broke new ground by proposing that the "chairman alone would direct the Joint Staff. He would determine the issues for study and initiate staff actions through the director of the Joint Staff."

Of the army chief's more radical proposals, Jones later said, "I appreciated General Meyer making me look more reasonable." Although the army chief pushed for more extreme reforms, he received little criticism from those opposed to change. They continued to focus their energies on denouncing Jones.[20]

Between April 21 and July 28, the Investigations Subcommittee compiled nearly a thousand pages of testimony from forty-three witnesses in twenty hearings. Barrett's expertise permitted the subcommittee to conduct the most rigorous examination of the JCS ever. With the hearings only two-thirds over, the *Armed Forces Journal* reported, "The hearings . . . are going into more depth than *AFJ* has seen a congressional committee go on any defense issue since the TFX [F-111 aircraft] hearings of the early 1960s."[21] When the subcommittee released the hearings' printed record, Vessey wrote White, "Whatever happens with JCS reorganization, the record of your subcommittee's hearings will stand for many years to come as the definitive reference document on the subject." In orchestrating these hearings, Barrett demonstrated why fellow West Pointers called him a hive.[22]

The subcommittee chairman and his staff aimed high when recruiting witnesses. White invited the three living former presidents—Nixon, Ford, and Carter—to testify. None accepted. White, Barrett, and Lally also targeted former defense secretaries. Although they had more success at that level, White and his staffers struck out with the incumbent secretary. In an April 2 letter, Weinberger declined the invitation: "Until my office receives a formal proposal from the chairman and the chiefs outlining their views for reorganization, and until it is properly staffed and reviewed, it would be inappropriate for me to comment or to appear as a witness on this subject."[23]

The subcommittee scheduled the joint chiefs to be among the first witnesses. Weinberger explained to the president that he had met with JCS representatives "to ensure that their testimony on the widely diverse proposals for reorganization does not present the picture of an organization unable to carry out plans or policies, and to ensure that the point is made that we will have a new chairman and two new chiefs in July."[24]

Turnover of three joint chiefs gave the secretary an excuse for not taking a position. He may also have anticipated that Vessey would not push reforms to the same extent as Jones. In any case, wait-and-see appears to have been a coordinated approach. After observing that a new Joint Chiefs of Staff—in which General Meyer and Gen. Robert H. Barrow of the Marine Corps would be the only holdovers—would be taking over later that summer, SASC chairman John Tower said, "We need to see how they work out before we think about any statutory mandate for reorganization."[25]

When subcommittee hearings started, Barrett remembered: "A lot of the time, we did not even have a Republican representative there. Just the chairman." Because White knew little about defense organization, he asked Barrett and Lally to conduct much of the questioning in early sessions. (The House permitted staff to question witnesses; the Senate did not.) As the hearings progressed, White's participation and commitment grew, according to Barrett. As evidence of disarray in the JCS mounted, the chairman "gets caught up in the issues and comes to believe that Jones is right. And then there was hell to pay. He just wouldn't let go until he did all he could do to take care of his responsibilities as chairman."

The subcommittee scheduled Cong. Newt Gingrich, a junior Republican from Georgia, as its first witness. Although Gingrich had shown an interest in JCS reform, permitting him to testify first represented only congressional courtesy.[26] However, when Gingrich did not arrive on time, White asked General Meyer to kick off the hearings. The army chief testified on ideas in his *Armed Forces Journal* article and warned the committee: "tinkering will not suffice. Only by taking on some of the issues which in the past have been put in the box which says, 'Too tough to handle,' are we going to be able to have the kind of operational advice and military advisers that the next two decades out to the 21st century are going to demand."[27]

When finally delivered, Gingrich's statement revealed expertise on defense organization and military history. The two-term congressman and former history professor was credited with bringing "a new supply of intellectual vitality to a House GOP bloc that had been accused of lacking it in the past." Gingrich, viewed as a "brash newcomer," had "a tempestuous first term in which he regularly offered strategy advice to his party's leadership and plotted out scenarios for Republican political dominance." He received "generous amounts of press attention" but drew "hostility from some older conservatives who felt his ideas amounted to personal fantasy."[28]

Gingrich began his testimony by declaring: "These hearings may well be the most important hearings of the year or many years in defense. The central problems of American survival are not budget, resource, or hardware problems. The real threats to our ability to survive are intellectual and organizational." He quickly aligned himself with reformers by stating, "the current system is not working."

Gingrich proposed eight forceful remedies: a single chief of the Joint Staff, a military advisory council separate from the JCS, focusing the service chiefs on preparing for war, a general staff system, joint training for all generals and admirals, strengthened CINC control of subordinate commands and their budgets, substantial strengthening of the Readiness Command's ability to direct joint training and develop joint doctrine, and a separate budget for command and control and joint training.

"Historically countries reform their military only after major defeats," Gingrich concluded. "I think the great challenge to this Congress as it looks at spending more on defense is to also spend more time thinking about defense, because we desperately need reform without defeat."

Only a handful of members could have articulated such insightful views on JCS reorganization. Gingrich contributed ideas—on the Joint Staff, Readiness Command, and a budget for joint activities—that would later become part of the reform debate, but some of his ideas were more than a decade ahead of their time. Despite its thoughtfulness, Gingrich's testimony did not influence the subcommittee or its staff. Seeing the Georgia congressman's testimony as pro forma, they were not open to his ideas.

The subcommittee reconvened that afternoon with General Jones testifying first. His testimony represented an intellectual leap. In his February testimony and *Journal* article, Jones addressed only symptoms. Now, he shifted the discussion to four fundamental problems: "First, responsibility and authority are diffused, both in Washington and in the field. . . . Second, the corporate advice provided by the Joint Chiefs of Staff is not crisp, timely, very useful or very influential. . . . Third, individual service interests too often dominate JCS recommendations and actions at the expense of broader defense interests. . . . And fourth, a service chief does not have enough time to perform his two roles . . . and these two roles have a built-in conflict of interest." Jones used Truman and Eisenhower quotations and forty years of reorganization studies to demonstrate the persistence of these problems.[29]

For the first time, Jones articulated specific solutions. He noted that all studies of the joint system had proposed two basic remedies: "strengthen the chairman" and "go to senior military advisers." Jones said, "General Meyer opts for the latter; I go for the former . . . but either one, I think, would make major progress."[30]

Jones's testimony detailed specific legislative changes to strengthen the JCS chairman. His initial proposal had enormous implications. "First, I would make the chairman the principal military adviser." To bring an end to the stranglehold that service interests had on joint decisions, Jones proposed that the chairman replace the JCS. The newly elevated chairman, Jones said, "would receive his counsel from the chiefs of the services and also, and very importantly, from unified and specified commanders." Although the air force general did not address the revised status of the other joint chiefs, his comments indicated that one role would be advisers to the chairman.

Jones's second specific proposal "would give the chairman oversight of the unified and specified commands." He did not explain this recommendation in detail, but selected the term "oversight" carefully. Stronger terms, such as "supervision," would have suggested infringement on the chain of command.

Jones noted that a DoD directive specified that the chain of command runs from the president to the secretary of defense through the JCS to the unified and specified commands. Jones's third specific proposal would have the chain run through the chairman rather than the JCS "and I would put it in the statute, not just in the directive."

Jones next made two recommendations to protect the JCS role of the service chiefs. In line with a more general notion advanced in his *Journal* article, he "would also have a provision whereby the secretary of defense and the president, and I could foresee the Congress, have the right to ask the corporate group for their advice on an issue." Jones cited arms control as an area where national leaders might want such advice.

To reassure each chief that he would have an opportunity to air his service's perspective before the secretary made a major decision, Jones proposed that if a chief "strongly disagreed with the chairman, he would have the right to provide his advice directly to the secretary of defense on that issue."

"I would also have the Joint Staff work directly for the chairman," Jones testified, restating a powerful idea offered by Meyer.

Although Jones had somewhat refined his ideas for joint personnel policies, they were still generalities: "I would have more people coming out of joint schools going to the joint system." This was designed to overcome the low percentage of officers who had joint schooling—then only 13 percent of middle-grade officers—serving in joint positions. Jones would "try to reprogram" officers promoted to one-star rank with "a capstone course . . . of about three to four months." The goal was "an individual capable of taking a very broad look at the problems rather than one who perceives only the narrow service problem." The chairman talked about promotions and stressed, "We need to do more from a rewards standpoint."

Jones's April 21 testimony represented another major step in the JCS reorganization battle. Many of his ideas would withstand years of inquiry and debate.

Admiral Hayward followed Jones. The CNO's testimony was the antireform camp's first formal rebuttal. Observers described Hayward's testimony as "forcefully delivered, intense." An aide reported to Weinberger that Hayward, "as the only speaker today opposed to statutory reorganization, electrified those in attendance."[31]

Hayward defended the status quo: "The current organization is entirely adequate to the task and performs its functions well. I believe it would be effective in war and does not need major surgery." Moreover, he emphatically declared, "I firmly believe that there is no need to reorganize the Joint Chiefs of Staff in any major way." Hayward termed the proposed reorganization "the first, dangerous step toward a general staff which the Congress clearly has not supported in the past, and which I do not support now." He also told the subcommittee, "I am deeply offended by the slanderous criticisms which one frequently hears about the Joint Chiefs being an ineffective group of parochial service chiefs who spend most of their time bickering among themselves, horse trading to preserve turf and what is best for their service."[32]

The *Armed Forces Journal* reported, "Admiral Hayward's blunt testimony opposing *any* JCS reform initiatives left the House subcommittee members almost speechless when he finished his prepared statement, saying, 'Reorganization is simply not necessary' and 'no reorganization is needed' in about ten different ways."[33]

When White asked the admiral, "Is there *any* recommendation made by General Jones or by General Meyer that you *do* endorse?" Hayward gave a long negative answer which the *Journal* interpreted as saying, "Not one—except that I do agree we need to strengthen the role of the JCS."

After the hearing, Hayward told a *Journal* reporter with White, Lally, and Barrett listening, "You *know* that I did not want these hearings to happen." Of the inquiry, he predicted, "It will not come to any good."

The Investigations Subcommittee heard from the rest of the current joint chiefs when Generals Lew Allen and Bob Barrow, the air force chief and marine commandant, testified respectively on April 27 and 28. Allen stressed the need for service chiefs to remain an integral part of the joint process. Without naming names, he communicated his opposition to Meyer's proposals. Allen did agree that reform could be useful "to improve the effectiveness of the current system. The key feature is a strengthening of the role of the chairman, and I agree that such a shift is needed."[34]

Allen supported nearly all of Jones's proposals but did not align himself with the chairman. He recommended designating the chairman as principal military adviser, allowing the chain of command to run through the chairman, and having the Joint Staff work for the chairman. Allen even commented favorably on the deputy chairman. He had told the Chairman's Special Study Group a deputy chairman was "not unacceptable." The air force chief's testimony publicly added a third sitting joint chief to the list of reform proponents.

Barrow, appearing one week after Hayward, escalated the naval service's rhetorical counterattack. "The proposal set forth by General Jones would not only not improve Joint Chiefs of Staff effectiveness, it would do serious harm to the system," the marine general proclaimed. Barrow's views on JCS organization had done an about-face in the four and one-half months since his last meeting with the CSSG. Then he had been the service chief most supportive of reform; now the commandant was vying with Hayward for most recalcitrant.[35]

At the end of July, the three new joint chiefs—Vessey, Watkins, and Gabriel—testified at the last hearing. Between the old and new joint chiefs, thirty-four witnesses appeared. Each of ten former high-ranking defense civilians favored JCS reform. All active and retired army and air force officers called to testify supported reform except for Gen. Lyman L. Lemnitzer, a former JCS chairman. Excluding CSSG members, all marine witnesses and half of the navy witnesses opposed reorganization. The three admirals who favored reform—

A DISAGREEMENT? – **US?**

10. This Richard Allison cartoon appearing in the *Navy Times* on May 24, 1982, depicted how brutal the fight over JCS reorganization had become.

Harry Train, Bob Long, and Thor Hanson—were serving or had served in senior joint positions. Train commanded the Atlantic Command while Long headed the Pacific Command. Hanson had served as Joint Staff director.

Because these three navy proreformers appeared near the hearings' end, military opinion in the early hearings divided nearly exclusively along army–air force and navy–Marine Corps lines. The *Armed Forces Journal* reported on the early hearings under the headline: "Navy, Marines Adamantly Oppose JCS Reforms Most Others Tell Congress Are Long Overdue." The article noted that "Navy/Marine Corps opposition to the reform proposals has been united among both present and retired chiefs from those services—and at times almost brutal."[36]

As the hearings progressed, White began to draft legislation. The chairman tried out his legislative fixes at the hearings. According to Barrett: "Being very proud of a provision after we'd get it hammered out, White would go to a hearing, read his provision out to some unsuspecting witness, and ask, 'What do you think about that?'"

One senior staffer ridiculed White's legislative drafting habit: "Dick White had a reputation. People used to say that he would draft legislation on toilet paper. He loved to write legislation. He was a lawyer, and he thought he could do it better than anybody else. He would say, 'I've got a bill here that I think will accomplish just what you're talking about there, Mr. So and So.' Here would be this legislation, and everybody would roll their eyes."[37]

In the midst of the subcommittee's work, General Jones retired. On June 17, the day before his retirement, Jones sent Weinberger a memorandum presenting his views and recommendations and urging the secretary to act. "The need for change now is more critical than ever before. The only question is not if, but when and under what circumstances we will correct these organizational deficiencies."[38]

The impact of Jones's departure on the reorganization campaign was unclear. Meyer remained to advocate his more radical reforms, but how Vessey's appointment would shift the balance of sentiment was unknown. Meanwhile, Jones announced that he intended to stay engaged. Asked in a television interview what he planned to do about JCS reform, he declared, "I'm going to fight for it."[39]

On June 28, Judge William P. Clark, Reagan's national security adviser, brought the White House into the JCS reorganization issue and compelled Weinberger to act. Clark advised the secretary "it would be useful to apprise the president of this matter." He also asked that information "describing how this issue is being addressed by the Department of Defense" be provided to the president by mid-July.[40]

The National Security Council (NSC) staff had urged Clark to write to Weinberger, noting, "To date, the civilian leadership in DoD has remained silent." The staff argued: "The command structure of our forces, and with it, the JCS system and structure, belongs to the commander-in-chief. Official administration statements on the need for reform or legislative proposals regarding the JCS structure should not be offered until you [Clark] and the president have had the opportunity to study the issue." The staff designed Clark's memorandum to Weinberger to "preclude premature public discussion" by DoD.[41]

The JCS drafted Weinberger's report to Reagan, which was submitted on July 19. The memorandum prescribed "five paramount criteria" for measuring proposals: "would the change improve the nation's ability to wage war; would it assure that you and I and future presidents and defense secretaries receive better and more timely advice; would it ensure that the requirements of the commanders of our combatant commands are better met; would the proposal improve our ability to allocate resources for national defense more wisely and use them more efficiently; would the proposal be consistent with civilian control of the military." The JCS had proposed the first four criteria. Weinberger added the last one at the suggestion of White House Fellow Mary Anne Wood, who advised him of the obvious: "There really is no way to judge most of the proposals against the criteria."[42]

Weinberger's memorandum defended DoD's management record since 1981, noting three improvements: access to the Defense Resource Board for combatant commanders, budgetary priority for readiness, and efforts "systematically to modernize our forces and improve our overall military potential to implement national strategy." Weinberger told the president that "some contributors to the present debate may be uninformed of those DoD management improvements." Invoking the JCS as supportive of departmental management, the secretary declared, "The JCS agree that in these respects, the present 'system' has been improved."

Meyer did not agree with that statement. Vessey told Weinberger, "One chief disagrees . . . judging that the steps mentioned have not contributed measurably to correcting our longstanding problems, and will only lull the uninformed into believing that we are on the road to recovery."[43]

Weinberger's memorandum addressed four areas where the department could act without statutory changes. First, he explained how the Pentagon sought to better support the combatant commanders by looking to the JCS chairman "to be their spokesman on both requirements and operations." Second, the secretary revealed that to "assure increased continuity," the acting chairman duty would rotate among the service chiefs not more frequently than quarterly. Third, Weinberger suggested improving the qualifications of officers in joint positions through formal schooling and repetitive assignments, increased rewards, and a special training program for Joint Staff officers.

Regarding one central reform issue, Weinberger explained, "I have assured the JCS that you and I want and need good military advice that is timely, and that we recognize that unanimity on the complex national security issues addressed by the JCS is not expected." The secretary also proposed that the president and joint chiefs meet once every three or four months.

The memorandum listed six major proposals requiring legislative changes that Weinberger had asked the JCS to examine. The secretary set October 1 as the deadline for the review and November 1 as his deadline for reporting to the president.

The NSC staff's review called the memorandum "just what was intended: the start of a deliberate, focused, and coordinated analysis of the JCS structure." Noting that Congressman White had introduced a JCS reform bill, the staff saw "virtually no likelihood that the bill will get out of the House subcommittee during this session. Furthermore, there has not been any action on the Senate side." The NSC staff reported, "We are not being pressed by congressional action."[44]

National Security Adviser Clark made the same point to Reagan in forwarding Weinberger's memorandum: "There is no chance that Congress will act on the bill during this session." The White House would await Weinberger's November report "to determine the next steps that may be required."[45]

On July 28, the three new joint chiefs—Vessey, Watkins, and Gabriel—appeared as the subcommittee's last witnesses. Months earlier, when Vessey testified before the SASC during his nomination hearing for chairman, Sen. Barry Goldwater asked him if he "would be agreeable to changes if they had to be made?"[46]

"I agree with many of the things that General Jones and General Meyer have proposed," Vessey answered. The *Armed Forces Journal* interpreted this response as significant and reported that "Vessey has given their initiatives new impetus."[47]

On July 28, a more cautious Vessey refrained from commenting on specific proposals, revealing only that Weinberger had asked the JCS to review Jones's and Meyer's recommendations and report the results by October 1.[48] Watkins and Gabriel made perfunctory remarks that complemented the new chairman's statement, but provided no substantive information. Gabriel's statement totaled only ninety-two words.

With this nondescript testimony, the Investigations Subcommittee hearings ended on a whimper. After forty witnesses had offered their views and numerous fora had debated the issues for five months, the last three witnesses said the joint chiefs needed another two and one-half months before they could recommend a position to the secretary. If White waited until October 1, there would be almost no chance of enacting legislation before Congress adjourned. He decided to press ahead without a formal DoD position.[49]

On July 21, a week before Vessey's appearance, White introduced a JCS reorganization bill, designated H.R. 6828, which was referred to the HASC. ("H.R." designates a bill originating in the House of Representatives, while "S." identifies a Senate-originated bill.) The purpose of H.R. 6828 was to "amend title 10, United States Code, to provide for more efficient and effective operation of the Joint Chiefs of Staff." Title 10 contains the vast majority of laws governing DoD, including all statutes on organizations, officials, and authorities.[50]

Viewing a need for only limited legislation, White, Barrett, and Lally drafted a bill that contained just ten modest provisions. The bill would allow the JCS chairman to provide military advice to the president and defense secretary "in his own right." Although they wanted to give the chairman an independent voice, White and his two staffers decided not to go as far as Jones's recommendation to make the chairman the principal military adviser. As a check on the chairman's new authority, the bill also provided that a joint chief could submit an opinion in disagreement with the chairman's advice.

The bill would establish a deputy chairman to act in the chairman's absence or disability. Besides specifying four-star rank for the deputy and prohibiting the chairman and deputy being members of the same service, H.R. 6828 was silent on the multitude of questions posed by creation of this new position.

Existing law provided that Joint Staff officers were "selected by the Joint

Chiefs of Staff with the approval of the chairman." H.R. 6828 would make the chairman coequal with the joint chiefs in the selection of Joint Staff members. This provision's second part would require nominees for Joint Staff service to be "from among those officers considered to be the most outstanding officers of their armed force." The bill drafters wanted to encourage the services to assign more qualified people.

The next provision relaxed statutory restrictions on the tenure of Joint Staff officers. It prescribed, "Members of the Joint Staff serve at the pleasure of the secretary of defense." This represented the first explicit congressional acknowledgment that the secretary's authority extended to the Joint Staff. The draft provision would give the secretary discretion to extend the prescribed three-year tour to six years.

Existing law required that officers who had served on the Joint Staff could not be recalled for a second tour until three years had passed, with an exception for up to thirty officers. H.R. 6828 would increase this number to one hundred officers.

The next provision of White's bill had major implications. The extant statute prescribed that the chairman manages the Joint Staff and its director "on behalf of the Joint Chiefs of Staff." The bill would place the chairman solely in charge of the staff and director.

. Another major proposal would allow the service chiefs and unified and specified commanders the opportunity to comment on any Joint Staff report or recommendation, giving warfighting commanders a greater say in decisions that affected their commands.

The next Joint Staff provision proposed that the "secretary of defense shall ensure that the Joint Staff is independently organized and operated [to] support the chairman of the Joint Chiefs of Staff and the Joint Chiefs of Staff . . . to provide for the unified strategic direction of the combatant forces, for their operation under unified command, and for their integration into an efficient team of land, naval, and air forces." Its substantive clauses were "The secretary of defense shall ensure" and "the Joint Staff is independently organized and operated." The first clause emphasized the secretary's powers and his role in overcoming service parochialism in Joint Staff affairs. The second sought to free the Joint Staff from the services' control. The provision's language used "unified direction," "unified command," "integration," and "team" in rapid succession, expressing the drafters' intention that the four services be truly unified. This language paraphrased the declaration of policy of the National Security Act of 1947.

In an effort to ensure that officers were properly rewarded for Joint Staff service, H.R. 6828's last provision specified, "that personnel policies of the armed forces concerning promotion, retention, and assignment of officers give appropriate consideration to the performance of an officer as a member of the Joint Staff."

On August 5, White convened his subcommittee to mark up H.R. 6828. Only eight of fourteen members attended—six of the eight Democrats and only two Republicans. The absence of the ranking Republican, Cong. Robin Beard of Tennessee, indicated the legislation's limited support. Only a few members actively participated in discussions. The others evidenced unfamiliarity with the subject. Most had not bothered to attend the hearings.[51]

Congressman Les Aspin's active participation demonstrated his grasp of Pentagon organizational dynamics. From 1966 to 1968, the Wisconsin Democrat had served as an OSD systems analyst while an army lieutenant and captain, departing the systems analysis office just before I arrived. The subcommittee approved his three amendments. Members agreed to specify that "The deputy chairman may attend all meetings of the Joint Chiefs of Staff," but that he "may not vote on a matter before the Joint Chiefs of Staff except when acting as chairman."

The other two Aspin amendments focused on the chairman's role in personnel matters. He argued that having the chairman and other joint chiefs coequal in selection of the Joint Staff was not workable. He gained approval of an amendment that would specify that the chairman would select Joint Staff officers from lists submitted by the services.

Aspin's last amendment would require the chairman to evaluate for the president the Joint Staff performance of any officer nominated for three or four stars. His motive was "to give the chairman more authority over the Joint Staff."

The subcommittee approved one other amendment, this one offered by Cong. Samuel S. Stratton (D–New York). He proposed the creation of a Senior Strategy Advisory Board made up of ten retired four-star officers. Stratton, who had strong ties to the navy, compared this board to the sea service's General Board. Some speculated that the navy had proposed the idea to him, probably as an alternative to Meyer's National Military Advisory Council.

The eight attending members voted to approve and agreed to cosponsor the revised bill. White submitted a new bill with the markup revisions, designated H.R. 6954, for consideration by the full HASC.

The *Armed Forces Journal* interviewed White about H.R. 6954. Asked why the bill did not prescribe the chairman as the principal military adviser, White answered, "Such a bill wouldn't get through the Congress." Asked to name the bill's most important initiative, the Texas Democrat responded, "I think the deputy chairman is the most important part." What were the chances of both Houses acting on his bill before the session's end? "If I get this bill out of the committee before the first recess [in August, which he did]," he predicted, "I'd say the chances are better than fifty percent."[52] As to what was behind his allegation that the navy had lobbied to block changes, White speculated that the navy had "talked to some of the members and . . . maybe some members didn't come [to the hearings] because the Navy cooled them."

Members were not the only ones lobbied by the naval community. Brigadier General J. D. Hittle, USMC (Ret.), had tried to change Arch Barrett's thinking during a series of luncheons.

Before the full committee considered the bill, White and his subcommittee explained its provisions to Weinberger and Vessey at a Pentagon breakfast meeting on August 10. The subcommittee did not press the secretary or chairman for a commitment. Weinberger reported to Reagan: "The committee has been very cooperative in giving General Vessey an opportunity to spend some time in his new position before being committed to long-term, substantive reforms."[53]

On August 12, when the HASC took up H.R. 6954, members showed little enthusiasm. A senior staffer explained why: "A Dick White initiated issue would not automatically generate much interest. As a matter of fact, it would generate the reverse. People would just discard it as being most likely not substantive."[54]

Congressman Dan Daniel (D-Virginia) chaired the full committee session. After White briefly explained the bill's provisions, Daniel expressed "appreciation to Mr. White for the enormous amount of work that he has done on this very important function" and then proclaimed, "Without objection, the bill is approved, and Mr. White will handle it on the floor." The proceedings lasted a mere six minutes.[55]

Despite its disinterest and reservations, the committee approved the bill. The same senior staffer characterized the members' thinking: "Nothing was going to happen. They just figured that it would just die some other way. The HASC did not regard it as a serious issue."[56]

Four days after the HASC's disinterested approval, the House, under a suspension of the rules, approved the "Joint Chiefs of Staff Reorganization Act of 1982" by a voice vote. In Weinberger's weekly report, he told Reagan: "This bill was rushed through the House primarily as a courtesy to outgoing Subcommittee Chairman Dick White of Texas, who is retiring at the end of the session. The White bill is a much watered down version of some of the major JCS reorganization proposals that have been proposed in recent months."[57]

The modest bill disappointed reorganization supporters. On September 10, General Maxwell Taylor criticized H.R. 6954 in a *Washington Post* editorial, complaining that the bill "contains nothing resembling a fundamental change in the status quo at the top of the military hierarchy, where, [the bill's authors] concede, all is not well." Taylor blasted the provision to create a Senior Strategic Advisory Board.[58]

"Without a board that will offset the inadequacy of the Joint Chiefs, there is no justification for the bill itself. Most of the trivial undiscussed changes contained in it could be effected by the secretary of defense and the chairman of the Joint Chiefs without legislation," Taylor wrote. "Indeed, it would be damaging to national security if this bill, in its present form, became law. Its passage would foster a general belief that Congress, after months of study, has found and corrected such weaknesses as may have existed in the Joint Chiefs system and henceforth there will be no cause for public concern." The general hoped "that the Senate, before deciding to pass it, will give this bill the close attention it deserves."

On October 13, Barrett heard Jones speak to a group about the bill. "General Jones in effect damned the proposed legislation with faint praise," Barrett observed, and "noting the lack of opposition to the bill in the House, General Jones inferred that Congress would accept a stronger measure." Barrett disagreed: "More far-reaching legislation is by no means likely to pass both houses of Congress. In fact, the odds against any legislative reform are great and will probably increase in the 98th Congress. H.R. 6954 was carefully crafted with the bounds of the politically feasible in mind."[59]

Whether a stronger JCS reorganization bill could have passed the House in August, 1982, is problematic. At some level of discomfort with legislative proposals, the Pentagon would have broken its self-imposed silence and objected. At some lesser level of discomfort, service associations and retired communities would have weighed in more heavily on Capitol Hill with their opposition. Given White's limited support, a modest degree of opposition might have scuttled JCS reform altogether. As events played out in the Senate, White, Barrett, and Lally made the right decision by avoiding the risk.

White's success in gaining House approval of a JCS reorganization bill deceived most observers, including me. They and I perceived the House to be solidly in favor of reform. On the contrary, the House, HASC, and many Investigations Subcommittee members were not committed to these reforms. The legislation moved quickly primarily because the administration raised no objections. Barrett confirmed this situation when he observed: "The 1982 reorganization bill was a one-man bill." That few outside of the committee understood this worked to the proreformers' advantage. Supporters of reorganization both inside and outside of government took heart from the passage of H.R. 6954 and initiated complementary efforts.

On November 22, nearly two months later, the JCS submitted its reorganization analysis. The chiefs concluded that "sweeping changes to title 10 USC [United States Code] are unnecessary." This represented a pivotal event. It led the Pentagon to adopt a rigid antireform posture and eventually to bitterly confront Congress.[60]

In his memorandum to Weinberger, Vessey explained that the joint chiefs had "reached agreement that while there were flaws in JCS organization, other problems proceeded from relationships between OJCS [Organization of the Joint Chiefs of Staff] and OSD which over the years have obscured and diluted the military advice you and the president are by law entitled to receive." The chairman added, "We agreed that we can work with you to clarify staff roles and responsibilities so that your military and civilian staffs can serve you better." The JCS analysis had confused cause and effect. Presidents and defense secretaries had increasingly turned to civilian staffs for counsel in the absence of quality JCS advice. This practice would not end until the JCS improved the usefulness of its advice.

On November 26 Weinberger advised President Reagan: "The chiefs recommend only two legislative changes. First, they propose to ease the existing restrictions on the size of the Joint Staff and tenure of its officers. Second, they propose that the law be changed to reflect formally the existing practice of inserting the chairman of the Joint Chiefs of Staff in the chain of command between the secretary of defense and commanders in chief of the unified and specified commands." Weinberger said he agreed "that these changes are desirable."[61]

The secretary also informed the president that he agreed with the JCS "that we should not support additional statutory changes at this time. Specifically, I do not consider it desirable or necessary: a. To specify that the chairman is your principal military advisor; b. To seek authorization for a full-time, four-star vice chairman; c. To subordinate the Joint Staff specifically to the chairman vice the JCS; or d. To supplant the JCS with a Council of Advisors composed of senior officers other than chiefs of service at this time."

Weinberger's memorandum also advised that the JCS wanted "a larger role in staffing and advising on 'major decisions of strategy, policy, and force requirements' than they currently do, and that the role of the Office of the Secretary of Defense should be correspondingly diminished. This is a serious proposal and should, and will be, carefully considered." Nonetheless, the reforms the chiefs recommended offered little prospect that their advice on strategy, policy, and force requirements would improve.

Weinberger did not ask the president for his views, and the president did not respond until after the end of the year. As a result, the administration and DoD never took a position on JCS reorganization in 1982. On December 8, Weinberger responded to a request from Congressman White for the department's views: "I am currently reviewing the Chiefs' recommendations and, when I have completed this process, I plan to discuss the issue with the president." Weinberger said he would get back to White "once we have developed a firm administration position."[62]

Despite the modesty of H.R. 6954 and its limited support, White, Barrett, and Lally made significant contributions in 1982. They had kept the issue of organizational reform alive until others could initiate more powerful efforts. They had also begun the process of severing the forty-year alliance between Congress and the services on organization—a partnership that had inhibited needed advances.

The legislative efforts of White and his two staffers also advanced critical concepts. Key among these was a more appropriate recognition of the defense secretary's authority. For thirty-five years, Congress had denied the secretary a full measure of power in order to preserve the services' independence and ensure a strong military voice. Although H.R. 6954 would only slightly expand the secretary's authority, it had sown the seeds. The bill moved toward empowering the chairman to break the JCS's consensual approach. The legislation also recognized the need to better prepare and reward Joint Staff officers and remove statutory constraints that denied effective utilization of their expertise. Although the legislation did not address the weaknesses of the unified commands, it did endorse their increased involvement in Washington activities. Finally, H.R. 6954 drew attention to DoD's inadequate emphasis on strategy formulation.

Despite its intellectual contributions and foresighted interest, the HASC Investigations Subcommittee would be relegated by partisan politics to being a secondary theater in the reform struggle. Although the Democratic Party controlled the House, a Republican occupied the White House, and his party held a majority in the Senate. Whatever position the administration decided to take on reorganization, it would look to the Senate as its Capitol Hill ally. The SASC would be the battleground where this fight would be won or lost.

Before White left office, he wanted to make every effort to convince the Senate to act on the House bill. He focused his efforts on a fellow Texan, Republican senator John Tower. As adjournment approached, the Texas connection became White's only hope.

CHAPTER 4

Texas Politics

Politics makes strange bedfellows.

—Charles Dudley Warner,

My Summer in a Garden

Senator John Tower did not want to be doing this. The Armed Services Committee chairman had other important business to conclude in the final hectic days of the lame-duck session. His pressing agenda did not include Joint Chiefs of Staff reform, but he had been unable to say no. The four-term Texas Republican had promised to conduct a hearing on the subject. So, at ten minutes after ten on Thursday morning, December 16, 1982, the chairman gaveled the hearing to order.

Tower had equivocated for so long on scheduling the hearing that it was doomed to being chaotic and poorly attended. Committees did not normally inquire into a new subject in a session's dying days, when the Senate focused on important legislation ready for enactment. Only nine days remained until Christmas, and the Senate had critical bills to consider before it could adjourn. Majority Leader Howard Baker (R-Tennessee) anticipated an all-night session that Thursday evening, followed by a full day on Friday and possibly Saturday and Sunday sessions.

When Tower started the hearing, the Senate had already convened for the day and roll-call votes were expected throughout the morning. Given the press of business on the Senate floor, few members were expected to attend the hearing. Those who did would have to leave for each vote. Tower would likely have to repeatedly recess the hearing.

Several sources had pressured the Texas Republican for a JCS reform hearing. Although Tower had responded with promises, he had found reasons for not fulfilling them. But after vacillating for months, Tower found that there was one request he could not disregard: Cong. Dick White from El Paso was retiring at the end of the session, and he had been after Tower for months to raise the JCS reorganization issue in the Senate. He wanted Tower to at least hold a committee hearing on the subject before he retired. Tower told me he simply could not "ignore that request from a fellow Texan." Nonetheless, SASC staff director Rhett B. Dawson said that even though Tower had told White he would hold a hearing, Tower "did not take JCS reorganization seriously at that juncture." According to Dawson, Tower wanted "to put the hearing off to a point in the session where it would no longer be relevant." He also intended "to design the hearing so that it would not give comfort to those agitating for reform."[1]

Tower did not mention pressure he had received seven months earlier from Sen. Sam Nunn (D-Georgia), a SASC member. On May 13, during the floor debate on the defense authorization bill, Nunn sought a commitment from Tower for JCS reform hearings. To force the issue, Nunn offered an amendment requiring the defense secretary to submit a report analyzing proposed JCS reforms. After explaining his amendment, Nunn inquired, "I ask the chairman of the committee whether he plans to hold hearings on this issue."[2]

Tower agreed with Nunn that JCS reform was "an enormously important subject." Speaking of the JCS's role in the decision-making process, the chairman observed, "I think it leaves very much to be desired." Tower seemed to contradict his only other public pronouncement on the subject. Two months earlier, he had told journalists he did not expect Congress to "support the Draconian overhaul" suggested by General Jones.[3]

Now Tower made the commitment Nunn sought: "I give the senator from Georgia my assurance—and I think he will have virtually unanimous support of the committee—that we will have hearings at the earliest possible date."[4]

Having obtained this commitment, Nunn withdrew his amendment.

The summer passed without Tower making any move to fulfill his commitment. The Senate received and referred H.R. 6954, the House-passed JCS reorganization bill, to the SASC on August 17. Still, the chairman took no action.

In mid-September, I asked Rick Finn, a bright young staffer working with me, to prepare a memorandum to Tower reminding him of his floor statement. The key paragraph read: "In light of your assurance to Senator Nunn and the importance of this issue, we recommend that the committee conduct two or three hearings in the short time left in this session of Congress. These hearings would *not* be designed to prepare for the immediate markup of H.R. 6954 or any other similar proposals. Instead, they would be meant to begin to 'air out the issue.'"[5]

Tower agreed to schedule a hearing during the last week of September. From a list of ten possible witnesses, he selected Congressman White and three former JCS chairmen, Generals Jones and Taylor and Adm. Thomas H. Moorer. Finn's memorandum advised Tower not to invite Weinberger or any serving joint chiefs, reasoning that "before late October, these officials would have little to contribute simply because their own internal review would be unfinished."

But Tower had to postpone this hearing "due to the last-minute rush of Senate business [before adjourning for campaigning] and the unavailability of General David Jones." In late October, the *Armed Forces Journal* inquired about the chairman's plans. Tower's press aide, Linda Hill, assured the *Journal* that hearings would be "rescheduled during the lame-duck session." As to prospects for legislation, the *Journal* reported, "Hill strongly cautioned that the committee wouldn't necessarily 'take unilateral congressional action' or approve the House legislation without first hearing the views of the new JCS leadership."[6] In other words, "There is no way that there will be legislation this year."

I went to work for Tower when he became SASC chairman in January, 1981. Two and one-half years earlier, then Chairman John C. Stennis—the venerable Mississippi Democrat—hired me out of the Pentagon to serve as the committee's senior foreign policy adviser. Stennis was my nominal boss, but my real boss was Nunn. Nearing the end of his first six-year term, Nunn was building a reputation as a defense intellectual, and he was increasingly interested in international security affairs. With Stennis's blessing, Nunn tasked me with major projects on East Asia and the Persian Gulf.

The Republicans unexpectedly became the majority party in the Senate when Reagan won his landslide victory in 1980, and although Senate committee leaders rarely asked staffers to cross party lines, Tower asked me to work for him. He planned to assign me the same foreign policy responsibilities that I had performed for the Democrats.

I was not surprised that Tower agreed to White's plea for a hearing. He tenaciously fought public battles, but he was easily swayed in private. He did not like confrontation and often yielded quickly. Despite this weakness, the committee staff admired Tower. He was bright, knowledgeable, politically courageous, and accessible—key attributes that congressional staffers look for in a boss. Unlike most senators, Tower was not a lawyer. Before winning a special election in May, 1961, to fill Vice Pres. Lyndon B. Johnson's Senate seat, he had spent the previous ten years as a political science professor at Midwestern University in Wichita Falls, Texas.

Tower studied at the University of London in 1952. While there, he became an Anglophile, which was noticeable in many aspects of his life. He dressed in proper British style and ordered his suits and shirts from London. He also smoked British cigarettes, which he kept in a silver case in his breast pocket. When Tower first appeared in Washington, political commentator David Broder observed that "an implausibly dapper and polished English-looking gent was now speaking for the brawny Lone Star state."[7]

Tower listed his height as five foot five and one-half, but that figure probably stretched the truth by several inches. The thirty-five-year-old college professor turned senator wrote that upon his Washington arrival "every story seemed to dwell on my height—or lack thereof. The term 'diminutive' was firmly affixed to me in that period, and someone wrote that I often needed to stand on a wooden crate to see over the top of the podium. That isn't true, but it never stopped those who needed to fill a couple of column inches of newsprint."[8]

What Tower lacked in size, he made up in intellect. Besides his studies in England, which stirred his interest in foreign affairs, Tower had a bachelor's degree in political science from Southwestern University and a master's degree from Southern Methodist University. By the time he became chairman, Tower had studied defense and foreign policy issues for decades and knew key legislators from many countries, especially in Europe.

Tower was also a great public speaker. Speaking from notes instead of a prepared text enabled him to exploit the cadence and eloquence of his own speech. I wrote Tower's foreign policy speeches. He and I would sometimes prepare them in an unusual order. I would write the full text of a speech, and when the chairman was comfortable with the logic, I would reduce the speech to a two- or three-page outline. After he agreed with the outline, I would boil it down to one page. From that single piece of paper, Tower would deliver a brilliant speech.

The senator was also unparalleled as an extemporaneous speaker. During one visit to London, John Nott, the British secretary of state for defense, hosted an elegant, formal dinner in Tower's honor at Admiralty House. When Nott offered an after dinner toast, Tower responded with an extemporaneous speech on British-American relations. The Texan's poignant remarks brought tears to many eyes. When the dinner ended, Nott rushed over to me and said, "Congratulations on those remarks you prepared for the senator. You are an outstanding writer. He's fortunate to have you on his staff."

"That wasn't my work," I replied. "That was all Senator Tower."

Nott said as he walked off, "And modest, too."

Although Tower practiced sophisticated British behavior, he never overcame some habits he had formed as a young World War II sailor. Despite his upbringing as the son and grandson of Methodist ministers and his scripture-quoting ability, Tower frequently expressed himself in salty four-letter words. When he did so in front of women, he never tired of using the sophomoric expression, "Pardon my French."

Tower enlisted in the navy at age seventeen, serving in his terms as a "deck ape" on an amphibious gunship in the western Pacific. After his discharge at war's end, he remained in the Naval Reserve. Throughout his Senate career, he was viewed as a navy man. While serving as SASC chairman, Tower—then the most senior enlisted navy reservist—was proud to be promoted to senior chief boatswain's mate and later master chief boatswain's mate.

Shortly after the November election, Finn and I sent Tower a memorandum offering options on rescheduling JCS reform hearings. We recommended two hearings, but the chairman decided to hold only one and invite the same four witnesses planned for the postponed September hearing. Staff Director James F. McGovern, who had replaced Dawson in late October, selected December 16 for the hearing. This late date would clearly diminish the hearing's potential utility.[9]

Tower assigned me lead responsibility for the hearing. I invited each witness to appear and explained the planned approach. The three retired officers

11. Admiral Tom Hayward, chief of naval operations, promoting Sen. John Tower, chairman of the Armed Services Committee, to senior chief boatswain's mate in the Naval Reserve. (U.S. Navy photo.)

were placed on a single panel. Joint appearance of proponents and opponents provided opportunities for informative cross-examinations. When Admiral Moorer was unavailable, Adm. James L. Holloway became the navy witness. As I began to organize the hearing, a retired marine, Brig. Gen. J. D. Hittle, invited me to lunch to provide the navy/Marine Corps perspective on reform. Hittle's influence with SASC members compelled me to accept.

Organizing the hearing also meant preparing the chairman, informing him of the views of each witness, and preparing questions for him to ask at the hearing. Formulating these questions was an art. You wanted to compel the witness to respond with an informative, meaningful statement, but you needed to be careful not to get the chairman in over his head. He did not have time to study the issues in detail, and you did not want the questioning to publicly expose his lack of knowledge. One rule of thumb for avoiding unpleasant surprises advised: "Don't ask a question you don't already know the answer to." Why ask a question if you already know the answer? Hearings are not held to educate staffers, they are held to inform senators, media, and public.

As I reviewed prior statements made by the four witnesses, I read an observation by General Jones: "No one can really understand the complex nature of the Pentagon bureaucracy unless he or she has served there as an action officer." Having spent ten years as a Pentagon civilian action officer, I heartily agreed.

Working in the Pentagon is an experience. The building is huge, like the department it houses. It has more than seventeen miles of corridors and twelve hundred toilets. Its unending, rigid rows of straight lines equate architecturally to a precise military formation. Its stone is khaki—a traditional military color. Many corridors in Washington's largest office building look like the wings of a museum. Artifacts portray America's wars, warriors, and war machines. The portraits of civilian and military leaders—from the republic's beginning to the current day—stare down at all who pass by. The building reflects the tradition-bound nature of all militaries.

Jones understood the services' attachment to the past: "The very foundation of each service rests on imbuing its members with pride in its missions, its doctrine and its customs and discipline—all of which are steeped in traditions." But tradition had a downside: "While these deep-seated service distinctions are important in fostering a fighting spirit, cultivating them engenders tendencies to look inward and to insulate the institutions against outside challenges."[10]

As evidence, Jones cited resistance to ideas and inventions whose time had come: "The Navy kept building sailing ships long after the advent of steam power. Machine guns and tanks were developed in the United States, but our Army rejected them until long after they were accepted in Europe. The horse cavalry survived essentially unchanged right up until World War II despite evidence that its utility was greatly diminished decades earlier. Even Army Air Corps officers were required to wear spurs until the late 1930s. . . . The result of this rigidity has been an ever-widening gap between the need to adapt to changing conditions and our ability to do so."

When General Eisenhower first reported to the Pentagon as army chief of staff, he became lost in the "building's labyrinth of corridors." Accustomed to going to and from the general officers' mess with other officers, never paying much attention to the route, one day, he recalled, "I ventured the return trip alone. Although I reached the E ring safely, I discovered that this ring, the outermost corridor of the building, was an endless vista of doors, every one of them identical in appearance. I had not the slightest idea which was mine." Eisenhower observed that the building "had apparently been designed to confuse any enemy who might infiltrate it." Eisenhower might have been the most notable officer to get lost in the Pentagon's physical maze, but he had plenty of company.[11]

Ideas—even great ones—also had to negotiate the bureaucratic maze created by the building's twenty-four thousand employees. A staggering number of offices, representing dozens of diverse perspectives, reviewed each idea. Moving an idea along the path toward approval required enormous time, energy, and skill. Frustrations with this horrendous process sparked fitting nicknames for the Pentagon: Five-Sided Squirrel Cage, Potomac Puzzle Palace, Disneyland East, Concrete Carousel. When the Defense Department performed poorly, many referred to the Pentagon as Fort Fumble or Malfunction Junction.

Few military personnel wanted to serve in the Squirrel Cage. In 1982, a newspaper article reported that "distaste for the Pentagon and its methods is common within the military. Part of it is the natural resentment of the fighter pilot who has been reassigned to push memos. Part of it arises from a genuine worry as to whether the nation is managing its forces wisely."[12]

Pentagon work—with its frustrating paperwork, exhausting meetings, bureaucratic infighting, and slow progress—did not resemble military activity in the field. Uniformed personnel reported that Pentagon duty did not reward traditional soldierly virtues like "courage, self-reliance, decisiveness and a willingness to accept responsibility."[13] Officers viewed as fortunate any officer who could declare, "I never served a day in the Pentagon." But officers assigned there throw themselves into their work. Bright, dedicated, professional warrior-bureaucrats vigorously and relentlessly tried to carry out all assigned tasks.

Despite their commitment to the job, military workers harshly judged Pentagon organization and procedures: "The feeling that the military is run by committee instead of leaders is strong. In particular at the triservice [JCS] level the complaint is, as one officer put it, that no one is in charge. Each service jealously guards its autonomy. Little is done until a consensus is reached, which historically has meant waste and duplication."[14] Why this was the case was, as officers said to me, "Way above their pay grade."

During my ten years in the Pentagon, where I worked extensively with the Joint Staff and reviewed reams of JCS papers, I saw firsthand the intellectual constraints imposed by service dominance. My Joint Staff counterparts would complain: "We're working our butts off. But what are we achieving? Nothing. We can't objectively examine issues because the services won't let us." Most could not wait until their tours in the building were over.

One assignment that I undertook in 1976 at the direction of Defense Secretary Donald H. Rumsfeld revealed the suppressive grip of the services. Rumsfeld believed that the Joint Staff could and should provide independent military advice on key budget proposals. I was instructed to work with senior Joint Staff representatives in developing procedures to make Joint Staff resource expertise available to the secretary. But the Joint Staff wanted no part of these contentious issues in which services had strong interests. They objected to every possible approach. After two months of bureaucratic mud wrestling, the effort had to be abandoned. Having personally observed the brokenness of the joint system, I understood the heavy odds against the changes Jones sought.

On November 7, the *New York Times Magazine* published a long article by Jones titled "What's Wrong With Our Defense Establishment." When the former chairman told me that he planned to submit this article as his written statement for the hearing, I carefully studied and summarized it for Tower.[15]

Jones's article opened a new front in the debate. It moved beyond JCS reform and examined other Pentagon deficiencies. Jones gave prominent attention to problems in the department's Planning, Programming, and Budgeting System (PPBS). He charged that the "defense guidance" document, a key planning paper, "always demands greater force capabilities than the budget constraints will allow" and "does little to set meaningful priorities." In Jones's view, the programming and budgeting phases produced "a defense budget that is derived primarily from the disparate desires of the individual services rather than from a well-integrated plan."

Jones tackled an explosive subject when he judged civilian control "more often apparent than real" on nonoperational matters. He asserted that the lack of comprehensive military advice on alternative strategies or weapon systems weakened the defense secretary. "It is ironic that the services have . . . been able to defeat attempts to bring order out of chaos by arguing that a source of alternative military advice for the president and secretary of defense runs the risk of undermining civilian control," Jones noted.

The former JCS chairman quoted the Chairman's Special Study Group report's finding that "a certain amount of service independence is healthy and desirable, but the balance now favors the parochial interests of the services too much and the larger needs of the nation's defenses too little."

The retired general seemed to have Weinberger in mind when he stated, "Civilian defense leaders have been reluctant to push hard for changes, either because they thought they could not succeed or because they did not want to expend the necessary political capital, which they believed was better spent on gaining support for the defense budget." Jones added that many resisted "raising basic organizational issues," fearing that opponents "would use admissions of organizational inefficiency to argue for further budget cuts."

The article advocated four new changes. First, Jones recommended the transfer of systems analysts from OSD to the Joint Staff. Second, he advanced the view that many of OSD's five hundred military officer positions should be eliminated. Both proposals would strengthen the Joint Staff at OSD's expense. With respect to PPBS deficiencies, Jones envisioned more independent cost analyses, increased funding reserves for unexpected cost growth or contingency operations, and early, tough decisions to preclude starting unaffordable programs. His last recommendation was that "administrative matters should be decentralized to the services." Although Jones's proposals were weak, they broadened the debate to include comprehensive reorganization.

To help inform Tower, I collected prior statements by General Taylor, including excerpts from his landmark book, *The Uncertain Trumpet*, published in 1959. That work had advanced a new national security strategy called "flexible response," which the Kennedy administration adopted. Taylor's book also recommended abolishing the JCS and separating those "responsibilities of the Joint Chiefs of Staff which can be dealt with by committee methods from those which require one-man responsibility." Taylor suggested replacing the JCS with "a single defense chief of staff for the one-man functions and by a new advisory body called provisionally the Supreme Military Council."[16]

Tower was the only senator present when he started the hearing. The hearing would be more than half over before another senator joined him. Tower began by welcoming his "distinguished colleague from the State of Texas, Dick White, with whom it has been my pleasure to work over the years."[17] White then delivered a straightforward summary of the House bill, briefly answered two questions from Tower, and departed.

The chairman then announced that the panel of three former JCS chairmen would testify in the following order: Jones, Taylor, and Holloway. "As an old naval person, I always like to give the Navy the last word," Tower joked.

Jones, testifying on JCS reforms for the first time since his retirement six months earlier, termed the problem "the most important defense issue facing the Congress and the nation. It makes issues on the MX [intercontinental ballistic missile] and others pale in comparison." The retired general commented that while serving as chairman, he thought "it would be appropriate that I limit myself to the Joint Chiefs of Staff." In retirement, Jones did not feel so constrained. He urged the adoption of a broad reform perspective: "I do not think one can address the issue of the Joint Chiefs of Staff without looking at the bigger issue of what is wrong in defense and what are the problems, not only in the Pentagon, but here in Congress."

Jones's oral statement also advocated "strengthening the role of the secretary of defense" and providing him "better advice on alternatives" and pressed the need for changes to end "services dominating the joint system." The former chairman reiterated his belief that reform should be studied "in great depth and in a broad context of our overall defense to include the role of Congress." Noting the inadequacy of that day's environment, he recommended proceeding "in an atmosphere next year that is not quite as hectic as this crisis of the lame-duck session."

As soon as Jones finished characterizing the atmosphere as hectic, Tower recessed the hearing so he could race to the Senate floor for a vote.

When Tower reconvened the hearing, General Taylor presented his views on JCS deficiencies and recommended fixes. He criticized the House bill as "most disappointing because of the failure to come to grips with the major defects in the system" and advised the committee to "give the House bill the close attention it deserves and reject it."

Admiral Holloway did not like the House bill either. Not because it was too weak, but because it was unnecessary and would "violate the safeguards for the assurance of civilian control and substantially reduce the opportunity for arriving at the best military decisions crucial to our national survival."

Tower showed signs of discomfort as the admiral forcefully defended the status quo. This was beginning to look like 1947 again with the navy opposing army and air force proposals to strengthen unification.

After another recess in response to a floor vote, the chairman questioned the admiral: "I happen to be one of those who has been concerned in the past that our civilian officials have not relied enough on professional military advice. Now, if you don't support any organizational changes that have been proposed this morning, how will you enhance the role of military leaders in national security decision making?"

"The principal reason that the civilian leadership did not take the advice of the Joint Chiefs of Staff . . . was because the chiefs were not giving advice that the civilian leadership wanted to hear," Holloway responded. "I believe that the present organization and concept is a sound one."

As the admiral was providing this answer, Sen. John Warner (R-Virginia), a former navy secretary, arrived. His questioning of the witnesses further highlighted Holloway's divergence from Jones and Taylor. To one Warner question, Jones replied that "Admiral Holloway and I must be looking at a different bill because the way I interpret this bill is the way that General Taylor does, that the changes are trivial. . . . I agree with General Taylor that if we pass this bill the country might think we have solved the problem. The problems are far greater than this."

Nunn arrived just as Tower and Warner were departing for another floor vote. In an unusual move, instead of recessing, Republican Tower allowed Democrat Nunn to chair the hearing in his absence. The Georgia senator asked Jones and Holloway to clarify their differences. The admiral answered, "The disagreement is that I think the Joint Chiefs are doing their job properly. General Jones, I think, believes that they are not."

Turning to Taylor, Nunn asked, "Can we look back in our history to any point where we have functioned the way you would envision that we should function?"

"I do not think we ever have," the army general answered. "That does not forgive us today, because the danger has changed. The time factor has changed. The complexities of weapons have changed."

Tower returned to close the hearing. Senator Jeremiah Denton (D-Alabama), a former admiral, arrived just as the hearing was ending. When he asked if Denton had any questions, Tower called him "Admiral Denton." The powerful SASC chairman quickly corrected himself. "I'm sorry. Being only a chief petty officer, I am awed by rank," he said.

Adjourning the hearing, Tower announced, "This is only the first in what I expect to be a number of hearings that will be continued into the 98th Congress." It was a pledge that encouraged many reformers. I had been on the Senate staff for too long to put too much weight on such promises, most of which are never fulfilled. This hearing was a political courtesy to a retiring representative, and it had occurred only because the representative hailed from Texas.

The Joint Staff prepared a summary of the hearing for internal use. It included the following impressions: "General Jones and Admiral Holloway were forceful and clashed on most points. General Taylor's health is failing rapidly and his delivery was weak, but his responsiveness to questions showed his intellect is still great. Senator Nunn is clearly coming from a reformer's perspective and sees the issue in a larger DoD-government context. Senator Warner seems to lean somewhat [in the] same way. Senator Tower, except for his 'amen' about putting Congress' house in order on [the] defense budget, is hard to read."[18]

The hearing revealed little to me other than the fact that Jones had joined Taylor in opposing the House bill, but the House bill was gasping its last breaths. It would die when the Senate adjourned on December 23.

Although I learned little, Tower learned something important: the navy, as represented by Holloway's mainstream views, fiercely objected to even the weak House reforms. From his first foray onto the reorganization battlefield,

Tower understood the dangers posed by this issue. Observing Tower's discomfort, I did not expect him to take the initiative in the new Congress on reorganizing the JCS or any other Pentagon component. I was certain that, having fulfilled his commitment to White and shown good faith toward Nunn, the Texas Republican would not make additional moves without significant pressure.

Tower soon surprised me.

CHAPTER 5

Unfinished Business

Nothing great was ever achieved

without enthusiasm.

—Emerson, *The Selected Writings*

of Ralph Waldo Emerson

When the Ninety-Eighth Congress convened in January, 1983, Cong. Bill Nichols of Alabama decided to chair the Investigations Subcommittee of the House Armed Services Committee, where he ranked fourth among Democrats. Nichols was following in the footsteps of retired Texas congressman Dick White.

The HASC members respected Nichols much more than they had White. The Alabama congressman's views and fervent patriotism fit well with the panel's conservative, promilitary orientation. In his fourteen years on the committee, he had compiled a solid record. The work of the Investigations Subcommittee would benefit from Nichols's stature.

On February 2, Nichols and the subcommittee's new ranking Republican, Larry Hopkins of Kentucky, met with John Lally and Arch Barrett to identify areas of inquiry for the subcommittee during the Ninety-Eighth Congress. The staffers raised JCS reorganization as a potential topic. Knowing of the previous year's exhaustive efforts, the slow-talking Nichols said: "This is unfinished business. We need to put it on our agenda." Although the new chairman felt obligated to carry out this work, it was not his issue. Nichols saw the unfinished business belonging to Dick White.[1]

Quiet and slow to anger, the Alabamian was described as "a huge man, tall and shaped like a barrel." At Alabama Polytechnic Institute (later Auburn

University), Nichols starred in football, earning three letters and serving as team captain. He studied agriculture and received his bachelor's degree in 1939. Two years later, Nichols earned a master's degree in agronomy.[2]

World War II interrupted Nichols's agriculture career. An ROTC graduate, he entered the army in March, 1942, as an artillery second lieutenant. His first action came in the Allied invasion of France. On Nov. 30, 1944, during the Battle of the Hürtgen Forest, a land mine shattered his left foot. Complications developed, and he lost his leg. Although doctors expected him to die, Nichols recovered slowly. The army finally discharged him as a captain in early 1947.

Nichols returned to his hometown of Sylacauga, started farming, and embarked on a business career. He entered politics in 1958 and won a seat in the state House of Representatives. Four years later, the electorate placed him in the state Senate. Governor George Wallace asked Nichols to serve as a floor leader, handling education and agricultural legislation.

Nichols entered the U.S. House of Representatives in January, 1967, following his election to represent Alabama's Third District. He was not considered a legislative activist and was often reluctant to speak out on issues. As a result of his chairmanship of the Military Personnel Subcommittee, Nichols was best known as a protector of military personnel, especially enlisted men and women.

According to Barrett, "Bill Nichols inspired more loyalty and love among the people who worked for him than any other individual I have ever known in my life—absolute affection." G. Kim Wincup, an aide on the Military Personnel Subcommittee, called Nichols "absolutely one of the most wonderful guys I ever met."[3]

Barrett explained that Nichols always treated people "with tremendous dignity. Complete strangers could go into his office, and they would feel, in just a few minutes . . . that they had been brought into the circle of someone who was interested in what they had to say and the contribution they had to make." Barrett added, "He made every member of his staff feel very important to him."[4]

Nichols said that to do well in public office, you have to "like people. You've got to understand people. You've got to be able to be interested in people's problems."[5]

Regarding Nichols's work, Barrett observed, "Mr. Nichols had the best judgment of any man—certainly any congressman—that I have ever been associated with." He "did not juggle the thousand issues that a congressman had from day-to-day. You had to spin him up, remind him where you were the last time you talked about this issue, then bring him forward, and lay out a particular problem. But if you did that, and then told him the various options, pros and cons, Mr. Nichols would make a decision, and rather quickly. . . . Six months later I could look back at that decision, and he invariably made the right decision."[6]

12. Second Lieutenant William F. Nichols, USA, at Fort
Bragg, North Carolina, about 1941.
(Auburn University Archives.)

Nichols, Wincup commented, "was never really regarded as an intellectual on military thinking, but he pushed through the Defense Officer Personnel Management Act with all its intricate details. He spent the time and learned it. And he became willing to do the same thing on reorganization."[7]

Nichols and seven other members were newly appointed to the Investigations Subcommittee. Only six congressmen returned from the 1982 subcommittee that had passed the JCS reform bill. The sole Republican holdover was Hopkins, who had not participated in the earlier work.

On February 3, at the subcommittee's initial meeting, Nichols briefed members on the prospective agenda. He raised "completion of legislative action" on JCS reform as the initial topic. Nichols and Hopkins "agreed that we should solicit the views of Secretary Weinberger, General Vessey, chairman of the JCS, and the other members of the Joint Chiefs, on the reorganization legislation . . . immediately." Then further action would be planned. The subcommittee supported this course. Anticipating this outcome, Nichols had already written to Weinberger asking for DoD's views on H.R. 6954, the 1982 bill.[8]

In mid-January, President Reagan concurred with Secretary Weinberger's endorsement of the JCS's limited reorganization recommendations. The president wrote to the secretary: "We should take advantage of this opportunity to improve the ability of the national military command structure to respond to the challenges ahead."[9]

In late February, Weinberger responded to Nichols's letter, announcing that "the administration is currently in the process of preparing legislation on this subject [to] be submitted to Congress in the near future." He communicated for the first time that the administration did not favor major JCS reorganization: "The Joint Chiefs have not proposed and the administration is not at this time considering any major reforms in the statutes establishing the Joint Chiefs of Staff. This is because we feel that the existing provisions of title 10 create a generally satisfactory structure."[10]

Weinberger's letter finally established the battle lines. The administration had taken a full year to decide whether it did or did not favor major JCS reorganization. Weinberger had decided to support the recommendations of his new JCS chairman, and the president had decided to support his defense secretary. This legislative-executive split magnified the challenge of reforming the Pentagon.

Responding to Nichols's request for the administration's views on the House-passed bill, Weinberger said he would "provide the subcommittee with our evaluation of that bill at the same time as we forward our own legislative proposal."

On April 6, the subcommittee decided to schedule JCS reorganization hearings. "I believe that we should have Secretary Weinberger's views, the recommendations of the Joint Chiefs, and the administration's legislative proposal so that we can commence consideration of this very important issue at an early date," said Nichols.[11]

Despite their correspondence, neither Nichols nor Weinberger made the first move on reorganization legislation in 1983. That action belonged to Cong. Ike Skelton, a four-term Missouri Democrat whose interest in military affairs long predated his 1980 appointment to the HASC. Skelton was not an Investigations Subcommittee member, and he had not participated in the 1982 hearings or legislation. Nevertheless, on April 14, he introduced the "Military Command Reorganization Act of 1983," which the House designated H.R. 2560.

Skelton was especially interested in the reform proposals of Gen. Maxwell Taylor, a fellow Missourian. When Skelton decided to submit his own legislative proposal, he sent Barrett and Tommy Glakas from his personal staff to interview Taylor, and then asked Barrett to translate Taylor's broad ideas into concrete provisions. Before submitting the legislation, the congressman met with Taylor and "went over his bill line-by-line with General Taylor for two hours."[12]

House Resolution 2560 would abolish the JCS, including the chairman, and replace them with a single chief of staff, who would serve as the principal military adviser. Two deputy chiefs would assist the new chief. The bill's other major provision would create a National Military Council consisting of five or six distinguished officers recalled from retirement or on their last assignment to advise the president and defense secretary on policy, strategy, and command responsibilities and assess policy and program implementation.

The Skelton bill paralleled General Meyer's proposals. Both would end the dual-hatting of service chiefs, create an advisory council to perform the strategy and planning function, and vest other responsibilities in a single officer. Given Skelton's interest, Nichols invited him to attend the subcommittee's hearings. The Missouri congressman proved to be the chairman's biggest supporter on JCS reform.

On April 18, DoD's general counsel, William H. Taft IV, submitted to Congress the Pentagon's legislative proposal on JCS reorganization, designated H.R. 3145 by the House. Taft's transmittal letter said, "The proposal would place the chairman of the Joint Chiefs of Staff in the national military chain of command, and would promote the efficiency of the Joint Staff by eliminating statutory restrictions that are disadvantageous to the effectiveness of that organization." Three proposed changes would achieve the second purpose: The bill would increase the maximum peacetime tour on the Joint Staff, including the director's, from three to four years. It would reduce the minimum interval between Joint Staff assignments from three to two years. Last, it would remove the four-hundred-officer limit on the size of the Joint Staff. Each change was consistent with improvements sought in the 1982 House bill.[13]

The bill language and explanatory text placing the chairman in the chain of command did not achieve the same clarity. Although one part of the bill language added a new duty for the chairman to "serve in the national military chain of command," the most prominent language suggested that he was not actually "in" the chain: "The chain of command runs from the president to the secretary [of defense] and through the chairman, Joint Chiefs of Staff, to the combatant commands. Orders to combatant commands shall be issued by the president or the secretary through the chairman, Joint Chiefs of Staff." When I read the bill, I did not think "through the chairman" meant the same as "placed in the chain of command."

Joint Chiefs of Staff Publication 1, *Dictionary of Military and Associated Terms*, then defined chain of command as: "The succession of commanding officers from a superior to a subordinate through which command is exercised." On one hand, DoD's language said they wanted to make the chairman part of the succession of commanding officers. On the other hand, Taft's letter explained that this change would "make explicit his functions as a link between the secretary of defense and the unified and specified commands." It also explained that "The practice has been for the secretary of defense to communicate with the combatant commands through the chairman of the Joint Chiefs of Staff, and the proposed legislation would formalize this arrangement." The words *link* and *communicator* did not create for me the image of someone who was part of a succession of commanding officers. I thought the idea of clarifying the chairman's role as the link and communicator had merit, but I judged that giving the chairman command of all forces was not likely to sell, at least not in the Senate.[14]

The department's confused chain of command proposal raised doubts about the depth of its understanding of defense organization. Moreover, promoting placement of the chairman in the chain of command made the department appear schizophrenic. Just a few months before, many Pentagon elements had bitterly opposed a few modest changes to strengthen the chairman. Now the Pentagon was unanimously urging his designation as supreme military commander.

Reform supporters reacted negatively to the administration's proposal. *Armed Forces Journal* reported that "proponents of JCS reform contend that the administration's changes are 'cosmetic.'"[15]

Weinberger declined Nichols's March 17 and April 28 requests for him to appear before the Investigations Subcommittee on grounds that a defense secretary normally testified only to a full committee. After considerable to-ing and fro-ing, the secretary agreed that he and General Vessey would meet informally with Nichols and his subcommittee. General Counsel Taft and Assistant Secretary for Legislative Affairs Russell A. Rourke accompanied Weinberger and Vessey to the meeting on May 18. Nichols and eight other subcommittee members participated, as did Skelton.[16]

Weinberger opened with a brief review of events that included the subtle but pivotal observation: "General Jones, the former chairman and chief critic of the present JCS reorganization, retired and was replaced by General Vessey." Results of the requested review from the "newly constituted" JCS, Weinberger said, "are reflected, inasmuch as legislative action is required, in the administration's proposal."[17]

The secretary elaborated: "An anomaly in the present law, which restricts the JCS chairman from commanding, would be removed, and the chairman would be placed in the chain of command by law." As far as the secretary was

13. Secretary of Defense Caspar Weinberger and Cong. Bill Nichols meet in the congressman's office. (Auburn University Archives.)

concerned, the chairman was going to be placed in the succession of commanding officers. The administration's proposals, Weinberger acknowledged, "are modest proposals, but they represent all that is needed in legislation. . . . The JCS system is already working well. . . . Good people are what it takes to make the JCS system work."

Weinberger said he opposed "the detailed management changes contained in H.R. 6954," which the House had passed in 1982. Concerning a deputy chairman, the secretary said, "No need has been demonstrated for such a position." He added, "General Vessey has established a duty roster among the chiefs which provides for a three-month rotation of the position of 'acting deputy chairman.' That system works and is satisfactory." Weinberger said he objected to H.R. 6954's Senior Strategy Advisory Board as "not needed because the secretary of defense already has access to advice from people such as those envisioned for the advisory board."

Weinberger also commented on Meyer's proposal to replace the chiefs with a National Military Advisory Council: "Assignment of dual responsibilities to the chiefs is not a problem if the individuals are carefully chosen. There is no evidence, with the current group of chiefs, that a conflict exists between their service and joint roles." He said current cooperation between the air force and navy chiefs on bomber support of sea control exemplified the absence of conflict.

Vessey then explained that the chiefs had decided to "address JCS reform themselves and not delegate any part of the task to staff or deputies." From their discussions, Vessey said, "The JCS agreed that the law should not be changed with respect to the duties given to the JCS." He admitted, "The JCS wrestled with the other issues for several months and arrived at a number of conclusions, and several new insights."

The four-star general reported that "the JCS concluded that the most important role of the Joint Chiefs of Staff is the same as the secretary of defense's civilian staff: to make the secretary of defense as capable as possible in performing his job." Vessey discussed three key JCS relationships: with the president and secretary of defense, among the chiefs, and with unified and specified commanders. Regarding the first relationship, "The Joint Chiefs concluded that through the years their predecessors had tied their own hands with procedures and other limitations which are not necessary and not required under law. As a result, many things which should be accomplished by the Joint Chiefs of Staff have moved to the Office of the Secretary of Defense. This is not a criticism of OSD. The movement has been because the Joint Chiefs of Staff have shunned responsibilities which they should shoulder."

To fix this problem, Vessey said, "The Joint Chiefs intend to nurture their relationship with the president and the secretary of defense more diligently, and improve it." He added that the "chiefs have asked the secretary of defense to review the things currently accomplished in the Office of the Secretary of Defense that should be done by the Joint Chiefs and begin a movement to restore those responsibilities to the JCS."

The relationship among the Joint Chiefs, Vessey said, reflected the two aspects of a chief's responsibility: as a service chief and as a member of a body of advisers who should rise above service interest in providing advice. The chairman revealed that the joint chiefs had "wrestled with the conflicting aspects of their position in light of the testimony of both General Meyer and General Taylor last year. They also asked the question: Is there enough time for a chief to fulfill both roles?"

As to any conflict of interest, the chiefs decided "that the president must have advice in every instance from the officer most capable of giving advice based upon his knowledge of the capabilities of his service. That can be no other person than the chief of that service. And for that reason, it is necessary that chiefs of service remain members of the Joint Chiefs of Staff advisory body."

Regarding the time problem, Vessey said, "The chiefs referred back to the Eisenhower solution.[18] That is, the provision of vice chiefs to focus on the day-to-day operation of the services." In wartime a chief might focus on his advisory function "and leave service direction to the vice chief. In peacetime, however, there is time for a chief to perform both jobs."[19]

On the third relationship, between the JCS and unified and specified commanders, Vessey simply said, "The chiefs agreed that the role of the CINCs should be increased."

Vessey recounted the wide range of opinion expressed on Jones's proposal to establish a vice chairman. Almost all former chiefs of staff recommended against a vice chairman. Former chairmen were mixed in their response while former Joint Staff directors favored the idea. He revealed the stumbling block: "the relationship between the vice chairman and the other chiefs would be a difficult one." Vessey said, "The Joint Chiefs split on the issue." Since they were split, he asked them to assume that they had approved the vice chairman position and to attempt to write a charter for the job. "No member of the Joint Chiefs of Staff was able to write a satisfactory charter. Consequently, the JCS decided to oppose establishing a vice chairman."

The JCS chairman then explained that the duty roster for acting chairman "has benefited the chairman by assisting him when he is absent. It has broadened the perspective of the chiefs, deepening their experience and understanding because they act as JCS chairman at the highest levels of government not only as advisers to the secretary of defense, but to the National Security Council and the president." Vessey concluded, "This makes them better chiefs of staff and members of the JCS."

Nichols, responding to Weinberger's and Vessey's statements, said: "The subcommittee has been addressing the issue of JCS reorganization for more than a year. It is time to put it to bed." He noted his tremendous respect for Vessey and his views on the subject, but in his courteous manner, signaled skepticism about the Pentagon's proposal by telling Weinberger some of his changes were "cosmetic."

"I believe the subcommittee should accept the administration proposals, which reflect the Joint Chiefs of Staff views," Vessey commented. "If once accepted, these proposals do not result in improved performance—that is, if they don't work—then the Congress should move to a more radical solution such as the one Mr. Skelton has proposed."

Skelton seized the opportunity to explain his bill. On Joint Staff provisions, he said, "At present, the best officers—with justification—do not want to serve on the Joint Staff because this assignment hurts their career." He said that this indicated the relative unimportance of the Joint Staff.

"I am working on it," Weinberger told the subcommittee. "I have told the Joint Chiefs that any stigma which derives from working on the Joint Staff must be removed."

Vessey noted that the "Joint Chiefs of Staff have addressed this problem and that it is on the way to being corrected." The general admitted, "The Navy did not promote anyone to admiral from the Joint Staff on the last list. But the other services did promote officers to flag rank. Admiral Watkins is aware of this problem and has assured me that it will be corrected."

Weinberger had brought to the meeting a draft letter to Nichols clearly stating that the JCS had unanimously recommended the Pentagon's legislative proposal to him. The letter proclaimed that "it is the position of the Department of Defense, supported by the current Joint Chiefs of Staff, that improvements in the operation of the Joint Chiefs of Staff, to the extent they are necessary, can and should come primarily from management initiatives undertaken within the current statutory framework."[20] General Jones had retired, but General Meyer was still a joint chief. Many observers wondered what had been done to get the army chief to back off his forceful proposal and instead support the administration's limited ideas.

The meeting and follow-up letter left no doubt that the Pentagon would resist changes beyond the modest ones in its legislative proposal. During the session, both Nichols and Hopkins indicated that they were eager to finish this unfinished business. Weinberger's and Vessey's arguments appeared to significantly influence the two subcommittee leaders. But the secretary's and general's presentations had not changed Barrett's thinking. "I believed Weinberger and Vessey were offering little, if anything," he recalled. "Accepting their proposal would leave the joint establishment in the hands of service interests. Nothing would come from enacting the Pentagon-proposed legislation, and the issue would be put to rest for many more years."[21]

Barrett had quickly established a strong relationship with Nichols, who seemed "to place more and more confidence" in his staffer. Whether the chairman's confidence in Barrett would withstand the Alabama congressman's admiration for and deference to senior defense officials and officers was unknown. "Nichols had seldom, if ever, bucked the Pentagon," Barrett noted. "To do so would be new and painful for him."

Weinberger hoped that enactment of the administration's proposal would get rid of this pesky issue. The repeated airing of past failures and alleged structural deficiencies might make it difficult over the long run to maintain congressional and public support for the big Reagan defense buildup. On May 20 he reported to the president on his informal meeting with the Investigations Subcommittee. The secretary judged that Nichols would not challenge the Pentagon: "I expect the committee will again approve a bill with minor changes to the present system, a position with which we are comfortable."[22]

A month after meeting with Weinberger and Vessey, the Investigations Subcommittee began its 1983 reorganization hearings. "We don't need a lot of hearings," Nichols told Barrett. "We have a thousand pages of hearings, but we should inform a new subcommittee of the issues and have the Joint Chiefs over." Nichols planned only three hearings with a total of eight witnesses.[23]

At the first hearing, on the morning of June 14, the new chairman summarized his subcommittee's situation: "We have before us three alternatives: the administration's proposal, last year's bill, and a more far-reaching measure advanced by the Honorable Ike Skelton of Missouri." Nichols's next statement recorded his skepticism about the administration's legislation. "In exploring these alternatives, the members of the subcommittee should recall that the bill we reported last year was criticized as being too modest to overcome the problems identified by a majority of witnesses during the many weeks in which we received testimony last year. Yet the administration's proposal before us is much more timid than our 97th Congress bill. We shall need to find out why the administration believes that the few changes it is recommending will correct the rather fundamental flaws identified in the hearings last year."[24]

But he also did not believe in major surgery: "On the other hand, we will need to explore with Congressman Skelton and, later, General Maxwell Taylor why we should dissolve the present organization and start over, as they propose, without first attempting more moderate remedies within the present framework."

In line with congressional courtesy, Skelton was the subcommittee's first witness. He began by quoting a British military historian, Sir Basil Liddell Hart: "There are over 2,000 years of experience to tell us that the only thing harder than getting a new idea into the military mind is to get an old one out." The Missouri Democrat reviewed the long history of problems: "Many of the structural flaws that we will discuss today in the Joint Chiefs of Staff system came about as a result of those compromises made back in 1947 which had the effect of preserving autonomy for the individual services." Skelton devoted the remainder of his testimony to explaining his bill.[25]

All five joint chiefs testified immediately after Skelton. Two members—Meyer and Barrow—were retiring at the end of the month. The Senate had already confirmed their replacements: Gen. John Wickham, USA, and Gen. P. X. Kelley, USMC. During the confirmation process, when Senator Tower asked about JCS reform proposals, Kelley responded: "I see very little in these proposals which would improve the effectiveness of the JCS. I believe that the system under which we currently operate is sound and effective."[26]

The appointment of Wickham and Kelley meant that all of the joint chiefs would be Reagan men. This Reagan team, which could expect to serve together for the next three years, was seen as "heavy with safe players who would ordinarily be a low-profile, go-along group." Long-term acquaintances described Wickham as a "conservative, efficient, detached officer," and predicted that he, in contrast to Meyer, would do "little innovating or cage-rattling." Colleagues portrayed Watkins as "a deft political operator" but doubted he would "make waves for Reagan, partly because he is all but eclipsed by the highly vocal Navy secretary, John F. Lehman Jr." Described as "affable," Gabriel was judged as "unlikely to poke his head above the cockpit." Kelley, "extrovertish" and "well-connected politically," was viewed as "likely to emerge as the dominant personality on the chiefs, partly for lack of competition."[27]

In front of Nichols's panel, the five joint chiefs took a low profile. Only Vessey made an opening statement, repeating what he had said to the subcommittee in the informal session. The general's written statement made it clear that the chiefs would support only the administration's proposal.[28]

During members' questioning, Meyer attempted to explain the dramatic change in his position. Noting that he had been "an advocate of major surgery," he now believed "that the most important aspect of this issue . . . is an agreement on the part of the chiefs . . . that we need to do a better job of providing military advice to the president and secretary of defense. We all agree with that [and] since this group of chiefs was willing to agree on a way to come up with a solution as to how to provide better military advice, I was willing to join with them in a common approach toward the solution." Meyer never clarified exactly what solution he was talking about.[29]

Near the end of his long statement, Meyer observed, "It may be necessary in the future to make some additional changes, but I believe . . . that this is the proper approach at this time."[30]

Meyer's testimony infuriated Barrett. The staffer saw the historic opportunity to reform the JCS slipping away. Just a year earlier, three sitting chiefs had testified that reforms were needed. Now, two were retired and the other was recanting. The weakness of the Pentagon's legislative proposal also irritated Barrett. It represented exactly what reformers were criticizing the JCS for doing: recommending the lowest common denominator. Vessey and his colleagues had unanimously recommended the proposal, but stopped short of pushing any ideas where opinions diverged. And Meyer, the champion of bold reforms, had gone along with this watered-down set of recommendations.[31]

As Barrett waited for his chance to ask questions, he pondered whether or not he should challenge Meyer. "I had a long time to think about it," the former colonel recalled, "and I decided that I would."[32]

When Nichols gave Barrett the floor, he immediately went after the army chief. "I would like to return to General Meyer's testimony of last year because it certainly conflicts, I believe, with what he said today." Earlier, Barrett reminded him, Meyer had argued "that any change we adopt should do a number of things. One is that it must enhance 'the role of the chairman and permit him to take charge of what I consider to be elemental internal discussions.' He also said, 'I don't believe you can tinker with the issues any longer; tinkering will not suffice.'" The former colonel then quoted the army chief as criticizing "the divided loyalty we currently demand of the service chiefs' that must be ended."[33]

The rapid-fire, accusatory tone of Barrett's statements sounded impolite. He later recognized that in his questioning of Meyer "Nichols let him get away with murder."[34]

Barrett continued firing: "Now, it seems to me that, with those sorts of past statements, to come here and indicate four rather modest administration changes will accomplish any part of his proposed reform is really a change in one short year."[35]

"Is Meyer inconsistent with what he said last year?" the general responded, speaking of himself in the third person. "The answer is yes. I have tried to explain why. Not because I don't believe that at some point in time we have gone in the direction in which I have indicated, but rather I believe that this group of chiefs . . . has been able to come to grips with some of these problems." His next sentence suggested that part of his willingness to go along centered on a desire for the JCS to quickly gain a more influential role in the Reagan administration. "At this time, this provides a solution to the problem when you are trying to get political support from a group this far into an administration, where you would have to make any sort of management changes."[36]

Lally asked Vessey if he had been able to effect any changes that would improve the timeliness and quality of military advice. After Vessey responded, Marine Commandant Barrow jumped in: "Let me add to that question because I have been there four years and I think we have been dancing around a very key issue here, sir, and that is that the JCS is very personality sensitive." Putting his arm around Vessey and hugging him, the commandant continued, "The key to all that is this fellow sitting here." Barrow explained that the new chairman provided the kind of leadership to the JCS that makes things happen, causes advice to be timely, and avoids trying to seek unanimity at all costs. "But this fellow [Vessey] has not given himself enough credit," Barrow continued. "He came in a year ago with clear-cut objectives he wanted to achieve, and one of them was obviously to enhance the timeliness and the effectiveness of the advice we give to the secretary of defense and the president. In my judgment, that has been done."[37]

Barrow stated publicly what the Pentagon had been telling Capitol Hill in private: "Vessey knew how to make the current system work effectively." The Pentagon placed enormous trust in the new chairman to overcome past problems. Barrett sensed that Vessey's approach and style appealed to Investigations Subcommittee members, who seemed prepared to heed Vessey's advice as well.[38]

Noting that the JCS had effectively defended their views, the *Armed Forces Journal* reported, "A recent congressional appearance by all of the Joint Chiefs of Staff may well defuse the sensitive issue of JCS reorganization, some fifteen months after two prominent JCS members ignited it."[39]

On June 23, Gen. Maxwell Taylor's testimony put the subcommittee back in a reform mood. He said that since his appearance before the subcommittee in 1982, his views had "changed little, if at all, and are quite similar to those expressed by Congressman Skelton's bill, H.R. 2560, presently before you."[40]

The high-pitched voice of the eighty-two-year-old former JCS chairman signaled his failing health. The general's mind remained sharp, however, and his
testimony was persuasive.[41]

Taylor criticized the administration's bill, H.R. 3145. Its provision that
would replace the corporate JCS in the chain of command with the chairman,
which Weinberger called "an important defense initiative," Taylor termed "little
more than a legislative legitimation" of an existing DoD directive. "In fact, the
language of H.R. 3145 authorizes the chairman to do little more than forward
orders from the president and the secretary to field commanders, which, to me,
is pretty much a clerical function. If the intention is to elevate the chairman
notably above his colleagues, that result is not achieved."[42]

Taylor called H.R. 3145's proposed Joint Staff changes "reasonable but also
of little importance." The general noted that he had a quite different impression of the attitudes of Weinberger and Vessey toward the need for JCS reform.
"The secretary sees little, if any, need for change. . . . The chairman . . . is inclined to concede the existence of past faults in the system but believes that he
and his colleagues have agreed on a series of remedial actions, which, if allowed to run their course, will correct the defects." Of these, Taylor said, "They
make an impressive list, but unfortunately offer no remedy to old weaknesses,
such as the following: A. The excessive workload of the dual-hatted chiefs; B.
Their demonstrated inability to produce timely advice on matters much beyond next year's budget; C. The inevitable service bias they bring to the council
table; and D. The inherent defects of committee action—slowness, ponderosity,
indecisiveness, and compromise."

The next part of Taylor's testimony had a major impact on the subcommittee's thinking. "It is clear that the secretary is prepared to stand pat on the
Joint Chiefs of Staff system as it is and would strongly resist any major changes
such as those contained in Congressman Skelton's bill," the general observed.
"Even if Congress were to pass this latter bill, the cold reception it would receive in many parts of the Pentagon would nullify many of its basic purposes.
For any such drastic change in military organization to succeed, it must have
the support, cooperation and goodwill of the principal officials, legislative and
executive, responsible for it." If Skelton's reforms were unworkable, "What
should be done about H.R. 3145 and its pallid content?"

Taylor answered his own question: "It would be unfortunate, in my opinion, to pass it in its present form, if only because doing so would imply agreement with the secretary that all is well with the Joint Chiefs of Staff system. I
sincerely hope that this is not the view of this committee."

Instead, the general proposed "a better course," achievable with certain
amendments to give it more substance. "Since a major purpose of the bill is to
increase the authority of the chairman, let's give him something of real significance," he said.

Taylor recommended three amendments. Concerning the chain of command, his proposed language read: "The channel of command runs from the president to the secretary and through the chairman, Joint Chiefs of Staff, to the combatant commands. Orders to these commands from the president or the secretary pass through the chairman, Joint Chiefs of Staff, who is authorized to communicate as needed with the combatant commands to verify the execution of such orders and to assure the maintenance of the state of readiness required by the strategic tasks assigned the commands." He explained that "such a change would eliminate the impression that the chairman is merely a communications robot mechanically conveying military orders from the president or the secretary."

As his second amendment, Taylor proposed adding a new paragraph to the bill: "The chairman, JCS, in presiding over the Joint Chiefs of Staff, will be responsible for the timely conduct of business within that body, with authority to settle issues on which the members are divided. Any member may appeal the chairman's decision to the secretary of defense." In support, Taylor cited the Kennedy administration's successful use of executive chairmen to expedite the work of large standing committees.

The former chairman's last amendment would add another new paragraph making the chairman a regular National Security Council (NSC) member. These three changes, he said, "In combination, . . . should clarify and strengthen the position of the chairman and thereby facilitate the job of General Vessey in carrying out his in-house reform program."

Taylor offered "a final word about the Skelton bill, H.R. 2560. Although unhappily its time may not have come, it contains many features worthy of continuing study and further development."

Nichols's subcommittee called its last witness, Admiral Tom Moorer, on the morning of June 29. After delivering a laudatory summary of the career of the former JCS chairman, Nichols said, "I might add on a personal note that I am extremely proud to report that Admiral Moorer is a constituent of mine, coming from my congressional district. He has an illustrious family."

In his response, Moorer built upon his connection to the subcommittee chairman, adding: "I would also like to say that I am very pleased to have a gentleman like you as chairman of this committee conducting this investigation because there are so many people that recommend so many changes in the military that have never heard gunfire. On the other hand, you are a man that has been there. Consequently, I know that you will understand the overall problems and structures of a command establishment."

Turning to the substance of the hearing, Moorer challenged the recommendations of "some twenty studies, I believe, of the Joint Chiefs of Staff since it was set up by the National Security Act of 1947." He said that these studies recommended that "we should have an organization that will give a unified view" to the president and defense secretary. This statement inaccurately characterized previous studies' recommendations on military advice, but fit the point that Moorer wanted to make. He countered this alleged recommendation by asserting: "it is important, in my judgment, that the president of the United States receive not just a single recommendation but rather options as to what would be the best course of action from which we would choose."

Moorer next challenged the view that the chiefs should be removed from the JCS because they did not have time to perform dual assignments. He argued that if you "cannot find enough time to perform your duties as chief of a service and as a member of the Joint Chiefs of Staff, you are not qualified for the job."

Responding to General Jones's statement that the chairman lacked adequate authority, the admiral countered: "The chairman of the Joint Chiefs of Staff, with respect to those in uniform, has all the authority he is willing to take." Apparently in reference to proposals to ensure appropriate promotion rates for personnel in joint-duty positions, the admiral warned, "It is very unwise to penetrate, you might say, the service promotion system."

Concerning the pending legislation, Moorer said, "Now, I have studied General Vessey's statement [and] I support in toto everything that he has said. I think that General Vessey is a very mature officer with great experience and great intelligence and balance, and I would think that his statement provides the best guidance I have seen for reorganization of the Joint Chiefs of Staff. Therefore, I fully support H.R. 3145."

Of H.R. 2560, Moorer warned, "I must say with great respect to Congressman Skelton, I think that this proposal is filled with booby traps."

Although Nichols never revealed how he felt about his constituent's testimony, Barrett sensed that the admiral's arguments were backfiring. "I came to welcome Moorer's testimony year after year," Barrett recalled. "His poorly, though strongly, argued positions against any change probably resolved or converted many members to favor reform. The alternative would be to associate themselves with the untenable positions of an intellectually shallow, superficial, self-serving, and curmudgeonly witness."[43]

On July 28, the Investigations Subcommittee decided to report a clean bill in lieu of an amended H.R. 3145. Nichols and Barrett used the bill the House had passed in 1982 as the basis for new legislation. They added each provision of the administration's bill, using the administration's rather than General Taylor's language on placing the chairman in the chain of command. Where the 1982 bill and administration proposal addressed the same Joint Staff sections of law, the latter was substituted for the former.

The draft bill included three other new provisions. Taylor's idea to make the chairman a statutory member of the NSC was one addition. Nichols and

Barrett added a modified version of another Taylor idea, which would empower the JCS chairman to "determine when issues under consideration shall be decided." Taylor had wanted the chairman to decide issues when members were divided. Although not as forceful as the Taylor proposal, the adopted wording was designed to help the chairman improve the timeliness of military advice.

The third addition resulted in part from Vessey's testimony and in part from Jones's testimony the year before. Of the unified and specified commanders, Vessey said, "The secretary of defense has asked that I, as the chairman, become their spokesman on operational requirements."[44] Jones had recommended that the chairman oversee the unified and specified commanders. Nichols and Barrett included both ideas in a single provision and used the stronger "supervise" in lieu of Jones's "oversee."

Nichols and Barrett decided to drop three provisions from the 1982 House bill. In line with Weinberger's argument, language that would give a service chief the right to express his disagreement with a position by the chairman was removed. They deleted as well the provision establishing a Senior Strategy Advisory Board. The last provision dropped created a deputy chairman.

"I just couldn't believe that General Vessey didn't want a deputy," Barrett recalled. "I felt he was saying publicly something he really didn't believe. I didn't see how any JCS chairman, knowing what I knew, would not secretly want a deputy chairman. And I kept telling Mr. Nichols this. And he said, 'Well, he says he doesn't.' So, I persuaded Mr. Nichols to get Vessey's personal views, one on one. The markup was approaching, and I couldn't get them together. I finally got a telephone call arranged. Mr. Nichols . . . talked to General Vessey and told him, 'We're going to mark the bill without a deputy chairman.' Mr. Nichols would have marked it either way. Vessey told him privately what he said in public. He was against the deputy chairman. After that call, I gave up because I had no other recourse."[45]

All nine subcommittee members in attendance voted in favor of the new bill. Nichols, acting for himself and nine cosponsors, introduced the bill, to be called the "Joint Chiefs of Staff Reorganization Act of 1983," in the House on the following day. Surprisingly, three subcommittee Democrats who had cosponsored White's 1982 bill—Daniel, Aspin, and Nicholas Mavroules—did not participate in a single 1983 hearing on JCS reform. Aspin and Mavroules also did not cosponsor the 1983 bill.

Following its designation as H.R. 3718, the bill was referred to the Investigations Subcommittee on August 4. On that same day, the subcommittee referred it to DoD for its views. General Counsel Taft did not respond for the department until September 20. His letter stated that the department supported only those portions of the bill that were in the administration's proposal and opposed or found other provisions unnecessary.[46]

Undeterred by Pentagon opposition, Nichols asked the full committee to consider the bill the same day DoD responded. The Alabama Democrat briefly explained the bill to the committee. Skelton made a supporting statement. A few questions were asked. Then the full committee chairman, Mel Price of Illinois, said, "The question is on the approval of the bill. Those in favor vote aye." After the voice vote, Price announced, "The ayes have it. The bill is approved." The session lasted only ten minutes.[47]

The *Armed Forces Journal* judged H.R. 3718 to be a stronger JCS reform bill "than either the administration's proposal or a more modest JCS reorganization bill, the White bill, which the House overwhelming passed last year." The *Journal* may have rushed to judgment; H.R. 3718 made three big changes to the White bill. It would place the chairman in the chain of command, make the chairman an NSC member, and forego establishment of a deputy chairman. As General Taylor observed, the first change was inconsequential. Making the defense secretary and JCS chairman equal NSC members would adversely affect their superior-subordinate relationship. Deletion of the deputy chairman was obviously a step backward for JCS reform.[48]

On September 27, the HASC reported H.R. 3718 to the House. On October 17, the House considered H.R. 3718. No amendments were offered, and, as it had the previous year, the House suspended the rules and passed the bill by voice vote.[49]

Four days after the House approved H.R. 3718, Weinberger reported the result to Reagan: "By a unanimous voice vote, the House on Monday passed and sent to the Senate a bill promoted by the Armed Services Committee that would make limited structural changes to improve the functioning of the Joint Chiefs of Staff. In addition to expanding the authority of the chairman of the Joint Chiefs and making him a formal member of the National Security Council, the bill provided for an expanded Joint Staff to assist him in carrying out his responsibilities. As passed by the House, the department supports the bill, which is not as far-reaching as had been originally proposed. Hearings are now underway in the Senate on this issue, but the final outcome is uncertain."[50]

Weinberger's statement that "the department supports the bill" contradicted Taft's letter and DoD's overt opposition, which continued through 1984. Maybe the defense secretary did not want to admit to the president that the House had completely disregarded the Pentagon's opposition to H.R. 3718. Maybe the secretary did not feel as strongly as others in the Pentagon about JCS reform. Maybe the secretary would accept the modest provisions of the House bill as the price of getting past congressional fascination with reform of the joint system. In any case, the department's position on H.R. 3718 was not what Weinberger told Reagan.

For the second time in as many years, the House had passed a bill to reorganize the JCS. In 1983, the administration finally took a position on this controversial issue and DoD presented its own legislative proposal. Although the Pentagon poorly formulated and presented its limited ideas, Vessey considerably influenced the outcome of the second bill, particularly the decision to drop the deputy chairman provision. The House, however, ignored Pentagon opposition to enactment of any provision not included in its own proposal.

Under Bill Nichols's leadership, slightly more subcommittee members took an interest in JCS reform, but most considered it "to be one of the least understood, least interesting, most boring, and politically unrewarding issues the subcommittee could address." The vast majority of the HASC also continued to see this as Dick White's issue.[51]

Even Nichols did not yet see JCS reorganization as his issue. That would soon change. Six days after the House passed H.R. 3718, a military tragedy in the Middle East dramatically altered how Nichols felt about this legislation.

CHAPTER 6

Misfire in the Senate

No enemy is worse than bad advice.

—Sophocles, *Electra*

John Tower wanted to be secretary of defense long before Pres. George H. W. Bush nominated him for that position in January, 1989. Eight years earlier, he had angled for the job in Reagan's first cabinet. Tower made the short list of contenders, and the press briefly reported him as the leading candidate.[1] In the end, however, Reagan's old friend Cap Weinberger landed the job, and Tower assumed duties as the Senate Armed Services Committee's first Republican chairman in twenty-six years. Reagan reportedly passed over Tower, at least in part, because his strong leadership would be needed in the Senate to enact the new president's defense buildup.[2]

As the administration entered its third year, Tower remained "fixated on becoming secretary of defense."[3] By then he believed it was unlikely that Reagan would select him to lead the Pentagon as long as he was serving as the SASC chairman or ranking minority member. Senate defense votes were getting tougher, and the Pentagon was relying increasingly on Tower. Weinberger's report to Reagan on the defense authorization bill in 1983 emphasized the Texan's important role: "John Tower has done a superb job in managing the bill on the floor. His leadership and legislative expertise have once again been invaluable."[4] Tower concluded that retiring from the Senate would enhance his chances of becoming secretary of defense.[5]

Tower thought chances were excellent that Weinberger would step aside if Reagan were elected to a second term. Four years as DoD's head was an exhausting grind. Few had served longer. Tower also based his speculation on the secretary's low standing on Capitol Hill. Weinberger's unyielding, combative style had alienated many members. Tower judged the secretary's leadership of the Pentagon to be poor. He also knew that Weinberger's performance displeased White House aides who saw him as a political liability.[6] With these factors pointing toward an opening in the top Pentagon post, Tower wanted to position himself to be selected.

The grinding congressional routine and Tower's loss of interest in many Senate activities reinforced his thoughts of retirement. Foreign policy and defense issues held his attention, but Tower was losing interest in domestic affairs and the mundane demands of constituent services. For whatever reasons, he decided in July, 1983, not to stand for reelection in 1984. He waited until late summer to announce his decision.

In June, 1983, the Texas Republican decided to launch a major committee inquiry into defense reorganization. It was a step calculated to strengthen his credentials for secretary and might also expose what Tower saw as Weinberger's poor performance. Tower was determined to use this inquiry to show that he knew something about DoD organization and management. Ironically, his lack of knowledge on these subjects led to a misdirected, ill-fated inquiry.

Inspiration for the inquiry came from Lt. Gen. Victor H. "Brute" Krulak, a famous and highly regarded retired marine and father of the thirty-first Marine Corps commandant. Krulak resided in San Diego. His former mayor, Pete Wilson, a Republican SASC member, arranged a meeting with Tower. The general, two senators, and Jim McGovern, the SASC staff director, met briefly on the morning of May 4. There was a longer session the next evening without Wilson.[7]

Both meetings focused on Krulak's recent book, *Organization for National Security*, which rebutted the proposals of Generals Jones and Meyer. The book analyzed the military's deficiencies and offered forceful remedies. Like retired general J. D. Hittle, Krulak had worked on the National Security Act of 1947. He also participated in marine opposition to the 1949, 1953, and 1958 amendments. His book drew on these experiences as well as his service in World War II, Korea, and Vietnam during a distinguished thirty-four-year career.[8]

During the meetings, Krulak repeatedly emphasized one overarching theme: the need to move "away from centralization."[9] Of this evil, Krulak wrote: "There has grown up, in the complex called the Office of the Secretary of Defense, a self-nourishing, self-perpetuating bureaucracy which impedes and diffuses the essential warmaking functions . . . to a degree that gravely diminishes the ability of the United States to provide for its security."[10]

Krulak argued that the World War II structure had been effective. In his view, postwar modifications caused the "procession of disastrous performances" by the military. He criticized the expanded role of the defense secretary, creation of the position of JCS chairman, and the large, meddling OSD staff. Krulak called this top level of the Pentagon "a sort of institutional bloat that saps our soldierly strength."[11]

Krulak's book offered a simple fix: return to the World War II system with the service chiefs working directly with the president. He reminded readers that "The entire OSD complex is a creation that did not exist when we won the greatest war in history." Krulak recommended removing the secretary of defense from the chain of command so he could not interfere in the vital link between the president and chiefs. He wanted the secretary's staff to be drastically reduced in size and argued for elimination of the position of JCS chairman. "The overriding reality is, while the concept of a JCS has proven its case, the concept of a JCS chairman has not. It is time to acknowledge that reality and to eliminate the office."[12]

Krulak's arguments reinforced popular themes on Capitol Hill, where knowledge of the Pentagon's vast bureaucracy was limited and often superficial. Only when a committee or subcommittee undertook a specific investigation— such as the SASC's 1980 examination of the failed Iranian rescue mission— did members gain an improved understanding, and then only for a slice of the structure.

Many of Krulak's arguments appealed to Tower.[13] Like many other pro-defense members, Tower agreed with the general's assessment that the overinvolvement of civilians in military matters caused America's defeat in Vietnam. "57,900 Americans died in the Vietnam War," Krulak wrote. "A fair case can be made that the number of dead would have been fewer and the results more favorable had we fought the war the way our military leadership wanted."[14]

The four services, especially the navy and Marine Corps, sympathized with Krulak's arguments and possibly with some of his recommendations. Tower judged that his strong supporters—the uniformed services, especially the navy—would benefit from enactment of Krulak's ideas. By leading a crusade for this community, Tower could reasonably expect that the services' many supporters would lend their considerable weight, if and when the time came, to his candidacy for the Pentagon's top post.

Tower asked the SASC's top lawyer, Alan R. Yuspeh, for his thoughts on a reorganization inquiry. Law codified the Pentagon's structure. Tower wanted to know the magnitude of enacting statutory changes.

Yuspeh earned a business degree from Harvard and a law degree from Georgetown. Because I also had a Harvard M.B.A. and ten years of Pentagon experience, Yuspeh asked me to assist him in responding to the chairman. We recommended against a legislative effort to reorganize DoD for three reasons. First, it would be controversial. Reorganization battles had been among the Pentagon's most brutal and emotional fights. Even Marshall, Truman, and Eisenhower had been unable to reason with reform opponents. Second, the committee members and staff lacked the required expertise. Among staffers, only I had served in the Pentagon for a significant period and with duties that provided insights on reform issues. Finally, given its already full agenda, the committee did not have time for a project of this magnitude.

"I had some reservation about any committee staff of our size undertaking a difficult, time-consuming, consulting study," recalled Yuspeh, who had worked for McKinsey and Company, a management consulting firm. "If you were to approach defense reorganization as a McKinsey study, you probably would have had a four- or five-person team working on it for a year. So, you'd have five man years' worth of effort by people who are specifically trained in organizational analysis." Yet normal duties fully occupied the SASC's twenty-one-person professional staff. "The staff was struggling just to get the defense authorization bill done."[15]

Yuspeh and I were missing one key piece of information: We were unaware that Tower envisioned reorganization along the lines of Krulak's book, proposals that contradicted General Jones's recommendations and provisions of the House-passed bill.

Yuspeh forwarded our views to Tower in writing. We were not given the opportunity to speak with the chairman. Tower rejected our recommendation and decided to launch a major study.

At a press conference on June 21, 1983, Tower announced that "the Senate Armed Services Committee will begin a comprehensive series of hearings on the structure, organization, and decision making procedures of the Department of Defense." I helped draft the senator's three-page statement.[16]

I wanted Tower to announce that the committee would examine all major DoD components. This plan would differ from the House's approach of examining only the JCS. A Harvard Business School course on organizational design had taught me about the interdependence of an organization's components. One of my favorite textbooks argued that "an organization is not a mechanical system in which one part can be changed without a concomitant effect on the other parts. Rather, an organizational system shares with biological systems the property of an intense interdependence of parts such that a change in one part has an impact on others."[17] General Jones raised similar arguments during his appearance before the committee in December, 1982.[18]

Tower agreed with my arguments for a comprehensive approach.[19] The chairman's press statement identified six major areas for inquiry: OSD, the Organization of the Joint Chiefs of Staff (OJCS), unified commands, budget process, acquisition process, and interagency relations.

To lessen the blow on the administration, Tower said, "These proposed hearings . . . are not intended as a criticism of any presidential administration. The Department of Defense has grown under both Republican and Democratic administrations, and the complex bureaucracy at DoD is the result of a continuous, gradual organizational evolution."[20]

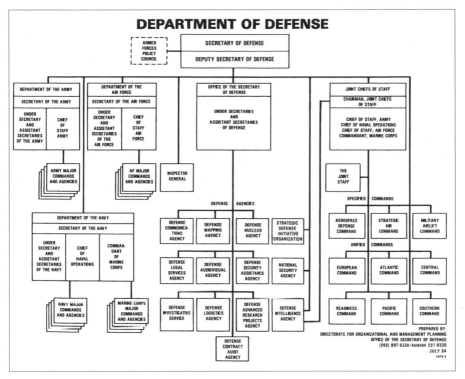

14. Defense Department Organizational Chart, July, 1984.

Tower planned that the full committee, not a subcommittee, would conduct the inquiry. Because the SASC did not have an investigations subcommittee, the full committee normally handled special inquiries. Full-committee hearings received more extensive media coverage than subcommittee sessions. With many nationally known members, the hearings would generate headlines and interest.

After Tower's announcement, I volunteered to organize the inquiry, and Tower and McGovern assigned me lead responsibility.[21] My background fit the task. After ten years in the Pentagon, I understood its structure and operations and had seen its problems up close. Academically, West Point had prepared me on military leadership and culture, and Harvard had provided me with a solid background on organization and management.

The Democratic staff that worked for the ranking minority member, Sen. Henry M. "Scoop" Jackson of Washington, selected Bruce D. Porter to be my counterpart. Prior to joining the committee in early 1983, Porter worked for Radio Free Europe in West Germany. He had earned both master's and doctoral degrees at Harvard following his graduation from Brigham Young University.

Given freedom to develop the inquiry, I settled on an approach with three key features. First, to the initial six areas to be studied, I added two more: military departments and congressional review and oversight. Some staff colleagues warned me I was "being too ambitious." Examining all major DoD components and processes simultaneously would be complicated and demanding, a "high-risk approach," they said. I understood their concerns, but a comprehensive approach offered the best chance for effective and lasting reform.

To augment the members' meager knowledge of defense organization, I determined that the staff should prepare a comprehensive report, synthesizing forty years of conflicting studies and testimony on military organization principles. This study proved to be an enormous burden, but it would play a pivotal role.

The third feature would involve the entire committee staff and military legislative assistants on SASC members' personal staffs in preparing the staff study. Because we had neither the expertise nor the time, the burdens of this project needed to be widely spread. Large-scale involvement also provided a better-informed staff when the inevitable controversy began to swirl around the committee members. Months later this widespread participation revealed an unforeseen advantage: it made the effort harder to kill.

Seven working groups would prepare the hearings and write chapters of the study. For each group, I recruited a majority staff coordinator and a minority staff counterpart. I headed the study group on OSD. Rick Finn would lead the OJCS team. Patrick A. Tucker, one of the majority counsels and a manpower specialist, assumed lead responsibility for studying the military departments. James C. Smith III, the longest-serving committee staffer, headed the team to examine the unified and specified commands. Michael B. Donley, the committee's budget and readiness guru, coordinated the work on the department's Planning, Programming, and Budgeting System. Yuspeh, the general counsel, headed two groups: National Security Council interagency system and procurement process. Each team had between three and eight members. Fifteen committee staffers and fourteen personal staffers participated, though none did so on a full-time basis.

A fourth feature of the inquiry originated with a colleague. As the staff began work, we prematurely focused on solutions. We were drawn in that direction by the debate on solutions under way in think tanks and universities. James G. Roche, the minority staff director, pointed out our error. "You need to focus on problems and their causes." Roche, who had a doctorate from the Harvard Business School, argued, "Only when you have precisely identified what needs to be fixed will you be able to formulate effective solutions."

Roche was right. My staff colleagues and I stopped thinking about solutions. We focused on problems and their causes. I revised the outline for each chapter of the staff study to emphasize this now-preeminent dimension.

In time, we came to understand why so many reorganization efforts fail. Nearly all reorganizers assume that they know what the problems are and immediately pursue solutions. They devote 5 percent of the effort to determining what is wrong and 95 percent to developing solutions. Then, when changes do not get to the heart of the problem, the organization experiences turbulence resulting in little benefit. Roche helped save us from that fate.

Late in the August recess, I briefed McGovern on my approach for the inquiry, proposed hearings, and preliminary results of our analysis. By then, Weinberger had already testified at the committee's first hearing. Our early staff work supported the views of Generals Jones and Meyer on joint system reform.

As I began to lay out the analytical results, McGovern interrupted me. "You're dead wrong," he declared. "Senator Tower was briefed by General Brute Krulak on his book on defense organization. Krulak recommends a return to the command system that worked so well during World War II. Tower is convinced that Krulak is right."

I was stunned. "I've never heard of Krulak's book," I replied. "But, from your description, his reforms are the last thing DoD needs. It's been clear since Pearl Harbor that the military needs a structure that will effectively integrate the capabilities of the four services."

"Bullshit," McGovern fired back. "This centralization crap has hamstrung the services. It's been the source of all operational problems. Tower's heard all the arguments, and he's made up his mind."

After a heated argument, I rose to depart. As I neared the door, McGovern firmly ordered, "And, Jim, I don't want you raising your views with Tower."

An Annapolis graduate, McGovern was a navy man even more so than Tower. McGovern was closely associated with John Lehman, the ambitious and ruthless navy secretary. Admiral William J. Crowe Jr. characterized Lehman as "the ultimate bureaucrat. He was unscrupulous. Didn't hesitate to lie."[22]

After his promotion from general counsel to staff director in late 1982, McGovern began isolating Tower from the Republican staff. The previous director, Rhett Dawson, had worked hard to ensure that the chairman heard all relevant ideas. McGovern took the opposite tack. He filtered all advice and information going to Tower and monitored all staff interaction with the chairman. Suddenly, Tower was not getting the full range of opinion.

At first, the Republican staff thought the new director was merely falling into the familiar trap of micromanagement. The staff designated Jim Smith and me to talk to McGovern about the problem. McGovern assured us that he had no intention of limiting the staff's access or the flow of information to Tower. He blamed his "newness to the duties of staff director." We accepted his explanation, but McGovern was misleading us.

One day when Tower had the majority staff assembled, the chairman told us, "Jim McGovern will be the single source through which all information from the committee will flow to me." Before the staff realized what was happening, McGovern had succeeded not only in isolating and controlling the chairman, but doing so with his blessing.

Following that meeting, the schism between McGovern and most Republican staffers widened. Every issue became a test of wills and bureaucratic skills. This split in the staff provided important support to me when McGovern and I later tangled on reorganization.

For nearly three years, Tower and I had worked closely on foreign policy issues. His fascination with international relations led Tower to covet the job of secretary of state. Believing that he could not achieve that position, he set his sights on secretary of defense, but his emphasis on foreign policy issues continued. After Tower and I had several foreign policy successes, he began calling me the SASC's foreign minister. During this period, I spent more time with the chairman than any other staffer except Rhett Dawson. I had great rapport with Tower, and I knew that he relied on my views. Although McGovern had told me not to talk to Tower about reorganization, I was determined to tell the chairman that he was heading in the wrong direction.

During September and October, I raised the issue with Tower five or six times. Each time he put me off by saying, "I'd like to hear your views, but at some other time." I began to sense that McGovern had succeeded in turning Tower against me on this issue. Eventually, I asked Tower to read several short analyses of key Pentagon problems I had written.

"McGovern said all papers should go through him," the chairman replied almost apologetically. That was the kiss of death. McGovern would never forward my papers to Tower. The chairman did not want to hear or read my views.

As courtesy and protocol dictated, Tower invited Weinberger to be the lead witness for the 1983 reorganization hearings. In an opening statement I had drafted for the July 28 hearing, Tower discussed the ambitious list of issues to be addressed. He then said, "The reason these hearings will sweep so broadly is that each of these subjects is, in my view, an inseparable part of an integrated whole. It makes no sense, for example, to consider how budgets are formulated without considering the extent to which the Joint Chiefs of Staff and unified commanders should be consulted on critical issues of resource allocation." The committee's intention was "to look comprehensively at the DoD structure and to assess whether or not that structure facilitates the formulation of a sound national security policy and the execution of that policy."[23]

In a letter written on July 14, Cong. Newt Gingrich warned Weinberger: "Your staff will be tempted to come to those hearings strategically on the defensive. They will want to counter by explaining how successful you have been at

15. Senator John Tower and Jim Locher meet in the senator's office in the Russell Senate Office Building in September, 1984. (U.S. Senate photo.)

cleaning up the Pentagon and by explaining your successes with specific examples. In doing that, they will be trying to communicate a message which, frankly, will not sell. If you enter those hearings defensively, you will have lost the battle before the first shot is fired. And you will be portrayed as the defender of big defense contractors, military bureaucrats and government waste."[24]

The Georgia Republican then told Weinberger: "This is a crucial opportunity for you to recast the entire debate. Your decision may be the most important political and public-relations decision you make in 1983. Will you come in focusing on past successes—putting you permanently on the defensive—or suggesting aggressive and fundamental reform which will put you permanently on the offensive?"

Weinberger did exactly what Gingrich had argued against. The first half of the secretary's statement explained improvements made and problems fixed. The second half described needed congressional reforms. The *Washington Post* reported that Weinberger claimed "he has run the Pentagon efficiently and that Congress is to blame for any remaining management problems."[25]

Weinberger's handling of questions on spare parts procurement epitomized his testimony. Two weeks before his appearance, a draft report by the Pentagon's inspector general was leaked to the press. A *Washington Post* article on this report published July 12 began: "The Defense Department is paying millions of dollars too much for aircraft engine spare parts and is giving far too little attention to cost increases." The news story cited examples: "In 1982, the Air Force paid $17.59 for a bolt that cost 67 cents in 1980. The price of one section of a Rolls-Royce ring assembly increased from $3.70 to $54.75 in the same period. In many cases, the report . . . found that 'little effort was being made to limit exorbitant cost growth,' while the Pentagon 'provided contractors with a "blank check" and no incentives to cut costs.'" The *Post* noted that "the draft report offers the most authoritative evidence so far of the widespread scope of the problem."[26]

Editorial cartoonists had a field day. In the week before Weinberger testified, one Herblock cartoon in the *Washington Post* showed him as a Pentagon watchman named "Rip van Weinberger"; another, as a spare part with a hole through the head in a room of "overpriced spare parts."[27]

Coverage of the inspector general's report sparked public and media interest in the Pentagon's management of its vast procurement activities. As media reporting over the next two years provided more evidence of waste, spare parts procurement became an explosive political issue. It also persuaded members to be more open to considering reorganization.

At the July 28 hearing, members questioned Weinberger about the leaked report. Senator William S. Cohen of Maine cited specific findings: "For example, the inspector general's report noted of 15,000 parts that they surveyed, 65 percent rose 50 percent or more in price between 1980 and 1982. More than 52 percent doubled in price during that period. Twenty-seven percent showed price increases of 500 percent or more in the same period the Consumer Price Index rose only 17 percent." Cohen asserted that such price increases "are beyond the realm of explanation."[28]

"We have changed our way of doing business," Weinberger replied. "We

16. This Herblock cartoon appeared in the *Washington Post* on July 20, 1983. (*Herblock Throught the Looking Glass,* W.W. Norton, 1984.)

did uncover all of these things that you mentioned and we discovered them before anyone else and took action to correct them immediately."[29]

Gingrich was right. Weinberger's message did not sell. Members did not know what the problems were or how to fix them, but they did not accept the secretary's arguments. In his first reorganization hearing, the secretary had succeeded in putting himself permanently on the defensive. Weinberger, however, did not sense his strategic blunder. Four days after the hearing, he wrote to Gingrich, "Your comments regarding the approach that the department should take to these hearings are well taken. I hope you felt the hearing results were useful."[30]

Despite his misreading of the outcome, Weinberger did understand that legislation would develop slowly. He reported to Reagan: "In coming weeks the committee will pursue this matter, but I expect no substantive changes in the immediate future."[31]

In projecting a slow pace, Weinberger may have been influenced by the poor understanding of issues displayed by senators. After reporting Nunn's tough questioning, the *Armed Forces Journal* stated that most "questions by committee members were vapid and they poorly addressed the serious issues involved and the challenges put forth in Weinberger's statement. The most pertinent and probing questions, other than Nunn's, were not even voiced in the hearing, but in written questions which Tower gave Weinberger to answer later."[32] Having written these questions, I was pleased by the praise. But there was little else to be pleased about. The hearing's inconclusiveness and senators' lack of a frame of reference convinced me that the staff report, when completed, would be crucial.

Two months passed before the SASC again examined reorganization. Two important events occurred in the interim. On August 23, in the chamber of the Texas House of Representatives in Austin, Tower informed the people of Texas that he would not seek reelection. Asked about his interest in becoming defense secretary in a second Reagan administration, Tower gave the only politically correct answer: "I have been offered no such appointment, nor do I expect one."[33]

Tower's retirement in sixteen months would leave a gaping hole in the administration's defense effort on Capitol Hill. Pat Towell, *Congressional Quarterly*'s defense expert, expressed the consensus view: "By any standard, Sen. John G. Tower's (R-TX) decision to retire from the Senate at the end of 1984 will deprive the defense establishment of one of its most eloquent advocates, a loss it can ill afford, given the evidently limited clout on Capitol Hill of most senior Reagan defense officials."[34]

On September 2, "Scoop" Jackson, a revered SASC member and its ranking Democrat, died. His death robbed the Senate of one of its giants. The Washington senator had served in Congress for forty-three years. Although he briefly attended the Weinberger hearing, the reorganization inquiry had not captured his attention. The new ranking minority member, Sam Nunn, wasted no time giving it priority. Earlier, at the Weinberger hearing, he announced, "I think this set of hearings may well in the long run be more important than any others we have."[35]

Many felt that Nunn would inherit Jackson's sobriquet "Mr. Defense" as the leading congressional expert on military matters.[36] One source reported: "Republicans as well as Democrats turn to Nunn as an authority on military manpower, strategy, tactics, and weapons."[37] Senator Cohen noted that Nunn "knows how to work across the political aisle."[38]

The forty-five-year-old Nunn had eleven years of congressional service, barely a fourth as long as Jackson. What had catapulted the relatively young and junior Nunn to such prominence as a defense expert? "Knowledge made Nunn a power in the Senate in a remarkably short time," answered one source.[39] The Georgia senator was described as having "a deeply personal compulsion to learn" and "an unquenchable fascination with the minutiae of defense issues."[40] In short, Nunn worked hard to be better informed than anyone else.

Having spent two and one-half years working for Nunn, I knew the intensity with which he studied issues. He would examine problems from every perspective, gather the best data, perform the most rigorous analysis, and hear from the best experts before making up his mind. Cohen said his "great strength is in holding back and waiting. He watches the dynamics in the committee play out, gives small pushes in various directions and then comes in with an intelligent proposal."[41]

Nunn demanded a great deal from himself intellectually and expected almost as much from his staff. I had prepared three three-inch notebooks filled with point papers and background material on each country and meeting for an eleven-day trip to East Asia with Nunn in January, 1979. As I handed Nunn his copy to peruse on the sixteen-hour flight from Washington to Manila, I thought, This will keep him busy for a while. Nunn finished studying the notebooks by the time the flight was only half over and asked, "Do you have anything else for me to read?"

A former member of Nunn's personal staff said, "Nunn wants to be a firm but friendly prodder of the military . . . and believes you cannot have lasting influence over an institution unless it respects you." Senator Carl Levin (D-Michigan) complimented Nunn's independence: "He is willing to disagree with the White House, even if it is occupied by his own party, and that is important."

Senate colleagues also admired Nunn's personal character. Senator David L. Boren (D-Oklahoma) said, "He has an excellent reputation for personal integrity."[42] Nunn could be counted on to consistently act in an honest, honorable, and fair way—an attribute that earned him trust. When it came to defense matters, an observer said, "Much of his credibility rests on his reputation for open-mindedness."[43]

Nunn's career followed in the footsteps of two other giants in military affairs from Georgia. The first was Sen. Richard Russell, the venerable SASC chairman who died in 1971. Seven years later, in my first months on the staff, Chairman John Stennis lectured me many times about the great Senator Russell. Nunn held the seat Russell once occupied.

The other Georgia giant was Nunn's great-uncle, Cong. Carl Vinson, a House member for a record fifty years. Vinson joined the Naval Affairs Committee when he arrived in 1914 and became its chairman in 1932. He was described as "one of the Navy's best friends on Capitol Hill."[44] When the House merged its Naval Affairs and Military Affairs Committees in 1946, Vinson served first as ranking Democrat of the new Armed Services Committee and then chairman until 1964. During the unification debates of the 1940s and 1950s, Vinson supported the navy, dominated the House debate, and was instrumental in preserving autonomy for the navy and other services. Nunn's interest in reorganization put him at odds with his legendary great-uncle.

By late September, I had gained approval for my proposed hearings. I suggested eleven more sessions. One would feature outside witnesses as a counterweight to Weinberger. The OSD, OJCS, and unified and specified commands would each warrant a hearing. Two sessions would address the military departments. Separate sessions would consider the department's resource allocation and acquisition processes. Looking to the larger national security community, another would consider the interagency system's impact on management of military affairs. Two sessions were left for broad commentary.

Eleven of thirty-one planned witnesses had appeared before the House Investigations Subcommittee in 1982 and 1983, but twenty would testify on reorganization for the first time, signifying the broader scope of the Senate inquiry. I grouped witnesses so the committee could hear conflicting views and recommendations in each sitting.

The second reorganization hearing, on September 20, presented three outside witnesses who provided alternative views to Weinberger's. General Krulak appeared to present positions expressed in his book. Philip A. Odeen and Richard Steadman had each prepared a report for President Carter's 1977–80 Defense Organization Study. Eight days later, former Defense Secretary Elliot L. Richardson, joined by former Deputy Defense Secretary W. Graham Claytor Jr., who had also served as navy secretary, testified on OSD. On October 4, General Jones and General Louis H. Wilson, a former Marine commandant and close friend of Senator Stennis, testified on the JCS. General Vessey, the incumbent chairman, followed them.

The first four hearings featured conflicting testimony and ended inconclusively. Widely varying descriptions of problems and solutions confused members. Of nine witnesses, five—Odeen, Steadman, Richardson, Claytor, and

Jones—supported significant reforms; three—Weinberger, Wilson, and Vessey—defended the status quo or offered only minor changes. Only one witness, Krulak, argued for turning the organizational clock back to a previous era. Tower did not comment on Krulak's intellectual isolation, but he at least began to understand that reorganization involved much more than the former marine general's simplistic remedies.

Four weeks passed before the committee held its fifth hearing. During this break, two incidents occurred that would profoundly affect the reorganization controversy.

On Sunday, October 23, 1983, a terrorist rammed a truck loaded with explosives into the barracks of the marine contingent of the multinational peacekeeping force in Lebanon. The blast had the force of six tons of dynamite, destroyed the building at the Beirut airport, and killed 241 servicemen, including 220 marines, the greatest number of marine deaths in a single day since the World War II battle of Iwo Jima and "the greatest peacetime tragedy to ever befall the Marine Corps."[45] Major General James M. Myatt described its effect: "I'll never forget it—Beirut is to Marines what Pearl Harbor is to Americans."[46] The tragedy was a major setback for America's foreign policy and international standing.

In hindsight, the disaster resulted from the Marine Corps's unpreparedness to deal with virulent terrorism. With DoD excessively focused on preparing for global war with the Soviet Union, lesser missions and threats received scant attention.

Although organizational deficiencies did not rank as the principal cause, the Beirut bombing had significant implications for reform. Adding another failure to the long list of postwar military setbacks, it enlarged the perception of an inept organization with ineffective leadership. Some began to question Vessey's leadership, and the bombing's aftermath markedly diminished Marine Commandant P. X. Kelley's standing.

The disaster placed a spotlight on command relationships within the U.S. European Command (EUCOM), the unified command responsible for the Lebanon mission, and revealed limited authority by the EUCOM commander and dysfunctional barriers imposed by the navy and marine chains of command.[47]

Still reeling from the news from Beirut, the nation awoke on the morning of October 25 to find that U.S. armed forces had invaded the tiny Caribbean island of Grenada. The island's Marxist government was building, with Cuban assistance, an airfield capable of handling large military aircraft. The Reagan administration feared that Grenada would permit Cuba and the Soviet Union to operate military aircraft from the field and that Grenada would attempt to destabilize its Caribbean neighbors.

17. Defense bureaucratic warfare is depicted in this cartoon that appeared in the *Armed Forces Journal* in August, 1983.

When the regime's leader and four government ministers were assassinated, chaos prevailed. The Organization of Eastern Caribbean States urged the United States to restore democracy to Grenada. Beyond regional security, Reagan and his advisers worried about the safety of nearly six hundred American medical students in Grenada.

Code-named Operation Urgent Fury, the surprise invasion posed a public relations challenge for the administration. Initially, the public reacted skeptically. Some charged that the administration had invaded Grenada to divert attention from its failed Lebanon policy.[48]

Tower focused the SASC's inquiries on the foreign policy issues of the Beirut bombing and Grenada incursion, not their implications for reorganization. The chairman was determined to defend administration policy in both cases.

The committee scheduled a closed hearing on Beirut with Weinberger for October 25, two days after the bombing. The Marine Corps's deputy chief of staff for plans, policies, and operations, Lt. Gen. Bernard E. "Mick" Trainor, accompanied the secretary. Trainor was substituting for Kelley, whom Reagan had sent to Beirut the day after the bombing.

Given the morning's news of the Grenada invasion, Weinberger was asked to address events in both Beirut and Grenada. With only fragmentary information available, the hearing contributed little to the committee's understanding of either incident. Addressing Trainor, Tower summed up the prevailing mood on the Beirut bombing: "It occurs to me that something was missing in the security element there. . . . you can see the concern of this committee that we didn't do everything, to the extent possible, to at least minimize the risk . . . we would like to talk to General Kelley at the earliest possible moment on his return."[49]

Nearly six thousand miles away in Beirut, Kelley was making headlines with ill-advised pronouncements. The next day's *Washington Post* announced: "Marine Chief 'Totally Satisfied' Beirut Had Adequate Security." The lead paragraph reported from Beirut: "Marine Commandant Gen. Paul X. Kelley said here today that he was 'totally satisfied' with security procedures in effect before Sunday's terrorist bombing that has left at least 214 marines and other U.S. servicemen dead [death toll at the time]."[50]

"I think we had adequate security measures," Kelley told reporters. "One has to realize if you have a determined individual who is willing to give up his life, chances are he's going to get through and do that."

The commandant's emotions were running high. On his way to Beirut, he made "an emotional stop" in Wiesbaden, West Germany, to visit Beirut casualties at an American military hospital. In Beirut, Kelley watched rescue workers "dig through the rubble for bodies, amid an increasingly strong stench."

Kelley's assessment stunned both administration and congressional officials. Tower made no effort to defend Beirut security arrangements or the commandant's statements. He expressed the SASC consensus "that the security was not adequate. It is difficult to defend against terrorist attacks, but that threat could have been minimized, in my judgment." Even Sen. Pete Wilson (R-California), a former marine, criticized protective measures: "What seems to have been lacking, plain and simple, is adequate security against an act of terror."[51]

Officers at Marine Corps headquarters were scrambling to figure out how to calm down the emotional commandant and minimize damage from his astounding statements.

On October 31, the SASC had its chance to hear from Kelley directly. General Bernie Rogers, an army officer and EUCOM commander in chief, also testified. The hearing started shortly after two o'clock in a closed session. A public session would follow. As the principal staffer for the hearing, I occupied a seat behind Tower and could observe the witnesses and sense members' reactions.

The top marine had been a favorite of many committee members for years. He had impressed them in hearings years earlier with bold, crisp testimony. Some members viewed Kelley as having a good chance to become the first marine to serve as JCS chairman. But Kelley's statements in Beirut had perplexed his committee admirers. The general had uncharacteristically lost his composure in trying circumstances. His emotional comments raised some senatorial eyebrows, but a solid performance before the committee would dissipate any concerns. Unfortunately, Kelley's performance that afternoon only enlarged concerns. By the end of the five-and-one-half-hour hearing, the marine commandant had killed whatever chance he had of becoming chairman.

Kelley meant to use his testimony to defend the Marine Corps's honor and defeat arguments that accused a fellow marine—Col. Timothy J. Geraghty, the on-scene commander—of failing to provide adequate security for his men. On his return from Beirut, the commandant found that "people in the media and people in the Congress and people all over Washington [had] assumed a lynch mob mentality." Calls for Geraghty or Kelley to be court-martialed came as a "great disappointment" and "hurt" the commandant. He felt "the institution [the Marine Corps] deserved a fair hearing."[52]

The commandant intensely spoke his first words. He stressed that it was "imperative" he give his opening statement before answering questions. His statement was unclassified, and the committee intended the closed session to address classified issues. But Kelley insisted on giving his statement. "I feel quite strongly about that. We have potentially 239 people [the death toll at the time] who have died for this country and I have to say, in all honesty, I have a story to tell, and I beg this committee to let me tell it in its entirety."[53]

Kelley's demeanor signaled that he had not calmed down. Members did not like calling distinguished officers before the committee to explain failures. Aware that they were going to have to take Kelley, and maybe Rogers, to the woodshed, the members were tense before the hearing started. The commandant quickly multiplied their anxiety.

Kelley spoke forcefully and dramatically while delivering his thirty-five-minute statement. He used twenty minutes to set the stage by describing events in Beirut over the previous twelve months. He then defended the security arrangements. "I believe that only extraordinary security could have met that massive and unanticipated threat." He repeated his view: "This represents a new and unique terrorist threat, one which could not have reasonably been anticipated by any commander." And again, "This flying truck bomb was an unprecedented escalation in our terrorist threat, both in size of the weapon and method of delivery."[54]

Emotion overcame Kelley as he approached the end of his statement. "You had to be there to see the devastation. For fifty hours prior to my arrival, day and night, our young Marines had clawed at steel and concrete, more to save the injured who were trapped at the time than to recover the dead. The emotional scars were already deep, and they are getting deeper. 'Why me?' they asked. 'Why am I alive and why are my buddies dead?'"[55]

Kelley broke down and had to pause to regain his composure. He continued, "Their commandant was asked, 'Was security adequate?' I replied, 'Yes.'
It was adequate to meet what any reasonable and prudent commander should
have expected prior to dawn on Sunday, October 23, 1983."[56]

Kelley finished with a theatrical flourish: "The perpetrators and supporters of this challenge to the rights of free men everywhere must be identified
and punished, and I will have little sleep until that happens." It was the most
dramatic presentation the SASC had seen in years, if not decades. Kelley
evoked a spectrum of emotion to sway the senators. But he was out of step
with them. The commandant was using high drama when the senators
wanted cold, hard facts.[57]

After Rogers briefly described his responsibility as the unified commander
and his deputy's postbombing trip to Beirut, Tower gave each senator three
minutes to ask classified questions. These brief exchanges began to convey that
Kelley's testimony had not convinced members. As Kelley sensed their skepticism, he became more combative. On occasion, his raised voice lacked proper
respect. From my vantage point, I sensed the members' early sympathy for the
commandant evaporating in the face of his hostile rhetoric. As the committee
adjourned to a larger hearing room for the open session, I judged that Kelley's
course, if unaltered, would lead to a stinging rebuke.

The public session began with Kelley again delivering his thirty-five-minute
statement. It lost even more of its appeal the second time around. In the questioning that followed, Nunn challenged Kelley's assertion that marine commanders could not reasonably anticipate the terrorists' use of a truck bomb.
He noted that terrorists had used a small truck to bomb the American embassy
in Beirut only six months before. Speaking of the five-ton Mercedes truck used
against the marine barracks, Nunn asked, "But did you say that that type truck
was seen often around airports?"

"Sir, that type truck is a common truck around the Beirut International
Airport," the commandant replied. "It is used all of the time. There would be
no reason for that sentry to be suspicious as that truck pulled into the commer-
cial parking lot."[58]

"If you could not have expected that size vehicle to come barreling
through," Nunn countered, "then it seems to me that that is not consistent
with the statement that that truck was seen all the time around the airport.
Why would it be unreasonable to assume that a truck that was in common use
around the airport might be utilized for this type of mission?"[59]

Cohen, one of the commandant's greatest admirers on the committee,
made the same point: "New meaning has been given to the words 'at dawn we
slept.' The fact that no one anticipated a terrorist attack of this magnitude and
precision, I think, is going to ring somewhat hollow to the parents of dead
Marines because there has been ample precedent for the loss of life in the re-

gion by car bombs, as you indicated. I do not know that it would take a vision-ary to foresee that a truck bomb might be used to take down an even more formidable structure."[60]

Nunn's and Cohen's logic devastated Kelley's arguments. Despite his erod-ing position, the commandant continued to vehemently defend his statements. In the process, the committee saw a Kelley it had never seen before. His testi-mony was not crisp and bold, but emotional and inconsistent. He was defend-ing the indefensible. Perhaps Kelley had determined that his duty was to shield the commander in the field. Perhaps Kelley defended this commander so deter-minedly because he had visited Beirut prior to the bombing and reviewed the security arrangements. His predecessor, General Barrow, had done the same just prior to his retirement. In fact, twenty-three generals or admirals had vis-ited the marine contingent in Beirut during the six months prior to the bomb-ing, including two other joint chiefs: General Vessey and Admiral Watkins, the CNO. Having reviewed this list of visitors, Tower and his committee realized that many officers in Washington and Europe had made the same error of judg-ment as a marine colonel in Beirut.

Kelley's reputation was shattered—with self-inflicted wounds causing the principal damage. His previous high standing with members cushioned his fall, but his influence would never be the same. The commandant's lesser standing would diminish the importance of his opposition to reorganization.

The hearing with Kelley did not satisfy the concerns of Congress and the public. To make matters worse, the American people had not yet signaled their support for the Grenada invasion. The White House and Tower began confer-ring about having the senator take a fact-finding trip to the Caribbean island to support administration policy.

However wide the first four reorganization hearings had opened Tower's eyes, he saw the light's full glare during a private meeting with former Secretary of Defense James R. Schlesinger on November 2. The committee scheduled Schlesinger, a highly regarded defense intellectual, to testify at ten o'clock that morning. Shortly before the hearing's start, Nunn asked for a one-hour delay to accommodate a last-minute request for his presence at the White House. Schlesinger was already en route, so I arranged for Tower to spend the hour meeting with him. I joined them.

Tower and Schlesinger were not friends and rarely, if ever, conferred. The secretary's persuasiveness that morning was not based upon personal relation-ship, but rather the power and clarity of his ideas. Schlesinger's analysis of JCS structural problems was compelling, and his use of examples from his Pentagon tenure transformed the problems from abstract to real. The secretary explained his strong support for the reforms proposed by General Jones. As Schlesinger talked, Tower's face communicated that he understood and believed his analysis.

At the hearing, Schlesinger's testimony provided the inquiry's most power-ful statement. "I applaud the committee's courage in taking on this particular issue," he began. "It is hoary, moss covered, and thorny. Your task is a formi-dable one."[61] The secretary then explained the need for reform: "Sound struc-ture will permit the release of energies and imagination now unduly constrained by the existing arrangements. Without such reform, I fear that the United States will obtain neither the best military advice, nor the effective execution of mili-tary plans, nor the provision of military capabilities commensurate with the fiscal resources provided, nor the most advantageous deterrence and defense posture available to the nation."[62]

In the postwar era, Schlesinger said, "We have sought to preserve a degree of service independence which has precluded effective integration of our mili-tary capabilities. . . . we are in my judgment no longer able to bear the luxury of arrangements which, whatever their advantages in preserving traditional in-stitutional roles, militate against the effective execution of military plans."[63]

The secretary identified the problem: "The central weakness of the exist-ing system lies in the structure of the Joint Chiefs of Staff. . . . The existing struc-ture, if it does not preclude the best military advice, provides a substantial, though not insurmountable, barrier to such advice. Suffice it to say that the recommendations and the plans of the chiefs must pass through a screen de-signed to protect the institutional interests of each of the separate services. The general rule is that no service ox may be gored. If on rare occasions dis-putes do break out that adversely affect the interests of one or more of the ser-vices, the subsequent turmoil within the institution will be such as to make a repetition appear ill-advised."

Schlesinger portrayed the result: "The unavoidable outcome is a structure in which log-rolling, back-scratching, marriage agreements, and the like flour-ish. It is important not to rock the boat."

"What comes up from the chiefs is a mutual endorsement of the individual desires of the several services," he said on the subject of budget formulation and force design. The former secretary elaborated on this in a sentence that was often repeated in subsequent debates: "The proffered advice is generally irrelevant, normally unread, and almost always disregarded."

Schlesinger then addressed unity of command: "In all of our military in-stitutions, the time-honored principle of 'unity of command' is inculcated. Yet at the national level it is firmly resisted and flagrantly violated. Unity of com-mand is endorsed, if and only if, it applies at the service level. The inevitable consequence is both the duplication of effort and the ultimate ambiguity of command."[64]

Turning to solutions, the secretary advised: "We are wisest to follow an evolutionary approach. I would move first to fix those things that now need fixing—and avoid the quest for an ideal military command system. In general, therefore, I would support the more modest reforms that have been suggested by General Jones for strengthening of the position of the chairman of the Joint Chiefs of Staff."

Schlesinger then addressed the defense secretary's staff: "The Office of the Secretary of Defense has grown substantially and has sometimes strayed beyond the appropriate boundaries of its authority. By and large, however, the growth of that office is a reflection of the weaknesses of the military command system."[65]

By the end of Schlesinger's appearance, Tower realized that he had put himself in the middle of a controversy whose outcome—if decided on the merits—might be unfavorable for the services. Regardless of how much Krulak's anachronistic ideas appealed to him, Tower now understood that they were intellectually unsupportable, had no meaningful constituency, and could never be enacted. The status quo, it now seemed evident, represented the best hope of the services and other reform opponents. By isolating the chairman, McGovern had permitted his boss to start a fight he could not finish.

Krulak's book even disappointed General Hittle, a like-minded retired marine. In a "very personal" memorandum to Navy Secretary Lehman, Hittle wrote: "As a longtime co-worker and admirer of General Krulak, and well aware of his rare abilities and contributions, I submit, as you requested, my comments and recommendations on his book. Regretfully, it is not, on the whole, up to his usually high standards." Of Krulak's proposal to take the defense secretary out of the chain of command, Hittle commented, "Such a proposal is fatally flawed." The general cited damage to the constitutional principle of civilian control of the military as a central drawback of Krulak's recommendation. Of the book's proposal to abolish the position of JCS chairman, Hittle observed: "The chairman is here to stay. The proposal is just not realistic."[66]

Hittle made two recommendations to Lehman: "That you do not, in any manner, be associated with a proposal to downgrade the secretary of defense," and "That your reaction to the book, if asked, be essentially: 'It has much useful reference material, as well as some omissions of material that would have strengthened it. However, I do not support, nor does the Department of the Navy, any proposal that would dilute or downgrade the status and role of the secretary of defense.'"

Hittle's tough memorandum soundly advised the navy secretary to hold Krulak's book at arms' length. McGovern had prevented Tower from receiving equally sound advice.

While Tower was trying to figure out how to extricate himself from his predicament, the committee members were trying to absorb the complex information with which they were being bombarded. That proved difficult. Schlesinger's appearance began a compressed schedule of eight hearings in fifteen days. Because each hearing focused on a different subject, the members were soon overwhelmed. I had to lower my expectations. Exposing them to the issues and building a solid record for future study became my new goals.

On Saturday morning, November 4, Tower traveled to Grenada on a two-day fact-finding trip. Public support for the invasion was improving but not overwhelming. Three committee staffers—Jim and Carl Smith and I—traveled with Tower. The trip's focus was on justifying the invasion. We devoted most of the time to meetings with the governor general of Grenada, Sir Paul Scoon, prime ministers of member nations of the Organization of Eastern Caribbean States, and American diplomats. These sessions provided powerful information in support of the operation, such as Scoon's calling the action "a liberation, not an invasion."[67]

But Tower also wanted to better understand the invasion's operational problems. He, the two Smiths, and I quickly sensed that the exhausted senior officers we encountered needed reassurance more than cross-examinations. Our efforts to gather information on the operation became discreet. We listened more than probed.

We learned that the army and Marine Corps had fought side-by-side under separate chains of command. The army had trouble coordinating with the navy for gunfire support, and the services had been unable to coordinate their air activities. Planners and soldiers and marines on the ground had been forced to rely on tourist maps. Worst of all, a third campus of American medical students—whose rescue was the rationale for the invasion in the first place—went undiscovered for days.

Upon our return to Washington, my fellow staffers and I prepared a lengthy paper for Tower's use in reporting to the White House, Congress, and the American people. Ninety percent of the paper was justification for the invasion. The 10 percent on conduct of the operation was carefully worded. This was not the time or place for the SASC chairman to blast the military's performance. The public relations battle remained Tower's first priority. Moreover, our examination of the military's performance was too incomplete and anecdotal to merit use.

Tower reported on the operation in a positive tone and without judgment: "The entire military incursion went quite well, considering the joint service nature of the operation and the very limited time available for planning." However, the chairman added: "Despite the overall success of the military operation, there are lessons to be learned. I intend for our committee to review this military operation in some depth."[68]

Committee efforts to find out exactly what happened in Grenada took years. The Defense Department did not want Congress uncovering further evidence of problems. The Pentagon's shielding of highly classified information on selected special operations forces complicated congressional attempts to comprehend the operation.

Tower released his Grenada report on November 9. He departed from the script the two Smiths and I had prepared for him, and said: "In spite of some flaws and glitches in the operation, one thing that strikes me is that this was almost a textbook example of how a joint operation should work. All four services involved, I think, did an outstanding job. It was organized on rather short notice, and I think the implementation of it was very professional. Any intimations of interservice rivalry, protection of turf, and differences of opinion, were subordinated to the greater goal of a successful operation. . . . I think we have to regard this as an extremely well implemented operation."[69]

Although the staff did not yet have sufficient evidence, we sensed that this had not been a textbook joint operation.

The committee's last two reorganization hearings on November 17 were the most informative ones of the seven following Schlesinger's appearance. In the morning, two former national security advisers, Zbigniew Brzezinski and Brent Scowcroft, a retired air force lieutenant general, dissected the interagency process. Both opposed making the JCS chairman a statutory NSC member. "In practice," Brzezinski reasoned, "attendance at the formal NSC meetings is at the president's discretion, and discussion is equally open to the statutory and nonstatutory members. The president calls upon those whose views he wants to hear. There is no vote and no de facto distinction between participants. Thus the views of the chairman of the JCS are heard as much as the president wishes to hear them."[70]

The former national security adviser considered the pivotal consideration "the relationship between the chairman of the JCS and the secretary of defense. . . . I would be concerned over changes which dilute the authority of the secretary of defense as the president's principal officer on defense matters." Years later, when the committee considered NSC membership for the chairman, Brzezinski's and Scowcroft's testimony proved decisive.[71]

Harold Brown, Weinberger's predecessor, drew his afternoon testimony from two chapters of his 1983 book, *Thinking About National Security*.[72] Although a proponent of significant reforms, Brown considered major change "not feasible at this time" and referenced his book: "If these radical JCS and military service reorganizations make sense, why have not previous DoD administrations (specifically my own) put them forward? The answer is simple: Ripeness is all. Such changes are best proposed by either a departing or recently departed administration, which cannot be accused of self-aggrandizement. They also require the informed support of the incumbent administration. All the organizational changes I have discussed are feasible, given an administration that is strong enough and a modicum of acceptance in the Congress. But until now they have not had a high enough political priority when that political strength was present."[73]

On JCS reform, Brown favored radical restructuring. "My own judgment is that what I will call a combined military staff, or general staff, headed by a single chief of military staff with a . . . deputy from a complementary . . . service background, should be created and given the responsibility for planning and direction for force application." Such a staff, in Brown's view, could engender a joint perspective and overcome the problems of strong service identification.[74] Brown's proposal for a general staff raised a highly controversial subject. Since the Second World War, Congress and service supremacists had created a "social myth" against the dangers of a "Prussian General Staff."[75] Few reformers were prepared to challenge this bias.

In sequence and substance, Brown's appearance provided the other bookend to Weinberger's testimony. The incumbent secretary defended the status quo while his predecessor called for radical change. The disparity between the two secretaries' views and divergent opinions from other witnesses left members perplexed. The hearings had not defined a clear course of action.

After the last hearing, Tower and McGovern quietly put reorganization on the back burner. During the remaining fourteen months of Tower's chairmanship, the committee held no more hearings on reorganization nor did it take any other initiatives.

Tower still wanted to be secretary of defense, but the Texas Republican believed that his chances lay in opposing, not proposing, defense reforms. Tower would stay out of the reorganization minefield—if he could

As 1983 ended, nearly two years had passed since General Jones had first called for JCS reform. Both houses of Congress had held lengthy series of hearings. Weinberger had asked the JCS to assess the need for reform. The administration had submitted its own modest bill. The House had twice passed JCS reorganization bills. The media had reported every step, yet no progress had been made.

Some analysts believed the prospects for meaningful reform had dimmed over the past two years. After a year of wavering, the Pentagon was digging in its heels, refusing to yield to anything beyond the token changes in the administration's proposal. With the popular Vessey joining Weinberger in opposition to broader reorganization, the Pentagon had solidified its position. Jones and Meyer had retired, and no uniformed crusader had emerged to push their proposals. The president appeared content to support his old pal, Weinberger.

The "progress" in the House deceived observers. White had been able to gain approval of a bill, but his subcommittee, his committee, and the House were not committed to reform. Nichols and many other Investigations Subcommittee members saw their 1983 bill as "unfinished Dick White business." That view would not produce commitment. White and Nichols believed that needed fixes required only limited legislation. The modesty of both House bills had disheartened reform advocates.

On the Senate side, Tower had erred in starting a reorganization inquiry. Following a midcourse correction, he was prepared to fight off DoD reorganization. His zigzags had only added to the confusion.

Amidst all this, principles for organizing the American military establishment remained confused. Nearly three decades of inattention to organizational issues and the parochialism of service supremacists had engulfed the debate in an impenetrable fog. Two years had passed, and the Pentagon's organizational defects were no closer to being fixed. Reorganization opponents seemed to be gaining momentum.

PART 2

Drawing
Battle Lines

CHAPTER 7

Beirut

Man is only truly great when he acts

from the passions.

—Benjamin Disraeli, *Coningsby*

E verything went wrong in Lebanon in 1983. In April, sixty-one people died
when the American embassy was destroyed by a car bomb; 1,250 Marines
were ashore struggling with a peacekeeping mission that the Pentagon opposed;
and one navy flier was killed and another was captured when two planes were
shot down while on perhaps the most inaccurate and stupidest bombing mission ever devised. Then, in October, a suicide terrorist attack leveled a four-
story reinforced concrete barracks and killed 241 servicemen, almost all of them
marines. Of all those mishaps, the one that lingers most painfully is the death
of all those marines—a tragedy known now simply as "Beirut."

The marine barracks bombing rocked Cong. Bill Nichols. Less than a month
earlier, the World War II veteran had visited those marines. "I had rapped with
them. We made pictures. I had written their mothers and fathers, those from
our district." Nichols had connected to those young men. The death of so many
was "a great personal loss."[1] The Alabama Democrat also regretted that he
had abandoned his earlier opposition to the Lebanon mission. In September,
military personnel in Beirut had persuaded Nichols to support a continuing
American role.[2]

Nichols chaired the Investigations Subcommittee of the House Armed Services Committee, which the House expected to investigate the disaster. He spent
the next two months examining painful facts.

Although the subcommittee possessed little expertise on terrorism, its two-
year study of JCS reform gave the members the confidence to question the per-

formance of the operational chain of command between Washington and the Beirut marines. The subcommittee's work on Beirut convinced Nichols of the need for reform.[3]

This tragedy and his personal connection to the dead and wounded marines galvanized Nichols on reorganization. "No member who took part in that investigation will ever forget it; the magnitude of the tragedy . . . seared our consciousness indelibly," he later observed. By December, when the investigation was finished, Nichols no longer viewed reforming the JCS system as Cong. Dick White's unfinished business. It was now his issue, and he was committed to fixing the organizational defects that had contributed to 241 deaths in Beirut.[4]

When the bomb exploded, marines had been deployed in Lebanon for nearly thirteen months. The second Multinational Force (MFO) for Lebanon—initially made up of French, Italian, and American forces and later including a small British component—assumed its duties on September 29, 1982. The shore-based contingent of the U.S. force was a marine amphibious unit (MAU) consisting of a 1,250-man battalion landing team (BLT), medium helicopter squadron, and logistics support group. Every six months, a new MAU rotated to Beirut.

The marines encamped at the international airport in south Beirut, "the lowest and least defensible terrain in the area, squeezed between rival Sunnis and Shiites on the north and south, against the Mediterranean Sea to the west and the Shouf Mountains to the east." Although this was an "obviously vulnerable" location, the basic assumption envisioned a "permissive environment."[5]

The U.S. European Command, a unified command headquartered in Stuttgart, West Germany, controlled American military activities in Lebanon. The command focused principally on NATO's defense of Western Europe, but its geographic area of responsibility included Israel, Syria, and Lebanon. The Beirut marines were assigned a two-part peacekeeping mission: "establish an environment that would facilitate the withdrawal of foreign military forces from Lebanon" and "assist the Lebanese government and the Lebanese armed forces in establishing sovereignty and authority over the Beirut area."[6]

In a major confrontation with the White House and State Department, Secretary Weinberger and the JCS had vehemently opposed participation in the Lebanon mission. The Pentagon, "playing the role of pacifist," had provoked an attitude of "near-contempt" by some civilian officials.[7] Responding to Weinberger's opposition to use of marines, "senior State Department officials jokingly offered to call for several hundred volunteers from the Foreign Service."[8] Critics of the military's attitude called the Pentagon the "Ministry of Pacifism" and the JCS the "Never-Again Club."[9]

The dispute centered on "serious differences about whether anything can be gained by using force and about conditions under which it is to be used." The State Department argued that the marine deployment exemplified "a great power's use [of] limited amounts of power judiciously at the right time" to back up diplomacy.[10] Weinberger and the military "never felt the use of force in Lebanon provided leverage to get a political-diplomatic solution." The Pentagon also saw the use of force against Arabs as "counter to our overall national security objectives in the Middle East."

Memories of the Vietnam quagmire contaminated the military's attitude toward the Beirut mission. Vietnam permanently scarred the American military psyche through "the sense of abandonment and betrayal, anguish at being depicted as moral monsters, and resentment at being scapegoated for a debacle not entirely of their making."[11] The military learned one overarching lesson from conflict in Indochina: no more Vietnams. Since the end of that disastrous debacle in Southeast Asia, the military had vigorously resisted involvement in ambiguous conflicts, such as Lebanon, for which the United States lacked understanding and skills and where its technological superiority offered little leverage. The Pentagon became increasingly reluctant to involve U.S. forces "without clear public support and a clearly defined mission."[12]

The White House overrode Pentagon objections to the Beirut mission, but it could not inspire its commitment. Throughout the deployment, the Department of Defense sought to end the mission, viewing it as excessively risky. Weinberger called it "a very dirty, very dirty, disagreeable and miserable job" and "one of the most miserable jobs ever assigned."[13]

The June, 1982, Israeli invasion had thrown Lebanon into turmoil. Beginning on August 25, marines participated for seventeen days in the first MFO operation: facilitating the withdrawal of Palestine Liberation Organization (PLO) forces from Beirut and helping to stabilize the city. The assassination of Pres.-elect Bashir Gemayel on September 14 and the slaughter of Palestinian refugees on September 17 plunged the Lebanese capital into chaos. The Lebanese government requested that the MFO return.

At first, the second MFO was "warmly greeted by the Lebanese people," and the leathernecks operated in a "low-threat environment." In November, the marines began training the Christian-dominated Lebanese armed forces, diminishing their neutrality in the eyes of some Muslim factions.

On March 16, 1983, a grenade tossed by members of an Islamic fundamentalist group wounded five marines. One month later, a large car bomb partially destroyed the U.S. embassy and caused sixty-one fatalities, including seventeen Americans. When ground fire struck a marine helicopter on May 5, the operating environment was recategorized as "high-threat."[14]

After terrorists in Europe had earlier attacked two four-star U.S. Army generals, Alexander Haig and Frederick Kroesen, Gen. William Y. Smith, an air force officer serving as EUCOM's deputy commander, established a EUCOM office on antiterrorism.[15] Colonel William T. Corbett, a former army Green Beret and

Vietnam veteran with a "profound grasp of America's politico-military problems and what caused them," headed this office.[16]

Three days after the embassy bombing, Smith sent Corbett to Beirut to review the security of the 130-man Office of Military Cooperation (OMC), primarily a Special Forces contingent, which was equipping and retraining the Lebanese army. Corbett established barricades and other defenses around the office's hotel and dispersed its personnel among many hotels.

Corbett saw the embassy bombing as "the start of a terrorist campaign against the American presence in Lebanon," while the JCS chairman, General Vessey, characterized it as "an inexplicable aberration." Corbett prophetically warned Smith: "Since [terrorist] organizations are motivated by an ideology seeking long-range ends, a single, random act of terrorism against U.S. interests in Lebanon is nonsensical. More applicable would be a series of terrorist acts, each, if possible, more spectacular and costly than the previous. Following [the American embassy] attack, U.S. military forces represent the most defined and logical terrorist target. . . . U.S. interests in Lebanon can expect an attack more spectacular than the action against the U.S. embassy."[17]

Smith told EUCOM's director of operations "to make damn sure those Marines are secure."[18] Lack of authority precluded fulfilling Smith's instruction. Although EUCOM could pressure its naval component on the marines' antiterrorism posture, the regulations in JCS Publication 2, *Unified Action Armed Forces*, did not permit it to direct specific actions.[19]

Noel C. Koch, the Pentagon's senior counterterrorism official, arrived in Beirut on the same aircraft with Corbett. During his short visit, Koch observed "serious shortcomings, particularly in managing intelligence related to the terrorist threat." Upon return to Washington, Koch arranged "for a small survey team to go to Beirut."[20]

The Pentagon sent an undercover military unit that specialized in clandestine activities. A marine, Lt. Col. William V. Cowan, led the team, which arrived in Beirut on May 26. Cowan's tasks included "a review of intelligence support to the U.S. Marines." He reported that "significant intelligence existed, but that reporting, correlation and analysis were not coordinated." The team recommended "a centralized intelligence support capability to the Marines, who were not augmented with the additional intelligence personnel and assets that their unique peacekeeping mission required, particularly in a hostile environment such as Beirut."[21]

The team's report "was received with bland apathy in the Pentagon and at Headquarters, Marine Corps" and was never seriously considered.[22] Koch blamed the fact that the team was "seen as having a special operations association, that their report reflected adversely on people who outranked them; and finally their work had been submitted with no opportunity for the military system to sanitize their findings. This led to denials, ass-covering, and all around

18. General P. X. Kelley visiting the 24th Marine Amphibious Unit in Beirut in August, 1983. Vice Admiral Edward H. Martin, Sixth Fleet commander, is at Kelley's left. (U.S. Marine Corps photo.)

outrage that the survey had been done at all. . . . The report was swept under the rug."[23]

Throughout the year before the bombing, Koch repeatedly briefed Joint Staff officers on the shift in the terrorist threat from hostage taking to assassinations and large bombs, but he was never given access to the JCS. After the bombing, Koch asked the Joint Staff director, the army's Lt. Gen. Jack N. Merritt, why, for nearly a year, "no time could be found on the Chiefs' agenda to discuss the subject." Merritt answered, "Well, you know, terrorism is an easy thing to ignore."

On May 30, the 24th MAU, commanded by Col. Timothy J. Geraghty, arrived to begin its six-month tour in Beirut. The colonel was viewed as "one of the finest officers in the Corps," and headed almost certainly for promotion to general.[24] His unit included BLT 1/8, commanded by Lt. Col. Howard L. "Larry" Gerlach, for which the 1st Battalion, 8th Marine Regiment formed the nucleus. As had previous units, the BLT headquarters and attached units housed themselves in the bombed-out, fire-damaged, four-story, reinforced concrete building once used by Lebanon's Aviation Administration Bureau. This well-built structure was repeatedly occupied because it "provided security from light to heavy hostile artillery, rocket and sniper fire."[25]

In June, 1983, Corbett found Geraghty "fully aware of the dangers" and informed about the "Syro-Iranian threat." Corbett knew nothing of the marines' tactical disposition and assumed they were spread out in perimeter bunkers. He had no idea that Geraghty and Gerlach had concentrated a large number of marines in a single building.[26] Given the threat, this concentration of troops was inconceivable to Corbett. "Had I known that these guys were living in that building with that flimsy fence they had around there, it would have blown my mind." Looking back, he realized that "the people who understood the threat didn't understand the tactical situation, and the people who understood the tactical situation didn't appreciate the threat."[27]

After a few stray rounds were fired at the marines in June and July, attacks on marine positions by Druze Muslims increased dramatically in August. Geraghty and Gerlach moved more of the BLT into the headquarters building "to provide protection from further barrages."[28] That brought the number of marines housed there to 350—more than a quarter of the BLT. Thus, while Corbett was emphasizing dispersion as an antiterrorism measure, marine commanders were concentrating their troops.

On August 29, heavy rocket, mortar, and artillery fire killed two marines and wounded fourteen others. For the first time, the leathernecks fired back, using their 155-mm artillery. On September 6, two more marines died and two were wounded in a rocket attack. Two days later the frigate USS *Bowen* fired its 5-inch guns in response to shelling of the airport. This was the first use of naval gunfire in support of the marines ashore.

These artillery and naval gunfire barrages began a de facto shifting of the mission from peacekeeping to peacemaking. In peacekeeping, force plays little or no role. Peacemaking employs force to discourage hostilities or restore order. President Reagan's decision to use naval gunfire to support Lebanese army troops under siege further shifted the marine mission toward peacemaking. On September 19, after two navy ships had fired 338 rounds, all Lebanese factions viewed the U.S. Marines not as neutral peacekeepers, but as "one of the factions firing on others."[29]

As casualties mounted, Congress began considering its role under the War Powers Act. Many members viewed the Lebanon mission as too vague and the situation as too volatile. Nichols agreed. On September 14—nearly a year after the deployment began—a Nichols press statement urged the president to "get Marines out of Lebanon." He recalled his "grave reservations about sending a United States Marine force there in the first place." Nichols saw the marines "in a no-win situation" which was "virtually hopeless."[30]

Two of Nichols's constituents, William J. and Peggy A. Stelpflug, agreed with his pronouncements. The Stelpflugs had a personal interest in the well-being of the deployed leathernecks: The youngest of their five children, Billy, was serving as an enlisted marine with BLT 1/8 in Beirut. The elder Stelpflug had spent twenty years in the air force and piloted F-4 aircraft in Vietnam. After retiring as a lieutenant colonel, he moved his family to Auburn, Alabama, where he and his wife taught at Auburn University, Nichols's alma mater.

The first four Stelpflug children had graduated from or were attending Auburn. Billy had decided to serve in the Marine Corps before going to college. His early years were typical of the life of an air force "brat," with family moves from base to base and friends left behind. Full of energy, he loved the outdoors—fishing, hunting for arrowheads, Boy Scout activities—and playing baseball as a catcher. Billy also had a quiet side and enjoyed writing poetry. In his junior and senior high school years, his academic performance had slipped from As to Bs and Cs, and he had become a "hard-core hell-raiser." Disappointed with his performance and behavior, Billy began "looking for discipline, a right way to do things, and to be tough." He saw his answer in the Marine Corps, "the toughest bunch of all."[31]

Shortly after he graduated in 1982, Billy started a three-year marine enlistment. Following his graduation from boot camp at Parris Island in December, Billy's transformation to a "tall, straight, strong, and quietly proud" young man amazed his brother. Several months later, Billy wrote to his brother from Beirut that "a strong family and hard Corps" had put him on his feet.

The youngest Stelpflug was proud of his service as a marine and of his unit. He wrote to his family, "I believe that I have wound up in the best possible group within the Marine Corps infantry." Trained to operate an antitank missile, the youngest Stelpflug was assigned to the Weapons Company of the 1st Battalion, 8th Marine Regiment.[32]

The significant casualty toll on August 29 compelled Colonel Stelpflug to write to Nichols urging withdrawal of the marines. "Lebanon has sunk so far into unreasoning hatred," he predicted, that the present policy "could well result in disaster and the useless loss of American troops . . . in a Mideast shooting gallery, in a crossfire between factions whose only interest is revenge and death for ancient wrongs."[33]

"Please be assured that I share your view on our American Marines stationed in Lebanon," Nichols replied. He also told the Stelpflugs that he had used a quote from their letter in his weekly radio program: "I felt it expressed the heartfelt emotion of parents directly concerned for the welfare of their nation, and their son."[34]

In September, the House—invoking provisions of the War Powers Act—was headed for a showdown on the marine presence in Lebanon. Speaker Thomas P. "Tip" O'Neill announced that the House would soon consider a resolution to keep marines in Lebanon for not more than another eighteen months. He said the resolution reflected "extensive consultations between congressional leaders and White House officials" and was "aimed at satisfying congressional opinion."[35]

Testifying to the Senate Foreign Relations Committee (SFRC) in mid-September, Secretary of State George Shultz, Marine Corps Commandant Gen. P. X. Kelley, and other administration witnesses "argued vehemently against setting any limit on the Marines' stay." Kelley declared, "There is not a significant danger at this time in terms of imminent hostilities to our Marines."

In preparation for the coming vote, the HASC decided to send a fact-finding delegation to Beirut to "assess the American participation in the peacekeeping role." A skeptical Nichols joined the ten-member delegation, headed by Cong. Sam Stratton (D–New York). The delegation spent September 24 and 25 on ships off the coast of Lebanon and an afternoon with "the troops in their sandbagged positions at the Beirut International Airport."[36]

While ashore, Nichols visited with several off-duty Alabama marines. Lance Corporal Billy Stelpflug was on-duty and not available to meet his congressman. As a combat veteran, Nichols easily related to the young men in uniform. The Alabama connection drew the old politician and young marines together. Nichols's genuine interest in people and political skills contributed to the warmth of their interaction.[37]

Nichols and his colleagues judged morale to be high among the officers and enlisted men. They found most military personnel "decidedly in favor of our remaining in Lebanon." Officers and diplomats communicated their conviction that "withdrawal would increase turmoil and perhaps damage America's credibility and effectiveness worldwide."[38]

The delegation's report endorsed these views but did not recommend the eighteen-month extension proposed by the House resolution, reasoning that "setting a deadline too short or too long might be detrimental."

In a separate statement, Nichols explained that his position had "moderated" as a result of his visit. Handwritten trip notes reveal that he feared that if the United States pulled out, the French and Italians would follow. "Vacuum would cause blood bath," he wrote. The marines "should remain there—for the time being."[39]

On September 28, the House debated for seven hours a resolution giving President Reagan authority to keep marine forces in Beirut for as long as eighteen months. Congressman Sam Gibbons (D-Florida) saw dangerous parallels to Vietnam: "[W]e are asking young men to fight and possibly die in a war our government is not committed to win. . . . If we are there to fight, we are far too few. If we are there to die, we are far too many."[40]

Speaker O'Neill countered that "this resolution clearly limits the scope and role of the United States forces in Lebanon so that the danger of a Vietnam-type escalation is avoided." The House backed the "Reagan-O'Neill agreement"

19. Congressman Bill Nichols with Alabama Marines in Lebanon twenty-eight days before the October, 1983, Beirut tragedy.
(Auburn University Archives.)

to extend the marines' stay by a vote of 270–161. Nichols voted against the resolution.[41] The Senate voted in favor of the resolution on the following day, although by a slimmer margin: 54–46.

The HASC's Beirut delegation judged that the mid-October attacks on marines were "deliberate" and "ominous." On October 20—three days before the bombing—Stratton, Nichols, and four other congressmen met with Weinberger "to express their concern" about the marines' increasing vulnerability.[42] The following day, Stratton detailed their concerns in commentary appearing in the *Washington Post*.[43]

Shortly after midnight on October 23, a flash message from the USS *Iwo Jima*, an amphibious helicopter carrier, shocked watch officers in the Pentagon's National Military Command Center. It said that "a large explosion at BLT 1/8 Hq. Bldg. [headquarters building] collapsed the roof and leveled the building. Large numbers of dead and injured." This message arrived in Washington about forty minutes after the blast.[44]

At 6:22 A.M. Beirut time, a lone terrorist drove a yellow Mercedes-Benz truck laden with explosives into the lobby of the BLT headquarters building where he triggered one of the biggest nonnuclear detonations ever. Pressurized gas containers forming the bomb's nucleus magnified its destructive power to equal twelve thousand pounds of explosives. The blast collapsed the four-story building into a "smoldering heap of rubble no more than fifteen feet high" and "burned, crushed, or smothered to death" 220 Marines, 18 sailors, 3 soldiers, a French paratrooper, and a Lebanese civilian. Another 112 Americans were wounded.[45]

The BLT commander, Lieutenant Colonel Gerlach, was in his room on the building's second floor. Blown clear by the explosion, he was one of the few survivors from his part of the building. Rescuers found Gerlach "unconscious, a total mess; no one expected him to survive." He suffered a broken neck, damage to his spinal cord, compound fractures of his left arm and right leg, and numerous facial fractures. He remained in a coma for three days. In a separate, but nearby building, Colonel Geraghty, the MAU commander, was "shaken but unhurt" by the blast.[46]

Americans reacted with outrage, consternation, and sorrow. Nichols grieved. His conviction that the tragedy could have been avoided deepened his sorrow. The failure of his and his colleagues' recent pleadings to Weinberger to end the mission haunted Nichols.[47]

To ensure accuracy, Marine Corps reporting of casualties was, in General Kelley's words, "excruciatingly slow." On Wednesday morning, three days after the blast, Washington received initial reports. Nichols's heart sank. Billy Stelpflug was among those reported missing. Nichols's staff told him that Billy's parents had "expressed great concern and are bitter about your stand that the Marines remain in Lebanon." In anguish, Nichols pressed the Marine Corps headquarters for more information. Three anxious days later, word came that Billy was dead. Five other Alabamians were dead or dying. Nichols was devastated. "The situation in Lebanon cut hard through Congressman Nichols' heart, spirit, and soul, and I could sense the real hurt in his voice," a friend reported.[48]

The day after the bombing, Reagan sent General Kelley to Beirut to assess the situation, but more importantly to determine how to shore up security. The commandant recommended that a commission investigate the bombing.[49] Kelley intended that something like a naval board of inquiry establish accountability and make recommendations for corrective or disciplinary action. Weinberger agreed with Kelley and on October 29 announced that he would create "an independent commission" to investigate the disaster and report to the president. On November 7, Weinberger convened a five-member commission headed by Adm. Robert L. J. Long, the recently retired commander of the Pacific Command.[50]

The HASC began full committee hearings on November 1 with Kelley as the lead Pentagon witness. His exchanges with members were sharp and volatile.

20. A view of the destruction following the bombing of the battalion landing team headquarters building. (U.S. Marine Corps photo.)

Arch Barrett, the HASC's reorganization expert, recalled that the commandant "dressed down the committee and was very belligerent." Kelley's surly responses to Richard Ray (D-Georgia) outraged members. Ray had visited Beirut in September with the Stratton delegation. Based upon the threat described to the delegation, Ray stated, "We should have been expecting just about anything."[51]

"Boy, you have a wilder imagination than I have, congressman, to ever think . . . that the terrorist threat . . . was going to be a five-ton truck going sixty miles an hour with 5,000 pounds of explosives, you have a better crystal ball than I have," Kelley responded.

When Ray began to reply, the commandant cut him off in mid-sentence: "Why don't we let the Long inquiry do its job, instead of speculating on that type of micro detail?"

Barrett believed such confrontational behavior "ruined P. X. Kelley" and "severely damaged" the remainder of his tenure as commandant. Kelley "never had any credibility before the committee anymore."[52] Members thought Kelley's "performance registered a greater dedication to the Marine Corps than to the truth." They blasted him for providing "often inaccurate, erroneous, and misleading information." Congressman Dan Daniel (D-Virginia), a strong military supporter, proposed citing Kelley for "conduct unbecoming to Marine Corps traditions."[53]

After two days of full committee hearings, Chairman Mel Price directed the Investigations Subcommittee to complete the inquiry. Nichols assembled six staffers, including Barrett, to guide the work. To conduct an on-site investigation, Democratic Congressman Nicholas Mavroules led a six-member delegation to Beirut. The delegation convened on November 12 and 13 aboard the *Iwo Jima* off the coast and heard twenty hours of testimony from eleven witnesses, including Colonel Geraghty.

The Investigations Subcommittee heard an additional twenty witnesses in Washington from December 8–15. Vessey and Gen. Bernie Rogers, the four-star EUCOM commander, appeared last. Rogers, a tough-minded military intellectual and former army chief of staff, was highly respected on Capitol Hill and in the Pentagon.

"Who was responsible for security oversight above the level of the Marine commander on the ground?" Nichols asked.[54]

"I am responsible as the theater commander for everything that happens in that theater," Rogers replied. "Those below me are responsible for everything that happens in their area of cognizance; those above me are responsible for the same."

Asked to comment on media-reported criticisms by unnamed officers that higher command echelons had failed to carry out their responsibilities to the marines, Rogers said, "I have been brought up in the school that when you get so far away from the battalion you should let the people on the ground command it, supervised by the next echelon of command." Rogers and Vessey had discussed "many times" that "it is impossible for him to command that battalion from Washington; it is impossible for me to command it from Belgium [his NATO headquarters]; it is impossible for my deputy to command it from Stuttgart."

Rogers continued, "I give the authority to the deputy commander in chief, European Command . . . to run that command within policy guidelines. But I cannot give him the responsibility. I bear that responsibility, and what you are really trying to determine here is not the responsible officer, but the culpable officer."

"The what?" asked Cong. Larry Hopkins.

"The culpable officer," said Rogers. "Every one of us in the chain of command bears the responsibility. What you have to determine is at what level is culpability." As to responsibility, "there is no way you can dilute it. Once you step into a command position, it is yours."

The subcommittee submitted its report on December 19. The media described it as "sharply critical" and "bluntly worded."[55] The report criticized "inadequate security measures taken to protect the Marine unit from the full spectrum of threats." Without naming Colonel Geraghty, it blamed the MAU commander for "serious errors in judgment in failing to provide better protection for his troops."[56] The subcommittee emphasized: *This is not a case of dereliction of duty, or of neglect. But it is a case of misjudgment with the most serious consequences.*"[57]

The report also criticized the performance of higher elements of the operational chain of command, which observers found "extraordinary."[58] Faulting the chain of command represented a rare undertaking for a congressional subcommittee. The Pentagon treated the chain of command as a sacred subject on which few officers considered congressmen to be experts.

For the subcommittee, decisions made in Washington—such as using naval gunfire to support the Lebanese army—and conflicts between American diplomats and on-scene commanders clouded any determination of accountability. The subcommittee gave little attention to issues beyond performance of the operational chain of command because it was "just difficult enough to try to find and put your finger on who was responsible."[59]

The subcommittee concluded that Rogers and his subordinate commanders had not fulfilled their responsibilities, and that "these higher command elements failed to exercise sufficient oversight of the MAU. Visits by higher-level commanders were commonly familiarization briefings and appeared not to provide positive oversight, such as directives to improve security. . . . The subcommittee is particularly concerned that the higher level commanders did not re-evaluate the MAU security posture in light of increasing vulnerability of the unit in the weeks before the bombing."[60]

Given the volatility of the environment and small size of the marine unit, the Washington-Beirut chain of command was excessively cumbersome and long. Eight layers existed between Reagan and the BLT commander, not including the JCS. Navy Secretary John Lehman described this command path as "bloated and paralyzed." Admiral Crowe, who had served in the Beirut chain of command until June, 1983, called it "long, complex, and clumsy."[61]

On December 20, the day after the Nichols subcommittee filed its report, the Long Commission submitted its report to Weinberger, although the White House did not release it until December 28. The report criticized the military's performance. But by also lambasting the mission, it sided with the Pentagon.

Although the two documents were "similar and equally critical," the Long Commission's report overshadowed the congressional report. The commission's membership—a retired four-star admiral, a former four-star-equivalent civilian, two retired three-star generals, and an active three-star general—assured this outcome. The group's collective expertise vastly exceeded that of Nichols and his colleagues.

The commission's "unusually blunt," "harsh," and "highly critical" assessments, especially of the president's Lebanon policy, astonished many in Washington.[62] Secretary Lehman later termed it a "blockbuster."[63] The commission's strong indictment of Reagan's policy reflected "the sharp rift between the Pentagon and White House."[64] Washington observers expected criticism from Congress, but these presidential critics were military men, and Reagan ranked as the military's best friend. He had staunchly supported the military and had given priority to the defense buildup. Despite Reagan's unwavering support, chilling memories of Vietnam caused the military to challenge their boss on Lebanon.

The Long Commission placed principal responsibility for the "catastrophic losses" on the BLT and MAU commanders. It faulted EUCOM's operational chain of command, citing "a lack of effective command supervision" and "failure . . . to inspect and supervise the defensive posture."[65] The commission report's last analytical section addressed terrorism as a form of warfare and said the military was unprepared to counter it.

The Long Commission judged the October 23 attack to be "an overwhelming success" for the terrorists, and that "the objective and the means of attack were beyond the imagination of those responsible for Marine security."[66] The commission further stated that "terrorism as a military threat to U.S. military forces is becoming increasingly serious." Suggesting the need for a new mindset, it declared that "systematic, carefully orchestrated terrorism . . . represents a new dimension of warfare."[67]

The Defense Department did not then consider terrorism to be a form of warfare. It did not even define terrorism in the JCS *Dictionary of Military and Associated Terms.* In fact, the Pentagon initially classified the servicemen killed in the Beirut bombing as "accidental deaths" and not battle casualties. Under pressure from Capitol Hill, DoD reclassified them as battle deaths. In announcing the change, Weinberger revealed the conventional war mind-set: "The casualties of the bombing attack in Beirut were not accountable as battle deaths in the classic military sense; however, the fact that they were not killed in an accident is painfully obvious."[68]

Long and his colleagues determined that the marines' mission statement and rules of engagement were "written to guide responses to a range of conventional military threats," and that the Marines were "not trained, organized, staffed or supported to deal effectively with the terrorist threat in Lebanon."[69] The commission judged the marine unit as not mission-ready, implying a failure by the Marine Corps.

A failure by naval forces off Lebanon in the early daylight of December 4 compounded the Pentagon's embarrassment. Forty-two days after the marine tragedy, the aircraft carriers *John F. Kennedy* and *Independence* launched twenty-eight fighter-bombers to attack Syrian and Druze antiaircraft and artillery positions near Beirut in response to attacks the previous day on two unarmed U.S. reconnaissance aircraft. However, communication blunders up and down the chain of command produced another disaster.[70]

The JCS ordered the aircraft launched "at first light" so that the retaliation would occur within twenty-four hours of the attack on the reconnaissance planes.[71] This order reached battle group commander, Rear Adm. Jerry O. Tuttle, at 5:30 A.M., one hour before the specified launch time. The chain of command denied Tuttle's repeated request for more time. "I told them three times I couldn't make it, and they said you've got to make it."[72]

This short notice did not provide time to adequately brief and prepare crews or load planes with the "right number or right types of bombs."[73] Moreover, Tuttle planned a midday strike "when there would be no shadows to mask the targets and the Syrian antiaircraft gunners would have to look straight into the sun." Under Washington's timetable, the morning sun would still be low in the east, "the targets would still be in shadow, and the pilots, not the antiaircraft gunners, would be looking directly into its glare."[74]

According to Tuttle, the JCS also instructed him to strike three sets of targets at once, placing "far too many aircraft in a very small target area directly above the antiaircraft positions."[75]

Unknowingly, by specifying details better left to the on-scene commander, the JCS had greatly increased the risk to raiding aircraft and diminished their chances of success. In the resulting "half-assed bombing mission," two modern U.S. aircraft were shot down by primitive shoulder-fired antiaircraft missiles.[76] One pilot was killed, and the Syrians, in a major coup, captured his navigator. Dismal bombing results contributed to making this a real fiasco. Only two Syrian gun emplacements were destroyed, and a radar site was put out of action for two days.[77]

Both the Investigations Subcommittee and the Long Commission focused their examinations of EUCOM's performance too narrowly. They only considered Rogers's responsibility for events in Beirut, not the adequacy of his authority. This mistake led to critical omissions and faulty conclusions. The Investigations Subcommittee's failure to assess the balance between Rogers's responsibility and authority was more understandable. Congress, which was focused on the defense budget and interacted primarily with Pentagon offices, knew little about the inner workings of warfighting commands. Permanent law reflected this inattention. In the two-inch-thick volume containing title 10 of the *U.S. Code*, which governs the armed forces, only one brief paragraph addressed the unified commands.[78] Only Pentagon regulations prescribed responsibilities and authorities of unified commanders. Congress did not examine such internal documents as long as they did not conflict with statute. The Investigations

Subcommittee thus had no reason to believe that an imbalance between responsibility and authority existed. Barrett observed that when the subcommittee saw all of the stars a unified commander wore, it "assumed he had authority." Although a number of earlier studies had decried the weakness of unified commanders, the subcommittee "didn't know this area."[79]

The Long Commission, especially Admiral Long, could not make a similar claim. As commander of the U.S. Pacific Command, Long had found an imbalance in his authority and responsibility. "I didn't have the requisite authority when I took over." The admiral discovered "an element of antagonism and enmity" between his service component commanders. Long also found his authority undermined by "inappropriate and improper" activity in the Pentagon. "There was an attitude of the service chiefs and their staffs in Washington that they were the ones that were really calling the shots, operationally." His staff sometimes "intercepted operational directives from service staffs in Washington." Long had experienced firsthand the handicaps hampering the effectiveness of the nation's frontline warfighting commanders.[80]

The Blue Ribbon Defense Panel's July, 1970, report revealed an imbalance between the responsibility and authority of unified commanders. The panel cited a 1958 statement by President Eisenhower: "Because I have often seen the evils of diluted command, I emphasize that each unified commander must have unquestioned authority over all units of his command. . . . Today a unified command is made up of component commands from each military department, each under a commander of that department. The commander's authority over these component commands is short of the full command required for maximum efficiency."[81]

The panel found, despite Eisenhower's arguments and resulting statutory changes in the Defense Reorganization Act of 1958, that the situation remained "substantially unchanged." It described "an organizational structure in which 'unification' of either command or of the forces is more cosmetic than substantive."[82]

With this earlier work as background, the SASC staff's initial thinking on the adequacy of a unified commander's authority was significantly influenced by a study completed in April, 1983, by a retired three-star army general, John H. Cushman. The general, who had commanded the Korean-American force defending the western sector of the Demilitarized Zone and approaches to Seoul in Korea prior to his 1978 retirement, had long studied defense organization. In the late 1950s he helped Gen. Maxwell Taylor, then serving as the army chief of staff, implement changes mandated by the 1958 act. During the Kennedy administration, Cushman worked for Cyrus Vance, DoD general counsel and later army secretary. Under Vance, Cushman "became deeply involved in how the Department of Defense was, or might be, organized and operated." Three tours in Vietnam further expanded Cushman's organizational insights.[83]

Cushman concluded that operational commanders' "authority and capacity . . . are very much out of balance with their responsibility and accountability."[84] Unfortunately, his comprehensive study was not widely read. Even the Pentagon library did not have a copy in 1983.[85]

Cushman explained that a unified commander's authority, as specified in *Unified Action Armed Forces*, had changed little since the JCS first prescribed it in 1948. The authority of the unified commander over his service component commands remained severely restricted.[86] During the Key West Agreement negotiations conducted in 1948, the CNO and air force chief of staff had sought to "protect the integrity of their service operations" in multiservice commands. They adopted service component commands as the device and insisted on a division of authority that ensured a weak unified commander and powerful service component commanders, which Cushman described as "powers with whom the multiservice commander conducts negotiations as equals more than as subordinates."[87]

Although Cushman's second theater command and control study was not published until March, 1986, he had formulated many ideas during 1984, including some on Beirut. In occasional meetings and telephone calls with me, Cushman analyzed the barrier between the unified commander and his service components created by *Unified Action Armed Forces* and service culture. Cushman called this barrier the "wall of the component" and concluded that it is "always inhibiting" and can be "devastating to mission readiness and mission performance."[88]

He considered the marine barracks bombing "a classic example of the devastating effect of the 'wall of the component.'" He believed General Rogers was inhibited by his limited authority, which "does not include such matters as administration, discipline, internal organization, and unit training except when a subordinate commander requests assistance." Rogers's authority also excluded "tactical employment of the forces" of a service component. Responsibility for these areas, including antiterrorism defense and training, was assigned to the marine administrative chain of command, beginning with the navy secretary and marine commandant and including the commanding generals of the Fleet Marine Force, Atlantic, in Norfolk, Virginia, and the 2d Marine Division at Camp Lejeune, North Carolina.[89] Both EUCOM and Headquarters, Marine Corps, saw antiterrorism defense and training as a Marine Corps responsibility.[90]

The European Command's different approaches to two subordinate units in Beirut—the marines and the OMC—illustrated the "wall of the component." After the embassy bombing in April, General Smith, the deputy EUCOM commander, immediately dispatched to Beirut the command's special assistant for security matters, Colonel Corbett, to evaluate OMC's security and implement antiterrorist measures. The Long Commission praised this "prompt, positive action" as "aggressive command involvement." In this instance, Rogers and Smith could be proactive because they did not have to overcome a service barrier.[91]

Rogers attempted to be similarly proactive in November, 1982, when he offered antiterrorism training to the Beirut marines. But the leathernecks declined the offer, saying that "training our troops for these kinds of things is a service responsibility."[92] Rogers was powerless to act. In Cushman's view, looking beyond the regulatory constraints, Rogers was further inhibited by a culture that produced both "tangible and intangible resistance" to a unified commander, especially from another service, when he seeks to inspect and impose standards on what were viewed as internal service matters. Cushman judged that marine generals in the administrative chain of command and navy admirals in the operational chain would have taken "a dim view" of a security inspection of the marines like the one given to OMC.[93]

General Smith also understood the limits of Rogers's authority: "I really felt the marines didn't work directly for me. On paper, they were under our command, but in reality, they worked for the commander in chief, U.S. Naval Forces Europe, our naval component. They had their own operational and administrative command lines, which flowed from the naval component commander. I felt that antiterrorism training was primarily a navy and marine service issue. We didn't have any control over that. We could advise, of course, but no more."[94]

In Beirut, Colonel Corbett knew he "really had no authority with the marines." The marines, he says, "worked for a chain of command which was not mine. So, it never occurred to me to ask Geraghty, a guy in a tactical position, to check his perimeter." If he had, "The problem of the concentration of marines in that building would have been immediately obvious."[95]

Rogers later confirmed—in line with Cushman's analysis and Smith's and Corbett's understandings—that he could not instruct the leathernecks on their antiterrorism posture and training. He also understood that he lacked the authority to modify the chain of command between himself and the marine unit and that his "headquarters was being bypassed too many times, and direct communication was going from the navy and Marine Corps, right down to the ships and to the forces ashore."[96] Long also suspected that Rogers had been bypassed just as the services had circumvented him in Hawaii.[97] Unfortunately, the commission report did not mention these circumventions or highlight how little control Rogers had of forces operating on his turf.

Washington was bypassing EUCOM to a much greater extent than either Rogers or Long imagined. An investigation uncovered thirty-one units in Beirut that reported directly to the Pentagon. Orders to the carrier battle group off Lebanon came "straight from the jury-rigged 'Navy only' chain of command" that originated with the CNO. Only after the navy had set plans for fleet operations were superiors in the operational chain of command informed. The navy's meddling "spoke volumes about the loss of discipline among the forces committed to Lebanon."[98]

In addition to his assignment as EUCOM commander, Rogers served as Supreme Allied Commander, Europe (SACEUR). His boss in the latter capacity, the NATO secretary general, would not permit him "to go outside of the NATO area." This prohibition prevented Rogers from visiting the marines in Beirut, unlike the twenty-three American generals and admirals who did travel to Lebanon before October 23. The "question that is always going to haunt me," he lamented, is "If I had been able to go there, would I—different from the others—have seen that there was danger and that we should do something about it?"[99]

The Beirut bombing fatally wounded American policy in Lebanon. Reagan did not want to abandon this commitment, but on February 6 the administration announced its decision to withdraw the marines. The last unit left the Beirut airport three weeks later. During the eighteen-month deployment, 238 Marines died, 151 were wounded, and 47 received nonbattle wounds or injuries—and the United States did not accomplish a single basic objective.[100]

This operational failure collapsed America's Middle East policy and forced a strategic withdrawal from the region with an attendant loss of influence. Adversaries viewed America as unwilling or incapable of effectively employing military force to protect its regional interests. Saddam Hussein's miscalculation in the 1990 invasion of Kuwait may have originated with America's retreat from Lebanon.

This "professional military debacle" further diminished the military's standing at home and abroad.[101] Preoccupation with conventional warfare had left the military unprepared for unconventional threats, like terrorism. Reacting to Vietnam, the Pentagon had excessively focused its planning and budget on defense of Western Europe. Even the Marine Corps was "heavying up" for potential action against the Warsaw Pact.

Unpreparedness for terrorism permeated the military from top to bottom.[102] There were only a few counterterrorism experts like Colonel Corbett, and none of them had much influence. The conventional war mind-set produced blinders at every level of the Beirut administrative chain of command and most levels of the operational chain. Colonel Geraghty and Lieutenant Colonel Gerlach could not see the terrorist threat or did not know what to do about it. It was the same with many of the twenty-three generals and admirals who visited the marines. The joint chiefs themselves were uninformed on terrorism and unwilling to listen to experts.

The JCS's liaison officer with the Lebanese army recalled the marines' landing at Beirut International Airport in September, 1982: "They ran from tree to tree with their rifles pointed, thinking they were going to be attacked by an army. I think they must have thought they were in Vietnam." He advised the marines: "Do not expect any classical offenses against you. Do not expect tanks or companies or battalions to attack. Here, the only threat is terrorism." Despite this warning, the marines in Beirut and their chain of command never considered terrorism as a primary threat.[103]

The marine force fit the original, low-threat mission. Sea-based support from amphibious ships was especially useful. As the level of hostility and terrorist threat increased, however, marine capabilities were less adequate. Immediately after the bombing, an analyst observed: "The Marines historically have placed little emphasis on acquiring the engineering and other skills associated with fortification and positional warfare. This comparative indifference to the art of defensive combat has persisted despite the Corps' experience in Vietnam, notably the siege of Khe Sanh."[104]

As the situation in Beirut deteriorated, the marines failed to prepare adequate defenses against terrorism. "Marine defensive arrangements featured limited dispersion, a dearth of barriers and protective reinforcements, and a contraction of local patrols in the face of an increasing threat."[105] The leathernecks erected few, "weak and largely symbolic" barriers. Deviations from security procedures further exposed the marines to tragedy. The Long Commission's report noted: "The security posture on 23 October 1983 . . . was not in compliance with published directives."[106] Interior guards were not permitted to have loaded weapons. One guard post was not manned. Light anti-tank weapons were removed from guard posts. Use of rooftop observers was discontinued. The reaction force was not on duty. The iron gate in front of the building was left open.[107] Geraghty and Gerlach failed "to take routine precautions that the commander of any deployed military force would have taken under normal circumstances."[108]

The two colonels received no help from the marine chain of command responsible for their manning, training, and equipping. The Marine Corps had failed to prepare for terrorism despite growth in the frequency and lethality of international terrorist attacks over the preceding fifteen years. Nevertheless, the commission did not condemn inadequate marine support to on-scene commanders despite substantial evidence of inferior support. The 24th MAU consisted of the same forces and mix of capabilities routinely deployed for Mediterranean Sea operations—a conventional force ill-suited for Lebanon's unconventional threats.

The Marine Corps provided only routine capabilities to its Beirut-bound units. When one of Geraghty's predecessors was asked how much specialized training his marines received before deploying, he answered, "Absolutely none." This remained the case, even after the April, 1983, embassy bombing.[109] In contrast, the Italian component of the MFO possessed a tailored mix of capabilities and underwent several months of special training prior to its deployment to Lebanon.[110]

Moreover, the marine chain of command claimed service prerogative to block proffered antiterrorism assistance from EUCOM. Had General Rogers been able to give Colonel Corbett the authority to order improvements in the marines' antiterrorism posture, the terrorists might have succeeded in attacking the airport compound in some manner, but they would not have found 350 marines bunched up in one building. Had Rogers challenged marine resistance to meaningful command oversight of antiterrorism preparedness, the issue would have gone to the Tank. There, the service-dominated JCS would have almost certainly rebuffed Rogers in defense of service authorities specified in existing regulations.

After the Office of Naval Intelligence (ONI) assessed all prebombing data to determine if the attack could have been predicted, Rear Adm. John Butts, director of naval intelligence, said, "We concluded the chances were pretty good we would have been able to predict." But naval intelligence reflected terrorism's low priority, failing to assign even a single full-time analyst to work on the Beirut threat.[111]

Despite such shortcomings, Colonel Corbett did not see the Beirut tragedy as an intelligence failure, but rather one of "commanders and managers neglecting their responsibility for security of their personnel in high-threat areas, against repeated, proven attack techniques."[112] One Middle East terrorist group had mounted at least 118 car-bomb attacks in the thirteen months prior to the marine bombing. "Any security professional who is waiting for intelligence to warn him is going to fail," said Corbett.[113]

Who deserved the blame for the Beirut tragedy? On the surface, the answer appeared clear-cut. Washington had assigned responsibility for the mission to the EUCOM operational chain of command, which began with Rogers and ended with Gerlach. The Long Commission and Investigations Subcommittee reports assigned blame based upon that responsibility. General Kelley, the marine commandant, sought to absolve himself of any blame by noting that he was not part of the operational chain of command.

The answer, however, is more complicated. Clearly, parts of the operational chain—Geraghty and Gerlach—mishandled key responsibilities. But, the marine administrative chain of command sent a not-mission-ready unit to Lebanon without the requisite training, assets, and assistance. Moreover, the Marine Corps rejected EUCOM's efforts to provide what would have been critical help by Colonel Corbett and others. The actions and inactions of the marines' administrative chain of command, beginning with the commandant, contributed most to the tragedy. That chain deserved the principal blame.

After a thorough investigation of the Pearl Harbor attack, a congressional committee enunciated twenty-five principles it hoped would aid our national defense and preclude a repetition of the failure of December 7, 1941. The final principle read: "In a well-balanced organization there is close correlation of responsibility and authority." Incorporating these principles into its operations field manual in 1949, the army expanded the final principle to say: "There must always be a close correlation between responsibility and authority, for to vest a commander or staff officer with responsibility and no corresponding authority is eminently unfair."[114]

The Long Commission forgot this principle. Its assessments and assignment of blame were "eminently unfair."

With General Cushman's assistance, my SASC staff colleagues and I had this principle in mind as we reviewed analyses of the Beirut bombing. We were convinced that serious imbalance in the responsibility and authority of each unified commander persisted despite the lessons of Pearl Harbor and more recent operational setbacks. We were also troubled by the long, confused operational chain of command. In February, 1984, having found the Beirut chain "cumbersome and slow to respond," the Pentagon cut out four naval command layers.[115]

President Reagan preempted serious disciplinary action against officers blamed by the Long Commission and HASC subcommittee. On December 27, the day before release of the commission's report, he accepted responsibility for the tragedy, saying any blame "properly rests here in this office and with this president." Reagan felt that local ground commanders had "already suffered quite enough" and should not be punished "for not fully comprehending the nature of today's terrorist threat."[116]

Some supported the president's "blame-stops-here attitude." Others worried about "what this will do to the system of military justice." The media viewed the president's action as a political "master stroke" because it "defused a critical Pentagon report on the incident, left Democratic critics sputtering and earned the gratitude of armed-forces careerists."[117] Many officers were also concerned about the potential compromise of military accountability. A former JCS member found it "very, very unfortunate that the president stepped in before the system could work." He considered it "a blow to military professionalism."[118]

While Reagan had ruled out courts-martial, his remarks did not preclude lesser punishment, such as disciplinary letters. In descending severity, these were letters of reprimand, admonition, or caution. After discussions characterized as "heated" and "intense," and over the objections of top navy officers, Secretary Lehman recommended that Geraghty and Gerlach receive formal letters of reprimand.[119] Weinberger discarded Lehman's recommendation and on February 9 ordered the navy secretary to issue mild nonpunitive letters of caution to Geraghty and Gerlach. Such a letter, placed in an officer's file to tell him how to perform his duties better in the future, served no purpose for either man. Both of their careers were over. When the Marine Corps delivered Gerlach's letter to his bedside at a Boston Veterans Administrations hospital, he "was virtually a quadriplegic whose ears were still ringing from the blast and whose vision was unfocused because the bones stabilizing one of his eyes had not yet healed in place."[120]

Long called punishment of only Geraghty and Gerlach "very inappropriate and grossly unfair, because there were other people who had equal responsibility to make sure the marines were better prepared."[121] General Meyer believed "that Pentagon leaders needed some fall guys, and so that got them." Although recognizing that the on-scene commanders had some responsibility, Meyer thought that the JCS and operational and administrative chains of command, especially the generals and admirals who had visited Beirut, were also responsible in that they failed to notice the marine barracks's vulnerability or do anything about it.[122]

Had Reagan permitted the system of military accountability to proceed, it was certain to make the same errors as the Long Commission. When responsibility and authority are so weakly defined, it is impossible to assign culpability.

Although DoD did not punish Kelley, and the Long and congressional reports did not admonish him for his role in the Beirut disaster, the commandant suffered professionally almost as much as the two colonels. Kelley's efforts to defend the Marine Corps for its indefensible failure backfired on Capitol Hill and among marines. Congress saw the commandant trying to "dodge responsibility."[123] His efforts to absolve himself "sent a shudder through the Corps"; his testimony "made him look cold, as if the leader of the Corps wasn't watching the backs of his men in the field."[124]

The operational failures and acquisition scandals of the preceding four years troubled Congressman Nichols. The Beirut episode scarred and motivated him. His personal connection to the bombing gave Nichols a "rock solid determination" to reorganize the Pentagon, beginning with the JCS.[125] Organizational deficiencies had plagued the marines' employment in Beirut. Although Nichols did not yet understand them, his commitment intensified as further study revealed these problems.

As 1983 ended, Bill Nichols was sure that he and his colleagues were on the right track with their House-passed JCS reform bill. The Alabama Democrat was anxious to begin working with Senate counterparts to enact legislation. He anticipated similar attitudes in the SASC, which had spent the last six months studying reorganization. Moreover, Senator Tower had promised action by his committee in the new year.[126]

Nichols had faith in Tower's commitment. Events would not meet his expectations.

CHAPTER 8

Scholars and Old Soldiers

The discovery of uncomfortable facts had never

been encouraged in armies, who treated their history

as a sentimental treasure rather than a field

of scientific research.

—Capt. Sir Basil Liddell Hart, *Thoughts on War*

W ith the government stalemated over defense reorganization, public policy institutions and universities became new battlegrounds for proreform crusades: scholars and practitioners—many former officials and officers—held conferences, convened study groups, commissioned papers, and published books. These activities added significant information and ideas and helped build political support for reform.

The navy quickly mobilized its own academic forces to defend the status quo. It also mounted attacks on reform research, recruiting or infiltrating spies into two proreform policy institutions to gather information. The navy succeeded in squashing publication of one scathing proreform paper, but its overall counterattack was weak. Reformers dominated the academic theater of operations.

Private nonprofit research institutions on the periphery of Washington's political process frequently defined policy options. The government often lacked time to do in-depth policy formulation; research institutions filled that void. Since the early twentieth century, nonprofit research centers have represented "one of the most distinctive ways in which Americans have sought to link knowledge and power."[1] They are "an American phenomena" because "no other country accords such significance to private institutions designed to influence public decisions."[2]

The first such institutions, founded around 1910, grew out of Progressive Era reform and the scientific management movement. The Brookings Institution's lineage dates to that era. A second generation emerged in the twenty years after World War II to provide the government "sophisticated technical expertise." These "think tanks" derived their name from World War II jargon for a secure room used to discuss plans and strategies. The term initially referred to military contract research organizations, such as the RAND Corporation, but came to refer to all kinds of private research centers.[3] The third, larger generation of think tanks emerged in the 1970s and 1980s. Generally operating with smaller budgets and staffs, these institutions focused more on political activism than scholarship. The Heritage Foundation and Institute for Policy Studies led this generation, which also included university research centers.

By the 1980s, more than a thousand think tanks operated in the United States. Of the roughly one hundred located in or around the nation's capital, sixty focused their research on foreign policy and national security. Two-thirds of Washington-based think tanks were created after 1970.

Beginning in 1963, the U.S. Military Academy at West Point annually sponsored the Senior Conference, "an informal seminar to facilitate an open exchange of ideas on a topic of immediate and significant national concern."[4] In September, 1981, conference organizers from the Department of Social Sciences, led by Lt. Col. Asa A. "Ace" Clark, selected military reform as the topic for the session to be held in June, 1982. At the time, they did not expect to include reorganization under the reform rubric.[5]

Senator Gary Hart (D-Colorado) introduced the term "military reform" in a commentary appearing in the *Wall Street Journal* in January, 1981.[6] By summer, he and Cong. G. William Whitehurst (R-Virginia) had formed the Congressional Military Reform Caucus (CMRC), a bicameral, bipartisan group advocating less complex, less costly, more numerous weapon systems and a shift of military doctrine from attrition warfare to maneuver warfare. The reformers focused on strategy, doctrine, force structure, and weapons acquisition issues. West Point's conference embraced three subjects: doctrinal innovation, quantity versus quality of weapons, and the mix of heavy and light forces.

Following calls for JCS reorganization by Generals Jones and Meyer, conference organizers decided to add a panel discussion on "The Question of DoD Organization: To Fine Tune or To Reorganize." Unlike West Point, the CMRC never addressed reorganization.

Besides West Point professors, the conference attracted seventy-three experts from the four services, Congress, academia, and media. Congressman Newt Gingrich, a leading CMRC member, gave the keynote address. General

Meyer devoted his banquet speech to JCS reform, arguing that such reform was necessary for the future success of a military "not organized to go to war when the big one happens."[7]

James Fallows, *Atlantic*'s Washington editor and author of a 1981 defense reform book;[8] Lt. Gen. Paul F. Gorman, an army officer serving as assistant to the JCS chairman; and Philip A. Odeen, a former senior defense and National Security Council official, comprised the organization panel and "generated sharply divisive discussion." Reformers argued that the JCS's practice of proffering unanimous advice reflected "self-serving, service-oriented bargains, not sound and coherent military advice." Antireformers countered that there was no compelling evidence anything was seriously wrong with the present system and that reform would destroy desirable redundancy and competition and create inefficient centralization.[9]

The conference did not have "time to consider the matter in detail," but its discussions did educate and catalyze participants. Fourteen conferees later played significant reorganization roles. The conference also inspired eight West Point professors. Four of them edited and wrote articles for *The Defense Reform Debate*, which gave significant attention to reorganization.[10] Three others contributed articles. Two of the book's editors, Jeffrey S. McKitrick and Peter W. Chiarelli, and an eighth professor—Daniel J. Kaufman, a West Point classmate of mine—continued to write on reorganization and became part of the Washington debate.

The Aspen Institute, a prestigious nonprofit institution dedicated to serving world leaders, annually held an arms control seminar at its forty-acre site on the edge of Aspen, Colorado. General Jones, retired for little more than a month, and General Meyer attended the August, 1982, seminar. Also present was Edwin A. Deagle, director of the Rockefeller Foundation's International Relations Program, which funded the seminar. Deagle, a West Point graduate and former professor and attendee at the academy's reform conference, had a strong interest in civil-military relations, the topic of his Harvard Ph.D. dissertation. His doctoral research had revealed flaws in JCS organization.[11] At an evening cookout at Aspen, Jones, Meyer, and Deagle talked about JCS reform and the prospects for legislation. Deagle told the generals that if they could mobilize "a hundred of the best folks" to aggressively press for legislation, he would provide the funding.

Later that year, Douglas J. Bennet, a former State Department assistant secretary and first president of the Roosevelt Center for American Policy Studies, a new Washington think tank focused on defense policy and disarmament, asked Deagle's advice on potential issues and collaborators. Deagle put Bennet in touch with Barry M. Blechman, a former assistant director of the Arms Control and Disarmament Agency. In a later meeting, he advised Bennet and

Blechman, who was already thinking of defense reorganization as a potential project to examine JCS reform.[12]

Six months later, Deagle funded a Bennet-Blechman proposal for the Roosevelt Center to undertake a reorganization study. Blechman would coordinate the Defense Organization Project on a part-time basis, and William J. Lynn, a young attorney just hired by the Roosevelt Center, would serve as the full-time executive director. Given Pentagon opposition, Blechman believed the project's leaders had to possess "impeccable credentials in the military establishment." He persuaded Phil Odeen to chair the project, and recruited former Defense Secretary Melvin Laird and Gen. Andrew J. Goodpaster, a former SACEUR and army aide to President Eisenhower, to serve as vice chairmen.[13] In June, 1983, Odeen announced the twenty-four-month project to prospective participants, identifying the work's primary target as "members of the next Congress and the administration that takes office in 1985."[14]

In addition to Odeen, Laird, and Goodpaster, the Roosevelt Center's steering committee of prominent defense experts would eventually total twenty-four members. By design, members were overwhelmingly proreform. It "was not a group to debate whether reform was desirable." Blechman and his colleagues believed that Pentagon reform was clearly needed. The steering committee's purpose was to determine "what should be done . . . what would be most helpful." By the first meeting on July 28, the committee numbered fifteen, including Jones and Meyer, Sen. Sam Nunn, Cong. Les Aspin, Bill Brehm, and Blechman. Shortly thereafter, the Roosevelt Center underwent a "change in management and philosophy" that put the reorganization project in limbo. Deagle encouraged Blechman to find a new institutional home for the work.[15]

Both Blechman and Deagle viewed the Center for Strategic and International Studies (CSIS), a conservative policy center then affiliated with Georgetown University, as a natural target. Founded in 1962, CSIS grew rapidly in the late 1970s and early 1980s. As the "most aristocratic" and "most ceremonial" of think tanks, it abounded with big names. Henry Kissinger, Zbigniew Brzezinski, and Jim Schlesinger served as "senior scholar-statesmen in residence." Other big names included former JCS chairman Adm. Tom Moorer, former Deputy CIA Director Ray Cline, and military analyst Edward Luttwak.[16] CSIS had "created a niche . . . as an intellectual resource for newly active congressmen and their staffs" and served "as a broker for discussion and accommodation." CSIS favored "an informal and consensual approach to policymaking."[17] According to Blechman, "CSIS seemed the logical place for the reorganization project with its strong connections, ability to convene high-level groups, and conservative credentials." There was also a West Point connection. The center's president and cofounder, David Abshire, graduated from the U.S. Military Academy, as did its vice president, Amos A. "Joe" Jordan Jr., Deagle's boss as head of the academy's Social Science Department. Other army and West

Point colleagues of Deagle's on the 150-person staff made CSIS "a hotbed of West Point intrigue."[18]

The reorganization project and its funding from Deagle's Rockefeller Foundation and the Ford Foundation shifted from the Roosevelt Center to CSIS in October. Four working groups were created: military command structure, defense planning and resource allocation, weapons acquisition, and congressional defense budget process. Steering committee members served on the working groups, but forty-five other senior defense experts were recruited to populate them. The project's seventy-five influential participants contributed to making reorganization "suddenly one of Washington's most talked-about political topics."[19]

In addition to Nunn and Aspin, four other members of Congress sat on the steering committee: William S. Cohen and Nancy L. Kassebaum from the Senate, and Newt Gingrich and Sam Stratton from the House. As a Republican on the SASC, Cohen's participation was particularly significant. A cerebral and independent senator, he was considered "a thoughtful critic of Ronald Reagan's foreign policy adventures."[20]

In 1983, the forty-three-year-old Cohen was serving his fifth year in the Senate following three House terms. Born in Bangor, Maine, to a Russian-Jewish immigrant father and Irish-Protestant mother, Cohen "voted his own way" in the "tradition of independent-minded representatives from Maine." He styled himself "as kind of a poet-philosopher." An all-state basketball player in high school and college, Cohen's bachelor's and law degrees were both cum laude. In 1974, as a freshman member of the House Judiciary Committee, Cohen was involved in President Nixon's impeachment inquiry. He joined "a small group of Republicans who were the first to break ranks with their party" to vote for impeachment. Cohen offered "a handsome profile in anguish, and he immediately attracted the media limelight."[21]

The SASC's senior Republican, John Tower, became Cohen's mentor and close friend. Reflecting Maine's maritime interests, Cohen chaired the Sea Power and Force Projection Subcommittee. Service on the Senate Select Committee on Intelligence broadened his national security knowledge.

When the CSIS project's steering committee reached its full strength of twenty-four, only Congressman Stratton, an infrequent participant, belonged to the antireform camp. Admiral Moorer, although connected to CSIS, was not invited to participate. According to Blechman, "Moorer was deliberately not involved" because of his antireform positions. A navy memorandum to Secretary John Lehman remarked: "Not much doubt how the reform will be structured with this lineup."[22]

The navy spied on the CSIS project. Commander Thomas R. Fedyszyn, the navy fellow at CSIS, sent written reports to Seth Cropsey, deputy navy under secretary for policy and Lehman's antireform point man. Despite the heavy

West Point influence at CSIS, the navy held a strong position as well. A former CNO, Adm. Arleigh A. Burke, "played a major, probably indispensable, role in founding, organizing, and developing" CSIS and served as its director for fifteen years.[23] Moorer maintained the large navy presence at CSIS once provided by Burke. Moorer also served as an important connection between CSIS and conservative foundations that helped to fund it.

The project leaders at CSIS eventually released a nearly sixty-page report entitled *Toward a More Effective Defense* in February, 1985. It summarized working group analyses. A 250-page book, containing the full steering committee and working group reports and other supporting papers, was published later in the year under the same title.[24]

The authors of the report questioned "the effectiveness and efficiency with which the United States plans, acquires, and operates its forces," and suggested substantial changes throughout the defense establishment. One of their ten major recommendations proposed designating the JCS chairman as the principal military adviser and emphasized the need for him to prepare fiscally realistic force planning proposals. The authors proposed that the Joint Staff report directly to the chairman and that the Joint Staff director be designated the deputy JCS chairman. They also recommended that each service establish a joint-specialty career path to prepare officers for joint duty, in line with the proposal made by the Chairman's Special Study Group in 1982. On JCS issues, the CSIS report paralleled Jones's proposals.[25]

Another recommendation envisioned expanding the budget role of the under secretary of defense for policy and providing an assistant secretary for each of three major missions: nuclear deterrence, European defense, and regional defense. Designating senior officials with mission responsibilities addressed the criticism that OSD was "ill-equipped to translate mission-oriented planning and programming guidance into force requirements and weapons programs." The SASC staff study had explored and written on this deficiency and proposed fix for several years.

On budgetary matters, the CSIS report's authors proposed that Congress shift from a one-year to a two-year defense budget cycle. They also favored a larger budget role for unified commanders, greater authority for them over their service component commanders, and a separate budget for them to fund the in-theater costs of their forces. The report's authors also recommended a new position in the OSD: under secretary of defense for force readiness and sustainability.

When a completed draft revealed the authors' proreform conclusions, Moorer launched a brutal assault on the project using his influence with conservative foundations as his principal tactic. He told Joe Jordan, serving as CSIS president while Abshire was posted as U.S. ambassador to NATO, that the "terrible" reorganization report would "jeopardize CSIS funding from conservative foundations, particularly the Scaife family foundations," then CSIS's biggest donor, having given at least $7 million in the preceding decade. Moorer's threat represented "a very serious problem for CSIS." Blechman recalled, "It was not something I had experienced in the think tank world before. I had never seen such blatant threats against funding sources."[26]

Moorer also "allegedly worked to have the Defense Department pressure CSIS to end support for the project by threatening a cutoff of defense funds to the think tank."[27] Such pressure would have been a mistake. Reorganization had become a visible issue, and powerful members of Congress were participating in the CSIS project. Weinberger and his advisers avoided this misstep.

Moorer later denied that he had tried to undermine the report, saying: "They had the deck packed. They say I tried to get money out of the hands of CSIS for this report, but . . . they told me to keep my mouth shut, tried to keep me from writing a dissent." When a writer questioned him on his opposition, Moorer angrily replied, "If you think American boys are going to execute orders from people who have never heard gunfire, you're full of shit and so are they."

Navy Secretary Lehman also was reportedly working "behind the scenes to block the CSIS report."[28] In a *Defense Week* interview, he characterized the report as "one more of those wrong-headed studies. It's the same old warmed-over, more-power-to-the-chairman, let's-create-a-general-staff idea." Blechman believed Lehman "was the *eminence grise* behind all these pressures on my project."[29]

Blechman was right. Lehman had instigated the attacks. To Moorer, Dan McMichael of the Scaife family foundations, and Morrie Liebman of CSIS's board, Lehman had sent an identical, caustic note: "Attached is the outline of your study at Georgetown. What is going on?"[30]

The project seemed caught between two influential foundations. When Jordan told Deagle "if Moorer had his way, he would suppress the study," Deagle replied: "You'll never get any money from me [Rockefeller Foundation] again if you let Moorer suppress it." But Blechman says Moorer was too late: "A complete draft of the report had been circulated throughout the steering committee, and many eminent people with impeccable conservative credentials had informally signed up to it. I couldn't imagine that the report could be withdrawn or very substantial changes made to it."[31]

To escape this predicament, Jordan asked Moorer, Schlesinger, and Lt. Gen. Brent Scowcroft, President Ford's national security adviser, to review the draft report. According to Blechman, this effort was designed to give Moorer "an opportunity to make his views known" as well as show "his ideas were favored by only a small group of people, wearing navy uniforms almost exclusively." Given the review group's composition, "The outcome was never in doubt."[32]

Schlesinger was "sympathetic to the thrust of the study and to many of its recommendations." Scowcroft was "enthusiastic in his praise." Jordan reported that Moorer argued that the "assignment of good people, both civilian and military, and a clear-cut designation of authority, responsibility, and accountability will ensure the best performance" rather than periodic reorganizations. Jordan also reported that Moorer particularly "disagrees with the proposals to strengthen joint military structures" and "disagrees strongly with the proposals to strengthen the unified and specified commanders." This mix of views permitted Jordan to endorse the report as a "high quality, but likely controversial, study."[33]

Eventually, CSIS was able to obtain the endorsement of six of seven living former secretaries of defense. Only Donald Rumsfeld was missing from the list. In the report's foreword, Harold Brown, Clark M. Clifford, Laird, Robert S. McNamara, Elliot Richardson, and Schlesinger spoke of "serious deficiencies in the organization and managerial procedures of the U.S. defense establishment." Of the report's recommendations, they were "united in support for the general thrust of its proposals." Besides greatly increasing the report's standing, this endorsement diminished the likelihood of retribution by conservative foundations.

Of seven think tank and university efforts, the CSIS project was "the most influential study in terms of the political debate then unfolding."[34] Blechman describes it as "probably my most successful project" over several decades of think-tank work. It unified the voice of numerous experts, including six former defense secretaries, in urging reorganization and articulating specific fixes. Having so many prominent former officials endorse reorganization made it a legitimate issue on Capitol Hill and "safe" for members to discuss. The project also helped educate members of Congress, especially Nunn, Cohen, and Aspin, each of whom would play critical roles in the coming legislative battles. Hearing directly from former senior officers about actual operational setbacks and petty interservice bickering especially impressed members.[35] The project's reports and papers provided important information to the Senate and House Armed Services Committees. Reformers were thankful that CSIS's project had withstood the navy assault.

The Heritage Foundation was not as fortunate. A navy attack on its reorganization project scuttled its most important paper. Heritage—even more conservative than CSIS—ultimately came out in favor of reform, providing cover for some conservative members of Congress who had been reticent to vote against the navy on this issue.[36]

Established in 1973, the Heritage Foundation flourished during the Carter years. It was "credited with having written the Reagan agenda in 1980." At the start of the Reagan administration in 1981, Heritage published *Mandate for Leadership: Policy Management in a Conservative Administration.* The book was "warmly welcomed by Reagan and his advisors." In the early and mid-1980s,

Heritage was closer to the center of power in the Reagan administration than any other think tank.[37]

Gingrich had pushed Heritage into undertaking its study and persuaded the think tank to hire Lt. Col. Theodore J. Crackel, a retiring army officer, to lead the project. Gingrich was a frequent lecturer at the Army War College in Carlisle, Pennsylvania, where Crackel served as the director of military history and strategic studies. Both had majored in history from undergraduate through doctoral studies and taught history, Crackel at West Point and Gingrich at West Georgia College. Initially, Gingrich had tried unsuccessfully to have Crackel hired as the executive director of the CMRC.[38]

On August 1, 1983, Crackel began an eighteen-month assignment at Heritage as a senior fellow and director of the Military Reform Project. The Smith Richardson Foundation helped to fund the project. When some conservatives objected to the term "military reform," Heritage quickly changed the name to Defense Assessment Project. The reason, said Crackel, was that "Some circles felt that people who really only wanted to cut costs regardless of the consequences had co-opted the term 'military reform.'"

Crackel's project dismayed some conservatives. In a meeting on September 9, Michelle Van Cleave of Cong. Jack Kemp's office told Crackel that his study would cause problems "because any 'criticism'—real or implied—of the administration or its programs will be used against them." She put Crackel on notice that "she and others were watching the project and me carefully and that they would attack if we stepped out of bounds." In his estimation, "The bounds seem to be any criticism—however voiced"—of the current administration.[39]

The project covered the entire range of reform issues, including weapons, doctrine, procurement process, personnel policies, and organization. Crackel hoped to arrive at a comprehensive blueprint that will "revolutionize the way we conduct our defense business" and shift the focus of military reform "from the current concern with specific weapons and doctrinal issues to more fundamental issues of process and structure." Crackel, the project's only Heritage staffer, created four working groups: defense management and planning, command and staff structure, service roles and missions, and defense and the nation. He recruited working-level people from Capitol Hill, the Pentagon, think tanks, and industry to serve on these groups.[40]

Richard V. Allen, Reagan's first national security adviser, chaired the project's eleven-member advisory board. Four Republican members of Congress joined the board: Senator Kassebaum and Congressmen Gingrich, Whitehurst, and James Courter. Efforts to recruit Senators Tower and Nunn failed. In addition to Kassebaum and Gingrich, two other advisory board members also served on the steering committee of the CSIS Defense Organization Project: Meyer and R. James Woolsey, a former navy under secretary.

In September, 1983, during Crackel's second month on the job, Edwin J. Feulner Jr., Heritage's president and cofounder, told him, "Secretary Lehman is going to give us a Navy fellow, and that fellow is going to work with you." A month later, Capt. William S. "Spencer" Johnson, arrived. He had been serving on Lehman's immediate staff as a special assistant. Johnson's high-level connections signaled that he was not a typical think-tank fellow. Crackel "was suspicious of the gift horse from the beginning."

"To the degree I could, I shared stuff with Johnson, like drafts for his comment, but I held back on some things I knew the navy would object to," recalled Crackel. "I don't think it was ever blatant. I don't think I ever charged Johnson with it, but it was my assumption that he was feeding stuff back to the navy."[41]

Johnson was sent to the think tank because "Lehman was very upset with Heritage. They had sent papers over to Capitol Hill that had, in Lehman's view, cost the navy 5 percent of its budget. Heritage was questioning the defense budget, especially John Lehman's six-hundred-ship navy." Johnson said, "I was sent to help educate Heritage on naval requirements, sea power, the defense budget, and the need for a strong navy." Johnson seemed well suited for this task. He had come to Lehman's attention after coauthoring the "Maritime Strategy," a controversial new scheme for how the navy would fight the Soviet Union. Johnson's instructions were "to keep close to what Heritage is doing" and "please help them understand some of the nuances of what they are writing. I wasn't invited into the heart of the Crackel's project because folks probably thought I was a 'white rat' for Lehman." Johnson spent half his time at Heritage and half in the Pentagon, where he could keep the navy informed of activities at Heritage and provide available papers.

Through Johnson and others, the navy obtained copies of Crackel's papers—even, on occasion, his rough drafts. One draft that reached Lehman's desk had the following note from one of his military assistants: "Seth [Cropsey] brought this by—it [is] from proposed Heritage report. You need to call R. V. A. [Richard V. Allen] Tuesday."[42]

Crackel planned to publish ten papers, which Heritage called "backgrounders," on various reform topics. In December, 1983, Heritage published the first, entitled "Reforming 'Military Reform.'" Written by Crackel, it addressed the potential of reform to "revitalize U.S. defense." In it he said, "'Military reform' may prove one of the most powerful sets of ideas of our time."[43]

Lehman did not like this backgrounder. He wrote to Dick Allen: "What *garbage!* Here we go again playing 'let's shoot ourselves in the foot' except that now it is a presidential election year." Lehman and Allen had been close since the Nixon administration's beginning in 1969 when Lehman started his Washington career at the NSC as Allen's junior staff member. Allen later helped Lehman secure his appointment as Navy secretary.[44]

Unaware of Lehman's attempt to intervene, Crackel focused his second backgrounder on JCS reorganization. The paper labeled joint planning and strategy making "wholly inadequate" and military advice of "little utility." Crackel recommended "dissolving" the JCS, designating the JCS chairman as the chief of the Joint Staff, assigning him the duties performed by the JCS, and giving him a four-star deputy. He also recommended giving "serious consideration" to "the elimination of all or part of the service secretariats."[45]

When he wrote this provocative paper, Crackel "knew it was going to be terribly controversial [and] would ruffle feathers." Warned of this controversy by Crackel, Burton Pines, Heritage's vice president for research, told Crackel to send the paper to "some key people for their comments." Among others, Arch Barrett on the HASC staff and I received copies. Crackel's letter to me advised that Heritage would release the backgrounder in two or three days and said it had been sent "for your information—and for any advice or counsel you would care to offer." He added: "The piece will be controversial. It goes somewhat beyond what the conventional wisdom says is politically possible. The purpose, of course, is to push the debate forward—and to raise issues that seem difficult for others to raise."[46] Crackel's paper impressed me, but Tower's antireorganization stance made it impossible for me to provide any advice or counsel.

When Crackel gave a copy of the backgrounder to Johnson, saying "It went to the print shop yesterday," Johnson reported the imminent release to Rear Adm. Paul David Miller, Lehman's senior military assistant. Miller responded, "We'll take it from here." Johnson gathered from the call that "Lehman had some sense of urgency that this paper had to be nipped in the bud."[47]

Heritage postponed releasing the JCS reorganization paper while others completed their review. It was on hold for more than two weeks. Crackel "began to hear rumors that Lehman, who was traveling, was trying to contact Feulner about the backgrounder." This possibility worried Crackel; Lehman and Feulner had been close friends for many years.

On April 16, after lunch with Lehman, Feulner distributed a memorandum: "Hold the JCS reorganization paper in the Defense Assessment Project until we have a chance to discuss it in detail. There are a number of sensitive areas that we must discuss before proceeding with it." Essentially, Feulner had killed the backgrounder Crackel considered "presenting the central theme of the whole project." Crackel was told, "We're not going to publish it. It's too controversial. The timing is not right."[48]

Like Crackel, Pines, chief of Heritage's publication program, "reacted strongly" to Lehman's pressuring Feulner to kill the JCS reorganization paper. Pines became "even more insistent that the reorganization message get out."

Word of Lehman's success in suppressing the Heritage paper spread quickly on Capitol Hill. The squashing of this report was a setback, but reformers worried more about the loss of Heritage's support for reorganization. This incident reminded my Senate colleagues and me of the services' power, especially the navy and its secretary.

Heritage eventually published Crackel's reorganization ideas. At Pines's urging, the project's report was summarized in the second edition of Heritage's flagship product: *Mandate for Leadership II: Continuing the Conservative Revolution*, released on December 7, 1984. Written by Crackel, the chapter addressed the full range of reorganization issues and "criticized Weinberger's marginal changes as insufficient."[49]

Crackel's chapter said DoD organization "sanctions and perpetuates institutionalized parochialisms." He added that "Service parochialism is as ubiquitous as it is legendary, and the services, which the [Joint] Chiefs individually represent, cooperate only grudgingly." Crackel's most forceful fixes centered on the JCS chairman, whom he would strengthen and provide a four-star deputy. He proposed that the chairman "be authorized to give military advice in his own right" and endorsed roles for the chairman that had appeared in House legislation: supervisor and spokesman for the unified commanders, a member of the chain of command, and sole manager of the Joint Staff. He added two new, controversial ideas: he would empower the chairman to select officers for all joint billets and recommend their promotions.

Also controversial, Crackel proposed assigning the chairman responsibility for the allocation of roles and missions among the services. He also proposed shifting the defense budget's focus from service aspirations to warfighting needs, recommending that programming and budgeting be "guided by requirements . . . identified by the combatant commands."[50]

Barrett praised the Defense Assessment chapter in a letter to Crackel. "The substance goes further than anything I could have anticipated and, as you know, I agree with most of it wholeheartedly." Barrett disagreed with placing "Heritage on record as favoring what amounts to a general staff," but admired its inclusion as a demonstration of "the breadth of your tour de force." Barrett thought the article was better than any other in giving "an excellent overview of the existing problems . . . and the opportunities for realignment."[51]

Secretary Lehman had delayed but not stopped Heritage's publication of proreform ideas. His intervention made the Heritage Foundation appear unreliable on reform, unable to withstand Pentagon pressure. Yet, its strongly proreform report gave some conservative members a rationale for ignoring navy lobbying.[52]

On October 15, 1982, in a meeting with Secretary Weinberger and Deputy Secretary Frank Carlucci, Lt. Gen. John S. Pustay, USAF, president of the National Defense University (NDU), proposed that NDU conduct two reorganization conferences in March and April, 1983. The first would feature scholars providing "historical and contemporary perspectives on military centralization," principally the experiences of other countries. Former Pentagon practitioners would present papers on key organizational issues at the second conference.[53]

Vincent Davis and Robert J. Art, two NDU consultants who had participated in the meeting, viewed reorganization as "an important issue."[54] Davis taught at the University of Kentucky and served as director of its Patterson School of Diplomacy and International Commerce. He had piloted carrier aircraft during the Korean War and retired as a captain after thirty-four years in the Naval Reserve. Davis's two books on the postwar navy gave him strong credentials on defense organization. Art, a professor and graduate dean at Brandeis University, had studied and written on the congressional budget process and its impact on the Pentagon.

When it appeared that the Pentagon and NDU were not going to conduct the conferences, Art, Davis, and Harvard professor Samuel P. Huntington, author of a classic book entitled *The Soldier and the State*, undertook the project on their own. All three belonged to the proreform camp. The Ford Foundation granted funds for their project, which Harvard and Kentucky would jointly administer. Harvard hosted the first conference in November, 1983, and Kentucky, the second less than a month later. Each session had about forty-five attendees, representing the ideological spectrum.

Bruce Porter and I from the SASC staff attended both conferences. Because the conferences were held in the midst of Senator Tower's reorganization inquiry hearings, many of the papers presented became valuable sources of information and ideas.

Art, Davis, and Huntington edited a book that included twenty conference articles. In the introduction, Art wrote: "The other nations analyzed in this volume—the Soviet Union, Israel, Great Britain, Canada, and the Federal Republic of Germany—have proceeded further in integrating their separate military services than has the United States. Each has forces more subject to central direction than does the United States, with an apparent increase in efficiency." Huntington said the project's major contribution, something that "really opened my eyes," was this comparison of the U.S. and foreign military establishments. "Our defense organization was so far removed from the types of organizations that others had. Ours was so pluralistic and decentralized."[55]

Unlike CSIS and Heritage publications, the Harvard-Kentucky book did not offer conclusions or recommendations. One commentator termed the book "academically the most respectable of the outside studies," but believed its influence was limited to helping to "place the debate in its international and historical context."[56]

In late 1983, Navy Secretary Lehman decided that the antireform camp needed its own academic and think-tank activities. He and J. D. Hittle, his reorganization watchdog, began forming a group to rebut proposed reforms. Just as most proreformers had done, Lehman and Hittle recruited only those who supported their view. They enlisted participation of a general or flag officer from each service: Lyman Lemnitzer from the army, Jim Holloway from the navy, John W. Vogt from the air force, and Louis Wilson from the Marine Corps. All but Vogt had served as service chiefs, and Lemnitzer had also been JCS chairman. Lehman personally recruited Vogt. He and Hittle added three other anti-reformers with varied congressional, veterans, and business connections.[57]

The Hudson Institute was chosen as the group's sponsor. Futurist Herman Kahn founded the Hudson Institute in a New York City suburb in 1961. Kahn epitomized the "popular stereotype of the think-tank 'type.'" One author described his role: "Kahn's full beard, capacious girth, and restless intellect typified the popular image of the think-tank intellectual—the crackpot genius, absent-minded misfit, and Strangelovian strategist." Following Kahn's 1983 death, the deeply in debt institute moved to Indianapolis, where a consortium of business and foundation executives had offered significant financial support.[58]

Also in 1983, Lehman awarded Hudson the contract to manage the Washington-based Center for Naval Analyses (CNA), replacing the University of Rochester, which had managed the center for many years. Because CNA's studies were challenging many of his policies and programs, "the institution had become a thorn in Lehman's side." In a highly controversial move, he decided to fire CNA president David Kassing. When Rochester told Lehman he lacked the authority to fire Kassing, the navy responded by putting CNA's contract out for bid and selected Hudson.[59]

As a result of this timely windfall, Hudson looked favorably upon navy causes. President Thomas D. Bell Jr. began speaking out against reorganization. In an opinion piece appearing in the *New York Times* in March, 1985, he termed JCS reorganization "generally esoteric, uninformed by history and very trendy." Bell maintained that "The existing system works and has long stood us in good stead."[60]

The Hudson study group, calling itself the Committee on Civilian-Military Relationships, issued its report, *An Analysis of Proposed Joint Chiefs of Staff Reorganization,* on September 17, 1984. The executive summary began: "In this report an eminently qualified group of Americans argues against proposed statutory changes in the structure of the Joint Chiefs of Staff, lest well-meaning 'reforms' leave the United States exposed to provincial Prussian-style military leadership. But . . . the group attacks decades of 'chronic inflation' in the Office of [the] Secretary of Defense [and] urges a twenty percent reduction in the OSD civilian-military bureaucracy."[61]

David O. "Doc" Cooke, Weinberger's deputy assistant secretary for administration, blasted the report as "lacking in analysis. Ninety percent of the contents are little more than 'cut and paste.'" He also thought the report was too oriented toward military experience: "None of the membership of the reporting committee have had working experience as a civilian in OSD or the NSC. . . . the report lacks a balanced perspective."[62] The report's lack of scholarship would have appalled Herman Kahn.

In a memorandum for Adm. James D. Watkins, Capt. Jake W. Stewart, executive director of the CNO Executive Panel—an internal think tank—attacked the Hudson report as "an unabashed piece of advocacy" and "more appropriate to the soapbox than to a 'detailed' study." To make his point, Stewart cited the following passage: "Never do proponents of a national general staff admit that their proposed system has flourished *only* when its roots sink deeply into the poisoned soil of militarism, dictatorship, and anti-democratic beliefs."[63]

Stewart recommended that Watkins "avoid participation in the current debate by slogan, but also that you consider the merits of redirecting the debate toward a higher caliber, more imaginative and less starkly framed level of discourse. . . . JCS/Defense reform need not be a zero-sum game." In light of the completion of the 1984 defense authorization conference, Watkins responded, "Issue resolved—at least for now." Reacting to the toughness of Stewart's message, the admiral decreed, "'Cool it!'"

In a letter to the editor of *Defense Week*, former Under Secretary of Defense Robert W. Komer described the Hudson report as a "one-sided and feeble . . . justification of the status quo." He called its recommendation to reduce OSD "a feature of the U.S. Navy's longstanding campaign against any defense organization measure which would reduce its prized autonomy."[64]

Not everyone saw the report as an embarrassment. Rear Adm. John M. Poindexter, the deputy national security adviser forwarded the report to his boss, Robert C. "Bud" McFarlane, Reagan's national security adviser, calling it "an interesting and timely study." Poindexter was "convinced that the correct model for JCS is corporate one. Due to the vagaries of the selection process [for JCS chairman] the United States needs insurance to guard against a bad selection." Eleven months after its release and despite Cooke's criticisms, Weinberger was still drawing the Hudson report to the attention of those outside the Pentagon who were studying reorganization.[65]

Shortly after the Hudson report's release, Admiral Watkins convened a select panel to review JCS reorganization proposals so he could "be prepared to take a balanced and thoughtful position."[66] Four retired officers and one on active duty comprised the CNO Select Panel. Admiral Bob Long served as chairman. The other members were Adm. Bobby R. Inman, Vice Adm. Frank W. Vannoy, Rear Adm. Samuel H. Packer, and Brigadier General Hittle.

When the panel completed its report on March 14, 1985, Watkins noted "the similarity between the views of the select panel and those provided by the secretary of defense, chairman of the Joint Chiefs of Staff, service secretaries and service chiefs." The panel opposed "any structural or procedural change in the Joint Chiefs of Staff that would modify or otherwise infringe upon the statutory responsibilities of the corporate Joint Chiefs of Staff." It recommended against designating the chairman as the principal military adviser, subordinating the Joint Staff solely to him, and providing him a deputy. The panel also opposed the administration's proposals to put the chairman in the chain of command and make him an NSC member.[67]

The CNO Select Panel supported strengthening the role of unified commanders, particularly on resource issues and readiness and sustainability matters, and stressed the need for the JCS to develop "a more comprehensive and coherent national military strategy." It recommended assigning more talented officers to joint billets and urged that the CNO "take an active role in overcoming the perception widely held by naval officers that joint duty is less rewarding."

Although the panel's report was intended to provide advice only to Watkins, the navy belatedly brought the work to attention of others, principally members of Congress.

Seth Cropsey arranged one last navy foray into the academic world: a "JCS Reform" conference hosted by the Naval War College in Newport, Rhode Island, in May, 1985. Inviting the college's president to sponsor this event, Cropsey said it would be "a genuine service [and] not only to the Navy which has long understood the problems of an overzealous centralization of military authority."[68] The conference attracted sixty participants, including Arch Barrett and Francis J. "Frank" Sullivan, who worked for Senator Stennis as the minority staff director of the Appropriations Committee. Most of the other Senate staffers planning to participate in the Friday-Saturday conference, including Rick Finn and me, were detained in Washington by Senate business.

The conference, like the Harvard-Kentucky project, focused its two parts on JCS reform proposals and organizational lessons from other countries. All speakers on JCS issues argued against reform except Gen. Bruce Palmer Jr., a retired former army vice chief and deputy commander of U.S. forces in Vietnam. Given this lineup, a staffer from Cong. Ike Skelton's office "complained that the conference was not sufficiently 'balanced.'"[69]

Robert J. Murray, a former navy under secretary, defended the status quo. The first of his three arguments centered on history. "The JCS system has taken us successfully through the most dangerous war [World War II] in our national life, and has subsequently carried us safely through four decades of the postwar nuclear era." His second argument lauded diversity of advice. "The present JCS enables . . . diverse military points of view to come forward." Murray's last point was that the existing system "has the important advantage of fitting both the letter and spirit of the Constitution." He cited the Founding Fathers' decision to distribute power widely, implying that they would be against proposals to strengthen the JCS chairman.[70]

Admiral Jim Holloway argued that the JCS system was not "paralyzed by the burden of service self-interest." He praised JCS advice on military operations while admitting that more deliberative advice "has not always been as precise, comprehensive, or as prompt as desired." The admiral criticized the CSIS report, saying its proposals to strengthen the JCS chairman "are completely contrary to the basic philosophy of our national military command structure."

David K. Hall, a Naval War College professor, pegged his antireform presentation on the belief that the quality of military advice and decisions "will continue to turn on technical expertise and interpersonal relations, not formal authority and organization charts."

A fourth antireformer, Jeffrey G. Barlow of the National Institute for Public Policy, argued that the "search for perfectibility . . . is simply not obtainable through defense reorganization." He judged that moving away from the corporate JCS system "will only add strategic inflexibilities and will further narrow the range of alternatives presented to civilian superiors."

Cropsey elatedly reported on the conference to Lehman: The quality of the papers and discussion was "quite excellent," "forceful, convincing," and "well-reasoned and equally persuasive."[71] Cropsey recommended that the Naval War College "publish a readable, shortened pamphlet of the best papers." Lehman agreed and provided the funding.

By volume of intellectual firepower, proreform academic forces overwhelmed the antireform forces. However, their mutual objective was not to defeat each other, but to influence decision makers in the Reagan administration and on Capitol Hill—two arenas where proreform scholars should have held the upper hand. The breadth and stature of their participants and endorsements, depth of their research, rigor of their scholarship, and volume of their books, reports, and articles were impressive. They were about to discover, however, that in an area as arcane and emotional as defense reorganization, the linking of knowledge and power was more problematic.

CHAPTER 9

Nichols Runs Tower's Blockade

Reformers have the idea that change

can be achieved by brute sanity.

—George Bernard Shaw

"Is the Senate going to do anything?" Cong. Bill Nichols asked in his Alabama drawl.[1]

"Senator Tower's staff director, Jim McGovern, said, 'Yes, the Senate will respond to your bill,'" staffer Arch Barrett responded.

"There's no excuse for the Senate *not* to be doing something this time," Nichols reasoned. "In 1982, the House sent the Joint Chiefs of Staff bill to the Senate during the second session. This time, we moved the bill during the first session."

The Investigations Subcommittee chairman was worried because the House's JCS reorganization bill was freestanding, not part of the defense authorization bill. If the Senate did not act, the JCS bill would die when the session adjourned at the end of 1984.

Nichols's early 1984 fretting about prospects for enacting JCS reforms reflected his recent concerns about the intentions of John Tower, chairman of the Senate Armed Services Committee. When Tower announced his committee's reorganization inquiry, the Senate seemed to become a partner in the reform crusade. The SASC's failure to produce legislation in 1983 did not trouble Nichols. Reorganization was a complex subject; it would take time for the Senate to formulate its ideas. But when no SASC activity was discernible in early 1984, Nichols became concerned.

Barrett's encouraging report led Nichols to accept Tower's and McGovern's promises.

Before the Senate and House Armed Services Committees began their 1984 work, two more naval embarrassments occurred in Lebanon. On February 6, in support of the Beirut marines, an A6 aircraft from the carrier *Kennedy* dropped two laser-guided bombs on gun positions firing at the leathernecks. The mission involved "two of the Navy's most skillful fliers flying the Navy's smartest bomber loaded with its smartest bombs against [an undefended] stationary target." Nevertheless, the bombs missed their target by more than a mile, hitting an apartment building and setting it on fire.[2]

Two days later, the World War II battleship *New Jersey* and another ship launched the largest naval gunfire barrage since Vietnam. The *New Jersey*'s nine 16-inch guns fired shells that weighed as much as a Volkswagen, traveled almost eighteen miles, and created a fifty-foot-wide and twenty-foot-deep crater. In one morning, the *New Jersey* fired 290 Volkswagens into Lebanon, and the other ship unleashed 450 5-inch rounds.

The day before, Navy Secretary Lehman testified to the HASC that 16-inch gunfire is "very accurate" and "great care is taken not to fire into civilian areas." But soon after the barrage, "administration officials" in Washington admitted "virtually all of the more than 700 huge shells fired at Druse and Syrian positions in Lebanon . . . missed their targets by very large distances and had little or no military or political impact." Poor accuracy resulted because "the Navy had no spotters, either on the ground or in airplanes above the target areas, who could [report] where the shells were dropping and how to readjust the aiming." Without a forward spotter, the *New Jersey*'s 16-inch rounds were "likely to land within 2,000 feet of their targets only fifty percent of the time."[3]

Poor gunfire results in Lebanon appear to have been the rule, not the exception. Facts suggest that "the firing from naval ships never destroyed a single military target." Lower-ranking naval officials conceded that naval gunfire had only "put big holes in mountainsides," killed civilians, and damaged property. Even the Druze militia, the gunfire's frequent targets, did not fear the barrages because "they never hit anything." According to one Druze commander, "Had they actually hit something, things might have been different."[4]

As with other failings, the embarrassing gunfire performance off Lebanon resulted because "the application of basic military technique was so poor."[5]

Although Tower and McGovern wished reorganization would disappear, the genie was too big to get back in the bottle. After a major public announcement of the inquiry, twelve hearings, work on a staff report, and heavy involvement of committee and senators' staffs, the issue was too visible to vanish. At the beginning of 1984, Tower and McGovern concocted a plausible reason for in-activity on reorganization: the unexpectedly heavy workload of other defense issues. The growing resistance in the Senate to the Reagan defense buildup and controversial weapon programs lent credence to this excuse.

But the staff study chugged along. Tower and McGovern could not easily concoct a reason to curtail it. Moreover, by the time they decided to apply the brakes, many staffers had become involved, and some were convinced of the need for reform. Interest in Pentagon problems was high.

McGovern implemented a three-pronged approach to negate the study. The first prong would strictly limit the number of staffers who had access to the study and prohibit anyone outside of the committee from seeing it. It was guarded more closely than a TOP SECRET document. McGovern apparently figured if no one knew what the study said, it could not do much damage.

McGovern's second prong sought to slow work on the study by piling other work on key participants. I was a central target of this approach. Fortunately, I had three talented research assistants working for me—Rick Finn, Drew A. Harker, and Judith A. Freedman—each of whom was anxious to assume in-creased responsibilities. Whatever extra work McGovern sent in my direction, I assigned to Finn, Harker, or Freedman with instructions to keep my desk free of McGovern's "make work" projects if at all possible.

On February 1, I wrote to McGovern: "Our DoD Organization Project is really struggling. Given all of the other work, I have not been able to devote the necessary time to redraft the OSD section; others are equally burdened. Some-how, we need to attempt to minimize lower priority work."[6] This report must have pleased McGovern.

Throughout 1984, I kept working on the staff report. Other staffers contin-ued to contribute as well. The pace of research and writing was slowed, but work continued.

McGovern's third prong envisioned altering the study's proreform direc-tion. He asked me for a copy for his review and comment, and then surrepti-tiously sent it to the navy for a detailed scrub. The marine officer who carried it to the Pentagon called me within moments of its delivery, saying, "You know that staff study that is being held so closely that no one can get a peek at it—well, I just delivered a copy from Jim McGovern to Secretary Lehman's office." I could not reveal this confidence, so I waited for McGovern's next move.

About two weeks later, McGovern sent me a twenty-page paper with de-tailed changes he wanted made. The paper reflected typical Pentagon style with the changes noted in a line-in/line-out format. The pages had been numbered by a special Pentagon machine.

When I gathered staffers to review McGovern's comments, the group ex-pressed a collective view: "What a charade. McGovern is trying to pass the navy's comments off as his own." We decided to resist.

I directly confronted McGovern: "These changes came from the Pentagon."
"This is my work," he replied. "I want these changes made in the staff study."

"The majority of staffers will not agree to these changes," I countered. "We
need to have a meeting of all staff from the committee and members' offices who
are working on the study to hear from you why these changes should be made."

I knew this would be too much visibility for McGovern. He was not knowledgeable enough to debate reorganization issues. He declined the offer and the
impasse continued.

When I went on a two-day trip on other committee business, McGovern
instructed my secretary, Barbara B. Brown, to type his changes into the study
master.[7] Upon my return I became infuriated when I discovered what McGovern
had done and had the offending comments removed. Considerable effort had to
be expended to reconstruct the study. Guerrilla warfare over the study and
McGovern's comments continued for months.

When his three-pronged approach didn't cripple the study, McGovern developed a fourth prong: Tower would ask one or more outside panels, each with
five to seven members, to review it. On May 9, Tower told Reagan's national
security adviser, Bud McFarlane, that the panels would "critique our staff report and offer legislative and administrative solutions to the committee in the
fall."[8] My reorganization colleagues and I feared that Tower and McGovern
would stack the panel with antireformers. Fortunately, other demands on the
committee precluded implementing this idea.

Under pressure from Nunn, Tower finally released a copy of the study to
each SASC member on May 15. His cover letter stated: "I have not yet had a
chance to read the report, therefore, it may not reflect my views or those of
other committee members. Because this could be a very sensitive issue—
particularly in an election year—I ask that you treat this as an 'eyes only'
document." Despite Tower's plea, copies were soon circulating in the Pentagon. Senator Dan Quayle's office had provided one of the copies.[9]

By the middle of May, when Tower had made no move to fulfill his promises,
Nichols determined that he would have to force Tower's hand by adding H.R.
3718, the reorganization bill passed by the House in October, 1983, as an amendment to the legislation authorizing the Pentagon's budget. This move would
require a Senate-House conference committee—formed to settle differences in
the two bills—to address JCS reform.

When the Pentagon learned of Nichols's plans, its general counsel,
Chapman B. Cox, wrote to HASC chairman Mel Price to express "grave reservations" about the substance of Nichols's amendment. Cox, asking Price to
withdraw Nichols's amendment, argued against attaching "such important
and substantial legislation to the DoD Authorization Act and thus overburden
an already important piece of legislation."[10]

Price rejected the Pentagon's request and instead on May 30 offered Nichols's amendment in a block of eleven "noncontroversial" provisions. Congressman Charles Bennett—the second-ranking HASC Democrat and a strong navy supporter—spoke against Nichols's amendment. He noted that H.R. 3718 would make "real changes" in JCS organization, "which are very much opposed by the Department of Defense." Bennett did not seek to defeat the amendment, believing that Pentagon objections "can be considered and handled in conference between the House and Senate."[11] The House accepted the block of amendments and passed the bill on June 1.

Three days later, Tower met with Secretary Weinberger to prepare for Senate consideration of the SASC's version of the authorization bill. Tower's point paper listed three subjects for the meeting: MX missile funding, seven possible controversial amendments, and defense organization. Reforming the JCS was identified as one of the controversial amendments that could be offered on the Senate floor. Tower said he might "need DoD to develop 'fallback' options in the event we need them" should amendments be offered in these areas.[12]

Tower suggested that Weinberger and the president "should decide whether it would be politically advantageous for you to embrace the *concept* of reorganizing the Department of Defense to neutralize the animus that presently exists between the Congress/media and the Department of Defense." Tower was on the hot seat, squeezed between the administration and reform-minded HASC. He hoped in vain that the administration would lift this burden.

Senator Sam Nunn was also thinking about how to handle the House's JCS reforms. His thoughts were much more positive than Tower's, although he saw two major flaws in the House's reforms: making the JCS chairman a statutory member of the NSC and inserting him in the chain of command. Nunn judged that "both proposals undermine the authority of the secretary of defense and should be deleted."[13]

Nunn suggested to Tower that they had two options. The first was to "stonewall" in the hope "that the House will recede in exchange for a promise from us to take up their bill promptly." However, Nunn realized that this option left the Senate little leverage in the conference committee if the House was "adamant." He also believed the "House might not buy our pledge to take up the bill" since the Senate already had a full legislative calendar. Barrett was concurrently advising Nichols to reject a Senate promise to take up the House bill separately, doubting that "with the best good will and good faith in the world, Senator Tower could deliver on this."[14]

Nunn's second option involved introducing a Tower-Nunn amendment on JCS reorganization during Senate consideration of the defense authorization bill. Having "now read the excellent study done by the committee staff," Nunn told Tower he was ready to discuss the contents of a possible amendment.[15]

Tower liked the first option. He had no interest in adding JCS reforms to the Senate bill.

On June 18, 1984, during floor action on the defense authorization bill, Sen. Thomas F. Eagleton (D-Missouri) offered a reorganization amendment that would replace the JCS with a chief of military staff and a National Military Advisory Council. Eagleton's amendment was similar to the bill submitted by his fellow Missouri Democrat, Cong. Ike Skelton.[16]

In response, Tower announced his "intention," in late July, "to convince the Armed Services Committee to consider legislation that would effect some fairly comprehensive reform." Tower said this approach would depend on completing the conference report on the authorization bill prior to the July 4 recess and asked Eagleton to await the results of the SASC's work before pressing his proposal.[17]

Offering a rare public glimpse of his thinking, Tower said, "While I agree with some of the observations of the Senator from Missouri, I do have some concerns with his proposal." He repeated the Pentagon's argument "that a great deal of power would actually be divested of the secretary of defense and, I think, would tend to militate against our tradition of civilian control of the military."

Nunn pressed Tower to make DoD reorganization "the top item for our committee during July."

Tower agreed. "That will be our priority effort then," he said.

"I do not know of anything more important, frankly, that we face in the whole defense arena," Nunn replied.[18]

Senator Barry Goldwater joined the debate, saying that Eagleton had targeted the conflict of interest "problem that has prevailed in the Joint Chiefs almost since its inception" and noting his interest in reorganization since statutory establishment of the JCS in 1947. "I do not know whether Senator Nunn will be chairman of the Armed Services Committee next year or whether I will be," he said, "but I think I am perfectly safe in saying that, whether he is chairman or I am chairman, this is a subject that is going to receive very deep study and, it is hoped, some resolution, so that our military services not only can perform better in military decisions, but also, just as important to me, perform better in procurement."

With these commitments, Eagleton withdrew his amendment.[19]

For almost a year, Tower had adroitly found reasons to put off JCS reorganization without having to declare his opposition. Jeffrey H. Smith, Nunn's staffer working on JCS reform, recalled: "I don't remember Tower personally expressing any opposition to reform in any meeting I ever attended. But, clearly, everybody knew Tower was against it; McGovern was against it; the navy was against it. This roadblock was going to make reform impossible."[20]

Rhett Dawson explained Tower's opposition: "As the Pentagon's spear carrier on the Hill, his job was to kill reorganization. Tower also had a disdainful view of the HASC work, seeing it as not well conceived and lacking a broad base of support. Importantly, the legislation would strike at Tower's uniformed constituencies, especially the navy and Marine Corps. In combination, these three factors exponentially increased his resistance. Moreover, Tower didn't see much upside to reorganization. During much of his career, he was not regarded as a reformer and was not adaptive to change. In addition, Tower was not close to any reform proponents."[21]

Tower's chairmanship of the House-Senate conference on the defense authorization bill enhanced his ability to defeat the JCS provisions. The chairmanship alternated between SASC and HASC chairmen for each major conference. The conference chairman decides the agenda for sessions, schedules issues for consideration, and leads the conference's reconciliation of differences in the Senate and House bills. In 1984, the two bills contained twelve hundred differences.

Two factors would magnify Tower's control as conference chairman. First, his extraordinary negotiating and parliamentary skills would enable him to exercise the chairman's full powers. Second, Tower's counterpart, seventy-nine-year-old HASC chairman Mel Price, was frail and "growing increasingly feeble." Because of his colleagues' great "respect and affection" for Price—the second most senior House member—most overlooked his "infirmities" and "diminished capabilities." One member bluntly stated the truth: "Mel drifts in and out."[22] Even on his best days, Price was no match for Tower.

Their chairmen's skills represented only one of many differences between the two committees. The SASC also contained several nationally known figures: Tower, Strom Thurmond, Goldwater, Nunn, John Stennis, Gary Hart, and Ted Kennedy. Few outside of Washington knew the names of the HASC members, who were described as representing the viewpoint of the average working man.[23] The two committees even looked different. The Senate side dressed in fine business suits with Tower always wearing an expensive three-piece British suit. The House side predominantly wore sports coats, with plaid being the most popular.

Traditionally, the hawkish, prodefense HASC was more unified than its Senate counterpart. The like-minded congressmen believed "that partisan political considerations take a back seat to national security issues." Republican member Jim Courter described private HASC sessions as "miraculously devoid" of partisan politics. Nichols said partisanship "just doesn't raise its head, and it shouldn't when you are talking about the defense of the country." The committee's bipartisan approach permitted it to have only one staff, "its most striking characteristic."[24] All other House and Senate committees had two staffs: one to serve majority party members and the other for minority members.

Tower would have difficulty cracking HASC unity. As a powerful chairman adept at playing hardball, he kept a tight rein on his committee, especially the

Republicans, and was certain to retain sufficient SASC votes to support his opposition to JCS reforms. Nunn's support for reform would complicate, but not seriously challenge, Tower's maneuvers. Understanding that "Tower basically didn't want anything to happen," Nunn focused his efforts on "using the House position as leverage to get something done, vis-à-vis Tower."[25]

To expedite its work, the conference committee organized a panel for each block of issues, such as strategic forces and manpower. These panels met informally and prepared recommendations for the committee. Before a panel met, staff discussions identified common ground and initiated resolution. Some issues were not assigned to a panel but were negotiated by the chairmen or under their supervision. Tower decided to handle JCS reform in that manner. He and Nichols would negotiate these issues. As the SASC's senior reorganization staffer, I expected to handle staff discussions and support Tower's negotiations.

Before the first conference session on June 22, McGovern asked to meet with me. He shocked me by saying: "Senator Tower has asked me to work the JCS issues for him. You're too proreform. I will handle the discussions with Arch Barrett. Rick Finn will assist me as needed. You will not be involved, and that's an order." I protested that this exclusion was inconsistent with my assigned responsibilities. The staff director harshly instructed me that Tower had already made his decision on staff support and that McGovern would not tolerate any interference from me. He gave me one final instruction: "I don't want you talking to Arch Barrett about this subject."

Putting McGovern in charge of JCS reform signaled my staff colleagues and me that Tower was committed to defeating Nichols's provisions. Tower's and McGovern's tactics centered on delaying consideration of the reorganization provisions. On the conference's first day, a Friday, Tower indicated that JCS reform would be addressed the following Wednesday, June 27. During that first week, McGovern refused to negotiate, saying he was not authorized to do so. This brought objections from the House staff director, Kim Wincup, and Barrett and forced Price to seek Tower's consent to staff discussions at the June 27 conference meeting. "If we do not start to confer we can hardly expect to finish," Nichols observed.[26]

Delaying consideration of JCS issues proved to be a major challenge for Tower and McGovern. Normally, a conference would last two to three weeks. This one lasted three months. Two unresolved major issues—the defense budget's size and the MX missile program—precluded progress. The White House and congressional leadership would have to resolve those issues. Failure to complete the conference before the July recess relieved Tower of his Senate floor commitment to have the SASC consider a reorganization bill in July.

The conference met five times in June, three in July, and then did not meet again for almost two months. Throughout that period, no member or staff negotiations were held on JCS reform.

Nichols and Barrett were kept busy defending the House bill from anti-reform attacks. In a commentary entitled "Let's Stop Trying to Be Prussians" appearing on June 10 in the *Washington Post*, Navy Secretary Lehman fired a broadside at the bill, saying it would create "a Prussian-style general staff." Lehman claimed that "a coalition of civilian arm-chair strategists, who don't really understand the Pentagon bureaucracy, and uniformed military staff officers, who understand it all too well" instigated the reforms.[27]

Lehman focused his attack on the same two provisions that troubled Nunn: having the JCS chairman serve as an NSC member and in the chain of command. He blasted the chain of command provision, saying it "violates every sound military axiom." Strangely, his criticisms focused on the central feature of the administration's proposal—to which Reagan, Weinberger, Vessey, and all the service chiefs had subscribed.

Despite shared objections, Senate reformers found Lehman's arguments erroneous. The secretary argued that the bill "called for more power to Washington staff officers and for severely diminished authority for field commanders and civilian leaders." He said the bill "subverts" two American military principles: civilian control and command responsibility. However, Lehman missed the mark because power was already overly concentrated in Washington staff officers: not the chairman and Joint Staff, but those in the service headquarters. That concentration undermined civilian control by the defense secretary and command responsibility of the unified commanders. But in the arcane world of defense organization, Lehman's slick arguments were not easy to refute.

In early July, an unsigned, undated letter attacking the House bill was sent to defense associations in Washington. It said the bill would elevate the chairman to "a supreme military commander," create "a Prussian-type national general staff," and "adopt the system that helped Germany lose World War II." The letter, repeating claims from the postwar unification fight, issued a five-bell alarm: "The proposed system means the end of naval aviation and, also, the Marine Corps." The Fleet Reserve Association provided a copy to Nichols and Barrett, who were troubled by the letter's "gross distortions."[28]

On July 12, the Association of Naval Aviation, where Admiral Moorer served as chairman of the board, issued the same letter to its members over the signature of its president, Admiral Holloway. He made only one significant change to the draft. He softened the alarm sentence to read: "This proposed system is a very real threat to naval aviation, and also to the Marine Corps." Holloway advocated a grassroots campaign to defeat the "Nichols bill." He asked association members to contact and write letters to senators, congressman, and local newspaper publishers and editors. The point paper he sent for use in these endeavors said the JCS chairman would become "a separate secretary of defense" and charged that civilian control over the military would be largely transferred to the chairman. It warned of "eventual elimination of Navy air and Marines."[29]

Speaker of the House "Tip" O'Neill and Senate Majority Leader Howard Baker broke the deadlock on the defense budget and MX missile on September 20. The conference convened later the same day with the goal of completing its work within days.

On Friday, September 21, after delaying for three months, McGovern and Finn met with Barrett for the first time for staff negotiations on JCS reforms. As reported by Barrett to Wincup, McGovern "began with the assertion that Senator Tower had made a major concession by virtue of merely allowing the House and Senate staffs to negotiate." Barrett "rejected that assertion out of hand as a basis for any concession by the House side, pointing out that our meeting finally consummated an agreement made by Senator Tower in the conference last June."[30]

Eighteen JCS reform issues were at stake. McGovern agreed to accept five minor provisions: authorize the JCS chairman to serve as spokesman for the unified commanders, relax assignment restrictions on the Joint Staff director, increase the maximum length of Joint Staff tours from three to four years, allow officers to be reassigned to the Joint Staff after a two-year interval rather than three, and require the defense secretary to ensure that service personnel policies give appropriate consideration to Joint Staff duty. Only the last provision was not contained in the administration's proposal or supported by the Pentagon. Barrett agreed to drop the provision giving service chiefs and unified commanders the right to comment on Joint Staff papers.[31] Noting that the Senate staffers had made only minor concessions, Barrett said: "What the Senate offered is completely unacceptable."[32]

Barrett told Wincup that Nichols "noted that some of the provisions that the Senate opposes are administration proposals." The Alabama congressman found McGovern's arguments to be unsupported by testimony before the HASC or SASC. Barrett said Nichols "is unwilling to allow the secretary of the navy, apparently without the imprimatur of either the Reagan administration or the uniformed navy or Marine Corps or the Joint Chiefs of Staff, to dictate the outcome of this conference." Nichols apparently believed that Lehman was instructing McGovern, and possibly Tower, on acceptable provisions.

Although other member and staff negotiations continued throughout the weekend, Barrett was unable to schedule additional meetings with McGovern and Finn. At 10 A.M. on Monday, September 24, the conference committee began a marathon session to settle all remaining differences. The meeting was held in the Senate Select Committee on Intelligence's small hearing room, S-407, on the fourth, attic floor of the Capitol, just outside the upper part of the Great Rotunda. A long table that extended nearly the length of the room was

used for conference sessions. The senators sat on one side and the congressmen on the other, with the two chairmen across from each other in the center.
Two rows of chairs for staffers ringed the table. The overly crowded room made
it difficult to move about.

Nichols repeatedly sought to raise the JCS provisions, but Tower kept de-
flecting him, saying, "We'll get to it." The senator's manipulations made JCS
reform the last remaining issue. Weary conferees turned their attention to this
contentious subject at 1 A.M. on Tuesday morning, after fifteen hours in session. Tower was positioned to crush Nichols. The House conferees had great
affection for Nichols, but for most, JCS reform was not "high on their agenda."[33]
If Tower showed determination, the tired conferees, anxious to finish, would
eventually abandon Nichols.

I presented nearly forty foreign policy issues to the conference just before it
considered the JCS provisions. McGovern let me remain in the room for this
last debate, but made it clear that I was not to speak.

As Nichols and Barrett anticipated, Tower began: "Everything else is done.
For God's sake, it's time to go home. It is particularly the wrong time to take up
a complicated issue like this." Tower argued with great success that changes to
the JCS should not be made in isolation. The components of the Pentagon were
interconnected and should be addressed only through a comprehensive set of
reforms. This argument was so powerful because it was right. The talented and
resourceful Texan did not want any changes in the Pentagon, at least not during his tenure, but he could use the all-or-nothing argument to his advantage.
Tower reiterated his theme: "Hey, let's go home. This is a big issue. It's after
midnight. We're all tired. We shouldn't be doing this on an authorization bill
in the first place."[34]

As the conference progressed, Nichols had become increasingly frustrated
with Tower. Barrett later reported: "It took us a little while to discern what Tower
was doing. Mr. Nichols felt that he had no recourse. He was not going to lose
his cool, his courtly southern demeanor, and he never did. He just sat there,
and that was his statement. He was at all conference meetings. When he would
bring up the JCS provisions, Tower would put them back down at the bottom.
In private, Mr. Nichols never forgave Tower. He loathed him for that. I never
heard Mr. Nichols curse, but once. In a private conversation with me, he referred to Tower as 'that little son of a bitch.' That was about as strong as he
would get, but he really felt Tower had not played fairly."[35]

In responding to Tower's statement, Nichols said: "I have tried to be patient. Four times, I have requested to be heard and have been put off. Now, the
hour is late. We have had only one meeting of staffs—last Friday. I am willing to compromise, but I have not been allowed to bring the issues up till the
twelfth hour."[36]

"Mr. Nichols," Barrett recalled, "wanted JCS reform bad enough to push it like he did and probably push it further in a conflict environment than anything he'd ever done."[37]

Barrett later described the dynamic: "Mr. Nichols had tremendous respect on the House committee, just overwhelming, but it only goes so far. Tower played his hand beautifully, and no matter how respected Mr. Nichols was, there was only a certain amount of time that he could hold the members on our side. I have never been under such pressure. I could see the House Republicans getting resistive. Tower and Nichols were arguing, and Tower finally offered this or that, a small point, and it began to look to the members that the Senate is being reasonable. Kim Wincup came and told me, 'We can't hold it much longer.'"[38]

In the midst of this struggle, Barrett looked to me for help. There was nothing I could do.

With six issues settled by the staff, Tower and Nichols debated the other twelve. Nunn's opposition to the two major provisions—JCS chairman in the chain of command and as an NSC member—essentially killed them. After prolonged debate, Tower accepted one and then another of the House provisions. The first would make the chairman responsible for determining when the JCS would decide issues. The second would provide that the chairman would select Joint Staff officers from among the most outstanding service officers. Nunn had pushed for adoption of the latter.[39]

"Tower was just meagering it out by one little point at a time," Barrett recalled. "Mr. Nichols even whispered to me at one point: 'This can't go on much longer.' I tried to compute in my head what we could take and what not, what would be some gain."

Wincup advised Barrett in a whisper: "Arch, you better take what they're offering, 'cause no one wants to stay much longer. This thing's going to crumble *soon.*"[40]

Every eye in the room was on Barrett. In contrast to earlier noise, members and staff were silent. "I just held out to the very last minute," Barrett recalled. "Mr. Nichols was taking the temperature of everybody. Finally, we settled for very little."[41]

"When John Tower rolled Bill Nichols, people on the House side felt badly about it," Wincup later said. "They felt it was personal, maybe not an insult, but close to it."[42]

After Nichols salvaged all that he could, Nunn proposed report language to accompany the bill that would commit the two committees to a comprehensive reorganization effort in 1985. "We turned the conference's work on JCS reform into a substantial report instead of a bill," he said later. Because he had based his opposition on the need for more informed study and a comprehensive package of reforms, Tower was unable to object to the proreform language. The report language praised the House for performing "an important service in bringing JCS reform to the fore." Citing the importance of reorganization, the report said that the conferees agreed "that both committees will make these issues high priority during the next session of Congress." It added, "Both committees consider themselves fully committed to studying the issues of JCS reform and of comprehensive DoD organizational reform with the intent of enacting legislation during the next legislative year."[43]

At Nunn's initiative, the report also included a long list of questions to be answered by the secretary of defense, JCS chairman, unified commanders, service chiefs, and service secretaries. "I felt like the questions were important because they would give us a foundation," Nunn recalled. "I considered their inclusion a significant move."[44] The report instructed responding officials to send their answers directly to the two committees not later than March 1, 1985. The conferees specified the requirement for direct responses in order to evade the Pentagon's thought police. Once the conference had approved the idea of posing questions, Nunn gained permission for me to take the lead in preparing them.

For the near-term, which was all he cared about, Tower had won a great victory on JCS reorganization. Although the conference approved eight of the House's eighteen proposals, they were all minor ones, and three were watered down before being adopted. Tower had turned aside the heart of the legislation. Significant reform was again thwarted. An internal Pentagon memorandum reported, "We came out of this very well."[45]

Nichols and Barrett felt that they had suffered a crushing defeat. Three years of work by Barrett and two by Nichols seemingly went down the drain. Nichols's commitment to reform in the aftermath of the Beirut bombing had been unequal to Tower's maneuvering. "I was just devastated, and Mr. Nichols was as unnerved as I was," Barrett recalled. "To me, it was the end."[46]

Congressman Ike Skelton, Nichols's strongest supporter, saw the outcome differently. "As we walked out of the conference room," said Barrett, "Skelton told me we had really done well. I just shook my head, and I probably lost some of my demeanor." Skelton persisted. "'No, I'm serious. Modest as it was, that was the first JCS reform that's passed Congress since 1958. We've broken the dam.'"[47]

The next day, Skelton called Barrett to his office and "recounted what he thought we had gained: 'We had cracked this thing that hadn't been cracked since 1958. This was only the first day. This was going to go further.' To Skelton, it was just a battle along the way."[48] Nunn and others felt as Skelton did.

Tower's distinguished Senate career ended several months later. Four years afterward, he was given his long-awaited shot at becoming the defense secretary when President Bush nominated him for that prestigious position. But the Senate rejected his nomination because of concerns about his personal conduct, and Tower's career of public service ended tragically.

The Texas senator's maneuvering on reorganization in 1983 and 1984 neither hurt nor helped his campaign for the Pentagon post, but the inquiry that he launched provided a solid foundation for the SASC's examination of reform in the following two years. Ironically, it was retired marine general "Brute" Krulak—wanting to dismantle the Pentagon's unifying elements—who started the SASC down a path that might eventually lead to a genuinely unified establishment. Whether that occurred would depend on the views and commitment of Tower's replacement, the new SASC chairman.

CHAPTER 10

Crowe Makes Waves

Nothing is more important in war

than unity of command.

—Napoleon, *The Military Maxims of Napoleon*

The Pacific Command (PACOM) had long been a navy stronghold. Its vast ocean area—stretching from the west coast of the United States to the east coast of Africa and encompassing half the earth's surface—required the naval service to lead American security efforts. Even after the post-Vietnam drawdown, the Pacific Fleet in 1984 remained an enormous entity: 220 ships, eighteen hundred aircraft, 220,000 sailors and marines, and fifty-five shore facilities. It dwarfed the air force and army forces in the Pacific.

Far removed from Washington, the Pacific theater nurtured some of the most parochial thinking in the Defense Department. It also had made little progress in improving its ability to conduct joint operations. From the beginning of World War II through the mid-1980s, bitter, petty service politics had precluded effective command arrangements. Disunity and disorganization weakened combat operations. Disaster often resulted.

Into the military's most anachronistic, fractured environment came a far-sighted, open-minded sailor: Adm. Bill Crowe, the new PACOM commander in chief. He belittled the parochialism of his own service: "The Navy has traditionally opposed anything that looked, sounded, or smelled joint." Crowe said, "I questioned that view."[1]

Throughout his career, Crowe had often developed bold, new ideas and voiced them firmly despite the objections of traditionalists. He rejected PACOM organizational tenets ingrained by forty years of interservice bickering. Crowe believed that the Pentagon and warfighting commands like his needed fundamental reorganization. When given the chance, he broke with DoD's official position and provided corroborating evidence and critical behind-the-scenes support.

In 1982, Adm. Stansfield Turner, a former director of central intelligence, called Crowe "an unconventional thinker, unhampered by traditional wisdom, who figures things out for himself." Crowe had been bucking conventional wisdom since his graduation from Annapolis in 1946. A diesel submariner, he decided not to enter Admiral Rickover's prestigious nuclear submarine program because he wanted to attend graduate school. He subsequently enrolled at Princeton University, where he earned a doctorate in politics, despite having been advised that "both moves would hurt his chances of promotion."[2]

Many recognized Crowe's intellectual skills. In the early 1980s, he was "widely regarded as among the most thoughtful naval officers." Nevertheless, numerous navy colleagues believed Crowe's 1980–83 tour as the four-star CINC, Allied Forces Southern Europe (and later CINC, U.S. Naval Forces Europe) would be his last. Their attitude did not surprise Turner, who said, "The Navy is a nonacademic organization that doesn't have too much use for intellectuals."

Crowe's powerful intellect more than made up for his lack of military bearing. Friends described him "as looking like an unmade bed." Crowe retained the drawl from his Oklahoma boyhood and often cast himself as a country boy. He was "a genuine raconteur with a fund of funny stories" that he used to entertain and instruct. I remember him joking about the frustration of dealing with Congress: "If Moses had gone up Capitol Hill rather than Mount Sinai, the two tablets he would have returned with would have been aspirin." After suffering through eleven banquets on an official trip to China, Crowe quipped, "I regret that I have but one stomach to give for my country."[3]

Crowe was caring and compassionate. In the 1970s, he and his wife Shirley housed an entire family of Vietnamese refugees—grandmother, parents, and children—who had fled to America. "He didn't have a big house," a friend recalled. "I expect it was quite crowded."

I first met Crowe in 1978 while he was serving in the Pentagon as a three-star deputy CNO. I had just joined the Senate Armed Services Committee staff. As a principal duty, I staffed the Pacific Study Group, a task force of four senators, headed by Senator Nunn. I was told that the first person I should talk to was Crowe. The admiral's Pentagon office contained a collection of more than a hundred military and ceremonial hats from around the world. Some were quite peculiar, and Crowe had a great story for each. His collection included a nineteenth century British navy captain's fore-and-aft cap, a reminder of his Princeton thesis on the political roots of the Royal Navy. Crowe also had collected a Micronesian bead headband from his days running the Micronesian-status negotiations at the Interior Department.[4]

After Crowe departed the Pentagon to serve in Europe and then the Pacific, I remained in contact with him as the committee's senior foreign policy adviser.

When Congress adjourned in October, 1984, I called Crowe to ask if I could study PACOM for the SASC staff study on reorganization. Since the end of World War II, nearly all of America's significant military failures had occurred in the Pacific, and some experts believed that inept command arrangements played a major role in most of them. These conflicts and operations included the Korean and Vietnam Wars, the North Korean capture of the USS *Pueblo* in 1968 and shoot-down of a navy EC-121 aircraft in 1969, and the evacuation of Saigon and seizure of the *Mayaguez*, both in 1975. The Pacific Command offered the richest environment for learning about organizational problems in the field, and an officer I knew well commanded it.

"Admiral, reorganization has become an explosive issue in Washington," I warned Crowe. You may not want congressional staffers poking around your command on this topic."

"Jim," he replied, "I don't know if you'll learn anything, but you're welcome."

Before I departed for Hawaii, Russ Rourke, assistant secretary of defense for legislative affairs, asked to see me. The gregarious redheaded former marine effectively handled his duties as the Pentagon's chief lobbyist with Congress. Rourke's outgoing personality won friends and arguments on Capitol Hill. His savvy opinions on political issues were widely sought.

Much to my surprise, Rourke offered me a job as his deputy for Senate affairs. I was honored by his offer but wanted to stay on the committee staff. I explained that I had been working on reorganization for nearly eighteen months and wanted to press ahead with that work.

"Jim, I admire your commitment," said Rourke, "but reorganization is going nowhere. Weinberger is against it. Vessey is against it. No one is going to overcome their opposition."

I believed strongly in the need for reorganization, but Rourke's assessment had me feeling like Don Quixote mounting Rocinante. The conference report language had committed the two Armed Services Committees to seriously address this issue. But those were only words. I did not know what direction Sen. Barry Goldwater—the anticipated new committee chairman—might take on reorganization.

Rick Finn and Jeff Smith, fellow committee staffers, joined me on the Pacific trip. We traveled first to Hawaii where Crowe and his army, navy, and air force component commanders were headquartered. At the time of our trip, forty-three years had passed since the lack of coordination between the army and navy had contributed to Japan's success at Pearl Harbor.

"A humiliation without precedent in American history" is how military historian John Keegan characterized the December 7, 1941 attack.[5] Six Japanese aircraft carriers launched 350 planes to strike Pacific Fleet ships moored at Pearl Harbor and American airpower located elsewhere on Oahu. Eighteen warships, including eight battleships, were sunk, capsized, or damaged. Many factors contributed: On-scene army and navy commanders poorly executed their responsibilities. Low army and navy priority to intelligence gathering and processing also proved costly. But the lack of unity of command ranked as the foremost problem.

Two chains of command—one for the army, the other for the navy—controlled American military forces in Hawaii in 1941. The army chain ran from Lt. Gen. Walter C. Short, commanding general of the Hawaiian Department, to Gen. George C. Marshall, army chief of staff, to Secretary of War Henry L. Stimson, and finally to President Roosevelt. The navy chain of command went from Adm. Husband E. Kimmel, commander of the Pacific Fleet, to Adm. Harold S. Stark, CNO, to Navy Secretary Frank Knox, and ultimately to the president. These dual chains meant that no one below the president exercised authority over both commanders in Hawaii.

The attack surprised Short and Kimmel despite separate warnings from Marshall and Stark ten days earlier. Stark's top-secret message to Kimmel began: "This dispatch is to be considered a war warning. Negotiations with Japan . . . have ceased and an aggressive move by Japan is expected within the next few days."[6] Stark's message foresaw a Japanese attack in Southeast Asia as most likely but alerted Kimmel to the potential of hostilities throughout the Pacific Fleet's area of responsibility. Likewise, Marshall told Short: "Japanese future action unpredictable but hostile action possible at any moment."[7]

The attack succeeded because the Japanese achieved strategic and tactical surprise. Washington did not expect an attack on Hawaii, and the American military failed to detect approaching Japanese forces. Dual command lines contributed to intelligence shortcomings in the weeks before the attack. No one below the White House was privy to all incoming intelligence. But no one at that level had the time or even the responsibility for comprehensively analyzing available intelligence. Peter P. Wallace concludes: "There was nowhere, short of the president, that intelligence could be joined with the command authority to take action on a joint basis, based on that intelligence."[8]

During the year before Pearl Harbor, the army and navy had been unable to agree on arrangements for unity of command at forward bases. Responsibility for defense of Hawaii was unclear.[9] With no unified commander, Short and Kimmel commanded by mutual cooperation, the prescribed method of coordination between the services. Neither questioned the other's plans or operations. Short assumed that the navy was conducting long-range air reconnaissance, while Kimmel assumed that the army's early warning radar was fully operational. Neither assumption was correct. A congressional investigating committee found "a complete failure in Hawaii of effective Army-Navy liaison during the critical period November 27–December 7. There was but little coordination and no integration of Army and Navy facilities and efforts for defense. Neither of the responsible commanders knew what the other was doing with respect to essential military activities."[10]

The congressional investigating committee asserted: "It was only in the wake of the Pearl Harbor disaster that the inherent and intolerable weaknesses of command by mutual cooperation were exposed."[11] This was not really true. The importance of unity of command had been recognized as a maxim of war at least since Napoleon's time.

The disaster alerted Roosevelt to the "dangers of divided command." On December 12, "determined that there should be no repetition of the confusion of responsibility that existed in Hawaii," he ordered establishment of a unified command in Panama under the army. Some senior navy officers were opposed to that order, but they accepted it, according to meeting minutes, because "unless unified control was effected by joint agreement between the Army and Navy, the establishment of a Department of National Defense . . . might be considered a certainty." On December 17, a unified command was established in Hawaii with the navy in charge. This time the navy did not object.[12]

Despite these early unifying moves and Pearl Harbor's searing lesson, the Joint Chiefs of Staff were never able to place the Pacific theater under a single supreme commander. Service mistrust and jealousies prevailed. General Douglas MacArthur, "a hero of towering stature," was the most logical choice for a supreme Pacific commander. He would greatly outrank in grade and seniority any admiral who might be nominated. MacArthur was believed to have "the support of the president, the Army, the American people, and the Australians." The navy vehemently opposed his selection and "would never have entrusted the fleet to a general unschooled in the mysteries of seapower." A chief navy planner warned that MacArthur would probably "use his naval force and air forces in the wrong manner, since he has shown clear unfamiliarity with proper naval and air functions."[13]

Outside navy circles, significant support existed for a single commander. Roosevelt "evidently had in mind a single commander for the entire area and had so stated in his recent message to the Prime Minister [Winston Churchill]."[14] Marshall, who firmly believed in the importance of unified command in all theaters, argued in late December, 1941: "I am convinced that there must be one man in command of the entire theater—air, ground, and ships. We can not manage by cooperation. Human frailties are such that there would be emphatic unwillingness to place portions of troops under another service. If we make a plan for unified command now, it will solve nine-tenths of our troubles."[15]

Even though Marshall's arguments persuaded Roosevelt and Churchill, the president did not force his preference on the navy. Unable to settle this army-navy dispute, the JCS split the Pacific into two commands in March, 1942. Roosevelt acquiesced by failing to overrule the arrangement. This decision doomed the Pacific theater to four decades of discord among the services and underachievement or failure on the battlefield.

The JCS designated MacArthur commander of the Southwest Pacific Area (SWPA) and Adm. Chester Nimitz commander of the remainder, entitled the Pacific Ocean Areas. The dividing line was labeled the "Pope's Line," after the line drawn by Pope Alexander IV in 1494 to split the New World between Spain and Portugal.[16] MacArthur and Nimitz reported through their respective service chief to the four-man JCS, which was immediately below Roosevelt in the chain of command. That meant a military committee, becoming "in effect a supreme command," directed Pacific operations.[17] Historian Ronald Spector observed of this ill-conceived arrangement that "traditional elements of careerism and doctrinal differences within the armed forces had combined to produce a monstrosity."[18]

Continuous army-navy bickering over strategy, command, and resources flared into major fights. One such confrontation erupted in June, 1942, over command of an offensive to capture the major Japanese base at Rabaul on New Britain. Because the offensive would be conducted in MacArthur's SWPA, the army argued that he should conduct it. The navy countered that the operation should proceed under Nimitz's command because it would be "primarily amphibious in character."[19]

The JCS hotly debated this issue for a week. King bluntly warned Marshall that he would instruct Nimitz to conduct the operation using only navy and marine forces. MacArthur asserted that the navy's stand reflected a longtime scheme to effect "the complete absorption of the national defense function by the Navy, the Army being relegated to merely base, training, garrisoning, and supply purposes."[20]

Marshall's proposal to segment the operation into three tasks provided the basis for a solution. Nimitz commanded the first task, and MacArthur the other two.[21]

Divided command in the Pacific precluded an overall strategy for fighting the Japanese and nearly caused a naval disaster in October, 1944, at the Battle of Leyte Gulf in the Philippines—the greatest naval battle in history. It was also the last major fleet action of World War II. Although Leyte Gulf resulted in an overwhelming U.S. victory, mistakes permitted by divided command endangered American naval forces and nearly led to a crushing defeat that would have rivaled Pearl Harbor.

The American landing on the island of Leyte during MacArthur's return to the Philippines led to the Battle of Leyte Gulf. The Japanese, fearing interruption of supply lines and loss of their most important captured territories, saw the fight for the Philippines as vital. They thus committed to the battle three naval fleets, a force that included almost every remaining Japanese warship.

American naval forces supporting and protecting the landing were divided into two fleets: the Third Fleet, commanded by Adm. William F. "Bull" Halsey, and the Seventh Fleet, commanded by Adm. Thomas C. Kinkaid. Halsey's chain of command consisted of Nimitz in Hawaii, CNO Adm. Ernest King in Washington, and the JCS. Kinkaid's Seventh Fleet, "MacArthur's Navy," reported directly to the army general. MacArthur, in turn, reported to Marshall, the army chief, and then to the JCS. Thus, the two fleets supporting the American landing at Leyte had no common superior below the JCS. The lack of unity of command in the field, coupled with communications complications caused by separate reporting chains, led to potentially disastrous misunderstandings.

One pivotal misunderstanding centered on "Task Force 34." Confusing transmissions, beginning with Halsey's plans to form a new unit, Task Force 34, to engage heavy Japanese surface forces, led Kinkaid and Nimitz to assume that Task Force 34 would be used to guard San Bernardino Strait, one of the two possible Japanese approaches to Leyte Gulf. This would leave Kinkaid's Seventh Fleet free to concentrate on the other major entrance, Surigao Strait.

Halsey was supposed to cover the Leyte beachhead, but his orders from Nimitz, possibly at King's direction, contained an ill-considered caveat: "In case opportunity for destruction of major portion of the enemy fleet offers or can be created, such destruction becomes the primary task."[22] Halsey seized upon this caveat and entered the battle offensively minded.

MacArthur, still afloat off Leyte's landing beaches, "was stunned by a tentative request of Halsey's regarding the possible withdrawal of fleet units from the Leyte operation." Halsey said an end to his covering mission "will permit me to execute orderly rearming program for my groups and allow further offensive operations." Within minutes, MacArthur replied firmly: "Our mass of shipping is subject to enemy air and surface raiding during this critical period. Consider your mission to cover this operation is essential and paramount."[23]

Despite MacArthur's message, when Halsey discovered Japanese carriers three hundred miles to the north, he left the Leyte Gulf region to attack them, a move some called the "battle of Bull's run."[24] The Japanese carriers, nearly devoid of aircraft, were a decoy to draw Halsey's fleet away from the battle. The vessels intended for Task Force 34 went with Halsey. He compounded his error by not telling Kinkaid that he had never formed Task Force 34.

This lack of coordination between Halsey and Kinkaid left San Bernardino Strait and Kinkaid's northern flank open to the Japanese. Japan's strongest fleet—consisting of four battleships, six heavy cruisers, two light cruisers, and eleven destroyers—sailed unopposed into Leyte Gulf. The only force blocking the path to the landing area was a fragile "jeep"-carrier unit. The Japanese hoped to smash this unit, then "wreak havoc on MacArthur's beachheads only a hundred miles to the south."[25]

By the time Kinkaid became worried about Task Force 34's whereabouts, the Japanese were coming through the strait and Halsey was 350 miles away. Worse still, Halsey ignored Kinkaid's desperate messages asking him to return. Only when Nimitz sent Halsey the famous message—"WHERE IS TASK FORCE THIRTY FOUR THE WORLD WONDERS"—did Halsey turn back. The last three words of the message were added as padding to complicate enemy decryption efforts. When Halsey's decoding officer left them in the message, it turned Nimitz's "gentle nudge" into what Halsey perceived as a "sarcastic slap."[26]

By the time Halsey arrived at Leyte Gulf, the battle had been won. King and Nimitz "concluded that Halsey had made a crucial error of judgment and tactical leadership in swallowing the bait dangled before him."[27] Divided command, exacerbated by King and Nimitz's orders, had permitted Halsey to make his error. Had he embraced MacArthur's mission and been fully under his command, the admiral would not have left San Bernardino Strait unguarded.

MacArthur did not criticize Halsey after the battle. In response to critical remarks by his staff, MacArthur said, "Leave the Bull alone. He's still a fighting admiral in my book."[28]

Fortunately for the United States, heroic fighting by the jeep-carrier unit and confusion and bad judgment by the Japanese overcame the problems created by divided command. During the sea battle, however, MacArthur's troops were denied adequate air cover, which the Japanese exploited. The loss of escort-carrier aircraft destroyed the air umbrella for subsequent ground operations, leaving MacArthur's invasion force "in gravest danger."[29] Of the Halsey-Kinkaid misunderstandings, naval historian Nathan Miller concludes: "None of these errors would have occurred had operations off Leyte been in the hands of a single supreme commander."[30]

MacArthur, in a view widely shared by historians, later criticized divided command in the Pacific: "Of all the faulty decisions of the war, perhaps the most inexplicable one was the failure to unify the command in the Pacific. The principle involved is perhaps the most fundamental one in the doctrine and tradition of command. . . . It was accepted and entirely successful in the other great theaters. The failure to do so in the Pacific cannot be defended in logic, in theory or even in common sense. Other motives must be ascribed. It resulted in divided effort, the waste of diffusion and duplication of force, undue extension of the war with added casualties and cost."[31]

MacArthur thought the Battle of Leyte Gulf "produced the greatest jeopardy" of all the "handicaps and hazards unnecessarily resulting" from divided command. "Leyte came out all right," he said, "but the hazards would all have been avoided by unity of command."[32]

Nine years later, the Naval War College initiated a special project to perform a "strategic and tactical analysis" and identify lessons from this great sea battle. The CNO, Adm. Arleigh Burke, terminated the project after four years before it reached the phase beginning with Halsey's controversial pursuit of the Japanese decoy. The project's fifth and final volume explained: "For reasons beyond the control of the Naval War College, the chief of naval operations decided to conclude the battle analyses with the Battle of Surigao Strait and to discontinue all other planned volumes."[33] Burke, who was chief of staff of one of Halsey's task forces at Leyte Gulf, had been convinced that heading after the Japanese carriers was a mistake.[34] Whatever Burke's reasons, his premature termination of the project denied the navy the opportunity to examine the battle's powerful lessons on the perils of divided command.

Despite the near disaster at Leyte Gulf, even the planned invasion of Japan could not bring the army and navy to accept a unified command. The JCS further compounded the problem: MacArthur would command the land campaign, Nimitz would direct the sea battle, and Gen. Henry H. Arnold, commanding general of the Army Air Forces, would command the Twentieth Air Force's bombers as executive agent for the JCS.[35]

The Japanese surrender on August 14, 1945, did not end the interservice bickering over Pacific command responsibilities. The JCS struggled with this controversial issue until September, 1946, when General Eisenhower, who succeeded Marshall as army chief of staff, presented a worldwide command plan. His proposal became the basis for the first Unified Command Plan, which President Truman approved on December 14.

The plan established two unified commands for the Pacific: Far East Command (FECOM) under MacArthur and PACOM under Adm. John H. Towers, Nimitz's successor. The Far East Command included forces in Japan, Korea, the Philippines, adjacent islands, and those in China in an emergency. The Pacific Command was assigned responsibility for security and operations in the remaining Pacific areas. In 1951, as FECOM focused on directing American operations in the Korean War, Washington transferred many of its geographic responsibilities, including the Philippines, to PACOM.

In 1956, the joint chiefs were again divided on the issue of Pacific command. Four chiefs wanted to disestablish FECOM and transfer its functions to PACOM, "particularly in view of the dwindling U.S. military strength in Japan and Korea, which cast doubt on the advisability of a separate command for that region." Predictably, the army chief dissented. The secretary of defense sided with the majority, and FECOM was disestablished in July, 1957.[36]

The long-sought creation of a supreme commander in the Pacific was finally achieved. Although this move should have improved interservice planning and operations, the desire of the services for independence destroyed the arrangement's potential. Command in Northeast Asia was more fractured after FECOM's disestablishment than before, and a new rival in Hawaii undermined the commander in chief, Pacific Command's (CINCPAC) authority.

As part of the newly enlarged PACOM, smaller unified commands, known as subordinate unified commands, were created in Japan and Korea. An air force three-star general headed U.S. Forces, Japan (USFJ), which reported directly to PACOM in Hawaii. He also commanded the Fifth Air Force, USFJ's air force component. He did not exercise operational control over his army and navy components, only "planning and coordination" authority. Despite his description as a subordinate unified commander, the USFJ commander commanded only air force units.

Arrangements in Korea were even less favorable for unified operations. The subordinate unified command, U.S. Forces, Korea (USFK), was commanded by a four-star army officer who reported directly to the commanding general, U.S. Army, Pacific (USARPAC), PACOM's army component. Forces in Korea thus were not under PACOM's firm control, and the commander in Korea suffered the same limited authority over other service components as his counterpart in Japan.

The 1957 changes also diluted command authority in Hawaii. In response to CINCPAC's enlarged responsibilities, Washington instructed him to give up command of the Pacific Fleet. He initially assigned this duty to his deputy, but in 1958, a separate position—the commander in chief, Pacific Fleet (CINCPACFLT)—was created to exercise command over all naval forces in the Pacific. This subordinate commander soon became a powerful competitor to, if not equal of, his boss.

Ten years later, an incident on the high seas highlighted the continuing disunity in PACOM and exacted a high price for not having truly unified the commands in Japan and Korea. On January 23, 1968, North Korean gunboats seized the USS *Pueblo*, a small, slow, virtually unarmed intelligence-gathering ship, in the Sea of Japan, approximately fifteen miles off the North Korean coast. This incident represented the first capture of a U.S. Navy ship on the high seas in peacetime in over 160 years. Because U.S. military forces failed to assist the *Pueblo* from the beginning of the crisis until its arrival in Wonsan Harbor about four hours later, the North Koreans seized sensitive information and gear and imprisoned the vessel's crew for eleven months. More important, the JCS privately assessed that foreign seizure of a U.S. Navy ship "damages severely the prestige of the United States" and said "the credibility of the United States as a defender of the principle of freedom of the seas is in jeopardy."[37] Organizational problems, especially the lack of command unity in Northeast Asia, precluded timely action to rescue the *Pueblo*.

At the time it was seized, the *Pueblo*, operating under cover as an oceanographic research ship, was executing its first operational deployment. The USS *Banner*, a sister ship, had previously conducted sixteen spy missions. Ten had targeted the Soviet Union, three were conducted off China's coast, and three observed reactions to U.S. Navy transits of the Sea of Japan. Two of the Soviet missions involved sailing up North Korea's east coast. During these sixteen missions, the *Banner* experienced ten incidents of "harassment/interference": one collision, one "heave to or I will fire" signal, three closing situations with guns trained, two surroundings by trawlers, two instances of dangerous maneuvers, and one shouldering. There was, however, "no record of harassment, surveillance, or interference by North Korean ships."[38]

Because of harassment, on two occasions a destroyer and two fighter aircraft on five-minute alert were dedicated to protecting *Banner* if the ship were threatened. Planning for one mission envisioned assigning one cruiser and thirty-one aircraft to provide round-the-clock defense for *Banner*.[39]

The *Pueblo*'s chain of command had assessed its mission as one involving minimal risk. Accordingly, Rear Adm. Frank L. Johnson, commander of U.S. Naval Forces, Japan—who exercised operational control over the *Pueblo*—did not earmark specific air and naval forces to assist the ship if attacked. However, twenty-five days before the ship was seized, the National Security Agency (NSA)—an intelligence agency that eavesdrops on foreign communications—sent a message to the Joint Reconnaissance Center, which worked for the JCS, warning of the danger of an attack on the *Pueblo*. The message said the North Koreans would likely take offensive action and suggested an evaluation of the "requirement for ship protective measures."[40]

Four days later, the Joint Reconnaissance Center retransmitted the message to CINCPAC with an information copy to the CNO. The Pacific Command took no action and did not pass the warning to subordinate commands. During the congressional inquiry on the *Pueblo* seizure, Adm. U. S. Grant Sharp, CINCPAC, explained that no action was taken because the message was "for information and not for action." Junior officers, recognizing no new information, did not bring it to Sharp's or other senior officers' attention.[41]

American officers in South Korea were not so passive. In early January, Brig. Gen. John W. Harrell Jr., the USFK air force component commander, was "becoming concerned about the belligerency of the North Koreans in the Demilitarized Zone" between the two Koreas. He had read a copy of the *Pueblo*'s sailing order and routine mission assessment. Although Harrell and others in South Korea had not seen the NSA's warning message, he thought the navy "was adopting a fairly cavalier attitude about the North Koreans." On January 8, he asked his staff to check with Fifth Air Force headquarters in Japan to ensure that he did not need "to prepare a strip alert or take any other precautionary measures on the ship's behalf." The response from U.S. Naval Forces, Japan, was that there was no need for a strip alert. Three days later, the navy repeated its negative response to a second air force inquiry.[42]

Totally unaware of the peril awaiting it, the *Pueblo* departed Japan on January 11 for its area of operation off the North Korean coast. Around noon on

January 23, the *Pueblo* noticed an approaching patrol boat. Within an hour, four North Korean submarine chasers had surrounded the U.S. spy ship. Soon, two North Korean MIG aircraft were overhead. *Pueblo* alerted its shore base in Japan at 12:54 P.M. that this activity was not routine harassment. More than ninety minutes later, at 2:32 P.M., the ship sent its last message: "Have been directed to come to all stop and being boarded at this time." The captured ship arrived in Wonsan harbor at 4:45 P.M. Sunset occurred at 5:41 P.M. with total darkness twelve minutes later. According to Peter Wallace, "The seizure was rapid, but there was some appreciable time for reaction if forces and commanders acted quickly."[43]

Back in Washington, Capt. Bill Crowe, fifteen years prior to becoming CINCPAC, was handling policy issues on the *Pueblo*'s seizure for navy headquarters. He later observed that the crew's lack of resistance had shortened the reaction time for U.S. forces. "The crew had not, for example, steamed away and forced the North Koreans to make a decision about sinking them. They had not put the engines out of commission, which would have forced their captors to tow them in (and would also have provided more time to mount a rescue mission)."[44]

Admiral Johnson in Japan did not command any forces capable of assisting the *Pueblo*. He had to request assistance from Lt. Gen. Seth J. McKee, dual-hatted as commander of both USFJ and the Fifth Air Force. This request took more than forty minutes to be communicated "because of the failure of the two commands to previously establish and exercise emergency telephone procedures."[45]

Air force aircraft on alert in South Korea were ruled out because they were armed with nuclear weapons, and the forty-one air force fighter aircraft in Japan were assumed to be unavailable because the Status of Forces Agreement governing USFJ's presence in Japan prohibited mounting combat operations from the home islands. McKee believed his only option was the air force wing on Okinawa, about three hundred miles farther south and seven hundred miles from the *Pueblo*. He ordered his commander there: "You are to launch aircraft as soon as possible. You are to proceed to Osan, South Korea, refuel as soon as possible, proceed to the scene at Wonsan Harbor and strike in her [*Pueblo*] support at any forces opposing her." Two F- 105 aircraft launched one hour and twenty-three minutes after the order was received. By the time they reached Osan, however, it was clear that they would not reach the *Pueblo* before dark. Although their efforts proved futile, the air force commanders had at least acted decisively. They were the only ones to do so.[46]

Two squadrons of marine fighter/attack aircraft based in Japan while undergoing air-to-surface training were only an hour's flight time away from the *Pueblo* and could have been used to respond. Unfortunately, these units—which reported to a forward command element of the Fleet Marine Force, Pacific, on Okinawa—were not in the same communications net as the *Pueblo* and did not even hear of the crisis until the following day.[47]

General McKee knew of the marine squadrons, though. However, despite being commander of USFJ, he had no authority over them. To employ marine aircraft he would have had to ask the Pacific Air Forces (PACAF) commander in Hawaii to work the issue with either CINCPAC or CINCPACFLT.[48]

The aircraft carrier *Enterprise*, which as part of the Seventh Fleet was conducting maneuvers approximately five hundred miles from the *Pueblo*, offered another avenue of assistance. Admiral Johnson in Japan assumed Washington would direct the Seventh Fleet commander, Vice Adm. William F. Bringle, to assist the *Pueblo*. Accordingly, he did not request the carrier's assistance. Meanwhile, *Enterprise*'s chain of command knew of *Pueblo*'s distress at 2:30 P.M., but took no action. Thirty-five of *Enterprise*'s fifty-nine fighter aircraft were operational. An appropriate strike force could have been launched within ninety minutes and been over the *Pueblo* an hour later. At 3:06 P.M., Admiral Bringle directed that "no ship or aircraft take any overt action until further informed." He did, however, order the *Enterprise* to change course and head toward Korea—but not until almost three hours after the crisis began.

Of the navy's inaction and his mistreatment by the North Koreans, a *Pueblo* crew member said more than a year later at the navy court of inquiry, "All the beatings that I and the rest of the crew took didn't hurt half as much as the fact that when we were pleading for help, we got none from the largest Navy in the world."[49]

The *Pueblo* incident showed critical flaws in U.S. military organization in Northeast Asia. Operational command remained divided in Japan and Korea. Although air force and army forces were unified under a subordinate unified commander in each country, navy and marine forces maintained separate reporting chains. Even naval command was divided between the Seventh Fleet and local commanders. Because navy, air force, and marine commanders in Japan worked for three separate chains, they did not work with each other. In essence, no unity of command existed below CINCPAC. The absence of such unity proved insurmountable in the *Pueblo* crisis.

This divided command also had a geographic dimension. The authority of the subordinate unified commanders in Japan and Korea stopped at the water's edge. Naval commanders retained responsibility for adjacent seas. This meant that the commander of USFK—the most knowledgeable officer on the military situation on the Korean peninsula—had no involvement in *Pueblo*'s mission.

The special congressional subcommittee said its *Pueblo* inquiry "has resulted in the unanimous view that there exist serious deficiencies in the organizational and administrative military command structure of both the Department of the Navy and Department of Defense."[50] Despite the dangers demonstrated by this crisis, neither Washington nor Honolulu did anything to correct the problems. At the time of my October, 1984, Pacific trip, organizational arrangements in Northeast Asia remained as they had been during the *Pueblo* tragedy.

As Finn, Smith, and I prepared for our trip to Hawaii, our studies suggested that poor interservice coordination continued to be a serious problem throughout PACOM. We also concluded that the Pacific theater never learned the organizational lessons of past operations: Leyte Gulf repeated Pearl Harbor, Vietnam repeated Korea, *Mayaguez* repeated *Pueblo*. Early in our travels, we discovered ample evidence to support these preliminary views.

On the trip's first day, October 29, 1984, we met privately with Crowe and his executive assistant, Capt. Joseph Strasser, USN. We agreed that Crowe's comments would be off-the-record and closely held. Only such arrangements would make it possible for Crowe to break with the Pentagon's official line if he were inclined to do so. And he was inclined to do so. What he was about to tell us would have made the Pentagon, especially his own service, furious with him. During his last several assignments, Crowe had expressed to colleagues his views on the need for organizational changes. But he had never spoken about the issue outside of the military.[51] Although Crowe then believed and told us his career would end after the tour in Hawaii, the admiral knew that the Pentagon, if it learned of his comments to us, would show its displeasure throughout the rest of his tour.

Crowe later said he had agreed to our visit because he "felt strongly that there was a need to do something on defense reorganization." He explained his openness: "Most people didn't want change. Occasionally, I would run into somebody who really thought there was a need for change. But Locher was the first person that . . . really had in mind doing something and was in a position to do something—given the senators he was working for. That's the reason I was so open with him, because there was really a chance that something would come out of it."[52]

Crowe set aside sixty minutes for our meeting. It lasted six hours.

I began by laying out the results of our research and outlining reform options. Crowe liked what he heard and quickly jumped into the discussion. His views on problems harmonized with ours. The admiral's bold, candid assessments contrasted sharply with the don't-offend-anyone comments from nearly all officers in Washington. "In my meetings with Jim Locher I discussed the need to streamline the cumbersome command setup," he recalled. "I was even more vocal about the need to assure the loyalty of the component commanders to their unified commander rather than to their service chiefs. Component commanders had to have a single boss. I also favored more jointness throughout the operational world and a further centralization of authority under the chairman of the Joint Chiefs."[53]

I questioned Crowe about his control over service logistics, which he had said were key to his command's warfighting capabilities. Finn, Smith, and I had heard a horror story in Washington that suggested logistics was a serious problem. As reported in Washington, Pacific war plans developed by Crowe and his headquarters staff specified the locations for the services' war reserve stocks. Reportedly, the Pacific Fleet refused to comply because it envisioned different conflict scenarios. Claiming that logistics remained a service matter, the Pacific Fleet put its stocks where it wanted them. Crowe confirmed this story and said it exemplified his inability to prepare his command for its missions.

Crowe's later writings paralleled his comments to us. "Like every other unified commander, I could only operate through the army, navy, air force, and marine component commanders, who stood between me and the forces in the field. The problem with this arrangement was that though the unified commander had all the responsibility, he did not have sufficient authority. His component commanders reported to their own service chiefs for administration, logistics, and training matters, and the service chiefs could use this channel to outflank the unified commander. There was a sizable potential for confusion and conflict."

For nearly ten years, Crowe had watched the services circumvent unified commanders. "I noticed it when I was the Navy operations deputy and then saw it again when I was commander in chief in Hawaii. The component commanders were always fighting the unified commander with back channels to their service chiefs to try and get the JCS chairman to change some things that the unified commander was doing. I never liked that very well. That just didn't seem right to me." [54]

The admiral also had powerful insights on Pentagon problems, especially in the JCS system. Crowe's service as the navy operations deputy in the JCS arena from 1977 to 1980 exposed him to the deficiencies of this committee system. He said he "had gradually developed my own conviction on the need for reform" during this tour. Later, he summarized these ills: "The main problems with the Joint Staff were not enough jointness and too much compromise. Each service habitually saw every issue exclusively from its own standpoint and in many instances held up the release of papers until its concerns were accommodated in some fashion. This typically resulted in watered-down positions that took too long to formulate." [55]

Crowe also believed that joint work suffered from poor officer management: "I was likewise convinced that the quality of officers detailed to the Joint Staff could use substantial upgrading. It was unusual to find the most highly regarded officers laboring in the Joint Staff vineyard; many considered a tour there as a hurdle on the career path."

At the end of the meeting, Crowe asked us to meet with him again in two days, after we had met with his army, navy, and air force component commanders. Responding to Crowe's openness, I gave him a copy of the staff study's chapter on the unified commands. He promised to read it and provide his thoughts at our second meeting.

At that subsequent meeting, Crowe said: "Don't change a word in this chapter. I am amazed that congressional staffers in Washington have been able to precisely capture the problems plaguing major commanders in the field."

After our meetings with Crowe, Finn, Smith, and I decided not to summarize the discussions in memoranda for the record. We were uncertain as to the SASC's direction on reorganization and feared that our memoranda might fall into unfriendly hands and create troubles for Crowe. We kept only a brief list of topics discussed.

Although Crowe had expected his Hawaii command to be the final assignment of his naval career, President Reagan and his advisers were eyeing the fifty-nine-year-old admiral for JCS chairman. In April, 1984, Reagan had stopped in Hawaii en route to China. Crowe said he was told he "would have thirty minutes with the president and that I ought to cover anything I thought important for him to know before he left for China."[56]

Reacting favorably to Crowe's informal style and insightful presentation, an "attentive and interested" Reagan extended the meeting to an hour and one-half. After the session, Secretary of State George Shultz told Crowe: "The President was very impressed." Back in Washington, Defense Secretary Weinberger asked Reagan, "How did my commander do out in Hawaii?" Reagan responded that if they needed another chairman, he had found him.[57]

In addition to meeting with the senior army, navy, and air force commanders in the Pacific, we also traveled to Crowe's subordinate unified commands in Japan and Korea. Our reception in four of these five commands was coolly polite, but we ran into a buzz saw at the Pacific Fleet headquarters at Pearl Harbor: Adm. Sylvester R. Foley Jr. Our visit with him convinced us that the Pacific Fleet had earned its reputation as DoD's most parochial organization.

After keeping us waiting, a scowling Foley swaggered into the room and barked, "I've read your bios and I know your biases." The short, crewcut four-star sailor was referring to the fact that Jeff Smith and I had strong army backgrounds as West Point graduates and must share the army's traditional bent for greater unification. As an army brat, Rick Finn was probably under suspicion as well. "The meeting deteriorated from there," Smith recalled. Foley responded harshly to each issue we raised and "lectured us about how he knew everything, and we didn't know anything."[58] The admiral gave us a first-class tongue-lashing.

Rear Admiral J. A. "Jack" Baldwin, Foley's deputy chief of staff for plans, sat in on the meeting. I knew Baldwin from my Pentagon service. He had a first-class reputation among navy thinkers and analysts. During the meeting, Baldwin did not speak. He had served on Foley's staff for only two weeks and did not know his boss well. Although Baldwin did not open his mouth, the proceedings opened his eyes widely.

Baldwin later recalled that Foley "came in hot." He was "surprised" by his boss's "abrasive" manner, which he said was "uncharacteristic" of him. According to Baldwin, Foley gave us the "rough hide of his tongue," and he thought that Foley's "straightforward, tough" message should have been "phrased differently." Baldwin recalled Foley repeating his basic in-your-face theme over and over: "Why should a bunch of civilians from back in Washington be telling the military how to do its business?"[59]

I abandoned efforts to explain Congress' role as prescribed by the Constitution when it became clear that Foley found my explanation more irritating than enlightening.

Toward the end of the meeting, I asked Foley about the logistics horror story we had discussed with Crowe. Foley confirmed that the navy had not put its war reserve stocks where Crowe had directed. "Logistics is none of Crowe's damn business." According to Foley, "Logistics always has been and always will be the sole prerogative of each individual service." He added, "Crowe is always trying to butt in where he doesn't belong."

Foley treated us more rudely than anyone we encountered during our reorganization work (and we had confronted plenty of unpleasant behavior). As the meeting was wrapping up, I was anxious just to escape. But not Jeff Smith. Foley's behavior angered Smith, a quiet, dignified gentleman. As the admiral began to stomp out of the room, Smith quickly rose and blocked his path. For a moment, they stood nose-to-nose (being shorter, Foley's nose was somewhat lower). In two rapid sentences, the West Pointer told the admiral: "Serious organizational problems exist in DoD. Parochial views such as yours are blocking necessary reforms." After having his say, Smith stepped aside, and Foley stormed out.

Foley had invited us to have lunch and tour Pearl Harbor with him on his barge. However, given the stormy nature of the meeting and the admiral's fiery exit, I guessed we would not be eating together. I was right.

Despite the admiral's unpleasant behavior, Smith found the meeting with Foley invaluable. "It made a point that Foley never intended," he said later. "The meeting conveyed that service component commanders like Foley were not only unresponsive to their unified commander, they were also arrogant and powerful. That's where the power was. And by God, they were running things for the navy in the Pacific. Foley, not Crowe, was the real power in Hawaii. His staff radiated that reality, and he reinforced it. Learning that made the meeting with Foley in some respects of equal value, if not more valuable, than the meeting with Crowe."[60]

Although Foley had beaten up three congressional staffers that day in October, 1984, a day of reckoning occurred a little more than a year later. After Foley retired from the navy, President Reagan nominated him to serve as assistant secretary of energy for defense programs. This civilian presidential appointment required the advice and consent of the Senate, and the committee with jurisdiction happened to be the SASC. Jeff Smith, the top minority staff lawyer, handled Foley's nomination and hearing for the Democrats.

"I remember the sweetness of it when Admiral Foley had to sit down in front of me and go through his finances and conflicts of interest," Smith recalled. "He treated me like I was his best friend, saying, 'Hey, Jeff, how are you? Great to see you again. Defense reorganization is a good thing.' He was all for it then."

During Foley's confirmation hearing on December 12, 1985, Sen. John Warner scolded the admiral for his treatment of the committee staff during the 1984 trip. Warner opposed reorganization, and as a former navy secretary, he did not relish dressing down an admiral in public. But Foley's challenge to the SASC's institutional prerogatives had forced Warner's hand. After explaining that the committee asks staff members to make visits when senators are not able to do so, Warner said to Foley, "I expect—but I would like to have you say for the record—that you will cooperate fully with staff persons at such times as you are visited on work in connection with this committee."[61]

Smith remembered Foley's expression when Warner finished: "It looked as if he'd eaten the world's most sour pickle. I tried not to smile, but I know I wanted to smile."[62]

In the context of Foley's nomination, this was a minor issue. On larger issues, the SASC found Foley fully qualified and recommended the Senate approve his nomination.

Seven years later, Jeff Smith still had not forgotten Sylvester Foley. After the election in November, 1992, President-elect Bill Clinton selected Smith to head his DoD transition team. When I first saw Smith after he assumed those duties in the Pentagon, he grinned at me and asked, "Where is Admiral Foley now, and how can we get at him?"

Our Pacific trip ended with a flight from Korea to Washington on November 5, the day before the presidential and congressional elections. Finn, Smith, and I were elated by the results of our trip, especially the meetings with Admiral Crowe. Although Generals Jones and Meyer and others had addressed problems in the JCS system, senior officers had not yet articulated problems in the unified commands. Crowe had reinforced the conclusions of our research. His praise of the staff study's chapter on the unified commands—much of which represented new thinking—reassured us.

Although Finn, Smith, and I had learned a great deal from our trip, we did not know whether the SASC would ever use the information. Three questions had to be answered first. Would the Republicans maintain control of the Senate? If so, would Goldwater replace Tower as SASC chairman? If he did, would Goldwater give priority to reorganization or would he bury the issue?

CHAPTER 11

Goldwater and Nunn Close Ranks

In battle, two moral forces, even more than

two material forces, are in conflict.

The stronger conquers.

—Col. Ardant du Picq, *Battle Studies*

"**J**im, I've got some great news," began a mid-December 1984 call from Gerald J. Smith of Sen. Barry Goldwater's personal staff. "The old man has decided to make defense reorganization his number-one priority. He views Pentagon reform as a critical issue and one where he might be able to make a lasting contribution before he retires." Smith explained that Goldwater knew "that if there is to be any chance of enacting meaningful reforms, partisan politics must be avoided. He's decided to take a truly bipartisan approach.

"You know the boss gets along well with Senator Nunn and has the greatest respect for him. Goldwater believes that he and Nunn will work well together on reorganization. He will approach Nunn with his ideas as soon as he can in the new year."

When Goldwater's intentions later became publicly known, reorganization opponents made relentless efforts to persuade him to forfeit his planned role.

The Republicans maintained control of the Senate in the 1984 elections. Tower's retirement put Goldwater—the GOP presidential candidate twenty years earlier—in line to chair the Armed Services Committee. The Arizona Republican, a pilot during World War II, retired from the Air Force Reserve as a major general in 1967. He had celebrity status in the defense community.

Despite his promilitary disposition, Goldwater's powerful new role did not please everyone in the Pentagon. He was opinionated, independent, and unpredictable. Secretary Weinberger privately confided that Goldwater concerned him more than House Democrats. One defense official reported "very deep concern" about Goldwater, while a lobbyist described the Pentagon mood: "Not despairing, but sober. Minor alarm, I guess."

Senator Cohen clarified why Weinberger and others were worried: "Barry has enough of the maverick in him to say that something is not a good idea. The Pentagon can't count on him to be a rubber stamp. He can always surprise you. His conservatism is not knee-jerk."

"When a program needs criticizing," Goldwater explained, "I don't hesitate to criticize. In that respect, I guess I'm not what you'd call a politician. I've never particularly worried whether what I said cost me votes or didn't cost me votes. I'm more worried whether if what I'm doing is best for the country. I have a tendency to say what I think. I don't think I would ever stop doing that. It's gotten me into trouble, but it hasn't been the kind of trouble I couldn't get myself out of."[1]

Goldwater did not automatically accept the SASC chairmanship. His health and age—seventy-six by the time he assumed the post—caused him to doubt his ability to carry out the duties. With Senate resistance to the Reagan defense program increasing, the Arizonan did not want to let the president and his party down. "I think it is really too big a job for me," Goldwater told intimates. "I'm worried. There haven't been many things in my life that I have worried like hell about. I just don't think I can do it."[2]

Goldwater underestimated his capabilities. During his 1964 presidential campaign, he said, "I'm not sure I've even got the brains to be president." Five months into his job as chairman, Goldwater wrote to Nunn: "I don't mind telling you I took that job with a lot of trepidation. I have been in the Senate now for almost thirty years, and while I have held some minor jobs, I have never held anything with the quality and authority of the Armed Services Committee."[3]

Goldwater credited Tower with convincing him to take the job. "I had a couple of good long conversations with John Tower," he said, "and old John was full of bullshit, but we would sit there and talk, and I was finally thinking I could do it." With other friends and colleagues also encouraging him, Goldwater decided to chair the committee for the last two years of his Senate career.[4]

On December 3, several weeks after the elections, Goldwater met with the entire committee staff. His request for both Republican and Democratic staffers to attend was unusual, for in one month he would become the boss of only those who worked for the majority party. To my surprise, Goldwater spoke with a warm bipartisan tone. I had expected the crusty Arizonan to be a Republican crusader. A few days later, he reinforced his bipartisan approach in a memorandum to the staff: "I think we can do a great job together and I think the best way to start is to forget about being Republicans or Democrats or liberals or conservatives. We should concentrate on just being good old Americans who want to move along with the idea of providing the best defense for America that we can. My door is always open and my mind will stay the same, open." These proved to be much more than idle words.[5]

"I'm the only Republican that ever lived in my family. My uncle started the Democratic Party in Arizona," said Goldwater, explaining the roots of his bipartisanship. When he entered politics, Goldwater found working with Democrats imperative. "Arizona was a strong Democratic state—had a lot of counties that were 100 percent Democratic. I was a Republican, and I had to get elected." Even while campaigning for president in 1964, Goldwater admitted, "I don't necessarily vote a straight ticket in my own state because there are sometimes Democrats out there who are better than Republicans. It's hard to believe but it's true."[6]

Goldwater surprised us near the end of the staff meeting when he said: "I know that the committee staff is in the habit of sending papers and talking points to the chairman for each and every issue. I've been in the defense business my entire life, and I don't need anybody telling me what to think or say. So, don't send me any of those papers. I don't want them. If I need your help, which is unlikely, I'll ask for it."

To a staff that prepared papers on every issue for the chairman, our new instructions were an about-face. Goldwater's feisty independence was legendary, but no one had expected him to diminish the staff's role so quickly.

Goldwater had been closely connected to the military throughout his life. "Arizona's history is very military," he said. "At one time, we had half of the United States Army stationed in the State just to support the action against two hundred Indians, and the Indians kicked the shit out of us. Arizona has always been military."[7]

The future senator's interest in the military started early. "I grew up knowing military people," he said. "I liked the military. I went to the Staunton Military Academy when I was fourteen. I kept wanting to go to West Point"[8] His Staunton instructors told Goldwater that he had qualified for a West Point appointment. "The idea appealed to me, but my father was not well. Mun [his mother] wanted me to come home."[9] Goldwater enrolled at the University of Arizona in the fall of 1928, but his college days and dreams of West Point ended with his father's death the following March. Goldwater decided that he "should leave college and prepare to take his place at the family store."[10]

In 1930, Goldwater was commissioned as an infantry second lieutenant in the army reserve and earned a private airplane pilot's license. In 1932, he attempted to join the Army Air Corps. Substandard eyesight caused his rejection. In 1941, with war approaching, Goldwater maneuvered onto active duty and was assigned as an aerial gunnery instructor. However, his age and eyesight ruled out his becoming an aviation cadet.

In 1943, Goldwater's request for transfer to the Air Transport Command was approved. The Air Corps had organized a group of overage pilots known as "the Over-the-Hill Gang" to deliver aircraft and supplies overseas, and Goldwater piloted aircraft to war zones in Europe, Africa, and Asia. He also served as a flight instructor for Chinese pilots in Burma. After the war, he became chief of staff of the Arizona National Guard with the rank of colonel and ended his career as a two-star general in the reserve. The ever-honest Goldwater told Tower his promotion to major general was "not important because you know and I know that I would never have gotten that promotion had I not been a senator."[11]

Preparing for his new duties, Goldwater agreed to take reorganization briefings from two proreform public policy organizations: Georgetown University's Center for Strategic and International Studies and the Heritage Foundation.

On December 5, Goldwater took the CSIS briefing, presented by General Goodpaster, a vice chairman of the reorganization project. Goodpaster was a good choice to make this presentation. The retired army general was approaching seventy, so he and Goldwater were of the same generation. Goodpaster had served as staff secretary to President Eisenhower—connecting him to the last defense reorganization, in 1958. Moreover, Goodpaster had recently completed a four-year tour as superintendent of his alma mater, West Point. Goldwater, who maintained his deep affection for "the Point," wrote: "One of the greatest frustrations of my life is that I did not take advantage of an appointment to West Point and attend that school. I hold West Point in the highest regard and always will."[12]

Gerry Smith arranged for me to sit in on Goodpaster's briefing. Goldwater, who had not been involved in the SASC's reorganization work, took a keen interest in the presentation. From his long military association, Goldwater recognized many of the problems that Goodpaster described. The senator was most animated regarding unnecessary duplication of military capabilities. As early as 1973, he berated the Pentagon on duplication. "My pet gripe is that we have four tactical air forces: Army, Navy and Marines, as well as the Air Force itself. This is one of the glaring examples of repetition that we don't need."[13]

I concurred with much of Goodpaster's presentation. Many of its themes agreed with preliminary results of the staff study. After the briefing, I informed Goldwater of the status of the staff's reorganization work. The senator showed genuine interest in the briefing and my status report but made no commitments.

Ted Crackel briefed Goldwater on the Heritage Foundation's study the following week. Its analysis and recommendations paralleled CSIS's. Heritage's conservatism heightened the importance of its support for reform. With the conservative military and conservative administration opposing reform, Heritage's

21. Senator Goldwater as a cadet captain at Staunton
Military Academy in 1928. (Arizona Historical
Foundation, Arizona State University.)

proreform stance helped prevent reorganization from dividing along ideological lines. Again, Goldwater was interested and actively participated, but he did not reveal his thinking.

Although Goldwater was guarding his plans, the two briefings reinforced his longstanding interest in reorganization. In 1958, Goldwater, then an Air Force Reserve colonel, wrote a seventy-five-page paper titled, "A Concept for the Future Organization of the United States Armed Forces." In it he argued that the military's "weak spot" was "our scheme of organization." Colonel Goldwater suggested that reorganization be guided by the signs at the North American Air Defense headquarters: "Our mission is to defend the United States, Canada, Alaska, and the northeast area from an attack: NOT TO DEFEND THE ROLES OF THE RESPECTIVE SERVICES."[14]

The Vietnam War had deeply troubled Goldwater. He said that after his 1964 presidential election defeat "the war became one of the driving forces in my life. I regularly spoke with American troops in Vietnam through the MARS

[Military Affiliate Radio System] network that had been patched into the ham radio shack next to our home. I also toured our military bases on five visits to Vietnam, getting the views of many old friends and acquaintances—military commanders, pilots, and GIs in the field."[15]

In a newspaper article published in March, 1985, Goldwater criticized America's performance in Indochina: "Blunder followed upon blunder. It is impossible to list all the mistakes that were made. For example, it took us almost five years to understand what the Viet Cong was, what it was all about and how they operated. From that knowledge, we eventually but too late, gained an understanding of how we would have to use our forces to successfully combat them."[16]

Goldwater placed much of the blame for Vietnam on civilian meddling in tactical military issues. While supporting President Johnson's and Defense Secretary McNamara's need for "broad war powers," he disputed "their military competence in making extensively detailed decisions about how to fight the war." Goldwater cited a SASC report published in 1967 that said civilians had discounted the "unanimous professional judgment of our military commanders and the Joint Chiefs, and substituted civilian judgment in the details of target selection and the timing of strikes." He asserted, "My own belief in civilian control of the armed forces is unshakeable." But he agonized over the question: "To what degree may the limited competence of civilians be allowed to dominate professional military decisions?"[17]

The Arizona senator also faulted military leaders of the Vietnam era for not protesting, a view also expressed by Gen. Edward Rowny: "In the end, there was no one of stature in the military who stood up to [McNamara]. They could have done so—not in public, because that was against tradition—but internally. They could have said, 'Either you support us or we quit.'"[18]

Goldwater discussed repeated operational setbacks and "the need for some sort of reorganization" with Smith, a retired air force colonel serving as the senator's military legislative assistant. He saw the Iranian rescue as "plagued with planning, training, and organizational problems. It was an ad hoc, improvised operation from start to finish." Searching for reasons for the failure, Goldwater talked at length with Col. Charles A. Beckwith, the army officer commanding the mission's ground force, who told Goldwater: "We didn't have [a] team. We got the four services reaching up on a shelf and giving us different outfits. I believe it would have been a different story in Iran—and . . . in Vietnam—if the four services had fought under a unified command."[19]

"The terrorist killing of Marines disturbed me greatly," Goldwater revealed. Of the Beirut tragedy, he said: "The fault was in the Pentagon command structure. The cumbersome chain of command imposed on the general [in charge] by the JCS and services precluded effective control." Five years after the bombing, Goldwater fumed, "I'm still outraged by the whole military mess."[20]

The chairman labeled the Grenada invasion "a minefield of errors." Communications foul-ups in Grenada had "piqued" the senator's interest. Goldwater reported, "Most Army and Navy units could not communicate with one another. Nor could they coordinate with [Vice Adm. Joseph] Metcalf, the overall commander. Communication between the two was, in fact, poor to almost nonexistent. There were similar problems between the Army and Marine forces. The reason was that all four services continue to purchase independent, incompatible communications equipment." Goldwater told Smith, "We have to do something."[21]

According to Smith, the new chairman saw the work the staff had done when Tower was chairman as "an opportunity to do something worthwhile." Goldwater also thought that the "synergism" between himself and Nunn made reorganization "doable." Goldwater decided to make this his highest priority because "he saw an opportunity to finally make some changes that would have a significant impact on downstream operational capabilities of the military."[22]

Goldwater's commitment to a long, demanding legislative campaign was unusual for him. He did not like the details of major legislation. Former Arizona congressman John Rhodes said, "That was not his thing. Barry has always painted with a broad brush, and I say that without criticism." Congressman Morris K. Udall agreed: Details bored Goldwater. "He always focused on the big picture." A journalist observed, "Goldwater was not a enthusiastic legislator. He preferred the public work of an evangelist to the private labor of pushing a bill to passage."[23]

Smith played a critical role in supporting Goldwater's reorganization inclinations. The former air force pilot had served on the Joint Staff in the late 1970s and seen its crippling problems firsthand. Goldwater used Smith as a sounding board, and the retired colonel urged the chairman on.

Smith was an affable storyteller of Irish ancestry with a great sense of humor. At work, he focused on getting the job done and did not worry about who got the credit. Smith had many friends on Capitol Hill, and a few enemies. His unyielding loyalty to Goldwater threatened some of the chairman's friends and subordinates. Smith sought to protect Goldwater from those who would use the senator's power for personal gain. In response, opportunists worked to discredit Smith in Goldwater's eyes. Struggles like this one for credibility and influence with a major public figure are the hand-to-hand combat of Washington politics.

In addition to reassuring the chairman on reorganization, Smith promoted Goldwater's confidence in me. Smith had previously headed the air force's Senate liaison office. During that time, he and I became well acquainted and traveled together on trips. "Locher will do an unbelievably good job on reorganization," Smith reassured Goldwater. "He's worked for Republicans and Democrats, which will be a big plus when the committee addresses this issue."[24]

The fact that I was a West Pointer also helped. Whenever Goldwater introduced me, he would say, "This is Jim Locher. He graduated from West Point."

In late January, Goldwater and Nunn agreed to be partners on reorganization. The chairman understood the long odds: "When Nunn and I began to make our move, I wouldn't have bet more than a sawbuck on our chances of success. History and tradition were against us. Yet I had made up my mind that I would not retire from the Senate without giving reorganization my best shot."[25]

Of the chairman's decision, Nunn said, "He derived it independently himself." Nunn "urged" Goldwater to pursue his plans, but their partnership "would not have been successful if Goldwater had not in his own independent thinking come to the conclusion that things could be dramatically improved and there were going to be big problems the way we were operating."[26]

In two sessions, Goldwater and Nunn—assisted by Gerry Smith and two of Nunn's staffers, Arnold Punaro and Jeff Smith—formed their approach. Goldwater later said he had "wanted to establish two things—equality and trust." They agreed to create a task force of SASC members to examine the issues and draft legislation. To ensure a bipartisan effort and equality between them, Goldwater proposed that he and Nunn cochair the task force.[27]

The cochairmen had to decide what to do about Jim McGovern, whom Goldwater, at Tower's urging, had kept on as the majority staff director. Knowing Goldwater's concerns about becoming committee leader, Tower had portrayed McGovern as "somebody who has experience here, can provide continuity, who knows the program, and somebody who will be very supportive." Goldwater, caught cold by his predecessor's appeal, promised to retain McGovern as staff director.[28]

Nunn briefed Goldwater on the staff director's history of antireform activities: "McGovern is taking Locher's work and giving it to Navy Secretary Lehman. Lehman is editing it and sending it back through McGovern, who makes it look like his work. If McGovern is heading up the staff on this issue, defense reorganization is a dead duck."[29]

Determined not to allow McGovern to interfere, Goldwater said, "Well, we'll just have to remove McGovern from the process. I'll have Locher report directly to me."[30]

"Well, I'll take my staff director, Arnold Punaro, out of it too, and we'll just have Jim Locher report to you and me," Nunn graciously replied. "Is that all right with you, Barry?"

"Fine," Goldwater answered.

Nunn proposed this evenhanded approach so no one could complain, and it did not look as if they were singling out McGovern. Punaro supported reform, but removing him was the price that had to be paid to exclude McGovern. Punaro had originated the idea and discussed it with Gerry Smith.[31] Nunn praised Punaro's sacrifice, saying: "The poison pill he was swallowing was also going to have to be swallowed by Jim McGovern. The two staff directors were not going to be in the chain of command on this project."

Of my role, Nunn said: "The background that Jim Locher and I had together gave me tremendous confidence that he would be objective, analytical, fair, and bipartisan. I had no hesitancy at all about not only agreeing, but I think recommending, that he be the person to lead the staff. In effect, Jim had the confidence uniquely of both Goldwater as chairman and me as the ranking Democrat. That was a very important element in this. Nobody else could have filled that role."

Nunn also had confidence in Gerry Smith and his ability to facilitate a good relationship between the two leaders. In case of Republican opposition to Goldwater's efforts, Nunn figured, "Gerry would be able to keep me and the re organization staff informed about what was going on on the Republican side."[32]

Near the end of January, Goldwater and Nunn designated me as the head of the task force's staff. Goldwater assigned Rick Finn and Barbara Brown, my secretary, from the Republican staff, and Nunn selected Jeff Smith from the minority staff as the fourth member. The chairman instructed Brown and me to work full-time on reorganization. He assigned my foreign policy and defense budget responsibilities to others. Goldwater and Nunn expected Finn and Smith to devote 50 percent of their time to task force work. Finn, a member of the larger majority staff, worked nearly full-time on this assignment. This proved critical, because Smith could allot only a small portion of his time due to the press of other minority staff business. While Punaro was not in our reorganization chain of command, Finn, Smith, and I kept him informed as our work progressed and occasionally sought his advice and assistance.

On January 28, Goldwater wrote a letter to McGovern outlining his plans. A chairman usually does not write to his staff director, but Goldwater apparently did not want to discuss this sore subject with McGovern. He also probably wanted a written record of his instructions. "Jim Locher," explained Goldwater, "whom I've known for some time and who has a keen interest in this subject is, in my opinion and Sam's also the most knowledgeable man we have available, and is the man I want to be the staff leader. He should . . . report directly to Senator Nunn and me." Given McGovern's history of providing the navy copies of the committee's work, Goldwater bluntly told him: "I don't want any staff leaks. I don't want the services to know any more about our studies than we want them to know."[33]

McGovern fumed about this arrangement, blaming me for Goldwater's decisions. Reorganization was the most important issue the SASC had addressed in several decades, and Goldwater was denying him, the most senior staffer, a role. The staff director would also be less able to protect the interests of the navy and his close friend, Secretary Lehman.

On January 31, Goldwater and Nunn informed members of their plans through a "Dear Committee Colleague" letter. Although they mentioned adding members to the task force, Goldwater and Nunn delayed taking that step. The two leaders figured that they could count on only two or three other senators to support reform. They would need to take a deliberate approach to the long uphill struggle ahead.[34]

Goldwater and Nunn formed a powerful team. Both had strong conservative and prodefense credentials. But in other respects, they were opposites. Goldwater was bold, almost reckless. Nunn was cautious, almost too careful. Goldwater made up his mind quickly. Nunn decided slowly. Goldwater relied on instinct and feel. Nunn depended on hard work and superior information. Their opposite characteristics complicated the work of opponents. Nunn could outthink you. Goldwater could outshoot you. Nunn could remain cool while Goldwater flashed his temper. Their opponents had to prepare for both Nunn's proficient jabs and Goldwater's knockout punch.

While Goldwater and Nunn were planning their approach, CSIS study leaders revealed the results of their work in press interviews. Although CSIS would not release its study until the end of February, it wanted to capture the new Congress' attention.

On January 22, 1985, two days after President Reagan's second inauguration, the *New York Times* reported on the study in a front-page article, "Overhaul Is Urged for Top Military." The article began, "A diverse group of experts, including some of the members of Congress who are most influential on military matters, has agreed to push this year for a sweeping restructuring of the American military operation." The article then summarized the study's thrust: "Current military organization is paralyzed by rivalries between the Army, Navy, Air Force and Marine Corps and is the underlying cause of bloated budgets, poor combat readiness and a lack of coordination in operations."[35]

The *Times* highlighted the report's proposal "to give the chairman of the Joint Chiefs of Staff new powers as a presidential adviser in an effort to override squabbling among the military services." The article described recommendations, to be published the following month, to "strengthen the powers of the regional military commanders who conduct combat operations, streamline the budgeting and planning operations of the Defense Department and alter the role of Congress in handling the military budget."

The *Times* also reported that Secretary Lehman "called the Georgetown proposals 'a very foolish way to organize a democracy's decision-making,' arguing that they would centralize too much power in Washington and diminish civilian control."

The day the *New York Times* article appeared, Pentagon spokesman Michael Burch said, "We may consider some reforms. But, we basically think the Joint

Chiefs of Staff structure as it exists is adequate." Burch described Weinberger as "very pleased with the service and contributions the Joint Chiefs give him."[36]

About a week later, two newspaper editorials supported the study. "The trouble with the ossified U.S. military command structure is that too many vested interests have a vital stake in the status quo," The *Atlanta Constitution* argued. "What Defense Department bureaucrats and the chiefs of the various services have come to defend best is their own turf, not to mention their own posteriors." The editorial said that Weinberger, "rather than trying to tame the beast, has allowed it to graze unchecked in the green pastures of the U.S. Treasury."[37]

A *Chicago Tribune* editorial advised: "Mr. Reagan should heed this [CSIS] report. His and Defense Secretary Caspar Weinberger's next four years should be devoted in large part to implementing recommendations like these."[38]

The short burst of press attention produced a standoff. The study received only modest attention, and the newspapers gave equal space to Pentagon criticisms.

On February 4, Goldwater and Nunn wrote to Weinberger announcing their plans and soliciting his cooperation: "It is our sincere hope that the task force, and eventually the full committee, will have the opportunity to work closely with you in an objective analysis of potential improvements to organizational arrangements and decision making procedures within the Department of Defense and within the Congress." Noting the long-term nature of the problems, the senators emphasized, "You should be assured that the committee's study is not a criticism of you, of any other official of the Department of Defense, or of this administration."

Alluding to the Pentagon's unfavorable press statements on the CSIS study, Goldwater and Nunn continued: "We have not yet taken a position on any of the issues that the committee has studied. This does not appear to be the case with certain vocal elements of the Department of Defense. In general, we are troubled by the negative public stance that the Department of Defense has taken on various organizational proposals that are beginning to surface in the defense academic community. These premature reactions are likely to complicate efforts by the Congress and executive branch to develop a cooperative approach on this subject. In addition, we are disturbed by reports that some officials of the Department of Defense are working behind the scenes to discredit the work of private organizations that are studying these important topics."

The letter ended: "Candidly, we intend to use the answers [to the 1984 authorization report questions] due by March 1 and the department's preliminary reaction to the Center for Strategic and International Studies draft report as key yardsticks in assessing whether the Department of Defense is prepared to enter into a constructive dialogue with the committee on organizational and decision making issues."[39]

Goldwater and Nunn believed that the SASC staff study provided the best vehicle for examining problems. My two bosses directed me to refine each chapter and submit them for their review. I met separately with them to discuss each submission and obtain guidance for additional research and revisions.

Goldwater would complete his review within twenty-four hours and was always anxious to meet with me early in the morning for our discussion. The study fascinated him. For the first time, he had a comprehensive framework for problems he had seen over five decades. A strong believer in using history to illuminate current problems, he liked the study's emphasis on historical analysis. Goldwater marked up each chapter with comments and questions. Of the chapter on the unified commands, he wrote, "A good, very good study but it frightens me—there are places I see no easy answers for. Thanks—It's really great."[40]

Gerry Smith had warned me about the chairman's early morning work habits. Goldwater would get to work after they arrived in the office at 6:30 A.M. A few minutes later, the chairman would typically say to him, "Get Dole on the phone."[41]

"Senator, he's not here," Smith would say.

"Well," the chairman would fume, "where in the hell is he?"

"He's probably in bed like every other normal senator around here," Smith would answer. "How many senators do you think are sitting in their office at 6:40 in the morning looking to call somebody?"

Goldwater enjoyed the early morning hours and did his best work then. He read newspapers and incoming mail first, and then he would fire off responses, including letters to newspaper editors. The chairman fired off letters at a prolific rate, not long epistles, but one-paragraph zingers—a dozen or so each day. When I arrived for our seven o'clock meetings, Goldwater was just finishing his correspondence.

During our first morning meeting, I was surprised to see the senator's door open with a secretary sitting just outside, noisily typing letters he had just dictated while Goldwater monitored her activity. She brought him the finished letters and he signed them and stuffed them into their envelopes. Then, grabbing his cane, Goldwater asked me to accompany him out into the marble-floored hallway on the fourth floor of the Russell Senate Office Building, where he dropped the letters down the mail chute.

The senator's performance of these clerical tasks amazed me. "Is there something special about these letters?" I asked.

"I want certain letters sent *exactly* as I dictated them," he replied. "If I give my office staff a chance, they'll revise my letters to make them more diplomatic and remove the cuss words. Now, that's okay for much of my correspondence, but certain letters I don't want altered in any way. What I say in these letters is what I mean, and how I say it is how I mean to say it. To ensure nothing is changed, I have to watch those letters like a hawk."

Goldwater's explanation made me think of a letter he wrote in April, 1984, that received considerable attention. Written to William Casey, director of central intelligence, the letter addressed the CIA's mining of Nicaraguan harbors. The *Washington Post* printed the entire letter under the headline, "Goldwater Writes CIA Director Scorching Letter." The letter began, "Dear Bill . . . I am pissed off . . . this is no way to run a railroad . . . I don't like this. I don't like it one bit from the president or from you. . . . [I]n the future, if anything like this happens, I'm going to raise one hell of a lot of fuss about it in public."[42] It must have been one of the letters the senator sealed and mailed himself.

As Goldwater's commitment to reorganization became publicly known, active and retired officers began to lobby him incessantly. "They're after me again," he would say sadly. "Several more friends of mine, retired generals, called today to tell me, 'You're making a terrible mistake. You'll regret what you're doing.'"

I once said to Goldwater: "You have always loved the military and have great respect for military leaders. They're all telling you reorganization isn't needed. How are you able to take on the entire military establishment and your friends? It must take a tremendous amount of courage."

"I wouldn't say it has taken courage," he replied. "You know, when you believe in something, courage doesn't mean a goddamn thing. If you think you're right, then go ahead and do it. And if you're wrong, you're wrong. I've had more damn experiences like that than you can count. I just have this gut feeling about defense reorganization, and it is growing stronger."[43]

On March 5, Weinberger submitted to Goldwater and Cong. Les Aspin, the new chairman of the House Armed Services Committee, the Pentagon's answers to the organization questions posed in the preceding year's defense authorization bill. This 142-page, one-and-one-half-pound package communicated that Pentagon thinking had not changed. Senior officials remained opposed to reform.[44]

The *Armed Forces Journal* reported, "Secretary of Defense Caspar Weinberger, the secretaries of the Army, Navy, and Air Force, and the chairman of the Joint Chiefs of Staff are agreed on one point—Capitol Hill proposals to reorganize the U.S. military establishment aren't necessary." The *Journal* added that Weinberger and the service secretaries "suggest that if any tinkering is necessary, it should be from within DoD and not from Congress, however well-intentioned."[45]

The questions did not spark the objective review for which proreform members had been hoping. But all was not lost. Three unified commanders—Adm. Bill Crowe of the Pacific Command and the army's Gen. Bernie Rogers of the European Command and Gen. Wallace Nutting of the Readiness Command—provided ammunition for the staff study by breaking with the Pentagon line.

Crowe spoke out most forcefully. He questioned "whether the unified commander has the requisite authority to ensure the readiness of his forces and, in times of crisis (or hostilities), to bring his subordinate commands together without undue disruption to conduct timely, imaginative and efficient operations." The admiral said that regulations imposing "single-service operational chains of command within the unified commands require the unified command to remain a rather loose confederation of single-service forces." Crowe complained about service dominance of resource decisions: "On occasion the results of major service decisions, not previously coordinated with me, have affected my ability to execute USPACOM [U.S. Pacific Command] strategy."[46]

I had heard Crowe privately express these views in Hawaii, but his public outspokenness was surprising, given that senior Washington officials were eyeing him for the top military job. In January, *Newsweek* reported: "In June, according to Pentagon and White House sources, General John W. Vessey will step down from his position as chairman of the Joint Chiefs of Staff after serving only half of his second two-year term. . . . The leading candidate to succeed Vessey is Adm. William J. Crowe . . . (a Navy man is due to get the job under normal rotation)."[47]

Crowe's frontrunner status was believable, given the stories of how he had impressed Reagan during the president's visit to Hawaii nine months earlier. But it was too early to assume that Crowe would be the next chairman. The selection process for such positions is long and grueling with many unexpected turns. Furthermore, the admiral was speaking out on reorganization. Weinberger opposed reorganization, and experts viewed Reagan's silence as unqualified support for his secretary's position.

In late February, the admiral came to Washington to testify to the SASC on the defense budget. I arranged for the two senators to meet privately with Crowe to hear his reorganization views. I briefed Goldwater and Nunn on my meetings with him in Hawaii the previous October. Both senators looked forward to talking with Crowe.

Minutes before the meeting started, Goldwater called me and said: "Jim, I'm in so much pain from my arthritis I can't come to the meeting with Crowe. You tell Sam to go ahead without me. You and he can fill me in later."

When Nunn arrived, he didn't like the idea of holding the meeting without the chairman. He understood that he and Goldwater needed to do and be seen doing things together. "Okay, we'll go ahead with this meeting with Crowe," the ranking Democrat said. "But from now on, if Senator Goldwater's health does not permit him to attend, we'll put off the meeting until he's ready to go."

For years, arthritis had indeed taken a tremendous toll on Goldwater's health and stamina. Knowing that the workload and pressures of reorganization would intensify, Nunn was concerned about the chairman's staying power. After an early meeting with Goldwater, Nunn told Jeff Smith: "This is so important, and I really want to do this right. But I'm afraid I'm going to have to carry the burden because I don't think Barry is physically up to it."[48]

"Nunn was clearly worried," said Smith. "Was he going to take this on, then . . . have the whole thing fall to him? He wouldn't have the votes and Barry wouldn't be able to deliver enough Republicans. Was this going to be a situation where Nunn took all the beatings and got nothing done?"[49]

Crowe's thinking impressed Nunn, as I knew it would. After being briefed on the session, Goldwater also viewed Crowe favorably. The two senators agreed that if reorganization legislation were ever enacted, Crowe would be the ideal JCS chairman to implement it. Goldwater and Nunn instructed us that when they went to the White House to meet with Reagan or his national security adviser, the last bullet on their talking points should suggest that Crowe would make an excellent chairman.

Unknown to Goldwater, Nunn, or the other committee members, Crowe had received static at his Hawaii headquarters from people in the Pentagon about his written answers to Capitol Hill's questions. "Oh my God, do you really believe all that?" he was asked. Callers also advised the admiral: "You are really sticking your neck in something. You shouldn't do that. Because there is just too much opposition back in Washington, and they won't appreciate you speaking out."[50]

Although the SASC's antireform faction had the upper hand, its members were concerned about the Goldwater-Nunn partnership. They were determined to break it. McGovern was quietly scheming to get Goldwater to step aside as task force cochairman in favor of Sen. Phil Gramm (R-Texas). The scheme would end the bipartisan cochairmanship. There would be only one chairman: Gramm.

The SASC Republicans and McGovern claimed that Nunn was taking advantage of Goldwater and intended to use defense reorganization to embarrass the Reagan administration and Republican Party. These fabrications became the rallying cries of the Republican opposition. They were repeated so often that many observers believed them.

On Thursday night, May 2, during a particularly long legislative week, McGovern made his move. Goldwater, dispirited by a Senate vote to cut the defense budget and worried about the vigor of his leadership, was suffering from an arthritis attack. Although the chairman had a high pain threshold, these attacks shortened his attention span and made him willing to go along rather than argue.

Succumbing to McGovern's arguments, Goldwater signed a letter to Nunn stating: "I am establishing an ad hoc task force that will consist of five majority and four minority members. Senator Gramm has agreed to chair this group and report directly and frequently to me. . . . I have asked Senators Cohen,

Quayle, Wilson and Denton to fill out our side." Goldwater also sent a letter to each of the task force's five Republicans.[51]

A flabbergasted Nunn called me the following afternoon after receiving his copy through the Senate mail system. In shock, Rick Finn, Jeff Smith, and I read the letter in Nunn's office.

"What do you think is behind this?" Nunn asked me.

"Senator, as you know, antireform Republicans are trying to make reorganization a partisan issue," I replied. "We've heard that they're saying that you and Congressman Aspin are conspiring to make this a Democratic issue, that you are taking advantage of Senator Goldwater, and that you are dominating the committee staff. I don't have the slightest idea if the chairman heard any of these lies or why he signed that letter."

"If Gramm takes over, we can forget about reorganizing the Pentagon," Nunn predicted.

After the meeting, I called Gerry Smith in Goldwater's office. "I need to see the chairman right away. He's signed a letter putting Senator Gramm in charge of reorganization—"

"What?" Smith said, cutting me off. "The boss hasn't said a word about changing his approach. Where did you see this letter?"

"I saw Senator Nunn's copy. He was blindsided. I don't know why the chairman has done this. Do you have any ideas?"

"I think I smell a rat," replied Smith, "and that rat's name is McGovern."

"The same thought crossed my mind," I volunteered.

"The chairman is traveling today, but he'll be back in the office first thing Monday morning. I'll put you on his calendar for 7 A.M."

Nunn also tried to talk to Goldwater on Friday. Having found the chairman unavailable, he fired off a letter to him criticizing McGovern and denying that he and Aspin were working together. The closing paragraph argued: "Barry, I believe if this [reorganization] is delegated to a task force not headed by the two of us, the chances of a meaningful bill emerging this year are greatly reduced. . . . If this issue becomes partisan, the chances of passage will be nearly zero. I am afraid we are heading rapidly in that direction. I did want you to know my feelings."[52]

As Finn and I headed back to our offices, we pondered our future. "If Gramm becomes the task force chairman and our boss, we're in deep trouble," Finn predicted. "Moreover, if we lose our direct connection to Goldwater, McGovern will make our lives unpleasant, to put it mildly."

By the time we reached my cluttered office we both were beginning to think about where we would go if we had to leave the committee. "We won't be able to find jobs anywhere in the defense community," I said. "The military is so worked up about reform that no organization will risk ruining its relationship with the Pentagon by hiring us."

With reorganization and our futures hanging in the balance, Saturday and Sunday passed slowly.

When I arrived at Senator Goldwater's office Monday morning, I knew that the coming minutes would be momentous. If I could not convince Goldwater to change his mind, our cause would be lost. The seriousness of the situation demanded a boldly candid conversation. "Reorganization is dead if Senator Gramm takes over the task force," I told him. "Navy Secretary John Lehman, who is—as you know—strongly antireform, has influenced Senator Gramm on this issue. Senator Gramm and Senator Nunn will be at loggerheads. Nothing good will come from that stalemate."

"Why are you stepping aside in favor of Senator Gramm?" I inquired.

"I've been informed that Senator Nunn is planning to make reorganization a partisan issue and that he's going to embarrass President Reagan and Secretary Weinberger with all of the information that the staff study is developing," Goldwater replied. "I've been urged to appoint a young, energetic Republican like Gramm to fight off Nunn's partisan attack." Goldwater explained the influence of the Senate vote to cut defense spending, "I was disappointed that I had not been able to make more persuasive arguments and turn the vote. At that moment, the call for a younger senator to protect the interests of the Republican Party seemed like a damn good idea."

After hearing Goldwater's rationale, I said: "Mr. Chairman, for months, I've witnessed every move that you and Senator Nunn have made on reorganization. At no time have I seen Senator Nunn do anything of a partisan nature. In fact, he has always bent over backward to make certain that there was not even the slightest appearance of party politics. Moreover, throughout the entire process, Senator Nunn has been highly deferential to your desires on how to proceed. The push to get you to step aside has nothing to do with Senator Nunn and partisan politics and everything to do with attempting to break your partnership with him. If this partnership is broken, the Pentagon will defeat reorganization."

We sat in silence for several minutes after I finished. Goldwater studied me. He was measuring me as much as my arguments. My boss—with his chiseled jaw, horn-rimmed glasses, and white hair—had a legendary face. His weathered hands, with an Indian tattoo on his left one, were even more fascinating. He held his hands close to his face as he scrutinized me.

Finally, Goldwater broke the silence, slowly lamenting, "My God, what have I done?" Seized by the need to correct his mistake, Goldwater declared, "I'm going to remain cochairman of the task force." Now fully back in the saddle, his voice swelled into a stern, vigorous instruction, "Forget all of the commotion of the last several days and get back to work on that damn staff study." He wrote to each senator who had received his earlier letter to tell them of his change of plans.

Two weeks passed before McGovern again tried to get Gramm appointed as task force chairman. Chris Cowart, the committee's chief clerk, found a letter making this assignment in a stack of minor administrative matters that Goldwater had signed at McGovern's request. She brought me a copy.

Goldwater was on the Senate floor, and Nunn was leaving his office to join him. I gave Nunn the letter. When he showed it to Goldwater, the chairman exclaimed, "I'll be goddamned! I didn't realize I had signed anything like that."[53]

McGovern must have felt Goldwater's wrath because he and Carl Smith rushed off in a panic to retrieve the letters from the Senate post office.

The rest of the staff gathered in the SASC's main hearing room to discuss this bizarre and disturbing development. After expressing our disbelief, we laughed when someone said, "I can picture Jim McGovern and Carl Smith, down on their hands and knees in the mailroom, madly looking for those eighteen letters."

Afterward, I asked Gerry Smith, "Why doesn't Senator Goldwater fire McGovern? Why is he tolerating such insubordination?"

"I don't really know," he replied. "Probably because he gave his word to Tower that he would keep McGovern. Maybe, he wants to show that he's up to controlling his staff director. But I don't think that the boss understands the depths that McGovern will go to. You know, the chairman always tries to see the good in people. When we most recently talked about McGovern, he said, 'Well, he really isn't that bad.' Goldwater knows that McGovern can't always be trusted. I said to him, 'You know, you rely on McGovern an awful lot, and he's not above doing things that are not right in your name.' He said, 'Well, he has a little larceny in him. I'll keep an eye on him.'"[54]

The retired colonel added wryly, "Goldwater thinks he can manage McGovern." Smith and I looked at each other and rolled our eyes.

McGovern's latest scheme convinced Goldwater and Nunn that they needed to settle the task force leadership and membership. They added seven members—four Republicans and three Democrats. Maintaining a true bipartisan approach required adding an equal number of Republicans and Democrats, but Goldwater and Nunn decided not to aggravate the committee's Republicans, who were already showing antireform tendencies.

The two senators decided that the committee's antireform faction should be well represented on the task force. Goldwater was determined to add Bill Cohen, and he accepted Dan Quayle, Pete Wilson, and Phil Gramm as the representatives of the opposition. Nunn added Jeff Bingaman, Carl Levin, and Ted Kennedy, each of whom had an open mind on the subject.

I liked Gramm and thought that meeting with him to explain reorganization issues might be useful. His military legislative assistant, Alan Ptak, had been a friend for many years. Before coming to the Senate, Ptak worked in the CIA's legislative affairs office. One of his duties was serving as the agency's liaison with the SASC, where I served as his principal contact. Ptak arranged for me to meet with Gramm on the morning of June 6. Formerly a Boll Weevil Democrat, the Texas senator switched parties in January, 1983, after resigning the House seat to which he had just been elected. He was reelected to his old seat as a Republican in a special election held one month later. In the next general election, Gramm ran for the Senate seat vacated by Tower. Smart and savvy, Gramm quickly demonstrated that he was a political force to be reckoned with. His doctorate in economics and early career as a college professor found expression in his highly visible work on the complex Gramm-Rudman-Hollings budget deficit legislation.

I explained to Gramm DoD's organizational problems and why the services, especially the navy, resisted reform. Gramm appeared unpersuaded. He responded with some of Lehman's themes. The Texas senator and navy secretary were building a close relationship. Lehman had designated several Texas ports as new locations for navy ships as part of the Strategic Homeporting Initiative. The secretary's decision generated a political windfall for the new senator. Not surprisingly, Gramm was receptive to Lehman's arguments on reorganization.

Even though my meeting with Gramm failed to produce anything tangible, I appreciated the chance to express my views to him. He did not agree that day, but maybe I gave him something to think about. Moreover, I did not walk away from the session empty-handed. Gramm laid down a challenge that I could use—like a coach—to motivate a key player on our team. As the meeting ended, Gramm said, "Tell Senator Nunn that I am going to be smarter on reorganization than anybody on the committee." Knowing how the competitive Georgia senator would react, I did tell him. If Nunn had maintained a locker in the Senate, I would have taped Gramm's challenge on it.

The first six months of Goldwater and Nunn's examination of reorganization had been a roller-coaster ride. Near disasters followed moments of great promise. In the pivotal development, the two senators were forming a strong bond. Although Goldwater and Nunn always had a good relationship, their leadership roles forced them to work more closely and depend on each other. The help that Nunn gave Goldwater in his early critical months as chairman catalyzed the building of a stronger relationship.[55]

The two senators quickly became comfortable communicating openly and candidly with each other. Nunn characterized their discussions: "He and I always shot straight. If I said or thought something strongly and I told him, Barry would always appreciate that. I never did go around him. I never did try to go through staff or any of that business. He knew when I told him something it was going to be my frank and honest opinion of it."[56]

22. Senators Goldwater and Nunn, chairman and ranking minority member of the Senate Armed Services Committee. (U.S. Senate photo.)

Attacks on Goldwater and Nunn's partnership tested their relationship. Rough moments of doubt occurred, but a strong, more resilient relationship emerged from these crises. Before long, they developed extraordinary trust in each other. "Goldwater developed more trust in me than anybody else on the committee," Nunn recalled. In an early June letter to Nunn, Goldwater wrote, "I have, in you, a ranking member whose ability and dedication I could not conceive of a way on which to improve."[57]

Looking back on the partnership, Goldwater said: "In going into this battle, I placed absolute trust in Nunn. He never disappointed me, not once. With Sam, I'd take on the devil in hell."[58]

The two senators instinctively divided the work to maximize their individual strengths. Goldwater focused on shaping the major thrusts of reform and serving as a bulwark against the unending condemnation from the Pentagon and its allies. "Because of his credibility and reputation for being so pro-military," Nunn said, "nobody was going to be able to say of what Goldwater was championing, 'It was subversive or that it was anti-military, or he was coming from some position of trying to harm the military.' The only thing they could say was, 'We don't agree with him.' Goldwater was immune from any kind of attack from the right. So, having Goldwater out front was crucial."[59]

While Goldwater kept the work on course and protected the project, the ranking Democrat zeroed in on more detailed analyses and solutions. Nunn's work would give full expression to the organization principles that he and Goldwater were formulating. The Georgia senator possessed exceptional analytical skills, and he had studied Pentagon problems for years.

Goldwater emerged as the moral force behind reorganization, and Nunn became the intellectual force. Nunn's contribution made the senators' work profound; Goldwater's made it possible.

Both reform proponents and opponents understood the importance of the Goldwater-Nunn partnership. If it were broken and partisan politics injected as a major factor, everyone knew that reorganization would die. If the senators' partnership remained solid, reorganizing the Pentagon might be possible. John G. Kester, a savvy proreformer, did not think so. In February, 1985, he predicted: "Congress will hold hearings on reorganizing the Pentagon; they will end in stalemate and minor adjustments."[60]

Opponents would hammer furiously at the link between Goldwater and Nunn. Having twice failed to get Goldwater to abandon his task force cochairmanship, they were likely to abandon that tactic. With the first meeting of the nine-member Task Force on Defense Organization approaching, reformers wondered what new attacks their opponents would mount.

CHAPTER 12

Weinberger Stonewalls

If ignorant both of your enemy and yourself,

you are certain in every battle to be in peril.

—Sun Tzu, *The Art of War*

While Goldwater and Nunn were searching for ways to give momentum to defense reorganization, Secretary of Defense Cap Weinberger just wanted the issue to go away. The secretary was never a behind-the-scenes antireform activist. Initially, he opposed reorganization only moderately. As time passed, his opposition grew, and he stubbornly resisted until the end. Weinberger doggedly defended the Pentagon's performance and organization. A journalist noted, "Weinberger fought more assiduously against the perception of problems in the Pentagon than he did against the problems themselves."[1]

The secretary resisted reorganization by stonewalling. He could not have selected a worse strategy. In doing so he played right into the hands of the reformers. His in-your-face rigidity created both the incentive and the ideal environment for the reformers to mount a crusade. Had Weinberger shown some flexibility during the first four years of debate, he could have undermined, if not curtailed, congressional efforts. Had he agreed to a few meaningful reforms and then asked Congress for three or four years to evaluate them before taking further steps, Weinberger could have defused the issue. Nunn later judged that if the secretary had compromised early, "it would have taken twenty years to achieve needed reforms."[2] An early compromise from Weinberger would have appealed to Capitol Hill, where a solid reason for delaying action on a controversial measure is often popular. Moreover, in a less confrontational environment, Senate reformers would not have been able to hold the attention of colleagues long enough to educate them on reorganization.

Weinberger proved to be an infuriating opponent. An adversary who evokes a strong emotional response always helps to rally the troops. Weinberger played that role to perfection. By refusing to admit the existence of so much as a single problem, he exasperated even members who were neutral on reorganization.

In Washington politics, author Hedrick Smith wrote, "Credibility—trust—is the most important key to survival and influence. . . . [T]he advocate who is too parochial, too partisan, or too political to be credible is not heard or heeded as time wears on." Weinberger was all three. His overzealous advocacy reinforced his low credibility on Capitol Hill. Added Smith, "Congress lost faith in Weinberger's credibility" during his second year as secretary.[3]

Weinberger's attitude encouraged other Pentagon officials, especially Navy Secretary John Lehman, to become unyielding antireform activists. The virulence of the Pentagon's campaign on Capitol Hill alienated many members of Congress and produced a backlash on the National Security Council staff.

A San Francisco native, Weinberger, who majored in government, graduated from Harvard College in 1938 and Harvard Law School three years later. His undergraduate honors included magna cum laude, Phi Beta Kappa, and president of the *Harvard Crimson* newspaper. Weinberger credits his long hours of writing at the *Crimson* as "instrumental in my learning to express, both orally and in writing, my pronounced views on both domestic and foreign policy."[4] His editorials were "fierce, biting, heavily ironic. One side was completely right and the other completely wrong." The editorial chairman warned Weinberger, "It is impossible to have your editorial message effective unless the pill of bias is coated with a little bit of the sugar of reason." The undergraduate spokesman for conservative, anti–New Deal positions saw "the world in black and white."[5]

Having failed an eye examination for the Royal Canadian Air Force during law school, after graduation Weinberger enlisted as a private in the U.S. Army. Following officer candidate school, the new second lieutenant was assigned as a platoon leader with the 41st Infantry Division. He spent almost three years patrolling New Guinea jungles, rose in rank to captain, and commanded an infantry company before being reassigned to General MacArthur's intelligence staff.

After the war, Weinberger clerked for a federal appeals judge for two years before starting his law practice. In 1952 he was elected to the California Assembly as a Republican from San Francisco and served three two-year terms. Journalists named him the most effective legislator in 1956.[6] "In the legislature," an acquaintance recalled, "he could be abrasive, stepping on toes, but no one really disliked him. But not many trusted him either. There was the feeling of hidden ruthlessness in his ambition."[7] A state official said Weinberger "was considered a leader of the liberal wing of the party in those days." Others described him and his San Francisco political associates as moderates.

Weinberger was so fervently moderate that his friends could not believe he had been a conservative in college. In 1958, Weinberger lost the Republican primary for California attorney general and never again ran for elected office.[8]

From 1959 to 1968, Weinberger hosted a weekly San Francisco television show on public affairs called "Profile: Bay Area," and remained active in Republican politics. He chaired the party's state central committee during Richard Nixon's defeat in the 1962 gubernatorial race and, two years later, the bitter fight between Barry Goldwater and Nelson Rockefeller in the 1964 California presidential primary. Weinberger backed Rockefeller. In 1966 he backed moderate George Christopher, a former San Francisco mayor, over conservative Ronald Reagan in the Republican gubernatorial primary. Weinberger served as Christopher's campaign chairman in northern California "on the grounds of old friendship and as part of the continuing battle to beat down the right."

In 1967, overlooking earlier political battles, Governor Reagan appointed Weinberger chairman of the Commission on California State Government and Economy, an independent agency that investigates government operations. In February, 1968, Reagan asked him to serve as the state's director of finance. Reagan and Weinberger soon developed a close association. Weinberger worked "tirelessly and unswervingly" to achieve the budget cuts Reagan had promised. He was "the kind of official who doggedly carried out his superior's wishes without much questioning them."

In January, 1970, President Nixon appointed Weinberger chairman of the Federal Trade Commission and tasked him with reforming the agency. Weinberger hired a young lawyer, William Howard Taft IV, from consumer advocate Ralph Nader's staff to work for him. Throughout Weinberger's career in Washington, Taft remained at his side. Weinberger moved "swiftly" and "ruthlessly" to implement massive reform. His operating method was described as "Get the brief. Set a course right away. Be tough with the opposition. Never waver. Make the president look good."[9]

In July, 1970, Nixon designated Weinberger as George Shultz's deputy director at the Office of Management and Budget (OMB). When Shultz became secretary of the treasury in 1972, Weinberger moved up to the top job. He selected Frank Carlucci, a foreign-service officer, as his deputy. When Nixon ordered government spending cut, Weinberger's "enthusiasm for the task knew no bounds," and defense spending steadily declined as a result. He earned the nickname "Cap the Knife" for his budget-cutting prowess.[10]

In February, 1973, Weinberger moved to the Department of Health, Education, and Welfare as its secretary, taking Carlucci along to serve as his deputy. A department official observed: "His technique is to repeat his point, to adopt a line and not deviate. He'd listen to an argument, but then respond by reiterating his original position. Infuriating, but effective."[11]

Weinberger left government service in August, 1975, and joined the Bechtel Corporation, a multinational company based in California, where George Shultz served as president. Weinberger was vice president and general counsel at Bechtel when Reagan selected him to serve as defense secretary. Weinberger's political and business credentials were impressive, but he had "little background in defense."[12]

His selection did not please conservative Republicans, many of whom remembered that he had backed Rockefeller over Goldwater in 1964. Journalist Robert Toth called Weinberger "a professed conservative who cannot rid himself of a liberal tinge."[13] Meanwhile, conservatives criticized his lack of defense experience and moderate positions and feared he would bring budget cutting to a Pentagon they viewed as underfunded. Weinberger's standing dropped even farther when he named Carlucci—neither a defense expert nor a member of the conservative circle—as his deputy.

A few days after the December 12 announcement of his selection, a Rowland Evans and Robert Novak commentary in the *Washington Post* entitled "Why Weinberger? Why Carlucci?" asked, "Why is Reagan getting a secretary and deputy secretary at defense who both need remedial courses in military nuts and bolts? Why did he pick a reputed budget-cutter ("Cap the Knife") to rebuild the nation's leaky defense structure?"[14]

On January 9, three days after Weinberger's Senate Armed Services Committee confirmation hearing, the two pundits opined, "Unease within the defense community over Caspar Weinberger has blossomed into panic." They cited his "nearly total ignorance on defense questions, which was fully revealed in his Senate confirmation hearing." The columnists criticized Weinberger's appointment of his longtime assistant Taft, "a Washington lawyer who knows even less about defense than Weinberger and Carlucci," to head the Pentagon transition team.[15]

If there was panic, it was short-lived. Senator John Tower, the new SASC chairman, kept Weinberger's confirmation on track and produced a unanimous committee vote in favor of his nomination. Commentators who believed that Weinberger's nomination could be undermined may not have understood his high standing with Reagan. "You can't overstate how close Reagan and Weinberger are," said a Republican leader who helped select the cabinet. Reagan referred to Weinberger as "my Disraeli."[16] Moreover, the Republican Senate was not about to undermine the president.

A leading conservative, Sen. Jesse Helms (R–North Carolina), carried the fight against Weinberger to the Senate floor. He launched a forty-minute attack in which he called the Weinberger and Carlucci nominations "particularly troublesome not only to me, who will vote against them, but also to a great number of my colleagues who plan to vote for confirmation." Helms added that "Mr. Weinberger has yet to demonstrate . . . that he has either that resolution or that vision" required to end Soviet nuclear superiority. He charged that numerous defense experts believed Weinberger comprehended neither "the decline of U.S. military power, nor the rise of Soviet strength." Of Weinberger's confirmation testimony, Helms said, "He did not seem to have a theoretical grasp" of the issues. In the end, however, only Helms and fellow North Carolina Republican John East voted against Weinberger.[17]

This controversy and Helm's attack shocked Weinberger. He apparently decided never to allow anyone to get to the political right of him on a defense or foreign policy issue, becoming "the ultimate hard-liner in a rather hard-line administration."[18] The new secretary jettisoned his previously moderate defense views "to focus singlemindedly on selling a major defense buildup to the Congress and the nation." As Reagan's top adviser on budgetary policy during the presidential campaign, Weinberger had recommended only a 5 percent hike in defense spending—the same level proposed by President Carter.[19] Following the conservative attack, Weinberger, now an "impassioned convert," pushed for more than a 20 percent increase in Reagan's first budget, "the largest and swiftest rise in defense spending during peacetime in our history."[20] A Senate staffer explained: "Cap Weinberger was heavily influenced by the opposition which surfaced during the confirmation process. He was stung and has never forgotten it. He must show the Congress that he is a 'defense advocate.'"[21]

Characteristically, Weinberger's enthusiasm for his defense-rebuilding task knew no bounds. He became a messianic protector of military spending. Taft later commented, "Nothing ever diverted Secretary Weinberger from his advocacy of higher defense budgets."[22] With huge federal deficits looming, administration officials and Congress fought Weinberger over the rapid pace of the defense buildup. Even though Congress voted sizable reductions in the 1982–1984 budget requests, during Reagan's first term, Weinberger secured a 50 percent increase in defense spending. This funding bought many weapons and fixed other deficiencies. This pleased the Pentagon's top brass, some of whom rated Weinberger as the best recent defense secretary and called his tenure "a golden era of defense."[23]

Beyond the budget, Weinberger worried about the conservatives' attitudes on every issue. Admiral Crowe later said: "Weinberger considered himself the guardian of the right in the Reagan administration, and he applied the political test to every major question: 'What will the right think about this?' If the right didn't have any views on it, then you could talk to him about it. But if it was something that was dear to their hearts, you were dead. He carried around some ideological baggage that was pretty fierce."[24]

While Weinberger's hard-line positions made many conservatives and military officers happy, he quickly alienated almost everyone else in Washington, especially on Capitol Hill. The greatest complaint was his rigidity. Weinberger would not budge even slightly from any position he had taken. Former boss

George Shultz said this was "a technique [Weinberger] used on many issues before and after: take a position and never change. He seemed to feel that the outcome, even if different from his position, would likely move further in his direction when he was difficult and intransigent. In many a battle, this technique served him well. But over time, as more and more people understood the technique, its effectiveness waned, and Cap's capacity to be part of final solutions declined."[25]

Weinberger's uncompromising style infuriated members of Congress. House Armed Services Committee chairman Les Aspin exploded, "Jesus, Cap, negotiating with you is like negotiating with the Russians. All you do is keep repeating your position." Senator Bill Cohen observed, "I don't think Cap particularly has the time, the patience, the inclination to want to sit down and try to take into account congressional concerns or proposals. . . . He has a mindset which precludes, for the most part, taking into account diversity of opinion or at least recognizing the legitimacy of a diverse opinion."[26]

Weinberger's stonewalling perplexed Tower. As the administration's foremost defense champion on the Hill, Tower found supporting the secretary increasingly difficult. I handled an issue in November, 1982, that exemplified Tower's frustrations with the defense secretary. Reacting to the failure of European nations to spend more on defense, the Senate Defense Appropriations Subcommittee had proposed a 23,900-man or 7 percent cut in planned U.S. military strength in Europe. The administration strongly objected to this provision, as did Tower. In preparation for a Senate floor fight, he sent me to Europe for discussions with U.S. and allied officials.

On my return, Tower asked me to poll each senator's office for a position on this issue. Results showed that thirty-five senators favored the proposed cut, fifteen senators supported the administration, and fifty senators were somewhere in between. These middle-ground senators were not comfortable with administration plans, but they did not favor a big cut. Tower knew that without a compromise position, the Appropriations Committee would win. He asked me to determine the cut in U.S. personnel in Europe that a majority of senators would support and then to work this compromise with the Defense Department.

After explaining the issue and proposing a 4,100-man cut to my Pentagon counterpart, G. Mike Andricos, he said he and Russ Rourke, assistant defense secretary for legislative affairs, would need Weinberger's approval. They could not obtain it. He refused to compromise. When I informed Tower, he believed that Weinberger did not understand our predicament. He asked that I again explain the situation to the Pentagon. Andricos and Rourke's more detailed explanation to the secretary elicited the same answer: compromising was out of the question. When I told Tower, he cursed, "Screw Weinberger." The Senate approved Tower's compromise amendment.

Tower held a low opinion of Weinberger from the beginning. In a meeting shortly after the secretary's confirmation hearing, Weinberger's lack of knowledge and judgment on defense issues stunned Tower.[27] Nunn shared Tower's low opinion, saying, "Some of [Weinberger's] statements are just preposterous." Goldwater was equally unimpressed. In a letter to Tower, he lamented, "With all due respect to Cap, he's never had it; he never will." In early 1982, Robert "Bob" Helm, the NSC's defense budget expert, had alerted his superiors to "Weinberger's loss of credibility on Capitol Hill on the defense budget."[28]

The secretary's laissez-faire management style also earned him low marks. "Weinberger believed in delegating authority. He deliberately gave the services ample leeway. When his own staff tried to impose central discipline, Weinberger often stopped them." Senior aides warned the secretary that the independence he had given the services would make it "almost impossible to control them." Weinberger replied that it "was how he had run the Department of Health, Education, and Welfare." But extreme decentralization did not work in the Pentagon, which was already excessively fractured. Weinberger's civilian assistants saw him "as a weak manager who pressured the services only when Congress or public controversy forced his hand."[29]

Weinberger was also intransigent in dealing with White House and NSC staffers. A senior White House official said, "Cap is probably the least flexible man on the team. Cap sets a path and simply does not get off of it."[30] His unpopularity was reflected in a White House senior staff meeting in December, 1982, shortly after the House rejected Weinberger's plan for basing the MX missile. As reported in the *New York Times:* "Someone brought a cartoon showing the defense secretary talking about the need for a missile silo that would be utterly impenetrable and impervious to outside forces. In the last panel, the missile was seen lodged in Mr. Weinberger's head. Staff members reportedly laughed uproariously on seeing the cartoon."[31]

National Security Adviser Robert C. "Bud" McFarlane, who clashed often with Weinberger, observed: "The secretary of defense has two jobs: develop sensible military strategy and spend money wisely. Secretary Weinberger was not qualified by training or experience for either role and never developed the least qualification in either domain." McFarlane judged that Weinberger's mismanagement and poor relations with Congress squandered the opportunity for a bigger defense buildup: "What was bound to be a post–Jimmy Carter renewal of our defense was less successful than it might have been as a consequence of his ineptitude."[32]

Despite his combative style, Weinberger exhibited "unfailing courtesy and graciousness" in personal relations. "Cap values civility in his daily life," said an associate. "He doesn't raise his voice in anger, and there are few confrontations."[33] General Colin L. Powell, who served as Weinberger's senior military assistant, described Weinberger as "a cultured man" with a "polished, Old World

23. This Steve Sack cartoon appearing in the *Chicago Tribune* on December 13, 1982, caused White House staffers to laugh "uproariously."

manner." According to Powell, "His tastes ran to the classics in literature and music. . . . [H]e worked when alone to the accompaniment of Bach and Beethoven."[34] The fact that Weinberger and Reagan both were gracious gentlemen strengthened their relationship.

A longtime associate saw Weinberger as "a reticent person, more comfortable at large cocktail parties than at small ones because there's not the risk of getting to know people deeply." Weinberger's dour public demeanor contrasts with "a quick and playful sense of humor, about himself as well as others" that he showed in private. At one staff meeting, when told that a member of the Pentagon's elite counterterrorism force had been arrested for indecent exposure, Weinberger quipped, "I thought they weren't even supposed to show their faces."[35]

Many who worked for Weinberger held him in high regard. Powell wrote that he had "the warmest feelings toward the man I had served. Cap Weinberger had his little quirks, but at the core, he was a great fighter, a brilliant advocate, a man, who, like his president, set a few simple objectives and did not deviate from them. He projected strength, unflappability, and supreme self-confidence."[36]

Yet Powell also noted that he found the secretary unwilling to back down on any position he had taken. He described Weinberger's approach as "all sails up, full speed ahead, where is the brick wall—I wish to run into it now." Powell later wrote: "Frank Carlucci had once counseled me that wise subordinates picked their fights with Weinberger selectively. 'If it's small potatoes,' Frank had warned, 'don't waste your energy. Even if he's dead wrong. Save yourself for the serious stuff, and even then you'll probably hit a stone wall.'"[37]

Although Weinberger was embattled throughout Washington, he still had Reagan's strong backing. The secretary himself admitted that he had a constituency of one. Returning from White House battles, Weinberger would often tell his staff, "There was only one vote in the room that was on my side, and that's the one that mattered." He felt as if he had no allies. It was "him versus the world, and the only person on his side was Reagan."[38]

Just before the 1984 election, in an interview with journalist Nicholas Lemann, Weinberger revealed parallels between his unyielding behavior as secretary and his lonely stands at Harvard: "He constantly described the stand he was taking as unpopular, implying an equation of unpopularity with virtue. He used words like *facile* and *comfortable* to describe his opponents' positions, and *difficult, long,* and *disagreeable* to describe his own. He told me that we had let our defenses lapse because 'nobody was willing to make the strong, unpopular fight against it.' Though he obviously felt the sting of the constant criticism of defense spending, he had always experienced attacks as a part of holding high office; naturally, in his highest office he experienced the strongest attacks."[39]

Lou Cannon reported that despite widespread pressure, Reagan "refused to replace Weinberger as defense secretary, a change keenly desired by key congressional Republicans who resented his intransigence on budgetary matters, and which White House officials told me was urged by Nancy Reagan after the 1984 election." Political consultant Ed Rollins noted that "Cap Weinberger was the most indomitable infighter I ever saw—the only member of the inner circle Nancy Reagan couldn't trump."[40]

Weinberger later wrote, "I was told by some that my 'stubbornness' was hurting the president, so I was particularly grateful and pleased when in 1984 he was re-elected by one of the largest margins in our history."[41]

Since the end of World War II, efforts to achieve greater military unification had originated with presidents and defense secretaries. The formidable alliance of Congress and the services consistently opposed and weakened the proposals of these two officials. This time, the roles were reversed: elements of Congress were pushing for unifying reforms, and Weinberger had inexplicably allied himself with the services in opposition. As one of its overarching objectives, reorganization sought to strengthen the ability of the defense secretary to lead and manage DoD. This fact makes Weinberger's opposition even more difficult to comprehend.

24. Defense Secretary Weinberger presents President Reagan with a copy
of *Soviet Military Power* in the Oval Office, March 3, 1983.
(Courtesy Ronald Reagan Library.)

In 1939, Sir Winston S. Churchill, one of Weinberger's heroes, said Russia "is a riddle wrapped in a mystery inside an enigma."[42] He could just as easily have been describing Caspar Weinberger. Weinberger exhibited many paradoxes: He had spent much of his life in politics, but he was unskilled as a politician. He was well educated but never became a defense intellectual. He was amiable but developed few friends. He was a public official but maintained the style of a private person.

Why did Weinberger oppose reorganization? Admiral Crowe says, "Weinberger didn't really understand how the department operated." Focusing on his advocacy role and key policy issues, he saw organizational concerns as "less important." Taft believed that Weinberger "was undoubtedly right that the department's most serious problems had been created by a combination of inadequate funding and irresolute political leadership and were well on their way to being solved by increased budgets and President Reagan's consistent approach to security policy."[43]

Weinberger viewed reorganization proposals as an excuse for cutting the defense budget: "Reorganization was put forth frequently by many people as a substitute for defense spending. They'd say, 'If we just had reorganization, we wouldn't need so much money,' which was quite absurd. You can't buy airplanes and bullets and rifles and submarines and things like that with reorganization plans."[44]

Weinberger's laissez faire management style gave the military departments leeway to pursue their own interests. Rather than shaping, integrating, and controlling the services' diverse programs, Weinberger saw the promotion of service desires as his principal duty. When the services rejected reorganization, he sided with them. Moreover, given his neglect of the secretary's integrating function, Weinberger was not attuned to reform's central tenet: the need for greater unification.

Weinberger's dislike of Congress was factored into his opposition to congressional reform proposals. His hostility may have originated in bitter memories of the Senate's consideration of his nomination. Taft later observed, "Secretary Weinberger was not always able to conceal his lack of confidence in many legislators who had either caused, acquiesced in or, at the least, failed to prevent the 'decade of neglect' preceding his term in office." For whatever reason, throughout his tenure, Weinberger resisted congressional initiatives and worked poorly with Congress. He "never really built the essential political networks" on Capitol Hill.[45]

As the administration's early consensus on defense spending disappeared, Weinberger experienced increasing resistance from Congress on Pentagon budget levels. He feared that the reform debate's focus on departmental problems would further erode support for defense spending.[46]

Moreover, Weinberger viewed reorganization as a harsh criticism of his tenure.[47] No matter how hard defense reform proponents stressed the long-term nature of organizational problems, Weinberger took their efforts personally. Given his enormous pride in his accomplishments, Weinberger was not about to accept such criticism.[48]

Only General Jack Vessey, JCS chairman, could have changed Weinberger's views on reorganization. The secretary says, "My relationship with General Vessey was very close, very warm, very friendly. We met every day, and I never had anything but good advice from him and good, frank, and candid reactions." In November, 1982, Vessey and the other joint chiefs completed a study requested by Weinberger on JCS reorganization that concluded that sweeping changes were "unnecessary." This study "had a substantial impact" on the secretary's thinking. He explains why: "I have enormous respect for General Vessey. He and I were the last two people in the Pentagon who had active service in World War II. I thought his advice was always sound. His judgment was extraordinary, and his understanding of the whole military was invaluable."[49]

Vessey equally admired Weinberger as "an exceptional secretary of defense. Nobody worked harder at the job than he did."[50] The chairman thought that criticisms of the secretary as a spendthrift were misplaced. "If everybody had the same concern for the taxpayer's dollar that Cap Weinberger had, we'd be in great shape."[51]

When the wiry, five-foot-nine, unassuming, plainspoken Vessey became chairman, he was confronted by the JCS reorganization controversy. Given his "nonconfrontational" operating style, he was an unlikely champion of that cause.[52] Vessey was a consensus builder, not a visionary reformer. Once on the job, even his supporters noticed "his reluctance to tangle with the Pentagon's feuding factions." One official conceded, "He hasn't gone in there and taken over the Joint Staff. He hasn't knocked any heads together."[53]

Vessey was "careful to cultivate smooth relations" with the four service chiefs. Compared to General Jones, his activist predecessor, Vessey was "more comfortable yielding to consensus." When program budgets needed to be trimmed, Vessey rarely recommended cuts himself, but would "pass on the services' inflated wish lists to the congressional chopping block." When it came to JCS reorganization, Vessey "refused to get out in front of his colleagues—preferring to lobby behind the scenes for a JCS consensus."

The army general was committed to making improvements, but did not see the need for statutory changes. He "thought there was more room inside the law for improvement and change than there was by changing the law." General Meyer observed, "Vessey, much like Admiral Moorer, believed you could change the system if you were strong. This belief didn't take into account the way the services were so dominant and could block you."[54]

Vessey's 1976–79 tour as the four-star commander of U.S. Forces, Korea, a subordinate unified command in the Pacific Command, had exposed him to the excessive power of the services and their ability to undermine his command authority. One dispute between Vessey and the Marine Corps illustrates these realities.

For many years, the 3d Marine Division on Okinawa had sent one artillery battalion at a time to Korea for practice firing at Nightmare Range, fifteen miles from the ever-tense Demilitarized Zone. The range was in the sector of I Corps Group, commanded by Lt. Gen. John H. Cushman, an army officer who reported to Vessey. Cushman told the marine division commander that he intended "if the North Koreans should attack while the Marine artillery battalion was in his area of responsibility, to place the battalion under operational control of the [U.S. Army] 2d Infantry Division Artillery so that the battalion's fires could be most effectively used in the defense of Korea."[55]

According to Cushman, "The Marine division commander demurred, pointing out that it was Marine Corps doctrine that Marine units fight together under the Marine division-wing command concept."

Cushman remarked, "If war should come, I would be surprised indeed to find the Marine artillery battalion waiting for a Marine division or other Marine formation headquarters to show up, before the battalion engaged the attacking enemy." Cushman added, "The former Marine Corps commandant, the famous Major General John A. Lejeune, who had commanded a Marine brigade under the same 2nd Division in World War I, and who later commanded the full Army division, might if he were alive take exception to having the Marine artillery either sit out the battle or operate without higher artillery headquarters' fire direction."

Despite military logic, Cushman was unable to resolve this issue. Vessey struck out as well, unable "to get the Marines to agree" to command arrangements in a crisis. In Cushman's view, Vessey did not press the issue with higher headquarters because it "would have taken him into a tangled web of doctrine, precedent, and service suspicion profitless to enter."

In one of the world's hottest spots, Vessey had a marine battalion—far from the sea, hundreds of miles from any naval force, but close to North Korean lines—with which he had no command relationship. This situation continued throughout Vessey's tour as chairman.

Beyond his weak command situation, Vessey could cite many historical examples of poor American interservice coordination on the Korean Peninsula going back to the Korean War, the first wartime test of the new Department of Defense.

American forces had occupied Korea south of the thirty-eighth parallel after the Japanese surrender in 1945. South Korea was part of the geographic area of responsibility of the Far East Command, a unified command led by General MacArthur. After helping to build internal security forces for the new Republic of Korea, the United States withdrew its forces, except for a small advisory group, in July, 1949. The South Koreans would have to defend themselves. Before dawn on June 25, 1950, the North Koreans attacked South Korea in a naked act of aggression.

In 1946, the JCS had directed all unified theater commanders to establish a "joint staff with appropriate members from the various components of the services . . . in key positions of responsibility." MacArthur did not act on this directive until nearly three years later, and then only to create a Joint Strategic Plans and Operations Group under his assistant chief of staff for operations. At the outbreak of the Korean War, "unification had never reached the Far East" at the highest headquarters level. The Far East Command operated for the first two and one-half years after the outbreak of hostilities without a joint headquarters. Manned almost completely by army personnel and focused on army operations, FECOM headquarters was "dominated by Army thinking and prone to honor Army concepts."[56]

Interservice problems proliferated in the absence of a joint staff. Coordination of air operations proved particularly troublesome. When the Korean conflict erupted, no centralized control of air force, navy, and marine aviation existed. Commanders could not effectively employ airpower, and pilots faced hazardous flying over the limited Korean airspace. The navy and

Marine Corps grudgingly agreed to give the air force limited authority over their air assets, called "coordination control." "Differences of opinion, misunderstandings of channels of communications, and disagreements over the wording of important operations orders" ensued. By the end of July, "improvised procedures brought some order to the fantastically confused command situation in the Far East, but . . . never achieved the full fruits of unification."[57]

Differences in army–air force and navy–Marine Corps doctrine for close air support "triggered a controversy that lasted virtually throughout the war." Army–air force doctrine envisioned close air support primarily beyond the range of army artillery, a distance of a thousand yards or more in front of the troops. Navy–Marine Corps doctrine substituted close air support for artillery, an approach driven by limited marine artillery.[58]

On July 22 and 25, navy attempts to provide air strikes in support of the beleaguered Eighth Army inside the Pusan pocket were "tremendously frustrated." Doctrinal differences, communications problems, and incompatible maps produced "total confusion." Radio discipline was poor, and "basic incompatibilities" existed between army–air force and navy radios. Navy aeronautical maps were "delineated in latitude and longitude" while gridded air force charts permitted controllers to "pinpoint targets by a combination of numbers and letters." Because of the confusion, "most Navy planes gave up [working with controllers], roaming the front on their own, looking for targets." In August, the navy scratched 30 percent of its sorties because planes could not contact [frontline] controllers.[59]

Assessing these organizational deficiencies, an air force historian later wrote: "Certainly, at the outset of the Korean war, the defective theater command system prevented the fullest employment of airpower, delayed the beginning of a comprehensive air-interdiction program for more than a month, and . . . caused confusion and loss of effectiveness at the very time that every single aircraft sortie was vital to the survival of the Eighth Army in Korea."[60]

The Pentagon also evidenced disarray. At the outbreak of fighting, the unified military establishment, less than three years old, "was an unfinished creation." The Pentagon continued to be plagued by "strong-willed interservice competition for men, money, weapons, and missions" and "resistance by the military services to the authority of the secretary of defense." Despite the role of the defense secretary and his staff, the services "retained much power." They "enjoyed remarkable success in holding onto many functions and prerogatives" by controlling "the military essentials—money, men, material, research and development, choice of weapons, and, above all, the assignment and promotion of personnel."[61]

Moreover, a series of "petty actions and frustrations" complicated interservice cooperation. The air force sometimes could not find a plane to fly the army chief, while "most Air Force generals had their individual, luxury-equipped aircraft." On the day of the critical Inchon landing in Korea, Acting Defense Secretary Robert A. Lovett had to settle an issue that had stymied the JCS: the allocation of parking spaces to marine officers at the Pentagon's Mall Entrance. On occasion, the JCS was able to resolve bitter disagreements over funding of major weapon systems only by flipping a coin.[62]

In the field, unified commanders like MacArthur had little say in shaping the force and weapons capabilities of service forces assigned to their commands. Such capabilities, dictated by the services, often "had more to do with the overall interests of the services than with the operational needs of the combat commands." The air force gave priority to strategic bombers, the army to guided missiles and atomic weapons, and the navy to supercarriers and large carrier aircraft when the unified commanders wanted more tactical fighters and transports, more divisions and tanks, and more nonaviation naval capabilities.[63]

Strategic planning, supposedly the province of the JCS and unified commands, was "dominated" by the services "through their review of JCS plans and the assignment to the Joint Staff of officers whose first loyalty was to their services." During this period, "allegiance to service above other entities remained the norm."

On Vessey's first day as chairman, the joint chiefs agreed to review their duties and performance and Jones's and Meyer's proposals for fundamental reform.[64] Meyer, who was still a member of the JCS, termed the review "very superficial. They didn't want to confront me. I didn't want to confront them. I didn't choose to make that a battlefield because I realized very quickly that change was not going to happen with Weinberger there. The best thing for me was to get out and take it on from the outside."[65]

Meyer judged that the secretary had a closed mind on reform. "Weinberger was a World War II veteran and had narrow blinders on. He had little imagination as to what should be done." Said Meyer of the secretary's thinking: "We had an Army that won World War II. There's no reason we can't win this war with the same approach." He found Weinberger unwilling to look at the need for greater "jointness."

Meyer's own relationship with Vessey also dissuaded him from forcing the issue. "I was leaving, and I didn't want to make Jack's job any harder. I knew I was going to fight this problem outside," he recalled.

When completed, the joint chiefs' review targeted OSD as the organization that needed reform. As they briefed that conclusion, a dispute erupted between the secretary's civilian and military advisers.[66]

Vessey did, however, help strengthen the JCS's ties with the president and defense secretary. When Reagan interviewed him for the chairman's job, they talked "about the importance of the president's getting military advice from the Joint Chiefs." When Vessey later accepted the job, he and Reagan "instituted regular quarterly meetings with the chiefs." Elated by this regular connection to the commander in chief, the JCS often ballyhooed this as a great organizational improvement, the fix that Admiral Hayward and other naval officers had argued would solve JCS problems.

The NSC staff believed the joint chiefs' presentations to the president offered little substance. Michael B. Donley, the NSC staffer in charge of arranging these meetings, said, "The Joint Chiefs always leaned in favor of absolute pap." Donley's colleague, John Douglass, termed the briefings "fluff."[67]

In terms of JCS performance, Vessey said, "The most important thing I felt that the chiefs needed to do was operate more as Joint Chiefs." By this, he meant emphasizing their duties as JCS members over their service roles. Vessey told each service chief that as a joint chief, "he had to hang his service cap on the peg outside the door and come in and take up a different set of duties."[68] Described as "a firm but fatherly squad leader," Vessey produced a more cooperative approach among the chiefs. His consensus-building lectures did not, however, resolve underlying differences.[69]

Early in his tenure, Vessey was credited with making the JCS "more influential than any of their predecessors in 20 years."[70] But his tenure was soon beset by operational and budgetary problems. One journalist observed: "As defense budgets soar, even some Pentagon officials complain that the Joint Chiefs have failed to overcome parochial interests and offer a coherent strategy for using the funds. Glitches in the Grenada invasion illustrated that the military services still have trouble operating in unison, and in both Grenada and Beirut, civilians have been frustrated by their inability to cut through the military's cumbersome chain of command."[71]

Yet Vessey continued to share Weinberger's conviction that no statutory changes in organization were needed. Of their views on reorganization, a former Pentagon official says, "I never saw any daylight between them."[72]

In June, 1984, Taft—who had been appointed deputy defense secretary in January—created an Ad Hoc Task Group on Defense Organization to "consider the options available to the department in the current legislative environment and present them for decision by the secretary."[73] Chapman B. Cox, the new OSD general counsel, chaired the seven-member group. Russ Rourke was one of two assistant defense secretaries on the panel. The other, Richard L. Armitage, handled international security affairs. A senior official represented each military department: Army Under Secretary James R. Ambrose, Navy Deputy Under Secretary Seth Cropsey, and Air Force Assistant Secretary Tidal W. McCoy. The final member, Vice Adm. Arthur S. Moreau, Vessey's special assistant, provided the joint perspective.

Despite its balanced appearance, the Cox Committee, as the group became known, heavily favored navy positions. Cox had come from the navy as an assistant secretary. David Berteau, the group's executive secretary, said, "Cox was seen as pro-Navy because that's where he came from, that's where his heart was, and everybody knew that's where he ultimately wanted to go as Lehman's replacement."[74]

McCoy, the air force representative, had worked closely with Lehman during the 1980 presidential campaign, and Lehman helped him land his assistant secretary position.[75] As a deputy CNO, Moreau had handled the navy's antireform efforts when Jones and Meyer initially pushed for reorganization. Along with Cropsey, Lehman's antireform henchman, these three gave the navy effective control of the group. *Defense Week* reported that the "group is dominated by Navy partisans."[76]

Berteau said that "the Pentagon established this group with a clear intention of 'if we can deep six this whole thing we've got to, and we can't do it without some kind of structure that is going to coordinate and unify our response.' . . . It could have been called the Ad Hoc Task Group to Prevent Defense Reorganization." The Pentagon assembled the right group: "None of the group's members was pro-reorganization."[77]

The group's meetings reflected this bias. According to Berteau, "We were trying to replace something with nothing." One initiative sought to have the Justice Department declare "congressional tampering with the chain of command" unconstitutional. Berteau described this undertaking as a "frontal assault on reorganization's legitimacy." The Justice Department rebuffed the Pentagon.[78]

The CSIS Defense Organization Project made a determined effort to work with the Cox Committee. "CSIS was reaching out to us to attempt to get us to embrace, or at least understand, some of what it was going to say in its report," said Berteau. "We didn't accept any of their ideas in any way, shape, or form." The Cox Committee responded by writing press statements and correspondence to Congress rebutting the CSIS report.

The committee also coordinated responses to congressional questions on reorganization—even after Congress prohibited such coordination. In 1984, Congress directed that answers to questions posed in the defense authorization act be sent directly by the responsible officials to the Senate and House Armed Services Committees without review by any intervening authority. "The Cox Committee complied with the letter of that requirement, but probably not with the spirit," said Berteau. "There were a number of discussions about what those answers might say before they were written. The JCS chairman's answers were not finalized until we had read the unified commanders' answers [in order] to counter any ill-advised comments." The committee, by ensuring the department's answers were "milk toast," made no intellectual contribution to the reorganization debate.

"Weinberger was badly served by the Cox Committee," said Barry Blechman of the CSIS project. "He received a very skewed, antireform view of the issues. If Weinberger had established a group more representative of various reform perspectives, he might have adopted a more responsible posture."[79] Given Weinberger's personality, however, it is unlikely that the Cox Committee could have changed his mind.

Weinberger did not have to wear down his key Pentagon colleagues on reorganization. They reinforced his stonewalling stance. Vessey, the top officer, fully supported the secretary, and so did the special group created to handle the issue.

With this backing and the president's unwavering support, Weinberger was ready to battle reformers in Congress and elsewhere.

CHAPTER 13

Naval Gunfire

The Navy, much more than any of the other services,

has cherished and clung to tradition.

—Carl H. Builder, *The Masks of War*

Brash, bright, feisty, Navy Secretary John F. Lehman Jr. was the Pentagon's foremost antireform hyperactivist. A chart in his 1985 posture statement symbolized his assault on Congress. To show the accuracy of 16-inch guns, it superimposed over Capitol Hill the results of test firings from the battleship *Iowa*. In the chart, according to a reporter, "The Capitol has been virtually obliterated and the nearby Rayburn House Office Building has taken its share of hits." Lehman said, "I thought it would be effective to take the actual data and transpose it over the Capitol so that they would get an idea of what the accuracy would look like . . . The tongue-in-cheek needling was intended as well."[1]

Members of Congress did not need the graphic reminder that the navy secretary was firing at them. In his early years at the navy's helm, Lehman often battled and defeated Congress.[2]

Lehman had vigorously opposed reorganization from the beginning, seeing it as a momentous issue whose outcome would determine whether the navy would maintain its independence and prerogatives. Having masterfully led an effort to revitalize the navy, Lehman was not about to see this resurgence undone by directives from the powerful central authority that reformers intended to create. The navy secretary entered this battle confidently, exhibiting his "undisguised zest for the forward attack in any contest."[3] His ruthless tactics normally prevailed. He aspired to emulate one predecessor, James V. Forrestal, who had defeated postwar unification reforms that the navy opposed. As he mounted his attack, Lehman "was at the pinnacle of his power, and arguably one of the most influential men in the capital."[4]

Lehman was "called everything from a maverick to a prima donna to the most dynamic secretary the Navy has ever had."[5] He ascended to the top navy job at age thirty-eight, one of the youngest navy secretaries ever. His Washington career began twelve years earlier on Henry Kissinger's National Security Council staff. After five years there, he joined the U.S. delegation to the Mutual Balanced Force Reduction talks in Vienna and later served as deputy director of the U.S. Arms Control and Disarmament Agency.

A native of Philadelphia, Lehman possessed impressive academic credentials. A 1964 graduate of St. Joseph's College, he attended Cambridge University in England for two years, departing with a bachelor's degree in honors law and a master's degree in international law and diplomacy. Returning to Philadelphia, Lehman completed doctoral coursework in international relations before heading to Washington and received his Ph.D. in 1974. By 1981, he had authored or coauthored five books on foreign policy, arms control, and aircraft carriers.

Upon graduation from St. Joseph's, Lehman enlisted in the Air Force Reserve. He transferred to the Naval Reserve in January, 1968, after retired admiral Arleigh Burke, who had befriended Lehman, arranged a direct appointment for him as an ensign.[6] Lehman qualified as both a helicopter pilot and a navigator-bombardier on A-6E aircraft and wore two sets of wings on his uniform. By the time he was sworn in as navy secretary, Lehman held the rank of lieutenant commander.

The conservative attack on Weinberger's nomination catapulted Lehman into the navy secretary job. After the uproar that followed Weinberger's selection of Frank Carlucci as his deputy and William Taft as his transition team head, hawks in the Republican Party, led by Senate Armed Services Committee members, reportedly were "allowed to make one key Pentagon appointment for each one made by Weinberger." The hawks placed Richard Perle, Fred Ikle, and John Lehman in key Pentagon posts.[7] At President-elect Reagan's December reception for the congressional leadership, Sens. John Tower and Scoop Jackson "cornered Reagan and said, 'Lehman is the guy you have to put in as Navy secretary.'" Lehman wanted the job because of "My deep concern for what was happening to the Navy, and my certain conviction that I knew how to fix it."[8]

Lehman entered the Pentagon on February 5, 1981, "as the darling of the hawks, the personal symbol to right-wing conservatives of Reagan's military buildup."[9] He had powerful patrons in the White House—including Vice Pres. George Bush and his old friend, Richard V. Allen, Reagan's national security adviser—and on Capitol Hill. Lehman effectively used these connections to advance his navy agenda. Conservative support also permitted him to take an independent stance in the Pentagon. Weinberger, especially in the beginning, did not want to anger conservatives by challenging Lehman.

Weinberger was no match for Lehman. One was a defense novice; the other was an expert. Weinberger was concerned only with his relationship with the president; Lehman tended a vast network of alliances. Also unlike Weinberger, Lehman demonstrated political savvy. When the defense secretary or other Pentagon powers tried to force decisions on Lehman, he "covertly ran to allies in the White House or in Congress and got his superiors overturned." Events in August, 1983, exemplified his guile.

Deputy Defense Secretary Paul Thayer, who had replaced Carlucci, instructed the navy secretary to cut one of two aircraft carriers in the next budget. Lehman instead used his White House allies, who were unaware of the Pentagon infighting, to obtain Reagan's approval of names for the two new carriers: *George Washington* and *Abraham Lincoln.* Weinberger was forced to overrule Thayer. In the White House press release announcing the names, the president also embraced for the first time the goal of having a six-hundred-ship navy.

Weinberger's laissez faire management style worked to Lehman's advantage. The defense secretary called his approach "controlled decentralization," but in reality it was uncontrolled. Weinberger gave the services "a relatively free hand" in setting priorities and allocating resources. He gave no firm policy or budget guidance and he was not adept at forcing the services to comply with his goals. A group of Democratic critics said, "It is like having traffic at a busy intersection directed by a blind man." Lehman often "took advantage of Weinberger's passiveness," without fear of retribution. Despite Lehman's transgressions, Weinberger—disdainful of confrontation—seldom scolded the navy secretary.[10]

General Colin Powell, who served as Weinberger's senior military assistant, later called Lehman "probably the ablest infighter in the building. Lehman would never budge an inch in the competition among the services. To him, the Navy position was always the Alamo." Hedrick Smith judges that Lehman accumulated more "real power and won more of what he was after than any other major figure in the Pentagon, including Weinberger."[11]

Weinberger later said, "Lehman was a very strong advocate of a very powerful navy. . . . He was extremely effective and very knowledgeable, but very vigorous and abrasive in his advocacy. [He left] a few victims and enemies along the path. . . . But he was helpful in building up the navy which was what we had to do." Weinberger's quick qualification, "Not all of it, but part of it," implied that Lehman's buildup was excessive.[12]

The navy's admirals also were no match for Lehman. Admiral King, the World War II CNO, and his successors usually turned navy secretaries, no matter how well qualified, into figureheads. Prior to the war, the department's civilian heads had wielded the real power, with the "top admirals having to defer all major decisions to the secretary." Lehman wanted "to reinstate the concept that it was the political leaders, not the sovereigns with stars on their shoulders, who should reign supreme over the Navy."[13]

Lehman instructed his lawyer to prepare a comprehensive account of the secretary's statutory powers, including laws that had been long forgotten. Lehman "wanted all the authority he could get." He would start by operating within the law, but "he would bend and circumvent the rules if need be and use every political means available to become the undisputed chief executive of the entire Navy." His power grab principally targeted the CNO, Adm. Thomas B. Hayward, whose character—reserved, gracious, and principled—was the opposite of Lehman's. The navy secretary "planned to take from Hayward as much power and responsibility as the law would allow and place it under his own control."[14]

The takeover was ruthless. Lehman exhibited "an uncompromising streak of independence, and an intellectual arrogance that brooked little internal disagreement or argument." The secretary repeatedly told naval officers: "Loyalty is agreeing with me." The careers of those who exhibited loyalty soared while those who challenged Lehman suffered. Of Lehman's first meeting with the admirals at navy headquarters, Adm. Stasser Holcomb later said: "It was a jarring experience. We had an activist secretary who was rude, who was arrogant." As his power grew, Lehman became more strident, especially with subordinate naval officers.[15]

Hayward and his fellow officers had nowhere to turn for help. Lehman had better connections at the White House and on Capitol Hill. Weinberger, who could have protected the uniformed navy, would not challenge Lehman, the favorite of conservatives. The defense secretary's novice status in the Pentagon also kept him from understanding the problem. Moreover, reigning in Lehman would clash with his management philosophy. Nor could Hayward appeal to the retired navy community: its most prominent members had backed Lehman's candidacy for secretary.

By early 1982, after just a year on the job, Lehman was in control of the sea service. He had relegated Hayward to "little more than a powerless, ceremonial figurehead." Many naval officers "hung their heads in shame and felt like fools for not standing up to Lehman. They resented his meddling, his cronyism, and his arrogant attitude that his decisions were the only ones that mattered. Now it was too late." Gloating over the way he had seized control, Lehman once told a journalist in an off-the-record setting: "The admirals don't understand that I've got *all* the power—money and promotions. I control their budget, and no one gets three or four stars without my OK."[16] Lehman would eventually accumulate more authority than he could use wisely.

Hayward retired in mid-1982 at the end of his four-year tour as CNO. He supported Adm. Jim Watkins as his replacement "because he felt Watkins would best be able to stand up to Lehman." According to colleagues, dealing with Lehman proved to be the toughest part of Watkins's job. Their stormy run-ins were known throughout the Pentagon. Watkins believed that Lehman was interfering in the CNO's legal responsibilities for personnel and operations.[17]

Lehman pushed a new naval strategy, called the Maritime Strategy, which envisioned U.S. aircraft carriers conducting strikes deep into the Soviet heartland. Watkins, so outspoken he was nicknamed "Radio Free Watkins," told reporters that Lehman's plan would bring the carriers "too close" to Soviet shores with great risks. He also said this decision belonged to either the CNO or JCS, not the navy secretary. Lehman disputed that view and later read to Watkins the duties of the navy secretary.[18]

The JCS also did not think Lehman's authority extended to naval strategy and operations. Calling the navy secretary "a noisy drum beater," General Vessey later said, "What annoyed the chiefs was that Lehman spoke as though he were the operator of the navy, when in fact Lehman was the man charged with organizing, training, recruiting, and equipping the navy for use by the unified and specified commands."[19]

Watkins won some battles with Lehman, such as when the secretary tried to alter *Seawolf* submarine specifications. The CNO "stormed into Lehman's office, irreverently pounding a fist on his boss's desk." Then, Lehman recalled, "He told me he didn't think I knew what I was talking about, that I was intruding where I had no business. In retrospect, he was right."[20] Congressional staffers attributed Lehman's desire to make all the decisions to his failure to understand that civilian control means keeping the military out of civilian decisions, not putting civilians into military decisions.

Lehman was also dealt aggressively with those outside the navy he believed were obstructing or criticizing his plans. He was so self-confident that he invited confrontation; he looked upon every critic as a potential convert. A journalist reported Lehman "curling his lip contemptuously at the 'petty bureaucrats' on Capitol Hill and 'lounge lizards in the Pentagon' who made his job difficult."[21]

Apparently, one of those lounge lizards was General Powell, whom Lehman attempted to have fired because he limited Lehman's access to Weinberger. Powell later wrote: "Not content to run the Navy, Lehman was forever pressing on Weinberger his ideas for running the entire defense establishment. Weinberger did not enjoy Lehman's aggressiveness, and I had to play the heavy, keeping him at bay. Not surprisingly, Lehman blamed me for depriving the secretary of the benefit of his brilliance. He went around the building claiming that I was not serving the secretary, but ingratiating myself with the Joint Chiefs of Staff to guarantee my future." Lehman urged Taft to have Weinberger fire Powell.[22]

Lehman did not shy from fights with members of Congress. His response to a letter from Cong. William J. Coyne (D-Pennsylvania) complaining about plans to name a new nuclear submarine *Pittsburgh* typified his creed of "fire back when fired upon." Coyne wrote, "If this administration wants to do something for Pittsburgh, it could do so by taking steps to reduce the [area's] double-digit unemployment." Lehman replied, "Thank you for your snide, tasteless letter. As a fellow Pennsylvanian, I know your extremist views do not represent those of the people of Pennsylvania or Pittsburgh."[23]

The navy secretary also boldly attacked Pentagon superiors in public. When Thayer attempted to reduce the navy's budget, Lehman complained to the *Washington Post*, "I'm sick and tired of spending 98 percent of my time up on the Hill undoing the damage that senior defense officials are doing to the president's budget. What I am trying to do is simply counter the guerrilla warfare by these defense officials who don't seem to understand what the president's program is all about." Although Thayer "hit the roof" and suggested he or Lehman had to go, Weinberger downplayed the navy secretary's attack, saying that he did not think Lehman was "guilty of outright insubordination."[24]

The navy prospered during Lehman's reign. In his first four years, its budget increased by 68 percent, and its fleet grew by fifty ships. Lehman had successfully sold the Maritime Strategy and a six-hundred-ship navy—121 more than the 1981 inventory. He also had elevated the navy's status, making it the most favored and visible service. "He's got a ready, fire, aim approach to everything," said a retired admiral, "but he's done more for the Navy than the last six or eight secretaries put together." Even Admiral Watkins concurred: "Perhaps he breaks china excessively, but to me the pluses so outweigh the negatives as to make the negatives irrelevant."[25]

Even critics marveled at Lehman's accomplishments. "Lehman is not a man to trifle with," said Rear Adm. Eugene J. Carroll Jr. "He's aggressive, confident, a real master of the bureaucratic process. He has an outstanding record in getting support for Navy programs, getting budget action to fund a major expansion. He has been more active and more effective in that role than any secretary of the Navy in modern memory." Senator Cohen agreed, calling Lehman the "most effective individual in the administration on defense policy . . . and probably the most effective service chief that I have seen, or anyone has seen, in a long, long time."[26]

Lehman also sought favorable press coverage. His public affairs officer's strategy "heaped so much positive press on Lehman" that Weinberger regularly sent "orders for Lehman to tone down his public image." Media reports "had painted Lehman as a golden boy, a man destined to go on to bigger and better things in the administration." Reporters touted Lehman as a future secretary of defense, national security adviser, senator, or even vice presidential candidate.[27]

The navy secretary became the Pentagon's media star. Hedrick Smith described his colorful reputation as "slick, cocky, rough-and-tumble operator, a self-proclaimed naval strategist and a showboater who enjoys making waves, thrives on controversy, knows his stuff, and has few peers as a bureaucratic infighter." Lehman craved the limelight. The flood of publicity often addressed

25. Secretary of the Navy John Lehman in front of a 16-inch gun
turret on the *New Jersey* battleship, September, 1982.
(U.S. Navy photo.)

"his irreverence, propensity for self-promotion, and outright arrogance."[28]
Negative coverage did not concern Lehman. I often heard him say, "There is no
such thing as bad publicity."

But Lehman also accumulated enemies. A veteran of three administrations
called him "one of the two or three slimiest men in Washington." A congressional staffer observed that Lehman will "generally do whatever is necessary, or
say whatever is necessary, to win the point." A journalist said he "used a dazzling array of creative tricks to get what he wants. He is famous for knifing his
enemies." Racking up victories, Lehman "wrecked careers, snookered Congress,
and lied to his bosses."[29]

Despite its successful buildup, the navy began experiencing "an endless number of foul-ups and disasters that began with the October 1983 bombing of the
Marine barracks." During the Grenada invasion, the navy "experienced problems on almost every front." Next, Vice Adm. Joseph Metcalf, commander of
the Grenada operation, botched the handling of the smuggling of Soviet-made
assault rifles into the United States. Then there was the Syrian shoot down of
navy jets in the Bekaa Valley, errant gunfire into Lebanon from the battleship
New Jersey, horror stories about astronomical prices paid for common items
following the ill-advised decision to eliminate the Naval Matériel Command
(which oversaw procurement), and irregularities in navy promotion boards.
The worst bad news, however, broke on May 20, 1985, when banner headlines
announced that FBI agents had arrested John Walker, his son, his brother, and
another man who had spied on the navy for eighteen years for the Soviet Union.
Earlier miscues blemished Lehman's record, but the last one was his undoing.[30]

This unprecedented security breach dragged the navy into its worst crisis
in years. After five months of stinging media and congressional criticism,
Weinberger, Lehman, and others met to discuss a plea bargain that would im-
prison John Walker for life and his son for twenty-five years. Although no one
at the meeting liked the plea bargain, they all agreed to it. However, when Justice Department lawyers announced the arrangement, Lehman lashed out,
saying it sent "the wrong message to the nation and to the fleet." He claimed
that he had objected to the deal: "We in the Navy are disappointed at the plea
bargain."[31]

Weinberger, who was surprised and angered by Lehman's double-cross,
fired back two days later: "Secretary Lehman now understands that he did not
have all the facts concerning the matter before he made several injudicious
and incorrect statements with respect to the plea-bargain."[32]

Lehman's backstabbing was the last straw. Weinberger "decided not to tolerate another of his affronts." Sixteen months later, on February 16, 1987, with
Lehman again meddling in a promotion board, Weinberger finally mustered
the courage to fire him. The navy secretary, who was on vacation with his family, was startled by the television news report that he had announced plans to
leave the Pentagon.

Lehman tells a different story: "In early February . . . I told Cap of my plan
to leave about the end of March, thereby giving him time to select my successor and to provide for a smooth transition. This turned out to be a serious miscalculation. Two days later, my intentions were leaked from Cap's office and
headlined in the press. Instantly, I was beset by resistance, rudeness, controversy, and downright insubordination . . . instead of a stately departure, I felt
like the retiring marshal of the Old West, backing out of the saloon with guns
blazing because every punk wants to take a shot at him on the way out."[33]

The admirals got in their digs when it came time for Lehman's farewell dinner: They declined their invitations. Only marine officers, led by the commandant, General Kelley, attended.[34]

Just before leaving office, Lehman took an off-the-cuff swipe at Senator Nunn, infuriating the new CNO, Adm. Carlisle A. H. Trost, who had replaced Watkins the previous summer. In a press interview several weeks afterward, Trost said Lehman's departure was "like a fresh breeze" because Lehman "was not a balanced human being." The admiral revealed that "The things that annoyed people about John Lehman were his disdain of senior military personnel, his tendency to override anyone who had a disagreement with him or contrary thought, and his habit of playing favorites: 'Play ball with me and you'll do well. Don't play ball with me and you're out.'" Trost added, "There was a saying he had: 'Loyalty is agreeing with me.' Well, that's not the military definition of loyalty. Loyalty is not to the individual, but to the service."[35]

"The admirals got a taste of real civilian control," a Lehman associate retorted, "and you know what? They found they didn't like it one little bit."[36]

The biggest blow to Lehman's reputation came more than a year after he left government service. On June 14, 1988, the FBI conducted raids in its largest investigation ever, Operation Illwind. The investigation's principal target was one of Lehman's closest associates, former Assistant Secretary of the Navy Melvyn Paisley. Eventually, more than ninety companies and individuals were convicted of felonies. Attorney General Richard Thornburgh called the investigation "the most sweeping and successful operation against white-collar fraud and defense procurement ever carried out by the Justice Department."[37]

Although Lehman was never connected to any wrongdoing, he was blamed for having "failed to keep closer track of the service's cumbersome procurement machinery." Andy Pasztor wrote: "The former Navy secretary's reputation has been stained forever by the scandal. His golden boy image has been equally tarnished, and his political aspirations may never recover. For years after the scandal broke, his mentor George Bush wanted nothing to do with him. Dreams of serving in the cabinet of some future Republican president have all but evaporated."[38]

But in early 1985, there was no inkling of Lehman's dazzling fall from grace. The secretary and his navy were riding high, gunning for Capitol Hill reformers. In February, during an air force flight bringing the American delegation home from the Wehrkunde security conference in Munich, West Germany, Lehman brainstormed his antireform attack. Joining him were Sen. Pete Wilson, who mostly listened, SASC staffers Jim McGovern and Carl Smith, and Capt. Thomas C. Lynch, head of the navy's Senate liaison office. So "cocky and confident" that they would defeat the reorganization effort, Lehman and his cabal brazenly plotted in front of a "shocked" Benjamin F. Schemmer, editor of *Armed Forces Journal.* Schemmer, a proreformer with close ties to Senator Goldwater, could not report on or mention this plotting because all discussions on the flight were off the record.[39]

Schemmer said the cabal mostly attacked Goldwater, who in their view "didn't have the foggiest notion as to what kind of buzz saw he was running into." Schemmer said McGovern and Smith showed "no loyalty or respect for Goldwater." Their attitude toward their boss was "almost contempt."[40]

"This is going to be the damnedest coup ever pulled on Capitol Hill or the Pentagon," Lehman and his plotters exulted. They were going to handily defeat reorganization by themselves. They did not need Secretary Weinberger or the JCS chairman, General Vessey. The cabal "already had lots of crap under way" with much more to follow. They envisioned an active role for Sen. Phil Gramm, who, they claimed, "We've got in our pocket." Schemmer found the group's plotting "blatant, gross, sinister, disgusting." The scheming and bragging apparently became too much for Senator Wilson, who excused himself after forty-five minutes. Lehman and others repeatedly taunted Schemmer with their blustering of how they would crush the reform campaign. Of this coming defeat, they boasted, "There's nothing you or anyone else can do about it, Schemmer."[41]

Lehman admired Navy Secretary James Forrestal, who later became the first secretary of defense. The Soviet newspaper *Pravda*'s comparison of Forrestal and him delighted Lehman, who said the paper "denounced me, saying in effect another maniac like Jim Forrestal has taken over the Navy. And if he keeps on this way, he will end up just like Forrestal. Which I thought was great."[42]

Recalling his predecessor's role in the unification battle, Lehman wrote: "Thanks to . . . Forrestal, the Navy had won very significant compromises in retaining some independence within the new department."[43] However, less than a year later Forrestal called those compromises a terrible mistake. Lehman ignored Forrestal's confession. Navy attitudes had changed little during the thirty-four years between its two most powerful postwar secretaries. Fears and prejudices ingrained during the unification fight fueled Lehman's antireform crusade.

A Princeton graduate, Forrestal had served as president of a New York investment firm before coming to Washington. He started in June, 1940, as an administrative assistant to President Roosevelt. Three months later, Roosevelt appointed Forrestal to the new post of navy under secretary, where he served during most of World War II.

As the army-navy debate over the unification of the War and Navy Departments intensified in the spring of 1944, Secretary of the Navy Frank Knox surprised Secretary of War Henry L. Stimson by privately saying he "strongly favored" a single department. Then, in one of those twists of history, the day Knox was scheduled to formally state his views on unification to a House committee, he died of heart failure.[44] Forrestal succeeded Knox and took the opposite position. His testimony was "cautious but firm, arguing against unification, yet asking not for rejection but only postponement and further study."

Throughout 1944 and 1945, Forrestal and other navy witnesses testified against unification. The hearings created a public perception of the navy position as "negative and defensive." Forrestal became "increasingly aware of a profound emotional resistance to [army-navy] integration within the Navy officer corps," a group, however, that "seemed incapable of a persuasive defense." By the fall of 1945, the navy secretary was resigned that "some form of unification legislation was inevitable" but he was determined to prevent "a shotgun marriage."[45]

In November, Forrestal brought Rear Adm. Arthur W. Radford, who later became the second JCS chairman, to the Pentagon to lead antiunification efforts. Radford, described as "confident and combative to the point of recklessness," played "hardball politics all day every day." He recruited other hard-chargers, including Forrest P. Sherman, who later served as CNO.[46] This group, especially Radford, became excessively uncompromising and complicated Forrestal's efforts.

In a message to Congress on December 19, 1945, President Truman endorsed the army's approach and proposed a single department led by a single cabinet-level officer, a single chief of staff, and assistant secretaries for land, naval, and air forces. Truman's naval aide and later special counsel, Clark Clifford, described these proposals as "the most radical reorganization of our armed forces in the nation's history." Clifford later wrote that Truman's recommendations, despite their merit, "never had a chance" because of opposition from the navy and Cong. Carl Vinson, chairman of the House Naval Affairs Committee.[47]

The president's proposals made two major concessions to the navy. Although Truman had wanted to consolidate all aviation in the new air force, he agreed to allow the navy to retain its aviation. "He also agreed, reluctantly, to maintain the Marine Corps as a separate military branch within the Navy, instead of abolishing it, as both he and the Army desired." Clifford adds, "In his heart, he always felt that there was no need for a separate Marine Corps; over time, I reached the same conclusion. But the political power of the Marine Corps was overwhelming."[48]

Forrestal's greatest apprehension centered on Truman's plans to create a single chief of staff to command all forces. He also "feared that the creation of a separate Air Force would make the Navy the odd man out in interservice fights." The navy secretary told Clifford: "We are fighting for the very life of the Navy."[49]

Freed by Truman to present his personal views to Congress, Forrestal's testimony countered the president's proposals but avoided emotional rhetoric. The Marine Corps commandant, Gen. Alexander A. Vandegrift, did not show equal restraint. On May 6, 1946, he charged that the proposals "will in all probability spell extinction for the Marine Corps" because its "very existence" represented "a continuing affront to the War Department General Staff." Vandegrift's testimony "opened up a highly emotional issue in almost inflammatory terms, one which was to complicate and distort the debate from that day forward."[50]

On May 12, Clifford advised Truman that "the Army's position might be correct on its merits, but was politically out of reach" and that he had to choose between concessions to the navy or no bill at all. The next day, the president pressed Forrestal and Secretary of War Robert Patterson to quickly agree on a "mutually acceptable plan of unification." Two weeks later, the secretaries reported they had failed to resolve four issues: creation of a separate air force, navy retention of land-based aircraft, Marine Corps roles and missions, and unification of the services under a single secretary. When he read this report, Truman "all but snorted in annoyance and contempt."[51]

Seeking common ground, the president conceded the idea of a single chief of staff, granted the navy the right to operate land-based aircraft, and accepted the Marine Corps with its own aviation as a separate navy entity. The president reaffirmed his goal of a single department headed by a single cabinet-level secretary.

Scorning these concessions, Forrestal replied that he "was totally opposed to the idea of a single Department of National Defense." He also suggested, for the first time, that he might resign rather than support unification.[52]

Clifford wrote that "letting Forrestal go may have tempted the president, but it would have enraged the Navy's powerful supporters in Congress, further entrenched the rest of the Navy, turned Forrestal into a martyr, and doomed hope for military unification on *any* basis. Knowing this, the president began a slow, patient, and skillful strategy designed to move Forrestal as far as possible without losing him." Noting his own original pronavy sentiments, Clifford began to feel that Forrestal "was showing excessive rigidity."

Forrestal apparently agreed. His negotiations with War Department officials left him feeling that "further flexibility in the Navy position was necessary." At the same time, however, he seemed increasingly "under the influence of Radford and his band of hot-eyed true believers." While Forrestal was edging toward the War Department's logic, naval officers maintained their "powerful desire to remain totally independent." The secretary was trapped "between his instincts and his loyalty to the Navy."

Following the lead of the Radford group, naval officers adopted "narrow, rigid perspectives" and an "increasingly strident, reckless stance" that Forrestal "seemed unable to moderate." Attitudes and actions by Army Air Forces officers had driven the navy "further into defensiveness and paranoia." Officers at the new Air University proclaimed the soon-to-be-created air force's primary objective to be "complete domination of all military air activities in the United States."[53] In an off-the-record speech to a heavily navy audience, an Air Corps brigadier general said the "Army Air Forces is tired of being a subordinate outfit." He advised that it would be the predominant force in war and peace and "is going to run the show." Calling the marines "a small bitched-up army talking Navy lingo," he said, "We are going to put those Marines in the Regular Army and make efficient soldiers out of them."[54]

In November, 1946, finally realizing that Radford was "incapable of compromise," Forrestal turned to Sherman for help in negotiating a settlement. On January 16, the war and navy secretaries announced an agreement. To placate Forrestal, the army dropped the idea of a single department. Instead, a "Secretary of National Defense" would direct a loose organization of autonomous departments, later strangely titled the National Military Establishment (NME). The three military departments would retain their status as individual executive departments and continue to function independently. The service secretaries would lose their cabinet seats, but would sit on the new National Security Council. Of the agreement, Clifford writes, "It left real power in the hands of the services, and gave the Secretary of National Defense almost no real authority, but this was the best the president could get at the time, and he decided to accept it."[55]

On February 26, Truman sent legislation embodying the agreement to Congress and "heartily recommended" passage. According to Clifford, despite the magnitude of the concessions they had won, "the Marines and Navy were still very unhappy." General Vandegrift felt "the Navy sold out to the Army" by not insisting that the law codify service roles and missions.[56]

As Congress considered the proposed bill, only naval aviators and marines continued active opposition.[57] The admirals had pushed Forrestal farther than he wanted to go; when they could not push him any farther, they refused to honor his compromise.

Vandegrift testified that the bill's failure to specify Marine Corps functions was "a source of grave concern" to him, and dramatically proclaimed that it allowed "the corps to be stripped of everything but name—to reduce it to a role of military impotence." Naval aviators, including Radford, testified against creating "a separate department for the Army Air Forces," or establishing a secretary of defense, preferring instead a presidential deputy or assistant for national security affairs. The naval aviators also pushed for a second naval officer on the JCS who, by law, would be an aviator.[58]

Unrestrained opposition by naval and marine officers weakened the compromise and "had a significant impact on the final legislation." Amendments "diluted the authority of the secretary of defense." Other amendments gave naval aviation and the Marine Corps statutory protection.[59]

Army officials, including Patterson and the chief of staff, General Eisenhower, "expressed disappointment . . . about the final bill and their private disgust at the behavior of the Navy." They felt that the navy's conduct violated the compromise agreement. Also disappointed, Truman said, "Maybe we can strengthen it as time goes on."[60]

On July 26, after nearly four years of exhausting bureaucratic conflict, Truman signed the National Security Act of 1947. Two Forrestal biographers later judged the law "a victory for paranoia and narrow, institutional self-interest."[61]

The navy and Marine Corps were dragged kicking and screaming into the new NME. Moreover, Air Force Secretary W. Stuart Symington's aggressive campaign for a large air force "created a near-siege mentality in the Navy, anxious to find weapons and missions" to ensure its equality with the army and air force.[62] The air force and navy battled "with all of the skill and tenacity that their planners and analysts could muster." In early 1948, navy leaders judged that they were losing ground "to a better organized Air Force campaign."[63] The B-36 bomber was the air force's premier new weapon system. A War Department press release extolled its capabilities: "The six-engine . . . B-36 heavy bomber could carry an atomic bomb to any inhabited region in the world and return home without refueling."[64]

Air force aspirations represented a major threat to the navy, whose "leaders, both aviators and nonaviators had emerged from the war convinced of carrier aviation's importance to the fleet's offensive and defensive effectiveness." The navy pinned its hopes on a new supercarrier capable of launching long-range attack aircraft carrying atomic weapons.[65]

While this fight raged, Forrestal attempted to make the NME work. He encountered services with "strong differences over the division of appropriated funds, kinds of military forces needed, roles and missions, and how the new NME should operate." The services' "traditional parochialism and distrust of each other" magnified these disputes. Unable to exercise effective control, Forrestal concluded that "the National Security Act would have to be amended to enhance the secretary's authority." The army and air force encouraged Forrestal. The navy strongly opposed the thinking of its former secretary.[66]

With its fight against the air force faltering and greater unification efforts under way, navy morale was low. Two personnel changes in early 1949 further depressed it. In January, Eisenhower, who had just retired, was asked to serve part-time as "presiding officer" of the JCS, replacing Admiral Leahy, who was ill and soon to retire. In late March, Louis A. Johnson succeeded Forrestal, who was having a nervous breakdown. "A hard-nosed West Virginia millionaire lawyer," Johnson had served as a World War I army officer, assistant secretary of war, and director of an aircraft corporation. He announced plans to "build up the Air Force and trim the Navy."[67]

On April 15, Johnson asked Eisenhower and the three joint chiefs if he should go ahead with building the navy's supercarrier, the *United States*. When only the CNO, Adm. Louis E. Denfeld, argued for construction, Johnson canceled it. The secretary had cleared this action with Truman, but he never consulted with anyone in the navy or on Capitol Hill. As soon as he heard the news, Navy Secretary John L. Sullivan resigned in protest. Naval leaders and congressional supporters were infuriated by Johnson's "highhanded" action, and the navy responded by attacking the B-36. General Omar N. Bradley, the army chief, described the atmosphere: "All hell was breaking loose in the Navy. The pent-up rage and frustration exploded in public."[68]

In early May, 1949, an "anonymous document" leaked to members of Congress alleged that serious improprieties had occurred during the air force's procurement of the B-36 and implied that Johnson and Symington had financially benefited. The document also declared that the bomber could not achieve its performance specifications. Cedric R. Worth, special assistant to the navy under secretary, was later identified as the document's author. "The leak was a shocking charge and it generated screaming headlines nationwide," Bradley said. After extensive hearings in August, the House Armed Services Committee dismissed the charges "as utterly without credence."[69] This verdict damaged the navy's credibility.

A navy court of inquiry investigated the circumstances behind the "Anonymous Document." Officers working in the CNO's office admitted helping Worth write it. The court decided not to punish them because they did not know the paper would be sent outside the navy. After the court recessed, Capt. John G. Crommelin, a distinguished naval aviator and critic of unification then serving on the Joint Staff, issued a statement to reporters at his home "alleging that members of the Joint Chiefs of Staff and Secretary Johnson were intent on eliminating the Navy as a separate service." He asserted that the navy was being "nibbled to death."[70]

Other naval officers, including Fleet Adm. William F. Halsey, supported Crommelin's statements. These developments angered the new navy secretary, Francis P. Matthews. To him, they indicated an antiunification attitude.[71]

The HASC convened a second round of hearings in October. In a campaign that came to be known as the "Revolt of the Admirals," uniformed navy leaders, including Denfeld, testified that strategic bombing served no useful purpose and was morally wrong. They attacked the B-36 as a mistake but argued that the supercarrier was vital. Refutations by air force witnesses "convinced the majority of the committee." Bradley, who had become the first JCS chairman in August, testified that the real issue was the navy's refusal to accept unification "in spirit as well as deed."[72]

Secretary Matthews dismissed Denfeld as CNO for his testimony. He retired rather than take another assignment.

Bradley later harshly criticized the naval officers: "Never in our military history has there been anything comparable—not even the Billy Mitchell rebellion of the 1920s. A complete breakdown in discipline occurred. Neither Matthews nor Denfeld could control his subordinates. Most naval officers despised Matthews. Denfeld, in my judgment, had abandoned, or at least grossly neglected, his disciplinary responsibilities in an apparent, and unwise, effort to straddle the fence. Denfeld gave lip service to unification, yet he allowed his admirals to run amok. It was utterly disgraceful."

From such beginnings, the navy remained a reluctant partner in the Department of Defense through the mid-1980s. On nearly every issue, the navy sought to retain its independence. A 1960 effort by President Eisenhower and Defense Secretary Thomas S. Gates Jr. to institute new arrangements for strategic forces exemplified the navy's resistance. Gates devised a plan for a National Strategic Target List and a Single Integrated Operational Plan (SIOP) to be prepared by the Strategic Air Command staff, augmented by officers from all services. He could not obtain JCS approval. The navy's lone dissent blocked approval. With Eisenhower's consent, Gates overrode the navy's objections.[73]

Its tradition of poor interservice cooperation and resistance to unification made the navy the butt of many barbs. While Admiral Moorer was CNO, he boasted to the other joint chiefs about a successful naval operation: "Once again the Navy has saved the nation." A civilian retorted, "Well, Admiral, now that you have saved the nation, how about joining it?"[74]

Weinberger saw Lehman's attitudes as consistent with forty years of navy resistance: "Carrying on the naval tradition, Lehman resented hotly the whole idea of the creation of the Office of the Secretary of Defense and the Defense Department. He wanted to be completely independent, deal directly with Congress and the president, which was not the role of the service secretary. . . . But, basically, what bothered him most was the fact that there was a Department of Defense over him and over the other service secretaries."[75]

In the reorganization battle with Congress, Lehman wanted Weinberger to shift from defensive stonewalling to active crusading. A January, 1985, memorandum to Lehman from Seth Cropsey suggested that this was unlikely: "The real issue is still Weinberger's unwillingness to deal with this problem, publicly, seriously, forcefully. Chapman [Cox] and I have discussed this, and he believes that SECDEF will do nothing to cross Vessey, and that CJCS will do nothing to cross Weinberger. I am, of course, thrilled at their warm personal relationship. But for us, it simply means gridlock. And, as long as it persists, we will be fighting a rearguard action, one that leaves too much influence over the outcome in the hands of our active antagonists on the Hill. In short, Chapman will not push Weinberger hard to get mean, and we will have to leave more to Fate than I think we have any right to expect she will provide us."[76]

In the absence of an active role by Weinberger, Lehman had developed his own antireform strategy. Making reorganization a partisan issue represented its centerpiece. In private lobbying, Lehman repeatedly charged that Democrats were going to make reform a political issue. Like Goldwater and Nunn, he understood that the reorganization campaign could not withstand the burdens of partisan politics. The navy secretary saw partisanship as the stake he could drive through the heart of reorganization. He began publicly claiming that the Democratic agenda was driving reform. "The reason this is such a big issue now is that the Democrats, . . . Sam Nunn and Les Aspin, have realized this is the way to steal the defense issue from the Republicans and make it the number-one issue in the next presidential campaign."[77]

A campaign speech by Democratic presidential candidate Walter Mondale provided evidence. Speaking to the American Legion in September 1984, Mondale promised: "I will reform the Joint Chiefs of Staff system. I will streamline its operation with a stronger chairman and clear lines of command authority to ensure better management of our defense buildup, a better match between strategy and resources, and better prepared fighting forces. I want the commanders who will actually face the fight in Europe and in Asia and elsewhere to have a bigger say in our defense policies. And I want the chairman of the Joint Chiefs to sit as an equal partner on the National Security Council."[78]

Aspin gave Lehman additional ammunition. In a speech to the Committee for a Democratic Majority on April 17, 1985, he identified Pentagon reform as an area of Democratic opportunity. "The Democratic party should be out front beating the drum for change, to give the chairman of the JCS and the Joint Staff more authority so they won't always be pushed around by the services. It makes sense politically, because the public is eager for proposals to cut down on service bickering."[79]

Washington Post journalist Mary McGrory reported similar Aspin comments in a July column. She said that he promised the Democratic Policy Commission "that if they concerned themselves with such questions as the reform of the Joint Chiefs of Staff system, the 'prize is the presidency.'" A Lehman memorandum to Weinberger called Aspin's statement "surely the most blatant admission by an advocate of JCS reorganization of the partisan, political motives of the movement."[80]

Congressman Bill Nichols closely watched Aspin's partisan tendencies. Nichols had labored hard to keep the reorganization work of his Investigations Subcommittee bipartisan. According to HASC staffer Arch Barrett, after Aspin became HASC chairman, anytime things started to look partisan, "Nichols would often have a meeting of the principals, including Aspin, and he'd get it back on a bipartisan track."[81]

Lehman attempted to convince Republican senators that Nunn was taking advantage of Goldwater. The staff grapevine repeatedly reported to me that

Lehman was making this argument privately in Senate offices. Lehman and his colleagues could not openly make this charge, which belittled Goldwater's capabilities as SASC chairman. Lehman cruelly and unfairly criticized the Arizona senator, saying his age and health problems had diminished his capacities and made him vulnerable to manipulation.

Lehman's strategy involved rallying the navy faithful on Capitol Hill. In 1984, eighteen senators had served in the navy, and nine in the Marine Corps. But the forty senators who once wore army green and the eleven who once wore air force blue were also susceptible to Pentagon antireform arguments. Lehman also sought to garner support from those states and districts with significant naval interests. The navy secretary had increased his congressional support with his Strategic Homeporting Initiative. Ostensibly to reduce their vulnerability to Soviet nuclear attack, new navy ships would be dispersed in ten to twelve new ports. Lehman "had politicians all over the country eating out of his hand, angling for new naval bases, construction, and jobs." Seeing the expensive initiative as traditional pork-barrel politics, critics called it "Strategic Homeporking." Goldwater told Weinberger the scheme was "pure unadulterated politics." Despite many objections, Lehman sustained this initiative and expanded the circle of navy supporters in Congress.[82]

Lehman relied on dozens of service and veterans associations for lobbying help on Capitol Hill. A journalist assessed them as playing "a significant, if typically subtle and little-noticed, role in the complex, protracted process by which defense policy is made." Most associations were headquartered in or near the nation's capital with chapters throughout the United States. The Navy League, Fleet Reserve Association, Association of Naval Aviation, Marine Corps League, and Marine Corps Association were top Navy Department supporters. Their nonprofit status caused them to downplay their lobbying efforts and "vigorously reiterate the educational nature of their mission." The Navy League's mission statement is typical: "dedicated to the education of our citizens, including our elected officials, and the support of the men and women of the sea services and their families."[83]

The associations found numerous ways to lobby without lobbying. They prepared and distributed issue reports, published articles in their magazines, and urged members to contact their congressmen. The Association of Naval Aviation "fought so vociferously" for congressional approval of the aircraft carrier *Theodore Roosevelt* that Lehman called it "the ANA carrier." Following the February, 1985, release of the CSIS report, Lehman asked General Barrow, a retired former commandant, if he would mobilize the marine associations. He also asked Barrow if he would be willing to write a commentary for the *Washington Post*, do other writing and speaking, and contact congresspersons.[84]

Lehman's antireform strategy included generating publicity. A memorandum by his special assistant for public affairs outlining immediate plans described four print media activities. The Chief of Naval Information would place a Lehman antireform article in as many newspapers as possible across the country. An article by Seth Cropsey would be delivered to the *American Spectator.* A Lehman commentary would appear in the next *Navy Times,* and Chief of Naval Information Branch Offices at navy bases—which were viewed as key to keeping this issue "visible"— would deliver reprints to editorial writers at *most* newspapers in their districts and "encourage their editorial consideration." The navy secretary would meet with *USA Today*'s editorial board the following week, and meetings with editorial boards from *Forbes* and *Newsweek* were to be conducted soon.[85]

The memorandum advised that an appearance without opposition on a CNN talk show could be arranged. The three major network Sunday talk shows would want opposing viewpoints. Other possibilities were John McLaughlin's *One on One* program and Larry King's *Let's Talk.*

Asked to comment on reorganization's prospects during one press interview, Lehman said, "I think it will perk along for a few more years. It's the kind of thing think tanks like to hold seminars on, so it will go on and on. I don't think any substantial changes will come of it, because the current system works." Lehman thought reformers failed to focus on the real problems.[86]

Lehman used six basic arguments to counter reorganization. Three sought to shift the focus of debate to organizational problems—Congress, excessive bureaucracy, and overcentralization—that Lehman argued should have the highest priority. His three other arguments sought to rebut reorganization proposals. These topics let Lehman go on the offensive rather than defend the status quo. The navy secretary asserted that Congress should be the first target of reform, saying, "The principal cause of military inefficiency is the micromanagement and the anarchy in Congress." He described its dimensions: "Ten years ago four committees wrote legislation on defense. Today 24 committees and 40 subcommittees oversee defense. By actual measurement, current law and regulation on defense procurement fill 1,152 linear feet of law library shelf space. Thousands of new pages are enacted yearly and almost none removed." Finally, Lehman argued, "The proliferation of legislative participation has reached the point where it is impossible to carry out what was intended by the Founding Fathers."[87]

The navy secretary prescribed two fixes for Capitol Hill. First, "We need no new legislation; we need the repeal of hundreds of linear feet of existing statutes and regulations." Second, he urged: "We need Congress to end the current chaos of subcommittees and reassert an orderly, strong role in meeting its constitutional responsibilities through a reasonable number of serious subcommittees."[88]

Lehman's second argument claimed that one problem behind organizational deficiencies was "too much bureaucracy." He said, "What has been created over the past 40 years is an incredible and unwieldy monster" born under the names of "reform, interservice unity, jointness, and reform progress." He repeatedly cited staff growth: "The Office of the Secretary of Defense, originally 50 people, is now 2,000 people. The Joint Staff, originally to be not more than 100 people, is now 2,000 people. The Office of the Secretary of the Navy, the Chief of Naval Operations and the Commandant of the Marine Corps, originally to be 300 people, is now 2,000 people. The Defense Logistics Agency, originally to be the 'coordinator' of commodities, is now 50,000 people. There are eleven defense agencies, nine joint and specified commands with staffs that run into the thousands each."[89]

Echoing debates of forty years earlier, Lehman said, "This vast bloat has all been done over the past 30 years in the name of reformation at the altar of the false idols of centralization and unification." His fix for "bureaucratic elephantiasis" was simple: "We need no new bureaucratic entities; we need a large reduction in the number and size of existing ones."[90]

Related to Lehman's bureaucratic growth argument was his charge of "too much centralization." While praising Weinberger for decentralizing authority to the service secretaries, he criticized reformers for wanting more centralization. "For 30 years," he said, "the reform movement has had one needle stuck in one groove, which is centralize, centralize, centralize. Talk about 'Johnny One-Notes'!" Lehman cited decentralization trends in successful American businesses as examples for the Pentagon, then added: "We need no more centralization and unification; we need more decentralization and accountability through which the strong secretary of defense can unify all efforts to a central policy."[91]

Lehman's arguments about Congress and excessive bureaucracy identified legitimate problems. The SASC was addressing both. The first had high priority. The second had appropriately been placed in the second tier of issues.

His charge about overcentralization, while effective, was false. Reorganization targeted the lack of sufficient central authority, both civilian and military, to make DoD function effectively. Lehman's arguments would have been valid for a well-organized entity, such as leading American businesses, but they did not fit an excessively decentralized Pentagon.

In attacking reorganization proposals, Lehman claimed proposed fixes would subvert civilian control, suppress disagreements among senior military advisers, and dilute the authority of operational commanders. He threw out one-liners about proposed reforms creating a Prussian general staff, but he did not dwell on that accusation. The navy secretary sneered at reformers, calling them "armchair academics," "parlor-room Pershings," and "amateur Bismarcks." Of civilian control, he argued that a new "super-chairman," offering only one military view, "would become the de facto commander-in-chief with the secretary of defense made irrelevant and the president kicked upstairs as a kind of chairman of the board on military matters."[92]

Lehman said making the JCS chairman the principal military adviser would make him the "sole source" of military advice. Moreover, he asserted that this one man would be "served by 'purple suiters' removed from operational responsibility and increasingly remote from operational experience." The navy secretary also warned that "suppressing the full range of ideas and information the Joint Chiefs provide will isolate civilian authorities from the critical issues and thus hamper, rather than enhance, wise decision making." The end result "would be radically to reduce civilian control of the military, and eliminate the freedom of choice of the president in making defense decisions."[93]

According to Lehman, a strengthened JCS chairman also endangered the unified commanders. "To interpose a super-chairman and his general staff in Washington between the CINCs and the secretary of defense and president," he argued, "adds yet another layer of bureaucracy to the chain of command and encourages second-guessing by remote, over-eager Pentagon staffers who lack both the on-scene judgment and the ultimate responsibility for our forces."

Lehman's first two arguments against reform repeated decades-old navy themes, only with more extreme rhetoric. The navy secretary's discussion of a strengthened chairman endangering the unified commanders was a stretch. In the existing system, the JCS, collectively and individually, had a stranglehold on the emasculated unified commanders. Much of his script was second-rate; Lehman's dynamic salesmanship generated more support and interest than he had a right to expect.

As with all other navy activities, Lehman called the shots in the antireform fight. The uniformed navy "broadly supported" his efforts, although some admirals and other officers "were worried about the potential backlash to Lehman's uncompromising resistance." The secretary was making powerful enemies on Capitol Hill, where memories lasted "far longer than the tenure of even the most durable service secretaries." In the 1940s, the admirals had pushed Forrestal farther than he wanted to go. In the 1980s, Lehman was going farther than the admirals thought advisable.[94]

Forrestal's success in shaping the National Security Act more to the navy's liking represented the climax of his career with the Navy Department. His achievements were grand: "He had defended his beloved Navy with brilliance and tenacity and . . . preserved for the Navy a large measure of freedom from unwanted interference."[95]

Lehman sought a similar historic success. He had reason to be optimistic. His position appeared more favorable than Forrestal's. The Defense Department was united in opposing reorganization and had strong allies on Capitol Hill and in the influential retired military community. The president was strongly connected to the military and consistently supported Weinberger and the Pentagon's opposition to reorganization. Most in Congress were ignorant on defense organization and reluctant to challenge the military on this sacred subject.

In fourteen years in government, Lehman had never lost a "big fight." His "genius for bureaucratic politics" enabled his extraordinary successes.[96] With his unbeaten streak intact, Lehman prepared for combat with Congress.

PART 3

Marshaling Forces

CHAPTER 14

McFarlane Outflanks the Pentagon

It is axiomatic that you must secure your own flanks

and rear, and turn those of the enemy.

—Frederick the Great,

Instructions for His Generals

Bud McFarlane, Reagan's national security adviser, recalls that defense decision making had concerned him "since March 8, 1965, when I commanded a Marine battery in the first landing of American forces in Vietnam. In that war, the military's lack of preparedness for guerrilla warfare and inability to apply its strategic advantage represented a dysfunctional planning and decision-making system. Since that day, trying to improve Pentagon planning and management has been an important goal for me."[1]

As interest in defense reorganization grew, McFarlane wanted the administration to play a constructive role. But Defense Secretary Weinberger, Reagan's close friend, remained unyieldingly opposed to reform. He was also McFarlane's nemesis. After their policy dispute over the marine deployment to Lebanon, Weinberger viewed McFarlane as an enemy and repeatedly clashed with him.[2] In deference to his agenda of other critical issues and the coming presidential election, McFarlane shied away from tangling with Weinberger on reorganization.

However, two members of McFarlane's National Security Council staff—Mike Donley and Lt. Col. John W. Douglass, USAF—were convinced that defense reform was so important to the president that McFarlane had to take on and defeat Weinberger. For ten months, Donley and Douglass fruitlessly schemed and prodded McFarlane.

Then Douglass covertly gained congressional support for a presidential commission, creating an opening whereby McFarlane might possibly prevail. The national security adviser decided to fight the defense secretary in what became an epic struggle for the commander in chief's support.

McFarlane, a soft-spoken workaholic, had risen rapidly through the civilian ranks of government after retiring from the military in 1979. While on active duty, the short, trim, marine lieutenant colonel and former White House Fellow had served for five years as an assistant to two national security advisers: Henry Kissinger and Lt. Gen. Brent Scowcroft.

McFarlane began his civilian career as a Republican staffer on the Senate Armed Services Committee, arriving about a year after I joined the Democratic staff. We were often counterparts on foreign policy issues. After a year and a half with the committee, McFarlane joined the incoming Reagan administration. He was first posted at the State Department in an under-secretary-level position focusing on special projects and troubleshooting. He moved to the White House a year later as the deputy national security adviser before being promoted to the top NSC position in October, 1983.

McFarlane knew key SASC members like Goldwater and Nunn, and he understood congressional politics like few others in the executive branch. During his committee service, senators and staffers viewed McFarlane as a superstar. They trusted him and respected his broad knowledge, professionalism, and serious, quiet, self-effacing style. His boss, Senator Tower, called McFarlane "one of the best geopolitical minds in this town."[3] Two combat tours in Vietnam and NSC staff jobs gave him expertise and experience that were rare on Capitol Hill.

With McFarlane at the NSC, SASC members and staff felt that they had someone at the White House with whom they could talk. Weinberger's limited repertoire of shallow refrains had consistently disappointed members.

McFarlane had high standing with his NSC staff. Donley compared him to Scowcroft in his integrity and demeanor and how he handled things. Similarities to Scowcroft were understandable. McFarlane viewed the former air force general as "my mentor, and kind of like my father."[4]

In May, 1984, Tower provided McFarlane a draft of the SASC staff study on defense reorganization. During their meeting, Tower "strongly urged the administration to launch an initiative on Pentagon reform or else risk being overtaken by congressional action." He also argued there was a need to "address the growing congressional cynicism [of] the Department of Defense" and urged a broad study.[5]

"Cap Weinberger is not sympathetic to the idea and will oppose it," McFarlane replied.[6]

Although parts of the draft committee study were incomplete and others inconclusive, some problems were well documented. The study reinforced many of McFarlane's concerns about Pentagon performance. He judged it "analytically sound."[7]

The Defense Department's recommendations during crises especially troubled McFarlane. During his first two weeks as national security adviser he had found the Pentagon's operational plans to be lax and inadequate. The marine barracks bombing in Beirut and the sloppy conduct of the Grenada incursion had demonstrated crucial flaws in Pentagon planning and operations.

Although principally blaming policy "paralysis" in Washington for the Beirut tragedy, McFarlane believes that the marines should have recognized "the vulnerabilities to terrorism of a force that remained fixed in one spot." In Grenada, he says, "It was dispiriting to see purely parochial service arguments over organization of that landing. Each service was seeking a larger role instead of focusing jointly on how to accomplish the mission."

The inability of acting JCS chairmen (a position that rotated among the service chiefs during the chairman's absence from Washington) to provide the president quality advice led McFarlane to "consider the need for a vice chairman."

Beyond observations gleaned as Reagan's NSC chief, the former marine had a historical perspective on Pentagon problems from prior service. In 1975, as a "bookend" to his early landing in Vietnam, he had been on the White House radio to Ambassador Graham Martin as the United States evacuated its embassy in Vietnam, culminating "a ten-year history of dysfunction in military planning, programming, and budgeting." A month later, he served as the NSC crisis action officer during the *Mayaguez* seizure off the coast of Cambodia, where the military made "a dysfunctional response purely as a consequence of service parochialism."[8] While serving on the SASC staff, McFarlane investigated the failed Iranian hostage rescue mission for the Republicans.

Despite his long military affiliation, McFarlane set aside Pentagon politics and service loyalty to focus on reforms needed to better meet the president's needs. The Pentagon's knee-jerk opposition and an intensifying confrontation between the executive and legislative branches chagrined the national security adviser. McFarlane saw no way to convince the president to overrule his longtime friend, Cap Weinberger. The former marine did not have the kind of personal relationship with Reagan that Weinberger enjoyed. McFarlane's source of influence was his "knowledge of substance and an understanding of how the bureaucracy works." As *New York Times* columnist Les Gelb wrote in 1984, when it came to meetings with the president, "detailed knowledge does not regularly prevail over personal ties." McFarlane simply did not "have the stature or presidential backing to challenge" Weinberger.[9]

Donley and Douglass both joined the NSC's defense office in mid-1984. Douglass, an air force acquisition expert, arrived in May. His NSC duties included strategic modernization programs, major weapon systems, and special access or "black" programs like low-observable stealth technology.

Donley moved from the SASC staff to the NSC in July. He had served the committee for nearly four years after a stint on the personal staff of SASC member Sen. Roger Jepsen (R-Iowa), and a brief tour at the Heritage Foundation. Involved in reorganization under Tower, Donley wrote initial drafts of the staff study's chapter on the Planning, Programming, and Budgeting System. His NSC responsibilities included the defense budget, policy planning, and organization and management.

Donley and Douglass worked for Ronald F. Lehman (not related to Navy Secretary John Lehman), another former SASC staffer. Lehman had left the Senate at the end of 1982 to become a deputy to Assistant Secretary of Defense Richard Perle.

In the summer of 1984, Congress and the media began heavily criticizing the Pentagon's management of acquisition. Horror stories emerged regarding "$500 hammers and $1,000 toilet seats." Douglass wanted to find solutions. As an adjunct to his duties, he began to "badger" McFarlane with acquisition reform ideas.[10]

Later in the summer, a group led by Richard Cook, head of the Washington office of the Lockheed Corporation, visited Douglass in his office in the Old Executive Office Building. Douglass described Cook as "a renaissance man" who did not think in the prevailing "narrow groove."

A discussion ensued about the "screwed up" Pentagon acquisition system and "how dangerous this was to the president." Cook blurted out: "You know what you ought to do, John? You ought to get somebody like Dave Packard to do a study of this thing. Some person with a perfect reputation, and Dave's the guy. He did wonderful things at the Pentagon as deputy secretary. He's been a wonderful industrial leader at Hewlett-Packard."

The idea of a figure above partisan politics to investigate the acquisition mess intrigued Douglass.

Shortly after assuming his new duties, Donley advanced forceful reorganization proposals. On July 27, he and Ron Lehman sent McFarlane a "TOP SECRET, EYES ONLY" memorandum proposing a National Security Decision Directive on reorganization. The high classification prevented anyone other than their boss from knowing about its existence. The memorandum envisioned the president tasking DoD to "develop a comprehensive plan for improving current management and decision-making procedures" for implementation "within the first one hundred days of 1985."[11] The specified areas of study paralleled the topics being examined by the SASC.

On August 7, McFarlane, still reluctant to challenge Weinberger, sent word to Donley that he was still "working on the approach" and "trying to figure out how to work-in outside help." Donley and Lehman were not "comfortable with the tone of the message."[12]

In August, Donley proposed that the president appoint a small group of outside "wise men" to advise him on reorganization, but no action was taken.[13]

By then, Donley and Lehman were viewing reorganization as a potential campaign issue. According to Donley, it became part of a process of laying out "a vision for what we wanted to do in national defense in the second term . . . recognizing that second terms provide opportunities to make institutional changes." He added that "it wasn't just that we were going to ask for more money or that the Soviets were going to be a bigger threat in the second term, but that we needed to do some work on institutions for which the president was responsible." Donley listed four pre-election objectives: "keep the process moving; make it public; make it our issue, and commit to further action in the second term." He envisioned action to "direct the Office of the Secretary of Defense or a 'blue ribbon' advisory group to undertake a formal review."[14]

In early October, Donley suggested that the president issue guidance on reorganization and appoint a "senior policy group" composed of the national security adviser, defense secretary, and JCS chairman to coordinate administration positions. No action was taken on these ideas.

As the 1984 presidential election approached, Donley and Douglass put McFarlane and his deputy, Rear Adm. John M. Poindexter, on notice: "Soon, you'll be too late. You'll be inside the window. Between then and the election, it is going to be perceived as a political partisan gambit of some sort."[15]

When this maneuver produced no reaction, Donley grew pessimistic: "It is slowly becoming apparent that the promise to address difficult issues after the election will, around November 7, be replaced with the promise to address these issues 'after the New Year,' 'after Congress settles down,' or 'after the personnel situation is resolved.' Nevertheless, my response to these arguments will continue to be that the strategic direction of the president's defense program should be set in motion from the NSC and its essential elements must endure any personnel shakeups in DoD."[16]

On January 2, 1985, the NSC staff took its first external step on reform. Poindexter wrote to Deputy Defense Secretary Taft proposing a senior policy group, arguing that the group would help "seize the initiative from Congress" and "develop a credible and forward-looking position for the president." Taft rejected the proposal, although he did "welcome" NSC staff representation on the Pentagon's Ad Hoc Task Group on Defense Organization, known as the Cox Committee. Poindexter designated Donley as the representative.[17] Six months into their campaign, all Donley and Douglass had to show for their efforts was Donley's membership on a Pentagon group.

McFarlane remained committed to reorganization, but he knew that the timing was not right. He also knew that "gaining the president's support would be achievable only through the combination of intellectual argument with the president and Congress' conveying . . . to him . . . how serious the situation was. But that combination had to be presented in a way and at a time where we could get results."[18]

Toward the end of 1983, anticipating Reagan's reelection, McFarlane "thought a long time about what can we do in the remaining five years." Engaging the Russians topped the list, but defense reorganization ranked high. Concrete action on any new policy initiatives would have to await the 1984 election since "the president's and staff's attention was focused on the election, almost from the beginning."

The national security adviser saw reorganization as a poor election-year topic. "It would have just drawn attention to a failing of the administration . . . Nothing was going to happen in an election year, in the way of self-criticism."

McFarlane "had the parallel frustration of knowing that Weinberger, who was conscious of the emergent groundswell of criticism in Congress, would fight like the dickens to avoid a White House initiative on defense reform. Weinberger simply wouldn't have it, and because of the president's affection for Weinberger, he would yield to him."

Members of Congress were busily blasting Weinberger "on the emergent scandal and dysfunction in the Pentagon." Tower and his committee colleagues were leading the charge. McFarlane remembers one senator telling the president: "You probably could have had another $60 billion in defense spending if you had somebody who could testify effectively for you and not demean the Senate by coming up here and lecturing us with incoherent testimony."[19] The degree to which Weinberger mishandled his budget relations with Congress is reflected in Senate Majority Leader Bob Dole's quip: "Cap Weinberger is the first person in history to overdraw a blank check."[20]

McFarlane confronted the president with these problems at morning briefings "because I had a responsibility to. Tower, with his study, made it pretty clear to Reagan that things were not right in the Pentagon and that the time was near when the president would be criticized for ignoring Weinberger's ineptitude."[21]

By the summer of 1984, with infighting between State and Defense Department leaders over national security issues paralyzing much of the policy process, McFarlane gained Reagan's approval "to engage people outside of government to study" critical issues, including defense reform. The NSC staff reached out to a few "old lions," but before they were fully engaged on defense reform, McFarlane's approach was overtaken by three developments in early 1985.

First, Donley's participation on the Cox Committee clarified for the NSC staff the Pentagon's inability to address reform issues. Second, Goldwater and Nunn's joint commitment to reorganization convinced those in the Old Executive Office Building of the potential for sweeping legislation. Third and most important, Reagan was increasingly disturbed by continuing defense acquisition horror stories and the resulting erosion of support for his military buildup.

On the Cox Committee, Donley became convinced that the Pentagon's inability to address reform created an intolerable situation for the president. Pentagon attitudes toward reform proponents also troubled Donley. Critics of the department's organization or functioning "were viewed as foes of the administration or Cap Weinberger. The Pentagon was unable to separate its animosity toward critics from the institutional issues that the Hill was beginning to raise and General Jones had stirred up."[22]

Deputy Secretary Taft communicated to Donley the depth and unreasonableness of the Pentagon's opposition: "If the Hill doesn't produce something that Cap can support and that would be acceptable to DoD, we would recommend that the president veto it."

To Donley, that statement starkly revealed "the depths to which the department was committed to opposing the Hill's efforts and its total disregard for the politics of the issue." As to the politics, "The department was so disconnected that it believed the president would veto a product that represented years of work by the Hill and by Goldwater and Nunn, two revered figures."

As Goldwater and Nunn began their reorganization campaign in January 1985, Donley and I frequently discussed their concerns about Weinberger's intransigence and compared notes about our perception that the secretary lacked an understanding of how the Pentagon operated and its organizational problems. Weinberger's testimony that he had "particularly tried to strengthen the role of the services" flabbergasted both of us in light of the services' excessive power and influence. Donley also noted "that the Hill was souring on Weinberger" and that he was "less and less a cabinet member to be feared on the Hill" had factored into NSC staff thinking.[23]

Because of the Pentagon's hostility, Goldwater, Nunn, and I agreed that I should maintain a dialogue with Donley and through him with the two other former SASC staffers at the NSC, Ron Lehman and McFarlane. Donley and I were friends, but we also represented powerful institutions placed in competition by the Constitution. Given the stakes, our conversations sometimes were testy. One heated debate centered on Congress' constitutional authority "to make rules for the government and regulation of the land and naval forces" versus the president's prerogatives as commander in chief.

When the two senators wrote to Weinberger on February 4, 1985, about their reorganization plans, they sent a copy of the letter to McFarlane. Donley understood this move: "Letter to us reflects NSC as potential surrogate for DoD."

He observed, "Because we kept channels open to all sides, we're in a position to know what's going on on all fronts, *but* now everyone wants to know what role the National Security Council will play."[24]

By early 1985, defense acquisition horror stories had become a major political problem for the president. In September, 1984, it was revealed that the air force had spent $7,622 for a coffee pot for C-5A cargo planes "that would go right on brewing coffee even if the plane's cabin pressure was lost in the air, yea, even though the plane was subjected to enough of gravity's G-forces to kill the entire crew."[25]

Under headlines like "Aerial Brew Haha," the media jumped on the story of what the air force called a "hot beverage unit." The *New York Times* observed: "Seventy-six-hundred-dollar coffee-pots, with 2,000 parts, capable of making fresh coffee after everyone is dead—this is the sort of thing the most frivolous billionaire would blush to own. Only the Pentagon could possibly buy such a machine."[26]

Another *Times* article examined other overpriced items on C-5 aircraft. "Every taxpayer should visit one of the Air Force's C-5 transport planes. He should climb the flimsy $74,000 aluminum folding ladder, sink into the $13,000 crew chief's seat, and rest his arm on the $670 foam-rubber-and-Naugahyde armrest."[27]

The air force was also ridiculed for paying $180 for an "emergency lighting system"—something everyone else calls a flashlight. "Even at $180 the flashlights don't work properly," a newspaper reported an air force officer testifying at a Senate hearing.[28]

On February 4, 1985, Weinberger appeared before the SASC and downplayed these stories by pointing out that the Pentagon had been the first to uncover excessive prices. "We identified the overcharges, and we got the refund," he told the senators. The secretary ended his defense by saying, "We don't want to spend a nickel more than we have to for anything."[29]

"I was interested to hear your remark about the $1,100 plastic cap, $400 hammer and $7,000 coffee pot," responded Senator Cohen. "I am told there will be a new story with a $600 toilet seat for P-3 aircraft," Cohen related and then deadpanned, "which I think gives new meaning to the word 'throne.'" *Time* magazine reported this exchange under the headline "Adjusting the Bottom Line."[30]

The Pentagon responded to this story by saying it was not really a toilet seat but a "toilet cover assembly." Created for use in navy P-3C Orion submarine-hunter airplanes, the plastic case, which fit over a toilet was "designed to be of light weight, corrosive resistant, thermoformed, polycarbonate material, seamless, and sufficiently durable to withstand repeated usage and aircraft landings."[31] The $640 toilet seat became a nightmare for the Pentagon and Weinberger, around whose neck editorial cartoonist Herblock of the *Washington Post* often drew a toilet seat.

When the president read about these stories in the press, he demanded that DoD tell him "what the hell this is all about." Each time such a story appeared, the NSC staff sent the Pentagon a memorandum requiring an answer within twenty-four hours.[32]

"No matter what happened," Douglass recalled, "the Pentagon replies would start out with something like: 'Last year, we bought 8,942 toilet seats. The average price was 89 cents, but this one—'" Another Pentagon approach, according to Donley and Douglass, was to claim: "It's not really a toilet seat; it's a human waste elimination dispersion device."[33]

The president was not pleased with the Pentagon's convoluted replies, said Donley and Douglass. Reagan "got tired of his administration being beat over the head with these stories."[34]

Criticism of DoD's acquisition performance caught the eye of many members of Congress and sparked various proposals and studies. Douglass belonged to a generation of officers that bridled at Congress "intruding on defense issues." Suggesting "that if we don't do something, the Hill is going to do it for us, that was second only to the Russians raising their flag over Washington. To have the Hill tell us how to do our business, that was the most hated, odious thing that you could suggest to a professional military guy." He found himself thinking: "For God's sake, don't let that crowd, who are inclined to pork and special interests and are advised by a bunch of staff guys that don't understand the acquisition system at all, handle this."[35]

Douglass concluded that a direct congressional threat to establish a defense acquisition commission might motivate the president to seize the initiative by forming his own commission. The lieutenant colonel decided that he would need to create that threat. He and his good friend and former air force colleague, Alan C. Chase, who worked for the senior Republican on the House Armed Services Committee, Cong. William L. Dickinson of Alabama, "cooked up this idea of having Dickinson write to the president and try to convince him that we needed a commission." Dickinson's view would carry considerable weight in the White House.

On March 27, before Dickinson could write his letter, Sen. William V. Roth Jr. (R-Delaware) announced his plans for a bill that would create a high-level defense reform advisory committee that would report to the defense secretary and examine the department's structure and operation. Roth saw acquisition reform as a key area. The senator wrote to Weinberger: "A genuinely bipartisan committee, headed by well-respected leaders such as David Packard and Melvin Laird, could dramatically strengthen your hand in instituting fundamental reforms." Weinberger apparently did not agree: he waited more than three months before answering Roth's letter.[36]

On April 1, Dickinson sent the president a strongly worded letter that contained many of Douglass's arguments. "I feel that the present situation regarding the perceptions of the government procurement process, especially in the defense sector, is intolerable," he wrote. Striking a theme that would resonate with Reagan, Dickinson argued, "Reasoned debate about the need for a strong defense is lost in the rhetoric surrounding waste, fraud, and abuse." He recommended "a Presidential Blue Ribbon Panel on Government Procurement Reform."[37]

The next day, before the White House received Dickinson's letter, Douglass sent McFarlane a memorandum outlining a presidential alternative to a congressionally mandated commission. Douglass admitted "that we have too often in the past substituted studies, panels and commissions for some badly needed fanny-kicking to obtain the attention of the acquisition community." He felt, however, that this initiative was needed to preclude "disjointed and inflammatory legislation." The memorandum's talking points had McFarlane telling the president that NSC staffers with extensive experience in acquisition had "come up with the idea of a presidential commission to review the entire process from stem to stern. They envision a commission led by a nationally known figure and staffed by leaders from business, academia, Congress, and defense."[38]

Dickinson kept up the pressure. On April 11, M. B. Oglesby Jr., assistant to the president for legislative affairs, reported that "Dickinson has called our office to press for prompt review and response to his letter." According to Oglesby, "Bill states that the president can tell him 'no,' but failing to hear that *directly* from the president, he is moving forward with his proposal—having already talked with Senators Goldwater (R-Arizona), Warner (R-Virginia), and Nunn (D-Georgia)."[39]

The horror stories about acquisition management made Reagan receptive to Dickinson's idea, but he remained reluctant to overrule Weinberger.

Given personal dynamics, only McFarlane was able to work the commission issue with the president and secretary. McFarlane and his staff took an intricate set of steps to advance their goals. "It took several months to lay the groundwork," Donley recalled. Weinberger needed to see that Reagan and McFarlane were ready to make a decision, "so that he could get on board at the last minute and change his view from opposing a commission, to being a shaper of what the commission would work on."

Donley said he and Douglass could envision "that eventually Bud would have to say to the president, 'Cap isn't going to like this, but we're going to have to do it anyway.' He had to work the president into the position where the president understood it on a level that separated it from his friendship with Weinberger." Donley believed that "Cap would have to have some meetings with the president first to air views. Then the Reagan-McFarlane meeting would have to take place during which the decision would be eased over the goal line. Then Bud would have to convey that to Cap."

As Douglass's proposal for an acquisition commission gained momentum, Donley introduced the idea of a broader commission. "At the beginning, I wasn't sure that was a good idea," Douglass said. After much discussion and "a fair amount of time," the air force lieutenant colonel "came around to Mike's point of view that Pentagon problems really were bigger than just contracting methods."[40]

On April 25, Donley and Douglass sent McFarlane a memorandum proposing a broad scope for the commission, noting: "Despite the real improvements we have made, the achievement of sustained increases in the defense budget is proving once again that money alone will not solve all our defense problems." They argued: "The current efforts of the Department of Defense fall short and have come too late to restore confidence in the department and deter further debilitating investigations and meddlesome legislation from Congress." They proposed "an offensive plan to break the current cycle of painful and embarrassing hearings and investigations which, while causing some improvements in DoD management, continue to drain confidence in our stewardship."[41] McFarlane agreed with their arguments and began presenting this idea to Reagan.

In early May, Reagan and McFarlane traveled to Bonn for the Group of Seven (G-7) summit meeting. Between sessions, they talked about a commission. McFarlane recalls saying, "When you get back, you're going to see Bill Dickinson. He's going to talk about his idea for an acquisition commission. Political criticism and genuine public airing of serious problems in the Pentagon are going to get worse and worse and worse. I think we have to create a commission, Mr. President."[42] Reagan apparently agreed.

The White House scheduled the meeting between Reagan and Dickinson for May 15. In preparation, Donley and Douglass met with Al Chase of Dickinson's staff to listen "without committing the president." After the meeting, they reported: "Dickinson believes that the president is in favor of the commission and will agree to its formation." As to opposition, "Dickinson is aware that DoD may not support the idea of a commission (based on a meeting he had with Deputy Secretary of Defense Taft)."[43]

Predictably, Weinberger remained opposed. Years later, Taft recalled that Weinberger "didn't think that it would help to improve the management of the department, which he felt was being improved all along. And I think he was also concerned about the political fallout of the president's appointing a commission in year five or six. He was worried about the political implications of the fellow who's been on the job for five years coming in and saying, 'How am I doing?' If you need to be told, you are already in trouble, and if you are told and it's not absolutely favorable, then you are in a bit of a pickle. If you are told and it is favorable, everyone will say it is a whitewash. So he didn't see, from that point of view, much advantage in it."[44]

Vice President George Bush, Weinberger, and Admiral Poindexter attended the twenty-two-minute Reagan-Dickinson meeting on May 15. McFarlane was still in Europe. The president's talking points, prepared by Donley and Douglass, envisioned him commenting favorably on the acquisition commission idea, but saying to Dickinson, "We'll get back to you." Despite the script, Reagan was ready to decide and "agreed to the formation of a blue ribbon commission in principle." The president did not mention the idea of a broad-chartered commission. Poindexter's meeting notes observed, "President not on broader approach yet." In light of the president's unexpected move, Donley and Douglass "visualized Weinberger going back to the Pentagon with flames coming out of the back of his limousine."[45]

McFarlane, Donley, and Douglass used the president's agreement to create an acquisition commission as a springboard for gaining approval of a broader commission. McFarlane raised the issue with Weinberger at a breakfast meeting on May 16. His justification centered on the advantages of killing "two or more birds [acquisition and organization] with one stone" and being able to argue that Hill action "should be postponed until we see the commission's recommendations next year."[46]

The McFarlane-Weinberger dispute on a broad versus narrow scope for the commission raged for twenty days. Throughout this period, the secretary maintained a "suspicious, but not overtly hostile" attitude toward the national security adviser. McFarlane met with Weinberger and General Vessey in the secretary's Pentagon office on May 17. He gave Weinberger a two-page "SECRET/SENSITIVE" memorandum and a draft National Security Decision Directive for a broad-chartered commission. Knowing the memorandum would be repugnant to Weinberger, McFarlane did not sign it.[47] The memorandum bluntly stated:

> This morning the President told me he wanted to go ahead and establish a Commission on Defense with a charter broad enough to cover the areas in which we are being criticized. . . . We have a whole range of issues that are affecting DoD's relationship with Congress and our credibility in the public's eyes. Acquisition is the area of most interest to the public because of allegations involving very high prices for what appear to be common household items. . . . The most important thing is that a bipartisan, credible, outside group reach conclusions that have a calming and stabilizing effect on our relations with Congress and which enhance our credibility with the American people.[48]

Unlike other correspondence, which usually moved quickly across the secretary's desk, this unsigned memorandum stayed in Weinberger's office for six months.

In retrospect, Weinberger said: "I just thought that the goals of the people creating the commission were basically to take a substantial amount of authority from the secretary and give it to Congress or military leadership." The secretary "thought the commission would be a repository for a number of criticisms of the costly coffee-makers and toilets and all that stuff that we'd turned up ourselves in the audits but which got presented by the press as another excess of defense waste and why we didn't need the kind of budgets we were talking about."[49]

Of the political environment, including proposals to create a commission, Weinberger said: "Having gotten one defense increase through the first year, there were a lot of people who felt that was more than enough. There were a lot of people who simply don't like spending money on the military. There's no way that you can get the kind of military strength that we needed at that time without strong, passionate advocacy because of the inherent opposition."

Weinberger saw creation of a commission as the opposition's work: "All of these things were, one way or another, designed to try to slow the momentum of the defense buildup or to turn it in a somewhat different direction."

Moreover, the secretary saw McFarlane as part of this opposition: "Basically, I gathered, certainly from McFarlane, that he and other civilian people on the White House staff were unhappy with the president's devotion to getting a strong defense."[50] He found the former marine "strange, indrawn, moody," and later called McFarlane "a man of evident limitations. He could not hide them, but he did attempt to conceal them, by an enigmatic manner, featuring heavily measured, pretentious and usually nearly impenetrable prose, and a great desire to be perceived as 'better than Henry [Kissinger].'"[51]

While Weinberger and McFarlane battled, Weinberger's and Vessey's assistants pressured Douglass and Donley. Douglass recalls that Maj. Gen. Colin Powell, the secretary's senior military assistant, "was giving me a hard time and was calling me up and chewing me out for not being more on Weinberger's side, for putting ideas in the president's head."

Donley said that he received the same message from Brig. Gen. George A. Joulwan, Vessey's executive assistant. Deputy Secretary Taft also scolded Douglass, who thought that it gnawed on the secretary that "these two guys at the White House—one of whom was a lowly colonel—had the gall to suggest that the department didn't know what it was doing in these areas."

"It was a difficult time for us," the two staffers related. "The Pentagon had fingered us: 'That's who the troublemakers are.'"[52]

With skirmishes ongoing behind closed administration doors, Senator Roth pressed ahead. On May 22, he gained unanimous Senate approval of an amendment to the defense authorization bill that would create a twenty-one-member commission.[53]

"The Senate accepted, by voice vote, a provision to establish an independent Commission on Defense Procurement," Weinberger informed Reagan in his weekly report. "You recall Bill Dickinson's interest in a similar concept. Should Congress finally enact such a panel, it could perhaps highlight our management improvements and savings, which receive far too little public attention." Reagan, McFarlane, and their staff exploited Weinberger's illusion that the commission might vindicate Pentagon management. "We went out of our way to try to make that point," recalled Douglass. "Over and over."[54]

The procurement horror stories triggered a rapid erosion of public and congressional support for a planned six percent increase in the defense budget. The House voted to freeze military spending at the previous year's level, while the Senate was headed toward a level that would add only enough money to cover inflation.[55]

On May 28, another horror story hit the newspapers. A House committee discovered that the navy had paid $659 each for ashtrays for E-2C electronic surveillance aircraft. Critics blasted these purchases as an "outrageous waste of money." In response, Weinberger jokingly suggested: "One of the fundamental ways of dealing with it is, first of all, not to have smoking on those planes. That's one way. And the other way is to use used, but relatively secure, old mayonnaise jars for ashtrays."[56]

On May 31, Dickinson called the White House legislative liaison office to urge action on the commission proposal as quickly as possible, "preferably before debate [on the DoD authorization bill] continues on the House floor." Other HASC members made similar pleas.[57]

"We basically agreed to disagree," McFarlane said of his showdown with Weinberger on June 1.[58] Of Weinberger's opposition, McFarlane observed:

One of government's worst features is the community in each political party that I would call 'them-and-us-ers.' Comity is alien to this group, which argues, 'It is them and us. They will always hate us. We will always be right, and you must never compromise because it shows weakness. It is better to go over the cliffs, flags flying, than to yield an inch to them.' Cap is a 'them-and-us-er.' . . . I would talk to Weinberger about Capitol Hill's evident unease on defense management—not that is was valid or invalid, but that it was real—and if we didn't engage in some fashion, we were breeding hostility in the relationship, and we would pay for it in terms of diminished budgets and so forth.

McFarlane recalled Weinberger responding: "You will lose more if you show weakness. When you are challenged, confront. Take your stand. Go to the people. Don't give an inch."[59]

26. This Herblock cartoon appeared in the *Washington Post* on May 31, 1985.

With the commission issue not yet resolved, Weinberger appeared to make a preemptive move. In early June, Pentagon legislative liaison personnel on Capitol Hill began talking about creation of a presidential commission on acquisition. Soon, press articles began repeating the Pentagon's slant. A *Wall Street Journal* headline announced, "Panel on Arms Procurement Considered." The *Washington Post* followed with "Presidential Panel to Assess Defense Purchasing Practices."[60] The Pentagon had convinced the press that only an acquisition commission was coming.

Reagan joined Weinberger and McFarlane on June 4 to air the dispute over the charter. The session lasted only nineteen minutes. "Cap gave a rather pointed criticism of the idea, saying this whole notion that there's something wrong is a misguided contrivance of people like Dickinson and others who are not really on the team," McFarlane recalled. He says Weinberger added: "This couldn't lead to anything constructive. Decision making and management of resources are coming along quite well. The only way to deal with it is essentially to dismiss it. By no means should we weaken the Pentagon and divert its attention by a unnecessary, time-consuming analysis."

McFarlane described the president saying, "Well, that kind of criticism is unwarranted, and you and I know that, Cap." At the same time, Reagan did not abandon the idea of a commission. "Cap was his friend," McFarlane explained. "He didn't want to embarrass him or express any lack of confidence because he, indeed, was confident in Cap. The president also came into the meeting sufficiently conscious of the legitimate problems at hand." McFarlane said the president was "appalled" by recent operational foul-ups, especially "the incredible snafus" in a retaliatory attack after the Beirut bombing. Two carrier aircraft had been shot down, one flier killed, and another taken prisoner in the Bekaa Valley raid on December 4, 1983. Chain of command blunders turned an uncomplicated operation into a fiasco. McFarlane said such blunders "set Reagan's teeth on edge. The president didn't want ever to embarrass his friend, but he wanted this system improved and was quite firm in that commitment."[61]

According to Donley, during this session "the possibility that the commission might vindicate the department's policies and management was one of the carrots held out to Weinberger." He said the president, hesitant to disappoint his old friend, "wrapped the idea of a commission as delicately as he [could] so that it [was] not offensive to Weinberger."[62]

Weinberger seized upon the president's statements. Three days later, at an Aspen Institute conference, the secretary declared that the commission was "formed to 'validate' DoD procurement and management reforms already under way." The *Armed Forces Journal* reported that the audience of former officials "gasped at Weinberger's perception of its purpose." Then, on June 7, Reagan met with McFarlane to address the two alternative charters—one narrow, one broad—prepared for his consideration.[63]

"What do you think, Bud?" asked Reagan.

"Mr. President," McFarlane replied, "there is a thoroughgoing need for reform of decision making in the Pentagon, in both policy formation and management of its budget accounts. And it isn't my judgment. It is that of Congress, outside critics, academic people, and people that have been in and out of government for years."

"Well, it's too bad, but it's something we've got to do," said Reagan. "I agree with you, Bud. We've got to find a cleaner way to make sure that timely decisions get done down at the working level and that we can make a better account of ourselves in how we handle money and decisions."[64] The president signed the broad charter.

The White House wanted to announce the commission as soon as possible to head off reform initiatives in the House. The NSC staff targeted June 17.

The search for a commission chairman focused on nine candidates, including David Packard; H. Ross Perot, chairman of EDS Corporation and later a presidential aspirant; Peter Ueberroth, Major League Baseball commissioner; Lee Iacocca, chairman of the board of Chrysler Corporation; and Jeane Kirkpatrick, former U.S. ambassador to the United Nations. Looking back at this list, Douglass exclaimed, "Oh my God, Ross Perot. Man, where would Mike and I be today if we had picked him?" Donley says that Packard was the leading candidate from the beginning "in part because of his deputy secretary reputation as having instituted important acquisition reforms."[65]

Packard—a basketball and football player in Stanford University's class of 1934—was a hulking athlete and rugged outdoorsman who stood six foot four inches tall and weighed 250 pounds. In 1939, he and Bill Hewlett, a college classmate, borrowed $538 and founded the Hewlett-Packard Company in their one-car garage—which California in 1989 designated as the birthplace of Silicon Valley. A coin flip determined whose name went first. An early order came from Walt Disney Studios, which used eight of the company's audio oscillators to produce the soundtrack for the movie *Fantasia*. The company became an electronics industry giant.[66]

While Hewlett handled engineering, Packard was viewed "as the company's dynamic manager, thinking strategically and making tough decisions." Packard developed innovative, highly regarded management practices known as "the HP Way." Packard's "renown as an administrator" keyed his appointment as deputy defense secretary in 1969. During his three Pentagon years, he "developed a reputation for candor and independent thinking and a tendency to challenge political influence."[67]

"David Packard is an unlikely revolutionary," began a 1970 article about him as deputy secretary. "He is too soft-spoken, too rich, and probably even too big, to fit the image." The "quiet revisionist" presided "over an upheaval in U.S. defense policy every bit as traumatic as when Robert Strange McNamara came to Washington nine years ago." Despite his role in defense budget cuts, he was "well-liked by the military chieftains." *Business Week* called him "the most powerful No. 2 man ever to hold the job."[68]

Before a decision on the commission chairman was made, McFarlane telephoned Packard in California. "The president is very concerned about the trouble we've been having between Congress and Defense Department on a whole range of issues," he explained. "Congress is in the process of taking control of procurement and management issues that should best be left to the executive branch. We need someone of your caliber to chair the commission." Packard demurred at first, saying, "I'm really kind of busy." Later he said, "Let me come and talk about it."[69]

The following evening, McFarlane, Packard, and Poindexter met. The national security adviser discussed "the dysfunction in Pentagon decision-making and management" and reiterated the president's request that Packard chair the commission. "Well, that's important stuff," Packard replied. "If the president wants me to do it, I'll do it." He later said he "wasn't terribly enthusiastic about it, but the president asked me to do it, and it was something I couldn't refuse."[70]

Weinberger supported the selection. "Dave Packard was a good personal friend. I'd known him for years in California before and after his service as deputy secretary of defense." The two Californians had also served together in the Nixon administration: Weinberger as deputy director of the Office of Management and Budget during Packard's Pentagon tenure. As to Weinberger's welcoming the "appointment of Laird's most notoriously cost-conscious assistant to head the study," one explanation was that the secretary "was apparently operating under the delusion that all Republicans believed in large defense budgets."[71]

Packard saw much that needed fixing: "There were stories of waste; the contractors were unhappy; the people on the Hill were unhappy. . . . I am not critical of Cap in terms of his overall contribution. I think that he did a very important job. But he didn't manage it very well; that was my concern. He turned the services loose and that made the competition, if anything, worse than it was before. The services, particularly the navy, threw their weight around. . . . The whole thing was not very well done."

When Reagan and Weinberger met with Packard on June 17, the president and defense secretary envisioned the commission validating ongoing management improvements. Packard believed the two "wanted the commission to come in, look things over, and tell everybody that everything was fine and not to worry."[72]

Packard, however, had different plans—something Weinberger may have begun to understand on June 24, when Chapman Cox advised the defense secretary that the industrialist, in testimony to the SASC in 1983, had enthusiastically voiced support for a number of reforms that continued to be anathema to the Pentagon.[73]

Goldwater and Nunn saw the impending commission as a positive development, portending improved executive-legislative cooperation. The senators also appreciated Donley's report that the NSC staff envisioned making "the committee's staff study the starting point for the commission's work."[74]

The two senators also saw risks. They feared use of the commission to curtail the committee's work. Goldwater and Nunn were just beginning their Task Force on Defense Organization. They worried that members might now be tempted to duck this hot issue.

Goldwater and Nunn also expected the White House to argue that Congress should wait for the commission's report before acting. The White House planned to give the commission about a year to complete its work. By then, only three months would remain in the 1986 legislative year, undermining prospects for legislation while Goldwater was chairman. To ensure they did not lose momentum, Goldwater and Nunn decided to "proceed as if the commission had not been established."

The senators saw a second risk in potential manipulation of the commission through the selection of members and staff and writing of the commission's terms of reference. The Pentagon had already asserted its right to have the biggest say in picking members. Donley reported that the NSC staff had thus far "fought off this effort." The senators decided to ask to "review the commission membership before it is announced."

Goldwater and Nunn informed the NSC staff that they were delighted with the formation of the commission and looked forward to working with it, but they would not alter their committee's schedule.

On June 12, the day after his selection, Packard met separately with Goldwater and Nunn. Goldwater described his partnership with Nunn and their "firm commitment to DoD reorganization." He stressed that they would act before he retired from the Senate. When Packard sought the chairman's input, Goldwater warned him to "carefully ensure" that the commission's composition, staff, and terms of reference "permit an objective evaluation of the issues." He offered the committee's support if Packard had problems on these matters. Both Goldwater and Nunn adopted a wait-and-see attitude while committing to "a close working relationship" with Packard and the commission.[75]

Packard also met that day with Senators Stennis and Bingaman and Congressmen Aspin and Dickinson. Each expressed support, although the pronavy Stennis "didn't feel a pressing need to significantly alter JCS organization."[76]

As the White House made final preparations for announcing the commission's appointment, the president received an emotional memorandum from General Vessey objecting that parts of the commission's charter fell "within the responsibilities of the Joint Chiefs of Staff." Vessey wrote that the commander in chief "should get the advice of the Joint Chiefs of Staff before he asks for advice from an outside commission. We know a great deal about those issues, at least as much as any commission that can be assembled." Donley characterized the memorandum as "unfortunate," its tone and content perhaps "intemperate or even in poor taste."[77]

The commission was announced on June 17 in a formal Rose Garden ceremony. Reagan devoted the first half of his statement to praising Weinberger as "an individual with unmatched management credentials" and who "has done a tremendous job at ferreting out waste and fraud." Somewhat undercutting the rationale for the commission, the president decried the "public misconception . . . born . . . of a drumbeat of propaganda and demagoguery that denies the real accomplishment of these last four years." Reagan said he was appointing the commission "at the recommendation of Secretary Weinberger."[78]

Packard perused the bland text prepared for him by White House staff then drafted his own statement. "I am pleased that you want us to do our job on a completely independent, nonpartisan basis," he told the president. "And that's exactly what we are going to do." Packard also noted that "The charter that you have given us will make possible a top-to-the-bottom and tough review."[79]

The two speeches portrayed different motivations. Reagan was focused on the politics of defense reform. He wanted to fix the political damage to his administration. Packard, on the other hand, understood that the magnitude of the issues overwhelmed the defense politics of one administration and that meaningful solutions would benefit the nation for generations.

Senators Goldwater and Nunn issued a joint statement commending the president and praising the selection of Packard. The senators added that they had been assured that "the commission will be bipartisan, well-balanced, and objective."[80]

Most members of Congress and the media commented favorably, but a spokesman for House Speaker Tip O'Neill said, "You don't need a commission to find a $7,700 coffeepot. For five years, the Pentagon has run like a supermarket sweepstakes: grab all you can, as fast as you can, price is no object."[81]

Congressman Edward J. Markey (D-Massachusetts) described the commission as "veneer. . . It is a gloss; it is a fig leaf."[82]

"If Reagan thinks his plan to name a presidential commission on wasteful military spending will cool off the critics, he's in for a surprise," said *U.S. News & World Report*. "Even Republicans in Congress who have been complaining about excessive costs scorn the panel as a mere public-relations device."[83]

Others were even more suspicious of the motives behind the commission's creation. Admiral Crowe later charged that "The behind-the-scenes purpose of this initiative was to undermine the reformers and fend off" reorganization.[84]

27. President Reagan announces the creation of the President's Blue Ribbon Commission on Defense Management with (*from left to right*) Congressman Aspin, Vice President Bush, Congressman Dickinson, Senator Roth, Senator Goldwater, Mr. Packard, Senator Nunn, and Defense Secretary Weinberger, June 17, 1985, in the Rose Garden. (White House photo.)

The Rose Garden announcement did not end the battling over the commission. The next skirmish centered on membership, which McFarlane, Weinberger, and Packard brokered. Suggestions for members came from the White House and NSC staffs, the Pentagon, Capitol Hill, former officials, and administration friends. Donley and Douglass compiled a list of 135 names, shortened by eight when Max L. Friedersdorf, the president's legislative strategy coordinator, insisted "absolutely no current members of Congress."[85]

"We tried not to pick any flamethrowers," said Douglass. "We wanted people with credibility but known to be reasonable and articulate, who could talk about reform in a positive way, not a negative way." The preclusion of flamethrowers ruled out Jones and Meyer. "Some people we thought met the criteria would get zipped off, no matter how many times Mike and I put them on." Former Defense Secretaries Laird, Schlesinger, and Brown were in this category.[86] Their exclusion probably resulted from Weinberger's reluctance to have predecessors evaluate his performance. Rather, he sought the appointment of two close associates, Frank Carlucci, his first deputy secretary, and Bill Clark, McFarlane's predecessor as national security adviser, to keep the commission under control.[87] The appointment of two retired officers—Adm. Jim Holloway and Gen. Bob Barrow of the Marine Corps, both known to be strongly antireform—also pleased Weinberger.

McFarlane and Packard succeeded in adding four proreform commissioners: Gen. Paul F. Gorman, USA (Ret.); William J. Perry; Lt. Gen. Brent Scowcroft, USAF (Ret.); and R. James Woolsey.

Although the makeup of the sixteen-member commission appeared to tilt slightly toward reform, the seven commissioners who were not defense experts represented a large swing block of votes and were viewed as wild cards. Few understood that Packard's hand was stronger than it appeared. Two of the "unknown" commissioners—Ernest C. Arbuckle and Louis W. Cabot—were close friends of Packard's.

On July 15, 1985, Reagan signed Executive Order 12526, creating the President's Blue Ribbon Commission on Defense Management, and announced its membership. The commission's beginnings in the Roth and Dickinson initiatives led many to believe that acquisition was its focus. Weinberger's moves to limit the commission's purview and the White House's emphasis on acquisition problems fueled the confusion. Despite the misperception, Reagan had assigned the commission the administration's lead on the entire range of reorganization issues.

This shift of responsibility for examining reorganization from DoD to the commission constrained the military in its fight with Congress. Although the Pentagon still packed a powerful wallop, McFarlane had succeeded in creating a more level playing field.

One outcome was clear: the Pentagon was now unable to make preemptive moves at the White House. Thus reassured, Goldwater and Nunn anticipated a constructive dialogue with the Packard Commission and hoped that it would become a helpful ally. But they had little time to worry about how the commission approached its work or its internal dynamics. They had enough worries of their own in the Senate Armed Services Committee.

CHAPTER 15

Trench Warfare

Without mobility an army is but a corpse—

awaiting burial in a trench.

—Capt. Air Basil Liddell Hart,

The Remaking of Modern Armies

S enators Goldwater and Nunn anxiously awaited the convening of their Task Force on Defense Organization. Its meetings would begin the long process of educating a core group of senators. The two leaders planned that the nine-member group would thoughtfully analyze and debate fundamental problems. They believed that the evidence gathered would support reform.

The chairman and ranking Democrat underestimated the challenge they faced. The majority of Republican members would give priority to defending the Pentagon and White House and would accept Department of Defense, especially navy, antireform arguments. On the Democratic side, the complexity of the issues and the fervor of Pentagon opposition would produce caution.

Goldwater and Nunn sensed the coming struggle when junior Republicans objected to the word *reorganization* in the task force's name, saying it prejudged the outcome. To appease them, Goldwater and Nunn adopted the neutral title Task Force on Defense Organization. Shortly after this initial skirmish, pro- and antireform members began to entrench in set positions. Soon, the task force was engaged in static, exhausting trench warfare. Barrages of arguments, research, and analysis did not alter frontline positions.

From mid-June through early October, when the Senate was in session, the task force met roughly once a week to discuss a chapter of the staff study or meet with former senior officers and defense officials. Member attendance was abnormally high. Usually, all nine members attended for every moment of the two- to three-hour sessions. No one wanted to risk missing a key debate on this high-stakes issue.

When a session focused on the study, one of my fellow staffers or I briefed the chapter under consideration and answered members' questions. We distributed a copy of the subject chapter for each task force member to read before the meeting. Each page contained the following disclaimer: "DRAFT STAFF DOCUMENT NOT APPROVED BY SASC NOR ANY OF ITS MEMBERS." Conclusions or recommendations were excluded from distributed chapters to put the focus "on whether the problem areas that have been identified do exist and whether the full range of possible solutions has been developed."[1]

To shelter members from external pressures while they were becoming informed, Goldwater and Nunn convened the task force in executive session, closing meetings to the Pentagon and public. They restricted committee staff attendance to only those who were working on the study and permitted each senator to bring only one member of his personal staff to meetings. The task force also adopted procedures recommended by Goldwater and Nunn for maintaining close control of all documents, including staff study chapters.[2]

By mid-June, Rick Finn and I had produced final drafts of five of the study's ten chapters. Goldwater and Nunn had reviewed earlier drafts of these and two others and provided guidance and comments. Several other staffers were helping to finish incomplete chapters. Colleen M. Getz was preparing the chapter on civilian control of the military under Jeff Smith's supervision; Alan Yuspeh was writing the chapter on the acquisition system; Pat Tucker continued to assist me in authoring the military departments chapter; John J. Hamre was writing much of the chapter on congressional review and oversight; and I was authoring the last chapter, an analytical overview. We were scurrying to finish these five chapters by the time the task force was ready to review them.

At its initial meeting on June 18, the task force established its procedures and schedule. All nine members attended. Senator Bill Cohen sat to Goldwater's right. Many judged the well-read and well-spoken Cohen to be the poet laureate of the Senate. I had the good fortune of working closely with him. He was easily engaged in policy issues, but he quickly lost interest in the more technical issues of Pentagon hardware. When I had such issues for Cohen to study, I wished that I could write about them in iambic pentameter.

Dan Quayle, the boyish senator from Indiana, sat next to Cohen. When he joined the committee in 1980, Quayle looked and acted younger than his age. Capable of book learning, Quayle never developed mature judgment in the view of most of his colleagues. Shortly after coming to the Senate, Quayle had shouted at Senator Tower, "You're not a chairman. You're a dictator." The scene was a Republican committee caucus on the sale of airborne warning and control system (AWACS) aircraft to Saudi Arabia, Reagan's first major foreign policy issue. Tower was pressuring colleagues to rally to the president's side. The chairman's glare in response to Quayle's comment could have burned a hole through armor. Committee members and staff viewed Quayle as a lightweight years before others tagged him with that label.

Unsmiling Pete Wilson occupied the next seat in the task force's Republican pecking order. The California senator and long-time mayor of San Diego gave the image of being all business and tough as nails. Wilson served as a rifle-platoon leader in the marines between earning an undergraduate degree at Yale and a law degree at Berkeley.

At the bottom of the Republican totem pole sat Texan Phil Gramm. Although last in seniority, the former college professor was near the head of the class in intellect and loquacity.

On the Democratic side of the dais, the former attorney general of New Mexico, Jeff Bingaman, sat next to Nunn. The two other Democratic senators, Carl Levin and Ted Kennedy, outranked Bingaman, but Nunn planned on using him as his deputy on reorganization. The young, soft-spoken Bingaman represented the new breed of Western legislator. Educated at Harvard and Stanford, he was intellectual, poised, and at ease with a wide range of national issues. Bingaman was especially interested in advanced technology issues.

Carl Levin, one of the SASC's three liberals, had inexhaustible energy and curiosity, which he used to search for better ideas and expose sloppy thinking. When other senators said, "This is good enough," the hard-working Levin pressed on in search of a better outcome for America and its taxpayers. Disheveled in dress and manner, the Harvard Law School graduate's mind was well ordered. Whether he agreed or not, the humble Michigan senator listened respectfully to what you had to say.

Ted Kennedy of Massachusetts sat next to Levin. The liberal philosophy of the youngest Kennedy brother often clashed with the perspectives of other committee members, but he had earned their respect through hard work.

Overall, the task force was composed of highly capable, intellectual senators. This group was well suited to the task of studying the exceedingly challenging world of defense organization.

When the task force met again on June 27, it entered the reorganization fray with its examination of the Joint Chiefs of Staff. I briefed the members on the three problems identified in the study's JCS chapter: the JCS's inability to provide useful and timely military advice, the inadequate quality of the Joint Staff, and insufficient review and oversight of contingency plans.[3] Studies conducted over a period of three decades had repeatedly criticized the quality of military advice. One of the earliest critiques, that of the 1949 Eberstadt Committee, paralleled the description of inadequate military advice identified thirty-five years later: "It has proved difficult to expedite decision on the part of the Joint Chiefs, or to secure from them soundly unified and integrated plans and programs and clear, prompt advice."[4]

My briefing presented considerable evidence on the JCS's inability to provide useful military advice. The joint chiefs had been unable to formulate military strategy, preferring instead to do fiscally unconstrained, pie-in-the-sky strategic planning. Their advice was virtually useless when it came time to prepare the budget because, as General Jones testified, "each service usually wants the Joint Staff merely to echo its views." The JCS had also failed to effectively represent the unified commanders on resource issues, even though a directive had stated the ultimate objective of resource allocation as providing "the operational commanders-in-chief the best mix of forces, equipment, and support attainable within fiscal constraints." In another area with resource implications, the JCS had been unable to settle disputes on service roles and missions.[5]

Parochialism in operational matters reflected the JCS's failure to rise above service interests. "Each of the services wants a piece of the action . . . and is demanding usually that it control its own forces," noted former defense secretary James Schlesinger. The joint chiefs themselves caused the organizational deficiencies in the unified commands when they released *JCS Publication 2: Unified Action Armed Forces,* which crippled the unified commanders. Similarly, the JCS had failed to objectively review the Unified Command Plan because "pride of service and allocation of four-star billets" impeded changes to the plan. Poorly developed joint doctrine represented another shortcoming. Lieutenant General Jack Cushman observed that the joint chiefs "have published no 'how to fight' doctrine at all."

The staff study identified eight causes of the JCS's poor performance in its advisory role. The dual responsibilities of service chiefs—as service head and JCS member—was foremost. This cause had two dimensions: the conflict of interest inherent in dual-hatting and insufficient time to perform both roles. The JCS chairman's limited authority was also judged a major cause. The study identified the desire for unanimity as a third cause. Robert W. Komer, a former under secretary of defense for policy, said this desire "must be regarded as mostly a self-inflicted wound." The joint chiefs also had to learn on the job, because few of them had education or experience in joint activities.[6]

The closed staff character of the JCS system added to advisory woes. The JCS system operated "relatively unfettered and unobserved" by outside officials. It was even sealed off from the rest of the Pentagon by its own guard force. The JCS area resembled a walled city within a city. The closed-staff character of the JCS system permitted perpetuation of practices and attitudes that could not have withstood outside scrutiny. Also contributing to poor advice were lengthy, cumbersome staffing procedures that gave the services a veto over every joint recommendation. Like the service chiefs, officers on the Joint Staff had a conflict of interest that impeded development of quality advice. Despite the staff's responsibility to provide a joint perspective, tremendous incentives existed for officers to protect the interests of their respective services. Finally, Joint Staff work failed to focus on missions, an orientation that could have provided a more useful framework for assessing service programs and considering each unified commander's needs.

The second major JCS problem identified by the staff study centered on the quality of the Joint Staff. Our analysis found that officers generally did not want joint duty, were pressured or monitored for loyalty by their services while assigned to a joint position, were not prepared by either education or experience to perform their joint duties, and served only briefly once they had learned their jobs. The Chairman's Special Study Group reported: "The general perception among officers is that a joint assignment is one to be avoided. In fact, within one service it is flatly believed to be the 'kiss of death' as far as a continued military career is concerned." The CSSG did not want to point fingers, but everyone knew that the unidentified service was the navy.[7]

The staff study further identified inadequate JCS review of contingency plans and oversight of the plans' preparation as a third problem area. Unified commanders develop contingency plans to guide force employment in potential crises or conflicts. These plans were not adequately informed of political and fiscal constraints. Komer believed that "the non-nuclear war planning process has become routinized, without much imaginative consideration at CINC or JCS level of strategic alternatives." John Kester observed that Joint Staff plans "often have dismayed outsiders who had occasion to read them."[8]

My briefing produced lively debate. Quayle, Wilson, and Gramm found my arguments to be less persuasive than the Pentagon's rebuttals. Other members were struggling to comprehend the enormous, complex Department of Defense. My first presentation to the Task Force on Defense Organization confirmed that reorganization was going to be a long, difficult, and painful process.

On July 9, the task force addressed the chapter on the unified commands, the one I had shared with Admiral Crowe the previous October. The Vietnam War provided powerful insights on organizational problems plaguing the unified commands, but that conflict remained shrouded in emotion, especially on Capitol Hill. Believing that it would not be possible to overcome this emotion and the superficial arguments that flowed from it, I did not use Vietnam as a case study. Instead, the staff prepared papers on the Spanish-American War, Pearl Harbor, the USS *Pueblo* capture, the Iranian hostage rescue mission, and the Grenada invasion.[9]

My briefing identified two overarching problems: a confused operational chain of command and weak unified commanders. Three causes combined to create the initial problem. First, the defense secretary's command role lacked statutory clarity. Whether he commanded the unified commanders remained open to interpretation. Peter Wallace commented, "Command is so critically important that one really has difficulty believing that Congress or the nation could rest very comfortably leaving the [secretary's] command authority open to argument. But this seems to be precisely what has happened."[10]

Second, the JCS occasionally exploited an ambiguous DoD directive to operate as part of the command chain. The directive prescribed the chain from the president and secretary of defense to the unified commanders as running through the JCS. Its intent was that the JCS serve as the channel of communication, but other interpretations were possible. A statement by Admiral Moorer, the CNO during hearings on the *Pueblo* crisis, illustrated the potential for confusion and opportunism. "The Joint Chiefs of Staff, of which the chief of naval operations is the Navy member, exercises command of all operating forces," he testified. "Thus in the case of the *Pueblo*, the command chain ran up from CTF 96; to commander-in-chief Pacific Fleet; commander-in-chief, Pacific; to the Joint Chiefs of Staff, who in turn report to the commander-in-chief of the armed forces through the secretary of defense." Moorer had transposed the responsibility of the defense secretary and JCS. His statement also reflected the navy's determination not to take orders from anybody other than the president.[11]

The third cause of the confused command chain was the de facto control that each service chief exercised over each unified commander from his service. President Eisenhower had attempted to remove the military departments from the operational chain of command. He succeeded in convincing Congress to mandate this change in the Defense Reorganization Act of 1958, but the service chiefs continued to call the shots. The chapter examined the Cuban missile crisis, during which the Navy Department ran operations at sea and Adm. George W. Anderson Jr., the CNO, showed his disdain for the defense secretary's operational role.

The crisis began on October 14, 1962, when an air force U-2 spy plane photographed Soviet missile sites in Cuba. President Kennedy publicly disclosed the discovery on October 22 and announced a "strict quarantine on all offensive military equipment under shipment to Cuba." He further demanded that Soviet chairman Nikita Khrushchev "halt and eliminate this clandestine, reckless, and provocative threat to world peace."[12]

This U.S.-Soviet showdown brought the world to the brink of nuclear war. Dean Rusk, Kennedy's secretary of state, called it "the most dangerous crisis the world has ever seen," the single instance when the nuclear superpowers came "eyeball to eyeball." Theodore Sorensen called it the "Gettysburg of the Cold War."[13]

Fearful that the navy's handling of the Cuba blockade would goad the Russians into retaliating, Defense Secretary McNamara went to its operations center to question the CNO:

McNamara returned to the line of detailed questioning. Who would make the first interception? Were Russian-speaking officers on board? How would submarines be dealt with? At one point, McNamara asked Anderson what he would do if a Soviet ship's captain refused to answer questions about his cargo. At that point the Navy man picked up the Manual of Naval Regulations and, waving it in McNamara's face, shouted, "It's all in there." To which McNamara replied, "I don't give a damn what John Paul Jones would have done. I want to know what you are going to do now." The encounter ended on Anderson's remark: "Now, Mr. Secretary, if you and your deputy will go back to your offices, the Navy will run the blockade." . . . [S]ome witnesses say that Anderson accused McNamara of "undue interference in naval matters." The admiral, thereafter ambassador to Portugal, said that was not his recollection, adding that he was brought up never to say such a thing even if he felt it.[14]

Senator Ted Kennedy read aloud the staff study's description of the Cuban missile crisis, beginning with the explanation of President Kennedy's concerns about the navy's activities in conducting the blockade. He spoke the words, but what he was saying was, "This was my beloved brother, and I am enormously proud of him and all that he accomplished." In the midst of the ongoing battle, this was a poignant moment.

After discussing the Cuban missile crisis, I summarized the study's analysis of the limited authority of each unified commander. I addressed their weak control of service component commanders, limited influence over resources, and little capacity for promoting unification at subordinate command levels. The study concluded: "The unified commands remain loose confederations of single-service forces which are unable to provide effective unified action across the spectrum of military missions."[15]

Evaluation of the 1983 invasion of Grenada, which Jeff Smith briefed, reinforced this conclusion. Nunn had repeatedly emphasized use of Grenada as a case study because its success avoided the sensitivities that surround a failure. The Atlantic Command (LANTCOM) conducted the invasion, code-named Operation Urgent Fury. Headquartered in Norfolk, Virginia, and commanded by Adm. Wesley L. McDonald, LANTCOM was ostensibly capable of integrating units from all four services into an effective force. The invasion demonstrated that LANTCOM's capabilities fell far short of what it should have been able to do as a unified command.

The nation of Grenada consists of three small islands with a land mass of 133 square miles, about twice the size of Washington, D.C. Seventy-five percent of its eighty-four thousand inhabitants are descended from Africa. Found at the southern extremity of the eastern Caribbean a hundred miles north of

Venezuela, Grenada is about two thousand miles from naval forces in Norfolk and major army and marine units in North Carolina.

A British colony for 140 years, Grenada gained full independence in 1974. Five years later, a bloodless coup overthrew Prime Minister Sir Eric Gairy—who was visiting New York City in part for a talk to the United Nations on unidentified flying objects[16]—and brought to power a Marxist government led by Maurice Bishop. The new regime ended democratic practices and came under Soviet and Cuban influence. In 1980, Cuban workers began construction of a nine-thousand-foot airport runway at Point Salines. This project concerned the Reagan administration because Soviet and Cuban advanced combat aircraft could operate from this runway.[17]

Weinberger later wrote that he began "receiving regular intelligence briefings on Grenada early in the new administration," which assumed office in January, 1981. By early 1983, Reagan "felt it necessary to tell the American people" about how a runway in Grenada threatened U.S. interests. He did so on March 23, in the same television address in which he proposed his Strategic Defense Initiative (SDI).[18] The president's message of alarm was apparently missed by the defense and intelligence communities, both of which would be caught unprepared seven months later.

A crisis erupted in Grenada on October 12, 1983, when the government's left-wing faction placed Bishop under house arrest. A week later, after Bishop's supporters had freed him, he was recaptured and executed along with seventeen others. An organization identifying itself as the Revolutionary Military Council replaced the civilian government, closed the airport, and threatened to shoot anyone violating a four-day, twenty-four-hour-a-day curfew. In Washington, State and Defense Department officials feared that the crisis would threaten the lives of the thousand or more American citizens in Grenada, including six hundred medical students.[19]

On October 14, the Joint Staff activated a response cell in the National Military Command Center (NMCC). The cell asked LANTCOM to provide a list of options for both a show of force and the evacuation of U.S. citizens. Four days later, the Joint Staff asked LANTCOM for options for evacuating American medical students in circumstances ranging from peaceful to armed resistance. On October 19, General Vessey sent Admiral McDonald a warning order for an evacuation operation.

Two years earlier, in August, 1981, LANTCOM had exercised a contingency plan for rescuing Americans from a Caribbean island. In this large joint exercise, army Rangers and marines conducted a landing on a small island. That experience informed the alternative courses of action McDonald submitted on October 20.

Later that day, Washington expanded LANTCOM's mission planning to include the neutralization of Grenada's armed forces and armed Cuban workers and the reconstitution of Grenada's civil government. On the evening of October 20, LANTCOM directed a marine amphibious ready group bound for Lebanon with nineteen hundred marines and the USS *Independence* carrier battle group, steaming for the Mediterranean, to alter their courses to head to areas within striking distance of Grenada. Following news reports of these diversions, intelligence reported that the Grenadians and Cubans were organizing to resist an American invasion.

Admiral McDonald's headquarters prepared two plans. One called for an assault by two battalions of army Rangers and other special operations forces (SOF) led by the army's Brig. Gen. Richard Scholtes, commander of the Joint Special Operations Command (JSOC). The second plan centered on a marine battalion landing team supported by navy SEALs. Both plans would reinforce the assault force with two battalions from the army's 82d Airborne Division.[20] When intelligence reported that the Grenadians were mobilizing two thousand reservists to augment fifteen hundred regular soldiers and six hundred armed Cubans, the JCS began pressuring McDonald to use both sets of forces. Vessey said the JCS wanted "to go in with enough force absolutely to get the job done . . . to minimize casualties, both on our side and on theirs. We wanted to intimidate the Cubans."[21]

At 11 A.M. on Sunday, October 23, McDonald briefed the joint chiefs on his concept of operations, which centered on a JSOC-led assault using Rangers and other SOF. This Pentagon meeting occurred only twelve hours after the terrorist bombing of the marine amphibious unit in Beirut had rocked the Marine Corps. The marine commandant, Gen. P. X. Kelley, pleaded for marine forces to have a role in the Grenada invasion.[22] His colleagues supported Kelley's plea, so "Vessey drew a boundary dividing Grenada into northern (Marine) and southern (Army) sectors."[23]

The final plan envisioned the operation beginning at 2 A.M. on October 25. It called for a coup de main, a surprise operation that would simultaneously execute supporting operations aimed at achieving success in one swift stroke. The assault forces were expected to accomplish all objectives by dawn. Planners also anticipated that participating SOF would "be out of Grenada by dawn or soon thereafter."[24]

McDonald designated the Second Fleet commander, Vice Adm. Joseph Metcalf III, to head the joint task force that would execute the plan. The Second Fleet's headquarters would provide the nucleus of the task force's staff. The plan called for four hundred marines to assault Pearls Airport and the nearby town of Grenville halfway up Grenada's east coast. Simultaneously, several hundred Rangers would parachute onto Point Salines Airfield, the nearly completed facility at the island's southwest tip. The Rangers would secure the airfield, rescue medical students at the adjacent True Blue campus, and capture Cuban headquarters at Camp Calivgny. Elements of the 82d Airborne

Division would quickly follow the Rangers into Point Salines, conduct mopping-up operations, and perform peacekeeping missions.[25]

In addition to the Rangers, other SOF were assigned roles. Navy SEALs would reconnoiter Pearls Airport prior to the marine assault. Elements of the Special Forces Operational Detachment-Delta would perform the same mission for the Rangers at Point Salines. Delta soldiers would assault the Richmond Hill Prison to rescue political prisoners while SEALs attempted to rescue the British governor general, Sir Paul Scoon, seize the Radio Free Grenada transmitter, and take control of the main power plant near Grand Mal Bay.[26]

On October 22, three days before the invasion, Weinberger inserted Vessey into the operational chain of command, implementing the statutory change that the administration had requested in April when it submitted its legislative proposal on JCS reorganization. The secretary authorized the JCS chairman to call upon backup forces and give strategic direction to LANTCOM and supporting commands. Washington's role in Operation Urgent Fury avoided many problems that had plagued previous operations. A Joint Staff after-action report concluded that "guidance and policy were concise and clear as were the orders" given by the chain of command. The report also noted: "The clearly defined rules of engagement permitted mission effectiveness with minimal civilian casualties." The Joint Staff added that Washington permitted field commands and forces to accomplish tasks "without undue intervention."[27]

Reagan, for his part, "placed full operational control of the mission in the hands . . . of the Joint Chiefs of Staff." The president gave Vessey and the service chiefs "a free hand in both planning and execution." He had taken this step to avoid another failure like the Iranian rescue mission, which he believed, incorrectly, the White House had caused by interfering. This time "from the very outset, Operation Urgent Fury was a military show; there would be no political interference."[28] The question thus became: Could the joint system effectively execute the operation?

The answer was no.

The operation did accomplish its objectives and was rated as an overall success in political and military terms. It rescued six hundred Americans and 120 other foreigners, restored democracy to Grenada, and eliminated threats to U.S. interests. Moreover, U.S. combat casualties were light. Nineteen American servicemen died during the operation, and 116 were wounded. Cuban losses totaled 25 killed, 59 wounded, and 638 captured. Forty-five Grenadian soldiers were killed and 358 wounded.[29]

The Reagan administration proclaimed the invasion was "a flawless triumph of American arms." The armed forces were "back on their feet and standing tall," according to the president. General John Wickham, the army chief of staff, called the operation "superb" and expressed confidence that the military was back "on the right track." Privately, most officers had a different view. They saw an operation full of flaws that exposed serious deficiencies in joint warfighting capabilities. Of this dichotomy between public expression and private belief, Mark Adkin writes: "The fact that the United States military had won their first clear-cut success since the Inchon landings in Korea over thirty years before was used as a smoke screen to conceal the unpalatable truth that it had been 'screwed up.' If ever the military had asked for a bloody nose, it had been in Grenada." Even the Joint History Office later admitted that Operation Urgent Fury "reinforced awareness of weaknesses in the joint system."[30]

The SASC staff initially heard about the flawed execution in informal discussions with Pentagon officers. Their commentary paralleled what two army generals who were well placed to observe the Grenada operation later wrote.

According to Maj. Gen. Colin Powell, serving as Weinberger's senior military assistant at the time of the invasion:

> We attacked with a combined force of Army paratroopers, Marines, and Navy SEALs. It should have been easy enough to take over a country of 84,000 population defended by a Third World militia of about two thousand poorly armed troops and a Cuban construction battalion. Yet, it took most of a week to subdue all resistance and rescue the medical students.
>
> The invasion was hardly a model of service cooperation. The campaign had started as a Navy-led operation, and only at the last minute was Major General H. Norman Schwarzkopf, then commanding the Army's 24th Infantry Division (Mechanized), added to Vice Admiral Joseph Metcalf's staff to make sure someone senior was on board who understood ground combat. Relations between the services were marred by poor communications, fractured command and control, interservice parochialism, and micromanagement from Washington. The operation demonstrated how far cooperation among the services still had to go. The invasion of Grenada succeeded, but it was a sloppy success.[31]

Schwarzkopf had a chance to see interservice rivalry up close. When he arrived in Norfolk the day before the invasion to join Metcalf's staff, he said he "felt about as welcome as a case of mumps." Schwarzkopf says that shortly after his arrival Admiral McDonald told him: "Now, for chrissakes, try and be helpful, would you? We've got a tough job to do and we don't need the Army giving us a hard time."

Service rivalry did not end when the invasion began. Schwarzkopf recalled that when army helicopters returning from battle landed on Metcalf's flagship, "Admiral Metcalf received an urgent message from the office of the Navy's comptroller in Washington warning that he should not refuel Army helicopters because the funds-transfer arrangements with the Army had not yet been worked out." Metcalf ignored the message.

Later, a marine colonel initially refused to obey Schwarzkopf's order to transport Ranger and airborne troops to rescue medical students saying, "We don't fly Army soldiers in Marine helicopters." Only after the general threatened to court-martial the colonel did the marine relent.

Schwarzkopf's assessment paralleled Powell's: "We had lost more lives than we needed to, and the brief war had revealed a lot of shortcomings—an abysmal lack of accurate intelligence, major deficiencies in communications, flareups of interservice rivalry, interference by higher headquarters in battlefield decisions, our alienation of the press, and more."[32]

In invading Grenada, the Pentagon had the operational initiative and employed an overwhelming force of eight thousand soldiers, sailors, airmen, and marines. American forces also had vast technological superiority, complete control of the sky and sea, and fire superiority with helicopters, air strikes, ground artillery, and naval guns. The invading force encountered only fifty Cuban regular soldiers along with 650 Cuban construction workers and fifteen hundred soldiers of the Grenadian People's Revolutionary Army, most of whom "never did engage U.S. forces in any significant way." Admiral McDonald described this force as a "third-rate, lightly armed, and poorly trained adversary." One estimate showed U.S. combat forces outnumbering defenders by approximately ten to one.[33] Such superiority predetermined the outcome, but it also served to put mistakes in stark relief.

Most notably, the U.S. military failed to execute its planned coup de main. Quick action was sought to rescue the medical students before the Grenadians or Cubans could seize them. Washington feared another hostage situation like Iran. The operation was not a swift stroke. It was not over in hours. It dragged on for five days. If the Grenadians or Cubans had intended to take hostages, they had ample opportunity.

The list of mistakes began with incredibly poor intelligence. The existence of two of the three medical student campuses was unknown to the invading force. Army forces learned of the second campus at Grand Anse only when students called to report that they were surrounded and request urgent rescue.[34] This was finally accomplished on the second day of the operation. Even more embarrassing, U.S. forces did not finally rescue all of the students until the fourth day, when units discovered a third campus with 202 students.[35] Other intelligence deficiencies included the absence of proper maps with grid coordinates and tactical information for U.S. forces. Poor intelligence was blamed for the "loss of surprise, slow development, tactical failures, and unnecessary casualties." Given four years of communist activity in Grenada, Reagan administration concern for several years, and the president's message of alarm to the American people, the total absence of intelligence is inexplicable.[36]

Glaring communications foul-ups marred the invasion. The services could not communicate with each other. Their continuing refusal to coordinate communications procurement principally caused this problem. The Joint History Office reports: "Navy radios could not communicate with the Vinson secure radio equipment used by the Army units, delaying and complicating requests for naval air and naval gunfire support. Soldiers in sight of warships delayed operations until distant Air Force gunships and Army helicopters could be summoned."[37]

Nunn heard of the army's frustrations over its inability to communicate with the navy when he attended Ranger Appreciation Day festivities at Hunter Army Airfield in Savannah, Georgia, on November 19, less than a month after the operation. He was told that the Rangers could not talk to navy ships in sight a few miles offshore. In need of naval gunfire support and finding his radio of no help, a Ranger officer stepped into a telephone booth, pulled out his AT&T calling card, and phoned Fort Bragg, which patched him through to Norfolk, which patched him through to the ships he could see. "The Army officer's use of his call to direct gunfire gave an entirely new meaning to the AT&T slogan, 'Reach Out and Touch Someone,'" said Nunn. More than any other story of service disunity, this one was remembered for years.[38]

Violating a fundamental principle of war, the operation did not have a single commander for ground operations. When army and marine forces were operating at a distance from each other in separate sectors, the absence of unity of command was less troubling. But even after marines landed at Grand Mal Bay in the army sector to assist in the heavier fighting in the south, no single commander was designated. This void led to friction and near disaster.

Some marine and army units were unaware of their close proximity. After the Grand Mal landing, the marine-army boundary was shifted south to accommodate marine operations. But word of this change did not reach all army units. In addition, army and marine units did not exchange liaison officers or establish a communications linkup, and they were not using joint fire support control measures. An army unit came upon a marine-held position and was surprised to find marines there. The soldiers were operating under the assumption that the area occupied by the marines was a free-fire zone.[39] Only good fortune prevented friendly fire casualties.

A friendly fire incident occurred on October 27, when an Air-Naval Gunfire Liaison Company (ANGLICO)—a team composed of marine and navy personnel specially qualified for shore control of naval gunfire and close air support—mistakenly vectored navy A-7 aircraft to attack a brigade headquarters of the 82d Airborne Division, wounding seventeen soldiers, three seriously. This tragedy occurred when the ANGLICO team, trying to coordinate an attack on a sniper position, lacked the army operating instructions and failed to coordinate its planned attack with the division's fire support element.[40]

Special operations forces were also misused during Operation Urgent Fury. Because special security compartments restricted information on many SOF

28. Paratroopers from the 82d Airborne Division move inland from their landing zone on the Caribbean island of Grenada. (U.S. Army Photo.)

activities for several years, Congress had only the sketchiest details of what had happened. Not until 1986, about a year after Jeff Smith's Grenada briefing to the Task Force on Defense Organization, did the SASC begin to obtain a better understanding of the special operations setbacks. Armed with that knowledge, the SASC passed major legislation—later called the Cohen-Nunn Amendment—to fix glaring SOF organizational problems. Key among the mistakes made was the decision by LANTCOM and the JCS to slip H-hour first by two hours and then by another hour to 5 A.M., only about thirty minutes before daylight. This decision by conventional force officers—unaware of the importance of surprise and darkness to a special operation—proved costly. Short warning times and inadequate cross-service training produced delays that forced special operators to conduct unsupported assaults in broad daylight. Failure resulted.[41]

How could so many things go wrong?

Arriving at the answer must begin with a discussion of LANTCOM's lack of unification. That command had navy, army, and air force component commands, but despite this unified appearance, LANTCOM was a "blue-water command" overwhelmingly staffed by naval officers. McDonald did have three subordinate unified commands, including Headquarters, U.S. Forces Caribbean at Key West, Florida. This organization was "responsible for the conduct of joint military operations within the Caribbean Sea, Gulf of Mexico, and portions of the Pacific Ocean bordering Central America." Officers from all four services staffed this truly joint headquarters. On October 20, LANTCOM planners recommended that the Key West headquarters coordinate the Grenada evacuation.[42]

This recommendation reflected existing Operational Plan (OPLAN) 2360 for an intervention in Grenada. In this plan, the Key West headquarters would exercise overall command of the operation with the on-scene commander being the commander of the army's XVIII Airborne Corps—at that time, Lt. Gen. Jack Mackmull. The plan listed available forces as an army division, an army brigade in reserve, a carrier battle group, and a marine amphibious unit. Its targets duplicated many of those that needed to be captured in October, 1983. Nonetheless, OPLAN 2360 was not used.[43]

Instead of the Key West commander, McDonald, as mentioned earlier, selected the Second Fleet commander, Vice Admiral Metcalf, to lead the joint task force. Two factors reportedly influenced McDonald's decision. First, Metcalf's headquarters was collocated with his. The distance between Norfolk and Key West would add time to coordination and make maintaining tight operational security more difficult. Second, the Key West headquarters, unlike the Second Fleet, had no assigned forces.[44]

The Second Fleet headquarters was not, however, prepared to command and control a joint task force. It was a naval staff "with little or no experience in planning and commanding large ground operations."[45] The Second Fleet staff did not include a single army officer. Schwarzkopf and two army majors were added during the last two days of planning, but the Joint Staff judged that the headquarters "still lacked needed ground and air expertise." Moreover, Metcalf, like McDonald, had limited joint experience. Neither had ever served a day in a joint military organization until McDonald arrived to command LANTCOM. Not surprisingly, the Grenada invasion began with several days of "uncoordinated ground operations by Rangers and Marines and the absence of unified air support."[46]

Effective unification did not exist at the unified command level, joint task force level, or subordinate levels. None of the forces employed had trained sufficiently together, established common doctrine and procedures, or made their communications equipment and other systems interoperable. Operation Urgent Fury required "meticulous planning, complete security, flexible and reliable communications, firm command and control, a high standard of interservice cooperation, plus a huge logistical backup."[47] Unfortunately, LANTCOM, its components, and assigned forces could not meet these requirements.

Jeff Smith's briefing to the task force on Grenada evidenced major deficiencies, but like our first briefing, the second presentation on the unified commands, Cuban missile crisis, Grenada, and other operations did not win converts to the proreform side. The task force found each issue to be contentious. Quayle, Wilson, and Gramm wanted equal time for antireform arguments to be heard. Goldwater and Nunn tried to accommodate their requests.

In the midst of the task force's struggles, Goldwater and Nunn received good news: on July 10 Reagan announced his intention to nominate Admiral Crowe to replace General Vessey as JCS chairman. Given their private knowledge of Crowe's proreform views, the two senators had lobbied for his selection. Vessey had decided to step down on October 1, eight months before the end of his second two-year term. According to a report in the *Washington Post*, "Crowe's associates predict that he will be more innovative as chairman than was Vessey, who had a low-profile, low-key style."[48]

The media speculated on Crowe's stance on reorganization. One editorial opined that, because Weinberger enthusiastically endorsed Crowe, he "is not likely to work toward the major structural reform that many analysts argue is necessary to face current challenges." The *New York Times* noted: "Admiral Crowe has an unusual amount of experience in joint positions, where his Navy loyalties were subordinated to responsibility to all the services." Meanwhile, *Newsweek* reported: "Vessey preferred the status quo at the JCS, and Crowe has yet to take a public stand on questions of reform. 'I suspect he may not have made up his mind,' says James Woolsey, former under secretary of the Navy."[49]

Goldwater and Nunn knew otherwise. Crowe was committed to reorganization. The senators did not know what the admiral might be able to do to promote the cause in the antireform Pentagon, but his selection elated them. During Crowe's confirmation hearing at the end of July, Nunn said, "I'm sure he's the right man for the job in the right place and the right time. I enthusiastically support his nomination."[50]

Goldwater occupied a lonely position as the reorganization point man. He could not confide in his Republican colleagues, most of whom were antireform. His military friends also did not support his efforts. The chairman turned to a few close friends for reassurance, including Ben Schemmer, editor of the *Armed Forces Journal*. On July 9, Goldwater sent Schemmer a copy of the staff study. An accompanying letter said, "What we have found, frankly, is frightening—not just in the Joint Chiefs of Staff or procurement—but in the whole Department of Defense structure."[51]

Goldwater had a second reason for sending Schemmer the study: "Now out of this whole effort, whether we decide to make any changes or whether the politics of the armed services will be too strong to allow it, will come a delineation of the problems that I think should be put into a textbook form some-time. With this thought in mind, I turn to you, because you know exactly what I am talking about."

Goldwater concluded by saying: "I think this study will have a bearing on the future of our country and a strong bearing on the future of freedom. About all I can leave this office with is the knowledge that I did something in 35 years to try to perpetuate freedom."

On July 30, Schemmer responded: "All I can say is 'Wow!' . . . let me express my strongest possible compliments to you and Sam Nunn and Jim Locher for a landmark work—clear, concise, eminently readable. As a professional word merchant, I'm jealous, Barry."[52]

Schemmer offered to help: "Barry, I would greatly look forward to helping you bring this whole problem into focus. Indeed, that could be one of your great-est services to this nation. If some action is not taken now, we are going to drown in our own bureaucracy or be strangled with our own rope."

The task force meeting on August 1 focused on the staff study's chapter on the Office of the Secretary of Defense. Having served in OSD for ten years, I knew its organizational problems. My briefing focused on four deficiencies. The first and foremost was OSD's limited ability to integrate the four services' capabili-ties along mission lines. In writing the OSD chapter, I had devoted considerable attention to the absence of a mission focus in the Pentagon. I coined the phrase "mission integration" to describe the desired "ability of the services to take unified action to discharge the major military missions of the United States." The staff study contended that mission integration—not unification or cen-tralization—was the real goal of reorganization. Comparing the three, the re-port argued that "unification relates to form; centralization relates to process; and mission integration relates to substance."[53] The OSD's organization along functional lines, such as manpower and research and development, had pro-duced an exclusive focus on managing functional activities.

The staff study targeted inadequate supervision and coordination of many OSD offices as a second deficiency. The defense secretary's extensive span of control—forty-one subordinates reported to him—caused this problem. Essen-tially, many senior officials reported to no one.

Personnel problems existed in OSD as well. Inexperienced political appoin-tees were a source of concern. High turnover rates and prolonged vacancies in such positions further undermined effective leadership. The turnover rate in the position of assistant secretary of defense for international security affairs exemplified the problem. Since the position's establishment in 1953, the length of service of appointees averaged only 1.6 years. The staff study also identified three problems in OSD's performance: micromanagement of service programs, lack of coalition-oriented planning and programming, and inadequate review of non-nuclear contingency plans.

In writing the OSD chapter, I had conducted extensive interviews in the Pentagon. These private sessions contrast sharply with public testimony and conversations. Publicly, officials and officers adhered to the department's formal opposition. In private, however, they expressed significant support for reform. In preparing our study, the staff privately interviewed more than five hundred officials and officers. Roughly three-fourths were troubled by the department's organizational deficiencies, but they were less certain as to the required fixes. Although these private views could not be made part of the public record, they did inform the staff's work. The knowledge that a significant number of Pentagon workers shared our perspective on the magnitude of the problems also reassured us.

After the four-week August recess, the task force reconvened on September 12. No senator had changed his view during the break. Antireform senators had developed a new line of attack, claiming that the staff study's analytical methodology was flawed. For the next session, I prepared a detailed rebuttal to that assertion, which satisfied a majority of the task force.[54]

This session examined organizational problems in the military departments. Their excessive power was causing problems in other components. But the staff study also focused on major problems in the military departments themselves. The most important deficiency centered on confusion about the role of the secretary of each department. When Congress passed the National Security Act of 1947, it did not prescribe the relationship between the secretary of defense and his service secretary subordinates. According to John Kester, "The role secretaries of defense have allocated for service secretaries has never been fixed." Most troubling, the absence of specificity had led to efforts by service secretaries to become independent from the defense secretary.[55]

A second problem focused on the existence of two headquarters staffs at the top of the Army and Air Force Departments and three at the apex of the Navy Department. One staff was the civilian secretariat; the other, a military staff, worked for the chief of staff. The Navy Department had three staffs because it had two military staffs, one under the CNO and a second under the marine commandant. This structure, essentially a holdover from World War II arrangements, was viewed as leading to unnecessary staff layers and duplication of effort.[56]

The task force met on September 17 to hear the staff's analysis on congressional review and oversight of defense. This chapter interested the members more than any other. They lived these problems every day. In examining deficiencies on Capitol Hill, senators did not have to worry about protecting the Pentagon, White House, or their party. In briefing the chapter on Congress,

John Hamre focused on how the budget process dominated Congress and overwhelmed other legislative tasks. He quoted an earlier Nunn statement that "the time and workload of the Senate—and of its committees—are being dominated and devoured by this task alone." Hamre explained how duplicative committee reviews and blurred committee jurisdictions were undermining the process and adding to its complexity and length. He talked about the budget review's focus on artificial accounting inputs, the problems of reviewing each service's budget in isolation, micromanagement, inadequate Senate review of presidential appointments in the Pentagon, and many other problems. The task force was unified in its view that serious congressional deficiencies demanded attention.[57]

Two chapters of the staff study dealt with DoD decision-making processes: the Planning, Programming, and Budgeting System (PPBS) and the acquisition system. The task force turned its attention to these chapters on September 26. The staff study addressed these primarily to provide background for the members on how the department operated. The task force's jurisdiction did not include acquisition, which a subcommittee under Quayle's leadership was addressing. Moreover, the task force was unlikely to recommend changes to internal Pentagon procedures, such as the PPBS.

On October 3, the task force held its seventh and final session on the staff study to consider the chapters on civilian control of the military and the overview analysis. Colleen Getz's work on civilian control revealed a "lack of consensus on a definition of civilian control" throughout American history. She found this ambiguity had "not undermined its effectiveness as one of the governing tenets of the American republic."[58]

Although the study concluded that "the concept of civilian control is unquestioned throughout the Department of Defense today," it argued against complacency: "Any changes to the U.S. military establishment must be carefully assessed for their impact on civil-military relations" and "No changes can be accepted which diminish civilian control." In applying this yardstick to the study's recommended changes, we concluded that they "either strengthen civilian control over the military or leave the balance as it currently exists."

The overview analysis looked across all of DoD's components and the staff study chapters in search of major problem themes. It identified ten: the imbalance of emphasis on functions versus missions, the imbalance of service versus joint interests, interservice logrolling, the predominance of programming and budgeting, the lack of clarity of strategic goals, insufficient mechanisms for change, the inadequate quality of political appointees and joint-duty military personnel, the failure to clarify the desired division of work among components, excessive spans of control by senior officials and the absence of effective hierarchical structures, and the insufficient power and influence of the secretary of defense.[59]

The overview analysis also established a historical context for these problems. It concluded, "The problems currently plaguing the Department of Defense have not just recently evolved. For the most part, they have been evident for much of this century."

During September, the magnitude of the reorganization challenge became clearer to Goldwater, Nunn, Finn, Smith, and me. After eight months of carefully laying the groundwork and more than three months of task force meetings, Goldwater, Nunn, and Cohen remained the only committed members. The three antireform senators—Quayle, Wilson, and Gramm—had not budged an inch. Bingaman, Levin, and Kennedy had exhibited open minds, but remained tentative. They were looking for reassurance before taking on the entire military establishment on this sacred issue. Bingaman's comment to me after one session reflected his concern: "Jim, your arguments and proposals appear sound, but all the generals and admirals across the river in the Pentagon are against this."

Although Goldwater and Nunn had gained ground during the summer, the pace was excruciatingly slow. Moreover, the energy expended—particularly by the few staffers—for every small step forward was enormous. Especially worrisome was the knowledge that our adversaries—the Pentagon and its supporters—had vastly greater resources to throw into the fight. They could write more papers, do more research, pose more questions, lobby harder, speak to more Rotary Clubs, influence more reporters, write more articles, and rally more retired generals and admirals.

The task force's meetings and members' individual inquiries generated a staggering workload for the staff. Only Rick Finn, Barbara Brown, and I were available full time to write the staff study, prepare task force sessions, and respond to members' questions and requests for research. The question-and-answer format of congressional hearings had popularized the saying, "One idiot can ask more questions than can be answered by ten angels." This saying took on new meaning for Finn and me as we fielded unending questions. The reorganization effort made us feel as if we were on a merry-go-round that was going faster and faster—and there was no getting off. The unbelievable pace forced Finn and me to work twelve-hour days seven days a week from mid-June through mid-September—eighty-nine days without a single day off.

That schedule ended when my doctor put me in the hospital for two days because of physical exhaustion. I slept for almost forty-eight hours. Finn, Brown, and I kept my hospitalization secret lest reform opponents recognize our weariness and redouble their efforts.

As Goldwater and Nunn looked beyond the task force to the full committee, the Republican side looked overwhelmingly antireform, and Democrats were not evidencing a groundswell of enthusiasm. John Stennis, the former chairman, appeared to be a reorganization opponent. The aged Mississippian's stance concerned Nunn. Stennis had taken Nunn under his wing when the Georgia Democrat was first elected to the Senate and took a special interest in his career. Nunn did not look forward to fighting his mentor over the emotional issue of Pentagon reform.[60]

Goldwater and Nunn were facing the same powerful parochial interests that had defeated Truman and Eisenhower. The senators were also heading for the same bitter setback—unless they could focus the debate on the issues and facts and thereby surmount the overwhelming power politics, partisan pleas, and emotional appeals of the Pentagon and its supporters.

Goldwater, Nunn, Finn, Smith, and I discerned that if we stayed in the trenches in a war of attrition, reorganization would be buried. We understood that we would have to adopt an innovative strategy to have any realistic chance of gaining sufficient support in the committee. Development of that strategy became a high-priority, do-or-die task.

CHAPTER 16

Playing the Media Card

Four hostile newspapers were more to be feared

than a thousand bayonets.

—Napoleon

By mid-September, Senators Goldwater and Nunn had pieced together a two-part strategy for breaking out of the trench warfare of reorganization. They planned to enlarge the battlefield beyond the halls of government by capturing the media's attention and to accelerate the education of members of the Task Force on Defense Organization and reassure them on this controversial undertaking.

The two senators believed that print and television reporting on reform would be overwhelmingly favorable, spark public interest, and build pressure for change. This would differ with the reporting of the postwar debates, when influential journalists had opposed unification. Engaging the media and the public, in Goldwater and Nunn's view, offered the best hope for breaking the Pentagon's stranglehold.

The media had dutifully reported each step since General Jones's call for reform in 1982, but reorganization was not considered a big story. Complex issues and conflicting testimony were not easily explained in short newspaper or television reports. Reorganization had initially lacked big-name sponsors. No key congressmen had led the House charge, where only a low-visibility subcommittee pursued reform. On the Senate side, where national figures were involved, Tower's abortive efforts had confused observers. The right ingredients were not there to grab headlines. With the clout and charisma Goldwater and Nunn could bring to bear, that situation was about to change.

The media generally had seen reorganization in a positive light. Favorable articles had emerged to balance self-serving Pentagon commentary. Service spokesmen, retired officers, and military associations had written numerous antireform articles and editorials. Intense service lobbying, especially by the navy, complemented these efforts. By the early fall of 1985, the public information battle had produced a stalemate.

Goldwater and Nunn could not afford a stalemate. That outcome meant victory for the status quo. They had to wage and win a public information battle the prize of which was votes in Congress. The two senators had to create a media drumbeat in favor of change. They needed front-page stories that educated opinion makers in the nation's capital and motivated people back home to write their senators. But what would arouse the media's interest? What kind of information did the media need?

The answer to these questions, Goldwater and Nunn decided, was to publicly release the Senate Armed Services Committee's staff study. Although designed for internal use, the study was not classified and could be released. In the two senators' view, the study comprehensively, intelligently, and fairly examined the full range of issues and evaluated every side of each of them. The study would make public all of the ammunition that Goldwater and Nunn had. They were convinced these materials told an explosive story.

Before releasing the study, however, Goldwater and Nunn needed to set the stage. They did not want to simply dump this massive document on the media and public. They had to be fed some tantalizing, bite-sized portions that would capture their attention and have them waiting eagerly for the next bite.

The chairman and ranking Democrat decided to deliver a series of speeches on the Senate floor, the setting where they could best reach and inform their colleagues, but also one where the large number of reporters in the Senate Press Gallery would hear their message. In a country colloquialism unusual for him, Nunn described the reason for the speeches with a favorite saying of Louisiana senator Russell Long: "You have to put the corn out for the hogs." Using the study's most powerful research and analysis, the floor speeches would vividly describe fundamental problems in the Department of Defense. Solutions would not be offered or discussed. This approach adhered to an old congressional dictum: "Don't solve a problem for people before they know they've got one." The speeches had to convince the Senate, media, opinion makers, and public that crippling problems existed. Selling solutions could wait.[1]

To magnify attention and demonstrate the bipartisan nature of their work, Goldwater and Nunn elected to present their statements jointly. They said their delivery would be like that of Chet Huntley and David Brinkley, referring to the popular and trusted television news coanchors of the 1950s and 1960s. Either senator by himself would have ranked as the public figure with the greatest stature on defense to call for Pentagon reform since President Eisenhower in 1958. Together, these two defense giants were sure to attract enormous attention.

In their efforts to generate favorable coverage, Goldwater and Nunn had two advantages that reorganizers of the 1940s and 1950s did not have. First, by 1985, the media had developed a critical attitude toward the Reagan administration's Pentagon. Repeated operational setbacks and procurement fiascos had helped build this negative view.

Strained relations with the Pentagon intensified the media's unfavorable attitude. An article appearing in the *National Journal* in February, 1985, described the press's viewpoint: "The Pentagon had become increasingly less forthcoming during the Reagan administration. Documents routinely released during the Carter administration are no longer available. The specter of polygraph tests has been used to discourage leaks to the press. Weinberger and Michael I. Burch, assistant defense secretary for public affairs, are markedly less forthcoming than their predecessors."[2]

The press blamed Weinberger for the rift. He was described as having "steadily become more reticent in public and has gradually sought, with some success, to tighten the controls over the flow of information from the Defense Department." Weinberger was seen as "fundamentally secretive" and "instinctively" prone to personally control the flow of information to the press.[3] In fact, repeated leaks of highly classified documents were the main force behind the secretary's efforts to clamp down on press access to Pentagon information.

Journalists' skepticism of the secretary and his department would provide Goldwater and Nunn a receptive audience for their thoroughly researched presentations.

Goldwater and Nunn's second advantage over their predecessors was the absence of influential opponents among journalists. In the immediate postwar period, strong press voices had opposed President Truman's plans for a unified military despite the fact that a large majority of newspapers and the public believed that some form of unification was desirable. This widespread opinion originated with the Pearl Harbor catastrophe, which "was seen to have proven the need for unification from the point of view of combat effectiveness." However, there was confusion over the preferred form of unification, and the number of people having firm opinions was "very small and divided." This indecisiveness provided an opening for negative press opinion.

Three leading military correspondents—Hanson W. Baldwin, Walter Millis, and George Fielding Eliot—had supported the navy's views on organization. Baldwin had won a Pulitzer Prize in 1943 for his World War II reporting from the Pacific. After the war, he became one of the most important and powerful civilian voices on military affairs. According to fellow journalist Arthur T. Hadley, Baldwin's reporting influenced the outcome of the unification fight: "The *New York Times* alone among the press had a full-time military affairs correspondent in addition to its Pentagon correspondent. That able man was

Hanson Baldwin, a 1924 graduate of the Naval Academy. Other reporters with less knowledge looked to him for guidance. His paper more than any other set the public stage for the defense debate." Hadley was certain that Baldwin "never consciously distorted the news." He found, however, that Baldwin's "unconscious pro-Navy bias time and again had a chilling effect on efforts of President Truman [and others] to unify the armed forces efficiently."[4]

In April, 1946, Baldwin castigated Truman for having "rapped the knuckles of the admirals" for opposing "his War Department-Navy Department merger project." He wrote that the president's "outburst" had "exacerbated . . . the long and bitter fight." Baldwin reported that some navy supporters felt that "the president, by his inferential invocation of the 'gag rule' over the Navy and his charges of Navy lobbying, so aroused congressional friends of the Navy that he administered, at least for this session of Congress, the coup de grace to the very legislation he espouses."

Of Truman's proposed legislation as revised by a Senate subcommittee, Baldwin opined, "The Navy has held out consistently—and, in this writer's opinion, correctly—for four fundamental principles." Baldwin's article elaborated on each of the four: opposition to a single chief of staff, separate administration of each military department, protection of the Marine Corps from elimination, and the navy's control of its own aviation. "These four points are major, not only to the Navy but to the nation," Baldwin argued.[5]

Goldwater and Nunn did not anticipate such determined journalistic opposition.

Throughout their reorganization work, Goldwater and Nunn had attempted to be low-key, objective, and fair. Anxious to find an opening for working constructively with the Pentagon, they refrained from overstating their case. Nevertheless, their floor statements would need some zing if the senators were to arouse the media's interest. Although colorful statements might risk further alienation of the Pentagon and its Capitol Hill supporters, Goldwater and Nunn decided to take that risk. They pressed Arnold Punaro into service to help create the needed zing. Before becoming the committee's minority staff director, Punaro had handled military public affairs on Nunn's personal staff. He had a keen eye for the turn of phrase that would make a headline or memorable quote.

Finn, Smith, Punaro, and I realized that Goldwater's and Nunn's speeches would require different styles. The bold, feisty Goldwater would prefer more colorful, blunt language. The cautious, meticulous Nunn would prefer more precise, diplomatic statements. Having worked for Nunn for thirteen years, Punaro could best judge language that Nunn would be comfortable using. In reading drafts, he would say, "Well, no, Senator Nunn won't ever say this, but we can get Senator Goldwater to say this." According to Nunn: "Locher slipped things into Goldwater's speeches that I was shocked with. Goldwater liked them, though. I remember seeing him reading those speeches, and every now and then he'd come to a corker and he'd kind of like it and he'd read it again."[6]

In six straight Senate sessions starting Tuesday, October 1, Goldwater and Nunn took the floor to focus attention on their crusade. Their first speeches addressed problems regarding the congressional role in national security. The two senators had decided that before criticizing the Pentagon, Congress's performance should be critically examined. The following day, they explained the long-term nature of America's military problems, starting with the Spanish-American War. The next three sets of statements hammered on deficiencies in the Joint Chiefs of Staff and unified commands, the Office of the Secretary of Defense, and the Pentagon budget process. Goldwater and Nunn devoted the last day to summarizing their earlier statements and describing the legislative process they had begun.

In introducing his first speech, Goldwater told his colleagues and all concerned Americans, "You will be shocked at the serious deficiencies in the organization and procedures of the Department of Defense and the Congress." He then uttered two sentences that the press and others often repeated: "If we have to fight tomorrow, these problems will cause Americans to die unnecessarily. Even more, they may cause us to lose the fight."[7]

"Congress is compounding the problems in the Department of Defense," said Goldwater, "and major changes in the way we conduct our business are long overdue." He addressed how the budget process dominated Congress's agenda and "is seriously degrading the quality of congressional oversight of the Defense Department." The Arizona Republican discussed Congress's repeated failure to enact a defense budget before the beginning of the fiscal year and the counterproductive duplicative reviews by the budget, authorization, and appropriations committees. "As we direct that changes be introduced into DoD to improve overall national security, we must make changes ourselves," he concluded. "I am casting the first stone and I am throwing it at our glass house here in the Congress."

Nunn's speech followed the same line: "We have found the enemy and it is us." He argued that the budgetary process "has led to the trivialization of Congress' responsibilities for oversight and . . . to excessive micromanagement." Nunn spoke of Capitol Hill's preoccupation with trivia: "Last year, Congress changed the number of smoke grenade launchers and muzzle boresights the Army requested. We directed the Navy to pare back its request for parachute flares, practice bombs, and passenger vehicles. Congress specified that the Air Force should cut its request for garbage trucks, street cleaners, and scoop loaders. This is a bit ridiculous. The current congressional review of the defense program would make a fitting version of the popular game, 'Trivial Pursuit.'"[8]

Being a strong believer in the use of history to understand current problems, Goldwater was enthusiastic about the second speeches' examination of past wars and crises. He said that he and Nunn would "discuss specific examples where the military services' inability, or unwillingness, to work together has led this nation to military disaster or near disaster." In another often-quoted line, he said, "As someone who has devoted his entire life to the military, I am saddened that the services are still unable to put national interest above parochial interest." Goldwater identified two problems: lack of true unity of command and inadequate cooperation among the services. On unity of command's importance to any operation, he said: "Every West Point plebe knows that. It means that there's only one commander. It means there is only one chief and he's over all the Indians—no matter what tribe." Goldwater spoke to the organizational problems evidenced by Pearl Harbor, Leyte Gulf, the Vietnam War, and the *Pueblo* seizure.[9]

Nunn's speech recounted the Iranian hostage rescue mission and the Grenada invasion. However, he began by talking about the unity of command problems in Vietnam, which he said "were never thoroughly discussed and never thoroughly understood by the media, the general public, or Congress." The Georgia Democrat also remarked that the *Pueblo* crisis "was never examined, at least in the public dialogue, from the point of view of what really went wrong." After reciting problems during the Desert One operation, ranging from the incompatibility of equipment to poorly coordinated joint training, he gave a detailed analysis of Grenada. "Grenada has been touted as a victory . . . But it is sobering to look at how many failures of coordination and communication there were. One cannot help but wonder what would have happened if the opposition on the island had been better armed, organized, or larger."[10]

The following day, Goldwater and Nunn addressed the deficiencies in the JCS and unified commands. "The shortcomings are not in the men, the shortcomings are in the office," Goldwater explained. "They are called on to do an almost impossible task: to represent their own service's viewpoint but, simultaneously, to sacrifice that view to the greater common good of joint considerations." On the liabilities of such arrangements, the chairman quoted Winston Churchill: "I am increasingly impressed with the disadvantages of the present system of having Naval, Army and Air Force officers equally represented at all points and on all combined subjects, whether in committees or in commands. This has resulted in a paralysis of the offensive spirit."[11]

Goldwater then listed the problems in the joint system: "The inability of the JCS to provide useful and timely military advice; the poor performance in joint operations; the inadequate quality of the staff of the Organization of the Joint Chiefs of Staff; the confused command lines; and the lack of adequate advocates for joint interests in budgetary matters." He also spoke of the dominance of the services in the joint system: "When the rope from the individual services pulls in one direction and the rope from the Joint Chiefs pulls in the other direction, the individual services invariably win that tug-of-war. . . . but the country loses."

Goldwater concluded by saying: "You will hear over and over again the old maxim: 'If it ain't broke, don't fix it.' Well, I say to my colleagues: It is broke, and we need to fix it."

Nunn began his speech by talking about JCS paralysis. To show how the JCS could not even easily resolve a minor personnel issue, he recounted an anecdote from General Jones describing how "the chiefs spent an entire afternoon arguing over which service should provide the new attaché at our embassy in Cairo."[12]

Turning to the unified commands, Nunn said, "I regret to report to you today that we have unified commanders but divided commands." He spoke at length about the lack of joint planning and coordination. One example that he used revealed a dangerous disconnect between the army and air force: "We learned that the Air Force was planning to evacuate a particular hospital in Europe in the event of war because it believed that the hospital would be destroyed almost immediately. At the same time, the Army was planning to move in and use the same hospital after the Air Force left. Now, who is in charge over there anyway? There is no excuse for this type of situation."

The fourth set of speeches addressed the absence of a focus on military missions in Pentagon planning and budgeting. Goldwater quoted Truman as saying in December, 1945: "With the coming of peace, it is clear that we must not only continue, but strengthen, our present facilities for integrated planning. We cannot have the sea, land, and air members of our defense team working at what may turn out to be cross-purposes, planning their programs on different assumptions as to the nature of the military establishment we need, and engaging for an open competition for funds." Goldwater said he agreed with Truman, adding that "in 1945, we needed a military establishment that could conduct integrated planning and resource allocation and, I am sorry to say, we still need it. Moreover, all of the things that President Truman said we do not need, we still have."[13]

Goldwater then offered the following analogy: "The absence of mission integration is like an orchestra that cannot play together. . . . The Department of Defense is like an orchestra with 41 sections [the number of officials reporting to the defense secretary], and many of them are the best in the business. But, because they're not integrated, they sound like Alexander's Ragtime Band, not the New York Philharmonic." When my boss finished that sentence, he paused and leaned over to me, seated next to him, and said, "I like ragtime music." From his tone, I sensed that he perceived that our analogy demeaned ragtime.

Nunn's speech criticized OSD, which he argued "has primary responsibility for ensuring that we have an integrated defense program and that the United

States is capable of performing its major military missions in the most effective and efficient manner." He judged that "they have failed to do this." Instead of concentrating on outputs, Nunn said OSD was focusing on inputs. "A number of people have responsibility for thousands upon thousands of individual inputs, but no one has responsibility for the single output."[14]

The fifth set of speeches addressed the Pentagon's budget process, which Goldwater said dominated activity: "The Department of Defense is preoccupied with chasing after resources. More time is spent preparing plans for the next budget than for the next war." In making his point, Goldwater quoted General MacArthur as saying, "There is no substitute for victory." Goldwater then lectured, "I say to the Pentagon, budget policy is no substitute for defense policy."[15]

Nunn addressed two consequences of flawed Pentagon budgeting. First, by always forecasting unrealistically high future budgets, it permitted programs to be started with limited funding in the budget year and the promise of more funding in the out years. "We have so many systems in production at inefficient rates because we start more programs than we can afford," Nunn argued. He also lamented the system's bias toward investment spending on hardware, research and development, and construction over readiness spending for munitions, spare parts, and similar items. "This is why we spent $2.6 billion on attack submarines last year but didn't buy enough torpedoes to give each of them a full load. This is why we have $45 million aircraft like the F 15 dropping World War II–era dumb bombs, because we cannot afford to buy sufficient quantities of modern munitions."[16]

The final set of speeches summarized the previous five and pointed the way ahead. Nunn spoke first, permitting the chairman to deliver the grand finale. "If we change these organizational weaknesses," said Nunn, "we will strengthen our military. That is what this effort is all about."[17]

Then it was Goldwater's turn: "I do believe that this is a terribly important subject. The reorganization of the Department of Defense may be the most important thing that Congress does in my lifetime. It will be the most important thing that I tried to do in mine." He urged "the Pentagon to work with us in a spirit of cooperation, not confrontation. We need their input and counsel. . . . If we are to fight a war, whether one starts tomorrow, ten years from now or fifty years in the future, we must have the organizations in place to defend this country. We owe this to the men and women in uniform who are the finest our country has ever produced. . . . They deserve a better system than we have now. . . . Congress must, and I am confident will, make the needed changes."[18]

Elated with his final statement, Goldwater said, "Damn, that was a good speech. Oh, I loved it."[19]

I agreed with him about the speech, but near the end, when Goldwater spoke about civilian control of the military, he ad-libbed the phrase "a principle of questionable constitutionality." I was stunned. Goldwater had often criticized civilian meddling in military operations. In 1983, at the first hearing of Tower's reorganization inquiry, he had said: "We have lost the last two wars we have fought because they have been run by civilians in Washington. . . . Now, I realize the sanctity of the idea of the civilian being supreme. It is a beautiful thing to think about. The question in my mind is, can we any longer afford to allow the expertise of men and women trained, at terrific expense, in what I consider to be the finest military academies in the world, to be set aside for the decisions of civilians."[20]

Goldwater's reorganization work had better informed him of all causes of the military's past failures. Although civilian meddling still troubled him, I had never before heard him question the constitutionality of the principle that had guided American civil-military relations since the creation of the republic. Did he earnestly hold that view, or was this a popular phrase from old stump speeches that just popped out? I had to find out. The reorganization effort could get sidetracked on a highly unproductive debate over Goldwater's comment.

After congratulating the chairman, I said, "There was one problem."

"What's that?" Goldwater asked, somewhat taken back.

"You called civilian control a principle of questionable constitutionality," I answered.

"I did?" he replied. Then, without further explanation, he said: "Sam and I must get back to the committee hearing. Jim, you know what to do."

Finn and I went to the Senate office of the Official Reporters of Debates, which is responsible for transcribing Senate floor statements and debates for the *Congressional Record*. There, as part of our normal duty to edit and correct transcription errors in Goldwater's floor statements, we struck the offending phrase.

Just as Goldwater and Nunn had hoped, their set of six speeches grabbed the media's attention. The print media reported extensively on them. The Associated Press and United Press International filed the first stories under headlines reading "Goldwater: Problems in Congress hinder military superiority," "Interservice Rivalries Still Plaguing Planners, Senators Say," and "Goldwater: Service loyalty hampers joint chiefs."[21] Soon, articles on the speeches appeared in all major newspapers and news magazines. The *New York Times* reported that the speeches "portrayed the military as a confusion of competing factions, quarreling over money in peacetime and tripping over one another in battle." *Time* related that when the senators gave their "sharply worded" speeches, "shock waves rippled clear across the Potomac to the innermost rings of the Pentagon." It summarized the speeches by reporting that "the two senators accused the military of endangering the nation's defense and squandering its assets with interservice bickering."[22]

The speeches had set the stage; the media and public were now anxiously awaiting release of the staff study.

Goldwater and Nunn initially intended to publish the study as a committee report, which would require a committee vote. They were highly uncertain that they could secure enough favorable votes. Moreover, opponents were likely to insist on debating every paragraph of the 645-page report—congressional trench warfare at its worst. To avoid these obstacles, Goldwater and Nunn decided to print the study as a staff report to the committee. Such an action required only the chairman's approval.

Releasing the study as a staff report had other important advantages. First, its ideas could form the starting point for deliberations without being explicitly endorsed by Goldwater and Nunn. This would greatly increase their flexibility in the politicking and negotiating that would be required to enact meaningful legislation.

A second advantage was greater freedom to use extreme recommendations as part of a negotiating strategy. In seven years on Capitol Hill I had repeatedly witnessed the central role of compromise in congressional politics. If our report recommended exactly what we thought was needed to fix those problems, the recommendations would become the starting point for prolonged negotiations and weakening compromises. We thus would likely end up with half a loaf: an incomplete and possibly unworkable set of reforms.

Nunn, also thinking about the need to include some extreme recommendations for posturing purposes, told Finn, Smith, and me, "We need staff recommendations that scare them so badly that when we do what we really intend to do, they will take out their handkerchiefs and wipe their brows and say, 'Boy, we sure are lucky.'"[23] Nunn envisioned some recommendations being more far-reaching than we truly believed appropriate so that he and Goldwater could use them as negotiating bait. With Goldwater's concurrence, Nunn asked me to go as far as I could in the report's recommendations and "still retain some plausibility." Because our posturing would do little good if others understood our strategy, only the two senators, Finn, Smith, Punaro, and I were privy to this scheme.

"When Jim Locher agreed with that tactic, he, in effect, became the point man," Nunn said. "He was willing to be the guy out front catching all the bullets. I thought it was a brave act on his part. It was intentional. It was our strategy."

Nunn recalled that he "was absolutely convinced that we had to put something out there stronger than we really wanted because if we didn't let the opponents knock down something, their blood thirst was never going to be satisfied."[24]

These few lightning-rod recommendations were the only changes we made to the staff study. We wanted the analyses of problems and evaluation of solutions to be as objective as possible.

As Finn, Smith, Punaro, and I began the process of selecting the right package of recommendations, we had Confederate general Thomas J. "Stonewall" Jackson's advice in mind: "Always mystify, mislead, and surprise the enemy."[25] We needed overly forceful proposals that were both believable in the minds of antireformers and defensible by us until the moment for compromise. I feared that our opponents would not be misled but would see through our maneuver. If that occurred, we would have climbed out on a limb with our extreme recommendations and achieved nothing. Fortunately, my fear never materialized.

The staff report contained seventy-nine specific recommendations for reforming the Pentagon. I used only seven for posturing, but some of those addressed highly visible and contentious issues. The most extreme recommendations called for disestablishing the JCS and replacing it with a joint military advisory council (JMAC)—a group made up of military elder statesmen without any service responsibilities serving on their last tour of duty. This concept was not new. General of the Army Omar Bradley, while serving as JCS chairman, had recommended it in 1952. Seven years later, Gen. Maxwell Taylor had pushed the idea. The Symington and Steadman reports in the 1960s and 1970s had also examined this option in detail. In 1982, Gen. Shy Meyer supported this structure. These earlier recommendations made the JMAC a believable option.

Although our desired outcome was to strengthen the JCS chairman along the lines of General Jones's proposals, recommending the JMAC provided the maximum negotiating room. It also sent two powerful messages to the Pentagon: We judged JCS performance as highly unsatisfactory, and we were making a serious effort to find meaningful solutions.

We knew that the recommendation to disestablish the JCS would be a lightning rod. The service chiefs and their supporters seemed certain to focus their full energy and attention on defeating it. And that is exactly what happened.

The first person outside of our six-man inner circle to decipher our posturing strategy was Senator Cohen. The second was Pat Towell, a *Congressional Quarterly* reporter. Cohen had decoded our scheme in early October. Towell's insights did not come until seven months later, well after we had successfully executed the strategy. Towell used the term "bullet traps" to refer to our overly forceful recommendations, especially the ones to disestablish the JCS and create a JMAC. He selected an accurate term. The Pentagon would expend a tremendous amount of ammunition trying to shoot down these ideas.

Four of the other five bullet traps focused on the services. One would reduce the service staffs that work on joint matters to not more than twenty-five officers. A second would increase the stature of the unified commanders by making them more senior in rank than the service chiefs. A third would remove the service component commanders in the unified commands from the operational chain of command. The last service-oriented bullet trap would merge the civilian secretariats and military headquarters staffs in the Army and Air Force Departments and partially merge them in the Navy Department. Even though I favored this idea, I had been unable to generate much support for it. Also, it occupied a lower position on our list of reorganization priorities. I added it to the list of bullet traps as great negotiating fodder.

The seventh bullet trap would establish three mission-oriented under secretaries of defense for nuclear deterrence, NATO defense, and regional defense and force projection. I had convinced some people of the need for an increased mission-focus in the Pentagon, but I could not convince Secretaries Schlesinger and Brown that these under secretaries were the answer. Without their support, I knew that Goldwater and Nunn would fight only so hard for this idea. Because approval of this recommendation was unlikely, I added it to the list. It also had the advantage of affecting seven lesser recommendations that were tied to it. When it came time to bargain the proposal for mission-oriented under secretaries away during negotiations, these lesser ones would follow and give the appearance of more concessions.

Punaro asked if we wanted to recommend changing the title of the chief of naval operations to chief of staff, U.S. Navy.[26] There was a valid reason for dropping the anachronistic title of CNO: it no longer reflected the position's duties. The CNO was no longer responsible for naval operations, a duty assigned to the unified commanders. Nevertheless, knowing what a hornet's nest changing the senior naval officer's title would stir up, I told Punaro, "I may be foolish, but I'm not suicidal."

As part of finishing the staff study, I prepared a cover letter that acknowledged those who had contributed to it. I called former committee staffer Mike Donley, then on the National Security Council staff, and asked, "Do you want me to acknowledge your contributions in my letter?"

"Reorganization is so controversial in the Pentagon that if you associate me with the staff study, I'll get the cold shoulder or worse," Donley replied. "My work on reorganization issues for the NSC staff will become much more difficult." After giving him a hard time, I let him off the hook.

Goldwater and Nunn decided to hold a committee hearing on the staff report to maximize the public impact of its release. In an unprecedented move, they decided to have Finn, Smith, and me testify. The committee had not previously taken testimony from its staff during an open hearing. Majority Staff Director Jim McGovern was "adamantly opposed" to having staff testimony.[27] Goldwater and Nunn dismissed his objections.

The senators planned to conduct the hearing in mid-October, but they had to complete other critical actions before they could take the dramatic step of releasing the study. Most important, they had to expand and solidify their base of support on the Task Force on Defense Organization, whose members were overly nervous and undereducated. Goldwater and Nunn needed to remedy this situation if the task force were to fulfill their expectation of providing the core support in the full committee. The two leaders had designed the second part of their strategy to meet this need.

CHAPTER 17

Gathering of Eagles

Some people live in the present, oblivious of the past

and blind to the future. Some dwell in the past.

A very few have the knack of applying the past

to the present in ways that show them the future.

—Pres. Richard M. Nixon

As the second part of their strategy to break out of the trenches, Senators Goldwater and Nunn decided to take the unusual step of sequestering the Task Force on Defense Organization at a distant army base in Virginia for an entire weekend. The senators planned to invite fifteen outside experts to join the gathering. This retreat would permit the task force to give its full attention to reorganization for two days and hear directly from experienced practitioners and distinguished scholars.

The task force's two- to three-hour weekly meetings had proved inadequate for comprehensive discussions. Not only were the issues numerous and complex, but the absence of agreement on fundamental principles for organizing, commanding, controlling, and administering the military had complicated their examination. Experts had debated various principles throughout the twentieth century but had reached lasting consensus on few. The competing demands of other Senate work had distracted members and prevented them from devoting more time to reorganization. Nunn had repeatedly expressed his frustration at these limitations. He often spoke of the need to get the task force out of Washington for several days.

"I was afraid that Barry and I were getting out in front of our own troops too much," Nunn recalled. He said we needed to "find a way to get other members involved in depth" so they would "be able to stick with it when the going got tough."[1]

Nunn sensed that the task force would benefit from increased discussions with former senior defense civilians and retired officers. The staff's analysis had impressed many members, but vocal opposition by the Pentagon's big guns and retired generals and admirals caused members to remain noncommittal. Hearing from those who had held top positions but were no longer constrained by Pentagon politics, Nunn thought, might both educate and reassure members.

Although the retreat would focus on the task force, Nunn believed that all Senate Armed Services Committee members should be invited. Eventually, the entire committee would have to be educated on reorganization. An early start with any who could attend would be useful. Goldwater endorsed Nunn's ideas, and the weekend retreat became part of their strategy.

Goldwater and Nunn scheduled the retreat for the first weekend in October at Fort A. P. Hill, an army base south of Fredericksburg, about seventy miles from Washington. A small, rustic lodge and six or seven austere cabins in a secluded part of the sixty-thousand-acre base would serve as the retreat's setting. I was familiar with these facilities. When Senator Tower was chairman, he had used them several times for staff retreats in January to examine major issues and plan the committee's work. This familiarity factored into the selection of Fort A. P. Hill. A second factor was our desire to have the army handle the retreat, which meant that we would have to use an army base. At the colonel level and below, the army had shown more support for reorganization than any other service. In our view, asking the navy to handle the retreat would have been sailing in harm's way. We amused ourselves imagining the awful places the navy might choose.

Given the divisions in the task force, deciding on the size and composition of the group of outside experts was a difficult, tedious undertaking. The members deliberated at length over whom to invite to ensure representation of all perspectives. They sought to balance numerous considerations: proreform vs. antireform, Republican vs. Democrat, civilian vs. military, Office of the Secretary of Defense vs. the military departments, and, among the four services, headquarters vs. field commands, and joint vs. service. The unavailability of certain invitees would reopen the bidding and further lengthen the process. The lists of invitees and substitutes and sets of alternatives became so complex that someone jested that I should ask one of the national laboratories for computer assistance.

Fifteen experts accepted invitations to the retreat, including former Defense Secretaries Jim Schlesinger and Harold Brown and two former JCS chairmen,

Adm. Tom Moorer and Gen. David Jones. The list of experts read like a *Who's Who in American Defense*. Goldwater called it "the most prestigious and knowledgeable group of experts in this area that has been assembled."[2] The group included two members of the Packard Commission: former senator Nicholas F. Brady and Gen. Paul Gorman, former commander in chief of the Southern Command (SOUTHCOM). In 1982, the New Jersey governor appointed Brady to fill the unexpired term of Sen. Harrison Williams, and Brady served on the SASC during this eight-month period. Gorman had earned the reputation of being one of the army's most brilliant leaders. Many considered him the father of the National Training Center at Fort Irwin, California. Gorman had served as Jones's special assistant when Jones launched his call for reform.

In addition to Moorer, Jones, and Gorman, two other retired officers were invited: Lt. Gen. Mick Trainor and Vice Adm. Thor Hanson. The cerebral, articulate Trainor had just retired after last serving as deputy chief of staff for plans, policies, and operations at Marine Corps Headquarters. He would soon begin to cover military affairs for the *New York Times*. Hanson, an old colleague of mine from the OSD systems analysis shop, was the president of the National Multiple Sclerosis Society. In his last two assignments before retiring in 1982 he had been posted as Brown's military assistant and Jones's Joint Staff director.

Harvard's Samuel P. Huntington and Texas A&M's Frank E. Vandiver represented the academic community. Huntington, a Harvard professor since 1950, ranked as the leading American scholar on civil-military relations. During the retreat, Huntington compared notes on reorganization with a former student: Sen. Ted Kennedy.[3] Vandiver, president of Texas A&M, was renowned as a military historian. Senator Gramm had pushed hard for Vandiver's participation.

The other five outside experts had garnered experience in Pentagon civilian posts. Robert J. Murray had served as a navy under secretary during the Carter administration. Bill Brehm, head of the Chairman's Special Study Group, had worked as an assistant secretary in the army and OSD. Lawyer John Kester, a prolific author on defense organization, had served as Brown's special assistant. RAND president Donald B. Rice, a deputy assistant secretary of defense in OSD systems analysis in the late 1960s, had also served as an assistant director at the Office of Management and Budget. Phil Odeen, chairman of the CSIS Defense Organization Project, had served as a deputy assistant secretary of defense with Rice and later worked for Henry Kissinger on the NSC staff.

Six experts were known to be strongly proreform: Schlesinger, Brown, Jones, Brehm, Kester, and Odeen. Three were expected to advocate antireform positions: Moorer, Murray, and Trainor. Some others—Gorman, Hanson, Rice, and Huntington—had commented favorably on some reform issues, but their broader views were unknown. Goldwater and Nunn wanted the meeting to tilt toward reorganization, but they also wanted opposing views aired.

All nine task force members agreed to participate. J. James Exon (D-Nebraska) accepted Goldwater's and Nunn's invitation to other SASC members. Finn, Smith, and I would attend with four other committee staffers: Jim McGovern, Arnold Punaro, Alan Yuspeh, and John Hamre. Eight military legislative assistants from the personal staffs of task force members would participate, as well as Frank Sullivan, who worked for Sen. John Stennis on the Appropriations Committee. In all, forty-one people would participate, plus a handful of army escorts.

At 9 A.M. on Saturday, October 5, all participants gathered at the Pentagon heliport. In an incredible site, the army had assembled eight UH-60 Blackhawk helicopters to transport the group to Fort A. P. Hill. The Blackhawk was the army's newest helicopter, and the brass was not about to miss this golden opportunity for show-and-tell.

Goldwater and I rode in the last Blackhawk. General Jones was also a passenger. As we were about to lift off the ground, Goldwater announced, "I'm going to fly this thing." He was famous for having flown almost every aircraft in the military inventory. The chairman's arthritis in his hips and knees limited his mobility, so getting him into the cockpit took some work. With the helicopter's crew doing a lot of pushing and shoving, Goldwater at last climbed into the copilot's seat and we took off. When Jones saw Goldwater in the cockpit, he moved quickly to the seat beside me and asked, "He's not going to fly, is he?" I nodded. Jones immediately looked out the door, but we were too high for him to jump.

This was a no-nonsense retreat. As soon as we stowed our gear, the work began. We met in the lodge's main room. The tables had been arranged in a large rectangle. The senators and outside experts sat along the outer side of the tables, and staffers occupied chairs behind them. Finn, Smith, and I had arranged the seating to intersperse experts and senators. Although we had to follow protocol, we had some flexibility to determine who sat next to whom. Knowing the senators and experts, we made a determination as to which expert might have the greatest influence with each member.

The weekend would be devoted to debating the completed staff study—a copy of which had been provided to each participant three days in advance. To promote candid discussions, Goldwater and Nunn had decided that all comments would be off the record. I started the discussion of each chapter by highlighting its findings, conclusions, and recommendations.

Most of the discussion focused on the study's analyses of organizational problems and their causes. The majority of the experts complimented these analyses and offered supporting evidence from personal experiences. Professor Sam Huntington graded the staff report as an outstanding dissertation for a Harvard doctoral candidate.

But the outside experts did not agree with the study's title: *Crisis in Defense Organization.* I had selected this title to communicate the situation's seriousness and the urgency for corrective action. Although many experts agreed with the need for major reforms, they thought that the title would come across, particularly in the Pentagon, as too strident. After the group discussed several alternatives, I proposed *Defense Organization: The Need for Change.* Nearly all participants thought this title was about right.

As the Saturday afternoon session began, Lt. Col. James Rooney, the head army escort, made an announcement. As was standard procedure for a gathering of such prominent officials, the army was providing physical security around the lodge and cabins. "I would like everyone to stay close to the lodge until further notice," Rooney said. "Two men wearing ski masks have been spotted in the woods by security personnel." Rooney paused, and then added, "It's probably Secretary Weinberger and Secretary Lehman." His quip got a big laugh—but not from everyone.

General Gorman's commentary about the unified commands significantly influenced the discussions. Having ending his tour as SOUTHCOM commander only seven months earlier, he could speak authoritatively on problems in the field. A 1950 West Point graduate, Gorman served his initial tour as an infantry second lieutenant in the Korean War. He earned more combat medals in Vietnam, where he gained a reputation as a "tough commander who pushed his troops hard." Once, from his unit's position, Gorman "directed an air strike of napalm bombs that landed so close they burned the map he was holding and singed his forehead."[4]

Gorman took over SOUTHCOM, headquartered in Panama, in May, 1983. He turned the once-sleepy outpost into one of the most important players in planning and executing the Reagan administration's Latin American policy. The army general was politically well connected in Washington. As special assistant to JCS Chairmen Jones and Vessey, he worked closely with the NSC and State Department. Earlier, Gorman had been assigned to the Central Intelligence Agency for a year. Gorman's major role in writing some of the documents included in the *Pentagon Papers,* a documentary history of the U.S. Government's involvement in the Vietnam conflict, had sharpened his understanding of Latin American insurgencies and how to counter them.

Gorman had also studied the Pentagon's organizational problems. He had assisted Jones's reorganization work in 1981 and 1982, served on the organization panel at the 1982 West Point conference, and testified on the subject to the SASC in 1983. In February, 1985, Gorman had answered the organization questions posed to commanders of the unified commands in the 1984 defense authorization bill. In July, President Reagan had appointed him to the Packard Commission.

Gorman's combined knowledge of the current state of the unified commands and defense organization enabled him to offer powerful insights. He provided vivid anecdotes and compelling evidence of how the services' power and independence had crippled his efforts to assist regional nations in their fights against insurgents, drug traffickers, and terrorists.

Gorman later recalled telling the conference participants of "some of the difficulties a CINC had with this curious notion of component commands and the prerogatives of the services." He began by explaining that he "was the only general officer assigned to SOUTHCOM headquarters. My next ranking assigned officer was a colonel." Gorman had argued for more senior officers to help him with his demanding missions, but "the chiefs couldn't muster the resolve or fortitude to redress this wrong."[5]

The retired four-star general also related, "My deputy CINC and air component commander, an air force major general, died on the job of cancer. The air force did not consider his job important, so they left him there. I was running several wars and was daily under the gun with the secretaries of state and defense, and I needed a hell of a lot more help than I got out of my air component commander. . . . I rarely saw him. He was not on the job. I didn't have a deputy."

Gorman revealed that his control of assigned forces was limited: "The army brigade in Panama was a Forces Command unit, and it received all of its resources from the Forces Command. As a result, I found myself under a series of dictates from the Forces Command commander dealing with operational tempo issues, like flying hours for army aviation." Gorman's ability to employ his force was constrained by a U.S.-based command having budgetary—but no operational—responsibility. His low priority for resources had also relegated Gorman to flying in an army propeller-driven C-12 aircraft. While modern transport jets flew other four-star officers, Gorman spent thirty-one days each year in the air flying long distances in his slow aircraft.

Service personnel policies undermined SOUTHCOM's ability to create interservice teams. "I discovered to my horror that all services had their own separate policies on how long SOUTHCOM temporary duty assignments should persist," Gorman said. "The army would say 120 days, the air force would say sixty days, and the navy would have a ninety-day policy. Every time I got a team together, they would disappear and be destroyed by these personnel policies over which the CINC had no control.

"We were at war in SOUTHCOM," Gorman told the retreat participants. "We were undertaking a series of operations to foreclose larger conflict, and we succeeded in that. But we did so despite the system, not because of it. I feel very strongly that this is a hell of a way to run a war, and it badly needs to be changed."

During the retreat, I had to defend the staff report's overly forceful recommendations. As expected, antireformers zeroed in on the proposal to disestablish the JCS. After one testy session on that recommendation, Senator Cohen, attuned to our strategy, grabbed me firmly and told me to defend it as long as I possibly could. In his view, the opposition had become fixated on that one proposal. I managed to defend that recommendation for more than four months, but it was not easy.

During meals, served family style at big tables, discussions about reorganization continued informally. Comments General Trainor made before dinner on Saturday irritated Goldwater. Everyone was congratulating Goldwater on his commitment to reorganization, saying how it would be his legacy to the country, the marine recalled. "Goldwater was just so full of himself with all this talk about his legacy, and I said, 'I hope you're not remembered for a legacy of folly.' Then I began about too much power in the hands of the chairman, and Goldwater really got pissed off, and for the rest of the conference he never acknowledged my existence."[6]

Goldwater orchestrated the retreat brilliantly. His masterstroke came during the discussion session after dinner on Saturday. Schlesinger and Brown were scheduled to return to Washington that evening. As they were preparing to depart, Goldwater asked them to summarize their thoughts on the day's discussions.

Schlesinger possessed impressive speaking skills. His talks were not spellbinding, but the logic of his arguments and the appeal of his words combined to leave a lasting impression. He carefully avoided overstatement and punctuated his talks with wit. "The organization of the Department of Defense is not logical," the former defense secretary began. "It reflects the compromises struck in 1958 which retained the power of the services. This creates a natural tension which you cannot resolve so long as the central compromise of 1958 is retained. . . . I am convinced you need to take an evolutionary approach. Things cannot be solved instantaneously. Gradual change has promise. Radical change does not."[7]

On the JCS, the Republican former secretary advised: "Don't ask people to deal with questions that they themselves cannot answer. The service chiefs of staff are unable to solve fundamental issues of roles and missions, budget shares, and so forth. Don't demand that they do what is beyond their abilities."

Schlesinger said the staff study "focused on the right problems and proposes useful, but, to some people, provocative solutions."[8] He recommended that "any changes for the OSD should avoid prescribing a management style for the secretary of defense."[9] Schlesinger said the present JCS structure "impedes efficient functioning." As to fixes, he advised, "I favor the modest evolutionary changes suggested by Jones: strengthen the JCS chairman, give him a deputy, give the Joint Staff to the chairman alone, improve the quality of the Joint Staff, retain the presence of the service chiefs on the JCS but don't give them authority over the staff."

The former secretary concluded: "These changes would improve the JCS, would help make the JCS more useful and, therefore, remove some of the needs for OSD interference, and would strengthen the unified commanders." Schlesinger had woven the day's disparate comments into powerful arguments.

Brown followed with an equally brilliant statement. He started by focusing on the imbalance in joint and service interests: "I believe that there is a continuing need for discrete military departments, but we have not achieved the desirable level of jointness in the Department of Defense. The services continue to be too strong.

"To correct the deficiencies that linger from the 1958 compromise," Brown asserted, "the JCS should clearly be the focus of current reform efforts." He spoke on his ideal solution: "I prefer a combined military staff [general staff] responsible to the JCS chairman. The chairman should have a deputy from the other service pair [army–air force versus navy–Marine Corps]."

Weinberger's predecessor continued: "There is substantial unanimity among all retreat participants that we need to strengthen the hand of the unified commanders. They need expanded control over staff resources and their component commanders."

After noting that he had served as a service secretary as well as defense secretary, Brown advised, " I agree that we should combine the staff of the service chiefs and service secretaries. If they don't work closely, they don't work well anyway."

Sensing the momentum created by the two secretaries, Goldwater continued around the table and asked the other experts for their thoughts. General Jones was seated beside Brown, so he spoke next and added to the momentum: "The current system can't handle the too-hard issues that lie ahead, like budget shares, roles and missions, the Unified Command Plan, and others."

Jones stressed the need of "getting better quality officers into the joint system." He cited statistics on inadequate experience: "Presently, only two percent of Joint Staff officers have ever had joint experience before." He summed up the problem in attracting better officers: "Joint work isn't interesting and the assignment contributes little to their careers. We need to change this."

Because Schlesinger had already outlined Jones's fixes for the JCS, the former JCS chairman emphasized only a few points, including his view that the service chiefs "should have the right to appeal recommendations of the chairman and Joint Staff. . . . The bulk of this should be done administratively rather than legislatively. But it is imperative that we convince DoD that unless we make these changes, congressional support of the defense program is threatened. If we don't make modest changes now, drastic changes will come later." I did not agree with Jones's political advice. We were beyond just threatening the Pentagon. Threats had not produced results. We were now engaged in a win-or-lose fight over legislation.

Texas A&M President Vandiver spoke next: "I don't think we should ignore the potential of a general staff. It should be a general staff that includes all military departments, not just the Army." Senator Gramm, startled by Vandiver's raising of this navy bugaboo, glanced at the historian seated next to him with a puzzled look that seemed to ask, "Who brought this person to the party?"

Odeen sought to counter the argument about improvements in the JCS over the preceding four years. He noted that good funding, no wars, and no critical issues had resulted in "an absence of friction." He thought the future would be different, and recent improvements would not substitute for organizational changes.

The CSIS project chairman spoke of the consensus on "a valid need to shift emphasis from inputs toward outputs and missions." He lamented, "Unfortunately, none of us has the answer how to do this."

"We are confronted with a dilemma," began Kester. "The opportunity for reform comes only one time per generation. This is now the time, and it calls for bold action. On the other hand, it isn't possible to legislate organizational details and outcomes. Consequently, we need to strike a balance in this dilemma, and I think the proper focus should be on the JCS. That is the center of the most persistent problems and flaws. That should be the focus of reform, and the key to reform there is to strengthen the chairman."

After this long string of proreform commentary, former Navy Under Secretary Murray threw cold water on reform notions: "As a society, we organize our institutions to support democracy, not efficiency. There will always be inefficiencies." His comments targeted criticisms of the JCS and other inefficiencies.

"The most important thing we can do is to find ways to increase cooperation and not competition among the services," said Murray. He thought the key was "to educate military officers on the strengths of their sister services," and added, "I am a fan of the military departments, and the service secretaries and their organizations. It is too hard for OSD to get close to the management issues that are unique to the individual services. The service secretaries are much closer and can make an indispensable contribution."

Admiral Hanson returned to proreform commentary, arguing "that the primary need is to strengthen the JCS chairman." He advocated a joint specialty for officers, a requirement that a unified commander must have served in a joint assignment, and a requirement that the JCS chairman must have served as a unified commander.

Professor Huntington recommended focusing "on what is currently missing in defense organization." He explained: "Two things are missing. We are missing an effective non-service military perspective—an alternative to the perspective of the service chiefs on joint matters. Second, we are missing the perspective that reflects missions rather than functions."

Huntington also noted that "the dynamic of the U.S. Government is to disperse power. The reform intended in 1958 was dissipated because the intended centralization of power was dispersed by the dynamic of the American political system.

"The conclusion of these two points in combination," Huntington said, "is that if you err in one direction or the other, err in giving more power to the secretary of defense, JCS chairman, and unified commanders because the dynamic of the system will always disperse power to the elements of separation as opposed to the elements of jointness."

Bill Brehm focused his comments on the relatively limited experience levels in key Pentagon positions: assistant defense secretaries and Joint Staff officers had served on the average only sixteen months, and general and flag officers in the joint system, only twelve months. "Inexperienced people are running a $300 billion company," he concluded. "We have got to make changes."

Don Rice supported the "modest evolutionary changes" already recommended. "None of these changes would threaten civilian control," he emphasized. "Indeed, they would strengthen civilian control." He also said he thought that Congress "needs to develop a careful legislative approach that is conducive to change, but avoids going overboard."

Admiral Moorer was the last expert to speak. As the retreat's most unyielding reform opponent, he was agitated by much of what he had heard and used emotion as a key element of his rebuttal. He asserted the need for preserving the service chiefs' stature: "If you lower the prestige of the service chief, you will create a negative effect on young officers. Young officers have to have a father image to look up to and that has to be the service chief."

The oldest living JCS chairman argued: "Leave the JCS as it is. I don't object to putting the staff under the chairman's control, though we didn't do that in the past, and I don't think it is required. . . . Don't cut the service chiefs out of the JCS. If a man can't be both a service chief and a member of the JCS, then fire him and get a man who can do both. Don't isolate the service chiefs from the president.

"It is critical that individuals in uniform have pride in their service," Moorer concluded. "Don't do anything that undermines that pride." His emotional pleas clashed with the day's serious, substantive debate and lessened his credibility.

Having heard from the experts, Goldwater then asked the senators for their thoughts. His request forced several members to summarize their views on reorganization for the first time, and in front of their colleagues and, more importantly, a distinguished panel of outsiders. Emboldened by the proreform comments of many experts, undecided senators spoke favorably about some reform proposals, especially strengthening the unified commanders. Even opponents were less adamant.

Bingaman rated the discussion as "very useful" and was anxious for clarification of "those things that can and should be done legislatively and those things which should be done through exhortation."

Caught up in the moment, Gramm said: "I am surprised at how much has been said today with which I agree. I think there is consensus on the following things: to strengthen the unified commanders, strengthen the JCS chairman, bring the Joint Staff under the jurisdiction and control of the JCS chairman, and make the Joint Staff more professional." In the months that followed, Gramm remained firm on strengthening the unified commanders, but he regressed on other positions.

That night, the Texas senator also espoused some antireform views: "I think the service secretaries are here to stay and should be strengthened. We should give to the service secretaries all responsibilities for recruiting, training, supplying, and procuring for their services, and we should do away with any redundancy that exists on the OSD staff."

"We want to preserve all the positive strengths of the services," Levin opined, "but we need more prominence for jointness than the current system permits."

Cohen offered the last views: "We are not in a crisis, but it is like a crisis. When the Grenada operation is hailed as a success, but was [close to] the edge of catastrophe, you know that we have to make changes. The key point is that unless we make serious changes now it could well undermine support for defense in the future. . . . It is naive to think that we can accomplish this without legislation. Unless we have the threat of legislation, there will be no movement. I agree with John Kester that we should be bold, but careful."

As the session broke up, Goldwater and Nunn compared notes. They were elated by the results. If they could have, they would have raked their chips off the table, packed up the whole kit and caboodle, and headed back to Washington that night.

After the Saturday night session, the Sunday morning presentations and discussions were anticlimactic. After lunch, we returned to the Pentagon by helicopter.

From Goldwater's and Nunn's perspective, the retreat was an overwhelming success. Goldwater told the participants that it was the best meeting he had ever attended.[10] The sessions had improved members' understanding of the issues, and they had heard directly from seasoned experts. To maximize the benefit of the experts' commentary, Goldwater and Nunn asked me to prepare a nonattribution summary of the experts' major areas of consensus to include in the staff study.

"The meeting was a great success," said Goldwater. "It was an extraordinarily productive session. Not all of the experts agreed on all points and, at times, the discussion got rather heated. But there was a consensus that there were serious problems that needed to be fixed and that the analysis in the study was essentially correct."[11]

The outcome also pleased many of the experts who participated. Huntington later called it "a very successful meeting. People were voicing questions and objections, but it seemed to me a very positive tone."[12] Brehm recalled that the "Fort A. P. Hill retreat was an astonishing experience, and in some sense a watershed because a lot of the anecdotal stuff that does really make impressions came out there. The give-and-take was good, and the senators made it easy to talk. The openness of the dinner table discussion was remarkable. . . . The turnout was extraordinary—testimony to the seriousness of the issues and interest of the people."[13]

Not everyone was pleased, however. General Trainor later complained, "The meeting was loaded in favor of reorganization." He said he thought Moorer's presence as the most senior opponent handicapped the antireformers because "Moorer was not an articulate spokesman." Nevertheless, admitted Trainor, "It was a good conference, and I had the opportunity to make the points and get across the dangers that I wanted to."[14]

Admiral Moorer wrote a two-page summary of the retreat, which he provided to the navy. Because the session was off the record, he attempted to hide the source by writing in third person, but a covering note to Admiral Watkins said the summary came from Moorer. The former JCS chairman wrote that Goldwater returned "to his lifelong campaign against the Navy's separate air arm, saying that we have four air forces, and we need only one. Dave Jones picked this up and said we had five air forces in Vietnam . . . and because the Air Force did not have control of all of them, it was all wrong."[15]

Moorer criticized my proposals to increase the Pentagon's focus on missions: "Locher—former McNamara systems analyst—would . . . organize DoD along mission lines. Their idea—(i.e., the idea of the Enthoven [former assistant secretary of defense for systems analysis] group still around, such as Locher, Phil Odeen, who was present, and Les Aspin)—is that the end game of DoD should be to concentrate on the missions." The admiral exulted, "The mission element approach—i.e., the PA&E [program analysis and evaluation, the new name for the systems analysis office] structure—was shot down." Moorer would have been apoplectic if he had known that three other attendees—Rice, Brehm, and Hanson—were also systems analysis alumni.

Although the admiral reported that "Locher kept referring to the crisis in the military," he said that there was no crisis—that we had been operating in the same way since the National Security Act was first passed in 1947. His notes ended with a quotation from a statement he made at the retreat: "The National Security Act of 1947 was purposely ambiguous, we didn't want it to be rigid."

Despite the adverse commentary, the retreat had gone as well as Goldwater and Nunn could have hoped. Bingaman, Levin, and Kennedy had voiced proreform views and were now solid backers of Goldwater and Nunn's campaign. This gave the senators six proreformers on the nine-member task force. The hope of a transformation by Gramm was short-lived. Someplace between Fort A. P. Hill and Washington he lost his proreform zeal. Nevertheless, during the retreat, he and Sen. Pete Wilson had become believers in the need to strengthen the unified commanders.

Goldwater later identified the retreat at Fort A. P. Hill as the pivotal moment during which the pendulum began to swing in the right direction.[16] He and Nunn still viewed themselves as underdogs, but they had busted out of the trenches and now had real hope for their campaign. Although the Fort A. P. Hill retreat ranked as a critical skirmish, several monumental clashes loomed ahead.

CHAPTER 18

Expedition into Hostile Territory

We must free ourselves of emotional attachments to

service systems of an era that is no more.

—Pres. Dwight D. Eisenhower, 1958

Public release of the staff study would be the next major step in the campaign of Senators Goldwater and Nunn. Before taking that step, however, they felt the need to arrange a courtesy briefing for Defense Secretary Weinberger. They did not want to give him further reason—such as hearing secondhand about the study—to oppose reorganization. Although briefing the study to the secretary and other senior defense officials might provide insights on their thinking, no one looked forward to going to the Pentagon for a showdown with reform's most determined adversaries.

The Fort A. P. Hill retreat convinced Goldwater and Nunn that the staff study could be a powerful instrument for change. Most outside experts had praised the report's quality and thoroughness. High marks from Secretaries Schlesinger and Brown had particularly impressed the two senators. The report's ideas had held up well under rigorous questioning. Even the so-called extreme recommendations had weathered the debate. Few supported them, but the retreat participants had accepted them as viable alternatives.

Goldwater and Nunn were determined to convene the committee hearing to release the study as soon as possible. The urgency reflected their fear that the report's message would leak out in the press and be poorly or inaccurately presented. In the contentious atmosphere of the reform debate, leaks were a distinct possibility. Each retreat participant had been given a copy of the report and Goldwater and Nunn had asked the recipients not to reveal the contents. Nevertheless, they understood that confidentiality was not Washington's strong suit. They were especially worried that opponents would try to neutralize the report by planting negative stories.

Setting the hearing date had to await printing of the study by the Government Printing Office. Goldwater and Nunn also had other critical tasks to accomplish before they could release the report. Besides Weinberger, they needed to arrange courtesy briefings for three other audiences: the House Armed Services Committee, the Packard Commission, and Bud McFarlane and his National Security Council staff. Goldwater and Nunn were working well with these three organizations. They did not want their allies to be caught cold by public discussion of the report.

Goldwater and Nunn decided to attend the briefings to Weinberger and the Packard Commission and instructed me to handle the other two. The senators selected the crucial briefings to attend. The other two proved uneventful.

My House staff counterparts—Arch Barrett and John Lally from the HASC and Tommy Glakas from Representative Skelton's office—took the first briefing on behalf of their members on the morning of Monday, October 7. Although the breadth and depth of the report's analysis impressed them, Barrett said, "We remain convinced that a massive and controversial reorganization—with several hundred major changes in law—is far too much for our committees to handle at one time. Our best chance of success is to take one component at a time. The House will continue its bite-size approach." Other than this major process issue, Barrett, Lally, and Glakas agreed with the problems identified in our briefing and acquiesced in many of the proposed solutions.

The NSC courtesy briefing was equally trouble free. McFarlane assigned his deputy, Vice Admiral Poindexter, and Mike Donley to hear my presentation. The session was held on Wednesday afternoon, October 9, in the White House Situation Room. Although I knew Poindexter from service together in the Pentagon, I was not aware of his position on reform. For months, I had heard rumors that the navy was leaning on him to help derail reorganization, but during my presentation, the admiral did not make any waves. In fact, he struck a positive tone, listened carefully, and asked insightful questions. Afterward, I reported to Goldwater and Nunn, "The NSC staff remains supportive."

Sandwiched between these briefings were sessions with the Packard Commission and Weinberger. Both were conducted on Tuesday, October 8. In the morning, Goldwater, Nunn, Rick Finn, Jeff Smith, Gerry Smith, and I went to the commission's offices near the White House. The attendance at the Fort A. P. Hill retreat of two commissioners—Sen. Nick Brady and Gen. Paul Gorman—paid dividends. They helped to break down attitude and communication barriers. Their prior involvement with our report seemed to make other commissioners more open to our ideas. Brady and Gorman usefully commented on my briefing and helped translate the report's concepts into ones more familiar to the commission.

I had incorporated a number of editorial changes in my briefing as suggested during the Fort A. P. Hill retreat, including many from Gorman. These changes removed some sharp elbows from my presentation. This proved to be valuable for the session with the commission, which, having just begun its own reorganization work, was not ready to accept strong language.

As I briefed the commission, Lt. Gen. Brent Scowcroft, who had been President Ford's national security adviser, encouraged me. Scowcroft's animated facial expressions showed agreement with the briefing's key points. Every few minutes he also gave me an energetic thumb's up or an okay sign.

My message did not please everyone, however. Antireform commissioners, especially the former marine commandant, Gen. Bob Barrow, posed sharp questions, but David Packard and other reform supporters appeared to hold the upper hand.

That afternoon, Goldwater, Nunn, Finn, Jeff Smith, and I traveled to the Pentagon to brief Weinberger and his senior colleagues. Our reform crusade personally offended the secretary. Despite the long history of structural deficiencies, he viewed our effort as a direct, unwarranted attack on his tenure. Weinberger was particularly unhappy with me. He viewed me as the principal transgressor. I anticipated a long and grueling afternoon.

En route to the Pentagon, Goldwater and Nunn unexpectedly began to laugh as they visualized the coming showdown. Their lighthearted approach did not match their normally serious nature. They found my plight as the point man for our expedition into hostile territory particularly amusing. "Jim," Goldwater laughed as he addressed me, "Sam and I are going to give you one hell of an introduction. Then, by God, we're going to get out of the line of fire." With a soft chuckle, he added, "Whatever happens, don't take it easy on them."

"I bet Cap Weinberger just can't wait for your briefing to start," Nunn chimed in. He probably has had a team of a hundred of his brightest colonels preparing killer questions for you." Nunn even had me laughing when he joked, "By the time you're done, you're going to look like Johnny Carson doing his imitation of General Custer with forty-seven arrows in his back."

When our car halted at the Pentagon's River Entrance, the laughter abruptly ended.

The five of us stepped out of the car and began climbing the steps into the massive building. The offices of the defense secretary are located in one of the Pentagon's museum-like halls: the Dwight David Eisenhower Commemorative Corridor. Memorabilia of the former president's military career—from West Point cadet to five-star general—are displayed there. As Goldwater, Nunn, my fellow staffers, and I were escorted to Weinberger's conference room, we walked through this corridor and passed by two Eisenhower portraits. One depicted him as president. In the other, he was wearing an Eisenhower jacket with five stars on each epaulet.

The portraits reminded me of Eisenhower's incomplete defense reorganization campaigns. Throughout his two White House terms, he pressed for improved coordination and cooperation in the Pentagon. Eisenhower had seen bitter interservice rivalry up close during his twenty-seven-month tour as army chief staff beginning in November, 1945. Later, while serving as a part-time military consultant to Defense Secretary James Forrestal, he watched even more vicious service infighting—especially between the navy and air force.

In January, 1949, Truman asked Eisenhower to preside over JCS meetings as an informal chairman. Even though Eisenhower was then serving as president of Columbia University, as a five-star general, he was on active duty for life, and thus available for part-time assignments from the president. Despite Eisenhower's best efforts, he was unable to curtail the bickering among the service chiefs. He noted in his diary in March, 1949: "The situation grows intolerable. I am so weary of this interservice struggle for position, prestige and power that this morning I practically 'blew my top.'" In October, he wrote: "The whole performance is humiliating—I've seriously considered resigning my commission, so that I could say what I pleased, publicly."[1]

Continuing interservice rivalries and the JCS's inability to achieve a national outlook disturbed Eisenhower throughout his presidency. On four occasions, he gave the joint chiefs his "lecture" on how they should operate. On a fifth occasion, he lectured Defense Secretary Charles E. Wilson and Admiral Radford, the JCS chairman. In December, 1954, he told the JCS: "All must resist efforts to create dissensions. Must work as a team, not fight among themselves." In February, 1956, he lectured, "Chiefs should avoid headline seeking—they should not be advocates of particular service." A month later, the president instructed the JCS, "Each chief should subordinate his position as champion of one particular service to position as one of overall national military advisors."[2]

On November 4, 1957, Eisenhower dined with the service secretaries and joint chiefs. Afterward, he held a "seminar" on defense organization. The president "began by saying that he had had three conferences earlier in the day, all of them greatly stressing that our people are deeply concerned over rivalry in our military establishment. The question was repeatedly raised, are we sufficiently unified? Are we getting the best personal judgment of our officers, rather than a parroting of service party lines?"

Eisenhower said "that the Joint Chiefs must be above narrow service considerations. . . . He said each one should try to approach problems from a national standpoint. . . . It is wrong to stress, or simply to press for, Army, Navy, and other service interests. He recalled that in 1947 he had favored a tight merger of the services, but this had not been adopted. He indicated that he still holds that view as the soundest solution."

The president added that the service chiefs "should remove operational functions from the service staffs which thereafter would concern themselves with mobilization administration, logistics, etc." Determined to make assignment to joint positions desirable, he spoke in favor of giving every man on the Joint Staff "some special recognition." Eisenhower said "he thought the members of the JCS should turn over the executive direction of their service to their deputy and should concentrate on their joint responsibilities." He ended his introductory comments by recalling "previous discussions with them urging them to take the stance of soldier-statesmen."

Admiral Arleigh Burke, chief of naval operations, said he disagreed "on some aspects of the president's proposal," and explained that "disagreements in the JCS do not arise because of service, but because of the individual experiences of the members." As to the JCS's reliance on an integrated Joint Staff, Burke said "he must have staff help and advice, for which he had to look to his own office."

Eisenhower "intervened strongly asking why it would not be better to have composite, well-thought out positions, reflecting the experience of many people of differing backgrounds and of differing services brought to him [Burke] rather than the views of his own service." Burke responded that he saw the potential for the Joint Staff becoming nothing more than "yes men," which would preclude having "all angles presented at the JCS table."

According to Goodpaster, the president also told the chiefs: "He wanted the American people to have a complete faith in the services . . . he hates to see the services rush into print, each trying to better its own position, often at the expense of the others. As a result of this, the American public has lost a large measure of confidence in the services. . . . He would like to see the step taken which would bring out that the first and the great loyalty of all members of the defense establishment is to the Defense Department, which means the United States of America. . . . He thinks that our people now believe the services are more interested in the struggle with each other than against an outside foe."[3]

Deeply troubled by the debilitating effects of service rivalry, Eisenhower privately commented, "I simply must find men who have the breadth of understanding and devotion to their country rather than to a single service that will bring about better solutions than I get now."[4] He also worried about how future presidents would deal with the lack of useful advice on military budgets from the chiefs: "Some day there is going to be a man sitting in my present chair who had not been raised in the military services and who will have little understanding of where slashes in their estimates can be made with little or no damage." While Eisenhower's specific concern was budgetary, his comments proved to be true on all military subjects. In less than three months, President Kennedy lost confidence in JCS advice and wanted nothing more to do with them.[5]

Despite many years of trying, Eisenhower failed to change the behavior of the service chiefs. His reorganization efforts in 1953 and 1958 were only partially successful, and they sought only limited objectives. Some of Eisenhower's key reforms enacted in 1958—removing the military departments from the operational chain of command and giving the unified commanders full operational command of assignment forces—were never meaningfully implemented by the services.

Goldwater and Nunn's reorganization work picked up where Eisenhower's had left off twenty-eight years earlier. The staff study's proposals encompassed many of the former president's unrealized plans for reform. Eisenhower's portraits reassured me as we headed for the showdown with the Pentagon's brass.

When we entered the conference room, Weinberger was seated at the end of a small table facing the briefing screen. After a courteous, but not warm, greeting, he placed Goldwater and Nunn to his left. Deputy Defense Secretary Will Taft sat to the secretary's right with the new JCS chairman, Admiral Crowe, beside him. Fifteen senior officials and officers—including Weinberger's top military assistant, Maj. Gen. Colin Powell—occupied seats against the wall. Finn and Smith joined them.

I had given my briefing dozens of times and knew it well. Without questions, the briefing lasted forty-five minutes. But questions and comments had lengthened every presentation to about two hours. That was not the case with Weinberger and his crew. After I started, not a single interruption occurred. Only my voice broke the silence. As I was speaking, I remember thinking, I can't believe that I am standing before the secretary of defense and telling him how screwed up his organization is. I don't think Weinberger could believe it either.

After I finished, I moved to my seat at the table next to Crowe. As I did so, Weinberger turned his chair to his left so he did not have to look at me.

"It is always useful, in my view, to conduct such reviews," the secretary began. "Of course, there is a wide range of opinion on these important matters. As you know, our internal reviews here at the Pentagon have been more positive. As always, we are most anxious to hear your views."

Goldwater, displaying his best behavior, thanked Weinberger for his comments. He then sought for the umpteenth time to reassure him. "Now, Cap," he said, "the problems identified in this briefing have existed for a long time. Some go as far back as the Spanish-American War. So, this work is in no way a criticism of the present administration."

At that point, things had gone as well as could be expected. It did not last. Deputy Secretary Taft commented next, and explosions started immediately thereafter.

Goldwater did not like William Howard Taft IV. In his view, President Taft's great-grandson was unqualified to serve in the Pentagon's number-two post. During Taft's confirmation hearing for this position twenty months earlier, in

January, 1984, both Goldwater and Nunn had criticized his qualifications. The low regard the senators had for Weinberger's management skills heightened their concerns about Taft's qualifications. They felt that a tough, knowledgeable, business-experienced deputy secretary was needed. Taft was a highly qualified lawyer capable of performing many Pentagon jobs, but the two senators judged that his skills and experience did not match the demands of the deputy position.

Nunn began the attack during Taft's confirmation hearing by noting that the deputy secretary normally runs the Defense Department. He then hammered at the nominee's lack of experience in "broad management responsibilities."[6]

Goldwater pursued the same theme. With his great admiration for former senator Robert Taft especially in mind, he started, "I come here with a respect for you and your forebears in the field of law that is very great." He then quickly added: "But my problem is that we are not looking for lawyers. We are looking for a man who can fill what, in my opinion, is about the toughest job in the Pentagon."

Nunn added another barb, "It takes a lot more than a law degree and an HEW [Department of Health, Education, and Welfare] background and adding machine to run the Department of Defense."

Taft's nomination so upset Goldwater that he carried the fight to the Senate floor. There, after complimenting Taft and his skills as an attorney, the senator argued, "He does not possess, however, the necessary qualifications needed to adequately carry out the duties of deputy secretary of defense." Many others had felt the same. But, as often was the case, only Goldwater said so.[7]

Although the heat of the confirmation battle had dissipated during the intervening months, tempers quickly rekindled in Weinberger's office.

About my presentation, Taft complained, "This briefing makes it seem like the Defense Department couldn't even defend the Pentagon's River Entrance."

In typical gunslinger fashion, Goldwater let Taft have it: "Your operational performance has been so piss poor, you guys would have trouble defending the River Entrance from an attack by a troop of Boy Scouts."

I do not know why Goldwater said that. He did not believe it. But he sure picked a fight.

Taft rebuked Goldwater: "That's the kind of statement I would expect from members of the media, not from the chairman of the Senate Armed Services Committee. This whole reorganization campaign has been built on exaggeration."

With that, Nunn—who angers slowly—blew his top. As his face grew redder than I had ever seen it, Nunn came to Goldwater's defense. "How much evidence do you want?" Nunn snapped. "For forty years, the Pentagon's problems have been repeatedly cited by one presidential commission after another. And each operational failure has served to reinforce the conclusions of these studies."

The two secretaries and two senators sparred for the next fifteen minutes. While this was going on, I remembered the humorous comments Goldwater and Nunn had made in the car, and was glad that they, not I, were tangling with Weinberger and Taft. Crowe, in only his eighth day as chairman, and I tried to become wallflowers, but that was hard to do given our proximity to the action.

After the four leaders tired of pounding on each other, the meeting ended in typical Washington fashion with everyone saying how useful it had been.

As we stood up from the table, the officials and officers in the chairs along the wall treated me like a leper. Not a single person extended a hand or even came near me, except one. General Powell strode up, shook my hand, and said, "Good briefing." Given Weinberger's hostile attitude toward my briefing and me, that gesture took some guts.

As the two senators stepped into the hallway, Goldwater hit Nunn in the ribs with his elbow and said, without explanation, "See what I mean—worthless."

PART
4

March
to Victory

CHAPTER 19

Seizing the High Ground

There is in every battlefield a decisive point the

possession of which, more than any other,

helps to secure victory.

—Antoine-Henri Baron de Jomini; *The Art of War*

By publicly releasing the staff report at a Senate Armed Services Committee hearing, Senators Goldwater and Nunn believed they could boldly take the initiative on reorganization. They could seize the intellectual high ground and put their powerful adversaries on the defensive. Reform opponents—compelled to attack the position staked out by the two senators—would have to fight uphill and over unfavorable terrain.

Goldwater and Nunn understood that this critical move—like a daring military operation—had to be carefully planned and flawlessly executed. Although preparatory activities needed to be well handled, the outcome of the hearing would determine success or failure. The report's information and ideas had to be clearly communicated and effectively defended.

The two senators also understood the risks to their cause and themselves. If they failed, reorganization would suffer a devastating, maybe mortal, setback. Goldwater's career would end with a bitter failure that left him estranged from his beloved military. Nunn's rising star as a leading defense intellectual would be dimmed for years.

As they began to plan their next steps, the senators' objectives for the staff report remained unchanged. In Nunn's words, "We want the report to rally support from outside government and to frame the debate inside government." Goldwater's and Nunn's speeches in the Senate had aroused media and public interest. The report's release would expand the facts and analysis available to both audiences. The committee leaders believed that this powerful information would rightfully grab headlines, command attention, and change minds. "This report is the best history of our military problems ever written," said Goldwater. "I can't wait for the American people to read it. It will open a lot of eyes."

Goldwater and Nunn also believed that the report would help structure debate on this complex subject and overcome the often-chaotic discussions of preceding years. More importantly, they knew that forcing the debate to center on the staff study gave them an advantage. The report's detailed analyses of problems and underlying causes would complicate their opponents' efforts to obfuscate or divert attention from the real issues.

On October 10, two days after the briefing to Weinberger, the first leak of the staff study appeared in the press. A *Washington Post* article announced the study's imminent release and discussed its thrust and the Fort A. P. Hill retreat.[1] Goldwater fumed, "Damn leaks." Although he and Nunn did not like the premature publicity, the article was balanced and did no harm.

A few days later, an official notice informed members that the SASC would hold its hearing on the staff study on the morning of Wednesday, October 16. Goldwater and Nunn, wanting to be certain that the media understood precisely what was going to be discussed, instructed me to brief all interested reporters the afternoon before the hearing. "Brief those reporters carefully," said Goldwater. "Some of them have trouble getting it right."

On the morning of the media briefing, another *Washington Post* article about the study appeared. This one, however, merely rehashed Goldwater's and Nunn's floor speeches.[2]

Forty-three newspaper, magazine, and television reporters attended my briefing. I gave my standard presentation, described the study's contents, and answered questions. We then distributed printed copies of the staff study to enable reporters to do their homework for the hearing and prepare more comprehensive articles. Each reporter agreed to embargo information until after the hearing.

The reporters grasped the magnitude of the issues. They saw the study and its recommendations as a hot topic. Both the television and print media made plans to attend the hearing.

Usually, the SASC asked hearing witnesses to deliver an oral statement of not more than twenty minutes. Assuming that the hearing on October 16 would follow traditional practice, I struggled to prepare a clear and comprehensive twenty-minute statement.

Nunn had a different idea. He wanted me to give my full briefing. "If we are going to seize the high ground and make the staff report the framework for debating reorganization," he argued, "the briefing has to occupy center stage at the hearing." After a brief debate, we did it Nunn's way.

The SASC's main hearing room in the Russell Building, the oldest of the Senate's three office buildings, was far too small to accommodate the anticipated public and media interest. So, Chief Clerk Chris Cowart secured a large hearing room, SD-562, in the Dirksen Building.

Being an early riser, Goldwater started all morning hearings at nine o'clock—an hour earlier than the SASC's long-standing practice. With many other early morning demands on their time, members often griped about the chairman's starting time; in fact, they were lucky that Goldwater did not choose to start earlier.

When Rick Finn, Jeff Smith, and I arrived at Room SD-562 about fifteen minutes before the hearing, a long line of citizens hoping to attend had already formed outside. Inside, the room buzzed with excitement. All seats reserved for the public were taken. Anxious reporters jammed the press tables. Television cameras from all major private and public networks were positioned to film the proceedings.

As we moved to the witness table to organize our materials, we learned that several public networks would carry the hearing live. C-SPAN would show the entire hearing without interruption, going "gavel to gavel" in Capitol Hill terminology.

As I took my seat, I looked around at the dais where the name of each of the nineteen members was displayed in front of his seat. For the ten senators who did not serve on the Task Force on Defense Organization, this hearing would be their first engagement in the Goldwater-and-Nunn-led reorganization campaign. I was anxious to see where they stood.

The membership was nearly equally divided along party lines with ten Republicans and nine Democrats. Strom Thurmond, the second-ranking Republican, sat on Goldwater's right. Then approaching his eighty-third birthday, the South Carolina senator was a physical fitness nut. He worked hard to stay in great shape. At a Senate office party, I once saw Thurmond—feeling challenged by a young staffer—take off his suit jacket and easily do fifty pushups. He had more endurance for the long Senate workday than most of his younger colleagues.

Even though Goldwater had been elected to the Senate first, Thurmond outranked him in both seniority and years of service. As the Republican candidate for president in 1964, Goldwater did not concurrently stand for election to a third Senate term. When reelected as a senator four years later, Goldwater had to begin anew in terms of seniority.

On the other hand, Thurmond entered presidential politics before his Arizona colleague. In 1948, while serving as South Carolina's governor, Thurmond ran as the States' Rights Party candidate. He garnered thirty-nine electoral votes, only thirteen fewer than Goldwater received as a major-party candidate four elections later.

With his greater seniority, Thurmond could have led the SASC, but instead he chose to chair the Judiciary Committee. Thurmond, a retired major general with thirty-six years in the Army Reserve, seldom displayed his pro-army sentiments in public. But behind closed doors, officers in green uniforms had the greatest influence with him.

John Warner of Virginia occupied the next most senior Republican seat. Warner's strong naval background began with his service in the navy near the end of World War II. He also served as a marine during the Korean War. Nearly twenty years later, President Nixon appointed him as under secretary and then secretary of the navy. Virginia's strong business interest and local political involvement with the navy and Marine Corps reinforced the senator's naval orientation.

Distinguished looking and well dressed, Warner was a true gentleman. He was also—much to the consternation of his more combative Republican colleagues—a peacemaker. Warner worked hard to see the other side's point of view and find common ground for reconciliation. More than any other senator, Warner took a great interest in the staff members and their welfare. He was generous with his concern and praise. In response to a special effort made on his behalf, the Virginia senator often gave small gifts or would find another thoughtful way to return the favor.

Senator Gordon Humphrey sat beside Warner. The unpredictable New Hampshire Republican was sometimes referred to as a "strange duck." The former air force and airline pilot seemed over his head as a senator. Humphrey focused his Senate work on two major issues: abortion and Afghanistan. This prompted some colleagues to say that Humphrey never got beyond the letter *a* in the alphabet.

Bill Cohen and Dan Quayle, two task force members, ranked fifth and sixth among Republicans. Cohen, Warner, and Humphrey had been elected to the Senate in 1978. Cohen should have outranked the other two because he served three terms in the House. The Republican caucus put Cohen behind Warner and Humphrey because he made them uncomfortable with his moderate stances and streak of independence.

Like Warner, the next Republican senator, John East of North Carolina, also had served in the Marine Corps. Thin and pale, East had serious medical problems, including polio, which confined him to a wheelchair. Before his Senate election, East taught at East Carolina University for sixteen years. A staunch conservative and political sidekick of Jesse Helms, North Carolina's senior senator, East went about his senatorial duties in a quiet, professional manner. Tragically, eight months after the hearing, East's ills would lead to his death by suicide.

Senator Pete Wilson of California, another task force member, occupied the next seat, between East and Jeremiah Denton of Alabama.

A retired admiral, Denton spent nearly eight years in a North Vietnamese prisoner of war camp. This ordeal had scarred him. Denton angrily and fervidly supported each and every cause—usually conservative and controversial—that he took up. He delivered many passionate sermons during committee sessions—almost all somehow connected to Vietnam. In the beginning, Denton was honored by his colleagues. Over time, he came to be pitied.

The most junior committee Republican, Texas senator Phil Gramm, participated as the fifth majority member on the task force.

On the other side of the dais, the longtime committee chairman, John Stennis of Mississippi, now occupied the number-two Democratic seat. When the Republicans took control of the Senate in 1981, he gave up the most senior minority position to become the ranking Democrat on the more powerful Appropriations Committee. From the old school, Judge Stennis—as the old-timers called him—never fully adjusted to the passing of the era of powerful chairmen. A master parliamentarian and tactician, Stennis could—when he was chairman—tie the committee members in knots and deftly undo them at the most favorable moment for his side of the issue.

The Mississippi senator had a booming voice in the tradition of the great Southern orators. In my early years with the committee, I wrote some of Stennis's key speeches. He would instruct me to put in some "Mississippi mud." Partial to southerners, especially Mississippians, Stennis would say to me, "Boy, where are you from?"

I would respond, "Sir, I'm from *southern* Pennsylvania."

As the committee met that morning, Judge Stennis was serving his thirty-eighth year in the Senate at age eighty-four. He was merely a shadow of the former Senate great he had been. He lost a leg a year earlier following an illness and used a wheelchair. Despite his age and ills, Stennis was not to be taken lightly. He could still rise up and deliver a sharp lesson to any opponent.

Frank Sullivan, the shrewd staff director of the Appropriations Committee, helped Stennis remain powerful. Sullivan, who moved with Stennis from Armed Services to the Appropriations Committee, had earlier been instrumental in Nunn's rapid rise as a defense expert. Sullivan retained considerable influence with Nunn. From several discussions with Sullivan, I knew that he—perhaps reflecting Stennis's position—opposed reorganization.

Gary Hart sat next to Stennis. Tall, with chiseled good looks, the intellectual Colorado senator saw himself as a visionary reformer. He spent much of his time looking to the future and assessing how it should be shaped. Unfortunately, his horizon was often too far in the future and too erudite for most of the Senate to grasp. Hart was a loner who had few friends in the Senate. His work style reflected his individualistic nature. He seemed to prefer being the lone champion of hopeless, idealistic causes than a comrade in important, but less lofty, efforts.

Jim Exon of Nebraska ranked fourth on the Democratic side. The pipe-smoking former governor had served as a sergeant in the army Signal Corps during World War II. Big and ham-handed, Exon looked like a Nebraska corn farmer. But he was not. Before his eight-year stint as governor, Exon had spent nearly two decades as the founder and president of an office equipment firm. Only he and four other committee members were not lawyers.

The next three seats belonged to Democratic members of the Task Force on Defense Organization: Carl Levin, Ted Kennedy, and Jeff Bingaman.

Although fireplug Alan Dixon of Illinois occupied a seat near the end of the Democratic side of the table, he ranked at the top in terms of being colorful. His spirited personality made him a staff favorite. Dixon's thirty years in the Illinois state government had prepared him well for his Senate duties. He was adept at taking care of his constituents' interests, a skill that earned him the nicknames "Al the Pal" and "The Prince of Pork."

John Glenn, the famous astronaut, ranked last among Democrats. Although the Ohio senator had served nearly eleven years in the Senate, he had joined the SASC only ten months earlier. Glenn, a retired marine colonel and test pilot, demonstrated great interest in technical subjects, especially aviation.

As nine o'clock approached, members began to file in and take their places. Not only did the hearing on the staff study initiate a major inquiry, it embodied the high drama that members love. Senators also love television cameras, and they were numerous. Not surprisingly, thirteen members attended. The number would have been higher but for the absence of three task force members: Cohen, Quayle, and Kennedy. Having already reviewed the staff study in detail, they may not have seen the need to attend.

Typically, only the chairman and ranking minority member make statements at the beginning of a hearing. This hearing would not be typical. After Goldwater and Nunn's opening remarks, eight other senators delivered statements.

Goldwater attempted to preempt the naysayers by repeating key elements of his earlier speeches: "Oh, there will be those who say the system ain't broke, so don't fix it. However, it is broke, and we need to fix it. If we do not, our military effectiveness will be seriously impaired. If we have to fight tomorrow, these problems will cause Americans to die unnecessarily. And even worse, they may cause us to lose the fight."[3]

The chairman characterized the issue's importance: "If we are able to correct these serious organizational deficiencies in the Department of Defense, it may be the greatest contribution to the national security that many of us will make in our lifetimes. I feel that strongly about it."

Nunn reinforced Goldwater's themes and complimented the chairman for his "wise leadership."

Warner then sought recognition to make a statement. Speaking to Goldwater, the former navy secretary quickly revealed his position, "I admire your candor, but sir, I must say respectfully, I disagree with the bluntness in your statement that the system is broke. It is not broke. We are about to take under consideration this morning the incisions to perform open heart surgery on the Department of Defense, and I think we have got to proceed with extreme caution and care."

Warner had tried to stay out of the reorganization fight as long as possible. But the pressure for him to join the opposition had apparently finally become too great. His statement allied him with the antireformist navy.

As evidence that the system was not broken, Warner quoted the chief of naval operations, Admiral Watkins, as saying, "Today we have the finest Navy in the world bar none." He also warned of the adverse impact of criticism of the Pentagon on morale in the armed forces and congressional treatment of the defense budget.

I hated to see Warner on the opposing side. Before the committee completed its reorganization work, everyone expected a vicious political fight. I did not relish the thought of being at loggerheads with the gentleman from Virginia.

After Warner's forceful rebuttal, I expected other tough antireform speeches. To my surprise, the following seven statements were bland. Stennis spoke next, but only five circumspect sentences. After remarking that he had just arrived in the Senate when the storm over the National Security Act of 1947 was beginning to settle, the former chairman said, "I came to learn."

Following Stennis, Gramm elaborated on Warner's admonition that those who wanted to slash the defense budget might misuse the committee's criticism of the Pentagon's performance. In line with the position he first announced at the weekend retreat, the Texas senator repeated his support for strengthening unified commanders. On the other side of the issue, he mouthed several of Navy Secretary Lehman's favorite themes, "I think we should decentralize the Pentagon and give the service secretaries greater responsibility. I think we should strip away layers of federal bureaucrats in the Defense Department."

Hart was recognized next. He cited his long interest in basic military reforms and his instrumental role in forming the Military Reform Caucus. The Colorado senator supported the committee's reorganization work, calling it "an historic effort and a vitally needed one." He also expressed hope "that we do not forget the necessity to reform the way we think about defense." This last statement foreshadowed the cold water Hart would throw on Goldwater and Nunn's work later in the hearing.

Denton followed with a positive statement: "I am entirely with this effort, sir." The retired admiral also noted his four and one-half years of service as the commandant of the Armed Forces Staff College, one of three schools that prepared officers for joint assignments.

Democrats delivered the last three opening statements. Levin announced his strong, proreform views: "I am convinced that the security of the United States continues to be threatened by inadequate coordination of our armed services."

Bingaman praised the staff study as "a high-quality report."

Dixon did not want the study to get too much praise: "I am concerned about reports that some individuals have seemed to feel that this report is the final word on what our committee intends to do regarding reorganization of the Defense Department."

Goldwater then asked me to give my briefing—the same twenty-slide presentation that I had given to the Packard Commission and Secretary Weinberger. Ten minutes into my presentation, Hart inquired whether passing questions could be asked. Goldwater agreed to this benign request.

The floodgates opened after Hart's initial question. Warner and Denton began to pepper me with questions. Warner posed the most memorable one: "It seems to me that you are relegating a chief of service to the role of honorary chairman of the board. You are literally stripping his epaulets right in front of his troops, and little is left for him to do other than to be maybe a functionary. Now, would you care to disagree with that?"

I did disagree, but Warner had stirred the crowd with his colorful metaphor.

After the seventh interruption by either Warner or Denton—whose positive opening statement quickly gave way to angry confrontational rhetoric—Goldwater asked that further questions be held until the end of the briefing. After I had briefed the last slide, Goldwater turned to questions from members. In the first round, each senator would be given ten minutes. By then, it was nearly eleven o'clock. Normally, the question period would begin thirty or forty minutes after the hearing started. But ten opening statements and my long briefing—lengthened by interruptions—had consumed nearly two hours. With ten minutes allotted for each senator's questions, some members would not have a chance to ask questions until after noontime. Sensing this, senators slowly began to depart as questioning progressed.

One can never be fully prepared for a congressional hearing. Having watched members cross-examine witnesses for more than seven years, I knew that these senators were among the all-time pros as question-askers. Witnesses often cracked under their heated, penetrating interrogations. Warner, Denton, and other antireformers would clearly have this objective in mind in questioning me.

The senators' questions targeted me as leader of the staff effort and the principal witness. Despite my solid preparation, the questioning seemed long and grueling. The glare and heat of the television lights did not help.

Goldwater let Nunn ask the first questions. The ranking Democrat knew the answer for each of his questions. But he wanted to reinforce key points and get vital information on the record. He led me through a series of questions on service headquarters staffs, reform alternatives for the Joint Chiefs of Staff, and the operational chain of command.

Warner, looking extremely earnest, questioned next. The Virginia senator initially zeroed in on the origin of the JCS's rule of unanimity and then challenged my assertion that the services controlled military promotions. He then turned to defense procurement, which everyone viewed as a serious problem. Warner seemed to want to redirect the committee's work toward this complex area, where parochial service interests were less threatened. I responded that Senator Quayle's Defense Acquisition Policy Subcommittee would be the focus of needed procurement reforms.

Warner then attacked our proposed JMAC. His thrust was blunted by my testimony on the CNO's anachronistic status as the principal adviser to the president on naval matters. No other service chief had such special standing.

Throughout Warner's questions, he and I were like prizefighters at the start of a fifteen-rounder. Warner would come out swinging, miss with a couple of haymakers, and then we would end up in clinches. A ringside announcer would have summed up the first round this way: "Pretty good footwork, a few jabs landed, but no one connected with any real punches."

Stennis followed Warner. Instead of asking questions, the senator who "came to learn" delivered a statement—essentially the one he did not make at the hearing's beginning. To the untrained ear, Stennis's verbal bobbing and weaving said little. But three statements spoke loudly to me. He complimented Warner: "I remember him as one of the outstanding men that has been in the Pentagon." Seeming to reject the staff study's proposals, Stennis kept referring to the need to develop "a substitute plan." He opined, "Otherwise—and I do not want to look on the darker side of this thing—I do not see how we will ever get anything fixed."

Goldwater and Nunn both responded that they hoped the result of the hearings would be a committee-sponsored package of reorganization measures. "Well, it may not be," replied Stennis. "It may not be possible to be. The reaction to this thing is going to be terrific. You already know that." By the time Stennis finished, I knew he would oppose reorganization. Goldwater and Nunn knew it as well.

Goldwater then recognized Senator Hart. Given that Hart had preached military reform for eight years, I thought he would pursue supporting themes in his questions. I was soon disappointed. Zeroing in and favorably commenting on the study's critiques of the Pentagon's "insufficient mechanisms for change," Hart called them "the most depressing or perhaps I should say frustrating pages in your book." After talking about the Pentagon leadership's lack of will, he said, "We have got to change the way people think."

Hart then stunned us. He expressed his concerns with Goldwater and

Nunn's approach, which he inaccurately characterized as "focusing on rearranging the boxes at the top." Then Hart added another barb: "I just hope that somehow we do not make the traditional mistake of confusing efficiency with effectiveness."

"When we started this study it was the term 'effectiveness' that we had in mind," I fired back. "That was our entire focus."

Talk about being wounded by friendly fire. I had expected reform opponents to put us in their sights, but I did not anticipate incoming rounds from behind our own lines. I agreed with both of Hart's ideas. That was not the problem. My disappointment came from his assumption that only he understood these truths and from the condescending tone of his remarks to Goldwater and Nunn.

Absent at the beginning of the hearing, Senator Wilson used his questioning time to deliver a supportive statement. After congratulating Goldwater and Nunn, Wilson said, "I went to Senator Tower a couple of years ago and expressed concerns about the organization and the fact that I thought it would be healthy to undertake a reexamination."

I was surprised that Wilson referenced his role—arranging the meeting between Tower and retired marine general Brute Krulak—that had initiated Tower's reorganization fiasco. I was even more surprised when Wilson later added, "I congratulate the staff on a truly comprehensive examination . . . a document that will be the basis for, I think, perhaps the most enlightened and thorough examination the subject has had in a very long time."

Like Gramm, Wilson showed interest in strengthening the unified commanders, saying, "I think that the [report] chapters that focus upon the problems of the unified commanders are perhaps those of the greatest immediate interest and concern."

The next three questioners—Exon, Bingaman, and Goldwater—were proreform. Their questions provided the opportunity to expand on favorable themes. Goldwater, like Nunn, posed questions that had been carefully constructed for maximum effect. The chairman's turn ended the first round of questions.

Warner was ready for a second round. Turning to Goldwater, he said, "First I would like to say, you know my respect for you and Mr. Nunn, and I hope I have not been too obstreperous today. But I purposely have stayed out of the study so that I could be a free agent and to offer constructive criticism."

Warner then turned toward the witness table and continued: "And I pay respect to you, Mr. Locher, Mr. Smith, and Mr. Finn. As Harry Truman said, 'If you can't take the heat, get out of the kitchen.' You have taken the heat. You have taken it admirably. But we may disagree."

As Warner was speaking, I tried to calculate the session's impact. So far, I told myself, we've effectively presented and defended the staff study. I could tell that Goldwater and Nunn were pleased. But the hearing was not over yet. Warner was about to turn up the heat in the kitchen.

By then, the former navy secretary was carrying the entire load for the antireform side. Denton had departed before his turn to ask questions. Gramm and Wilson—reversing the hostility that marked their task force work—made supportive statements and did not ask any questions. Quayle did not attend. Although Warner must have been encouraged by Stennis's statement, the Mississippi senator had not helped to challenge the hearing's proreform message.

Warner's first question in the second round centered on who would select the senior personnel if the service secretary and chief had a common staff. When I replied, "The secretary," Warner responded, "Then you have really stripped the service chief down to his skivvy drawers, because that [his staff] is the source of his power." As the hearing progressed, Warner seemed to think less and less of our ideas. An hour earlier he had viewed us as just stripping the service chief's epaulets, now he saw us removing all but his undershorts.

Warner then skillfully presented two arguments. First, he addressed the issue of good people: "But sometimes it seems to me that if we have the right man in the right place at the right time, under the existing framework, I think they can do a credible job."

Had I been given the opportunity to respond, I would have said, "We don't need to choose between good people and good organization. We should emphasize both."

Turning to his second argument, Warner said: "We have singled out the *Pueblo*, we have singled out certain other chapters which are not distinguished in our military history, but nevertheless this system has given us forty years of peace in Europe."

On other occasions, I had heard Nunn pierce this argument with the short retort, "Are you saying because of this system or in spite of?" On this day, he did not go after his colleague from Virginia.

Warner saved his biggest question for last, "What authority do we in the legislative branch have in telling the commander-in-chief of the armed forces, the president, that his organizational structure is broken?"

My response buried that issue for good: "We have the responsibilities under the Constitution to provide for the rules and regulations of the armed forces. . . . The Department of Defense is a creation of the Congress. All of these positions are specified in law, and the Congress has essentially specified the current organizational arrangements." Nearly every other issue raised during the hearing would be debated many times, but not this one.

With only Goldwater, Warner, and himself remaining, Nunn decided to ask additional questions. He started by saying to Goldwater, "You and I and Senator Warner have about worn everybody else out here." I clearly was worn out, and I was certain that Finn and Smith were as well. By then we had been on the hot seat and under the camera lights for three hours. We were ready for the hearing to end. But Nunn—clearly pleased with how things were going—wanted to get more information on the record, particularly in front of the television audience. Fortunately, Nunn ran out of questions before we ran out of endurance.

At 12:12 P.M., Goldwater adjourned the hearing.

As Finn, Smith, and I finally stood up from our seats at the witness table, well-wishers surged around us to offer congratulations. Goldwater gave us a salute before he limped off. Nunn came down from the dais to praise our performance. Goldwater's aide, Gerry Smith, pushed his way to the front of the crowd and said, "You ought to be ashamed of yourself, Locher, for taking on and destroying your intellectual inferiors like that. That hearing was so much fun. I loved it. Goldwater loved it. There wasn't one thing that the Warners or the Dentons or any of the pronavy guys could say that you didn't have an absolute, very calm, reasoned response to."[4]

I was pleased with the outcome of the hearing. We had done our part. The hearing had gone well, better than we had anticipated. Although I felt that we had effectively articulated our message, I was uncertain how the media would react.

In the hours after the hearing, Finn, Smith, and I anxiously awaited "questions for the record" from antireform senators. When a senator does not have a chance to ask all of his questions during a hearing, he can submit them for written responses from the witnesses. We feared that senators might bombard us with questions, maybe as many as several hundred. Reform opponents knew that we were few in number and that we were already worn out. Preparing written answers could tie us up for weeks. We breathed a long sigh of relief when it became clear that opponents were not going to put us through that misery. Not a single question for the record was submitted.

The hearing generated enormous public interest in the staff study. The two thousand copies printed were gone in less than twenty-four hours. The committee had been unable to print more because Congress limits the amount of money that can be spent printing a staff report. Normally, this poses no obstacle. A staff report usually totals only fifteen to twenty pages. At that length, more than fifty thousand copies could be printed. But our 645-page tome constrained the print run. To meet the overwhelming demand, the committee began the several-month process of having the Senate and House pass a concurrent resolution authorizing the printing of more copies.

In the meantime, interested organizations and individuals made thousands of photocopies. This became a major activity at the Pentagon, where everyone wanted a personal copy. Earlier, we had given DoD the opportunity to extend the committee's print run at the Government Printing Office. This would have been an inexpensive way to obtain a large number of copies. But Pentagon officials—dismissing the staff report in advance—insisted they would need "only a few copies."

At 7 P.M., the committee's small reorganization staff gathered around the office television to see if the network evening news would cover the hearing. About ten minutes into the *CBS Evening News*, Dan Rather provided an answer. He opened a two-and-one-half-minute segment by saying: "A long-awaited and much-leaked Senate panel's study of the Pentagon chain of command is officially out tonight, and calling for top-to-bottom changes. And some supporters of the present system are reacting as if someone just tossed one of those $10,000 monkey wrenches into the works."[5]

Although we found Rather's characterization of the study as "much-leaked" to be bizarre, we were ecstatic about his report. With whoops and hollers, we turned the dial to catch *ABC World News Tonight*.

Peter Jennings was just starting his report on the hearing with a familiar quote: "'It is broke and we need to fix it.' That was Senator Barry Goldwater today commenting on the system by which this country defends itself, how the Pentagon runs itself, and how the Congress oversees the Pentagon." Jennings later said that the staff study "has raised up quite a hornets' nest."[6]

Both news programs presented the views of opponents: Warner and Secretary Lehman on CBS and Admiral Moorer on ABC. But overall, we judged that the television reports had put a positive spin on Goldwater and Nunn's reorganization work.

The next morning, when I picked up a copy of the *Washington Post* from the front steps of my home, I saw a front-page headline that read, "Pentagon Is Mismanaged, Report Says." A subtitle added, "Replacement of Joint Chiefs, Reorganization Urged by Senators." The article's lead paragraph reported: "The Defense Department's preparations for war and ability to fight are seriously hampered by interservice rivalry, poor Pentagon management, and congressional nitpicking, and needs a major overhaul, according to a Senate report released yesterday." As I read further down, I was encouraged to see that the article accurately and positively reported key ideas from the staff study.[7]

The article also noted the uphill nature of the reorganization struggle. Reflecting the committee's pro-Pentagon position in recent years, it labeled the SASC "a supporter of the status quo in the Defense Department." Based on the fireworks at the hearing, the article observed that Warner "signaled that the type of drastic reorganization envisioned by the report will not be achieved without a fight."

The *Post* article also reported the Pentagon's negative reaction. Based upon the previous week's interception by navy jets of an Egyptian airliner carrying

"WHAT DO THEY MEAN WE'RE NOT COMBAT-READY?"

29. Herblock cartoon in the *Washington Post,* October 18, 1985.
(*Herblock at Large,* Pantheon, 1987.)

suspected Palestinian terrorists, DoD "disparaged the report's critical tone." A Pentagon spokesman was quoted as saying, "These kind of conclusions without the data to back them up don't match up with our recent experience where we had a military mission assigned by the president on very short notice to our military forces, which was carried out with skill, excellence, flawlessly."

By the time I arrived at the office, Goldwater's and Nunn's press assistants were reporting that other newspapers were featuring articles similar to the *Post*'s. Page one of the *Atlanta Journal* declared, "Panel suggests dissolving Joint Chiefs of Staff." The *New York Times* titled its piece, "Proposed Revamping of Military Calls for Disbanding Joint Chiefs." The *Baltimore Sun* had two front-page articles: "Senate report suggests broad military reforms" and "Coordination said to be a problem." The *Wall Street Journal* reported, "Senators Clash Over Proposal to Shift Power at Pentagon Away From Services."[8] Within a few hours, we knew that the hearing and study had received the extensive and favorable coverage we had hoped for.

Our efforts to educate the public on reorganization received an unexpected boost. Viewer interest had prompted C-SPAN to continue to air their tape of the hearing. It was shown every other day or so for several months.

"What Command Problems?"

30. Tom Flannery cartoon in the *Baltimore Sun,* October 28, 1985.

31. Jim Dent cartoon in the *Charleston* (*West Virginia*) *Gazette*,
October 21, 1985.

32. Tony Auth cartoon of October 16, 1985 (©1985 *The Philadelphia
Inquirer.* Reprinted with permission of Universal Press Syndicate.
All rights reserved.)

The Pentagon took a few days before firing back. Two days after the hearing, a short article in the *Baltimore Sun* covered the DoD arguments.[9] The Pentagon's first long rebuttal, written by Seth Cropsey, deputy under secretary of the navy, appeared in the *New York Post* on October 23. Entitled "How Not to Reform Defense," the article began: "That most dangerous of alliances—inexperienced congressional staffers and the Washington think-tanks—has rumbled up to the ramparts, and the defenses they're aiming at are ours." By attacking people, not ideas, Cropsey's rebuttal got off to a poor start. The article argued that reform advocates merely wanted to reduce defense spending and to find a political "quick fix" for Pentagon problems. Cropsey judged that the proposed reforms would add more bureaucracy, isolate civilian leaders, reduce civilian control, and lead to far less competition of ideas.[10]

Just as newspaper columnists began to taper off their reporting, political cartoonists and editorial writers kept the topic alive. Cartoonists often found the military an attractive target, and the reorganization struggle sparked their imagination. Two days after the hearing, a Herblock cartoon in the *Washington Post* became the first of many to humorously promote Goldwater and Nunn's cause.

Editorial writers overwhelming supported the need for reform. The conservative *Washington Times*'s editorial page addressed the issue first, saying, "It's heartening to find defense-minded Sens. Barry Goldwater and Sam Nunn urging reform." Referencing Rambo movies and the flak the two senators were taking from the Pentagon, the *Times* editorial concluded, "The 'Rambo right' should remember that its hero was obliged to overcome the defense establishment before he could get down to serious business."[11]

Magazines also were soon running favorable articles about the report and hearing. In editions that hit the newsstands on October 22, *Newsweek* reported "The Pentagon Under Siege," and *U.S. News & World Report* announced "Pentagon Comes Under Fire From Its Friends."[12] Most notably, *Armed Forces Journal*, Ben Schemmer's magazine, which was widely read in defense circles, devoted an "extra"—only the third in the magazine's 122 years—to the staff study and Goldwater's and Nunn's floor speeches.[13] In an editorial, Schemmer wrote: "The editors and staff of *Armed Forces Journal* believe that staff study, *Defense Organization: The Need for Change,* is the single most important body of work on national security matters done so far this century. The Senate's deliberate action on its conclusions and recommendations may well endure as the greatest contribution to America's security we'll see in our lifetimes."

After the hearing and its favorable repercussions, Goldwater and Nunn were solidly entrenched on the high ground. As they prepared for a lengthy series of reorganization hearings, the two senators were still the underdogs with powerful enemies and significant obstacles yet to overcome. But the odds against them were not as long as they once were.

CHAPTER 20

Transition to the Offensive

A sudden powerful transition to the offensive—the

flashing sword of vengeance—is the

greatest moment for the defense.

—Carl von Clausewitz, *On War*

A fter releasing the staff report on October 16, 1985, the Senate Armed Services Committee paused for four weeks before continuing hearings. This delay allowed prospective witnesses time to study the staff report. Senators Goldwater and Nunn had instructed each witness to base his testimony on the report.

The two leaders came to the hearings in a defensive posture. They expected the Pentagon, especially the joint chiefs, to mount a full-scale counterattack, both in testimony and behind the scenes. Men in uniform enjoyed respect and credibility on Capitol Hill. Their arguments could persuade senators to doubt the wisdom of ignoring the advice of the nation's top officers.

To Goldwater's and Nunn's great surprise, Department of Defense witnesses offered weak, unconvincing testimony. As the hearings progressed, the two leaders and other proreform members—sensing the superiority of their arguments—transitioned to an offensive posture.

Goldwater and Nunn approved a plan for ten hearings, with Secretary Weinberger appearing first on November 14. The hearings' key objective was to solidify the staff report's role as the framework for debate. Defending its analyses and recommendations ranked second. Goldwater and Nunn hoped also to use the hearings to continue to influence members' thinking. Last, they wanted to build the public case in support of Pentagon reform. Hearings do not efficiently communicate ideas and information, so neither the two senators nor their staff harbored great expectations.

The staff report, soon called the Locher report, "created quite a stir" in the defense community. Two scholars later described it as "the most radical of the reform studies," observing that its extreme recommendations "made the Locher report the lightning rod for criticism of JCS reform and subjected Locher himself to a good deal of verbal abuse; interviewees referred to a 'lynch-Locher' mentality among many in the Pentagon after the report appeared." The Defense Department had become so hostile regarding the study that most of my Pentagon friends told me they could not afford to be seen with me in public. The two scholars add that "Locher's recommendations made those of other studies appear more moderate and appealing, suggesting that Locher helped pull the ongoing legislative effort toward more far-reaching reforms."[1]

Officially, the Pentagon had "stayed mum in advance of the hearings." Behind the scenes, however, Goldwater "caught flak from members of the military community." Nunn reported that the chairman "continues to be under . . . pressures . . . to back off." Goldwater reportedly had "been cornered at parties and been bombarded by calls from current and retired military personnel asking him to drop the reform issue." Retired admiral Robert J. Hanks vociferously criticized the chairman: "Goldwater's outlived his usefulness. The report goes too far. That, coupled with the fact that he's a heavy Air Force advocate, makes it clear there's as much parochial thought in Goldwater as there is in any service."[2]

To complement the hearings, Finn, Smith, and I arranged one-on-one meetings between committee members and former senior defense officials and officers who were proreform. Military legislative assistants on members' personal staffs advised us which former officials and officers had credibility with their bosses. For example, George K. "Ken" Johnson Jr. knew that his boss, Sen. Strom Thurmond, would be influenced by Gen. Shy Meyer's views on reorganization. At our urging, Meyer met several times with Thurmond.[3] Throughout the fall, Finn, Smith, and I encouraged such meetings with members.

Goldwater and Nunn also arranged a series of meetings during which I would brief senior officials on the study. The first meeting targeted key House Republican leaders, of whom only Minority Whip Trent Lott and Republican Conference Chairman Jack Kemp attended. Congressmen Bill Nichols and John Kasich, fearful that House Republicans might back the Pentagon, had urged Goldwater and Nunn to arrange this session. Congressmen Gingrich, Whitehurst, and Kasich attended to reinforce the senators' message. Lott appeared supportive, but Kemp communicated his opposition. At one point, Lott said to Kemp, "We all agree that we have problems, don't we, Jack?" Kemp shrugged.[4]

Goldwater and Nunn scheduled a session on November 13 with House Speaker Tip O'Neill. My briefing fascinated the speaker. When I finished, O'Neill was eager to know more. Finally, Goldwater and Nunn ran out of time, but they left me with the speaker for another hour to answer his questions and provide more details.

Another session was held with Vice Pres. George Bush on November 19 in his office just off the Senate floor. Bush's questions impressed me. He had quickly grasped the central issues presented in my briefing. I also remember being amused by the Mickey Mouse watch on his wrist.

The committee heard vintage Weinberger during his November 14 appearance. Despite the best efforts of Admiral Crowe and Assistant Secretary for Legislative Affairs Russ Rourke, Weinberger maintained his stonewalling stance. His story was simple: Nothing in the Pentagon is broken, so fixes are not needed. Weinberger said the staff study and other reports "seem to be talking about a Pentagon that was perhaps in existence before, which we do not fully recognize now. We think that . . . the practices and problems of the past have been corrected." When evidence of continuing problems was cited, Weinberger became an absolute bulldog. He admitted nothing, exasperating many members, and wore them down by his tenacity. The *Washington Post* correctly described Weinberger's testimony as "combative and obfuscatory."[5]

One key debate focused on whether the services had difficulty communicating with one another during the Grenada invasion. To a question from Senator Levin about inadequate communications, Weinberger replied, "In Grenada, there was adequate interoperability to enable us to do the job that we had to do."[6]

Nunn knew better. Shortly after the invasion, the Georgia Democrat had heard directly from the troops about communications problems. Nunn was also familiar with DoD's own after-action report, which criticized interservice communications. The ranking Democrat was not about to let Weinberger smooth over communications problems in Grenada, especially when they epitomized the services' inability to operate together.

Nunn rebutted the secretary's answer to Levin: "We have a classified report here from the Department of Defense . . . Mr. Secretary, that in all respects directly contradicts your assessment."

"Overall [the communications problems] were not of the nature that interfered with the success of the operation," replied Weinberger, repeating his earlier bottom line.

The senator and defense secretary went round and round. Each time Nunn cited serious communications problems, Weinberger responded that they had not interfered with the success of the operation.

Exasperated, Nunn belittled Weinberger's testimony: "That is very crafty wording; the operation was successful; therefore, nothing interfered with the success of the operation because it was successful. That is ridiculous."

Despite this clash, Nunn got Weinberger's help in discrediting Navy Secretary Lehman. The senator quoted Lehman as saying, "The Pentagon could be run at a twenty-percent savings if we could get rid of those 6,000 bureaucrats in OSD who are accountable essentially to nobody." Nunn then asked Weinberger: "Who are those 6,000 bureaucrats he is talking about? . . . Are they not directly under your control?"[7]

"The 6,000 have never been identified to me by name or function," the secretary answered. "I think there is a bit of hyperbole there." Citing the OSD's size as less than two thousand, Weinberger did not know how Lehman intended to cut six thousand or save $30 billion. He indirectly slammed Lehman by concluding: "John is perfectly free to make criticisms and the comments that he does and from them I think we all benefit, especially if we investigate them and find out they are not fully justified."

Senator Warner, a former navy secretary, spoke next. He pointed out that "he would have been beheaded" had he made comments like Lehman's during his time in the Pentagon.

"Occasionally you have to take executory measures," Weinberger quipped, "but we try to limit them."

Despite this moment of levity, by the hearing's end the faces of many senators were flushed from arguing with the intransigent secretary. Goldwater was clearly frustrated by Weinberger's uncooperative stance and lawyerly answers. As the hearing drew to a close, Goldwater exploded: "Mr. Secretary, I have to be honest with you, you did not answer the questions, you have not approached this thing right. I think you had better go back and read this report of ours. We are going to get you back again. We want your answers."[8]

"We are reading it very carefully," Weinberger replied. "I will be glad to come back."

"Read it again," Goldwater fired back, and slammed down the gavel to end the hearing.

Goldwater and Nunn later decided that the committee would not benefit from hearing Weinberger again.

The defense secretary scored many debating points during his appearance. He was elusive and evasive. Not a single senator nailed him. Yet despite the secretary's masterful performance, his testimony damaged DoD's position. Before the hearing, Weinberger had little credibility on Capitol Hill. After the hearing, he had less. The staff study's analyses were too hard-hitting and well documented to be dismissed by clever rhetoric. Weinberger's testimony conveyed to the committee either that his mind was closed on reorganization or that he did not comprehend the need or opportunity to make improvements. In the view of proreform members, if the Pentagon's top man was unyielding and unthinking, little could be expected from his subordinates. They began to write off DoD as a meaningful participant in the reform process.

Many in the Pentagon recognized problems with the secretary's testimony. A summary prepared for Admiral Crowe reported that the hearing "went poorly in its later stages . . . the secretary clearly hurt his case where he was unwilling to admit the severity of communications problems in Grenada that had already been documented in a DoD report."[9]

Lieutenant Colonel Daniel J. Kaufman, a West Point classmate of mine who was reviewing reorganization for the army chief of staff, recalled his reaction: "I was there, and the only way to describe it was that Weinberger took a spear in the chest. After that hearing, it was clear to all of us on the army chief's reorganization review committee that things were going to change. We made the argument to General Wickham that you can help craft the outcome or you can be run over by this truck, but it is very clear that we're going to get reorganization."[10] Although some in the Pentagon held this view, on Capitol Hill the perspective was that the outcome was still highly uncertain.

Weinberger gave President Reagan an upbeat account of his testimony "in opposition to the fundamental changes in the Joint Chiefs of Staff proposed by [the SASC] staff":

> I reported that the Joint Chiefs system was working well and that you and I felt that we had received good and timely advice from the Joint Chiefs. But, having put much staff work in this project, both Barry Goldwater and Sam Nunn seem determined to move ahead with proposals that would either seriously weaken, or abolish altogether, our Joint Chiefs. The staff report makes many other recommendations, and I offered our full assistance to work with the Senate committee to reach agreement on some of these recommendations. Given the momentum behind this, we must ensure the proposed changes are fully considered to avoid serious disruption to our system of command. I understand that you will be briefed on the committee's staff report. I have felt it important that I keep an open mind as we receive the committee's input, and I certainly have tried to avoid premature endorsement of all their recommendations. The Joint Chiefs organization is too valuable an asset for us lightly to cast aside on the say-so of a Senate staff report.[11]

Goldwater and Nunn devoted the next four sessions to hearing from thirteen former civilian and military officials who the senators believed would present more candid and constructive testimony. Such commentary, less constrained by the Pentagon party line, would provide a useful context before hearing again from DoD witnesses, particularly the service chiefs. Ten of the thirteen witnesses testified in support of major reorganization, with differences primarily over the potential effectiveness of various reforms.

On November 19, Gen. Shy Meyer, Adm. Harry D. Train II, and Gen. Russell E. Dougherty, USAF (Ret.), provided strong proreform testimony. There was only one dissenter: marine general Brute Krulak. Krulak said the staff "study does little more than nibble at the edges of stale concepts, offering more bureaucracy and more complexity."[12] The proreform drumbeat continued the next day when former defense secretaries Schlesinger and Brown testified.

Goldwater began the November 21 session with Admiral Moorer and General Jones by calling attention to the House's passage the preceding day of a JCS reorganization bill by an "overwhelming" vote of 383 to 27. "The House JCS vote is a very powerful one," said Goldwater. "I believe the House action will build momentum for substantial JCS reorganization."[13]

Weinberger reported the House action to Reagan, calling the legislation "a very moderate bill." Giving the situation an unwarranted positive spin, the secretary wrote: "While we did not publicly embrace the bill, we were able to have a significant impact in minimizing the changes and forestalling other more radical reorganization plans similar to those currently being discussed in the Senate and elsewhere. We will continue to work closely with the Congress on this sensitive issue to protect our vital interests. We must, however, guard against perhaps well-intentioned, but nonetheless overreactive legislative solutions."[14]

Shortly after the November 21 hearing started, Senator Warner, seeing an evolving pattern, commended Goldwater and Nunn for the selection of witnesses and the hearings schedule. "I am confident that the full committee will eventually come out with a unanimous decision on this difficult subject," he predicted.[15] At that moment, Warner may have been the only member or staffer who believed the process would end with unanimous agreement.

Admiral Moorer's testimony started where his criticisms of the staff study had left off at Fort A. P. Hill, saying, "I do not agree with many things in this staff study."[16] He began by attempting to impress members by outlining his career. This tactic might work at a Rotary Club luncheon, but it was ill suited for an audience of senators. The former naval aviator told of being at Pearl Harbor, where he "saw 2,000 American boys dead, laid out on the grass, ships burning and exploding." When he next said, "I was shot down during the war in flames," Goldwater leaned toward Nunn and whispered, "That's nothing to brag about."

Midway through Moorer's ten-minute biographical sketch, as he listed his medals, Nunn whispered to Goldwater, "When a witness believes that he has to spend all this time telling you who he is, he probably won't say much that's worth listening to."

After Moorer complained about the president and defense secretary not accepting JCS advice during the Vietnam War, he noted that people had said to him, "You could resign." He told the committee, "I thought about it, but the one thing that was driving me during that time was the POWs, and I was determined

I was going to stay until I got them free."[17] Moorer's argument was emotional but untenable: he allowed the POW issue to outweigh efforts to correct what he viewed as a flawed approach to the war.

Moorer's written statement ended with this observation: "I consider that the staff report is filled with overstatements based on opinions and hearsay rather than fact and, consequently, the majority of the corrective actions are excessive and often are aimed at solving problems that have been or are being progressively solved."[18]

Introducing General Jones, Goldwater said, "You are the fellow who sort of dreamed this all up, so take it away."[19] Jones's insightful testimony contradicted and overshadowed Moorer's. However, the admiral's passionate delivery had masked the intellectual weakness of his position.

After hearing from Moorer and Jones, the committee remained in session to hear from Admiral McDonald, the soon-to-retire commander of the Atlantic Command. McDonald gave a positive statement, commended the staff study, and endorsed many recommendations. He did not, however, support designating the chairman as the principal military adviser. Nonetheless, his qualified support came as a pleasant surprise.

In a letter to Goldwater on December 2, the day Congress returned from its Thanksgiving recess, Weinberger surprisingly agreed to implement a number of reforms. Sensing that DoD verged on irrelevance, the secretary's advisers had pleaded with him to take a more cooperative approach with Congress. Weinberger finally agreed.

"I always thought that Weinberger played it very dumbly," said Admiral Crowe. "I had some fierce arguments with him over reorganization. I actually thought I had won at one time. My argument in winning was, 'Look, Cap, it's going to happen, and you can march up and down over here and stomp your feet all you want to, but that's counterproductive. You ought to say, 'Yeah, we want it to happen,' and then try and shape it—if you've got some things you feel strongly about—try and shape it, but get on board. And one time he said, 'Okay, I'll do that.' But he didn't mean it. He just resisted."[20]

Weinberger's letter supported making the JCS chairman the principal military adviser. He also endorsed authorizing the secretary of defense to place the chairman in the operational chain of command—a bad idea in our view—and to use the chairman as the secretary's agent in supervising the unified commands. The secretary also supported statutory changes to make the chairman the Joint Staff's sole boss and to establish the position of vice chairman. Weinberger qualified this last idea by arguing: "The vice chairman should not outrank the JCS and he should not act as chairman in the absence of the chairman." The secretary was pushing the services' arguments for a vice chairman who was not a vice chairman.[21]

Weinberger's letter meant little to me because it offered little. The secretary addressed only a few of the many needed changes, and we disagreed, at least in part, with two of his five proposals. But to many committee members, the letter was much more significant than the few bones it contained. Senator Kennedy excitedly asked me, "Did you see Weinberger's letter?" When I told him I was nonplussed by what it offered, he answered, "Yes, yes, but the significance lies in Weinberger admitting—and remember he doesn't admit anything—that problems exist. His letter is the crack in the wall."

Weinberger informed Reagan of his letter: "We made our first initial report to the committee this week after testifying in November. By indicating to the committee we could support putting into law certain improvements, which we have already made in the Organization of the Joint Chiefs of Staff, we have demonstrated our continued willingness to work with the committee as they move toward almost certain legislative initiatives early next year."[22]

The fall of 1985 was a difficult one for Goldwater. The long, trying first session of the Ninety-ninth Congress had taken its toll on his health and stamina. Illness occasionally precluded his participation in planned reorganization activities. When this was the case, Nunn insisted that these activities be put off until Goldwater was ready.

The health of the senator's wife, Peggy, had taken a serious turn for the worse. She had been confined in an Arizona nursing home for many years. The senator would frequently travel to see her. In the late fall, Mrs. Goldwater's condition became more severe, and Senator Goldwater increasingly devoted his time and attention to her care. When the Senate reconvened on December 2, Goldwater remained in Arizona with his wife and asked Thurmond and Nunn to run the hearings in his absence. He missed the last five days of hearings, which ended on December 12, the day after Mrs. Goldwater died.

With half of the Goldwater-Nunn team missing, the effort lurched along out of balance. Moreover, not knowing the status of Mrs. Goldwater's health, we did not know how long the chairman would be gone. On the positive side, thrusting Thurmond into the role of acting chairman had long-term benefits. It brought him into the work's mainstream and made him responsible for keeping it on track.

On December 4, Thurmond chaired his first reorganization hearing, the fourth session with former officials. Four retired officers appeared: General Vessey, General Goodpaster, Admiral Long, and General McBride. Thurmond read a statement that Goldwater had sent from his wife's hospital. It ended with "a few remarks to every person in uniform:"

No matter what color uniform you wear, no matter what rank or insignia you carry, no matter what command you now have or might ever have, you are going to remember these hearings all of your days, and my guess is that you are going to thank God they came about.

I know how hard it is to find problems within your own organization. I was a corporate president myself once, and I was also the commander of different units during World War II. Since and before that time, if you ever wanted me to get mad, start making wisecracks about my outfit. But after leaving them and thinking back, I could think of times when criticism was deserved. Had I not been so wedded to my job and so parochial in my thinking, I could have understood it at the time. . . . Only by long, honest discussion between all of us will the matters that need correcting be brought to the surface. . . .

Please keep this one thought in mind. None of us live forever, but with proper care, allegiance, and adherence to basic principles, we have a country that will endure, so let us put our minds to that task.[23]

Vessey offered bland, neutral testimony highlighted by a plea "to make sure that we do not throw out the baby with the bath water." Goodpaster delivered a powerful statement that quickly brushed aside Vessey's more upbeat tone by speaking to "inherent and fundamental weaknesses" in the JCS system. Long emphasized the need to strengthen the unified commanders while recommending against making the JCS chairman the principal military adviser. McBride focused on the needs to improve joint officer management and streamline Joint Staff procedures. He based his testimony on the recommendations of the Chairman's Special Study Group, on which he had served.[24]

The strategy of hearing from retired officials had worked well. Of the thirteen, only Moorer and Krulak gave outright antireform testimony, while Vessey was neutral. All others favored reform. McDonald and Long qualified their support for reform more than any of the others, but they were passionately proreform on a number of important issues. These four hearings gave members the opportunity to explore many issues, and the improved understanding provided valuable context for the antireform arguments of the service chiefs.

On December 5, the committee, with Warner chairing, met to take testimony from the uniformed heads of the four services. Goldwater and Nunn had believed that this session would pose their biggest challenge. Surprisingly, the chiefs stumbled through weak and often confused testimony. Afterward, Nunn happily concluded, "The chiefs never laid a glove on us."

If anyone should have understood the Pentagon's organizational deficiencies, it was the army chief of staff, Gen. John Wickham. He had served—more than any other officer on active duty—in multiservice assignments that exposed him to the devastating consequences of organizational problems. More puzzling still, Wickham's resistance to reform clashed with the army's historic approach. The army had traditionally supported the organizational concepts that Goldwater and Nunn were championing. Wickham's predecessor, General Meyer, had openly supported reorganization. Goldwater and Nunn had continuously held out hope that Wickham would eventually come to support their efforts. While this had not occurred, they never expected the army chief to be a furious opponent.

Moreover, Wickham ignored the advice of the special study group that he had established: the U.S. Army Special Review Committee on Department of Defense Organization. Consisting of two colonels, three lieutenant colonels, one major, and two civilians, the committee was chartered to subject the SASC staff report to "an independent look, unconstrained by prior Army positions." The army had determined that such an effort was needed after a Joint Staff group had reviewed the report and "had nonconcurred in all of its recommendations."[25]

The special review committee worked for Lt. Gen. Carl Vuono, the army's deputy chief of staff for operations. Lieutenant Colonel Richard H. Witherspoon, another of my West Point classmates, served as Vuono's reorganization action officer. Vuono graduated from West Point in 1957. One of his classmates, Arch Barrett, was the lead reorganization staffer for the House Armed Services Committee. During the fall of 1985, Vuono and Witherspoon traded barbs as to whose classmate on Capitol Hill was the more outrageous.[26]

One of Vuono's deputies, Brig. Gen. Howard D. Graves Jr., instructed the special review committee: "Let's look at what the country needs. Let's get out of the green suit [a broader perspective than just the army]." The army might have to sacrifice some of its special interests for the greater good. "You have to rise above parochialism."[27] The committee followed Graves's instructions even after it was confronted by the antireform position papers prepared for Weinberger by the Cox Committee, which had "running throughout them . . . the theme that the current organization worked well and should not be changed." The army committee took a bold stand in favor of major reform. It recommended designating the JCS chairman as the principal military adviser and endorsed many of the staff study's major recommendations, only opposing creation of a JCS vice chairman.[28] Wickham did not accept his committee's recommendations, but his testimony was more proreform than that of the other service chiefs. The army committee "regarded that as a major victory."[29]

The marine commandant, Gen. P. X. Kelley, offered the strongest criticism of the reform effort. Although the SASC had expected this, Cohen and Nunn, both of whom had collaborated with Kelley in the early 1980s, had anticipated a different response.

Kelley was then a three-star general serving as the first commander of the Rapid Deployment Joint Task Force (RDJTF). President Carter had created that force to protect American interests in the Persian Gulf region following the 1979 revolution in Iran. As a joint command, the RDJTF struggled for resources and other support in a lopsided competition with powerful service bureaucracies. The SASC had been heavily involved in Persian Gulf issues, due both to a study group led by Nunn and a subcommittee chaired by Cohen. The committee took an active interest in Kelley's plight, strongly supported his budget, and jawboned with the services on his behalf. I had handled this work as the principal staffer for Persian Gulf issues.

In December, 1985, Kelley headed one of the powerful service bureaucracies against whom he had been pitted in a life-or-death struggle just years earlier. He had then watched the services attempt to choke off a high-priority initiative—mandated by the commander in chief—because it threatened their interests. Kelley acted as though his earlier frustrations with service power and parochialism had never occurred. Now, as marine commandant, he was determined to maintain his service's dominating power. Kelley's position especially disappointed Cohen, Nunn, and me.

Although Nunn felt that our reorganization effort had not been hurt in any way by the chiefs' appearance before the committee, the same could not be said for Kelley. The marine commandant rejected the testimony prepared for him by his staff and wrote his own. Although his emotional statement contained numerous flaws in logic, Kelley passionately delivered his remarks.

The commandant appeared to be highly offended by the staff study. I knew that he was hopping mad at me. He was so mad that eighteen months later he still had not cooled off. In his remarks during his retirement ceremony on June 15, 1987, the commandant said: "When I take off the uniform of a Marine for the last time later this month, I will do so with some haunting concerns. My first concern is with a growing attitude in the Congress which places more credence in the views of staff members on matters dealing with national security than in the views of the service chiefs."[30] Colonel Terry Murray later told me that Kelley had reorganization and me in mind when he penned those words.

During his committee appearance, Kelley gave every indication that he was raging inside. My long experience with the committee had taught me that emotional witnesses generally do poorly. Kelley's appearance added more evidence to that observation. During questioning, Cohen and Nunn exposed flaws in the marine's logic.

In his opening statement, Kelley argued, "The burden must be on the critics to prove beyond a reasonable doubt that tangible improvements will result from the recommendations for change." Cohen retorted: "The suggestion was made by General Kelley, that advocates of change . . . must carry the burden of proof beyond a reasonable doubt. I do not think that anybody on this committee, no one that I am aware of, is accusing you of criminal misconduct. That [proof beyond a reasonable doubt] is the standard we apply to criminal misbehavior, not to an opportunity to see whether improvements can be made."[31]

Kelley's face remained expressionless as Cohen made him look silly, but the aides seated behind the commandant winced.

Cohen next raised the issue of the RDJTF. Kelley had argued that the chiefs are able to subordinate the interests of their parent services to the larger interests of national defense, testifying, "I can find no significant shortcomings in the ability of our current system to address strategy, resource, operational, and organizational issues."[32]

Cohen responded that Kelley's statement "struck me as being somewhat in contrast to the enormous difficulties you had as the first commander of the Rapid Deployment Joint Task Force. Now in that particular case . . . there was great difficulty, serious infighting, [and] the current system had some shortcomings in addressing strategy and resource and operational and organizational issues. So is this one of the situations in which the Joint Chiefs were able to subordinate the interests of their parent services to the larger national interest?"[33]

Kelley had no real answer. Cohen had nailed him. The Maine senator had witnessed the infighting over the RDJTF, so Kelley could not deny it. The top marine responded with incomprehensible chain-of-command gobbledygook.[34] Cohen decided not to follow Kelley into the swamp of Pentagonese; he had made his point. Kelley's aides winced again.

Next it was Nunn's turn to spar with the commandant. In an effort to improve the quality of Joint Staff officers, one of the few changes in law resulting from the Tower-Nichols confrontation in 1984 required such officers to be among the most outstanding. Kelley argued that this requirement was ill considered. To deride it, he used a number of rhetorical questions, including, "And when a unit suffers casualties unnecessarily because it was not led by our 'most outstanding officers,' to whom will their families turn for accountability?"[35]

Nunn looked at Kelley and said, "You do not want to suggest that this requirement will mean the Marines will die because your best officers are on the Joint Staff and not in command. . . . It seems to me we have got a real challenge to either change the statute or you have got a challenge to get more outstanding officers in the Marine Corps." Nunn then covered his microphone and said informally to his colleagues, "When the Marine Corps said they were looking for 'a few good men,' I didn't realize how few."[36] Even the antireform senators chuckled. Kelley's aides looked on crestfallen as the committee members laughed at their boss.

Although I had sat in on hundreds of hearings, I had never before seen a witness fail to realize when he was whipped and attempt to cut his losses. Yet Kelley kept coming back with one foolish argument after another. Nunn and Cohen hammered him unmercifully. The hearing signaled the bitter end of what had been at one time a strong relationship between the general and key committee members.

The inability of the four service chiefs to rebut proreform arguments completely altered the dynamic of the hearings. The proreformers were no longer on the defensive; the Pentagon was. This became clear at the next session on December 6, when Deputy Secretary Taft, Army Secretary John O. Marsh Jr., Navy Secretary Lehman, and Air Force Under Secretary Edward C. "Pete" Aldridge Jr. appeared. Nunn, Levin, Exon, Kennedy, and Thurmond kept the witnesses off balance with tough questions. Among antireform members, only Warner attended.

During this hearing, Nunn destroyed Lehman's boast about how he alone had succeeded in reducing bureaucracy. The senator dramatically thumbed through the Pentagon telephone book's organizational index and noted that twenty-one pages were devoted to the OSD, JCS, and all defensewide and joint activities, twenty-nine pages to the army, fifteen pages to the air force, six pages to the Marine Corps, and fifty-two pages to the navy. Nunn recalled the scene: "Lehman talked about [how] the navy didn't have too much bureaucracy. It was slimmed down, but everybody else had excessive staffs and layers. I just started thumbing through the Pentagon telephone book. You should have seen Lehman. He just went through the floor. It was so much fun."[37]

Nunn finished his act by commenting, "Now I am not saying this is a statistically accurate survey of organizations, but it does indicate something." Lehman weakly quipped, "We have more telephones."[38]

Five proreform witnesses appeared during the last two days of hearings. Former defense secretary Mel Laird, former assistant defense secretary Lawrence J. Korb, and former NSC staffer Phil Odeen appeared on December 11. Admiral Crowe and General Rogers appeared separately the next day.

Crowe's position at the end was designed to protect him. I had convinced Goldwater and Nunn that we should leave Crowe out of this battle, which was a no-win proposition for him. We knew that he supported many reorganization ideas, but he would also play a critical role in implementing any enacted reforms. To draw him out and force him to openly oppose his colleagues, especially the chiefs, would be shortsighted. I had argued that many witnesses could present and defend proreform perspectives, but only Crowe would potentially play a key role in making the reforms work. Nunn's questions avoided the barnburner issues, and the admiral escaped without any obvious damage.

Rogers told me a few days before his appearance that he could not get his opening statement approved by the Pentagon. "Just have the chairman ask me a broad question," he said, "and I'll give my opening statement as the answer." Warner chaired the hearing, and Rogers proceeded to give his statement when Warner gave him an opening. In listing actions Congress should take, the general said, "The first thing is to eliminate the service secretaries."[39]

Almost swallowing his tongue, Warner garbled, "I beg your pardon?"

After bantering about how Rogers's recommendation had grabbed the former navy secretary's attention, Nunn inquired: "General, may I ask you for one little clarification, to ease Senator Warner's mind. You would not make that retroactive, would you?"[40]

After the last hearing, Rick Finn and I turned our attention to drafting a reorganization bill. Goldwater and Nunn intended it to be the SASC's first item of business in the new year. We began with a series of meetings with the two senators, following Goldwater's return from Arizona on December 17, to get their approval of our approach and specific provisions. Just before the Christmas holidays, Goldwater and Nunn approved a long list of conceptual changes to defense organization. By mid-January, Finn and I had translated these into a draft bill. On January 17 we met with General Jones, Bill Brehm, John Kester, and Phil Odeen to review the draft bill.[41] These four, later joined by General Gorman, served as the staff's informal advisers throughout 1986.

In January I began to assess in detail where the reorganization votes might lie in the committee. Some votes were easy to predict, but other members had carefully guarded their views. The situation on the Republican side did not look good: Goldwater and Cohen were the only certain supporters, and Thurmond was the only other Republican leaning in support. Warner, Wilson, Denton, and Gramm were solidly against reorganization. I put Humphrey, Quayle, and East in the leaning against category. With only two or three favorable GOP votes, Nunn's ability to corral his Democratic colleagues would be critical.

Nunn refrained from pursuing committee Democrats for much longer than the staff thought was advisable. Staffers worry excessively about their issues and often second-guess the political timing of members. Smith, Finn, and I were no exception to this rule. We fretted about Nunn's delay in putting the strong arm on his colleagues. Antireform agents were lobbying members. We needed to get firm commitments before those provocateurs undermined our position.

Finally, Nunn made his move. With Smith, Finn, and me in attendance, Nunn telephoned each committee Democrat and asked for his complete support. When the ranking Democrat was finished, he had a total of seven committed votes. Only Stennis and Glenn would be voting against reorganization.

With nineteen senators on the committee, Thurmond's position became pivotal. With him on their side, Goldwater and Nunn would start the bill's markup with a one-vote margin in favor. If Thurmond cast his vote in the other direction, reorganization could be dealt a severe—even possibly a fatal—blow. "Maybe you should get together with Senator Thurmond," I said to Goldwater, "and shore him up on this issue." The chairman answered, "Don't worry about Thurmond; he'll be there when we need him." Goldwater later explained their close relationship: "I got Strom Thurmond to become a Republican—that's years and years ago. His state voted for me for president, and that's when he changed and became a Republican. We've always gotten along. I wasn't the least bit worried about him."[42] Despite Goldwater's confidence, I worried.

Ken Johnson, Thurmond's staffer, strongly supported reorganization. Despite heavy flak, the Citadel graduate and former Special Forces officer continuously urged his boss to support Goldwater and Nunn. He also worked hard to inform Thurmond on these complex issues. Given the importance of Thurmond's vote, Johnson's role became critical.

On January 29, six days before the markup's start, Goldwater personally delivered copies of the draft bill to Weinberger and Crowe and asked for their comments. In a cover letter, he and Nunn wrote: "We have taken the unusual step of providing markup materials to you because of the importance of the issues addressed and the desire to have the best advice available before the committee acts." The senators requested that the secretary and admiral not distribute copies outside their offices.[43] Hoping to avoid intense lobbying by the entire Pentagon, Goldwater wanted all other copies to remain inside the committee. But even before he could make his deliveries, opposing senators leaked the bill to military allies. Copies were soon circulating throughout the Pentagon, where they caused major heartburn.

Also on January 29, Goldwater and Nunn issued a press release with a seven-page summary of the draft bill's provisions. The senators said they had "directed the staff to draft a bill that incorporated, as much as possible, the consensus views that had emerged during the committee's lengthy examination." Still maintaining maneuvering room, they added, "Although we may not agree with every provision of the draft bill, we do believe that it represents an excellent starting point for the committee's consideration."[44]

In drafting the bill, the staff, with the approval of Goldwater and Nunn, dropped five of the seven extreme recommendations advanced in the staff study, including proposals to disestablish the JCS and replace it with a JMAC. Goldwater and Nunn believed that the extreme recommendations had served their purpose. Opponents had spent several months trying to shoot them down, especially the one to disband the JCS. Now Goldwater and Nunn could appear statesmen-like, earn goodwill with opponents, and undercut antireform arguments by dropping the extreme proposals. "Goldwater and I are going to ride in on white horses and save the republic from the staff," said Nunn.

The draft's two remaining extreme recommendations would create three mission-oriented under secretaries of defense and merge the civilian secretariats and military headquarters staffs in the military departments. We believed in these ideas, and testimony had revealed the need for mission integration. Yet support for these recommendations was limited; they were near the top of the list of negotiating bait.

Goldwater and Nunn were firmly committed to other major provisions of the draft bill, including designating the JCS chairman as the principal military

33. Senators Strom Thurmond and Sam Nunn.
(Sam Nunn Archives, Emory University.)

adviser, assigning duties then performed by the JCS to the chairman, creating a JCS vice chairman and designating him the second-ranking officer, assigning the vice chairman the duty of serving as acting chairman in the chairman's absence, authorizing the chairman to manage the Joint Staff and prescribe its procedures, specifying that the chain of command—unless otherwise directed by the president—runs from the president to the secretary of defense to the combatant commanders, strengthening the authority of combatant commanders and giving them full operational command over assigned forces, specifying the responsibility of the service secretaries to the secretary of defense, making consistent the statutes governing the military departments, reducing the size of headquarters staffs, and repealing various congressional reporting requirements.

Nowhere in the Pentagon was the alarm over the draft bill greater than in the navy, which sent its analysis of the bill to all interested parties. On January 31, Lehman fired similar letters to Vice President Bush, Secretary Weinberger, and Vice Admiral Poindexter.[45] His letter to Weinberger read: "Here is my first cut at the Goldwater-Locher-Dave Jones Bill. It is even worse than before. It is a blatant indictment of all that we have done these last five years. In substance it is simply an updated return to McNamara. What supreme irony that Goldwater has become the unwitting tool of the liberal 'whiz-fogies.'"

In Bush's letter, Lehman added that the bill "is heavily directed against the Navy CNO and SecNav."

A few days after receiving the draft bill, Crowe called me with an invitation for Goldwater and Nunn to meet with the JCS on February 3, the eve of the start of the markup sessions. The vehemence of the services' reaction to the draft bill worried the admiral. He feared that the legislation would tear the fabric of the JCS by going too far too fast. Crowe wanted Goldwater and Nunn to hear the white-hot responses pouring forth from the Pentagon's power corridors.

I told Crowe that I expected Goldwater and Nunn to accept his invitation. The two senators had not given up hope that the chiefs would cooperate with their reform efforts. Their attempts to gain that cooperation had constantly been rebuffed, but they continued to hold out the olive branch. I also told Crowe that the two senators were certain to want their staffers to accompany them. Crowe said that would not be a problem.

On the day of the meeting, Crowe called me to change the terms of the invitation. The chiefs now believed that other SASC members, especially bill opponents, should also attend. Furthermore, the chiefs did not want staffers there. Before I could relay this information to Goldwater, his office received calls from John Warner, Jeremiah Denton, and Phil Gramm—then among the staunchest Republican opponents—indicating that they understood that they had been invited to meet with the JCS and wanting the details.

The chiefs' tactics were clear. They wanted to stack the deck against the two senators. Goldwater was no fool. He was not about to face the chiefs with his Republican colleagues sniping from behind and without staff support to handle questions on the bill's details. The chiefs were also angling to drive a wedge between the two senators and their staff. Because the proposed legislation had been termed a "staff draft," the chiefs hoped that Goldwater and Nunn were not committed to it and would abandon it in the face of fierce Pentagon opposition.

After conferring with Nunn, Goldwater ended the dispute. If the chiefs wanted this meeting, it would be on the two senators' terms: no other members were to be invited, and the three staffers—Finn, Smith, and I—who had drafted the legislation would be present. His Republican colleagues complained bitterly, but Goldwater was unyielding.

The two leaders met with the JCS on the evening of February 3, 1986. That explosive session removed all doubt from Goldwater's and Nunn's minds about the intensity of the fight they would face in the Senate Armed Services Committee.

CHAPTER 21

The Packard Commission Reinforces

A seasonable reinforcement renders the success

of a battle certain, because the enemy will always

imagine it stronger than it really is,

and lose courage accordingly.

—Napoleon

"There has been nothing but praise from members of my committee . . . for the obvious competent way in which you are handling your assignment," Senator Goldwater wrote in a letter to David Packard, chairman of the Packard Commission, on September 24, 1985. "It didn't come as a surprise to me because, in the years that I have known you, that has been the outstanding feature you possess—you get the job done. I thank you for this." He ended with: "Let's keep in touch. Getting this military in the shape to defend our country, to me, Dave, is the only thing of importance we have left to do."[1]

Six days earlier, eight of the nine senators on Goldwater and Nunn's Task Force on Defense Organization had held a breakfast meeting with Packard and ten others from the sixteen-member commission. Congressmen Les Aspin, Bill Dickinson, and Bill Nichols attended as well. Frank exchanges at the meeting convinced Goldwater and Nunn that Packard and his colleagues were serious about their work and that the SASC could look forward to a cooperative relationship with the commission. Packard concluded the meeting by agreeing "that it is time to do something fundamental and that Congress and the commission must keep in communication."[2]

Strong personal relationships enhanced communication between the commission and the SASC. Commissioner Nick Brady had been a Republican SASC member in 1982, and R. James Woolsey had served as the committee's general counsel from 1970 to 1973. Commissioner William J. Perry had maintained a close relationship with Nunn since Perry's service as under secretary of defense for research and engineering during the Carter administration. The participation of Brady and Gen. Paul Gorman in the Fort A. P. Hill retreat further strengthened SASC-commission ties.

Two commission staffers—Staff Director Rhett Dawson and Robert S. "Steve" Dotson—also had strong SASC ties. Dawson, who had spent six years on the SASC's Republican staff, served as Tower's minority staff director and his first majority staff director. In the latter capacity, he had been my boss for two years. He was also responsible for Tower offering me a position on the Republican staff after the 1980 elections. We remained close friends after Dawson departed the committee staff in late 1982. After Packard selected him to head the staff, Dawson and I met four times in July and August to discuss reorganization.

Dotson, a SASC Democratic staffer in the late 1970s and early 1980s, had been appointed to the commission staff to represent the Office of Management and Budget. He graduated from the Air Force Academy and Harvard Business School. Before Dotson left the committee, he and I often discussed the Pentagon's organizational problems. Our common business school education gave us a similar perspective.

Combined with the strong rapport among Packard, Goldwater, and Nunn, these relationships eased discussions. Throughout this dialogue, one common agenda united the commission and the SASC: achieving changes that would be best for the nation's security. There was never a hint of executive-legislative competition, partisan politics, or concern about who got the credit. The quality and openness of SASC discussions with the Packard Commission were refreshing after years of haggling with Pentagon officials.

The Packard Commission was composed of highly qualified businessmen, academics, and former officials. Usually, presidential commissions are peopled with members who are near the end of their career and who do not anticipate subsequent government appointments. This was not the case for six Packard Commissioners. Frank Carlucci went on to serve as national security adviser and then defense secretary in the last years of the Reagan administration. During the Bush presidency, retired lieutenant general Brent Scowcroft reprised the role of national security adviser he played for President Ford. Brady served as Bush's treasury secretary, and Carla A. Hills, a former secretary of housing and urban development, was his U.S. trade representative. President Clinton later appointed Perry as deputy defense secretary and then secretary, and Woolsey served as Clinton's director of central intelligence.

Executive Order 12526, dated July 15, 1985, instructed the commission to "first devote its attention to the procedures and activities of the department associated with the procurement of military equipment and material." President Reagan requested a report on this politically troubling area by the end of December. Given the tight deadline, the commission's August and September meetings focused on acquisition reform. In its first session on August 15, all sixteen commissioners met with Secretary Weinberger. Dawson recalled the outcome: "Each commissioner, including Frank Carlucci, was absolutely crestfallen and stunned by Weinberger's extraordinarily defensive performance. They were really discouraged."[3]

The commission's initial session on organization did not occur until October 8, when Goldwater, Nunn, and I briefed the SASC staff study. This delay permitted the commission to use the study as a principal resource. Two of the commission's five panels addressed the reorganization issues being considered by Congress. The Organization Issues Panel, headed by Gorman, focused on the most controversial issues: those involving the Joint Chiefs of Staff and unified commands. The Strategy and Resource Planning Panel, chaired by Scowcroft, addressed mechanisms for determining military force structure, weapons, and budgets. Two other panels worked exclusively on acquisition problems, and the fifth panel studied implementation.[4]

A powerful, activist, energetic chairman, Packard controlled the commission's agenda and work. David Berteau, recruited from the Pentagon to serve as the commission's executive secretary, later commented: "Packard drove the meetings. He drove the staff. He drove the whole process. . . . It's rare to have somebody of Packard's stature spend that much time on commission work and to do it as constructively as Packard did. He was also unique in the degree to which he tried to navigate that narrow space among the White House, Pentagon, and Capitol Hill and do it in such a way that the commission successfully participated and cooperated with all three."[5]

According to Berteau, Packard's first discussion with the staff communicated that he had set his sights on far-reaching reforms: "He did not want to put boundaries around alternatives or recommendations. There were no constraints. It was clear from the beginning that the commission would be serious about reform."

Five other commissioners—Brady, Louis W. Cabot, Admiral Holloway, Charles J. Pilliod Jr., and General Barrow—joined Gorman on the Organization Issues Panel. Packard probably selected Gorman to head the panel because he had "been more vocal on reorganization than others during the early proceedings." For years, Gorman had felt that the JCS system "left much to be desired." As the three-star assistant to General Jones, Gorman had been involved in reorganization from the beginning and had often written and lectured on the subject. Not only did Gorman's long discussions with Jones influence his thinking, but his "own struggles as a CINC," about which he spoke during the Fort A. P. Hill retreat, had educated him on organization problems.[6]

Vietnam, where Gorman said he had "focused six years of my life," played an important role as well. He had commanded a battalion and a brigade in that conflict, served as a division operations officer, worked as special assistant to the secretary of defense for counterinsurgency, and served as a member of the U.S. delegation to the Paris peace talks, where he worked for General Goodpaster. During this period, Gorman found organizational arrangements "professionally perplexing." He recalled: "My Vietnam experiences directly contributed to my puzzlement. It was a real education on our military's organizational and procedural shortcomings."

As the retired four-star army general began his commission work, he found himself in agreement with the problems identified in the SASC staff report and Goldwater's and Nunn's notions on how to fix them that he had heard discussed at Fort A. P. Hill. He called that gathering "an exceptional event," and said: "I was extraordinarily favorably impressed by the openness and candor of the members. I thought that the discussion was very elevated."

On November 14, 1985, the day Weinberger testified on the SASC staff study, Packard and Gorman gave Goldwater and Nunn a status report on the commission's work. The senators and commissioners also discussed the timing of their respective work. Goldwater and Nunn then thought that their committee would report a reorganization bill not later than mid-February. With an interim commission report on management and organization due at the end of March, a staff memorandum to Goldwater and Nunn advised, "We believe that there is some flexibility in the February-March time period for you to adjust the schedule to await inputs from the Packard Commission."[7] This possibility became more viable when the commission subsequently decided to include the interim management and organization report in a comprehensive interim report to be released on February 28.

Nunn later described his impression from this meeting and other conversations with Packard: "He told us they were going to concentrate on procurement and wanted to follow what we were doing on reorganization. The commission would not necessarily take what we had done, but it was clear that they wanted us to continue to lead and that they were going to try to be positive on reorganization."[8]

Dawson said that Packard gave priority to his meetings with SASC and HASC leaders because "he understood the importance of the Hill in making reforms happen." Of the Goldwater-Packard rapport, Dawson explained: "Packard played to his and Goldwater's mutual disdain for Cap Weinberger and Will Taft. Packard did not regard Weinberger as his equal or somebody who knew much about the military. He thought Weinberger had made a hash of defense acquisition and didn't know how to run the department."[9]

A potential setback for reorganization arose with Bud McFarlane's sudden resignation as national security adviser on December 4. His departure created unease among Senate reformers. Given McFarlane's central role in establishing the Packard Commission and his support for reorganization, his absence could prove troubling. McFarlane's replacement, Vice Admiral Poindexter, appeared supportive, but earlier concerns about his pronavy sentiments lingered.

Gorman said that Packard had definite ideas on reorganization: "Dave was convinced that the only way to solve acquisition problems—the fundamental deficiency confronting the commission—was to do away with the military departments and truly unify the armed forces. His arguments were very persuasive. He was a man ahead of his time. There was a lot of talk about the Canadian model [only one military service]. This thrust thoroughly alarmed commissioners like Barrow and Holloway and many others. Our panel had a real bear by the tail, and his name was Dave Packard."[10]

Moreover, said Gorman:

Because of Dave's position, we had to refer the Organization Panel's issues to the commission as a whole. The person who made the big difference in that debate was Navy Secretary John Lehman. In a lengthy session with the commission on December 10, he went through a detailed recitation of cases where he, as Navy secretary, had been able to intervene in acquisition processes gone sour, where there had been malfeasance in office or fumbling on the part of a program manager. Lehman went through instances—chapter and verse, names, places, dates—of actions that were close to criminal and programs that were misconceived from the beginning, but had acquired an invulnerability to correction, where he had acted. He cited a number of instances where he had been able to initiate worthwhile programs that the uniformed Navy had rejected.

Lehman felt very strongly that the service secretary had a real and important role to play and that the department needed the secretary for oversight and a guarantee of probity among political appointees and contractors. His forceful presentation foreclosed Dave Packard's efforts to get his own ideas into the final report. Lehman succeeded by creating a broad coalition among the commissioners that said, "No, no, Dave, that's too far. We don't want to come out for that."

After the commission rejected Packard's ideas, it found itself in agreement with many congressional proposals. According to Gorman, the "Commissioners interpreted what Goldwater and Nunn had put forward as being congruent with the notions they had been discussing."[11] By December, the commission was clearly "entertaining organizational reforms closely akin to those under serious discussion on Capitol Hill."[12]

Of the commission's process for making final decisions on its interim report, Berteau said: "It was the sixteen commissioners sitting around, hashing this out, piece-by-piece, item-by-item. Everybody was engaged. . . . There was a pretty strong emphasis on consensus, not unanimity, but 'Let's keep going until we reach agreement that this is the right thing to do and give everybody the chance to raise objections and voice concerns, and if we can't resolve them, we'll keep plugging at it.'" Gorman identified Carlucci, Woolsey, and Scowcroft as having significant influence on commission deliberations.[13]

According to Dawson, it was clear in early January, 1986, "after Holloway threw in the towel," that the commission would issue heavily proreform reports. "The process was a lot less difficult than I would have thought given our cast of characters," said Dawson. "Frankly, I was surprised that Holloway gave in as early as he did. I thought there would have been a minority report, which would have produced the serious issue of a divided commission."[14]

Early in the commission's work, the NSC staff, especially Mike Donley, began to understand that the commission's recommendations might produce changes that would "equal the importance" of President Eisenhower's 1958 initiatives.[15] In November, Donley traveled to the Eisenhower Library in Kansas to research the Eisenhower administration's work.

Information from Donley's trip sparked the commission's interest in the 1958 reorganization act. Packard asked Gorman to interview his former boss, General Goodpaster, who had been Eisenhower's staff secretary. Goodpaster told his interviewers:

> The degree of command exercised by unified commanders today is less than that desired for them by President Eisenhower . . . "operational command" with its present limitations falls far short of his intent. . . . [T]he service chiefs were to spend the bulk of their time and effort attending to duties as corporate members of the Joint Chiefs of Staff, with most of the day-to-day running of the services left to the service vice chiefs.
>
> Contrary to popular impressions today, command arrangements during World War II also had problems. As supreme commander, Allied Expeditionary Force in World War II, General Eisenhower insisted on command of naval and air corps units for the Normandy invasion. He told General Marshall that he could not continue as supreme commander otherwise.[16]

Packard, recalling the commission's interest in Eisenhower's initiatives, said: "We had a fairly good feeling of what he [Eisenhower] wanted to do and what he did not get done. That had an influence on what we tried to do."[17]

Donley said he made his trip to the Eisenhower Library for three reasons. First, he felt that "Reagan would probably resonate with Eisenhower as a good example for how to address reorganization." Second, Donley believed that providing the history of Eisenhower's role would "reinforce with Reagan that he had every right and reason to be interested in what was going on" and "make sure that he was personally involved." Last, he wanted to "get a handle on how Eisenhower bureaucratically handled reorganization."[18]

Poindexter sent the results of Donley's research to Reagan in a memorandum just before the commission submitted its February interim report. The memorandum favorably compared the Packard Commission's recommendations with Eisenhower's initiatives and drew other parallels. One parallel noted that Eisenhower also found his Pentagon working group "too eager to prove that things were perfect as they were."[19]

The memorandum did point out one major difference: "Ike faced a Congress that was opposed to change; today, it is Congress that is pushing for more extensive and detailed changes in defense management and organization. . . . So, where the Eisenhower initiatives were intended to push Congress into doing something they would otherwise resist, we hope to use the Packard Commission initiatives as a substitute for the more objectionable legislation being forcefully advanced by Congress."

The memorandum concluded:

> There are many parallels between the recommendations of the Packard Commission and the Eisenhower initiatives of 1958. The commission's conclusions are consistent with the historical trend of enhancing the authority of the secretary of defense and JCS as a means of improving the integration of the military departments in support of strategic plans, while still maintaining the integrity of the individual services and their responsibility for program execution. . . . While Packard's recommendations are significant, and to some may appear as a departure from current practice, they in fact represent a realignment back to the original intent of the National Security Act, which President Eisenhower tried so hard to implement.

Packard met with Goldwater and Nunn on February 6 to brief them on the planned contents of the interim report, which was issued on February 28. He said the commission would recommend greater authority for the unified commanders, more emphasis on missions, stronger representation in the JCS for the unified commanders, designation of the JCS chairman as principal military adviser, and creation of a JCS vice chairman. Packard noted that the commission would diverge from Goldwater and Nunn's thinking on the vice chairman's rank and role. He said a majority of commissioners favored making the service chiefs more senior than the vice chairman and retaining the system of rotating the acting chairman duty among the service chiefs. Packard expressed his private opinion that the vice chairman should be the second-ranking officer. At the senators' request, he agreed to reopen the vice chairman issue because the Senate and House bills "may be identical [on this issue] and it could be a close vote and veto-able."[20]

A commission-SASC dialogue on the vice-chairman issue continued for several weeks, especially between Arnold Punaro, Woolsey, and Dawson. On February 18, responding to the commission's request, Goldwater and Nunn sent Packard a four-page letter presenting the views of a "bipartisan majority" of SASC members on the issue. The letter stated that "arguments have convinced us that the most important officer in our armed forces—the *only* civilian or military official in the U.S. Government without a deputy—should finally be given a 'true' deputy."[21]

Whatever the outcome of the commission's reconsideration of its vice-chairman recommendations, the outline of its interim report pleased Goldwater and Nunn. They did not expect the report to offer new arguments or ideas. Given its three years of reorganization work, the SASC's research, analyses, and debates were far more advanced than the commission's. Instead, the senators' satisfaction derived from thoughts of the report's political impact. It would deliver a devastating blow to administration antireformers and complicate their efforts to stonewall reform proposals.

Goldwater and Nunn had known privately for several months that they had a potentially powerful ally in the Packard Commission. In just three weeks, that ally was scheduled to publicly state its proreform views. Although uncertainty remained about the commission's ability to resist political pressure, the clarity of its message, and White House and Pentagon reactions, Goldwater and Nunn looked forward to timely political reinforcement by the Packard Commission.

CHAPTER 22

The Decisive Battle

I propose to fight it out on this line,

if it takes all summer.

—Gen. Ulysses S. Grant, dispatch from

Spotsylvania Courthouse, May 11, 1864

A decisive battle in American military history began on the morning of February 4, 1986. It was not a conflict of arms, but a momentous clash of ideas and interests in a Senate hearing room. The adversaries were not armed with weapons, but with concepts, statutes, and amendments. This battle did not directly threaten anyone's life, but its outcome—depending on whether deeply entrenched, outmoded traditions and practices were reformed or sustained—could save or cost untold lives of American soldiers, sailors, airmen, and marines.

At 9 A.M. that day, the Senate Armed Services Committee initiated its long-awaited markup of a fifty-six-page defense reorganization bill. Earlier in the morning, the Pentagon delivered eight letters to the committee, one each from Admiral Crowe, the three service secretaries, and the four service chiefs. The letter from Crowe was reasonably argued, like the one received the night before from Secretary Weinberger after Senators Goldwater and Nunn met with the JCS. The letters from the seven service officials were quarrelsome and contentious. Perhaps seeking to neutralize Goldwater's and Nunn's strong defense credentials, they all took the line that the bill reflected only the views of headstrong staff and not those of the SASC leadership.

Navy Secretary Lehman's letter ranked as the most bellicose. "I am surprised and disappointed that the serious effort that the service secretaries and the service chiefs devoted to your hearings seems to have largely been ignored in the staff effort," he complained. After lauding Weinberger's management changes, Lehman wrote that the staff bill "charts a return to the discredited philosophy that led to the overcentralized bureaucracy we inherited in 1981."[1] Given the importance of the votes of the committee's nine Democrats, that slap at the Carter administration was ill considered.

Lehman added that the draft bill's proposed strengthening of the unified commanders "would make a hash of our defense structure." Five other service letters also strongly criticized increasing the authority of unified commanders. Only the air force chief, General Gabriel, did not object to those provisions. By attacking reforms that were supported by overwhelming evidence and a sizable majority of the committee, service officials undermined their credibility.

According to the navy secretary, the staff draft would "make the offices of the service secretary and service chief essentially ceremonial. In place of the former would be five CINC pro-consuls freed from civilian control; and in place of the latter, one single voice (with deputy) to provide military advice to the president, NSC, secretary of defense and Congress."

Lehman concluded by urging the committee members "to reject the staff draft, and consider true reform as recommended to you by Secretary Weinberger last year. We need less bureaucracy, not more; fewer bureaucratic layers, not more; less congressional micromanagement, not more; and more decentralization and accountability rather than a return to the 'whiz-kid' theories contained in your staff draft."

The marine commandant's letter matched Lehman's tough language. General Kelley repeated much of what he had told Goldwater and Nunn the night before, including: "If the 'draft bill' were to be enacted in its current form it would result in a significant degradation in the efficiency and effectiveness of the defense establishment—to the point where I would have deep concerns for the future security of the United States. In this regard, I know of no document which has concerned me more in my 36 years of uniformed service to my country."[2]

General Kelley said that he "was extremely disappointed by the obvious lack of balance and objectivity [in] the 645-page staff report." He accused the authors of the staff-drafted bill of having "been unfaithful to your [Goldwater and Nunn's] direction and have placed more emphasis on their own preconceived opinions than on 'consensus views.'" The commandant complained that "The 'draft bill' virtually destroys the corporate nature of the Joint Chiefs of Staff," and attacked General Jones by observing: "I know of only one former chairman who would support this chapter of the 'draft bill' as written, and his views must be carefully weighed against his performance while in office." He added that his own "views on the vice chairman being senior to the Joint Chiefs of Staff are a matter of record: I am strenuously opposed! Moreover, the Joint

Staff is currently a viable and efficient organization. I implore your indulgence to keep it that way."

Kelley castigated the proposed strengthening of the unified commanders, arguing: "In my professional view, this chapter of the 'draft bill' would create chaos between the duties and responsibilities of the service chiefs and those of the CINCs. It provides a complex, unworkable solution to an ill-defined problem. This is an exceptionally dangerous chapter, one which has resulted from little, if any, dialog. It will create more disharmony than jointness." Of the draft bill's changes to military department statutes, Kelley wrote, "My opinion is that these proposals are alien to good logic and common sense, and the only 'consensus' is among the drafters themselves!"

After noting that his comments did not represent all of his concerns, the commandant concluded, "I strongly urge you to consider additional hearings to achieve conscious addressal of these vital issues."

The CNO, Admiral Watkins, wrote: "I believe our nation would surely be standing into shoal water, with severe damage predictable, if we were to follow the course charted for us in the current draft bill now before your committee. In short, I consider the bill as drafted to be terribly flawed and certainly not in the best interests of national security."[3]

The letters from the army and air force secretaries and chiefs of staff were also critical, but they were less strident.

All nineteen SASC members were present for the decisive battle's opening moments. Ideologically, the committee tilted heavily to the political right. All Republicans were conservatives, except for Cohen, who was a moderate. Greater diversity was found on the Democratic side, where four conservatives outnumbered liberals by only one, and two moderates—Bingaman and Dixon—occupied the pivotal middle ground.

Reorganization was unlikely to be sorted out on the basis of ideology. The strength of the senators' connections to various services and their party affiliation would play more significant roles. Thirteen members had served in the military: four in the army, two in the air force, three in the navy, and four in the marines. Some members attached little importance to these previous relationships while others maintained strong ties. Still others maintained close connections with the services for entirely different reasons. For example, John Stennis tilted toward the navy because the Pascagoula Shipyard ranked as Mississippi's largest employer. Party affiliation prompted some Republican senators to defend the administration and Pentagon.

As the markup session began, Goldwater set the historical context: "The committee's action continues an evolutionary trend that began shortly after the Spanish-American War." He also established a Constitutional context, calling the work "a solemn responsibility assigned by the Constitution to the Congress." He added, "We have neglected this important responsibility for too long.

34. Members of the Senate Armed Services Committee gather in the main hearing room used for markup of the reorganization bill on June 18, 1986. *Seated (left to right)*: Gramm, Denton, Wilson, East, Quayle, Humphrey, Warner, Thurmond, Goldwater, Stennis, Levin, Kennedy, Bingaman, Dixon, and Glenn. Cohen and Nunn are absent. *Standing (left to right)*: McGovern and Punaro. (U.S. Senate photo.)

Many of the problems that we now seek to solve have been evident for decades." The chairman then urged the committee to "rise above narrow interests and emphasize genuine national security interests. This has been a problem for the Congress in the past. Narrow interests with strong constituencies have blocked or weakened necessary reforms."[4]

Goldwater announced that "the committee will conduct the markup in a deliberate and comprehensive manner. . . . We want to hear all points of view and carefully consider all aspects of these important decisions. We must exercise caution in mandating changes in the U.S. military establishment. At the same time, we must not shy away from correcting clearly identified deficiencies and from fulfilling our Constitutional responsibilities."

The chairman added: "I'd like to make one personal point. I know that some senior Pentagon officials have been opposing what I am trying to do by telling senators that this is not my initiative. Instead, I am supposed to just be going along with the staff and other senators. Frankly, these lies make me mad as hell! I have been deeply involved in this project from the outset. I have read every word of the staff report and the bill. I have attended every hearing, except when I had to be in Arizona. So I know these issues and I want to fix these problems."

In his opening statement, Nunn noted "that we have had nearly forty years of experience with the current arrangements. We have seen these arrangements in action and have many concrete examples of their shortcomings." Referencing the SASC's extensive reorganization work, Nunn said, "I do not know of any other set of issues since I joined the committee over thirteen years ago that the committee has been better prepared to address."[5]

Following the two leaders' presentations, each member made an opening statement outlining his starting position. These statements and readings from the Pentagon letters consumed the morning. By noon it was clear that the SASC was bitterly divided, with strongly held positions on both sides.

The morning session also featured a squabble over whether the committee would conduct the markup in open or closed sessions. Antireformers wanted the sessions open to the public, believing that the committee would be more cautious under the Pentagon's glare. Goldwater and Nunn knew the importance of proceeding in closed sessions and gained approval for doing so. Their arguments centered on the need to discuss classified information, which would happen seldom, if ever, during consideration of this bill.

Just before the end of the morning session, a message from Ben Schemmer, editor of the *Armed Forces Journal*, informed Gerry Smith of Goldwater's staff that the navy had established a "crisis management center on DoD reorganization." Schemmer also provided the center's telephone number.[6] The center's purported mission was to defeat the legislation, an activity of questionable legality. With mischief in his eye, Goldwater grabbed Smith and me and said, "Let's find out what this is all about."

Back in his office, Goldwater said, "I'm going to call this office and see what the Navy's up to." Smith offered to place the call, but the senator insisted on dialing it. When his call was answered, Smith and I saw a Goldwater we had never seen before: an actor. Disguising his voice, Goldwater asked the secretary who answered, "Is this the Navy office that is working to defeat the reorganization legislation?" When she said, "Yes," he inquired who worked there. She answered, "Captain Cohen, and there is a Lieutenant Colonel Dole, and a Major Robert Roach."[7] Goldwater repeated the names as he wrote them down.

Goldwater said he wanted to help and asked if she had an assignment for him. She said she did not have one at the moment, but if he would leave his name and number, the office would get right back to him.

Goldwater said he would have to call back later and thanked her. As he hung up, the senator said, "Can you believe that? They're not supposed to lobby Congress on legislation. I can't wait to tell the committee." At the start of the afternoon session, the chairman took great delight in recounting his telephone call.

After the committee adopted the draft bill as the basis for amendment, Goldwater asked me to give an overview briefing. This led to what the chairman called "a good discussion of a number of broad issues" that consumed the entire afternoon.[8]

The following afternoon, Goldwater—sensing that work on the bill would be highly confrontational and time-consuming—decided he did not want other SASC sessions competing with the markup: "I am reaffirming, after consulting with Senator Nunn, my direction that no other full committee or subcommittee hearings be scheduled until we finish this markup." Goldwater also noted that it might not be possible to finish in three days: "We will continue the markups mornings and afternoons every day if it takes one week, two weeks, or three weeks to finish." He also conveyed his determination: "I want everyone in this room to understand that I will not be deflected or sidetracked in this effort even if I get a letter a day from everyone in the Pentagon."

In a campaign organized by the Pentagon, military and veterans associations, such as the Reserve Officers Association and National Guard Association, were bombarding Goldwater with letters objecting to the bill. The chairman fired off a tough response to each letter and set up a meeting for me to brief the associations.

Goldwater and Nunn had decided to address unified command reforms first because there was wider support for them. When Goldwater opened the floor for the consideration of changes, Warner presented a package of thirteen amendments. The third-ranking Republican had accepted the role of opposition leader. Although he had tried to stay out of the reorganization battle as long as possible, the pressure for Warner to take the lead eventually became overwhelming. The pressure came from his status as a former navy secretary, former marine, and senator from Virginia, a state with a powerful navy lobby. Nevertheless, Warner appeared uncomfortable with the intellectual arguments of the antireform coalition. Nunn later said, "Warner always was concerned, I think, in his heart of hearts, that he wasn't on the right track basically taking the Navy's line."[9] Nevertheless, the Virginia senator threw himself full force into the role of opposition leader.

As the committee considered Warner's amendments, my role was to assess the impact of each and begin a discussion of its advantages and disadvantages. I also offered recommendations as to what action the committee should take. I made every effort to perform these tasks as objectively as possible and assist Warner with the presentation of his amendments. Some amendments or portions thereof had positive aspects that I recommended be adopted, such as clarifying how aspects of administration and support would be identified for inclusion under a unified commanders' authority. But many of Warner's

35. Secretary of Defense Melvin R. Laird (*back to camera*) presents the Department of Defense Distinguished Public Service Medal to Navy Secretary John W. Warner. (DoD photo.)

amendments would have weakened reform. Lengthy discussion of each amendment by the members clearly indicated to Warner that he would not be able to have his reform-weakening amendments adopted, so he did not force a vote on the first day. The approach of deliberately talking through each issue became the norm for the markup. By the end of the afternoon session, however, we had finished only about half of the package laid down by Warner, and it was clear that he had many more amendments.

The afternoon's developments displeased Goldwater. It was clear that the committee would never finish in three days, as he had hoped. The chairman also feared that the bill might face "death by amendment." He did not want to cut off debate, but he worried about how seemingly unending amendments might affect prospects for completing committee action. Goldwater asked me to consider how he might put some pressure on the committee's reorganization opponents and the Pentagon, which many believed was aiding Warner and his allies. Goldwater did not want to play an excessively heavy hand; he was looking for firm but not drastic responses that would create pressure and, equally important, demonstrate that he was serious.

I created a menu of SASC activities that the chairman could hold in abeyance while the markup sessions were still under way: no consideration of nominations for senior defense civilian and military positions, no consideration of promotions for military officers, no approval of reprogramming of monies from one defense budget account to another, no consideration of a supplemental authorization bill, and no approval for the navy to begin expending funds for its Strategic Homeporting Initiative. Goldwater especially liked holding up the navy's project, which he called "strategic homeporking."

As the chairman read down my list, a hint of a smile emerged. I had expected him to choose one or two. He looked up and said, "If Senator Nunn has no objection, do them all." Goldwater wanted to close down the committee while it was considering the reorganization bill. He did not want another piece of paper to move.

The next morning, Goldwater announced his actions to the committee and indicated that these prohibitions would remain in place at least until the committee had completed its work on the reorganization bill. If he sensed that obstacles—like a filibuster—might be employed in an effort to prevent the Senate's timely consideration of the bill, Goldwater said he might have to leave the prohibitions in place until the Senate had completed action on the bill.

The feisty chairman also announced that he was prepared to dedicate the entire year to working on reorganization. If this required the committee to forgo its traditional defense authorization bill, this would, in Goldwater's view, be an acceptable price for enacting critically needed Pentagon reform. Goldwater made clear that he and Nunn were prepared to hear and debate every argument in an effort to prevent the committee from making decisions on emotional and superficial bases like those that had dominated congressional action on defense organization in the 1940s and 1950s.

Later that morning, Warner forced a vote on one of his key amendments: to have acting JCS chairmanship in the chairman's absence rotate among the service chiefs rather than be performed by a newly created vice chairman. Fifteen senators were present for the vote, which Goldwater and Nunn won by a margin of ten to five, with Strom Thurmond providing the critical tenth vote. I told Goldwater that the four absent senators, who would have until 5 P.M. to record their votes, would likely vote with opponents. This would narrow the victory margin to one vote. Goldwater wanted a bigger margin for this first crucial vote. He was determined to secure a favorable vote from one of the four absent senators.

With the list of absent senators in hand, Goldwater and I headed for his office. By the time we arrived there, the chairman had decided to target the lightly regarded Dan Quayle. He placed a telephone call to a surprised Quayle and said that he wanted his vote. Goldwater played political hardball, warning Quayle that if the Indiana senator failed to support him he would first take the chairmanship of the Defense Acquisition Policy Subcommittee away from him. Then he would get him kicked off the Armed Services Committee. And then he would work for his defeat in the next election.

When he finished, Goldwater put down the receiver and said with a smile of satisfaction, "Quayle's voting with us."

When the committee convened that afternoon, however, Quayle's military legislative assistant, Henry Sokolski, approached me and said, "Senator Quayle wants to change his vote."

I directed him to speak to Goldwater, who responded, "I have personally spoken with Senator Quayle, and I will not change his vote unless we speak again." As Goldwater anticipated, the day ended without any further word from the Indiana senator. Although the proreform side won the first vote by a margin of eleven to seven, Goldwater's power play backfired: it increased the tension between the two sides and caused opponents to regroup. Normally, the chairman and ranking minority member would vote proxies from their party colleagues. However, because both Goldwater and Nunn were on the same side, antireform Republicans and Democrats collected their proxies and decided who would vote them.

Goldwater and Nunn's commitment to a patient, fair, everyone-gets-to-be-heard process provided the first important step in creating a high-quality dialogue on the bill. When Warner, a sincere and considerate gentleman, matched the two leaders' tone, the ingredients for a productive examination of the bill were present. Neither side lessened the intensity of its convictions, but after the initial trying days, a high degree of collegiality emerged. If a member asked for more research, opinion of a Pentagon official or officer, a briefing, or examination of additional options, Goldwater and Nunn made sure that the request was honored. Warner later commented, "At no time did the distinguished chairman or ranking minority member deny me any privilege under the procedures of the committee to make known my views and the views of those senators working with me." Levin observed that Goldwater "chaired the committee in a nonpartisan way; he has done it in the fairest way I have ever seen the chairman conduct the committee."[10]

Warner also won admiration for the way he led the opposition. He thoroughly challenged every idea and ensured that the Pentagon's perspective on each issue was well represented, but he was not intransigent. Christopher K. Mellon, Cohen's staffer, later said: "One thing about Senator Warner that I always admired and respected and caused me to feel a lot of regard and warmth toward him is that he maintained an open mind. He was willing to change his point of view based on new evidence and information. Senator Warner might go into something with a great deal of conviction on one side and argue furiously, and yet as new information would come to light, he always listened."[11]

In the lengthy debate of amendments and rewriting of bill provisions, Cohen and Levin emerged as Goldwater's and Nunn's lieutenants. Both were brilliant and articulate lawyers, and they made insightful, thoughtful contributions. They also helped to shoulder the burden of defending and strengthening the bill.

At the end of the first week of markup, Congress recessed for a week. When committee activity resumed, the tactics and battle lines were unchanged. Activity focused on the stack of amendments that Warner offered on each bill chapter. Warner's and Denton's military legislative assistants, retired army colonel Romee L. "Les" Brownlee and Allan W. Cameron, respectively, were preparing Warner's amendments. While Finn, Smith, and I were burning the midnight oil to defend the bill, Brownlee and Cameron worked late each night preparing amendments to attack it. Many staffers were convinced that the navy was helping Brownlee and Cameron, a charge they denied. Arnold Punaro later commented: "There's absolutely no question that the navy helped them. With their limited resources and lack of access to legislative counsel, who were helping Goldwater and Nunn, there's no way they could put that material together."[12]

Other members offered written amendments as well, but in combination, theirs totaled twenty-seven compared to Warner's fifty-three amendments. The committee debated each of Warner's amendments in exhausting detail. Warner forced only three roll-call votes, each of which he lost.[13]

As Thurmond's steadfastness to Goldwater and reorganization became clear, the opposition set a new goal. If the opponents could not defeat the bill in committee, they would set their sights on overturning it on the Senate floor. A one-vote margin in committee would serve as the springboard for convincing the full Senate that this legislation was ill considered. To antireform senators and their supporters in the Pentagon and elsewhere, it was imperative that they maintain nine votes in opposition. "Ten to nine" became the opponents' rallying cry, like "fifty-four-forty or fight" more than a century before.

Arnold Punaro, a marine reserve colonel, had to withstand withering antireform pressure from active and retired marines, but he also returned fire. After every markup session, Punaro took the long way back to his office just so he could let the antireform officers in the navy–Marine Corps legislative liaison office know that the proreform faction still had the upper hand on the committee. The officers responded with the "ten to nine" slogan and told Punaro to wait until the full Senate got its hands on the committee's bill.[14]

Although the solidarity of Goldwater and Nunn's ten votes convinced opponents that the SASC would report a bill, antireform senators were determined to make every effort to shape it more to their liking. The committee continued a detailed debate of each provision, addressing a staggering total of 140 written and oral amendments—nearly twice the average number of amendments during committee markup of a defense authorization bill.

In chairing the markup sessions, Goldwater continued to demonstrate that he was going to patiently allow the debate of each idea to go on as long as needed. But he also signaled that he would not tolerate delaying tactics or other mischief. Symbolic of Goldwater's preparedness to deal sharply with any disruptions was a small wooden rifle that he kept close at hand. My secretary, Barbara Brown, had given the rifle, a rubber-band shooter, to our boss. Goldwater called it his antiamendment weapon or "AAW." He kept it loaded at all times and more often than not held the rifle in his hands. Although he was tempted to fire it on numerous occasions, he only shot it once. After one session, Staff Director Jim McGovern came into the hearing room to speak with Goldwater. The chairman fired a rubber band at McGovern's crotch. "Didn't hit anything," the staff director responded. Goldwater, known among friends for a ribald sense of humor, replied, "Target too small."

Goldwater and Nunn's decision to ensure a full debate turned out to be a critical one. Proreform arguments proved to be more persuasive, and the debate slowly strengthened the position of reform proponents. It was clear that many opponents were finding the Pentagon's logic to be superficial and indefensible, even though not a single vote had yet changed sides.

Goldwater and Nunn decided when to offer compromises, including those on the two extreme recommendations in the draft bill: mission-oriented under secretaries and the merger of the two headquarters staffs in the military departments. These offers were well timed. Bargains were reached, and both sides were delighted. The opponents were relieved to have beat back an extreme provision; Goldwater and Nunn were pleased to have their desired outcome endorsed by the entire committee.

As the markup entered its third week, Goldwater and Nunn began slowly to pick up support in the debate. Gramm was the first member to switch sides. But soon after, another senator joined the proreform camp. When Goldwater and Nunn had thirteen or fourteen senators on their side, the opposition began to collapse.

Looking back at the committee's work, Mellon said: "It was an example of good government. It is the memory I would like to have of the Senate. There weren't parochial motives that I was able to discern. Members were motivated by national security considerations. People were dedicated; everybody was engaged; they were working with a great deal of vigor, energy, and commitment. Issues were decided on the merits and substance. It was the kind of experience that makes you want to go into government and be involved and participate."[15]

Although the committee was nearing the completion of its deliberations, Goldwater and Nunn slowed the pace to permit the committee to hear first-hand from the Packard Commission on February 28, the day the commission was slated to deliver its interim report to the president. During the meeting, Packard said that "the portions of the commission's report dealing with defense organization and the committee's bill are consistent and mutually supportive." The interim report dropped all mention of the JCS vice chairman's seniority. On the issue of who should serve as acting chairman, the report recommended, "The secretary of defense, subject to the direction of the president, should determine procedures under which an acting chairman is designated." Goldwater and Nunn's press statement announced: "We are absolutely delighted with the report that the Packard Commission submitted today to President Reagan."[16] The meeting with the commission did not produce any new ideas, but it reassured certain members and added to the rationale others could cite for their emerging proreform positions.

At the next SASC session, held on March 4, Warner offered an amendment to conform the provision on the JCS vice chairman to the Packard Commission's language. The amendment—on a priority issue for the Pentagon—was defeated twelve to four, with only Warner, East, Wilson, and Denton voting in favor.[17] The vote confirmed what the debate had signaled earlier: only a handful of senators continued to oppose key reorganization provisions.

The navy was outraged when it became clear that its supporters in the committee had been defeated on reorganization. Navy leaders blamed Warner, Wilson, and Denton, the three senators who had spearheaded the opposition, referring to them as the "three stooges." The criticism was self-serving and grossly unfair. The bill's opponents had put up a vigorous fight. Unfortunately for antireformers, much of the ammunition the Pentagon supplied had been duds.

The rigorous challenge to the draft bill carried important benefits. It forced the members to debate fully every word of the lengthy bill, question every idea, and thoroughly examine every issue. This rigorous process strengthened the bill and achieved consensus. Chris Mellon compared it to forging a sword. He said, "Warner and the Navy were the hammer, and Goldwater, Nunn, and the staff were the anvil. Warner kept firing in these amendments and concerns and objections to provisions. In a way, they helped to strengthen, sharpen, and harden some of the provisions and forged the bill in a hotter fire."[18]

The committee accepted about 60 percent of Warner's amendments in some form, many after significant modification.[19] None of the amendments that passed altered the basic thrust of the bill. Instead, they provided useful clarification, especially of roles and relationships, or provided safeguards governing the exercise of new authority. One major initiative by Warner required the president to submit an annual national security strategy report to Congress.

On the night before the markup's last day, Finn, Smith, Punaro, and I speculated about the final vote on the bill. Fifteen votes in favor seemed certain, but would there be more? I predicted a vote of seventeen to two, with Stennis and Denton casting the two nays.

The committee met on March 6 to conclude its work on the bill. Everyone present understood the historic significance of the coming vote. Goldwater did not rush this golden moment. He allowed the drama to build and for everyone to savor the committee's achievement at the end of a hard-fought battle. Finally, time for the last roll call came.

In line with practice, Chief Clerk Chris Cowart called the roll of the majority party first, starting with the most senior member after the chairman. It was fitting that Thurmond, who had represented the pivotal vote in the early going, cast the first aye. Warner voted yes next, then Humphrey, then Cohen, and all other Republicans, except for Denton, who passed.

Allan Cameron, Denton's military legislative assistant, assessed the final vote in a memorandum for the senator. Cameron himself opposed the bill, arguing that it "reverses nearly 200 years of American military history" and earlier legislation that had "concluded that a single military adviser was unwise and that the military advice in a democracy should be provided by a corporate body."[20]

Based upon input "from the staff members of the senators most likely to vote no," Cameron predicted the outcome as follows:

Warner: Will vote YES because he believes that the JCS compromise requires it and because he believes that the bill has been sufficiently improved.

Humphrey: Will probably vote YES for reasons of comity, although he is not happy with the bill.

Quayle: Will probably vote YES.

Wilson: Will vote YES. Believes the issue is politically sensitive for him, that "the train on defense reform has already left the station," and that he cannot afford to vote against "reform" in the context of California politics and his reelection campaign in 1988.

Gramm: Unknown, but apparently feels some pressure to vote YES for reasons of committee comity and relations with the chairman.

Stennis: Probably will vote NO because he believes the whole idea of JCS reform is bad; Stennis went through the [same] wars on the earlier occasions.

Glenn: Unknown, but much pressure to vote YES because of changes to the bill and the political realities of Ohio.

Cameron's memorandum summarized the situation: "I suspect a maximum of three or four NO votes, assuming you vote NO. I certainly believe that

SOMEONE should vote NO, but I would not recommend that you or any other senator do so ALONE." As Cowart began to call the roll of Democrats, Denton's decision to vote yes or no depended on Stennis's vote.

On the Democratic side, Nunn led off with his vote in favor. Stennis was next. He began by explaining the vote he was about to cast. Stennis revealed that Goldwater had asked to meet with him the night before and that they had discussed the fundamental issues at stake. "I reiterated that it was an extremely important vote for the future of the armed forces," Goldwater later recalled. "I told him I was not speaking that way because of my background, but because of what I've learned here and what I see."[21] Goldwater's final attempt to bring his longtime colleague onboard succeeded. Stennis voted in favor. All of the other Democrats also voted in the affirmative.

The clerk then asked the chairman for his vote; Goldwater proudly said, "Aye."

Only Denton's vote remained to be recorded. When the clerk returned to him, he voted in favor. His positive vote indicated prudence, not that he supported the bill. Nevertheless, when Cowart announced the tally, the committee had approved the bill by an astounding vote of nineteen to none.

News of the committee's historic unanimous vote was extensively reported in the print media the next day. The same newspaper editions carried a belated ill-informed attack against the legislation by syndicated columnists Rowland Evans and Robert Novak. They had accepted wholesale the superficial arguments of the Pentagon's reform opponents. The two columnists sought to characterize reorganization as "an attempt by serious Democratic politicians to regain military respectability through reform" and a "final victory for McNamara's Whiz Kids, the super-bureaucrats, against the uniformed professional military."[22]

Since I was the only former "whiz kid" on the committee staff, little doubt existed that Evans and Novak were shooting at me. The morning after the nineteen to zero vote, Evans and Novak looked foolish claiming that "Goldwater followed the lead of Sen. Sam Nunn, the committee's senior Democrat, and has been joined on key votes by only one other Republican, Sen. William Cohen of Maine." Had this attack appeared several weeks before it might have gathered some attention. Instead, it was merely an embarrassment to its authors.

Goldwater and Nunn had done it. In fourteen months of hard work, they had broken the military services' stranglehold and had forged new organizational concepts for the Defense Department. Many concepts were original—such as those strengthening the increasingly important, but long neglected, warfighting commands. Not only were Goldwater and Nunn able to gain approval of a comprehensive reform bill, they also achieved all of their desired reforms. The strategy of starting the process with extreme recommendations had succeeded in avoiding the watered-down results they feared. Overcoming the odds against them, Goldwater and Nunn produced a consensus on the entire spectrum of defense organization concepts, an agreement never before achieved during the nation's history.

Only later did I learn that after the committee's final vote, Punaro made his normal trek to the navy-marine liaison office. "Well fellas, you got your 'ten to nine' vote," he told them. "Ten Republicans for defense reorganization and nine Democrats for defense reorganization."[23]

CHAPTER 23

Mopping-Up Operations

A prompt and vigorous pursuit is the only means

of ensuring complete success.

—Gen. Philip Sheridan

The Senate Armed Services Committee's unanimous vote on its defense reorganization bill struck the decisive blow in a long campaign to reform the Pentagon. Congress was almost certain to enact comprehensive legislation. Even though a veto by President Reagan remained a possibility, sufficient votes would likely be available for an override. Accordingly, Capitol Hill shifted its attention from the issue of whether there would be a bill to what kind of bill it would be.

The intellectual challenges of charting the Pentagon's organizational future were daunting. Numerous battles remained, and any setback could prove costly. Strong pockets of resistance in the Pentagon and retired military community were capable of sowing conceptual land mines. The emotion of military issues can sway public opinion. Countering emotion with reason had gotten the reformers this far. They needed to be ready to respond quickly to the canards and red herrings that might now be thrown into the debate.

As the legislation progressed, the SASC would face competing pressures. The administration appeared determined to weaken the committee's bill on the Senate floor. Once past this hurdle, the SASC would have to play a different hand with its House counterpart, which had begun to draft more far-reaching legislation. Although the Senate-House conference committee to iron out differences between the two bills would feature a struggle among friends with common objectives, sharp disagreements on how to achieve those objectives were certain.

After the SASC's last vote on March 6, Rick Finn, Jeff Smith, and I turned our attention to two major tasks: putting the bill in final form and preparing the accompanying report. Hugh C. Evans, the senior defense lawyer in the Office of the Senate Legislative Counsel and a man with valuable legal drafting experience, assisted us. Having attended each markup session, Evans understood the bill and committee action. On March 28, the final bill, designated S. 2295, was circulated for the committee's review.

Finn, Smith, and I took our time writing the 161-page report. It represented important legislative history, and we wanted to clearly and precisely record the committee's intent.

On April 9, Goldwater and Nunn provided copies of our draft report to each member for review. They allotted three days for this review and informed members that the bill would be filed in the Senate on Monday, April 14.[1] Toward the end of that week, four or five senators who in the early going had been the most active opponents began complaining to me that they needed more time. On the afternoon of Thursday, April 10, Goldwater was scheduled to enter the hospital for minor surgery. Just prior to his departure, I told the chairman that several senators were demanding more time.

I asked for guidance, and Goldwater replied, "If that bill is not filed on Monday, you're going to need a new job." His words stiffened my spine for dealing with disgruntled senators.

In response to the chairman's immovable deadline, several senators huffily declared that they would have their say in additional views to be filed with the report. After all the bellyaching, however, only Denton submitted additional views.

For someone who had voted for the bill, Denton's additional views were highly critical—not only of the bill, but of the report and the entire process. "There remain serious questions about whether the bill would in fact lead to improvement of the organization and functioning of the Department of Defense or whether, in fact, it would make the situation worse," he asserted. It was unclear how Denton, after announcing that view, could justify his vote. I was amused to see that he was still firing heavy ammunition at the "bullet traps" in the staff report. "Whatever needs for change there might be," he argued, "the changes required were not, on the whole, those proposed in the staff study."[2]

On the night of April 15–16, U.S. aircraft struck targets in Libya. Code-named Operation El Dorado Canyon, the raid retaliated for a Libyan-backed terrorist bombing of a West Berlin disco ten days earlier. One American soldier was killed, and fifty were wounded. A Turkish woman also died, and 180 others were injured. Navy attack planes from the Sixth Fleet and air force F-111 aircraft based in England conducted the raid. The attack commenced at 2 A.M. local time, lasted twelve minutes, involved about one hundred strike and support aircraft, and delivered sixty tons of munitions.

Washington had assigned responsibility for the mission to the European Command, headed by four-star army general Bernie Rogers, a strong reorganization supporter. Having suffered through the organizational deficiencies that had crippled the marines' employment in Beirut in 1983, Rogers was determined to avoid the same cumbersome chain of command and service interference. He established a streamlined command arrangement for the operation and obtained a commitment from higher authority not to interfere: "I insisted and Crowe agreed that Washington would stay out of it."[3]

The SASC staff study's extensive criticism of JCS Publication 2, *Unified Action Armed Forces (UNAAF)* had led the JCS to initiate a review of that publication, beginning on October 7, 1985, at the end of Admiral Crowe's first week as chairman.[4] By the time of Operation El Dorado Canyon, Washington had circulated a draft *UNAAF* revision for comment that incorporated many of the expanded authorities for unified commanders contained in S. 2295.

Rogers operated as if the draft revision were already in effect. He designated the Sixth Fleet commander, Vice Adm. Frank B. Kelso II, as the operation's joint commander. Rogers gave Kelso the task, time frame, and authority to pull the operation together. The raid required only a limited degree of jointness because navy and air force strikes were "operationally and geographically divided."[5] Nevertheless, the authority given to local commanders and lack of Washington interference signaled the beginning of a new approach to warfighting.

Although the air force lost an F-111 aircraft, Admiral Crowe judged the operation "eminently successful."[6] Pentagon congressional liaisons were soon arguing that the success demonstrated that detailed reforms were not needed. Senate reformers arrived at a different conclusion. To their minds, the outcome confirmed the potential of the reforms mandated in S. 2295.

Five days after the attack, Rogers submitted comments on the draft *UNAAF.* In a ten-page message, he argued that the vice chairman should rank second on the JCS and should act as chairman in the chairman's absence. He urged that greater weight be given to successful performance by an officer serving on the Joint Staff. "'Successful' is defined as supporting what is best for the nation rather than best for service," Rogers added. He argued that unified commanders should be given the opportunity to review proposed service programs and budgets sufficiently early to influence their final construct. Rogers also wanted unified commanders to have the authority to "establish overall requirements for and direct the intelligence activities of the command."[7]

The navy did not like Rogers's submission. The CNO's executive assistant wrote to Admiral Watkins: "If he [Rogers] got all this stuff, 'CINC' would not be a strong enough title, 'Emperor' would be more descriptive."[8] Watkins concurred: "I do *not* agree with most of his inputs! The 'Emperor' must not have his way. This is worse than Locher!"[9]

Because Rogers had also argued—in line with his SASC testimony in December—that "service secretaries are no longer needed; creates an extra layer for obfuscation and delay," Watkins sent the message to Lehman. The secretary immediately fired the following message to nineteen senior officials and officers: "Ref A [message] from General Rogers calling for abolishing service secretaries and giving their powers and functions to unified CINCs calls to mind the quote from the recent gridiron speaker: 'Power corrupts, but absolute power is really neat.'" Rogers sent the message to Nunn as another example of navy misrepresentation, with a note that ended, "I didn't dignify the message with a response."[10] Pentagon sources reported that Lehman was so furious with Rogers about the original message that he planned to retaliate. At Nunn's direction, Arnold Punaro informed Assistant Secretary for Legislative Affairs Russ Rourke that the SASC would not tolerate any action against Rogers.[11]

On April 1, President Reagan signed National Security Decision Directive 219, a six-page "SECRET" document approving implementation of those initial recommendations of the Packard Commission that did not require legislation. In a covering memorandum, Vice Admiral Poindexter told Reagan: "In the midst of congressional uncertainty, the NSDD demonstrates our commitment to proceed with necessary reforms." However, on March 12, Poindexter had told Weinberger: "The NSDD is intended to strengthen your hand vis-à-vis the legislation now in both houses and maintain your control of the implementation process. . . . The [commission's] report thus gives the president considerable leverage in dealing with the more radical proposals for reform that now abound in both houses."[12]

Reagan devoted his weekly radio address on April 5 to defense reforms. He did not mention the SASC's bill, House-passed JCS reorganization bill, or any other congressional efforts. The president spoke as if the reform initiative belonged to the administration: "I will soon send a message to the Congress asking your senators and representatives to join me in reforming the defense establishment. . . . The changes our administration will request are based upon the recommendations made in February by the Packard Commission, a bipartisan group that spent months studying ways to give our nation stronger defenses more economically."[13]

The president transmitted his message on reorganization to Congress on April 24. The message contained the same theme as the radio address: the Packard Commission has recommended the necessary improvements, and Congress needs to take only a few legislative steps "for these improvements to be fully implemented." Reagan endorsed legislation, saying, "Certain changes in law are necessary to accomplish the objectives we seek." But he had a very short list of changes in mind. The president asked Congress to designate the JCS chairman as the principal military adviser, assign the chairman exclusive control over the Joint Staff, and create the new positions of JCS vice chairman and under secretary of defense for acquisition. Obliquely referring to the bills in Congress, Reagan continued, "Other proposed changes in law are, in my judgment, not required." The president asked Congress to retain the service chiefs as members of the JCS and permit the president and defense secretary to determine who should serve as acting chairman in the absence of the chairman.[14]

In forwarding the message on reorganization to Reagan for his approval, Poindexter noted that Congress was likely to rebuff the plea to refrain from legislating significant changes: "In this message we will attempt to convince the Congress that such changes are not necessary because they are already being implemented through executive action. Unfortunately, however, this will probably not succeed. We cannot expect the Congress to walk away from four years of work on defense reorganization. We also have to face the cold reality that Congress is deeply skeptical that the Department of Defense will follow your lead and take the actions needed to institute real reform."[15]

Poindexter was right. The two Armed Services Committees rejected Reagan's plea. Having little confidence in the Pentagon, the committees were convinced that all reforms would require the force of law to guarantee reasonable prospects for meaningful implementation. Goldwater wrote Reagan to tell him that "much more remains to be done" than his NSSD 219 directives.[16]

In the weeks leading up to Senate floor action, I met with key NSC and DoD representatives to discuss S. 2295. I learned that the administration would push three or four amendments. Because each would weaken the bill, I informed the executive branch emissaries that the committee would oppose them. The administration was also convinced that it could muster at least fifteen votes in opposition to the bill, but even this would not be enough to prevent a veto override.

On April 28, the Office of Management and Budget issued a Statement of Administration Policy on S. 2295 that began, "The administration supports Senate passage of S. 2295 provided that an amendment is adopted to delete the requirement that the term of the chairman of the Joint Chiefs of Staff expires no later than six months after the accession of a new president. This provision could have the effect of politicizing the military establishment." The SASC had added this provision to its bill to enable a president to have a chairman of his choosing shortly after he entered office without having to fire the incumbent. The administration's concern was overblown. A minor change to the provision—starting the chairman's term on October 1—resolved the issue.

The administration's policy statement also announced support for amendments to modify or delete eight provisions that limit the defense secretary's authority to manage personnel, procedures, and structure, delete provisions that require staff reductions and impose permanent personnel ceilings, and clarify the president's and defense secretary's authority to name an acting JCS chairman in the chairman's absence.[17]

On May 4, Sen. Daniel Patrick Moynihan (D–New York) called Nunn to report that the navy was waging a misinformation campaign against S. 2295. Other members had commented to Goldwater and Nunn about the navy's antireform lobbying, but Moynihan's detailed report of misstatements by Deputy Under Secretary of the Navy Seth Cropsey triggered a vigorous response from the two leaders. Instructed to prepare a letter to Weinberger, I wrote text that was midway between Goldwater's guns-blazing style and Nunn's cautious approach. Goldwater, who found my draft too weak, asked, "When's the staff going to get some balls?" Nunn labeled my draft too tough, asserting, "We can't say that." When I told each the other's position, they agreed to send the letter as drafted.

The senators' letter told Weinberger they were "extremely troubled," and reported:

> Although this [Cropsey's lobbying] is troubling enough in light of the support for the bill provided in the President's Message to the Congress on defense organization and the Administration's Policy Statement on the bill, we are even more disturbed because Mr. Cropsey is seriously misrepresenting the bill. . . . Mr. Cropsey characterized S. 2295 as being unconstitutional. He also charged that the bill would result in loss of civilian control; make the chairman of the Joint Chiefs of Staff a voting member of the National Security Council; and strengthen the combatant commanders to the extent they would become "proconsuls.". . . Mr. Cropsey's unprincipled efforts to misrepresent this bill are an affront to the integrity of the national political process.
>
> We do not believe for a moment that you are aware of Mr. Cropsey's activities or that you would condone them. We cannot say the same for the Secretary of the Navy. In our view, Secretary Lehman must be held fully accountable for Mr. Cropsey's activities. . . . We urge you to do everything within your power to correct this situation. While we could appeal to others or could use congressional authority to seek remedies, only you can deal effectively with this problem. We urge you to do so.[18]

The Senate devoted May 7 to considering S. 2295. In an early morning meeting, Secretary Lehman asked Senator Warner to offer an amendment that would exempt the navy from having to comply with the bill. Stunned by Lehman's request, Warner asked his assistant, Les Brownlee, for his thoughts. Brownlee said that the idea of excluding one of the three military departments was unworkable. He added that Senator Warner had carried so much water for the navy in the reorganization fight that it would be best if Lehman found another sponsor for his amendment.[19]

36. Senator Sam Nunn and Cong. Les Aspin.
(Sam Nunn Archives, Emory University.)

The Senate convened at 10 A.M. on May 7, and forty minutes later turned its attention to S. 2295. Although Goldwater and Nunn kept their guard up all day waiting for the administration's amendments to be presented, the Senate's activity was like a celebration. Seven minor clarifying amendments were offered and accepted, and three others were introduced and withdrawn. An extraneous amendment dealing with support to rebels in Afghanistan and Angola was tabled. Most of the day was devoted to explaining the bill and praising it and the SASC's two leaders. Over the preceding seven months, many senators who were not committee members had watched with amazement as prodefense conservatives Goldwater and Nunn clashed with the Pentagon's powerful brass. They understood the magnitude of political and intellectual challenges that the two committee leaders had overcome and took the floor to offer their congratulations.

Goldwater and Nunn had closely coordinated every move on the Senate floor. Thus, in midafternoon, when Nunn announced that he had a "revolutionary" amendment,[20] Goldwater grabbed me and said, "What is he doing?" Nunn's surprise amendment would name the bill after Goldwater.

I was as surprised as Goldwater. As Nunn was praising Goldwater's "wisdom, courage, and leadership," I was thinking that the two senators had worked as partners. The bill should be titled "Goldwater-Nunn." I wanted to mention that possibility to Goldwater, but he was overcome by emotion. Moreover, Nunn had cosponsors for his amendment, which suggested this was a well-coordinated move and that a staffer's suggestion to modify it would not be appreciated.

Nunn's magnanimous gesture so pleased Goldwater that the crusty old man cried. Nunn set aside his own interest to ensure that Goldwater got the credit he deserved.

At 5:50 P.M., when the clerk had finished calling the roll on final passage of the "Barry Goldwater Department of Defense Reorganization Act of 1986," the vote was ninety-five to none in favor. Like its amendments, the administration's fifteen opposing votes had evaporated. After the vote, Goldwater and Nunn went to the press gallery to answer reporters' questions. During this informal press conference, Goldwater said of the bill, "It's the only . . . damned thing I've done in the Senate that's worth a damn."[21]

For several years, the House had been far ahead of the Senate on reorganization. When the SASC staff report was released on October 16, 1985, the House found itself trailing the Senate by a considerable distance. The Senate's comprehensive reorganization effort now overshadowed the House's narrowly focused JCS reform proposals.

When Cong. Les Aspin became House Armed Services Committee chairman in January, 1985, he had placed JCS reorganization high on his agenda. The Wisconsin Democrat had risen to the top post by mounting a coup to unseat aged Chairman Melvin Price, jumping over five more senior Democrats. A reporter described the forty-six-year-old Aspin as "alternately charming and inconsiderate, a windmill of arms and shoulders when he speaks, a bluster of energy and goals and four-letter words." The new chairman—a former Rhodes scholar with a doctorate in economics from the Massachusetts Institute of Technology—was known as "a serious thinker who also loves political pit fights."[22]

Aspin was tall—six feet two inches—with prematurely silver hair and a bald spot. His rumpled suits hung "on his large frame like a loose sack." He was "notorious for his clumsy manners." Washington viewed him as "a defense intellectual, a member of the elite fraternity of experts on strategic weaponry, arms control, Soviet military strength and the arcana of the American defense system." His expertise, policy skills, and Pentagon service made him intellectually a better choice than Cong. Bill Nichols to lead a broad reorganization campaign. But Nichols rated as a better choice politically because of his conservative credentials, combat record, and standing with HASC members. Aspin understood this. He would prod Nichols and Arch Barrett to be more aggressive on JCS reform and eventually to explore other reorganization areas, but he was not about to usurp Nichols's leadership role.[23]

Having participated in the CSIS Defense Organization Project, Aspin favored a broad reorganization effort. With Nichols focused on JCS reform, Aspin put several other reorganization topics—the Pentagon's decision-making process, role of service secretaries, and influence of unified commanders—on the agenda of his newly formed Defense Policy Panel.[24]

On October 24, 1985, eight days after release of the SASC staff report, the HASC Investigations Subcommittee passed another JCS Reorganization Act, H.R. 3622. Due to Aspin's prodding and support, the bill contained more far-reaching provisions than the previous House bill.[25] These included making the chairman the principal military adviser and creating a deputy chairman. The full committee gave its approval on October 29, and the House passed the bill by a vote of 383–27 on November 20. Twenty-one Republicans voted against the bill, including Reps. Jack Kemp, John McCain, and Richard Armey.

The administration had opposed the bill, saying in a policy statement: "No legislative action should be taken until the recommendations of the Packard Blue Ribbon Commission have been evaluated and other congressional proposals have been reviewed. Therefore, the administration opposes enactment of H.R. 3622 at this time."[26] The overwhelming approval of the bill showed how little influence the administration had on this subject.

A few days later, Aspin was ready to shift into high gear and work through the Thanksgiving recess to prepare a comprehensive reorganization bill. At a meeting with Barrett, he said, "The Senate's coming, and it's coming with a broad bill. We're going to go for a very broad bill. We're going to pass a defense organization bill that will complement what we've just done on the JCS." Aspin's desire to move quickly shocked Barrett, who had just completed an exhausting effort on the JCS bill and did not see the need to match the Senate's broader legislation. He remembered telling Aspin: "You know, first of all, you only have me. I'm tired. I plan to go off for Thanksgiving, and I'm going." For the first time in his House career, Barrett dug in his heels with his boss: "It'll just have to wait until I get back."[27]

Aspin was notorious for forgetting staff vacations. Having approved them in advance, he was shocked when staffers were not available. He was known to ask, "Who said they could take vacations?" The day before another Thanksgiving, one of his office staff meetings "drifted into the dark hours." Finally, Aspin's administrative assistant nudged him, "Les, it's getting late. Some people have to get on the road."

"Why?" he asked blankly.

"It's Thanksgiving, Les. A national holiday. Remember the Pilgrims?"[28]

Barrett, recalling his disagreement with Aspin on whether or not the House needed a broad bill, said: "The way I was looking at it was: 'Okay, the Senate's going to do a whole broad range of things. We've done really good work on the JCS. So, we'll have a conference, and we'll put it all together.' But Mr. Aspin's view was: 'No, the House can't go in there naked on all of these issues.'"[29] Driven by Aspin, the Investigations Subcommittee initiated work on a broad bill.

The SASC and HASC leaders and staff communicated extensively throughout 1985 and 1986. Goldwater and Nunn often met or wrote to Aspin and ranking HASC Republican Bill Dickinson. Sometimes Nichols participated in these sessions. Staff level contacts were even more extensive. In an unusual session on January 9, Aspin asked Finn, Jeff Smith, and me to meet with him, Barrett, and Kim Wincup to discuss how the HASC might proceed. We described areas that the SASC bill would comprehensively address and those that needed additional attention where the HASC might consider focusing its limited time. One such area was personnel policies for joint officers.

While the Senate committee was marking up its bill during February and March, the HASC Investigations Subcommittee held a series of broad reorganization hearings. Starting on February 19, thirteen hearings were conducted, with the last occurring on March 12, six days after the final SASC vote. On February 26, Aspin, Nichols, Skelton, and a few other reformers introduced four bills dealing with unified commands, joint officer management, military departments, and defense agencies. Aspin commissioned a twenty-two-page staff report to justify and garner support for House action.[30] When Barrett saw that the desired product was what he called a proreform "polemic" rather than an objective presentation, he refused to work on it or allow his name to be associated with it. On March 11, these four bills were merged into a single bill, H.R. 4370, which Nichols introduced. Aspin provided the drive and intellectual leadership for preparation of these bills, leading Barrett to later say, "On the House side, Aspin is the unsung hero of defense reorganization."[31]

Building upon momentum created by the SASC bill, HASC reformers proposed more ambitious reforms in H.R. 4370. All of a sudden, the SASC bill looked more reasonable to the Pentagon. On May 9, Weinberger, congratulating Goldwater on the Senate-passed bill, wrote, "Please be assured that we will support the bill in its current form in conference, although we will seek amendments relating to the remaining issues we have discussed."[32]

The HASC planned to address H.R. 4370 on June 25. Hoping to influence the outcome, the JCS invited Nichols and his Investigations Subcommittee colleagues to a breakfast meeting on June 24. Barrett advised Aspin that the JCS had "pulled out all the stops" at the breakfast. He reported that the JCS had invited other HASC members at the last moment to produce a guest list that "was stacked against HASC members who support the bill. Both Mr. Nichols and Mr. Kasich went to the breakfast and came back telling me how acrimonious the exchanges became." Barrett also reported that the CNO, Adm. Jim Watkins, called provisions dealing with the consolidation of military department headquarters "un-American." Barrett wrote of the reaction of the patriotic Nichols, who had lost a leg in World War II combat: "Mr. Nichols took personal offense and so stated. I have never seen Mr. Nichols so upset as when he came by my office and told me what had happened. I think the JCS behavior will work in our favor."[33]

Admiral Crowe "vividly remembered" that breakfast meeting: "I could have shot Watkins, could have just shot him. If I hadn't shot him, Nichols would have. He truly offended Nichols, and I spent the next six weeks trying to get Nichols squared away. Of course, Watkins was just five days from retirement. So, he just marched away. Watkins has a tremendous ego. It never occurred to him that he offended anybody. But he called what Nichols was proposing 'un-American.' And Nichols didn't have that view of himself. . . . Nichols and his colleagues had a right to be upset."[34]

Barrett describes the scene for the markup of H.R. 4370: "We had opposition on the HASC, not anything like in the SASC, but the Pentagon was putting on a full-court press." He advised Aspin, "There's no question that we have significant pockets of strong resistance on the committee. Moreover, many members are uncommitted." With this opposition and the Senate naming its bill for Goldwater in mind, Barrett wrote to Aspin, "Sooner or later it is going to occur to members that the House should also have a name on the legislation, and the logical choice is Mr. Nichols. (Another choice, as you and I both know, is Les Aspin; but I surmise that this cannot be [because of Nichols's more visible leadership role and his higher standing with HASC colleagues].) If Mr. Nichols' name is going to be placed on the bill, I recommend that it be done in the committee because this is where it will have the most effect in diluting opposition."[35]

The next day, after Nichols had explained the bill to the committee, Aspin said, "I would like to offer the first amendment. My amendment would be to name . . . it the Bill Nichols Defense Reorganization Act of 1986." Of Aspin's move at the markup's beginning, Barrett recalled, "It just slew the opposition. A very few members brought up their amendments. Others just would read their amendments and withdraw them. It just emasculated whatever little opposition there was going to be."[36] The committee approved the bill by a thirty-nine to four vote. It addressed nearly all areas included in the Senate-passed bill, except for JCS reorganization, which the House had approved in H.R. 3622 the preceding November.

During his explanation of the unified command part of H.R. 4370, Nichols spoke of the marine barracks bombing: "We laid the blame for the tragedy in Beirut in 1983 on the shoulders of the commander on the ground and his superiors in the chain of command right up to the commander of the European Command [General Rogers]. . . . But responsibility is only one side of the coin. The other side is authority to carry out a responsibility. . . . After extensive hearings this year we can affirm that the combatant commanders—CINCs—the Bernie Rogerses—lack authority commensurate with their responsibilities. They are responsible for our very survival as a nation if war should come because they are our combat commanders. Yet, incredibly, their authority is limited." Barrett said this statement was "not an apology to Rogers, but an indication that Nichols knew more in 1986 than he did in 1983 about the whole situation."[37]

Unable to schedule floor time for the House to consider H.R. 4370, the HASC offered an amendment to attach H.R. 4370 to the defense authorization bill for Fiscal Year 1987, while the House was deliberating the latter bill on August 5. The House gave its approval to this amendment—and thereby to H.R. 4370— by a vote of 406–4. Democrats Samuel S. Stratton of New York, James Weaver of Oregon, and Henry B. Gonzalez of Texas and Republican William Carney of New York cast the four negative votes. In the entire Congress, these four votes were the only ones cast against the final version of either House's reorganization bill.

The House required additional parliamentary maneuvering before the two houses could begin to reconcile their reorganization bills. House Resolution 4370 had to be detached from the defense authorization bill and combined with H.R. 3622. The House approved these actions on August 11, clearing the way for a Senate-House conference committee.

By August 11, the SASC and HASC leaders were becoming increasingly concerned about the congressional calendar. With elections looming in November, Congress would recess in early October. To avoid a pocket veto and ensure that Capitol Hill had the chance to override a veto, Congress needed to send the bill to the White House not later than mid-September. With a congressional recess scheduled to begin on Friday, August 15, and last until September 8, work needed to start immediately on resolving differences between the Senate and House bills.

Shortly after the Senate's May 7 vote, I began preparing spreadsheets to show the differences in the two bills for use by the Senate-House conferees. This was not easy. The two bills were long, structured differently, and took different approaches to the same topic. After figuring out what to compare to what and how, brevity became a second challenge. I had to capture a provision's essence in a few words. With too many words, the spreadsheets lost their utility. I had the spreadsheets ready for Arch Barrett's review when the House completed action on August 11.

Although the two bills embodied similar themes, they contained more than two hundred significant differences and more than a thousand substantive wording differences. Convened on August 13, the conference committee consisted of all nineteen SASC members, but only seven HASC members: Aspin, Dickinson, Nichols, and Hopkins—full committee and Investigations Subcommittee chairmen and ranking members—and Skelton, Mavroules, and Kasich, each of whom had participated extensively in reorganization efforts.

The conference committee designated Goldwater and Nichols as chairman and vice chairman. "In my view," began Goldwater, "the conference committee is in an excellent position. We can select the best ideas from two outstanding bills. Furthermore, I don't expect this conference to be contentious. Our bills share thirteen fundamental objectives. We differ solely on how to best achieve these common goals." He asked the conferees to agree to four principles: "focus on the genuine needs of U.S. national security . . . carefully consider each issue and hear all points of view . . . each provision should rise or fall on its own merits . . . [and] ensure that provisions of law are not so detailed or specific that they cannot be adapted to the needs of the unforeseen future."[38]

The committee devoted its attention to resolving the twenty-three most significant differences before the August 15 recess. This list included the term and duties of the JCS chairman, details of establishing the vice chairman position, channel of command communications issues, specific authorities for unified commanders, qualifications required of unified commanders, joint officer personnel policies, and personnel reductions in defense agencies. The twenty-three issues were hotly contested over three grueling days of negotiations. Barrett and I presented each issue and each house's position. A normal conference is a madhouse. The complexity of the reorganization issues tripled the difficulty of having a twenty-six-member committee, divided by house and political party, reach agreement.

The more far-reaching provisions of the House bill created problems on the Senate side. The majority of Republican senators had accepted the SASC bill only after a bitter fight. They were not prepared to give another inch and vociferously opposed the House provisions. Goldwater and Nunn, even when they favored a House provision, felt compelled to honor major compromises struck during the SASC markup.

One such issue involved the House's proposal to merge the civilian and military headquarters staffs in the military departments. The staff-drafted SASC bill had contained a similar provision, but Goldwater and Nunn had negotiated it away. Despite sympathy for the House provision, they refused to accede to it. The conference finally approved a compromise that would consolidate seven functions in the civilian secretariats.

When the committee recessed on August 15, Barrett, Finn, Jeff Smith, and I began the painstaking process of resolving all other differences, preparing the bill, and writing the report. To guard against a veto, the conference committee had instructed us to complete our work and have it available for consideration on September 9, the day after the recess ended. We took the first weekend off to catch our breath. On Monday, August 18, we shifted into high gear: seven-day workweeks and fifteen-hour days.

The pressure was enormous. Four years of arduous work were on the line, and this legislation was a once-in-a-generation opportunity to revitalize the military by fixing its structural flaws. We had to get it right. Another thirty years might pass before Congress again made major legislative changes to defense organization.

Hugh Evans and his counterpart, Robert W. Cover from the House's Office of Legislative Counsel, worked with us. To provide the legal support that we needed, they adopted a work schedule even more onerous than our own. While we worked from nine in the morning until midnight, the two lawyers would start at noon and work until four or five every morning. When we adjourned at midnight, Evans and Cover would stay until they had produced a clean legal text of agreements reached that day. They would have the new drafts waiting for us when we arrived the following morning.

On the Senate side, we had two other lawyers and an organizational expert advising us. On a close-hold basis, I had asked the Pentagon's top reorganization lawyers—Andrew S. Effron and navy captain Rick DeBobes—and a key organizational specialist—Ralph Furtner—to review drafts of the legal text. Effron worked for the OSD general counsel, and DeBobes was the JCS's legal adviser and legislative assistant. Furtner served in the Pentagon's Office of Administration and Management.

Given the adversarial relationship between Congress and the Pentagon on reorganization, all parties needed to keep quiet about this arrangement. Many on Capitol Hill did not trust the Pentagon and would have opposed allowing defense personnel access to conference work. House knowledge of this arrangement could have strained Senate-House staff relations. Pentagon colleagues of Effron, DeBobes, and Furtner would have viewed working with the SASC staff as collaborating with the enemy. Although their immediate superiors had consented, few in the Pentagon knew of their activities.

This behind-the-scenes work with Pentagon counterparts paid dividends. Some heated debates occurred before we agreed that they were to refrain from commenting on fundamental decisions and limit their role to advising on how the Pentagon would legally interpret various provisions. They also brought to our attention unintended consequences of proposed statutory changes.

Barrett, Finn, Smith, and I had set Friday, August 29, as the deadline for settling all differences. When that day arrived, we had made excellent progress. Only a few issues remained. Unfortunately, they were among the toughest ones. We negotiated all day Friday, all day Saturday, all day Sunday, and we finally finished on Monday, Labor Day. Those four days were brutal. Both sides—convinced that they had a better vision of DoD's organizational needs and how to meet them—did not yield easily. By the time we finished, we were exhausted.

After members and staff had reviewed the resulting bill and report, the conference committee met at 2 P.M. on Thursday, September 11, to resolve six minor issues and take final action. The proposed bill fully satisfied an overwhelming majority of conferees, and the meeting was expected to last an hour.

However, the Pentagon's strongest supporters among Republican senators fussed about aspects of a number of provisions, especially ones consolidating certain functions in the military department headquarters and establishing joint officer policies. A heated debate broke out. I had arranged for a Senate photographer to capture the historic end of the conference with Goldwater and Nichols shaking hands across the table. The photographer departed after his allotted one hour without snapping a shot. Finally, Goldwater cut off his Republican colleagues, and the committee unanimously adopted the conference report on both the Senate and House sides. Nunn then moved to name the bill the "Goldwater-Nichols Department of Defense Reorganization Act of 1986," which the conferees unanimously approved.[39]

After the session, a HASC press release quoted Aspin as saying, "This is one of the landmark laws of American history. It is probably the greatest sea change in the history of the American military since the Continental Congress created the Continental Army in 1775." A few days later, a letter from Admiral Moorer to Barrett declared, "I just want to tell you once again, I think the Congress has made a serious mistake and that in very short time you will find it necessary to address your mistakes."[40]

Following approval of the bill, the staff rushed to prepare the conference report for filing. Four staffers—Barrett, Finn, Smith, and I—and two supporting lawyers—Evans and Cover—finished this task about 11 P.M. on Friday, September 12, and filed the bill with the Clerk of the House, who had remained available to receive it. On the following Monday and Tuesday, the Senate and then the House approved the conference report by voice vote.

Congress had done its part. Now the Goldwater-Nichols Act required only the president's signature to become law.

CHAPTER 24

The Commander in Chief Approves

All successful revolutions are

the kicking in of a rotten door.

—John Kenneth Galbraith, *The Age of Uncertainty*

G iven near unanimous congressional support, not even a veto by President Reagan could derail the Goldwater-Nichols Act. Senate and House leaders could easily muster the two-thirds vote required in each house to override a veto. Even though they had the votes, Senators Goldwater and Nunn wanted to avoid the damage a veto by the commander in chief could do. The act called for dramatic and painful changes in the way the Department of Defense would conduct operations, formulate plans, make program decisions, and manage officers. It also sought to gradually alter the military culture. Success of the reforms would depend on effective implementation. A veto might encourage foot-dragging or worse in the Pentagon.

On the surface, a veto seemed inconceivable. The Reagan administration, however, sometimes showed flashes of unpredictability. Secretary Weinberger's singular influence with Reagan meant that there was some chance that the president might be persuaded to veto the bill.

With those thoughts in mind, Goldwater and Nunn asked me to meet with Ron Lehman and Mike Donley of the National Security Council staff to check the White House's reaction to the bill. We expected it to be favorable. McFarlane and Poindexter had supported the reorganization effort, and Reagan had endorsed the Packard Commission's recommendations, which paralleled the provisions of the Goldwater-Nichols Act. I expected a pro forma trip to the Old

Executive Office Building, where it seemed certain that Lehman and Donley would tell me of rapid progress toward a presidential signature.

Instead, Lehman and Donley, who were both close friends of mine, received me with calculated coolness and refused to predict what course of action Reagan might take. I was stunned. After the lengthy congressional battle and exhausting work, the possibility of a veto unnerved me. I knew that Lehman and Donley personally supported Pentagon reorganization. Their equivocation communicated that they had not ruled out the president yielding to an appeal from his pal Weinberger and his beloved military. Soon the three of us were exchanging heated words. Donley later explained their position: "You never commit the president to a course of action before he has to decide. That's sort of an operating principle." But he also admitted, "You can't always be an accurate speaker for Weinberger in terms of what he would recommend at the very end."[1]

My report of the meeting discouraged Goldwater and Nunn.

After the Senate and House had passed the Goldwater-Nichols Act on September 16 and 17, it had to be enrolled before it could be submitted to the president. Enrolling involved printing the bill on parchment and having the speaker of the House and president of the Senate or their designees sign it. With the end of the session approaching, a backlog of bills awaited printing on parchment. Because of the Goldwater-Nichols Act's importance and concerns about having sufficient time before Congress adjourned for a veto override, the secretary of the House gave it sufficient priority to complete the printing in two days. After Cong. Thomas S. Foley signed the act for the House and Sen. Strom Thurmond for the Senate, the Goldwater-Nichols Act was submitted to the president on Friday, September 19.[2] The Constitution provides the president ten days—not counting Sundays—to act on a bill. That meant he would need to act not later than Wednesday, October 1.

The Office of Management and Budget exercises responsibility for recommending a position to the president on enacted legislation. Even before the enrolled bill arrived at the White House, OMB had requested the views of the NSC and Departments of Defense and Justice. The Pentagon responded first. Deputy Secretary Taft's letter to OMB advised, "The Department of Defense interposes no objections to presidential approval of H.R. 3622."[3] Taft did not go as far as recommending approval, but "no objections" registered as a positive response.

Chapman Cox had prepared the letter for Taft's signature. His covering memorandum stated: "While we have continuing concern with respect to the implementation of certain provisions of the bill which you should monitor closely, we recommend that the president sign the bill." Normally, Pentagon officials would widely coordinate a letter establishing DoD's position on major legislation. Cox did not follow that route. He advised Taft: "This memorandum and letter have *not* been coordinated with the military departments nor with the chairman of the Joint Chiefs of Staff." Only the new general counsel, H. L. "Larry" Garrett III, had coordinated.[4]

The navy's continued opposition may have convinced Cox to forgo normal coordination procedures. A draft memorandum from Lehman to Weinberger argued that the reorganization bill "will reduce your authority and dramatically increase Pentagon bureaucracy." After restating opposition to many provisions, the memorandum concluded, "These factors will reverse the trend toward effective defense management and successful military operations that has taken place under your leadership. I urge you to consider the serious consequences of H.R. 3622's enactment into law, and convey those concerns to the president."[5]

Fearing that Weinberger might acquiesce to the Goldwater-Nichols Act, Lehman's staff drafted two long letters for him to send directly to the White House: one to presidential assistant Patrick J. Buchanan and the other to the president. The highly political letter to Buchanan argued: "Simply put, the legislation aims to derail the president's policies as well as his accomplishments in strengthening national defense. Only time will tell if it actually endangers national security. Your consideration and help are requested to prevent these eventualities." The letter called the bill "a harsh attack" on the Reagan administration, "radical," and "privately being used for Democratic Party ends."[6]

The letter ended with the navy's strategy for securing a veto:

It is clear from the Packard report that virtually every needed change in defense structure can, under current law, be undertaken *without* additional legislation. In that light, given the conferees' failure to meet the administration's wishes on the bill, it would be entirely appropriate for the president to pocket [veto] it, promulgate an executive order on his own reforms, and let Congress know that politics will not stand in the way of a strong defense. At the same time, the leadership on these issues of such highly regarded legislators as Senator Goldwater should be strongly recognized, and they could be brought in to help implement the message. Or, alternatively, the president could ask for certain congressional actions required to implement the Packard Commission, which could also serve as a suitable legislative monument to Senator Goldwater.

The draft letter to Reagan, focusing on the substance of the bill and not on politics, restated the navy's objections. It ended by urging a veto: "While a number of provisions of H.R. 3622 are good ones, others are so flawed as to erode our national security. They not only restrict the authority of the president and secretary of defense, they also bottle-neck our combat forces in unneeded new bureaucracy—a prescription for future military failure. In the absence of a line-item veto, we must urge you to reject H.R. 3622, and implement its positive recommendations by executive means."[7]

Ever the wise politician, Lehman, apparently sensing no interest, did not sign the correspondence to Weinberger, Buchanan, and Reagan, and the letters were never sent.

On September 23, the NSC informed OMB that it "recommends that the president sign" the Goldwater-Nichols Act. Two days later, OMB director James C. Miller III forwarded his favorable recommendation to Reagan. He noted that the OMB and NSC recommended approval of the bill, DoD had no objection, and the Department of Justice had no comment. Miller concluded, "While Congress did not accommodate all of the administration's concerns, . . . H.R. 3622 is a significant step toward reforming the structure and management of the Defense Department as was strongly recommended by the Packard Commission."[8]

Six White House offices reviewed Miller's memorandum before it reached the president. All concurred except Buchanan's Office of Communications, which had "no objection."[9] An internal memorandum in the White House Counsel's Office, concurring with OMB's position, reveals the unending constitutional competition between the executive and legislative branches: "While the bill evidences a continuing trend on the part of the Congress to engage in micromanagement of military affairs, including a delineation of the authority of frontline commanders and the manner in which the president receives military advice, I do not believe they constitute a sufficient basis for a presidential veto. Furthermore, since the legislation consists, in large part, of measures recommended by the Packard Commission and approved by the president, I do not believe a veto would be appropriate."[10]

On September 30, David L. Chew, staff secretary and deputy assistant to the president, sent Reagan a brief note: "Attached for your approval is enrolled bill H.R. 3622, the Goldwater-Nichols Department of Defense Reorganization Act of 1986." The note informed the president of the positions of all departments and White House offices and advised him that the following day, October 1, was the last day for action.[11]

While the bill was making its way to the president, Donley began planning a signing ceremony with help from John Douglass. Donley's initial proposal totaled thirty-eight attendees for the ceremony including me, my wife, and our son.[12] By the third iteration, the list was down to eighteen: five senators, six congressman, three from the Pentagon, and four from the White House and NSC staffs. No congressional staff would be invited. The NSC staff also planned a side conversation between Reagan and Goldwater after the signing ceremony, with the president saying, "Congratulations, Barry; you are leaving a tremendous mark on our defense establishment. Only someone of your stature could get this accomplished."[13] I later learned that when the White House approached Goldwater and Nunn with the tentative plan for a small ceremony, the senators said if their staff was not invited, they would not attend.[14]

As part of the signing ceremony preparation, the NSC staff had drafted a forward-leaning, two-and-one-half-page statement for the president's use. The Pentagon objected, saying that the statement did "not accurately portray the history of this administration in acquisition and management improvement. The president and Secretary Weinberger have led an evolving and growing effort in this area since the early days of the administration." Instead, DoD recommended a much briefer statement that was less fulsome in its praise of the legislation and Packard Commission recommendations.[15]

Except for the exploratory calls to Goldwater, Nunn, and key House members about possible attendance at a signing ceremony, all executive branch activity had taken place without congressional knowledge. As the deadline for action approached, the two Armed Services Committees were in the dark as to what direction Reagan would take. The committees' leaders and staff were not sitting around waiting. We were fully engaged in the conference committee on the defense authorization bill.

On the morning of October 1, Reagan traveled to Atlanta to participate in the dedication ceremony for the Carter Presidential Center. He returned to Washington in midafternoon. With the afternoon hours passing, there still had been no word from the White House as to the president's intentions. Apparently, there was not going to be a signing ceremony. (The Pentagon's lack of interest scuttled plans for a ceremony.)[16]

By six o'clock, activity in Room SR-232, where my office was located, was beginning to slow. I was sitting at my desk working on conference issues when Chris Cowart, the chief clerk, opened my door and said, "Congratulations. The Senate bill clerk just called to say the president signed the Goldwater-Nichols Act. I'll let everyone else know."[17]

That was it. The momentous battle that had raged for four years and 241 days—longer than U.S. fighting in World War II—ended with a whimper.

The White House issued a terse, three-paragraph press statement. Reagan called the act "a milestone in the long evolution of defense organization since our national security establishment was created in 1947," and thanked six members of Congress—Goldwater, Nunn, Nichols, Skelton, Kasich, and Hopkins—and Weinberger, Packard, and the JCS for "their patience and perseverance." He concluded by saying: "After long and intense debate, we have set a responsible course of action by taking another important step forward, building on improvements underway since 1981, and affirming the basic wisdom of those who came before us—the Forrestals, Bradleys, Radfords, and Eisenhowers—advancing their legacy in light of our own experience."[18]

The Pentagon got its wish. The statement was short, bland, thanked opponents as well as architects, and in speaking of the wisdom of predecessors, cited two—Forrestal and Radford—who had done as much as anyone to delay needed organizational changes.

37. Senator Goldwater (*left to right*), Jim Locher, Barbara Brown, Jeff Smith, and Senator Nunn celebrate passage of the Goldwater-Nichols Act, October 16, 1986, in Goldwater's office. (U.S. Senate photo.)

In the absence of a White House ceremony, Rick Finn, Jeff Smith, and I decided to arrange a small gathering during which we would honor Goldwater and Nunn's historic achievement. October 16 would mark the first anniversary of their release of the staff study and commencement of their public campaign to achieve reform. We decided to have hard covers put on two copies of the study and inscribe them for presentation to Goldwater and Nunn on that anniversary date.

Goldwater, Nunn, Jeff Smith, Barbara Brown, and I gathered in Goldwater's office on the morning of October 16, 1986. We were missing Rick Finn, whose wife was giving birth to their first child. I opened the ceremony by making a speech about Goldwater's and Nunn's brilliant leadership, honesty and integrity, perseverance against long odds, intellectual contributions, wisdom, political acumen, and bipartisan spirit. It was an easy speech to give because I had two years' worth of great material to use. I talked about how their efforts would overcome problems that had plagued the military for decades and pave the way for a far-reaching revitalization of the armed forces. I also said how proud and honored their staff was to have served them in this historic undertaking. I then read the inscription in Goldwater's book, which included: "Your victory is now recognized as a great one, but only in the future will the magnitude of its greatness be fully understood and appreciated." To Nunn, we wrote that the legislation "would not have been possible without your outstanding leadership."

The two senators responded with their own observations about the legislation, the struggle to produce it, and their remarkable partnership. They also thanked the staff for their exceptional efforts. After these presentations, a Senate photographer took pictures. Normally, that would have ended a Senate ceremony. But Goldwater, Nunn, and their staff lingered. We all knew that this was our last gathering, the end of a once-in-a-lifetime experience that each of us cherished. Like a military unit getting ready to break up after a war, we wanted to relive one final time the skirmishes and crises of the past two years. We enjoyed telling story after story. Goldwater's telephone call to the navy's Defeat Reorganization Office. Nunn's devastating attacks on Lehman's and Kelley's testimony. The Senate floor speeches. The retreat at Fort A. P. Hill. The briefing to Weinberger at the Pentagon. The surprising unanimous vote in committee. After we had shared every story and enjoyed every laugh, we could not delay the end any longer. Warmly congratulating each other, we shook hands one last time and departed.

As I walked back to my office through the marbled halls of the Russell Senate Office Building, my mind shifted to the future. My own prospects were clouded. My relations with many Republican senators and staffers would never recover from the bruising reorganization fight. Goldwater's retirement left me exposed to ill feelings.

These worries were dwarfed by my excitement that the act was now law. I expected that the Pentagon's implementation would encounter rough spots, but I was confident that Admiral Crowe and other senior officers—then and in the future—would find the right path. They now had the edge to overcome the parochialism of service supremacists. As the far-reaching reforms took effect, I was convinced they would greatly improve the military's warfighting capabilities, enable the services to adapt more effectively to new challenges, and introduce a new era. The Goldwater-Nichols Act completed the reorganization efforts started eighty-five years earlier in the aftermath of the Spanish-American War. It finally corrected the distortions of power and influence that emerged during World War II and had troubled U.S. security for forty years thereafter.

As I reached my office and turned the handle of Room SR-232's massive door, I was exhilarated by anticipation. I could not wait to watch the Goldwater-Nichols Act revitalize and transform the military and improve the odds for American service members put in harm's way.

Epilogue

Unified at Last

Sound structure will permit the release of energies
and of imagination now unduly constrained by the
existing arrangements.

—Defense Secretary James R. Schlesinger, 1983

D espite negative Pentagon attitudes, the Senate and House Armed Services
Committees and other reorganization supporters had high expectations
for the Goldwater-Nichols Act. Have results matched these expectations? Comparing the Department of Defense's performance since 1986 with congressional
objectives provides a useful yardstick for assessing the act's contributions.

In reorganizing DoD, Congress' overarching concern centered on the excessive influence of the four services, which had inhibited the integration of
their separate capabilities into effective joint fighting units. With its desire to
balance joint and service interests as the backdrop, Congress declared nine
purposes for the act: strengthen civilian authority; improve military advice;
place clear responsibility on combatant commanders for accomplishment of
assigned missions; ensure that the authority of combatant commanders is
commensurate with their responsibility; increase attention to strategy
formulation and contingency planning; provide for the more efficient use of
resources; improve joint officer management; enhance the effectiveness of
military operations; and improve DoD management.[1] Some objectives were

more important than others. Congress gave priority to fixing problems in DoD's operational dimension: military advice, responsibility and authority of combatant commanders, contingency planning, joint officer management, and the effectiveness of military operations.

Congress found numerous obstacles impeding effective civilian authority. Members agreed with John Kester's characterization of the secretary of defense: "His real authority is not as great as it seems, and his vast responsibilities are not in reality matched by commensurate powers."[2]

Congress saw the secretary's efforts being "seriously hampered by the absence of . . . independent military advice." Joint Chiefs of Staff logrolling provided the secretary with watered-down advice. This forced the Office of the Secretary of Defense to carry the entire burden of challenging the services on policies and programs. The SASC staff study assessed the outcome: "The natural consequence has been a heightening of civil-military disagreement, an isolation of OSD, a loss of information critical to effective decision-making, and, most importantly, a political weakening of the secretary of defense and his OSD staff. The overall result of interservice logrolling has been a highly undesirable lessening of civilian control of the military."[3]

Confusion concerning the roles of the military department secretaries ranked next on Congress' list of problems hampering the defense secretary's authority. The National Security Act of 1947 never defined the new secretary's relationship to the service secretaries. Bitter controversy over unification precluded clarification. The 1947 law preserved considerable independence for the civilian heads of the military departments. Subsequent amendments strengthened the defense secretary's power and staff, but they did not prescribe his relationship to the service secretaries. Not surprisingly, service secretaries energetically advocated parochial positions, frequently at the expense of their boss' broader agenda.

Three Goldwater-Nichols prescriptions were most important in addressing these problems. First, to leave no doubt as to the defense secretary's authority, report language declared, "The secretary has sole and ultimate power within the Department of Defense on any matter on which the secretary chooses to act."[4] Congress meant this to end claims by defense officials to jurisdictions independent of the secretary's authority.

Second, Congress envisioned that making the JCS chairman the principal military adviser would provide the secretary a military ally who shared a department-wide, nonparochial perspective. Capitol Hill foresaw this alliance ending the civil-military nature of Pentagon disputes.

Third, the law specified each service secretary's responsibility to the defense secretary. These provisions filled a void that had existed for nearly forty years.

By empowering the secretary of defense to more effectively lead and manage the department, the Goldwater-Nichols Act achieved the objective of strengthening civilian authority. Disputes over the secretary's authority have ended; he is viewed as the ultimate power. Richard B. Cheney, the first defense secretary to fight a war under Goldwater-Nichols, found that "each service wants to do its own thing." He observed that "the Department of Defense is difficult enough to run without going back to a system that, in my mind, served to weaken the civilian authority of the secretary and the president. . . . Goldwater-Nichols helped pull it together in a coherent fashion so that it functions much better . . . than it ever did before."[5]

Despite Cheney's valid assertion, Goldwater-Nichols's impact on civilian authority has received more criticism than any other area. Critics claim that the enhanced role of the JCS chairman and improved Joint Staff capabilities have led "to the erosion of civilian control of the military." These naysayers do not suggest that the revitalized military is disobedient or making major decisions. They worry instead about "the relative weight or influence of the military in the decisions the government makes."[6]

There is no doubt that the Joint Staff now overshadows OSD, diminishing the civilian voice in the decision-making process. Two trends have produced this result: the improved quality of Joint Staff work and a weaker performance by OSD. Ineffective leadership in a fast-paced environment and inattention to personnel matters have contributed to OSD's decline. As worrisome as this imbalance may be, it does not match the seriousness of the more overt challenges to civilian authority during the pre-Goldwater-Nichols era. Then, the military often resisted the authority of the defense secretary. As Cheney noted, Goldwater-Nichols helped overcome that problem. Now the concern is that officers are helping the secretary too much by providing better, more timely information and more powerful ideas than their civilian counterparts.

The solution to this problem is not to weaken military staff work but to improve civilian contributions. Changes in law are not needed to achieve this outcome. The defense secretary already has sufficient authority to take the required actions. Creating a dynamic leadership culture and building a highly qualified civilian workforce are demanding, long-term tasks. Of the failure to act, Eliot Cohen advised, "It is the civilians, not the soldiers, who have abdicated their responsibilities."[7]

Recalling pre-1986 military advice, Gen. Colin Powell, the first JCS chairman to fight a war under Goldwater-Nichols, observed that "almost the only way" previous chiefs reached agreement on advice was "by scratching each other's back," while the Joint Staff "spent thousands of man-hours pumping out ponderous, least-common-denominator documents that every chief would accept but few secretaries of defense or presidents found useful." This partly explains "why the Joint Chiefs had never spoken out with a clear voice to prevent the deepening morass in Vietnam."[8]

In response to inadequate military advice, Congress crafted some of the Goldwater-Nichols Act's most far-reaching provisions. The act made the JCS chairman the principal military adviser, transferred to him the duties previously performed by the corporate JCS, and added new duties. To assist the chairman, Congress created the position of vice chairman as the second-ranking officer. Last, Congress gave the chairman full authority over the Joint Staff.

A comprehensive assessment concluded that the act "made a significant and positive contribution in improving the quality of military advice," a judgment shared by principal customers. Cheney said he regarded the chairman's uncompromised advice "a significant improvement" over the "lowest common denominator." Powell's successor as JCS chairman, Gen. John M. Shalikashvili, agreed, "We have been able to provide far better, more focused advice."[9]

Former navy secretary John Lehman disagreed with these assessments and the designation of the JCS chairman as principal military adviser. Repeating his mid-1980s arguments, he said the chairman's role has "limited not only the scope of military advice available to the political leadership, but also the policy- and priority-setting roles of the service chiefs and civilian service secretaries."[10]

Congress found pre-1986 operational chains of command confused and cumbersome. The chain of command roles of the defense secretary and JCS were unclear. Despite removal of the military departments from the chain in 1958, service chiefs retained de facto influence over combatant commands, increasing the confusion.

To achieve its objective of placing clear responsibility on combatant commanders, Capitol Hill clarified the chain of command to each commander and emphasized each commander's responsibility to the president and secretary of defense for mission performance. The Goldwater-Nichols Act directed that the chain of command run from the president to the secretary of defense to the combatant commander. The JCS, including the chairman, were explicitly removed.

Opinion is universal that this objective has been achieved. Senior officials and officers have repeatedly cited the benefits of a clear, short operational chain of command. Commenting on Operation Desert Storm, Gen. H. Norman Schwarzkopf stated, "Goldwater-Nichols established very, very clear lines of command authority and responsibilities over subordinate commanders, and that meant a much more effective fighting force." Secretary of Defense Bill Perry recalled that commentaries and after-action reports were unanimous in attributing that war's success "to the fundamental structural changes in the chain of command brought about by Goldwater-Nichols."[11]

Congress found the combatant commands weak, unified in name only. They were loose confederations of powerful service components and forces. The services used *Unified Action Armed Forces*, which established policies for joint operations, to restrict the authority of the combatant commander and give significant autonomy to his service component commanders.

To correct this violation of command principles, Congress modeled the law on the authority that the military had traditionally given to a unit commander. The Goldwater-Nichols Act empowered each combatant commander to give authoritative direction, prescribe the chain of command, organize commands and forces, employ forces, assign command functions to subordinate commanders, coordinate and approve aspects of administration and support, select and suspend subordinates, and convene courts-martial.

Service claims that the legislation would make warlords of the combatant commanders quickly ended as the soundness of balancing authority and responsibility at the combatant commander level—in line with military tradition—became apparent. Agreement is widespread that Goldwater-Nichols has ensured commensurate authority for combatant commanders. "This act," said Shalikashvili, "by providing both the responsibility and the authority needed by the CINCs, has made the combatant commanders vastly more capable of fulfilling their warfighting role."[12] Performance of these commands in operations and peacetime activities convincingly supports this judgment.

A minority view urges increased authority for combatant commanders through a greater resource-allocation role. Not wanting to divert these commands from their principal warfighting function, Congress intended that the JCS chairman and Joint Staff would represent their resource needs. To many, this approach continued to remain preferable to schemes that would require greater involvement by the commands. Recent JCS chairman Gen. Henry H. Shelton agreed: "More involvement by the combatant commanders in resourcing would not be healthy. We want to keep them focused on warfighting."[13]

In formulating Goldwater-Nichols, the two Armed Services Committees determined that strategic and contingency planning in DoD were underemphasized and ineffective. Because strategic planning was often fiscally unconstrained, it was also unrealistic. Moreover, strategy and resource allocation were weakly linked. Contingency plans had limited utility in crises; often they were based on invalid political assumptions.

To highlight strategy making and contingency planning, Congress formulated four principal Goldwater-Nichols provisions. First, it directed the president to submit an annual report on national security strategy. Second, it instructed the JCS chairman to prepare fiscally constrained strategic plans. Third, the act required the defense secretary to provide written policy guidance, including political assumptions, for preparation and review of contingency plans. The fourth provision directed the under secretary of defense for policy to assist the secretary on contingency plans.

Prior to Goldwater-Nichols, the JCS had so jealously guarded nonnuclear contingency plans that the only civilian briefed on them was the defense secretary. Additional civilian access was denied to prevent civilian "meddling" in operational matters and leaks—civilians weren't trusted with sensitive material. Alone, the secretary could not provide meaningful review or direction. The absence of rigorous civilian review led to plans based on unrealistic assumptions, sharply limiting their utility.[14]

Goldwater-Nichols increased attention to both strategy making and contingency planning. The quality of strategy documents has varied, but in every case their value has been superior to those predating Goldwater-Nichols.

Contingency planning consists of two categories: deliberate plans and crisis action plans. Deliberate plans are prepared for all potential wars and major crises and updated every year or so. Crisis action plans respond to unexpected crises, such as the famine in Somalia in 1992. Contingency planning improvements have occurred almost exclusively in the deliberate planning category. In 1996, Shalikashvili saw advances: "Our major war plans . . . are the best I have seen." Five years later, his successor, General Shelton, cited additional progress: "We have been able to better integrate the political-military, coalition, and interagency aspects into our plans." OSD eased into its oversight responsibilities, seeking to reassure a nervous joint system. A retired three-star general was hired to head the civilian review office, which was staffed by active-duty officers. A single civilian sat between the general and his staff. The office did not conduct its first contingency plan review until 1992; a year later, it had established a comprehensive review regime. Civilian involvement has increased, but military officers still dominate "civilian" review.[15]

For crisis action plans, progress on improving civilian review has been extremely limited. The joint chiefs have used traditional arguments of civilian meddling and untrustworthiness to deny access beyond the secretary, deputy secretary, and under secretary for policy. Occasionally, the price for the absence of rigorous civilian review is staggering: military planners failed to plan for postoperation law and order and restoration of government services in Operation Just Cause, the invasion of Panama in 1989. Lawlessness, looting, and slow recovery tarnished the operation's success. In modern conflicts and crises, policy and operations intertwine. The department's practice of separating them ignores the intent of Goldwater-Nichols, blocks essential collaboration between policy and operational planners, and will continue to produce unsatisfactory results.

Mid-1980s testimony before Congress revealed that DoD's ambiguous strategic goals gave service interests, not strategic needs, the dominant role in allocating resources. The lack of an independent military assessment of service programs and budgets also impaired the secretary of defense's resource management.

To achieve its objective of providing for more efficient use of resources, Congress turned to the JCS chairman for the lacking independent military perspective, assigning him six new resource-related duties. Two important ones were advising the secretary on combatant command priorities and assessing conformation of programs and budgets of the military departments and other defense components with strategic plans and combatant command priorities. The chairman was also empowered to recommend alternative programs and budgets.

The potential of resource allocation reforms has been realized only once, when General Powell used his new resource advisory role in 1990 to formulate the Base Force. Reducing the Cold War force structure by 25 percent represented DoD's most important and difficult resource issue since the passage of Goldwater-Nichols, so Powell's contribution was not insignificant. Besides this critical contribution, JCS chairmen have yet to provide definitive resource advice to defense secretaries.

The chairman has mechanisms for developing advice on resource allocation to best meet joint warfighting needs. Admiral William A. Owens, while serving as JCS vice chairman, instituted several innovative changes improving support by the Joint Requirements Oversight Council (JROC) for the formulation of resource advice. The council—consisting of the vice chairman and the four service vice chiefs—advises the chairman on requirements and acquisition. Owens introduced Joint Warfighting Capabilities Assessments (JWCAs), which cover such areas as sea, air, and space superiority and strategic mobility and sustainment, to assist the JROC in analyzing department-wide resource needs and priorities.

The JWCAs offer dramatic improvements in comparing service programs against mission requirements. Unfortunately, the JROC operates by consensus—just like the old Joint Chiefs of Staff. At a time when the Defense Department needs decisive priorities and tradeoffs, the JROC simply rubber-stamps service initiatives. Owens acknowledged that decisions still "squander enormous funds."[16]

Instead of informing the chairman's independent advice, the JROC prenegotiates the old logrolling way. The military has come full circle to the wasteful, bad old days. Its approach could result in the services locking arms on major resource issues to politically overpower the defense secretary and Congress. When the JCS chairman permits these activities and surrenders his independent perspective, he abandons the intentions of Goldwater-Nichols. If such practices go uncorrected, Congress will need to act.

On joint officer issues, Congress concluded: "For the most part, military officers do not want to be assigned to joint duty; are pressured or monitored for loyalty by their services while serving on joint assignments; are not prepared by either education or experience to perform their joint duties; and serve for only a relatively short period once they have learned their jobs."[17] Because the Joint Staff and combatant command headquarters staffs are the preeminent military staffs, Capitol Hill found this situation intolerable.

Title IV of the Goldwater-Nichols Act established procedures for the selection, education, assignment, and promotion of joint-duty officers. Congress and the Pentagon fought the last Goldwater-Nichols battles over this title. The services resisted a joint officer personnel system because loss of absolute control of officer promotions and assignments would weaken their domination of the Pentagon. Congress was equally determined to eliminate a system in which "joint thinkers are likely to be punished, and service promoters are likely to be rewarded."[18]

The joint officer incentives, requirements, and standards prescribed by Goldwater-Nichols have significantly improved the performance of joint duty. Cheney judged that requiring joint duty "prior to moving into senior leadership positions turned out to be beneficial." He also felt that joint officer policies made the Joint Staff "an absolutely vital part of the operation." Powell judged that the Joint Staff had "improved so dramatically" it had become "the premier military staff in the world." General Schwarzkopf commented that Goldwater-Nichols "changed dramatically" the quality of people "assigned to Central Command at all levels."[19]

These positive results were achieved despite the indifference of OSD, senior joint officers, and the Joint Staff, as well as efforts by the services to minimize title IV's impact. The JCS chairman at the time of Goldwater-Nichols's enactment, Admiral Crowe, later wrote of his unfavorable view of title IV: "The detailed legislation that mandated every aspect of the 'Joint Corps' from the selection process and the number of billets to promotional requirements was, I believed, a serious mistake that threatened a horrendous case of congressional micromanagement. In this instance the chiefs were unanimous in their opposition, and I agreed with them wholeheartedly." Not surprisingly, for many years, Joint Staff implementation reflected this sympathy toward service attitudes. "We probably have not advanced as far or as fast as we could have had more attention been directed toward joint officer management," admitted Shelton.[20]

The initiative of individual officers accounts for the success of the joint officer provisions. Seeing joint duty as career enhancing, qualified officers vigorously pursue joint assignments.

Congress had hoped that DoD, after several years of implementing title IV, would develop a better approach to joint officer management. That has not occurred. The Goldwater-Nichols objective of improving joint officer management has been achieved, but the Pentagon still lacks a vision of its needs for joint officers and how to prepare and reward them.

For forty years after World War II, service parochialism and independence denied DoD the unity of effort required to wage modern warfare. Congress found that the "operational deficiencies evident during the Vietnam War, the seizure of the *Pueblo*, the Iranian hostage rescue mission, and the incursion into Grenada were the result of the failure to adequately implement the concept of unified command."[21] To enhance the effectiveness of military operations, Congress' principal fix was to provide combatant commanders sufficient authority to ensure unity of command during operations and effective mission preparation. The Goldwater-Nichols Act also assigned to the JCS chairman responsibility for developing joint doctrine and joint training policies.

Overwhelming successes in Operations Just Cause in Panama and Desert Shield/Storm in the Persian Gulf region showed that the act had quickly unified American fighting forces. Of this improved performance, Powell said, "Goldwater-Nichols deserves much of the credit." Malcolm Forbes commented: "The extraordinary efficient, smooth way our military has functioned in the Gulf is a tribute to . . . the Goldwater-Nichols Reorganization Act, which shifted power from individual military services to officials responsible for coordinating them. . . . The extraordinary achievements of Secretary Cheney and Generals Powell and Schwarzkopf would not have been possible without Goldwater-Nichols." An article in *Washington Monthly* added, "Goldwater-Nichols helped

38. General H. Norman Schwarzkopf (*left to right*), Defense Secretary Richard Cheney, Pres. George Bush, and Gen. Colin Powell. (DoD photo by R. D. Ward.)

ensure that this war had less interservice infighting, less deadly bureaucracy, fewer needless casualties, and more military cohesion than any major operation in decades."[22]

Speaking in 1996, Secretary Perry observed that Goldwater-Nichols "dramatically changed the way that America's forces operate by streamlining the command process and empowering the chairman of the Joint Chiefs of Staff and the unified commanders." It produced "the resounding success of our forces in Desert Storm, in Haiti, and . . . in Bosnia."[23]

Joint doctrine and training have experienced more modest progress, especially in the early years. In 1994, General Shalikashvili said: "While we have *some* joint doctrine, it is really in its infancy, at best. It is not well-vetted; it is not well-understood at all; and it is certainly not disseminated out there. And most certainly, it is almost *never* used by anyone." The JCS chairman, calling joint training "an embarrassment," said, "We have an awful long way to go to bring us into the 21st century." A year later, the Commission on Roles and Missions characterized the first generation of joint doctrine as "a compendium of competing and sometimes incompatible concepts (often developed by one 'lead' service.)"[24] Attention has been given to these shortcomings, particularly joint training, which has benefited from establishment of the Joint Forces Command, Joint Training System, and Joint Warfighting Center.

The Joint Forces Command's role as the joint force integrator, trainer, provider, and experimenter has great potential for enhancing the effectiveness of military operations. To date, parochial attitudes by the services and some geographic unified commands and weak Joint Staff support have hamstrung the Joint Forces Command's progress. Inadequate resourcing has hindered the command's work. To carry DoD to the next level of jointness, Shelton argued, "The Joint Forces Command needs a funding line and acquisition authority." Shelton also believed that DoD should use a joint budget account to fund all joint activities rather than continuing to rely on funding by service executive agents. Mike Donley asserted that the executive agent system "has left the services with too much influence over joint funding priorities."[25]

Shelton recommended another dramatic change: "The next big step in jointness is to establish standing joint task forces and recognize that capability as a required core competency. We need to have the organization, training, and equipment that will allow us to move rapidly, have a common operational picture, and conduct rapid decisive operations as a joint force. That's a Ph.D. level of warfighting which you can't do with our current pickup team approach. We should designate four standing joint task force headquarters: East Coast, West Coast, Hawaii, and Europe."[26]

Despite remaining work, improvements in joint warfighting capabilities have been swift and dramatic. In 1996, Senator Nunn asserted, "The Pentagon's ability to prepare for and conduct joint operations has improved more in ten years—since passage of the Goldwater-Nichols Act—than in the entire period since the need for jointness was recognized by the creation of the Joint Army-Navy Board in 1903." Shalikashvili saw similar progress: "No other nation can match our ability to combine forces on the battlefield and fight jointly."[27] This was demonstrated at the small-unit level during the Afghanistan phase of the war on terrorism: army Special Forces soldiers directed punishing air force and navy air-strikes.

A few critics, mostly retired marines, have disputed these views. Retired colonel Mackubin T. Owens Jr. argued: "The contributions of the Goldwater-Nichols Act to the improved performance of the U.S. Armed Forces are marginal at best, and ... the unintended consequences of the act may well create problems in the future that outweigh any current benefits." Lieutenant General Paul K. Van Riper, USMC (Ret.), warned: "The path to 'jointness' some are advocating has grave implications for national defense. . . . The organizational structures brought about by Goldwater-Nichols are not necessarily appropriate for the future."[28]

Many Goldwater-Nichols provisions helped improve the department's management. But, in adding this objective, Congress had in mind specific structural problems hindering sound management, including excessive supervisory spans of control, unnecessary staff layers and duplication of effort, continued growth in headquarters staffs, poor supervision of defense agencies, and an unclear division of work among defense components.

The secretary of defense's span of control especially concerned Congress. Forty-one officials and officers, excluding his deputy and personal staff, reported directly to him. To reduce this span, Goldwater-Nichols required the secretary to delegate the supervision of each defense agency and field activity to a senior civilian or the JCS chairman. The chairman's role as overseer of the combatant commands also lightened the secretary's supervisory burdens.

Other provisions consolidated certain functions in the military department secretariats, limited the number of service deputy and assistant chiefs of staff, reduced by 15 percent the number of personnel and general and flag officers in the military department headquarters, and reduced certain other staffs by 10 or 15 percent.

Yet such remedies were largely ineffective. The defense bureaucracy remains far too large. Duplication of effort continues. Defense agencies—some with expenditures larger than the biggest defense contractors—receive negligible guidance or oversight. The department still lacks a concept for the appropriate division of work among components.

Beyond the unfinished business of the Goldwater-Nichols Act, DoD faces other organizational challenges. The act's strengthening of the JCS, Joint Staff, and combatant commands has produced dramatic results in one of the department's two dimensions: warfighting. Reforms of business activities—performed principally by OSD, the military departments, and defense agencies—have been fewer and less successful. This dimension requires rigorous attention.

Secretary of Defense Bill Cohen attempted to provide this attention with his Defense Reform Initiative, launched in 1997. Cohen envisioned "igniting a revolution in business affairs within DoD that will bring to the department management techniques and business practices that have restored American corporations to leadership in the marketplace."[29]

But the Defense Reform Initiative has focused on the lesser challenges of Cohen's revolution. The department needs to elevate the initiative's sights to major shortcomings. Of organizations like the Pentagon, business guru John Kotter wrote: "The typical twentieth-century organization has not operated well in a rapidly changing environment. Structure, systems, practices, and culture have often been more of a drag on change than a facilitator. If environmental volatility continues to increase, as most people now predict, the standard organization of the twentieth century will likely become a dinosaur."[30]

The Pentagon's change-resistant culture represents its greatest organizational weakness. Because of the Pentagon's immense success in wars cold and hot, it suffers from the "failure of success." It is an invincible giant who has fallen asleep. Given past successes, the Pentagon cannot break its embrace of past warfighting concepts and traditional weapon systems, as Secretary of Defense Donald Rumsfeld found in early 2001 during his troubled efforts to transform the military. This attachment leads to "preparing to fight the last war over again." Two business scholars observed, "Yesterday's winning formula ossifies into today's conventional wisdom before petrifying into tomorrow's tablets of stone."[31]

According to internal critics, long-range Pentagon plans "are not characterized by new operational concepts, or a new vision of how we might conduct military operations, or how we might respond to the wide array of possible future challenges." The department's plans for physical capital "largely continue the production of articles and polish ideas that triumphed during the Cold War."[32]

The Defense Department's change-resistant culture was less troubling during the relatively stable Cold War. But the twenty-first century world is experiencing an unprecedented rate of change. Michael Hammer explains that "change is happening exponentially. It's not that every bit of additional knowledge adds a little more change to the world. But rather, because it interacts with all the other knowledge and experience that we already have in so many domains, it has a cumulative effect. That's why the rate of change has become so astounding."[33] To anticipate and adapt to change, DoD needs to employ the change-enabling techniques of successful American businesses, like strategic visioning and a renewal process.

The Pentagon is choking on bureaucracy. The corporate headquarters totals thirty thousand, and staffs within twenty-five miles of the Pentagon swell to 150,000. Each military department has two headquarters staffs (three in the navy)—one civilian and one military—sharing one mission. This duplicative structure, which originated in World War II, cannot be justified in a fast-paced environment. If DoD merged these staffs, it could greatly improve efficiency and effectiveness. There has been movement on this issue: in December, 2001, the army and air force announced their intention to merge their two headquarters staffs.

The Pentagon's bureaucratic bloat creates enormous friction and increases time and energy expended. As the pace and complexity of work have increased, the department has added staff rather than adopting new, efficient work practices. In particular, the Pentagon makes poor use of horizontal process teams—multifunctional groupings of experts given a single set of objectives and empowered to produce results. Businesses find that such teams produce better results with 30 percent of the effort. The Pentagon continues to rely on outmoded hierarchical approaches based on the archaic premise that "all wisdom resides at the top." Peter Senge notes that such approaches produce "massive institutional breakdown and massive failure of the centralized nervous system of hierarchical authoritarian institutions in the face of growing interdependence and accelerating change."[34]

The department's focus on inputs rather than outcomes further hinders its performance. The Pentagon is organized along functional lines, such as research and engineering, intelligence, and health affairs. Organization specialists understand that a functional structure leads to an input focus that hinders integration of diverse inputs to produce desired outcomes, such as mission capabilities. The input categories of the Future Years Defense Plan, the department's accounting system, reinforce these tendencies.

The department also faces organizational challenges in its external environment. The Pentagon must strengthen its ability to work with other government departments and agencies. Contemporary crises are complex. They have military, diplomatic, economic, law enforcement, technological, and information dimensions. As Senator Nunn said, "The old days of the Pentagon doing the entire mission are gone for good."[35] Successful peacetime preparation and crisis management require the effective integration of many, diverse capabilities and unity of effort across the government. This is especially true for homeland security, where weak cross-government coordination was painfully revealed by the terrorist attacks on September 11, 2001. Two recent JCS chairmen, Generals Shalikashvili and Shelton, have recognized the need for better interagency harmonization. But the department is still too wedded to its traditional go-it-alone attitude. The need for improved national security planning and coordination across many departments and agencies has produced calls for a Goldwater-Nichols II to reform the interagency system.

The Pentagon must also learn how to work more effectively with international organizations like the United Nations and nongovernmental organizations like the Red Cross. Both will play significant roles in future crises and often interact with American military forces.

The Goldwater-Nichols Act ended a forty-five-year struggle to produce a unified military establishment. At the beginning of the twenty-first century, a new set of organizational changes is needed. Hopefully, the act has provided the tools and experience to enable a timely response by the Pentagon.

In the broad sweep of American military history, the post-Goldwater-Nichols era has been remarkable for the number and scope of significant DoD achievements and successes. Superb leadership played an important role, as did doctrine, training, education, and hardware developments. Nevertheless, a significant body of evidence and numerous assertions by senior officials and officers argue that the Goldwater-Nichols Act enormously contributed to these positive outcomes.

The act has attained most of the objectives established for it, helping to transform and revitalize the American military profession in the process. Goldwater-Nichols succeeded most in joint warfighting areas, to which Congress had given its highest priority. In some areas, act-inspired developments are still evolving and adding further luster to the legislation's achievements. In others, much remains to be done.

Secretary Perry used a historic yardstick to praise the legislation, calling the Goldwater-Nichols Act "perhaps the most important defense legislation since World War II." Admiral Owens saw the legislation in larger terms: "Goldwater-Nichols was the watershed event for the military since the second World War." In line with congressional expectations, the Goldwater-Nichols Act has profoundly improved the military's performance and warfighting capabilities. Even some critics have praised the act. In 1995, Gen. John Wickham said, "It has achieved eighty percent of its objectives and will go down in history as a major contribution to the nation's security."[36] That's high praise from a former opponent.

NOTES

Abbreviations

a.n.	accession number
AFJ	*Armed Forces Journal*
ADB	Private Papers of Archie D. Barrett, Monterey, Calif.
BMG	Barry M. Goldwater Collection, Arizona Historical Foundation, Hayden Library, Arizona State University, Tempe, Ariz.
CMH	U.S. Army Center of Military History, Fort McNair, Washington, D.C.
CNO	Records of Chief of Naval Operations, Operational Archives, Naval Historical Center, Washington Navy Yard, Washington, D.C.
DDEL	Dwight D. Eisenhower Library, Abilene, Kans.
DJB	Private Papers of David J. Berteau, Washington, D.C.
Donley	Private Papers of Michael B. Donley, Springfield, Va.
GPO	U.S. Government Printing Office
JCS	Official Files of the Joint Chiefs of Staff, National Archives and Records Administration, College Park, Md.
JFQ	*Joint Force Quarterly*
JGT	John G. Tower Papers, A. Frank Smith Jr. Library Center, Southwestern University, Georgetown, Tex.
JFL	John F. Lehman Jr. Papers, Operational Archives, Naval Historical Center, Washington Navy Yard, Washington, D.C.
JRL	James R. Locher III Papers, Special Collections, National Defense University Library, George C. Marshall Hall, Fort McNair, Washington, D.C.
JWD	John W. Douglass Papers, RRL
MBD	Michael B. Donley Papers, RRL
NYT	*New York Times*
OPNAV	Records of Chief of Naval Operations, Deputy Chief of Naval Operations (Plans, Policy, and Operations), Strategic Concepts Branch (OP-603)/Strategic Concepts Group (Op-605), boxes 10, 13, 15, 22, Operational Archives, Naval Historical Center, Washington Navy Yard, Washington, D.C.
RDF	Papers of Richard D. Finn Jr., included in the James R. Locher III Papers
RRL	Ronald Reagan Library, Simi Valley, Calif.
SASC	Official Files of the Senate Armed Services Committee, 98th Congress, Goldwater-Nichols DoD Reorganization, boxes 1902–49, National Archives and Records Administration, Center for Legislative Archives, Washington, D.C.
SD	Official Records of the Secretary of Defense, Deputy Secretary, and the Executive Secretary to the Secretary and Deputy Secretary of Defense,

> National Archives and Records Administration, Washington National
> Records Center, Suitland, Md.

PSt   Private Papers of Peggy Stelpflug, Auburn, Ala.

PSS   Paul Schott Stevens Papers, RRL

TJC   Private Papers of Theodore J. Crackel, Special Collections, National Defense University Library, George C. Marshall Hall, Fort McNair, Washington, D.C.

USN&WR *U.S. News & World Report*

WFN   William F. Nichols Papers, Special Collections, Ralph Brown Draughon Library, Auburn University, Auburn, Ala.

WKB   Private Papers of William K. Brehm, McLean, Va.

WP   *Washington Post*

WSJ   *Wall Street Journal*

Prologue. Turf, Power, Service

This chapter reconstructs the February 3, 1986, meeting from Goldwater's description in his autobiography, *Goldwater;* Carter's notes; Finn's notes; a one-page paper, "Chiefs' Objections," prepared immediately after the meeting by the author and Finn; a five-page paper, "Meeting with the Joint Chiefs of Staff," prepared by the author in the fall of 1986; a February 4, 1986, letter from each joint chief to Goldwater restating the views he presented at the meeting; interviews of eight participants: Goldwater, Nunn, Crowe, Wickham, Carter, DeBobes, Finn, and Smith; and an interview with Col. Richard Witherspoon, the Army Staff action officer for reorganization.

1. Gen. John A. Wickham Jr. to Barry Goldwater, Feb. 4, 1986, box 1943, folder "Wickham Letter—2/4/86," SASC.

2. Ibid.

3. Richard D. DeBobes during author interview of Sam Nunn, July 14, 1995; Powell F. Carter Jr., author interview, Aug. 14, 1995.

4. Wickham to Goldwater.

5. Gen. John A. Wickham Jr., author interview, May 9, 1995; Richard H. Witherspoon, author interview, December 1993.

6. William J. Crowe Jr. with David Chanoff, *The Line of Fire: From Washington to the Gulf, the Politics and Battles of the New Military* (New York: Simon and Schuster, 1993), 152.

7. Barry M. Goldwater with Jack Casserly, *Goldwater* (New York: Doubleday, 1988), 337.

8. Gen. P. X. Kelley to Barry Goldwater, Feb. 4, 1986, box 1943, folder "Kelley Letter—2/4/86," SASC.

9. Goldwater with Casserly, *Goldwater,* 338; Carter interview.

10. Adm. William J. Crowe Jr., author interview, April 26, 1994.

11. Adm. James D. Watkins to Barry Goldwater, Feb. 4, 1986, box 1943, folder "Watkins Letter—2/4/86," SASC.

12. Kelley to Goldwater.

13. Carter interview.

14. Watkins to Goldwater.

15. Kelley to Goldwater.

16. Author's recollection confirmed by Nunn.

17. Goldwater with Casserly, *Goldwater,* 337.

18. Ibid., 338; Wickham interview.

19. Colin Powell to Jim Locher, Feb. 3, 1983, box 1943, folder, "Weinberger Letter—2/3/86," SASC.

20. Goldwater with Casserly, *Goldwater,* 338.

21. DeBobes comments about the service chiefs near reorganization's end: "I was struck by how little the chiefs knew about other issues that were related to the Goldwater-Nichols Act, how uninformed they were." (author interview, May 2, 1994).

22. Goldwater with Casserly, *Goldwater,* 337.

23. Nunn interview.

24. Goldwater with Casserly, *Goldwater,* 338.

25. Ibid., 339.

26. Nunn interview.

Chapter 1. The Rise of Service Supremacists

1. Archie D. Barrett, *Reappraising Defense Organization: An Analysis Based on the Defense Organization Study of 1977–1980* (Washington: NDU Press, 1983), xix.

2. Samuel P. Huntington, *The Soldier and the State: The Theory and Politics of Civil-Military Relations,* Caravelle ed. (Cambridge, Mass.: Harvard University Press, 1957; reprint, New York: Vintage Books, 1957), 315; Paul Y. Hammond, *Organizing for Defense: The American Military Establishment in the Twentieth Century* (Princeton, N.J.: Princeton University Press, 1961; reprint, Westport, Conn.: Greenwood Press, 1977), 107; Roger R. Trask and Alfred Goldberg, *The Department of Defense, 1947–1997: Organization and Leaders* (Washington: OSD, 1997), 3.

3. Huntington, *Soldier and the State,* 143–62; James Clotfelter, *The Military in American Politics* (New York: Harper and Row, 1973), 10–27.

4. Huntington, *Soldier and the State,* 154.

5. Ibid., 200.

6. Hammond, *Organizing for Defense,* 53.

7. Huntington, *Soldier and the State,* 164, 251.

8. Demetrious Caraley, *The Politics of Military Unification: A Study of Conflict and the Policy Process* (New York: Columbia University Press, 1966), 5–6; Russell A. Alger, *The Spanish-American War* (New York: Harper, 1901; reprint, Freeport, N.Y.: Books for Libraries Press, 1971), 242–49; Walter Millis, *Arms and Men: A Study in American Military History* (New York: G. P. Putnam's Sons, 1956; reprint, New Brunswick: Rutgers University Press, 1984), 173.

9. Hammond, *Organizing for Defense,* 8–9, 12; Allan R. Millett and Peter Maslowski, *For the Common Defense: A Military History of the United States of America* (New York: Free Press, 1984), 263–64; James E. Hewes Jr., *From Root to McNamara: Army Organization and Administration, 1900–1963* (Washington: CMH, 1975), ix, 3–6.

10. Huntington, *Soldier and the State*, 195–203.

11. Caraley, *Politics of Military Unification*, 84, 237–39.

12. Huntington, *Soldier and the State*, 251: Millis, *Arms and Men*, 175.

13. Root, quoted in Hammond, *Organizing for Defense*, 18.

14. Vernon E. Davis, *The History of the Joint Chiefs of Staff in World War II: Organizational Development*, vol. 1, *Origin of the Joint and Combined Chiefs of Staff* (Washington: JCS, 1972), 7.

15. Ibid., 24, 42–43; Hewes, *From Root to McNamara*, 12–21.

16. Hammond, *Organizing for Defense*, 54, 61.

17. Ibid., 77, 81.

18. Edgar F. Raines Jr. and David R. Campbell, *The Army and the Joint Chiefs of Staff: Evolution of Army Ideas on the Command, Control, and Coordination of the U.S. Armed Forces, 1942–1985* (Washington: CMH, 1986), 1; Thomas D. Boettcher, *First Call: The Making of the Modern U.S. Military, 1945–1953* (Boston: Little, Brown, 1992), 7, 24, 58–59; Hammond, *Organizing for Defense*, 6.

19. Carl H. Builder, *The Masks of War: American Military Styles in Strategy and Analysis* (Baltimore: Johns Hopkins University Press, 1989), 18–19.

20. Davis, *History of the Joint Chiefs of Staff*, 1:11, 28–29.

21. Ibid., 1:37.

22. Hammond, *Organizing for Defense*, 8.

23. Ibid., 8,9, 30, 53, 61; Huntington, *Soldier and the State*, 247, 263.

24. Roger Burlingame, *General Billy Mitchell: Champion of Air Defense* (New York: McGraw-Hill, 1952), 109.

25. Davis, *History of the Joint Chiefs of Staff*, 1:37, 241–42.

26. Ibid., xi.

27. Davis, *History of the Joint Chiefs of Staff*, 1:245–46.

28. Hammond, *Organizing for Defense*, 113–22, 145–58.

29. Huntington, *Soldier and the State*, 318–24.

30. Eric Larrabee, *Commander in Chief: Franklin Delano Roosevelt, His Lieutenants, and Their War* (New York: Harper and Row, 1987), 17.

31. William Frye, *Marshall: Citizen Soldier* (Indianapolis: Bobbs-Merrill, 1947), 347, 325.

32. Ibid., 325.

33. Hammond, *Organizing for Defense*, 185.

34. JCS Special Committee for Reorganization of National Defense, *Report of the Joint Chiefs of Staff Special Committee for Reorganization of National Defense*, Apr., 1945, 5; Larrabee, *Commander in Chief*, 105.

35. Huntington, *Soldier and the State*, 315–24; 354–55.

36. Hammond, *Organizing for Defense*, 170–75, 349–51.

37. Ibid., 318–19; Boettcher, *First Call*, 21.

38. Huntington, *Soldier and the State*, 336; Townsend Hoopes and Douglas Brinkley, *Driven Patriot: The Life and Times of James Forrestal* (New York: Alfred A. Knopf, 1992), 345.

39. Huntington, *Soldier and the State*, 335–36; U.S. Congress, Senate, Committee on Military Affairs, *Department of Armed Forces, Department of Military Security: Hearings*

before the Committee on Military Affairs, 79th Cong., 1st sess., Oct. 17, 18, 19, 22, 23, 24, 30, and 31; Nov. 2, 7, 8, 9, 14, 15, 16, 17, 23, 29, and 30; and Dec. 4, 5, 6, 7, 10, 13, 14, 15, and 17, 1945, 521.

40. Victor Lasky, *J.F.K.: The Man and the Myth* (New York: Macmillan, 1963), facing 1.

41. Davis, *History of the Joint Chiefs of Staff,* 1:246–50.

42. Raines and Campbell, *Army and the Joint Chiefs,* 20–21.

43. Hoopes and Brinkley, *Driven Patriot,* 320.

44. Raines and Campbell, *Army and the Joint Chiefs,* 32–33.

45. Ibid., 33.

46. JCS Special Committee, *Report of the Joint Chiefs,* 1, 8, 17.

47. Raines and Campbell, *Army and the Joint Chiefs,* 36; Larrabee, *Commander in Chief,* 24; Leonard Mosley, *Marshall: Hero for Our Times* (New York: Hearst Books, 1982), 122; Caraley, *Politics of Military Unification,* 31–32, 90.

48. Raines and Campbell, *Army and the Joint Chiefs,* 37; Boettcher, *First Call,* 22.

49. Harry S. Truman, *Memoirs of Harry S. Truman: 1946–1952, Years of Trial and Hope* (Garden City, N.Y.: Doubleday, 1956; reprint, New York: Smithmark, 1996), 46–47; Truman, "Our Armed Forces Must Be Unified," *Collier's,* Aug. 26, 1944, reprinted in U.S. Congress, Senate, Committee on Military Affairs, *Department of Armed Forces, Department of Military Security,* 192.

50. Historical Division, Joint Secretariat, *Organizational Development of the Joint Chiefs of Staff, 1942–1989* (Washington: JCS, 1989), 12; Caraley, *Politics of Military Unification,* 38.

51. Trask and Goldberg, *Department of Defense,* 4; Hoopes and Brinkley, *Driven Patriot,* 319; Victor H. Krulak, *First to Fight: An Inside View of the U.S. Marine Corps* (Annapolis: Naval Institute Press, 1984; reprint, New York: Pocket Books, 1991), 26.

52. Henry L. Stimson and McGeorge Bundy, *On Active Service in Peace and War* (New York: Harper and Brothers, 1948), 506.

53. Ibid.

54. Hoopes and Brinkley, *Driven Patriot,* 325; Alice C. Cole et al., eds., *The Department of Defense: Documents on Establishment and Organization, 1949–1978* (Washington: OSD, 1978), 11.

55. Hoopes and Brinkley, *Driven Patriot,* 328.

56. Ibid., 328–29.

57. Caraley, *Politics of Military Unification,* 189–94; Huntington, *Soldier and the State,* 415, 422–23.

58. Huntington, *Soldier and the State,* 428–37.

59. Eisenhower, quoted in Cole et al., eds., *Department of Defense,* 177.

60. Walter Millis, ed., *The Forrestal Diaries* (New York: Viking Press, 1951), 299.

61. Trask and Goldberg, *Department of Defense,* 14; Hoopes and Brinkley, *Driven Patriot,* 423.

62. Hoopes and Brinkley, *Driven Patriot,* 423.

63. Ibid., 423–24.

64. Ibid., 424.

65. Hoover Commission, quoted in Hoopes and Brinkley, *Driven Patriot,* 424.

66. Trask and Goldberg, *Department of Defense,* 20–25.

67. Eisenhower, quoted in Cole et al., eds., *Department of Defense*, 175.

68. Trask and Goldberg, *Department of Defense*, 25–27.

69. Committee on the Defense Establishment, *Report to Senator Kennedy*, Dec. 5, 1960, 6.

70. Ibid., 9–14; Theodore C. Sorensen, *Kennedy* (New York: Harper and Row, 1965), 238, 269; Trask and Goldberg, *Department of Defense*, 32.

71. Arthur M. Schlesinger Jr., *A Thousand Days: John F. Kennedy in the White House* (Boston: Houghton Mifflin, 1965), 295; H. R. McMaster, *Dereliction of Duty: Lyndon Johnson, Robert McNamara, the Joint Chiefs of Staff, and the Lies That Led to Vietnam* (New York: Harper Collins, 1997), 6, 8–9; Peter Wyden, *Bay of Pigs: The Untold Story* (New York: Simon and Schuster, 1979), 307; Sorensen, *Kennedy*, 347.

72. David C. Jones, "What's Wrong With Our Defense Establishment," *NYT Magazine*, Nov. 7, 1982, 70.

73. Peter P. Wallace, *Military Command Authority: Constitutional, Statutory, and Regulatory Bases* (Cambridge, Mass.: Harvard University, Center for Information Policy Research, 1983), 55–56.

74. Trask and Goldberg, *Department of Defense*, 34–35.

75. Richard A. Gabriel, *Military Incompetence: Why the American Military Doesn't Win* (New York: Hill and Wang, 1985), 61–83.

76. Richard C. Steadman, *Report to the Secretary of Defense on the National Military Command Structure* (Washington: GPO, 1978), 52–53.

77. Harold Brown, *Thinking About National Security: Defense and Foreign Policy in a Dangerous World* (Boulder, Colo.: Westview Press, 1983), 207.

78. Gabriel, *Military Incompetence*, 85.

79. Donald Bruce Johnson, comp., *National Party Platforms of 1980* (Urbana: University of Illinois, 1982), 177, 206, 210.

80. U.S. Congress, House, Committee on Armed Services, *Reorganization Proposals for the Joint Chiefs of Staff—1985: Hearings before the Investigations Subcommittee*, 99th Cong., 1st sess., HASC no. 99-10, June 13, 19, and 26, 1985, 61.

Chapter 2. Jones Breaks Ranks

1. David C. Jones, author interview, Sept. 25, 1995.

2. Archie D. Barrett, author interview, Sept. 28, 1994.

3. Barrett quoted in Linda Head Flanagan, "The Goldwater-Nichols Act: The Politics of Defense Reorganization," case study, Kennedy School of Government, Harvard University, 1992.

4. Jones interview, Sept. 25, 1995.

5. David C. Jones and William K. Brehm, author interview, Feb. 15, 1996.

6. Jones interview, Sept. 25, 1995.

7. Jones also knew that the "firestorm" a year earlier over his potential dismissal shielded him against such action.

8. Jones interview, Sept. 25, 1995.

9. Congress, House, Committee on Armed Services, *Military Posture and H.R. 5968:*

Hearings before the Committee on Armed Services, 97th Cong., 2d sess., pt. 1, *Military Posture*, HASC no. 97-33, 337.

10. Raines and Campbell, *Army and the Joint Chiefs*, 149. General Marshall, the army chief of staff at the time, picked Collins to serve as the War Department spokesman on unification.

11. *Military Posture*, HASC no. 97-33, 337–40.

12. Jones interview, Sept. 25, 1995.

13. *Military Posture*, HASC no. 97-33, 471.

14. Jones and Brehm interview.

15. *Military Posture*, HASC no. 97-33, 504–505.

16. David C. Jones, "Why the Joint Chiefs of Staff Must Change," *Directors & Boards* 6, no. 3 (winter, 1982): 4–13.

17. Flanagan, "Goldwater-Nichols Act," 6.

18. Frank C. Carlucci, handwritten note to David C. Jones, Jan. 20, 1982, a.n. 330-84-0002, box 20, folder 020 JCS (Jan.–Apr.), SD.

19. A slightly abridged version of Jones's article appeared in *Directors & Boards*. References are to the full text of the article, which appeared in Jones, "Why the Joint Chiefs of Staff Must Change," *AFJ*, Mar., 1982, 62.

20. John Chancellor, "Joint Chiefs Called Cumbersome," *NBC Nightly News*, Feb. 17, 1982, as reported in *Radio-TV Defense Dialog*, DoD, Feb. 18, 1982.

21. Michael Getler, "Chairman Asks Major Changes in Joint Chiefs," *WP*, Feb. 18, 1982, 1; Walter S. Mossberg, "Joint Chiefs Chairman Seeks More Powers In Order to Offset Interservice Rivalries," *WSJ*, Feb. 18, 1982, 6; articles also appeared in the *NYT*, *Baltimore Sun*, *Los Angeles Times*, and *Philadelphia Inquirer*.

22. Richard Halloran, "Q.&A.: Gen. David C. Jones: Retiring Chief Speaks Out on Military Council," *NYT*, Feb. 25, 1982, B14; Drew Middleton, "Joint Chiefs: Changes Due," *NYT*, Mar. 1, 1982, D10.

23. Caspar W. Weinberger, "Weekly Report on Defense Activities," memorandum for the president, Feb. 26, 1982, a.n. 330-84-0002, box 18, folder 020 DoD (Jan.–Mar.), SD.

24. Jones interview, Sept. 25, 1995.

25. Undated draft attached to Weinberger, "Weekly Report on Defense Activities."

26. Caspar W. Weinberger, author interview, Oct. 27, 1998.

27. Lisa Myers, "Reagan to Dismiss Gen. Jones," *Washington Star*, Dec. 19, 1980, 1.

28. Jones interview, Sept. 25, 1995.

29. Michael Getler, "Brown Cautions Against Ousting Joint Chiefs Head," *WP*, Dec. 22, 1980, A1.

30. James R. Schlesinger, "The 'Charge' Against Gen. Jones," *WP*, Jan. 1, 1981, A21.

31. Caspar W. Weinberger, *Fighting For Peace: Seven Critical Years in the Pentagon* (New York: Warner Books, 1990), 86.

32. Edward C. Meyer quoted in Mark Perry, *Four Stars: The Inside Story of the Forty-Year Battle between the Joint Chiefs of Staff and America's Civilian Leaders* (Boston: Houghton Mifflin, 1989), 254.

33. Bernard Weinraub, "General Named Head of Chiefs: David Charles Jones," *NYT*, Apr. 6, 1978, B4.

34. "He Is Exasperated with People About Half the Time," *Time*, Oct. 29, 1979, 29.

35. William K. Brehm, handwritten notes of CSSG interview of Bob Barrow, July 22, 1981, WKB.

36. Perry, *Four Stars*, 254, 298.

37. "Team Player for the Joint Chiefs," *Time*, Apr. 17, 1978, 16.

38. Bernard Weinraub, "Joint Chiefs Losing Sway Under Carter," *NYT*, July 6, 1978, A11.

39. "Team Player," 14.

40. Fred S. Hoffman, "Gen. Jones to Be Retained As Joint Chiefs Chairman," *WP*, Feb. 10, 1981, A2.

41. Jones, "Why the Joint Chiefs of Staff Must Change."

42. Jones interview, Sept. 25, 1995.

43. "He Is Exasperated," 29.

44. Jones interview, Sept. 25, 1995.

45. Jones and Brehm interview.

46. Congress, Senate, Committee on Armed Services, *Nominations of David C. Jones, Thomas B. Hayward, and Lew Allen Jr.: Hearings before the Committee on Armed Services*, 95th Cong., 2d sess., May 18 and 22, 1978, 107–10.

47. Jones interviews, Sept. 25, 1995, and May 12, 1999.

48. The planning phase was named Operation Rice Bowl.

49. Paul B. Ryan, *The Iranian Rescue Mission: Why It Failed* (Annapolis: Naval Institute Press, 1985), 113.

50. Joint Staff, "Report on the Iranian Hostage Rescue Mission," undated draft, JCS.

51. The DoD definition of special operations: operations conducted by specially organized, trained, and equipped military and paramilitary force to achieve military, political, economic, or informational objectives by unconventional military means in hostile, denied, or politically sensitive areas.

52. Jones interview, May 12, 1999.

53. Special Operations Review Group, *Rescue Mission Report* (Washington: DoD, 1980), vi.

54. Otto Kreisher, "Desert One," *Air Force Magazine*, Jan., 1999, 60.

55. Gabriel, *Military Incompetence*, 107.

56. Ibid., 104.

57. Ryan, *Iranian Rescue Mission*, 28–29.

58. Gabriel, *Military Incompetence*, 103.

59. James H. Kyle, *The Guts to Try: the Untold Story of the Iran Hostage Rescue Mission by the On-Scene Desert Commander* (New York: Orion Books, 1990), 34.

60. Gabriel, *Military Incompetence*, 105.

61. Jones interview, May 12, 1999.

62. Gabriel, *Military Incompetence*, 106–107; Ryan, *Iranian Rescue Mission*, 12–13.

63. Ryan, *Iranian Rescue Mission*, 41.

64. Gabriel, *Military Incompetence*, 110–11.

65. Ibid., 99.

66. Kyle, *Guts to Try*, 283.

67. Special Operations Review Group, *Rescue Mission Report*, 50.

68. Jones interviews, Sept. 25, 1995, and May 12, 1999.

69. Congress, Senate, Committee on Armed Services, *Nomination of David C. Jones: Hearing before the Committee on Armed Services*, June 16, 1980, 13–14; Jones interview, Sept. 25, 1995.

70. *Nomination of David C. Jones*, 14–15.

71. Flanagan, "Goldwater-Nichols Act," 6.

72. Jones interview, Sept. 25, 1995.

73. Ibid., May 12, 1999 (emphasis in original).

74. Ibid., Sept. 25, 1995.

75. David C. Jones to Barry M. Goldwater, Jan. 29, 1981, provided by Gerald J. Smith.

76. Jones and Brehm interview.

77. Brehm interview.

78. Jones and Brehm interview.

79. Jones and Brehm interview; William K. Brehm to author, May 24, 1999.

80. William K. Brehm, "Meeting with the Chairman, JCS in regard to the Special Study of Joint Activities, May 28, 1981," memorandum for record, May 29, 1981, WKB.

81. William K. Brehm to author, Mar. 14, 1996.

82. Brehm interview.

83. William K. Brehm to Richard Danzig, June 15, 1981, WKB.

84. Jones and Brehm interview.

85. William K. Brehm, handwritten notes of meeting with Lew Allen, July 6, 1981, WKB.

86. William K. Brehm, handwritten notes of meeting with Tom Hayward, July 6, 1981, WKB.

87. Adm. Thomas B. Hayward, "Improving the Effectiveness of the Joint Chiefs of Staff," a concept paper forwarded by memorandum for General Jones, General Allen, General Meyer, General Barrow, "Joint Chiefs of Staff," Jan. 15, 1981, a.n. 330-84-0002, box 20, folder 020 JCS (May–Sept.), SD.

88. A. S. Moreau, "JCS," message to CNO, Dec. 24, 1980; and Capt. C. S. Campbell, USN, "How to Reestablish the JCS as a Creditable Agency," point paper, Dec. 22, 1980, both in box 15, folder "Review of JCS Credibility," OPNAV.

89. Hayward, "Improving the Effectiveness."

90. Jerry J. Burcham, handwritten notes of meeting with Adm. Moorer, July 7, 1981, WKB.

91. William K. Brehm to Gen. David C. Jones, July 21, 1981, WKB.

92. William K. Brehm, handwritten notes of meeting with Bob Barrow, July 22, 1981, WKB.

93. William K. Brehm, handwritten notes of meeting with Shy [Meyer], Oct. 7, 1981, WKB.

94. Donn A. Starry, "Review of Strategic Planning," critique of the Pentagon's strategic planning process, Sept. 3, 1981, WKB.

95. CSSG, "The JCS Organization—Talking Points—Meetings With the Service Chiefs," two-page outline, n.d., WKB.

96. William K. Brehm, handwritten notes of meetings with Lew Allen and Perry Smith, Dec. 4 and 11, 1981, WKB.

97. William K. Brehm, handwritten notes of meeting with Bob Barrow, Dec. 9, 1981, WKB.

98. William K. Brehm to David C. Jones, Dec. 10, 1981, WKB.

99. William K. Brehm, handwritten notes of meeting with Shy [Meyer] and Jack [Vessey], Dec. 23, 1981, WKB.

100. Burcham, "Meeting with CNO, December 28," typed summary of meeting, n.d., WKB.

101. Hayward, "Improving the Effectiveness."

102. Brehm to author, Mar. 14, 1996.

103. J. D. Hittle, "Defense Reorganization (memo #2)," memorandum for Secretary of the Navy, Sept. 10, 1981, box 7A, folder "Personnel Issues—Hittle memos," JFL (emphasis in original).

104. J. D. Hittle, "Defense Organization," memorandum for Secretary of the Navy, Oct. 22, 1981, ibid.

105. J. D. Hittle, "Defense Organizations," memorandum for Secretary of the Navy, Nov. 4, 1981, ibid.

106. J. D. Hittle, "Defense Reorganization," memorandum for Secretary of the Navy, n.d., ibid.

107. Thomas B. Hayward to author, Oct. 30, 1998.

108. Jones and Brehm interview.

109. CSSG, *The Organization and Functions of the JCS: Report for the Chairman, Joint Chiefs of Staff* (Arlington, Va.: Systems Research and Applications Corp., Apr., 1982).

110. Brehm interview.

111. Hayward to author.

112. Flanagan, "Goldwater-Nichols Act," 1.

113. Halloran, "Q.&A."

114. William K. Brehm, handwritten notes of meeting with Dave Jones and Paul Gorman, Jan. 27, 1982, WKB.

115. Jones and Brehm interview.

116. Ibid.

Chapter 3. The House Fires the First Shot

1. Except where otherwise noted, all quotations and observations by Archie D. Barrett are from author interviews conducted Sept. 28 and Nov. 1, 1994.

2. United States Military Academy, *The 1957 Howitzer* (New York: Comet Press, 1957), 308.

3. "Darts and Laurels," *AFJ*, Oct., 1983, 107.

4. Richard C. White, "Subcommittee to Consider Joint Chiefs of Staff Reorganization," press release, Mar. 11, 1982, ADB.

5. Author interview with former HASC staff member.

6. *Howitzer*, 308.

7. Barrett, *Reappraising Defense Organization*, xix–xx.

8. Ibid., 13.

9. Archie D. Barrett to Gen. David C. Jones, Apr. 14, 1982, ADB.

10. Gen. David C. Jones to Archie D. Barrett, May 10, 1982, ADB.

11. Barrett, *Reappraising Defense Organization,* xxv.

12. Richard Halloran, "Choice for Top U.S. Soldier," *NYT,* Mar. 5, 1982, B9.

13. Richard Halloran, "Needed: A Leader for the Joint Chiefs," *NYT,* Feb. 1, 1982, 12.

14. Charles W. Corddry, "Reagan picks Vessey to head Joint Chiefs," *Baltimore Sun,* Mar. 5, 1982, 1; Stephen Engelberg, "Military chairman chosen 'for leadership'," *Norfolk Virginian-Pilot,* Mar. 9, 1982, A1.

15. Caspar W. Weinberger, "Weekly Report on Defense Activities," memorandum for the president, Mar. 12, 1982, a.n. 330-84-0002, box 18, folder 020 DoD (Jan.–Mar.), SD.

16. Corddry, "Reagan picks Vessey," 1.

17. Phil Gailey, "Tough Submariner for Navy's Helm: James David Watkins," and Bernard Weinraub, "Fighter Pilot at the Top: Charles Alvin Gabriel," *NYT,* Mar. 19, 1982, B5.

18. Crowe, *Line of Fire,* 146–47.

19. Edward C. Meyer, "The JCS—How Much Reform Is Needed?," *AFJ,* Apr., 1982, 82–90.

20. Jones interview, Feb. 15, 1996.

21. Deborah M. Kyle and Benjamin F. Schemmer, "Navy, Marines Adamantly Oppose JCS Reforms Most Others Tell Congress Are Long Overdue," *AFJ,* June, 1982, 61.

22. John W. Vessey Jr., handwritten letter to Chairman White, Dec. 2, 1982, ADB.

23. Caspar W. Weinberger to Melvin Price, Apr. 2, 1982, a.n. 330-84-0002, box 20, folder 020 JCS (Jan.–Apr.), SD.

24. Caspar W. Weinberger, "Weekly Report on Defense Activities," memorandum for the president, Apr. 23, 1982, a.n. 330-84-0002, box 18, folder 020 DoD (Apr.–May), SD.

25. Quoted in Drew Middleton, "Army Chief of Staff Urges a Broad Reorganization," *NYT,* Mar. 31, 1982, 19.

26. Archie D. Barrett, author interview, Feb. 9, 1996.

27. Congress, House, Committee on Armed Services, Investigations Subcommittee, *Reorganization Proposals for the Joint Chiefs of Staff: Hearings before the Investigations Subcommittee,* 97th Cong., 2d sess., 1982, HASC no. 97-47, 3, 5.

28. Ibid., 42–46; Alan Ehrenhalt and Robert E. Healy, eds., *Politics in America: Members Of Congress in Washington and at Home, 1982* (Washington: Congressional Quarterly Press, 1981), 284.

29. *Reorganization Proposals,* HASC no. 97-47, 53–56.

30. Ibid., 49.

31. Kyle and Schemmer, "Navy, Marines Adamantly Oppose," 61; Mary Anne Wood, "JCS Hearings," memorandum for Secretary Weinberger, Apr. 21, 1982, a.n. 330-84-0002, box 20, folder 020 JCS (Jan.–Apr.), SD.

32. *Reorganization Proposals,* HASC no. 97-47, 100–101.

33. Kyle and Schemmer, "Navy, Marines Adamantly Oppose," 61.

34. *Reorganization Proposals,* HASC no. 97-47, 178.

35. Ibid., 195.

36. Kyle and Schemmer, "Navy, Marines Adamantly Oppose," 61.

37. Former HASC staff member interview.

38. David C. Jones, "Joint Organization," Memorandum for the Secretary of Defense," June 17, 1982, a.n. 330-84-0002, box 20, folder 020 JCS (May–Sept.), SD.

39. Deborah M. Kyle, "JCS Reform Legislation Imminent," *AFJ*, July, 1982, 12.

40. William P. Clark, "Current Hearings on the JCS System," memorandum for Caspar W. Weinberger, June 28, 1982, a.n. 330-84-0002, box 20, folder 020 JCS (May–Sept.), SD.

41. Allan A. Myer, "Reorganization of the Joint Chiefs of Staff," memorandum for William P. Clark, June 21, 1982, RRL.

42. Caspar W. Weinberger, "Hearings on JCS Reorganization," memorandum for the president, July 19, 1982; and Mary Anne Wood, "Memorandum for the President on JCS Reorganization," memorandum for Secretary Weinberger, July 16, 1982, both in a.n. 330-84-0002, box 20, folder 020 JCS (May–Sept.), SD.

43. John W. Vessey Jr., "Hearings on JCS Reorganization," memorandum for the secretary of defense, July 12, 1982, a.n. 330-84-0002, box 20, folder 020 JCS (May–Sept.), SD.

44. Allan A. Myer, "JCS Reorganization," memorandum for William P. Clark, July 27, 1982, RRL.

45. William P. Clark, "Hearings on JCS Reorganization," memorandum for the president, Aug. 7, 1982, RRL.

46. Congress, Senate, Committee on Armed Services, *Nomination of John W. Vessey Jr., to Be Chairman of the Joint Chiefs of Staff: Hearing before the Committee on Armed Services*, 97th Cong., 2d sess., May 11, 1982, 8.

47. Ibid., 9; Kyle and Schemmer, "Navy, Marines, Adamantly Oppose," 64.

48. *Reorganization Proposals*, HASC no. 97-47, 956–58.

49. Ibid., 958–60.

50. Congress, House, *Joint Chiefs of Staff Reorganization Act of 1982*, 97th Cong., 2d sess., H.R. 6828.

51. *Reorganization Proposals*, HASC no. 97-47, 971–93.

52. "*AFJ* Talks To Congress: Richard C. White," *AFJ*, Sept., 1982, 18.

53. Caspar W. Weinberger, "Weekly Report of Defense Activities," memorandum for the president, Aug. 13, 1982, a.n. 330-84-0002, box 18, folder 020 DoD (Aug.–Oct.), SD.

54. Former HASC staff member interview.

55. Congress, House, Committee on Armed Services, *Full Committee Consideration of H.R. 6954*, 97th Cong., 2d sess., Aug. 11, 1982.

56. Former HASC staff member interview.

57. Congress, House, *Joint Chiefs of Staff Reorganization Act, H.R. 6954*, 97th Cong., 2d sess., *Congressional Record—House* (Aug. 16, 1982): 21226–35; Caspar W. Weinberger, "Weekly Report of Defense Activities," memorandum for the president, Aug. 20, 1982, a.n. 330-84-0002, box 18, folder 020 DoD (Aug.–Oct.), SD.

58. Maxwell D. Taylor, "This Is No Way to Reform the Joint Chiefs," *WP*, Sept. 10, 1982, 27.

59. Barrett to Tim Ahern [Associated Press], Oct. 29, 1982, ADB.

60. John W. Vessey Jr., "JCS Reorganization," memorandum for the secretary of defense, Nov. 22, 1982, a.n. 330-84-0002, box 20, folder 020 JCS (Oct.–Dec.), SD.

61. Caspar W. Weinberger, "Organization of the Joint Chiefs of Staff (JCS)," memorandum for the president, Nov. 26, 1982, a.n. 330-84-0002, box 20, folder 020 JCS (Oct.–Dec.), SD.

62. Caspar W. Weinberger to Richard C. White, Dec. 8, 1982, ADB.

Chapter 4. Texas Politics

1. Rhett B. Dawson, author interview, Mar. 30, 2001. Dawson attended the meeting during which White put his request to Tower "on a personal basis."

2. Congress, Senate, Senator Nunn of Georgia speaking for an amendment requiring a JCS reorganization study, 97th Cong., 2d sess., *Congressional Record—Senate* (May 13, 1982), 10054–67.

3. Drew Middleton, "Army Chief of Staff Urges a Broad Reorganization," *NYT*, Mar. 31, 1982, 19. Tower made his quoted statement on March 25 to *AFJI*.

4. *Congressional Record*, May 13, 1982, 10067–68.

5. Rick Finn, "Hearings on the JCS Organization," memorandum to Senator Tower through Rhett Dawson and Jim Locher, Sept. 16, 1982, box 1938, folder "Initial Work on DOD Reorganization," SASC. Copy also in RDF.

6. Rick Finn, "Hearings on the JCS Organization," Memorandum for Senator Tower through Jim McGovern and Jim Locher, Nov. 15, 1982, RDF; Deborah M. Kyle, "Slow Go On JCS Reform: Service Rhetoric on Promoting Only the Best?," *AFJ*, Nov., 1982, 13.

7. David S. Broder, "Tower Exits The Senate," *WP*, Aug. 28, 1983, C7.

8. John G. Tower, *Consequences: A Personal and Political Memoir* (Boston: Little, Brown, 1991), 62.

9. Finn, "Hearings on the JCS Organization," Nov. 15, 1982; Finn, "Scheduling of JCS Hearing," memorandum to Jim McGovern, Nov. 19, 1982, RDF.

10. Jones, "What's Wrong," 38.

11. Dwight D. Eisenhower, *At Ease: Stories I Tell to Friends* (Garden City, N.Y.: Doubleday, 1967), 315.

12. Fred Reed, "Soldiering: Dislike for Pentagon Common in Military," *Washington Times*, Aug. 19, 1982, 3.

13. Ibid.

14. Ibid.

15. Jones, "What's Wrong," 38.

16. Maxwell D. Taylor, *The Uncertain Trumpet* (New York: Harper and Brothers, 1959), 175–76.

17. Congress, Senate, Committee on Armed Services, *Structure and Operating Procedures of the Joint Chiefs of Staff: Hearing before the Committee on Armed Services*, 97th Cong., 2d sess., Dec. 16, 1982, 2–54.

18. Lt. Col. Nevins [Joint Staff], "Summary of SASC Hearing on JCS Reorganization—16 December 1982," Dec. 16, 1982, included in briefing book for Weinberger, a.n. 330-85-0023, box 46, folder "020 JCS (May 13, 1983)," SD.

Chapter 5. Unfinished Business

1. Archie D. Barrett, author interview, Nov. 1, 1994.

2. Ehrenhalt and Healy, eds., *Politics in America*, 25; Kayla Barrett, "Auburn's Soldier Statesman," *The Auburn Alumnews*, Jan.-Feb., 1993, 6–8; Kayla Barrett, "Working the Mill Gate," *The Auburn Alumnews*, Mar., 1993, 12–14.

3. Barrett interview, Nov. 1, 1994; G. Kim Wincup, author interview, Sept. 21, 1995.

4. Barrett interview, Nov. 1, 1994.

5. Dwayne Cox and Barbara Nelson, eds., *William F. Nichols Oral History Transcripts* (Auburn, Ala.: Auburn University, 1991), 41, 387.

6. Barrett interview, Nov. 1, 1994.

7. Wincup interview.

8. Rep. Bill Nichols, Statement to Investigations Subcommittee, Feb. 3, 1983, a.n. 89-10, box 10, folder "Investigations Febr 1983," WFN; Rep. Bill Nichols to Caspar W. Weinberger, Feb. 1, 1983, a.n. 330-85-0023, box 46, folder "020 JCS (Jan.–)," SD.

9. Ronald Reagan, "JCS Reorganization," memorandum for Caspar W. Weinberger, Jan. 12, 1983, ibid.

10. Caspar W. Weinberger to Rep. Bill Nichols, Feb. 25, 1983, a.n. 89-10, box 10, folder "Investigations March 1983," WFN.

11. Rep. Bill Nichols, "Meeting to Discuss Subcommittee Agenda," Mar. 30, 1983, a.n. 89-10, box 10, folder "Investigations Apr., 1983," WFN.

12. Barrett interview, Feb. 2, 1996; Barrett to author, June 16, 1998; Barrett, memorandum for John Ford, Apr. 18, 1983, ADB. Of the Skelton bill, Barrett said: "I felt it would be tantamount to establishing a general staff, an outcome I heartily opposed as being just as bad as the organizational arrangements we were attempting to improve."

13. William H. Taft IV to Thomas P. O'Neill, Speaker of the House of Representatives, Apr. 18, 1983, a.n. 330-85-0023, box 46, folder "020 JCS (Jan.–)," SD,

14. JCS, *Dictionary of Military and Associated Terms* (Washington: JCS, 1979), 62.

15. Deborah M. Kyle, "JCS Message to Congress: People Key to JCS Reform, Not Changes," *AFJ*, July, 1983, 6.

16. Russell A. Rourke, "JCS Reorganization—Talking Points for Telephone Call to Representative Bill Nichols," memorandum for the Secretary of Defense, Apr. 29, 1983; and Carl R. Smith, note for Russ Rourke, May 5, 1983, both in a.n. 330-85-0023, box 46, folder "020 JCS (Jan.–)," SD.

17. Barrett, "Notes on the Meeting of the Investigations Subcommittee with the Secretary of Defense and Chairman of the Joint Chiefs of Staff Concerning JCS Reorganization, May 18, 1983," memorandum to Chairman Bill Nichols, May 31, 1983, ADB.

18. In 1958, President Eisenhower recommended that the service chiefs delegate major portions of their responsibilities to the vice chiefs so that they could give priority to their JCS duties.

19. Barrett, "Notes on the Meeting," May 31, 1983.

20. Weinberger to Nichols, May 19, 1983.

21. Barrett to author, June 16, 1998.

22. Caspar W. Weinberger, "Weekly Report of Defense Activities," memorandum for the president, May 20, 1983, a.n. 330-85-0023, box 46, folder 020 DOD (Mar.–July), SD.

23. Barrett interview, Nov. 1, 1994.

24. Congress, House, Committee on Armed Services, *Reorganization Proposals for the Joint Chiefs of Staff: Hearings before the Investigations Subcommittee*, 98th Cong., 1st sess., HASC no. 98-8, June 14, 23, and 29, 1983, 2.

25. Ibid., 46, 47.

26. Congress, Senate, Committee on Armed Services, *Nominations of General Paul X. Kelley, Richard L. Armitage, and Chapman B. Cox: Hearing before the Committee on Armed Services*, 98th Cong., 1st sess., S. Hrg. 98-153, May 24, 1983, 27.

27. George C. Wilson, "Inside: The Pentagon," *WP*, Apr. 6, 1983, A17.

28. *Reorganization Proposals*, HASC no. 98-8, 64.

29. Ibid., 69.

30. Ibid., 70.

31. Barrett interview, Feb. 2, 1996.

32. Ibid., Nov. 1, 1994.

33. *Reorganization Proposals*, HASC no. 98-8, 80.

34. Barrett interview, Feb. 2, 1996.

35. *Reorganization Proposals*, HASC no. 98-8, 80.

36. Ibid., 81.

37. Ibid., 79–80. Barrow hugging Vessey is from Barrett interview, Feb. 2, 1996.

38. Barrett interview, Nov. 1, 1994.

39. Kyle, "JCS Message to Congress," 6.

40. *Reorganization Proposals*, HASC no. 98-8, 88.

41. Barrett interview, Feb. 2, 1996.

42. *Reorganization Proposals*, HASC no. 98-8, 88–109.

43. Barrett to author, June 16, 1998.

44. *Reorganization Proposals*, HASC no. 98-8, 63.

45. Barrett interview, Nov. 1, 1994.

46. Congress, House, *Joint Chiefs of Staff Reorganization Act of 1983: Report [To accompany H.R. 3718]*, 98th Cong., 1st sess., Report no. 98-382, Sept. 27, 1983, 12–17.

47. Congress, House, Committee on Armed Services, *Full Committee Consideration of H.R. 3718, H.R. 3289, and Committee Resolution Honoring the Late Honorable Larry P. McDonald*, 98th Cong., 1st sess., HASC no. 98-18, Sept. 20, 1983, 1–13.

48. Deborah M. Kyle, "House Committee Strengthens JCS Chairman/System; DOD Protests," *AFJI* (November 1983), 8.

49. Congress, House, Joint Chiefs of Staff Reorganization Act of 1983, H.R. 3718, 98th Cong., 1st sess., *Congressional Record—House* (Oct. 17, 1983), 28016–24.

50. Caspar W. Weinberger, "Weekly Report on Defense Activities," memorandum for the president, Oct. 21, 1983, a.n. 330-85-0023, box 45, folder "020 DoD (Oct.–Dec.)," SD.

51. Barrett to author, June 16, 1998.

Chapter 6. Misfire in the Senate

1. Tower, *Consequences,* 12; Michael Getler, "Sen. Tower Reported Leading Choice for Secretary of Defense," *WP,* Nov. 18, 1980, A3; Richard Burt, "Senator Tower Eyes Position in Cabinet," *NYT,* Nov. 20, 1980, B12.

2. Ehrenhalt and Healy, eds., *Politics in America,* 1147; Michael Getler, "Tower Out of Running for Pentagon," *WP,* Nov. 21, 1980, A12.

3. Dawson interview.

4. Caspar W. Weinberger, "Weekly Report of Defense Activities," memorandum for the president, July 15, 1983, a.n. 330-85-0023, box 46, folder 020 DoD (Mar.–July), SD.

5. Dawson interview.

6. Tower and his staff frequently discussed Weinberger's performance with the White House and NSC staff.

7. Tower's daily schedules and scheduling forms for May 4 and 5, 1983, boxes 1162-1 and 1163-4, JGT; Victor H. Krulak to author, Feb. 10, 1994, and author interview, Apr. 4, 1994.

8. Victor H. Krulak, *Organization for National Security: A Study* (Washington: United States Strategic Institute, 1983).

9. Krulak interview.

10. Krulak, *Organization for National Security,* 131.

11. Ibid., 101–102.

12. Ibid., 118, 125.

13. Dawson interview.

14. Krulak, *Organization for National Security,* 87.

15. Alan R. Yuspeh, author interview, Nov. 13, 1995.

16. John G. Tower, "Statement of Senator Tower, June 21, 1983," Press Office Series, box 50, folder 28, JGT.

17. Paul R. Lawrence and Jay W. Lorsch, *Developing Organizations: Diagnosis and Action* (Reading, Mass.: Addison-Wesley, 1969), 10–11.

18. Congress, Senate, Committee on Armed Services, *Structure and Operating Procedures of the Joint Chiefs of Staff: Hearing before the Committee on Armed Services,* 97th Cong., 2d sess., Dec. 16, 1982, 14.

19. Tower, *Consequences,* 247.

20. Tower, "Statement, June 21, 1983."

21. Tower, *Consequences,* 247.

22. William J. Crowe Jr., author interview, Apr. 26, 1994.

23. Congress, Senate, Committee on Armed Services, *Organization, Structure, and Decisionmaking Procedures of the Department of Defense: Hearings before the Committee on Armed Services,* 98th Cong., 1st sess., S. Hrg. 98-375, pt. 1, July 28, 1983, 2.

24. Newt Gingrich to Caspar Weinberger, July 14, 1983, a.n. 330-85-0023, box 46, folder 020 DoD (Mar.–July), SD.

25. Fred Hiatt, "Weinberger Blames Congress for Pentagon Management Problems," *WP,* July 29, 1983, 6.

26. Fred Hiatt, "Auditors Report Pentagon Spending Too Much on Parts," *WP,* July 12, 1983, 15.

27. Herblock, "I believe I do see a little something—but, after all, I've only been on this job for two and a half years," *WP*, July 20, 1983, A22; Herblock, untitled cartoon, *WP*, July 27, 1983, A20.

28. *Organization, Structure, and Decisionmaking Procedures*, S. Hrg. 98-375, pt. 1, 22.

29. Ibid., 23.

30. Caspar W. Weinberger to Newt Gingrich, Aug. 1, 1983, a.n. 330-85-0023, box 45, folder 020 DoD (Aug.–Sept.), SD.

31. Caspar W. Weinberger, "Weekly Report of Defense Activities," memorandum for the president, July 29, 1983, a.n. 330-85-0023, box 46, folder 020 DoD (Mar.–July), SD.

32. Deborah M. Kyle, "Weinberger Challenges Senate Committee At Defense Reform Hearing: Ease Up," *AFJ*, Sept., 1983, 16.

33. Dan Balz, "Sen. Tower Won't Seek Reelection," *WP*, Aug. 24, 1983, A1.

34. Pat Towell, "Reagan Will Be Hard-pressed To Articulate His Defense Policy on Hill When Tower Steps Down," *AFJ*, Oct., 1983, 16.

35. *Organization, Structure, and Decisionmaking Procedures*, S. Hrg. 98-375, pt. 1, 18.

36. Steven V. Roberts, "Expertise on Military Budget," *NYT*, Apr. 15, 1985, 16.

37. Ehrenhalt and Healy, eds., *Politics in America*, 270.

38. Michael R. Gordon, "Sam Nunn for the Defense—Georgia Boy Makes Good as Gentle Pentagon Prodder," *National Journal*, Mar. 31, 1984, 612.

39. Ehrenhalt and Healy, eds., *Politics in America*, 270.

40. Steve Coll, "Sam Nunn, Insider from the Deep Southland," *WP*, Feb. 18, 1986, B11.

41. Gordon, "Sam Nunn for the Defense," 611.

42. Roberts, "Expertise on Military Budget," 16.

43. Ehrenhalt and Healy, eds., *Politics in America*, 270.

44. Maxine Bloch and E. Mary Trow, eds., *Current Biography: Who's News and Why 1942* (New York: H. W. Wilson, 1942), 857.

45. Benis M. Frank during interview of Gen. Paul X. Kelley, July 19, 1986, U.S. Marine Corps Oral History Program, 1.

46. James M. Myatt quoted in Richard F. Smith, "Nothing was predictable," *The (Jacksonville, N.C.) Daily News*, Oct. 22, 1993, A1.

47. Congress, House, Committee on Armed Services, *Adequacy of U.S. Marine Corps Security in Beirut: Report Together with Additional and Dissenting Views of the Investigations Subcommittee*, 98th Cong., 1st sess., Committee Print no. 11, Dec. 19, 1983, 43–54.

48. Ronald H. Cole, *Operation Urgent Fury: Grenada* (Washington: Joint History Office, 1997), 63.

49. Congress, Senate, Committee on Armed Services, *The Situation in Lebanon: Hearings before the Committee on Armed Services*, 98th Cong., 1st sess., S. Hrg. 98-612, Oct. 25 and 31, 1983, 39.

50. William Claiborne, "Marine Chief 'Totally Satisfied' Beirut Had Adequate Security," *WP*, Oct. 26, 1983, A1.

51. Michael Getler, "Congressional Leaders Question the Steps Taken to Protect Marines Before Attack," *WP*, Oct. 27, 1983, A25.

52. Kelley, interview by Frank, 40.

53. *Situation in Lebanon*, S. Hrg. 98-612, 46, 47.

54. Ibid., 53, 54, 55.

55. Ibid., 55–56.

56. Ibid., 56.

57. Ibid., 57.

58. Ibid., 87.

59. Ibid., 87–88.

60. Ibid., 100.

61. Congress, Senate, Committee on Armed Services, *Organization, Structure, and Decisionmaking Procedures of the Department of Defense: Hearings before the Committee on Armed Services*, 98th Cong., 1st sess., S. Hrg. 98-375, pt. 5, Nov. 2, 1983, 182.

62. Ibid., 186.

63. Ibid., 186–87.

64. Ibid., 187.

65. Ibid., 188.

66. J. D. Hittle, "*Organization for National Security*, by LTGEN Krulak; comments and recommendations," memorandum for the Secretary of the Navy, Feb. 16, 1983, box 7A, folder Personnel Issues—Hittle Memos, JFL.

67. John G. Tower, "Grenada," memorandum for the Senate Committee on Armed Services, Nov. 9, 1983, Press Office Series, box 51, folder 3, "Grenada Memorandum," JGT.

68. Ibid.

69. Congress, Senate, Committee on Armed Services, *Organization, Structure, and Decisionmaking Procedures of the Department of Defense: Hearings before the Committee on Armed Services*, 98th Cong., 1st sess., S. Hrg. 98-375, pt. 8, Nov. 9, 1983, 329.

70. Congress, Senate, Committee on Armed Services, *Organization, Structure, and Decisionmaking Procedures of the Department of Defense: Hearings before the Committee on Armed Services*, 98th Cong., 1st sess., S. Hrg. 98-375, pt. 11, Nov. 17, 1983, 488.

71. Ibid., 489.

72. Brown, *Thinking About National Security*, 199–224.

73. Congress, Senate, Committee on Armed Services, *Organization, Structure, and Decisionmaking Procedures of the Department of Defense: Hearings before the Committee on Armed Services*, 98th Cong., 1st sess., S. Hrg. 98-375, pt. 12, Nov. 17, 1983, 517; Brown, *Thinking About National Security*, 214.

74. *Organization, Structure, and Decisionmaking Procedures*, pt. 12, 522–23.

75. Robert L. Goldich, "The Evolution of Congressional Attitudes Toward a General Staff in the 20th Century," Senate Committee on Armed Services, *Defense Organization: The Need for Change*, 99th Cong., 1st sess., S. Prt. 99-86, Oct. 16, 1985, 244–74.

Chapter 7. Beirut

1. Cox and Nelson, eds., *Nichols Oral History Transcripts*, 366; Congress, House, Congressman Nichols speaking on the issue of continued Marine presence in Lebanon, 98th Cong., 1st sess., *Congressional Record–House* (Oct. 26, 1983), 29405; Peggy Stelpflug, "Don't Forget Beirut," *Birmingham News*, Oct. 17, 1993, C1.

2. Rep. Bill Nichols, press release, Sept. 28, 1983, a.n. 89-10, box 108, folder "Press Releases 1983," WFN.

3. Stelpflug, "Don't Forget Beirut;" Barrett, author interviews, Nov. 1, 1994, and Sept. 22, 1998.

4. Congress, House, Committee on Armed Services, *Full Committee Consideration of H.R. 4370*, 99th Cong., 2nd sess., HASC no. 99-69, June 25, 1986, 2–3; Barrett interview, Nov. 1, 1994.

5. Stansfield Turner, *Terrorism and Democracy* (Boston: Houghton Mifflin, 1991), 164; Benis M. Frank, *U.S. Marines in Lebanon: 1982–1984* (Washington: History and Museums Division, Headquarters, Marine Corps, 1987), 23.

6. *Report of the DoD Commission on Beirut International Airport Terrorist Act, October 23, 1983* (Washington, D.C.: DoD Commission on Beirut International Airport Terrorist Act, 1983), 2–3.

7. Morton Kondracke, "Wading In," *New Republic*, Oct. 10, 1983, 11.

8. Roy Gutman, "Battle over Lebanon," *Foreign Service Journal*, June, 1984, 12.

9. Kondracke, "Wading In," 11.

10. Michael Getler, "Lebanon Policy Fuels Debate: Diplomats Are Bold, Pentagon Wary," *WP*, Mar. 4, 1984, 1.

11. Andrew J. Bacevich, "Discord Still: Clinton and The Military," *WP*, Jan. 3, 1999, C1.

12. Robert C. McFarlane with Zofia Smardz, *Special Trust* (New York: Cadell and Davies, 1994), 211; Bernard W. Rogers, author interview, Dec. 10, 1998; Richard Halloran, "Reagan as Military Commander," *NYT Magazine*, Jan. 15, 1984, 24; Michael Getler, "Diplomats Are Bold, Pentagon Wary," *WP*, Mar. 4, 1984, 1.

13. Thomas L. Friedman, "Weinberger Faults Marine Mission," *NYT*, Mar. 1, 1984, 8; Robert S. Dudney, "Lebanon Fallout: Strains Between Reagan, Military," *USN&WR*, Jan. 9, 1984, 21.

14. Congress, Senate, Committee on Armed Services, *The Situation in Lebanon: Hearings before the Committee on Armed Services*, 98th Cong., 1st sess., S. Hrg. 98-612, Oct. 25 and 31, 1983, 49–51; Frank, *Marines in Lebanon*, 150–51.

15. William T. Corbett, author interview, June 28, 1999.

16. John K. Cooley, *Payback: America's Long War in the Middle East* (Washington: Brassey's, 1991), 79–80.

17. David C. Martin and John Walcott, *Best Laid Plans: The Inside Story of America's War Against Terrorism* (New York: Harper and Row, 1988), 107–108.

18. Ibid.

19. William Y. Smith, author interview, Nov. 23, 1999.

20. Noel C. Koch to Sam Nunn, n.d. (Sept. 15, 1986), JRL.

21. William V. Cowan, "Intelligence, Rescue, Retaliation, and Decision-making," undated paper provided by Peter Probst, Office of the Assistant Secretary of Defense for Special Operations and Low-Intensity Conflict, Washington, D.C.

22. Ibid.

23. Koch to Nunn. At the time, many conventional officers did not view special operations personnel favorably.

24. Mary McGrory, "Ousting Kelley Wouldn't Make U.S. Role in Lebanon Any

Wiser," *WP*, Jan. 3, 1984, 3; James Kitfield, *Prodigal Soldiers* (New York: Simon and Schuster, 1995), 261.

25. Frank, *Marines in Lebanon*, 30, 71–72.

26. Cooley, *Payback*, 80–81; Corbett interview.

27. Corbett interview.

28. Daniel P. Bolger, *Americans at War: 1975–1986, an Era of Violent Peace* (Novato, Calif.: Presidio Press, 1988), 213.

29. Ibid., 150–51; Turner, *Terrorism and Democracy*, 165; John M. Collins, *America's Small Wars* (Washington: Brassey's, 1991), 193–94.

30. Rep. Bill Nichols, press release, Sept. 14, 1983, a.n. 89-10, box 108, folder "Press Releases 1983," WFN.

31. Peggy A. Stelpflug to author, Feb. 5, 1999; Joe Stelpflug, "Brother Bill," n.d.

32. Stelpflug, "Don't Forget Beirut;" Joe Stelpflug, "'Peacekeeping' endangers lives," *Auburn (Alabama) Plainsman*, Nov. 3, 1983, A5.

33. William J. Stelpflug to Rep. Bill Nichols, n.d. (late Aug./early Sept., 1983), PSt.

34. Rep. Bill Nichols to Mr. and Mrs. William J. Stelpflug, Sept. 19, 1983, PSt.

35. John M. Goshko, "House Will Consider Marines' Stay in Lebanon," *WP*, Sept. 14, 1983, A29.

36. Congress, House, Committee on Armed Services, *Full Committee Hearings on the Use of U.S. Military Personnel in Lebanon and Consideration of Report from September 24–25 Committee Delegation to Lebanon*, 98th Cong., 1st sess., HASC no. 98-28, Sept. 27 and 28, 1983, 29–30.

37. Peggy Stelpflug, notes on WFN, July 21, 1992, PSt.

38. *Full Committee Hearings*, HASC no. 98-28, 30, 35–36.

39. Nichols, press release, Sept. 28, 1983; Stelpflug, "Don't Forget Beirut."

40. T. R. Reid, "House Votes 18-Month Limit On Marines' Use in Lebanon," *WP*, Sept. 29, 1983, A1.

41. Ibid.

42. Congress, House, Committee on Armed Services, *Adequacy of U.S. Marine Corps Security in Beirut: Report together with Additional and Dissenting Views of the Investigations Subcommittee*, Committee Print No. 11, 98th Cong., 1st sess., Dec. 19, 1983, 52.

43. Samuel S. Stratton, "Let's Get Out of Lebanon," *WP*, Oct. 21, 1983, A19.

44. Frank, *Marines in Lebanon*, 94.

45. Ibid., 2–3; Michael Petit, *Peacekeepers at War: A Marine's Account of the Beirut Catastrophe* (Boston: Faber and Faber, 1986), 6; David Zucchino, "Recalling those who came in peace: Blast scarred those present, thousands more who were not," *Daily News (Jacksonville, N.C.)*, Oct. 22, 1993, 1A.

46. Eric Hammel, *The Root: The Marines in Beirut, August 1982–February 1984* (San Diego: Harcourt Brace Jovanovich, 1985), 320, 350, 381, 385.

47. Barrett interview, Sept. 22, 1998.

48. Congress, House, Committee on Armed Services, *Review of Adequacy of Security Arrangements for Marines in Lebanon and Plans for Improving That Security: Hearings before the Committee on Armed Services and the Investigations Subcommittee*, 98th Cong., 1st sess., HASC no. 98-58, Nov. 1, 2, 12, and 13; Dec. 8, 9, 14, and 15, 1983, 26; "Congressman Nichols," staff typed note, n.d., PSt; Billy Atkinson to Ms. Peggy Stelpflug, Oct. 27, 1993, PSt.

49. Kelley, interview by Frank, 41.

50. Gen. Paul X. Kelley, author interview, July 2, 1999. The commission was titled the "DoD Commission on Beirut International Airport Terrorist Act of October 23, 1983."

51. Barrett interview, Sept. 22, 1998; *Review of Adequacy of Security*, HASC no. 98-58, 82–83.

52. Barrett interview, Sept. 22, 1998.

53. McGrory, "Ousting Kelley"; Congress, House, Committee on Armed Services, *Adequacy of U.S. Marine Corps Security in Beirut: Summary of Findings and Conclusions (To Accompany Committee Print no. 11—Basic Report) of the Investigations Subcommittee*, Committee Print no. 11A, 98th Cong., 1st sess., Dec. 19, 1983, 2.

54. *Review of Adequacy of Security*, HASC no. 98-58, 592, 620, 603, 622.

55. David Rogers, "House Panel Faults Marine Commander for Errors in Beirut Truck-Bomb Attack," *WSJ*, Dec. 20, 1983, 5; Margaret Shapiro, "House Unit Faults U.S. Security in Oct. 23 Bombing," *WP*, Dec. 20, 1983, 1.

56. HASC, *Adequacy of U.S. Marine Corps Security in Beirut: Summary of Findings and Conclusions*, 1.

57. HASC, *Adequacy of U.S. Marine Corps Security in Beirut: Report*, 47 (emphasis in original).

58. Shapiro, "House Unit Faults U.S. Security."

59. Barrett interviews, Nov. 1, 1994, and Sept. 22, 1998.

60. Ibid., Nov. 1, 1994; HASC, *Adequacy of U.S. Marine Corps Security in Beirut: Summary of Findings and Conclusions*, 1.

61. John F. Lehman Jr., *Command of the Seas* (New York: Charles Scribner's Sons, 1988), 324; Crowe, *Line of Fire*, 150.

62. See Fred Hiatt, "President Accepts Blame in Attack On Marine Base: Pentagon Is Critical of Security in Beirut," *WP*, Dec. 28, 1983, 1, and "Report Hits U.S. Reliance on Force in Lebanon," *WP*, Dec. 29, 1983, A1; and James Wallace, "Time to Pull Out of Lebanon?" *USN&WR*, Jan. 9, 1984, 18.

63. Lehman, *Command of the Seas*, 320.

64. Hiatt, "Report Hits U.S. Reliance."

65. DoD Commission, *Report*, 6–7, 56.

66. Ibid., 122, 123, 130.

67. Ibid., 128, 127.

68. "Marines Reclassify 241 Killed in Lebanon as Battle Deaths," *NYT*, Jan. 17, 1984, 15; "Marine Deaths Reclassified," *WP*, Jan. 17, 1984, 13.

69. DoD Commission, *Report*, 130, 133.

70. Gabriel, Military Incompetence, 140–41; George C. Wilson, *Super Carrier: An Inside Account of Life Aboard the World's Most Powerful Ship, the USS John F. Kennedy* (New York: Macmillan, 1986), 155.

71. Ibid., 129.

72. Quoted in Martin and Walcott, *Best Laid Plans*, 142.

73. Wilson, *Super Carrier*, 133, 144.

74. Martin and Walcott, *Best Laid Plans*, 141.

75. Wilson, *Super Carrier*, 151–52; Gabriel, *Military Incompetence*, 142 (quotation).

76. Wilson, *Super Carrier*, 133, 155.

77. Martin and Walcott, *Best Laid Plans*, 144.

78. Title 10, *U.S. Code*, sec. 124: Combatant commands: establishment; composition; functions; administration and support.

79. Barrett interview, Sept. 22, 1998.

80. Robert L. J. Long, author interview, Jan. 9, 1999.

81. Dwight D. Eisenhower, "Message to the Congress," Apr. 3, 1958, in Cole et al., eds., *Department of Defense*, 179.

82. Blue Ribbon Defense Panel, *Report to the President and the Secretary of Defense on the Department of Defense* (Washington: GPO, 1970), 50.

83. John H. Cushman, *Command and Control of Theater Forces: The Korea Command and Other Cases* (Cambridge, Mass.: Harvard University, 1986), ii.

84. John H. Cushman, *Command and Control of Theater Forces: Adequacy* (Cambridge, Mass.: Harvard University, 1983), ES-3 and ES-6.

85. John H. Cushman to author, July 8, 1999.

86. Cushman, *Adequacy*, 3-49.

87. Ibid., 3-48–3-58.

88. Cushman, *Korea Command and Other Cases*, 5-23.

89. Ibid., 5-29, 5-39; *Unified Action Armed Forces* (Washington: JCS, 1974), 49 (changes 1–4 included).

90. William Y. Smith interview, Nov. 23, 1999; Bernard E. Trainor, author interview, Nov. 22, 1999.

91. DoD Commission, *Report*, 54–55, 131–32.

92. Rogers interview, Dec. 10, 1998; HASC, *Adequacy of U.S. Marine Corps Security in Beirut: Report*, 36.

93. Cushman, *Korea Command and Other Cases*, 5-39, 5-40.

94. William Y. Smith, author interviews, Nov. 23, 1999, and Jan. 14, 2000.

95. Corbett interview.

96. Rogers interview, Dec. 10, 1998.

97. Long interview.

98. Martin and Walcott, *Best Laid Plans*, 134–37.

99. Rogers interview, Dec. 10, 1998.

100. Collins, *America's Small Wars*, 194; "Failure in Lebanon," *WP*, Feb. 17, 1984, A22.

101. Jeffrey Record, "The Beirut Disaster Could Have Been Avoided," *WP*, Nov. 16, 1983, A27.

102. Trainor interview, Nov. 22, 1999.

103. Philip Taubman and Joel Brinkley, "The U.S. Marine Tragedy: Causes and Responsibilities," *NYT*, Dec. 11, 1983, 49.

104. Record, "Beirut Disaster."

105. Bolger, *Americans at War*, 244, 246.

106. DoD Commission, *Report*, 88.

107. Ibid., 248.

108. Gabriel, *Military Incompetence*, 139.

109. Philip Taubman and Joel Brinkley, "Security: As Threats Grew, Defenses Were Improvised," *NYT*, Dec. 11, 1983, 49.

110. Ralph A. Hallenbeck, *Military Force as an Instrument of U.S. Foreign Policy:*

Intervention in Lebanon, August 1982–February 1984 (New York: Praeger, 1991), 151;
DoD Commission, *Report*, 130; HASC, *Adequacy of U.S. Marine Corps Security in Beirut:
Summary of Findings and Conclusions*, 2.

111. Martin and Walcott, *Best Laid Plans*, 130.

112. Cooley, *Payback*, 81.

113. Martin and Walcott, *Best Laid Plans*, 108, 366 (quotation).

114. *Field Manual 100-5: Field Service Regulations, Operations* (Washington: Department of the Army, 1949), 264–65.

115. Richard Halloran, "Pentagon Moves to Simplify Chain of Command to Beirut," *NYT*, Feb. 23, 1984, 10.

116. Ronald Reagan, "Remarks and a Question-and-Answer Session With Reporters on the Pentagon Report on the Security of United States Marines in Lebanon," Dec. 27, 1983, *Public Papers of the Presidents of the United States: Ronald Reagan, 1983, Book 2, July 2 to December 31, 1983* (Washington: GPO, 1985), 1748.

117. "The Easy Way Out," *WSJ*, Dec. 29, 1983, 12; "Blame, but No Answer," *Los Angeles Times*, Dec. 28, 1983, II-4; "Accepting Blame," *Christian Science Monitor*, Dec. 29, 1983, 13; "Washington Whispers," *USN&WR*, Jan. 9, 1984, 12.

118. Dudney, "Lebanon Fallout," 21.

119. Fred Hiatt and David Hoffman, "Shelling Restraint Ordered By 'Surprised' Weinberger," *WP*, Feb. 14, 1984, 1; Philip Taubman, "Navy Secretary Said to Favor Reprimands for Beirut Blast," *NYT*, Jan. 10, 1984, 1; Fred Hiatt, "Military Officials Respond to Marine Report," *WP*, Jan. 10, 1984, 13.

120. Weinberger, *Fighting for Peace*, 166; Lehman, *Command of the Seas*, 325–26; Hammel, *Root*, 424.

121. Long interview.

122. Gen. Edward C. "Shy" Meyer, author interview, Feb. 1, 1999.

123. Trainor interview, Nov. 22, 1999.

124. Thomas E. Ricks, *Making the Corps* (New York: Scribner, 1997), 142.

125. Barrett interview, Sept. 22, 1998.

126. Ibid., Nov. 1, 1994.

Chapter 8. Scholars and Old Soldiers

1. James A. Smith, *The Idea Brokers: Think Tanks and the Rise of the New Policy Elite* (New York: Free Press, 1991), xiii and xv.

2. Gregg Easterbrook, "Ideas Move Nations: How Conservative Think Tanks Have Helped to Transform the Terms of Political Debate," *Atlantic*, Jan., 1986, 66.

3. Smith, *Idea Brokers*, xv, xiii, xiv, xv–xvi, 211, 214, 215.

4. Peter W. Chiarelli, "Introduction" in U. S. Military Academy, *Final Proceedings, Senior Conference XX: The "Military Reform" Debate: Directions for the Defense Establishment for the Remainder of the Century: Final Proceedings*, ed. Peter W. Chiarelli (West Point, N.Y.: United States Military Academy, 1983), 1.

5. Daniel J. Kaufman, author interview, Dec. 10, 1997.

6. Gary Hart, "The Case for Military Reform," *WSJ*, Jan. 23, 1981, 20.

7. George C. Wilson, "Military Pessimism Aired," *WP*, June 6, 1982, 7.

8. James Fallows, *National Defense* (New York: Random House, 1981).

9. Chiarelli, ed., *Final Proceedings, Senior Conference XX*, 47.

10. Asa A. Clark IV et al., eds., *The Defense Reform Debate: Issues and Analysis* (Baltimore: Johns Hopkins University Press, 1984).

11. Edwin A. Deagle, author interview, Nov. 20, 1995.

12. Barry M. Blechman, author interview, Dec. 16, 1999.

13. Ibid.

14. Philip A. Odeen to William Brehm, June 20, 1983, WKB.

15. Blechman interview; Barry M. Blechman to Sam Nunn, Oct. 14, 1983, JRL; Deagle interview.

16. Easterbrook, "Ideas Move Nations."

17. Smith, *Idea Brokers*, 210, 212.

18. Blechman interview; Deagle interview.

19. Perry, *Four Stars*, 329.

20. Lloyd Grove, "For Bill Cohen, A Midlife Correction," *WP*, Jan. 26, 1996, F1.

21. Biographical Note in the William S. Cohen Papers at the Raymond H. Fogler Library, University of Maine; Grove, "For Bill Cohen."

22. Blechman interview; William Spencer Johnson, "Center for Strategic and International Studies (CSIS), Georgetown University, Military Reform Project," memorandum for the Secretary of the Navy, Nov. 16, 1984, JFL.

23. T. R. Fedyszyn, "CSIS Defense Organization Project, Status of," memorandum for the Deputy Undersecretary of the Navy (Policy), n.d., and "AEI Public Policy Week: DoD Management, Organization and Resource Allocation Panel," memorandum for the Deputy Undersecretary of the Navy (Policy), n.d. (Dec., 1984), both in box 10, folder "CSIS Defense Organization Project (1985-018)," OPNAV; E. B. Potter, *Admiral Arleigh Burke* (New York: Random House, 1990), 445.

24. CSIS Defense Organization Project, *Toward a More Effective Defense: The Final Report of the Defense Organization Project* (Washington: Center for Strategic and International Studies, Georgetown University, 1985); Barry M. Blechman and William J. Lynn, eds., *Toward a More Effective Defense: Report of the Defense Organization Project* (Cambridge, Mass.: Ballinger, 1985).

25. CSIS Defense Organization Project, *Toward a More Effective Defense*, 1–3, 13–15, 25–26.

26. Blechman interview; Easterbrook, "Ideas Move Nations."

27. Mark Perry, "How Cap Weinberger Lost the Fight over Defense Reform," *American Politics*, Feb., 1988, 4.

28. Easterbrook, "Ideas Move Nations."

29. Melissa Healy and Michael Duffy, "Joint Chiefs Draw Defense," *Defense Week*, Feb. 4, 1985, 14; Blechman interview.

30. John F. Lehman Jr. to Admiral Moorer, Dan McMichael, and Morrie Liebman, n.d., box 5, folder "OI [Organizational Issues]—JCS Reorg—1985" (folder 7 of 8), JFL.

31. Deagle interview; Blechman interview.

32. CSIS Defense Organization Project, *Toward a More Effective Defense*, 56; Blechman interview.

33. CSIS Defense Organization Project, *Toward a More Effective Defense*, v–vi, 56–57.

34. Thomas L. McNaugher with Roger L. Sperry, "Improving Military Coordination: The Goldwater-Nichols Reorganization of the Department of Defense," in *Who Makes Public Policy: The Struggle for Control Between Congress and the Executive*, ed. Robert S. Gilmour and Alexis A. Halley (Chatham, N.J.: Chatham House, 1994), 232.

35. Blechman interview.

36. Theodore J. Crackel to author, Nov. 21, 2000.

37. "Vying for the President's Ear," *The Middle East*, June, 1985, 53.

38. Theodore J. Crackel, author interview, Sept. 3, 1998.

39. Theodore J. Crackel, "Meeting with Michelle Van Cleave," memorandum to Burt Pines, Sept. 13, 1983, TJC.

40. Crackel interview; Theodore J. Crackel, "Defense Assessment Project: Quarterly Report," memoranda to Burt Pines, Nov. 17, 1983, and Mar. 14, 1984, TJC.

41. Crackel interview.

42. William Spencer Johnson, author interview, Jan. 11, 2000.

43. Theodore J. Crackel, undated draft of paper identified as FILE: B:CRACK6.MSS— FIFTH DRAFT, box 3, folder "OI—Defense Reorganization, 1984" (folder 2 of 5), JFL; Theodore J. Crackel, "Reforming 'Military Reform,'" *The Heritage Foundation Backgrounder*, Dec. 12, 1983.

44. John F. Lehman Jr., undated note to Dick Allen with Heritage backgrounder, "Reforming 'Military Reform,'" attached, box 7A, folder "Personnel Issues—Allen, Richard," JFL (quotation, emphasis in original); Lehman, *Command of the Seas*, 66–67, 106–109.

45. Crackel, untitled draft of paper, n.d., box 3, folder "OI—Defense Reorganization, 1984" (folder 2 of 5), JFL.

46. Crackel interview; Theodore J. Crackel to author, Mar. 26, 1984, TJC.

47. Johnson, author interviews, Jan. 11 and Feb. 2, 2000.

48. Crackel interview; Ed Feulner, untitled memorandum to Burt Pines, Apr. 16, 1984 (2:30 P.M.), TJC.

49. Theodore J. Crackel, "Defense Assessment," in Stuart M. Butler et al., *Mandate for Leadership II: Continuing the Conservative Revolution* (Washington: Heritage Foundation, 1984), 431–48; McNaugher with Sperry, "Improving Military Coordination," 232 (quotation).

50. Crackel, "Defense Assessment," 433, 442–43.

51. Archie D. Barrett to Ted Crackel, Dec. 13, 1984, TJC.

52. Crackel to author, Nov. 21, 2000.

53. Robert J. Art, author interview, Nov. 14, 1994; "Talking Paper on the NDU-Proposed Conference on DoD," a.n. 330-84-0002, box 20, folder 020 JCS (Oct.–Dec.) 1982, SD (quotation).

54. Art interview.

55. Robert J. Art, "Introduction: Pentagon Reform in Comparative and Historical Perspective," in *Reorganizing America's Defense: Leadership in War and Peace*, ed. Robert J. Art et al. (Washington: Pergamon-Brassey's, 1985), xi–xii; Samuel P. Huntington, author interview, Nov. 14, 1994.

56. McNaugher with Sperry, "Improving Military Coordination," 232.

57. J. D. Hittle, "'Defense Study,'" memorandum for the Secretary of the Navy, Dec. 2, 1983, box 3, folder "OI—Defense Reorganization, 1983" (folder 1 of 5), JFL.

58. Smith, *Idea Brokers*, 154, 158.

59. Gregory L. Vistica, *Fall from Glory: The Men Who Sank the U.S. Navy* (New York: Simon and Schuster, 1995), 166–67.

60. Thomas D. Bell Jr., "The Joint Chiefs Should Remain Joint," *NYT*, Mar. 22, 1985, 31.

61. Committee on Civilian-Military Relationships, *An Analysis of Proposed Joint Chiefs of Staff Reorganization* (Indianapolis: Hudson Institute, 1984), ii.

62. D. O. Cooke, "Report by the Committee on Civilian/Military Relationship—Hudson Institute," memorandum for record, Oct. 2, 1984, a.n. 330-86-0046, box 16, folder "020 JCS," SD.

63. Jake W. Stewart, "JCS Reform: Hudson Institute Study," memorandum for Admiral Watkins, Sept. 26, 1984, CNO (emphasis in original).

64. R. W. Komer, "Opposing View on JCS," letter to the editor, *Defense Week*, Oct. 1, 1984, 3.

65. John M. Poindexter, note to Robert C. McFarlane, n.d., attached on top of Philip A. Dur, "Hudson Institute Report," RRL; Colin L. Powell [Weinberger's senior military assistant], note for Rhett Dawson [staff director of the Packard Commission], Aug. 23, 1985, a.n. 330-87-006, box 15, folder "020 JCS," SD. Note reads: "SecDef wanted to make sure this [attached Hudson report] was available to the [Packard] Commission."

66. James D. Watkins, "Reorganization of the Joint Chiefs of Staff," memorandum to the Deputy Chief of Naval Operations (Plans, Policy and Operations), n.d., CNO.

67. James D. Watkins to Senator Nunn, Mar. 29, 1985, SASC; CNO Select Panel, *Report of the Chief of Naval Operations Select Panel: Reorganization of the National Security Organization* (Washington: Office of the CNO, 1985), I-5–I-8, I-10, I-12–I-13.

68. Seth Cropsey to Rear Adm. James E. Service, Oct. 17, 1984, OPNAV.

69. Seth Cropsey, "Newport JCS Conference," memorandum for the Secretary of the Navy, May 8, 1985, box 5, folder OI—JCS Reorg—1985 (folder 2 of 8), JFL.

70. Naval War College, *JCS Reform: Proceedings of the Conference* (Newport, R.I.: Naval War College, 1985), 3–4, 11–15, 47, 57.

71. Cropsey, "Newport JCS Conference."

Chapter 9. Nichols Runs Tower's Blockade

1. Barrett interview, Nov. 1, 1994.

2. Wilson, *Super Carrier*, 214–15.

3. Fred Kaplan, "Naval firepower and its impact," *Boston Globe*, Feb. 10, 1984, 9; idem., "US shelling of Lebanon is called ineffective," *Boston Globe*, Feb. 18, 1984, 1.

4. Gabriel, *Military Incompetence*, 145; Kaplan, "US shelling of Lebanon."

5. Gabriel, *Military Incompetence*, 144.

6. James Locher, "Schedule for DoD Organization Project," memorandum for Jim McGovern, Feb. 1, 1984, box 1918, folder "Locher Chron File—Jan.–Mar., 1984," SASC.

7. Barbara B. Brown, author interview, Dec. 1, 1998.

8. James McGovern, "Committee Staff Report on the Organizational Structure and Decision-making Process of the Department of Defense," memorandum to Senator

Tower and Senator Nunn, Pre- and Post-Senate Papers, folder "Staff Report on the Organization and Decision-Making Procedures of the DoD," JGT; "Agenda for Chairman Tower's Meeting with Bud McFarlane (5/9/84)," talking points, n.d., Defense, Foreign Relations, and Armed Services Committee Series, box 972, folder 7, JGT.

9. John Tower to Barry Goldwater, May 15, 1984, box 1905, SASC; David J. Berteau, author interview, Sept. 16, 1999.

10. Chapman B. Cox to Melvin Price, May 24, 1984, box 1, 1984 conference, "JCS FY1985 Authorization Bill H.R. 5167" (1984 changes to title 10), ADB.

11. House, Congressman Price of Illinois speaking for a block of eleven amendments, H.R. 5167, Department of Defense Authorization Act, 1985, 98th Cong., 2d sess., *Congressional Record* (May 30, 1984): 14478, 14482.

12. "Talking Points for Chairman's Meeting with Secretary Weinberger, June 4, 1984," undated point paper, Defense, Foreign Relations, Armed Services Committee Series, box 972, folder 7, JGT (emphasis in original).

13. Sen. Sam Nunn, "Provision on JCS Re-organization in the House Authorization Act," memorandum to Senator Tower, June 6, 1984, RDF (emphasis in original).

14. Ibid.; Archie D. Barrett, "Legislative Workload," memorandum to Chairman Bill Nichols, June 7, 1984, box 1, file "JCS FY1985 Authorization Bill H.R. 5167" (1984 changes to title 10), ADB.

15. Nunn, "Provision on JCS Re-organization."

16. Congress, Senate, Senator Eagleton of Missouri speaking for an amendment for improvement in system for providing military advice to the president, NSC, and secretary of defense, 98th Cong., 2d sess., *Congressional Record* (June 18, 1984): 16924–29.

17. Ibid., 16929.

18. Ibid., 16930.

19. Ibid., 16931.

20. Jeffrey H. Smith, author interview, June 16, 1998.

21. Dawson interview.

22. Michael Glennon, "Democrats' Panel Defends More for Defense," *Congressional Quarterly*, Mar. 31, 1984, 730, 732, 735.

23. Ibid., 730.

24. Ibid.

25. Sen. Sam Nunn, Oral History, Sept. 9, 1996, the Sam Nunn Archive, Special Collections, Robert W. Woodruff Library, Emory University, Atlanta, Ga. The author interviewed Senator Nunn, and Arnold L. Punaro, Jeffrey H. Smith, Richard D. Finn Jr., and Richard DeBobes provided additional comments.

26. Archie D. Barrett, "Outline of Remarks to Authorization Conference Initiating JCS Discussion," memorandum to Chairman Bill Nichols, June 27, 1984, box 1, file "JCS FY1985 Authorization Bill H.R. 5167" (1984 changes to title 10), ADB; Archie D. Barrett, "Prospects for Agreement Between House and Senate Conferees on Specific JCS Provisions," memorandum to Chairman Bill Nichols, June 26, 1984, and "Conference Statement of Honorable Melvin Price: JCS," undated statement, both in ibid.

27. John Lehman, "Let's Stop Trying to Be Prussians: An Old Bad Idea Surfaces Again," *WP*, June 10, 1984.

28. Archie D. Barrett, "Attached Communication on the JCS Bill," memorandum to Chairman Bill Nichols, July 17, 1984, a.n. 89-10, box 20, untitled folder (includes 1984 defense authorization conference materials), WFN.

29. J. L. Holloway III to Commodore Paul D. Miller, USN, with Association of Naval Aviation Blue Stripe #6, dated July 12, 1984, attached, July 23, 1984, box 4, folder "OI—JCS Reorg—1984" (folder 4 of 4), JFL.

30. Archie D. Barrett, "Staff Negotiations on the JCS Issue," memorandum to G. Kim Wincup, Sept. 22, 1984, box 1, file "JCS FY1985 Authorization Bill H.R. 5167" (1984 changes to title 10), ADB.

31. "Status of Negotiations on JCS Reorganization," undated point paper, a.n. 89-10, box 20, untitled folder (includes 1984 defense authorization conference materials), WFN; Rick Finn, "Status of Negotiations on JCS Reorganization," point paper, Sept. 22, 1984, RDF.

32. Barrett, "Staff Negotiations."

33. Wincup interview.

34. Barrett interviews, Nov. 1, 1994, and July 29, 1999.

35. Ibid., Nov. 1, 1994.

36. Rep. Bill Nichols, handwritten talking points, n.d., a.n. 89-10, box 20, untitled folder (includes 1984 defense authorization conference materials), WFN.

37. Barrett interview, July 29, 1999.

38. Ibid., Nov. 1, 1994.

39. Bruce Porter, Phil Odeen, and Bill Lynn, "DoD Organizational Reform and the House-Senate Conference," memorandum for Senator Nunn, Sept. 22, 1984, box 1, folder "JCS FY1985 Authorization Bill H.R. 5167" (1984 changes to title 10), ADB.

40. Kitfield, *Prodigal Soldiers*, 279–80; Wincup interview.

41. Barrett interview, Nov. 1, 1994.

42. Wincup interview.

43. Sam Nunn, Oral History, Sept. 9, 1996; Congress, House, *Department of Defense Authorization Act, 1985*, 98th Cong., 2d sess., report 98-1080, Sept. 26, 1984, 330–31. Bruce Porter, Phil Odeen, and Bill Lynn prepared the first draft of the report language.

44. Nunn Oral History. Nunn had originated the idea of the questions. Bruce Porter, Phil Odeen, and Bill Lynn provided a draft of these questions for Nunn.

45. David J. Berteau, "JCS Reorganization," memorandum for the Deputy Secretary of Defense, Sept. 25, 1984, DJB.

46. Barrett interview, Nov. 1, 1994.

47. Kitfield, *Prodigal Soldiers*, 282.

48. Barrett interview, Nov. 1, 1994.

Chapter 10. Crowe Makes Waves

1. Crowe, *Line of Fire*, 148–49.

2. Neil Ulman, "Four-Star Fighter: Adm. William Crowe Battles for Recognition Of His NATO Area," *WSJ*, Aug. 31, 1982, 1.

3. "William Crowe: A Diplomat Among Warriors," *USN&WR*, Oct. 7, 1985, 13.

4. Jennet Conant with John Barry, "An Officer and Intellectual," *Newsweek*, July 22, 1985, 29.

5. John Keegan, *The Second World War* (New York: Viking Penguin, 1990), 255.

6. Congress, Joint Committee on the Investigation of the Pearl Harbor Attack, *Hearings before Joint Committee on the Investigation of the Pearl Harbor Attack*, 79th Cong., 1st and 2d sess., pt. 14 (1946): 1406.

7. Ibid., 1328.

8. Wallace, *Military Command Authority*, 44.

9. Roberta Wohlstetter, *Pearl Harbor: Warning and Decision* (Stanford: Stanford University Press, 1962), 10.

10. Congress, Joint Committee on the Investigation of the Pearl Harbor Attack, *Investigation of the Pearl Harbor Attack: Report of the Joint Committee on the Investigation of the Pearl Harbor Attack*, 79th Cong., 2d sess., 1946, 153.

11. Ibid., 245.

12. Louis Morton, *Strategy and Command: The First Two Years* (Washington: Office of the Chief of Military History, Department of the Army), 144.

13. Ronald H. Spector, *Eagle Against the Sun: The American War with Japan* (New York: Free Press, 1985), 144–45.

14. Robert E. Sherwood, *Roosevelt and Hopkins: An Intimate History* (New York: Harper and Brothers, 1948), 455 (emphasis in original).

15. Morton, *Strategy and Command*, 244.

16. Nathan Miller, *War at Sea: A Naval History of World War II* (New York: Scribner, 1995), 232.

17. Morton, *Strategy and Command*, 225.

18. Spector, *Eagle Against the Sun*, 145.

19. Ibid., 185; Morton, *Strategy and Command*, 294–301.

20. Spector, *Eagle Against the Sun*, 185.

21. Ibid., 185–86; Morton, *Strategy and Command*, 301–304.

22. Thomas J. Cutler, *The Battle of Leyte Gulf, 23–26 October 1944: The Dramatic Full Story, Based on the Latest Research, of the Greatest Naval Battle in History* (New York: HarperCollins, 1994), 60.

23. Charles A. Willoughby and John Chamberlain, *MacArthur, 1941–1951* (New York: McGraw-Hill, 1954), 246.

24. Ibid., 250.

25. Miller, *War at Sea*, 468.

26. Cutler, *Battle of Leyte Gulf*, 251.

27. Miller, *War at Sea*, 474.

28. Willoughby and Chamberlain, *MacArthur*, 255–56.

29. Ibid., 255.

30. Miller, *War at Sea*, 475.

31. Willoughby and Chamberlain, *MacArthur*, 254–55.

32. Ibid., 255.

33. Cutler, *Battle of Leyte Gulf*, 295.

34. Ibid., 212.

35. Grace Person Hayes, *The History of the Joint Chiefs of Staff in World War II: The*

War Against Japan (Annapolis: Naval Institute Press, 1982), 693; Spector, *Eagle Against the Sun*, 541.

36. Ronald H. Cole et al., *The History of the Unified Command Plan: 1946–1993* (Washington: Joint History Office, 1995), 26.

37. *Commander in Chief Pacific Command History*, vol. 4, 1969 (Camp H. M. Smith, Hi.: Historical Branch, Headquarters, Pacific Command, 1970), 170.

38. *Commander in Chief Pacific Command History*, vol. 4, 1968 (Camp H. M. Smith, Hi.: Historical Branch, Headquarters, Pacific Command, 1969), 230–31.

39. Wallace, *Military Command Authority*, 52; "*Banner* Operations (Action No. 1)," undated point paper, FOIA Mandatory Review, case no. NLJ 97-309, doc. no. 22a, Lyndon Baines Johnson Library, Austin, Tex.

40. House Committee on Armed Services, Special Subcommittee on the USS *Pueblo, Inquiry into the U.S.S. Pueblo and EC-121 Plane Incidents*, Report of the Special Subcommittee on the USS *Pueblo*, 91st Cong., 1st sess., July 28, 1969, HASC no. 91-12, 1654; Thomas P. Coakley, ed., *C3I: Issues of Command and Control* (Washington: NDU, 1991), 9.

41. *Inquiry into the U.S.S. Pueblo*, HASC no. 91-12, 1655.

42. Trevor Armbrister, *A Matter of Accountability: The True Story of the Pueblo Affair* (New York: Coward-McCann, 1970), 10, 13.

43. *Inquiry into the U.S.S. Pueblo*, HASC no. 91-12, 1661; Wallace, *Military Command Authority*, 53.

44. Crowe, *Line of Fire*, 66.

45. *Inquiry into the U.S.S. Pueblo*, HASC no. 91-12, 1622.

46. Ibid., 1669.

47. Robert R. Simmons, *The Pueblo, EC-121, and Mayaguez Incidents: Some Continuities and Changes* (Baltimore: Occasional Papers/Reprints Series in Contemporary Asian Studies, 1978), 6.

48. Wallace, *Military Command Authority*, 54.

49. Edward R. Murphy Jr. with Curt Gentry, *Second in Command: The Uncensored Account of the Capture of the Spy Ship Pueblo* (New York: Holt, Rinehart, and Winston, 1971), 379.

50. *Inquiry into the U.S.S. Pueblo*, HASC no. 91-12, 1619.

51. William J. Crowe Jr., author interview, Nov. 3, 1999.

52. Ibid., Apr. 26, 1994.

53. Crowe, *Line of Fire*, 150.

54. Crowe interview.

55. Crowe, *Line of Fire*, 148, 150.

56. Ibid., 117.

57. Ibid., 118; Robert C. McFarlane, author interview, Feb. 8, 1999.

58. Jeffrey Smith interview.

59. J. A. Baldwin, author interview, Sept. 7, 1999.

60. Jeffrey Smith interview.

61. Congress, Senate, Committee on Armed Services, *Nominations of Chapman B. Cox To Be Assistant Secretary of Defense for Force Management and Personnel and Sylvester R. Foley Jr. To Be Assistant Secretary of Energy for Defense Programs: Hearings before the Committee on Armed Services*, 99th Cong., 1st sess., Dec. 12, 1985, S. Hrg. 99-509, 25.

62. Jeffrey Smith interview.

Chapter 11. Goldwater and Nunn Close Ranks

1. David Shribman, "Sen. Goldwater, More Unpredictable Than Ever, Troubles Pentagon Brass on the Military Budget," *Wall Street Journal*, Feb. 20, 1985, 64; Bill Keller, "Rattling the Pentagon's Coffee Cups," *NYT*, Dec. 17, 1984, B12.

2. Barry M. Goldwater, author interview, May 8, 1995.

3. Robert Byrne, *1,911 Best Things Anybody Ever Said* (New York: Fawcett Columbine, 1988), 227; Barry Goldwater to Sam Nunn, June 9, 1985, box C-1, folder 11, BMG.

4. Goldwater interview.

5. Barry Goldwater, "Memo to the Staff of the Senate Armed Services Committee," n.d., SASC.

6. Goldwater interview; Goldwater quoted in *Sacramento Bee*, Jan. 8, 1964.

7. Goldwater interview.

8. Ibid.

9. Barry M. Goldwater, *With No Apologies: The Personal and Political Memoirs of United States Senator Barry M. Goldwater* (New York: William Morrow, 1979), 23.

10. Lee Edwards, *Goldwater: The Man Who Made a Revolution* (Washington: Regnery, 1995), 16.

11. Barry Goldwater to John Tower, Aug. 27, 1984, JGT.

12. Barry Goldwater to Carl F. Ullrich, June 27, 1985, box C-1, folder 11, BMG.

13. "We Should Be Spending More," *USN&WR*, Oct. 15, 1973, 76.

14. Barry Goldwater, Colonel, USAFR, "A Concept for the Future Organization of the United States Armed Forces," 1958, BMG.

15. Goldwater with Casserly, *Goldwater*, 221.

16. Barry Goldwater, "The Vietnam War," undated article for a Georgia newspaper attached to a letter to Mack Mattingly, Mar. 13, 1985, box C-1, folder 15, BMG.

17. Goldwater with Casserly, *Goldwater*, 227–30.

18. Ibid., 246.

19. Gerald J. Smith, author interview, May, 1994; Goldwater with Casserly, *Goldwater*, 344, 347 (Beckwith quotation).

20. Ibid., 348.

21. Ibid., 349; Gerald J. Smith interview; Goldwater with Casserly, *Goldwater*, 349.

22. Gerald J. Smith interview.

23. Anne Q. Hoy, "A Leader, Not a Legislator," *Arizona Republic*, Jan. 18, 1987, 49 (Rhodes and Udall quotations); Jerry Kramer, "1953: Matt Dillon goes to Washington," *Arizona Republic*, Jan. 18, 1987, 22–23.

24. Gerald J. Smith interview.

25. Goldwater with Casserly, *Goldwater*, 340.

26. Nunn Oral History.

27. Goldwater with Casserly, *Goldwater*, 342; Jeffrey Smith interview.

28. Gerald J. Smith interview.

29. Ibid.; Nunn Oral History.

30. Gerald J. Smith interview.

31. Arnold L. Punaro, author interview, Mar. 29, 2001.

32. Nunn Oral History.

33. Barry Goldwater to James F. McGovern, Jan. 28, 1985, SASC.

34. Barry Goldwater and Sam Nunn, "Dear Committee Colleague," Jan. 31, 1985, SASC.

35. Bill Keller, "Overhaul Is Urged for Top Military: Panel Seeks to Expand Power of Chairman of Joint Chiefs," NYT, Jan. 22, 1985, 1.

36. Walter Andrews, "Reagan, Weinberger happy with form of Joint Chiefs of Staff," Washington Times, Jan. 23, 1985, 2.

37. "Military-Reform Study on Target," Atlanta Constitution, Jan. 25, 1985, 18A.

38. "A Real Defense Need," Chicago Tribune, Jan. 28, 1985, 14.

39. Barry Goldwater and Sam Nunn to Caspar W. Weinberger, Feb. 4, 1985, SASC.

40. Barry Goldwater, handwritten notes on Locher, Finn, and Smith, "Chapter on the Unified and Specified Commands," memorandum for Senator Goldwater and Senator Nunn, Apr. 24, 1985, SASC. Goldwater's interest in the use of history was confirmed in a discussion with Terry Emerson, a longtime member of Goldwater's personal staff.

41. Gerald J. Smith interview.

42. Barry Goldwater, "Goldwater Writes CIA Director Scorching Letter," WP, Apr. 11, 1984, A17.

43. Goldwater interview.

44. Caspar Weinberger to Barry M. Goldwater, Mar. 5, 1985, SASC.

45. Michael Ganley, "DoD Leaders Defend Command Structure, But Joint Commanders Ask for More Say," AFJ, June, 1985, 26.

46. Weinberger to Goldwater, Mar. 5, 1985.

47. "A New Chief for the Joint Chiefs," Newsweek, Jan. 28, 1985, 17.

48. Sam Nunn, author interview, July 14, 1995; Nunn Oral History; Jeffrey Smith interview.

49. Jeffrey Smith interview.

50. Crowe interview.

51. Gerald J. Smith interview; Barry Goldwater to Sam Nunn, May 3, 1985, box C-1, folder 12, BMG.

52. Sam Nunn to Barry Goldwater, May 3, 1985, box C-1, folder 12, BMG.

53. Nunn Oral History.

54. Gerald J. Smith interview.

55. Nunn interview; Goldwater to Nunn, June 9, 1985.

56. Nunn interview.

57. Ibid.; Goldwater to Nunn, June 9, 1985.

58. Goldwater with Casserly, Goldwater, 342.

59. Nunn Oral History; Nunn interview.

60. John G. Kester, "Caution: Leaner Times Ahead," Military Logistics Forum, Jan.–Feb., 1985, 8.

Chapter 12. Weinberger Stonewalls

1. Nicholas Lemann, "The Peacetime War," Atlantic, Oct., 1984, 88.

2. Nunn Oral History.

3. Hedrick Smith, The Power Game: How Washington Works (New York: Random House, 1988), 46.

4. Weinberger, *Fighting for Peace*, 5.

5. Ibid.; Lemann, "Peacetime War," 78.

6. Richard A. Stubbing with Richard A. Mendel, *The Defense Game: An Insider Explores the Astonishing Realities of America's Defense Establishment* (New York: Harper and Row, 1986), 368–69.

7. Robert C. Toth, "Weinberger: Deep Man, Complex Job," *Los Angeles Times*, Aug. 9, 1981, 1.

8. Lemann, "Peacetime War," 80, 82.

9. Stubbing with Mendel, *Defense Game*, 369; Lemann, "Peacetime War," 82.

10. Stubbing with Mendel, *Defense Game*, 370.

11. Toth, "Weinberger."

12. Stubbing with Mendel, *Defense Game*, 372–73.

13. Lou Cannon, *President Reagan: The Role of a Lifetime* (New York: Touchstone, 1991), 83; Toth, "Weinberger."

14. Rowland Evans and Robert Novak, "Why Weinberger? Why Carlucci?" *WP*, Dec. 19, 1980, A21.

15. Rowland Evans and Robert Novak, "Antidotes to Weinberger," *WP*, Jan. 9, 1981, A15.

16. George C. Wilson, "Weinberger: Pentagon Chief to Be Something of Contradiction," *WP*, Dec. 12, 1980, A8.

17. Congress, Senate, Senator Helms of North Carolina speaking against the nomination of Mr. Caspar W. Weinberger to be secretary of defense, 97th Cong., 1st sess., *Congressional Record—Senate* (Jan. 20, 1981): 554–58.

18. Walter S. Mossberg, "Pentagon's Captain: A Big Winner in 1981, Weinberger Is Having a Tougher Time Now," *WSJ*, May 25, 1982, 1.

19. Stubbing with Mendel, *Defense Game*, 376.

20. Lemann, "Peacetime War," 76, 72.

21. Stubbing with Mendel, *Defense Game*, 376.

22. William H. Taft IV, "Counterpoint to History: Basis of Opposition," (speech presented at the Louis A. Bantle Symposium, "Goldwater-Nichols from 1986 to 2006: The Department of Defense Reorganization Act Past, Present, Future," Oct. 15, 1998, Syracuse University).

23. Stubbing with Mendel, *Defense Game*, 381; Smith, *Power Game*, 204.

24. Crowe interview.

25. George P. Shultz, *Turmoil and Triumph: My Years as Secretary of State* (New York: Charles Scribner's Sons, 1993), 144.

26. Smith, *Power Game*, 209–10.

27. Dawson interview.

28. Smith, *Power Game*, 209; Barry Goldwater to John Tower, Aug. 27, 1984, JGT; Robert Helms Papers, RRL.

29. Smith, *Power Game*, 204, 207.

30. Martin Schram, "Caspar One-Note's Military March," *WP*, Apr. 18, 1982, B1.

31. Phil Gailey and Warren Weaver Jr., "Briefing: Backfire from MX," *NYT*, Dec. 18, 1982, 14.

32. McFarlane interview, Feb. 8, 1999.

33. Stubbing with Mendel, *Defense Game*, 380.

34. Colin L. Powell with Joseph E. Persico, *My American Journey* (New York: Random House, 1995), 256, 294.

35. Toth, "Weinberger."

36. Powell with Persico, *My American Journey*, 314.

37. Colin Powell, quoted in Cannon, *President Reagan*, 405; Powell with Persico, *My American Journey*, 294.

38. Berteau interview, Sept. 16, 1999.

39. Lemann, "Peacetime War," 90.

40. Cannon, *President Reagan*, 187; Ed Rollins with Tom DeFrank, *Bare Knuckles and Back Rooms: My Life in American Politics* (New York: Broadway Books, 1996), 105.

41. Weinberger, *Fighting for Peace*, 71.

42. John Bartlett, *Familiar Quotations*, ed. Emily Morrison Beck et al., 15th ed. (Boston: Little, Brown, 1980), 743.

43. Crowe interview, Apr. 26, 1994; Taft, "Counterpoint to History."

44. Weinberger interview.

45. Taft, "Counterpoint to History"; Smith, *Power Game*, 209.

46. Weinberger interview.

47. Berteau interview, Sept. 16, 1999.

48. Crowe, *Line of Fire*, 151.

49. Weinberger interview.

50. John W. Vessey, interview by Alfred Goldberg and Stuart Rochester, Jan. 29, 1993, OSD Historical Office, Arlington, Va.

51. John W. Vessey, interview by Alfred Goldberg and Maurice Matloff, Mar. 21, 1990, ibid.

52. Gen. Edward C. "Shy" Meyer, author interview, June 25, 1998.

53. Steven Strasser, "Reagan's Kind of Hero," *Newsweek*, Nov. 14, 1983, 41.

54. Vessey interview, Mar. 21, 1990; Meyer interview, June 25, 1998.

55. Cushman, *Korea Command and Other Cases*, 5-74–5-83.

56. Robert F. Futrell, *The United States Air Force in Korea: 1950–1953* (Washington: Office of Air Force History, 1983), 44–45, 693.

57. Ibid., 48–50, 55.

58. Richard P. Hallion, *The Naval Air War in Korea* (Baltimore: Nautical and Aviation, 1986), 41–44.

59. Ibid., 44–45.

60. Futrell, *United States Air Force in Korea*, 55.

61. Doris Condit, *History of the Office of the Secretary of Defense*, vol. II, *The Test of War: 1950–1953* (Arlington, Va.: OSD Historical Office, 1988), 13, 513, 518.

62. Arthur T. Hadley, *The Straw Giant: Triumph and Failure: America's Armed Forces* (New York: Random House, 1986), 111–12.

63. Condit, *History*, 518–19.

64. Vessey interview, Mar. 21, 1990.

65. Meyer interview, June 25, 1998.

66. Vessey interview, Mar. 21, 1990.

67. Michael B. Donley and John W. Douglass, author interview, Aug. 16, 1995.

68. Vessey interview, Mar. 21, 1990.

69. Richard Halloran, "A Commanding Voice for the Military," *NYT*, July 15, 1984, sec. 6, 18.

70. Ibid.

71. Gerald F. Seib, "Top General: Vessey of Joint Chiefs Helps Give the Military Clout in White House," *WSJ*, Mar. 22, 1984, 1.

72. Berteau interview, Sept. 16, 1999.

73. William H. Taft IV, "Senate Hearings on Organization of the Department of Defense," Memorandum for the Secretaries of the Military Departments, Chairman of the Joint Chiefs of Staff, and Under Secretary of Defense for Policy, June 20, 1984, a.n. 330-86-0046, box 16, folder "020 JCS," SD.

74. David J. Berteau, author interview, Sept. 21, 1995.

75. Blechman interview.

76. Healy and Duffy, "Joint Chiefs Draw Defense," 14.

77. Berteau interviews, Sept. 21, 1995, and Sept. 16, 1999.

78. Berteau interview, Sept. 16, 1999; "Minutes of the February 5, 1985, Meeting of the Ad Hoc Task Group on DoD Organization," DJB.

79. Blechman interview.

Chapter 13. Naval Gunfire

1. Department of the Navy, *Report to the Congress: Fiscal Year 1986* (Alexandria, Va.: Naval Internal Relations Activity, 1985), 9; Michael R. Gordon, "Lehman's Navy Riding High, But Critics Question Its Strategy and Rapid Growth," *National Journal*, Sept. 21, 1985, 2120.

2. Tower, *Consequences*, 239; Gordon, "Lehman's Navy Riding High."

3. Cathryn Donohoe, "Lehman Power: The Navy secretary's hard sell for the seas," *Washington Times*, Aug. 20, 1985, 1B.

4. Kitfield, *Prodigal Soldiers*, 285.

5. Deborah G. Meyer and Benjamin F. Schemmer, "An exclusive *AFJ* interview with John F. Lehman, Secretary of the Navy," *AFJ*, Nov., 1983, 66.

6. Bill Keller, "The Navy's Brash Leader," *NYT*, Dec. 15, 1985, sec. 6, 31.

7. Stubbing with Mendel, *Defense Game*, 374.

8. Dawson interview; Lehman, *Command of the Seas*, 103.

9. Smith, *Power Game*, 187, 189, 193.

10. Stubbing with Mendel, *Defense Game*, 392–93; Michael Duffy, ". . . But Democrats Call Request 'Bloated'," *Defense Week*, Feb. 11, 1985, 6; Vistica, *Fall from Glory*, 162.

11. Powell with Persico, *My American Journey*, 298; Smith, *Power Game*, 187.

12. Weinberger interview.

13. Vistica, *Fall from Glory*, 28–29.

14. Ibid., 19, 21, 23.

15. Kitfield, *Prodigal Soldiers*, 286; Vistica, *Fall from Glory*, 13, 22.

16. Vistica, *Fall from Glory*, 146; Benjamin F. Schemmer, written statement, Mar. 3, 2000.

17. Vistica, *Fall from Glory*, 137; Bernard E. Trainor, "Man in the News: James David Watkins; A Compassionate Pragmatist," *NYT*, June 4, 1988, sec. 1, 7.

18. Sally Squires, "Setting the Course on AIDS; How an Admiral Turned Around the President's AIDS Commission," *WP,* June 7, 1988, Z14.

19. Vessey interview, Jan. 29, 1993.

20. Stephen J. Hedges, Andy Plattner, and Marianna I. Knight, "Admiral Watkins's Toughest Command," *USN&WR,* Aug. 14, 1989, 29.

21. Keller, "Navy's Brash Leader."

22. Powell with Persico, *My American Journey,* 298.

23. Trevor Armbrister, "The Man Who Shaped Up the Navy," *Reader's Digest,* Dec., 1985, 133.

24. Fred Hiatt, "Feud Erupts on Navy's Future: Pentagon Officials Tangle," *WP,* Oct. 11, 1983, A1; idem., "Weinberger Asked to Mediate: Battle Rages with Navy," *WP,* Oct. 12, 1983, A1.

25. Keller, "Navy's Brash Leader."

26. Donohoe, "Lehman Power," 1B ; Smith, *Power Game,* 188.

27. Vistica, *Fall from Glory,* 100, 166.

28. Andy Pasztor, *When the Pentagon Was for Sale: Inside America's Biggest Defense Scandal* (New York: Scribner, 1995), 28; Smith, *Power Game,* 187.

29. Tina Rosenberg, "Fool of Ships: How one of Washington's slickest operators keeps the Navy abloat," *New Republic,* June 3, 1985, 20; Donohoe, "Lehman Power," 1B.

30. Vistica, *Fall from Glory,* 179–85.

31. Ibid., 184–88; Lehman quoted in Ruth Marcus and George C. Wilson, "Spies' Plea Bargains Irk Navy Secretary: Sentences Sent 'Wrong Message' to Fleet," *WP,* Oct. 30, 1985, A6.

32. Michael Weisskopf, "Weinberger Scolds Aide: Lehman's Remarks Called 'Injudicious'," *WP,* Nov. 2, 1985, A1; Vistica, *Fall from Glory,* 188.

33. Lehman, *Command of the Seas,* 418.

34. Vistica, *Fall from Glory,* 251; Kitfield, *Prodigal Soldiers,* 298.

35. Associated Press, "Top Admiral Calls Lehman's Departure 'Fresh Breeze,'" Apr. 29, 1987.

36. Rowland Evans and Robert Novak, "The Admirals Strike Back," *WP,* May 6, 1987, A19.

37. Pasztor, *When the Pentagon,* 38.

38. Ibid., 35–36.

39. Benjamin F. Schemmer, author interview, Apr. 26, 2001.

40. Ibid.

41. Ibid.

42. Vistica, *Fall from Glory,* 133.

43. Lehman, *Command of the Seas,* 94.

44. Stimson and Bundy, *On Active Service,* 519; Hammond, *Organizing for Defense,* 191–92.

45. Hoopes and Brinkley, *Driven Patriot,* 324–25.

46. Ibid., 325.

47. Clark Clifford with Richard Holbrooke, *Counsel to the President: A Memoir* (New York: Random House, 1991), 147, 149.

48. Ibid., 148–49.

49. Ibid., 149.

50. Hoopes and Brinkley, *Driven Patriot*, 330.

51. Clifford, *Counsel to the President*, 150.

52. Ibid., 151 (emphasis in original).

53. Hoopes and Brinkley, *Driven Patriot*, 335, 342, 343 (emphasis in original).

54. Caraley, *Politics of Military Unification*, 151 n.

55. Hoopes and Brinkley, *Driven Patriot*, 343; Clifford, *Counsel to the President*, 154–55.

56. Clifford, *Counsel to the President*, 155; Vandergrift quoted in Gordon W. Keiser, *The US Marine Corps and Defense Unification: 1944–1947: The Politics of Survival* (Washington: NDU Press, 1982), 72.

57. Caraley, *Politics of Military Unification*, 268.

58. Ibid., 164–65, 175–76.

59. Hoopes and Brinkley, *Driven Patriot*, 343–49.

60. Clifford, *Counsel to the President*, 157.

61. Hoopes and Brinkley, *Driven Patriot*, 349.

62. Trask and Goldberg, *Department of Defense*, 17.

63. Jeffrey G. Barlow, *The Revolt of the Admirals: The Fight for Naval Aviation, 1945–1950* (Washington: Naval Historical Center, 1994), 293.

64. Ibid., 148.

65. Ibid., 292–93.

66. Trask and Goldberg, *Department of Defense*, 11, 14.

67. Potter, *Admiral Arleigh Burke*, 319–20.

68. Omar N. Bradley and Clay Blair, *A General's Life* (New York: Simon and Schuster, 1983), 507.

69. Bradley quoted in Barlow, *Revolt of the Admirals*, 1; Trask and Goldberg, *Department of Defense*, 17.

70. Steven L. Rearden, *History of the Office of the Secretary of Defense*, vol. 1, *The Formative Years: 1947–1950* (Washington: OSD Historical Office, 1984), 415.

71. Barlow, *Revolt of the Admirals*, 236.

72. Trask and Goldberg, *Department of Defense*, 17–18.

73. Ibid., 30–31.

74. Gordon, "Lehman's Navy Riding High."

75. Weinberger interview.

76. Seth Cropsey, "Offense," memorandum for the Secretary of the Navy," Jan. 18, 1985, box 5, folder "OI—JCS Reorg—1985" (folder 1 of 8), JFL.

77. "Primary cause of military inefficiency is meddling Congress," *San Diego Union-Tribune*, Oct. 27, 1985, C6.

78. "Transcript: Mondale—American Legion," Sept. 5, 1984, box 4, folder "OI—JCS Reorg—1984" (folder 4 of 4), JFL.

79. Les Aspin, "A Democratic Defense Policy: Defense without nonsense," speech text for delivery to Committee for a Democratic Majority, Apr. 17, 1985, WKB.

80. Mary McGrory, "Democrats' Party Is a Flop," *WP*, July 11, 1985, A2; John Lehman, "Democrats Politicize Joint Chiefs Issue—Action Memorandum,"

memorandum for the secretary of defense, Sept. 10, 1985, a.n. 330-87-0006, box 15, folder "020 JCS," SD.

81. Barrett interview, July 29, 1999.

82. Millard I. Barger and Deborah M. Kyle, "Over Three-fourths of Senators Are Military Alumni; Half Served in Army," *AFJ*, Apr., 1984, 12; Smith, *Power Game*, 191.

83. David C. Morrison, "Backstopping Defense," *National Journal*, Oct. 17, 1987, 2597.

84. Ibid.; "For SECNAV Lunch with General Barrow," three-by-five-inch note card with talking points attached to Admiral Moorer's rebuttal of CSIS report, box 3, folder "OI—Defense Organization—1985" (folder 4 of 5), JFL.

85. J. B. Finkelstein, "JCS Reorganization Plan/Action," memorandum for Secretary Lehman, May 10, 1985, box 5, folder "OI—JCS Reorg—1985" (folder 3 of 8), JFL.

86. James D. Hessman and Vincent C. Thomas Jr., "'An Absolute Requirement for Every American': Interview with Secretary of the Navy John Lehman," *Seapower*, Apr., 1985, 5.

87. "Primary cause of military inefficiency"; John Lehman, "What Defense Needs: 'De-Organization'," *WP*, May 26, 1985, C7; "Required Reading: Entities of Democracy: Excerpts from a speech by the Secretary of the Navy, John F. Lehman Jr., to the Sea-Air-Space Exposition Banquet in Washington, April 3, 1985," *NYT*, Apr. 6, 1985, 6.

88. Lehman, "What Defense Needs."

89. George C. Wilson, "Navy Secretary Declares War on Bureaucracy: Crystal City Unit Shutting Down," *WP*, Apr. 5, 1985, A6; "Required Reading," *NYT*.

90. Lehman, "What Defense Needs."

91. Hessman and Thomas, "'An Absolute Requirement'"; Lehman, "What Defense Needs."

92. John Lehman, "JCS Reorganization Idea Is Not New or Improved," *Navy Times*, Dec. 16, 1985, 27.

93. John Lehman, "Trendy bureaucrat could beach Navy," *Cleveland Plain Dealer*, May 25, 1985, 13; idem., "JCS Reorganization Idea."

94. Kitfield, *Prodigal Soldiers*, 286, 288; Carlisle A. H. Trost, author interview, Mar. 27, 2001.

95. Hoopes and Brinkley, *Driven Patriot*, 349.

96. Rosenberg, "Fool of Ships," 20.

Chapter 14. McFarlane Outflanks the Pentagon

1. McFarlane interview, Feb. 8, 1999.

2. Cannon, *President Reagan*, 596–97.

3. Brock Brower, "Bud McFarlane: Semper Fi," *NYT Magazine*, Jan. 22, 1989, 27.

4. Michael B. Donley, author interview, May 24, 1994; McFarlane interview, Feb. 8, 1999.

5. Tower, *Consequences*, 247–48; "Agenda for Chairman Tower's Meeting with Bud McFarlane (5/9/84)," talking points, n.d., Defense, Foreign Relations, and Armed Services Committee Series, box 972, folder 7, JGT.

6. Tower, *Consequences*, 248.

7. McFarlane interview, Feb. 8, 1999.

8. McFarlane coauthored a book on the *Mayaguez* incident: Richard G. Head, Frisco W. Short, and McFarlane, *Crisis Resolution: Presidential Decision Making in the Mayaguez and Korean Confrontations* (Boulder, Colo.: Westview Press, 1978).

9. Leslie H. Gelb, "McFarlane Carving His Niche," *NYT*, Mar. 28, 1984, B10; Lou Cannon, "McFarlane's Hidden Hand Guides U.S. Foreign Policy," *WP*, Feb. 15, 1985, 1.

10. John W. Douglass and Michael B. Donley, author interview, Aug. 16, 1995.

11. "Draft NSDD on Defense Reorganization," undated paper, box 91726, folder "NSDD DOD Reorganization," MBD. A National Security Decision Directive announces a presidential decision implementing policy objectives in all areas of national security.

12. Michael B. Donley, "Draft NSDD on DOD Reorganization," memorandum for record, Aug. 7, 1984, ibid.

13. "Previously Considered Options/Proposals," point paper, n.d., box 91726, folder "Defense Reorganization," MBD.

14. Donley interview, May 24, 1994; Michael B. Donley, handwritten notes, box 90961, [President's Blue Ribbon Commission on Defense Management, unfoldered material] (9), MBD.

15. Donley and Douglass interview.

16. Michael B. Donley, two handwritten notes, box 90961, folder [President's Blue Ribbon Commission on Defense Management, unfoldered material] (2), MBD.

17. John M. Poindexter, "Defense Organization," memorandum for William H. Taft IV, Jan. 2, 1985, and William H. Taft IV, "Defense Organization," memorandum for John M. Poindexter, Jan. 16, 1985, both in a.n. 330-87-0006, box 15, folder "020 DOD (Jan.–Feb.)," SD.

18. McFarlane interview, Feb. 8, 1999.

19. Ibid.

20. Bob Dole, quoted in Smith, *Power Game*, 208.

21. McFarlane interview, Feb. 8, 1999.

22. Donley interview.

23. Congress, Senate, Committee on Armed Services, *Organization, Structure, and Decisionmaking Procedures of the Department of Defense: Hearings before the Committee on Armed Services*, 98th Cong., 1st sess., S. Hrg. 98-375, pt. 1, July 28, 1983, 5; Donley interview.

24. Donley, handwritten notes, n.d. (preparatory notes for memorandum dated Feb. 7, 1985), MBD (emphasis in original).

25. Russell Baker, "Aerial Brew Haha," *NYT*, Oct. 10, 1984, 27.

26. Ibid.; "Cap the Knife," *Norfolk Virginian-Pilot*, Sept. 23, 1984, C4.

27. "The Pentagon Brew," *NYT*, Oct. 10, 1984, 26.

28. "Cap the Knife," *Norfolk Virginian-Pilot*.

29. Congress, Senate, Committee on Armed Services, *Department of Defense Authorization for Appropriations for Fiscal Year 1986: Hearings before the Committee on Armed Services*, 99th Cong., 1st sess., S. Hrg. 99-58, pt. 1, Feb. 4, 1985, 26.

30. Ibid., 60–61; "Adjusting the Bottom Line," *Time*, Feb. 18, 1985, 23.

31. Fred Hiatt, "Now, the $600 Toilet Seat," *WP*, Feb. 5, 1985, 5; Wayne Biddle, "Price of Toilet Seat Is Cut for Navy," *NYT*, Feb. 6, 1985, D15.

32. Donley interview.

33. Donley and Douglass interview.

34. Ibid.; Donley interview.

35. Donley and Douglass interview.

36. William V. Roth Jr. to Caspar Weinberger, Mar. 27, 1985, a.n. 330-87-0006, box 14, folder "020 DoD (May–June)," SD.

37. William L. Dickinson to the president, Apr. 1, 1985, box 92040, folder "Blue Ribbon Commission," JWD.

38. John W. Douglass, "Presidential Commission on Acquisition Reform," memorandum for Robert C. McFarlane, Apr. 2, 1985, and "Talking Points on Presidential Acquisition Reform Commission," prepared for Robert C. McFarlane, n.d., both in box 92055, folder for Apr., 1985, JWD.

39. M. B. Oglesby Jr., "Bill Dickinson (R-Alabama) Letter to the President on DOD Procurement Reform," memorandum for Don Regan and Bud McFarlane, Apr. 11, 1985, box 92040, folder "Blue Ribbon Commission," JWD (emphasis in original).

40. Donley and Douglass interview.

41. Michael B. Donley and John W. Douglass, "A Broader Perspective re Ongoing Problems in Defense Management," memorandum for Robert C. McFarlane, Apr. 25, 1985, box 91762, folder "Packard (5)," MBD.

42. Robert C. McFarlane, author interview, May 18, 1999.

43. John W. Douglass and Michael B. Donley, "Meeting with Allen Chase of Congressman Bill Dickinson's Staff Re: Presidential Commission Issue," memorandum for John M. Poindexter, May 10, 1985, box 91726, folder 3318 (2 of 3), MBD.

44. William H. Taft IV, interview by Alfred Goldberg and Maurice Matloff, May 3, 1989, OSD Historical Office, Arlington, Va.

45. John W. Douglass and Michael B. Donley, "Talking Points for Meeting with Congressman Bill Dickinson," attachment to presidential briefing paper by Max Friedersdorf and M. B. Oglesby Jr., "Meeting with Congressman Bill Dickinson," May 15, 1985, Christopher M. Lehman Papers, box 90513, folder "Blue Ribbon Commission on Ntl Defense (Congressman Dickinson)," RRL; idem., "Meeting with SecDef re Blue Ribbon Commission on National Defense," memorandum for Robert C. McFarlane, May 15, 1985, box 92055, folder for May, 1985, JWD; John M. Poindexter, handwritten notes of president's meeting with Congressman Dickinson on May 15, 1985, n.d., RRL; Donley interview.

46. Douglass and Donley, "Meeting with SecDef re Blue Ribbon Commission."

47. McFarlane interview, May 18, 1999.

48. "Establishment of a Blue Ribbon Commission on Defense Management," memorandum for Caspar W. Weinberger, n.d., a.n. 330-87-0006, box 14, folder "020 DoD (Nov.)," SD.

49. Weinberger interview.

50. Weinberger's view of McFarlane as an opponent was reported in "Washington Whispers," USN&WR, Mar. 10, 1986, 15. "Defense Secretary Weinberger at first resisted the Packard Commission report on reforming the Pentagon, because he feared rivals such as former National Security Adviser Robert McFarlane would use it to undermine him" (ibid.).

51. Weinberger, Fighting for Peace, 360.

52. Donley and Douglass interview.

53. Congress, Senate, Senator Roth of Delaware speaking for an amendment to establish a Commission on Defense Procurement, 99th Cong., 2d sess., *Congressional Record* (May 22, 1985): 13181–85.

54. Caspar W. Weinberger, "Weekly Report on Defense Activities," memorandum for the president, May 24, 1985, a.n. 330-87-0006, box 14, folder "020 DoD (May–June)," SD; Donley and Douglass interview.

55. Wayne Biddle, "'Horror Stories' and Pentagon's Budget," *NYT*, May 24, 1985, 13.

56. Michael Weisskopf, "Navy Probes Grumman Prices," *WP*, May 29, 1985, 3; Caspar W. Weinberger, interview with ABC News, May 30, 1985, as quoted in *Radio-TV Defense Dialog*, DoD, May 31, 1985, 4.

57. Alan M. Kranowitz, memorandum to Robert C. McFarlane, May 31, 1985, box 91762, folder "Packard (4)," MBD.

58. Robert C. McFarlane, "Readout on meeting w/Sec Weinberger," E-mail, June 1, 1985, ibid.

59. McFarlane interview, Feb. 8, 1999.

60. Tim Carrington, "Panel on Arms Procurement Is Considered," *WSJ*, June 5, 1985, 4; Michael Weisskopf, "Presidential Panel to Assess Defense Purchasing Practices," *WP*, June 8, 1985, 2.

61. McFarlane interview, May 18, 1999.

62. Michael B. Donley, "Packard Commission and Goldwater-Nichols," paper prepared for Alfred Goldberg, Jan., 1995, Donley; Donley and Douglass interview.

63. McNaugher with Sperry, "Improving Military Coordination," 240 and n 56; Michael Ganley, "Packard Panel on DOD Management May Derail DOD Reforms in Congress," *AFJ*, Aug., 1985, 16; Robert M. Kimmitt, memorandum, June 8, 1985, Kimmitt Papers, RRL; McFarlane interview, Feb. 8, 1999.

64. McFarlane interviews, Feb. 8 and May 18, 1999.

65. "Potential Chairman for the Blue Ribbon Commission on National Defense," n.d., box 91762, folder "Packard (5)," MBD; Donley and Douglass interview; Donley interview.

66. David Packard, *The HP Way: How Bill Hewlett and I Built Our Company* (New York: HarperBusiness, 1995), 13, 35–46.

67. Julie Pitta, "Electronics pioneer's innovative practices are legend," *Detroit News*, Mar. 27, 1996, 2A; Bart Barnes, "David Packard Dies at 83; Founded Hewlett-Packard," *WP*, Mar. 27, 1996, D4.

68. Michael Getler, "David Packard: presiding over a revolution," *Armed Forces Management*, Mar., 1970, 24; "The Pentagon's powerful No. 2 man," *Business Week*, Mar. 21, 1970, 94.

69. "Talking Points for Discussion with Potential Chairman of the Blue Ribbon Commission on National Defense," n.d., box 91762, folder "Packard (5)," MBD; McFarlane interview, Feb. 8, 1999.

70. McFarlane interview, Feb. 8, 1999; David Packard, interview by Alfred Goldberg and Maurice Matloff, Nov. 28, 1988, OSD Historical Office, Arlington, Va.

71. Weinberger interview; Perry, *Four Stars*, 333.

72. Packard interview.

73. Chapman Cox, note for SECDEF, June 24, 1985, a.n. 330-87-0006, box 14, folder "020 DoD (May–June)," SD.

74. Jim Locher, Rick Finn, and Jeff Smith, "Presidential Commission on DoD Organization and Procurement," memorandum for Senator Goldwater and Senator Nunn, June 4, 1985, box 1939, folder "Memo to Goldwater/Nunn, Presidential Commission, 6/4/85," SASC.

75. Jim Locher, Rick Finn, and Jeff Smith, "Meeting with David Packard," memorandum for Senator Goldwater and Senator Nunn, June 12, 1985, box 1939, folder "Meeting with Packard, 6/12/85," SASC.

76. John H. Dressendorfer, "Presidential Commission on Defense Management and Organization," memorandum to Adm. John M. Poindexter, June 13, 1985, Donley.

77. John W. Vessey Jr., "Draft NSDD—Establishment of a Blue Ribbon Panel on Defense Management," memorandum for the president, June 14, 1985, a.n. 330-87-0006, folder "020 DoD (May–June)," SD; Michael B. Donley, "JCS Memo to the President re Blue Ribbon Commission," memorandum for Robert C. McFarlane, June 15, 1985, box 91762, folder "Packard (1)," MBD.

78. Ronald Reagan, "Remarks Announcing the Establishment of the Blue Ribbon Commission on Defense Management," June 17, 1985, *Public Papers of the Presidents of the United States: Ronald Reagan, 1985*, Book 1, *January 1–June 28, 1985* (Washington: GPO, 1988), 775–76.

79. David Packard, "Mr. Packard's Remarks," n.d., box 91762, folder "Packard (2)," MBD.

80. Barry Goldwater and Sam Nunn, "Goldwater and Nunn Respond to President's Commission on Defense Management," press release, June 17, 1985, box C-1, folder 11, BMG.

81. Quoted in Gerald M. Boyd, "President Establishes Panel to Review Military Spending," *NYT*, June 18, 1985, 15.

82. Quoted in Ganley, "Packard Panel on DoD Management."

83. "Washington Whispers," *USN&WR*, June 24, 1985, 17.

84. Crowe, *Line of Fire*, 152.

85. Max L. Friedersdorf, handwritten note, n.d., MBD.

86. Donley and Douglass interview.

87. Donley, "Packard Commission and Goldwater-Nichols."

Chapter 15. Trench Warfare

1. James Locher, Rick Finn, and Jeff Smith, "Chapters 1, 4, and 5 of the Staff Study on DoD Organization," memorandum for the Task Force on Defense Organization, June 18, 1985, SASC.

2. Barry Goldwater and Sam Nunn to William S. Cohen, June 12, 1985, SASC; "Procedures of the Task Force," attachment to "Overall Approach for the Committee's Work," June 18, 1985, SASC.

3. Senate Committee on Armed Services, *Defense Organization: The Need for Change: Staff Report to the Committee on Armed Services*, 99th Cong., 1st sess., Committee Print, S. Prt. 99-86, Oct. 16, 1985, 139–274.

4. Ibid., 159.

5. Ibid., 160–65.

6. Ibid., 165–79.

7. Ibid., 179–84.

8. Ibid., 184–87.

9. Ibid., 354–70.

10. Ibid., 303–304.

11. Ibid., 304–306.

12. Graham T. Allison, *Essence of Decision: Explaining the Cuban Missile Crisis* (Boston: Little, Brown, 1971), 117–18.

13. Quoted in James G. Blight, Joseph S. Nye Jr., and David A. Welch, "The Cuban Missile Crisis Revisited," *Foreign Affairs,* fall, 1987, 170.

14. Allison, *Essence of Decision,* 131–32, 309. Walter S. Poole, formerly of the Joint History Office, provided an alternative account: "Years ago, I interviewed Admiral Anderson precisely about this passage and he vehemently denied the accuracy of it. By his telling, McNamara came to Flag Plot along with two Public Affairs officials and asked why one destroyer was well away from the quarantine line. When McNamara became insistent, Anderson took him to a secure area and explained that the destroyer was shadowing a Soviet sub by means which the Public Affairs men were not cleared to know. Anderson then said in what he thought was a jocular tone: 'Why don't you go back to your quarters and let us handle this?' He was convinced that the TFX controversy was the real reason for his dismissal" (Walter S. Poole, memorandum for James Locher, July 10, 2000, copy in author's collection).

15. SASC, *Defense Organization,* S. Prt. 99-86, 307–19.

16. Weinberger, *Fighting for Peace,* 101.

17. Cole, *Operation Urgent Fury,* 10.

18. Weinberger, *Fighting for Peace,* 105.

19. Cole, *Operation Urgent Fury,* 11.

20. Ibid., 23.

21. Ibid., 26.

22. Maj. Gen. Richard A. Scholtes, USA (Ret.), meeting with Senators Cohen, Exon, Nunn and Warner, Aug. 5, 1986. General Scholtes testified before the SASC Subcommittee on Sea Power and Force Projection in open and closed sessions during a hearing on combating terrorism and other forms of unconventional warfare. His testimony focused on the misemployment of special operations force in Operation Urgent Fury. Cohen arranged a private meeting with General Scholtes later in the day. This material also derives from the author's discussion with Jeff Smith and Hen Johnson, who both attended the meeting. The meeting with Scholtes's testimony is also discussed in Susan L. Marquis, *Unconventional Warfare: Rebuilding U.S. Special Operations Forces* (Washington: Brookings, 1997).

23. Cole, *Operation Urgent Fury,* 31.

24. Marquis, *Unconventional Warfare,* 95–96.

25. Cole, *Operation Urgent Fury,* 41; Marquis, *Unconventional Warfare,* 96.

26. Gabriel, *Military Incompetence,* 152.

27. Joint Staff, "Joint Overview of Operation Urgent Fury," May 1, 1985, JCS.

28. Gabriel, *Military Incompetence*, 150–51.

29. Cole, *Operation Urgent Fury*, 6.

30. Ibid.; Mark Adkin, *Urgent Fury: The Battle for Grenada* (Lexington, Mass.: Lexington Books, 1989), 335.

31. Powell with Persico, *My American Journey*, 292.

32. H. Norman Schwarzkopf with Peter Petre, *It Doesn't Take a Hero* (New York: Linda Grey Bantam Books, 1992), 246, 250, 254, 258.

33. Cole, *Operation Urgent Fury*, 6, 35 (McDonald quote); Gabriel, *Military Incompetence*, 154, 173.

34. SASC, *Defense Organization*, S. Prt. 99-86, 365–66.

35. Cole, *Operation Urgent Fury*, 1, 2, 56.

36. Adkin, *Urgent Fury*, 336.

37. Cole, *Operation Urgent Fury*, 66.

38. Author's recollection confirmed by Punaro.

39. Ronald H. Spector, *U.S. Marines in Grenada, 1983* (Washington: Marine Corps History and Museums Division, 1987), 21–22.

40. Cole, *Operation Urgent Fury*, 4–5, 53.

41. Adkin, *Urgent Fury*, 169–70.

42. Cole, *Operation Urgent Fury*, 16, 31, 66; Adm. Wesley L. McDonald, "U.S. Atlantic Command: Implementing the Vital Strategy of Forward Deployment," *Defense 84*, Nov.–Dec., 1984, 28.

43. Adkin, *Urgent Fury*, 131–32.

44. Cole, *Operation Urgent Fury*, 66–67.

45. Ibid., 6.

46. Ibid., 66.

47. Adkin, *Urgent Fury*, 128.

48. George C. Wilson, "Admiral To Head Joint Chiefs," *WP*, July 10, 1985, 1.

49. Bill Keller, "Politically Attuned Admiral: William James Crowe Jr.," *NYT*, July 11. 1985, 8; Conant with Barry, "An Officer and Intellectual," 29.

50. Associated Press, "Panel Recommends Confirming Crowe," *WP*, July 31, 1985, 10.

51. Barry Goldwater to Ben Schemmer, July 9, 1985, box C-1, folder 10, BMG.

52. Benjamin F. Schemmer to Sen. Barry Goldwater, July 30, 1985, box C-1, folder 9, BMG.

53. SASC, *Defense Organization*, S. Prt. 99-86, 77

54. James Locher, "Validity of Analytical Methodology," undated point paper, box 1941, folder "Analytical Methodology," SASC.

55. SASC, *Defense Organization*, S. Prt. 99-86, 416–27.

56. Ibid., 427–31.

57. Ibid., 569–612.

58. Ibid., 45.

59. Ibid., 613–38.

60. Nunn interview.

Chapter 16. Playing the Media Card

1. Nunn quoted by Arnold L. Punaro in Nunn Oral History; Punaro interview.

2. Michael R. Gordon, "Uneasy Truce Prevails Between Pentagon and Reporters Who Cover Defense News," *National Journal*, Feb. 16, 1985, 360.

3. Richard Halloran, "The Pentagon; Weinberger and the Press: An Ebb in the Flow," *NYT*, Aug. 25, 1984, 6.

4. Caraley, *Politics of Military Unification*, 146, 236, 331 n 81; Gale Group, "Hanson W(eightman) Baldwin," *Contemporary Authors Online*, www.galenet.com, 1999; Hadley, *Straw Giant*, 90.

5. Hanson W. Baldwin, "Service Merger Battle: Remarks by Truman Enlarge Arena; 'Compromise' Legislation Is Assailed," *NYT*, Apr. 14, 1946, 22.

6. Nunn Oral History.

7. Congress, Senate, Senator Goldwater of Arizona speaking on congressional oversight of national defense, 99th Congress, 1st sess., *Congressional Record* (Oct. 1, 1985): 25348–50.

8. Congress, Senate, Senator Nunn of Georgia speaking on congressional oversight of national defense, 99th Congress, 1st sess., *Congressional Record* (Oct. 1, 1985): 25350–54.

9. Ibid., Goldwater, Oct. 2, 1985, 25539–41.

10. Ibid., Nunn, Oct. 2, 1985, 25541–43.

11. Ibid., Goldwater, Oct. 3, 1985: 25804–806.

12. Ibid., Nunn, Oct. 3, 1985, 25806–808.

13. Ibid., Goldwater Oct. 4, 1985, 26159–61.

14. Ibid., Nunn, Oct. 4, 1985, 26161–63.

15. Ibid., Goldwater, Oct. 7, 1985, 26345–48.

16. Ibid., Nunn, Oct. 7, 1985, 26348–50.

17. Ibid., Nunn, Oct. 8, 1985, 26693–95.

18. Ibid., Goldwater, Oct. 8, 1985, 26695–96.

19. Jeffrey H. Smith quoting Goldwater, Nunn Oral History.

20. Congress, Senate, Committee on Armed Services, *Organization, Structure and Decisionmaking Procedures of the Department of Defense: Hearings before the Committee on Armed Services*, 98th Cong., 1st sess., pt. 1, July 28, 1983, 3.

21. Eliot Brenner, "Goldwater: Problems in Congress hinder military superiority," UPI, Oct. 2, 1985; Lawrence L. Knutson, "Interservice Rivalries Still Plaguing Planners, Senators Say," Associated Press, Oct. 3, 1985; Eliot Brenner, "Goldwater: Service loyalty hampers joint chiefs," UPI, Oct. 3, 1985.

22. Bill Keller, "2 Key Senators Join in Assault on the Military," *NYT*, Oct. 6, 1985, 1; Evan Thomas and Bruce van Voorst, "Drums along the Potomac: The military establishment is besieged by some of its staunchest supporters," *Time*, Oct. 21, 1985, 34.

23. Nunn interview.

24. Nunn Oral History.

25. Thomas J. "Stonewall" Jackson quoted in G. F. R. Henderson, *Stonewall Jackson and the American Civil War*, vol. 1 (London: Longman's, Green, 1926).

26. Punaro interview.

27. Punaro in Nunn Oral History.

Chapter 17. Gathering of Eagles

1. Nunn Oral History.

2. Goldwater, *Congressional Record—Senate* (Oct. 8, 1985): 26695.

3. Huntington interview.

4. Robert S. Greenberger, "Soldier on the Spot: U.S. General Is Playing Crucial Role in Setting Central America Policy—Army's Paul Gorman Keeps Strong Military Presence Via 'Training Exercises'—Is It a 'Backdoor' Buildup?" *WSJ*, June 26, 1984, 1.

5. Paul F. Gorman, author interview, May 17, 2000.

6. Bernard E. Trainor, author interview, Nov. 14, 1994.

7. John Hamre, "Wrapup Session," typed notes of wrap-up session comments, Oct. 6, 1985, JRL.

8. James Locher, "Secretary Schlesinger's comments," handwritten notes, n.d., JRL.

9. Hamre, "Wrapup Session."

10. Goldwater quoted in Thomas H. Moorer, "Notes on Camp Hill," Oct. 7, 1985. This two-page paper was attached to a memorandum to Admiral Watkins from Vice Adm. D. S. Jones, Oct. 8, 1985, CNO. A copy is also in box 5, folder "OI—JCS Reorg—1985" (folder 5 of 8), JFL.

11. Goldwater, *Congressional Record—Senate* (Oct. 7, 1985): 26345.

12. Huntington interview.

13. William K. Brehm, author interview, Oct. 30, 1995.

14. Trainor interview, Nov. 14, 1994.

15. Moorer, "Notes on Camp Hill."

16. Goldwater interview.

Chapter 18. Expedition into Hostile Territory

1. Quoted in Stephen E. Ambrose, *Eisenhower,* vol. 1, *Soldier, General of the Army, President-Elect: 1890–1952* (New York: Simon and Schuster, 1983), 487.

2. Diary entry, Jan. 6, 1958, DDEL. An attachment listed five major meetings during which Eisenhower discussed "interservice rivalries."

3. A. J. Goodpaster, memorandum for record, Nov. 6, 1957, DDEL.

4. Dwight D. Eisenhower to Everett Hazlett, Aug. 20, 1956, reproduced in Eisenhower, *Mandate for Change: 1953–1956* (Garden City, N.Y.: Doubleday, 1963), 455.

5. Richard Reeves, *President Kennedy: Profile of Power* (New York: Touchstone, 1993), 183.

6. Congress, Senate, Committee on Armed Services, *Nomination of William H. Taft IV, to Be Deputy Secretary of Defense: Hearing before the Committee on Armed Services,* 98th Cong., 2d sess., S. Hrg. 98-611, Jan. 24, 1984, 3, 12, 24.

7. Congress, Senate, Senator Goldwater of Arizona speaking against the nomination of William H. Taft IV, of Virginia, to be Deputy Secretary of Defense, 98th Cong., 2d sess., *Congressional Record—Senate* (Feb. 2, 1984): 1643.

Chapter 19. Seizing the High Ground

1. George C. Wilson, "Senate Study Suggests Reorganizing Pentagon: Need for Accountability Is Cited," *WP,* Oct. 10, 1985, 13.

2. George C. Wilson, "Military Reform to Be Unveiled," *WP,* Oct. 15, 1985, 1.

3. Congress, Senate, Committee on Armed Services, *Reorganization of the Department of Defense: Hearings before the Committee on Armed Services,* 99th Cong., 1st sess., S. Hrg. 99-1083, Oct. 16; Nov. 14, 19, 20, 21; Dec. 4, 5, 6, 11, 12, 1985, 4–63.

4. Gerald J. Smith interview.

5. Department of Defense, "Radio-TV Defense Dialog," Oct. 17, 1985 (broadcasts of Oct. 16, 1985); Vanderbilt Television News Archive, *Television News Index and Abstracts,* Oct., 1985, 1934. Also available at www.tvnews.vanderbilt.edu.

6. "Radio-TV Defense Dialog," 2; *Television News Index and Abstracts,* 1931–32.

7. Michael Weisskopf, "Pentagon Is Mismanaged, Report Says: Replacement of Joint Chiefs, Reorganization Urged by Senators," *WP,* Oct. 17, 1985, 1.

8. Jim Stewart, "Panel suggests dissolving Joint Chiefs of Staff," Oct. 17, 1985, *Atlanta Journal,* 1; Bill Keller, "Proposed Revamping of Military Calls for Disbanding Joint Chiefs," *NYT,* Oct. 17, 1985, 20; Charles W. Corddry, "Senate report suggests broad military reforms: Panel opens probe of Pentagon, forces," *Baltimore Sun,* Oct. 17, 1985, 1; Vernon A. Guidry Jr., "Coordination said to be a problem," *Baltimore Sun,* Oct. 17, 1985, 1; Tim Carrington, "Senators Clash Over Proposal to Shift Power at Pentagon Away From Services," *WSJ,* Oct. 17, 1985, 14.

9. Reuters, "Pentagon assails notion of reorganizing military," *Baltimore Sun,* Oct. 18, 1985, 21.

10. Seth Cropsey, "How Not to Reform Defense," *New York Post,* Oct. 23, 1985, 39.

11. "Redoing defense," *Washington Times,* Oct. 18, 1985, 9A.

12. Robert A. Kittle with Melissa Healy and Orr Kelly, "Pentagon Comes Under Fire from Its Friends," *USN&WR,* Oct. 28, 1985, 24; Tom Morganthau with Kim Willenson and John Barry, "The Pentagon Under Siege," *Newsweek,* Oct. 28, 1985, 38.

13. "Defense Organization: The Need for Change," *AFJ,* Oct., 1985.

Chapter 20. Transition to the Offensive

1. McNaugher with Sperry, "Improving Military Coordination," 235–36.

2. Mark Sullivan, untitled article, States News Service, Nov. 13, 1985.

3. Meyer, author interview, June 25, 1998.

4. Archie D. Barrett, "Meeting with Republican leaders—10-30-85," handwritten notes, ADB.

5. *Reorganization of the Department of Defense,* S. Hrg. 99-1083, 77; George C. Wilson, "Weinberger Surrounded by Snipers," *WP,* Nov. 19, 1985, 22.

6. *Reorganization of the Department of Defense,* S. Hrg. 99-1083, 124, 126, 127.

7. Ibid., 109–10.

8. Ibid., 137.

9. Capt. Richard DeBobes, "SecDef Testimony Before SASC," memorandum for Admiral Crowe, Nov. 15, 1985, JCS.

10. Kaufman interview.

11. Caspar W. Weinberger, "Weekly Report of Defense Activities," memorandum for the president, Nov. 15, 1985, a.n. 330-87-0006, box 14, folder "020 DoD (Nov.)," SD.

12. *Reorganization of the Department of Defense,* S. Hrg. 99-1083, 165.

13. Ibid., 275.

14. Caspar W. Weinberger, "Weekly Report of Defense Activities," memorandum for the president, Nov. 22, 1985, a.n. 330-87-0006, box 14, folder "020 DoD (Nov.)," SD.

15. *Reorganization of the Department of Defense,* S. Hrg. 99-1083, 276.

16. Ibid., 277.

17. Ibid., 279.

18. Ibid., 287.

19. Ibid., 288.

20. Crowe interview.

21. Weinberger to Barry Goldwater, Dec. 2, 1985, a.n. 330-87-0006, box 13, folder "020 DoD (Dec.)," SD.

22. Caspar W. Weinberger, "Weekly Report of Defense Activities," memorandum for the president, Dec. 6, 1985, ibid.

23. *Reorganization of the Department of Defense,* S. Hrg. 99-1083, 335–36.

24. Ibid., 353, 357.

25. Edgar F. Raines Jr., "Report on the Proceedings of the U.S. Army Special Review Committee on the Department of Defense Organization, 4–22 November 1985," memorandum for record, Dec. 11, 1985, CHM.

26. Story related by Richard H. Witherspoon.

27. Raines, "Report."

28. "Army Special Review Committee on DoD Organization," briefing, Nov. 20, 1985, personal papers of Daniel J. Kaufman.

29. Kaufman interview.

30. P. X. Kelley, "Remarks by General P. X. Kelley," June 15, 1987, JRL.

31. *Reorganization of the Department of Defense,* S. Hrg. 99-1083, 513–14, 535–36.

32. Ibid., 518.

33. Ibid., 536.

34. Ibid., 536–37.

35. Ibid., 518.

36. Ibid., 566; Nunn Oral History.

37. *Reorganization of the Department of Defense,* S. Hrg. 99-1083, 614; Nunn interview.

38. *Reorganization of the Department of Defense,* S. Hrg. 99-1083, 614.

39. Ibid., 742.

40. Ibid., 743.

41. James Locher, Richard Finn, and Jeff Smith, "Draft Defense Organization Bill," memorandum to General Jones, Bill Brehm, John Kester, Phil Odeen, Jan. 14, 1986, WKB.

42. Goldwater interview.

43. Barry Goldwater and Sam Nunn to Adm. William J. Crowe Jr., Jan. 29, 1986, JCS.

44. Committee on Armed Services, U.S. Senate, "Goldwater and Nunn Release Summary of Staff Proposal on Defense Reorganization," Jan. 29, 1986, SASC.

45. John Lehman, handwritten letters to Bush, Weinberger, and Poindexter, Jan. 31, 1986, box 6, folder "OI—JCS Reorg—1986" (folder 1), JFL.

Chapter 21. The Packard Commission Reinforces

1. Barry Goldwater to David Packard, Sept. 24, 1985, box C-1, folder 8, BMG.

2. "President's Blue Ribbon Commission on Defense Management, Organizational Working Notes, September 1985," box 91473, file "President's Blue Ribbon Commission on Defense Management [Meetings: Minutes and Notes]," PSS.

3. Ronald Reagan, "President's Blue Ribbon Commission on Defense Management," Executive Order 12526, July 15, 1985, box 0A12657, file "JGR (John G. Roberts Jr.)/Blue Ribbon Commission on Defense Management," RRL; Dawson interview.

4. David Packard, "Talking Points," press statement, Oct. 10, 1985, box 92228, folder "President's Blue Ribbon Cmsn on Defense Management," JWD.

5. Berteau interview, Sept. 16, 1999.

6. Gorman interview, May 17, 2000.

7. James Locher, Richard Finn, and Jeff Smith, "Meeting with Mr. Packard," memorandum for Senator Goldwater and Senator Nunn, Nov. 14, 1985, SASC.

8. Nunn Oral History.

9. Dawson interview.

10. Gorman interview.

11. Ibid.

12. McNaugher with Sperry, "Improving Military Coordination," 240.

13. Berteau interview, Sept. 16, 1999; Gorman interview.

14. Dawson interview.

15. Michael B. Donley, author interview, May 17, 2000.

16. "Memorandum for the Record," Jan. 15, 1986, box 91474, folder "Eisenhower materials," PSS.

17. Packard interview.

18. Donley interview, May 17, 2000.

19. John M. Poindexter, "Comparing the Packard Commission with the Eisenhower Initiatives in Defense Management," memorandum for the president, Feb. 24, 1986, JWD.

20. "Outline of Commission Report," undated paper, box 92043, folder "Jan., 1986 [Selected Documents]," JWD; "Rank of the JCS Vice Chairman," undated paper, SASC; Rhett Dawson, "Meeting with Nunn & Goldwater, 2/6/86," handwritten notes, Dawson Papers, 0A14162; Goldwater and Nunn, box 14162, RLL.

21. Nunn Oral History; Barry Goldwater and Sam Nunn to David Packard, Feb. 18, 1986, SASC.

Chapter 22. The Decisive Battle

1. John Lehman to Barry Goldwater, Feb. 4, 1986, SASC.

2. Kelley to Goldwater, Feb. 4, 1986.

3. Watkins to Goldwater, Feb. 4, 1986.

4. "Opening Statement by Senator Barry Goldwater (R-AZ.), Chairman, Committee on Armed Services, for the Markup Session on the Legislative Proposal on Defense Reorganization, February 4, 1986," SASC.

5. "Opening Statement by Senator Sam Nunn (D-GA.), Ranking Minority Member, Committee on Armed Services, for the Markup Session on the Legislative Proposal on Defense Reorganization, February 4, 1986," SASC.

6. Gerald J. Smith interview.

7. Michael Ganley, "How's That Again? You're Opposed to *What?*" *AFJ,* Mar., 1986, 18.

8. "Opening Statement by Senator Barry Goldwater (R-Arizona), Chairman, Committee on Armed Services, for the Markup Session on the Legislative Proposal on Defense Reorganization, February 5, 1986," SASC.

9. Nunn Oral History.

10. Congress, Senate, Senator Warner of Virginia speaking on the Department of Defense Reorganization Act of 1986, S. 2295, 99th Cong., 2d sess., *Congressional Record* (May 7, 1986): 5481; Senator Levin, ibid., 5500.

11. Christopher K. Mellon, author interview, Aug. 25, 1998.

12. Punaro interview.

13. Richard Finn, "Written Amendments Considered during Markup," table, Mar. 6, 1986, RDF; Chuck Alsup, "Summary of Executive Markup of DoD Reorganization Act of 1986," June 21, 2000, JRL.

14. Punaro interview.

15. Mellon interview.

16. James Locher, Richard Finn, and Jeff Smith, "Comparison of the Packard Commission's Recommendations and the Committee's Draft Bill on Defense Reorganization," memorandum for the SASC, Mar. 3, 1986, SASC; President's Blue Ribbon Commission on Defense Management, *An Interim Report to the President* (Washington: President's Blue Ribbon Commission on Defense Management, 1986), 11; SASC, "Goldwater and Nunn Praise Packard Commission Report," Feb. 28, 1986, SASC.

17. Chuck Alsup, telephone conversation with author, Feb. 23, 2001.

18. Mellon interview.

19. Finn, "Written Amendments;" Alsup, "Summary."

20. Allan W. Cameron, "Final Vote on Defense Organization Bill," memorandum to Senator Denton, Mar. 5, 1986, SASC.

21. Goldwater interview.

22. Rowland Evans and Robert Novak, "Goldwater and the Whiz Kids," *WP,* Mar. 7, 1986, A19.

23. Punaro interview.

Chapter 23. Mopping-Up Operations

1. Barry Goldwater and Sam Nunn to Committee Colleagues, Apr. 9, 1986, SASC.

2. Senate Committee on Armed Services, *Department of Defense Reorganization Act of 1986: Report [To accompany S. 2295] together with Additional Views*, 99th Cong., 2d sess., Apr. 14, 1986, Report 99-280, 163.

3. Gen. Bernard W. Rogers, author interview, Sept. 12, 2000.

4. *Reorganization of the Department of Defense*, S. Hrg. 99-1083, 708.

5. Stephen E. Anno and William E. Einspahr, *Command and Control and Communications Lessons Learned: Iranian Rescue, Falklands Conflict, Grenada Invasion, Libya Raid* (Maxwell AFB, Ala.: Air War College, 1988), 51.

6. Crowe, *Line of Fire*, 145.

7. USCINCEUR, "Draft Strawman Unified Action Armed Forces (JCS Pub2)," message to JCS, Apr. 21, 1986, CNO.

8. CNO executive assistant to CNO, Apr. 26, 1986, CNO (emphasis in original).

9. Adm. James D. Watkins, "Draft Strawman Unified Action Armed Forces (JCS Pub 2), CNO Comment Sheet, Apr. 28, 1986, CNO (emphasis in original).

10. Gen. Bernard W. Rogers to Sam Nunn with Secretary Lehman's message attached, May 12, 1986, SASC.

11. Punaro interview.

12. Vice Adm. John M. Poindexter, "Implementation of the Recommendations of Your Commission on Defense Management," memorandum for the president, n.d., MBD; idem., "Implementation of the Recommendations of the President's Commission on Defense Management," memorandum for Caspar W. Weinberger, Mar. 12, 1986, RRL.

13. "Radio Address to the Nation on Defense Establishment Reform," Apr. 5, 1986, *Public Papers of the Presidents of the United States: Ronald Reagan, 1986*, Book 1, *January 1 to June 27, 1986* (Washington: GPO, 1988), 422–23.

14. "Message to the Congress Outlining Proposals for Improving the Organization of the Defense Establishment," Apr. 24, 1986, ibid., 517–24.

15. John M. Poindexter, "Special Message to Congress on Defense Reorganization," memorandum for the president, Apr. 24, 1986, MBD.

16. Barry Goldwater to the president, Apr. 9, 1986, box C-5, folder 10, BMG.

17. "S. 2295—Department of Defense Reorganization Act of 1986," statement of administration policy, Apr. 28, 1986, Ronald K. Sable Papers, box 90644, file "DoD Reorganization [2 of 6]," RRL.

18. Barry Goldwater and Sam Nunn to Caspar W. Weinberger, May 5, 1986, SASC.

19. Romee L. Brownlee, author interview, Mar. 15, 2000.

20. Congress, Senate, Senator Nunn of Georgia speaking on the Department of Defense Reorganization Act of 1986, S. 2295, 99th Cong., 2d sess., *Congressional Record* (May 7, 1986): 5500.

21. Goldwater quoted in George C. Wilson, "Pentagon Reform Bill Sweeps Through Senate," *WP*, May 8, 1986, A9.

22. Peter Ross Range, "Aspin's Ambition: The upstart head of the House Armed Services Committee is determined to change the way the Pentagon thinks," *WP Magazine*, May 26, 1985, 10.

23. Archie D. Barrett, author interview, May 19, 2000.

24. Range, "Aspin's Ambition."

25. Barrett interview, July 29, 1999.

26. "H. R. 3622—Joint Chiefs of Staff Reorganization Act of 1985," statement of administration policy, Nov. 18, 1985, ADB.

27. Barrett interview, July 29, 1999.

28. Range, "Aspin's Ambition."

29. Barrett interview, July 29, 1999.

30. Congress, House, Committee on Armed Services, *Background Material on Structural Reform of the Department of Defense Compiled by the Staff of the Committee on Armed Services*, 99th Cong., 2d sess., March 1986, Committee Print no. 15.

31. Barrett interviews, July 29, 1999, and May 19, 2000.

32. Weinberger to Barry M. Goldwater, May 9, 1986, SASC.

33. Barrett, "Mark up of defense organization bill," memorandum for Chairman Aspin, June 24, 1986, ADB.

34. Crowe interview.

35. Barrett interview, July 29, 1999; Barrett, "Mark up of defense organization bill."

36. *Full Committee Consideration*, HASC no. 99-69, 86; Barrett interview, July 29, 1999.

37. *Full Committee Consideration*, HASC no. 99-69, 3; Barrett interview, Sept. 22, 1998.

38. Barry Goldwater, "Opening Statement by Senator Barry Goldwater (R-Arizona), Chairman, Committee on Armed Services, for the Conference Committee Meeting, August 13, 1986," SASC.

39. John F. Lally, "House-Senate Committee of Conference on H.R. 3622," minutes, Sept. 11, 1986, JRL.

40. HASC, "House-Senate Conference Wraps Up Defense Reorganization Bill," News Release, Sept. 11, 1986, box 56, folder "Mr. Nichols," WFN; Thomas H. Moorer to Arch Barrett, Oct. 1, 1986, box 1986, folder "Administration," ADB.

Chapter 24. The Commander in Chief Approves

1. Donley, author interview, May 24, 1994.

2. Congress, House, Congressman Annunzio of Illinois speaking on bills and joint resolutions presented to the president, 99th Cong., 2d sess., *Congressional Record* (Sept. 19, 1986): 25373.

3. William H. Taft IV to James C. Miller III, Sept. 19, 1986, a.n. 330-88-0038, box 13, folder "020 DoD (Aug.–Sept.)," SD.

4. Chapman B. Cox, "The Goldwater-Nichols Defense Reorganization Act of 1986—ACTION MEMORANDUM," memorandum for the deputy secretary of defense, Sept. 18, 1986, ibid.

5. "Defense Reorganization," unsigned memorandum for the secretary of defense, filed on Sept. 30, 1986, box 6, folder "OI—JSC Reorg—1986" (folder 7 of 8), JFL.

6. Unsigned letter to Patrick J. Buchanan, n.d., box 6, folder "OI—JSC Reorg—1986" (folder 8 of 8), JFL (emphasis in original).

7. Unsigned letter to Ronald W. Reagan, n.d., ibid (emphasis in original).

8. James C. Miller III, "Enrolled Bill H.R. 3622—Goldwater-Nichols Department of Defense Reorganization Act of 1986," memorandum for the president, Sept. 25, 1986, White House Office of the Executive Clerk: Bill Reports, box 67, Oct. 1, 1986 [H.R. 3622], RRL.

9. David L. Chew, note for Mr. President, Sept. 30, 1986, attached to ibid.

10. C. Dean McGrath Jr., "Enrolled Bill H.R. 3622: Goldwater-Nichols Department of Defense Reorganization Act of 1986," memorandum for Peter J. Wallison, Sept. 29, 1986, McGrath Papers, box 15540, folder "CDM/Defense Reorganization/Goldwater-Nichols (1)," RRL.

11. Chew note.

12. "Draft List of Attendees: Godwin Photo/Signing Ceremony," Rodney B. McDaniel Papers, box 90667, RRL.

13. John W. Douglass, "Signing Ceremony for the Defense Reorganization Bill and Meeting with Dick Godwin," memorandum for John M. Poindexter, Sept. 25, 1986, JWD.

14. Punaro interview.

15. Rodney B. McDaniel, "Signing Ceremony for the Defense Reorganization Bill and Meeting with Dick Godwin," memorandum for David L. Chew, n.d., box 90961, folder "Proposed DoD Reorganization Signing Ceremony and President's Meeting with Godwin," MBD.

16. William L. Ball III, assistant to Reagan for congressional affairs, discussion with author, Jan., 2001.

17. Christine E. Cowart, author interview, Mar. 7, 2000.

18. *Public Papers of the Presidents of the United States: Ronald Reagan: 1986*, Book 2, *June 28 to December 31, 1986* (Washington, GPO, 1989), 1312.

Epilogue. Unified at Last

1. Congress, House, *Goldwater-Nichols Department of Defense Reorganization Act of 1986: Conference Report [To accompany H.R. 3622]*, 99th Cong., 2d sess., Report 99-824, sec. 3.

2. John G. Kester, "The Office of the Secretary of Defense With a Strengthened Joint Staff System," in *Toward a More Effective Defense*, ed. Blechman and Lynn, 187.

3. Congress, Senate, Committee on Armed Services, *Defense Organization: The Need for Change: Staff Report to the Committee on Armed Services*, 99th Cong., 1st sess., S. Prt. 99-86, Oct. 16, 1985, 620, 629.

4. *Goldwater-Nichols Department of Defense Reorganization Act*, Report 99-824, 101.

5. "About Fighting and Winning Wars—An Interview with Dick Cheney," *U.S. Naval Institute Proceedings* 122, no. 5 (May, 1996): 33.

6. Richard H. Kohn, "The Crisis in Military-Civilian Relations," *National Interest*, spring, 1994, 3–17.

7. Eliot A. Cohen, "What To Do About National Defense," *Commentary* 98, no. 5 (Nov., 1994): 21–32.

8. Powell with Persico, *My American Journey*, 410–11.

9. Christopher Allan Yuknis, "The Goldwater-Nichols Act of 1986—An Interim Assessment," in *Essays on Strategy X,* ed. Mary A. Sommerville (Washington: NDU Press, 1993), 97; "About Fighting," *U.S. Naval Institute Proceedings,* 33; Gen. John M. Shalikashvili, "Goldwater-Nichols: Ten Years From Now," remarks, NDU Goldwater-Nichols Symposium, Dec. 3, 1996.

10. John F. Lehman and Harvey Sicherman, "America's Military Problems and How to Fix Them," *Foreign Policy Research Institute WIRE: A Catalyst for Ideas* 9, no. 3 (Feb., 2001), www.fpri.org.

11. Congress, Senate, Committee on Armed Services, *Operation Desert Shield/Desert Storm: Hearings before the Committee on Armed Services,* 102d Cong., 1st sess., Apr. 24, May 8, 9, 16, 21, June 4, 12, 20, 1991, 318; idem., *Nominations Before the Senate Armed Services Committee, First Session, 103rd Congress: Hearings before the Committee on Armed Services,* 103rd Cong., 1st sess., S. Hrg. 103-414, Jan.–Nov., 1993, 343.

12. Shalikashvili, "Goldwater-Nichols."

13. Gen. Henry H. Shelton, author interview, Apr. 27, 2001.

14. Robert W. Komer, "Strategymaking in the Pentagon," in *Reorganizing America's Defense,* ed. Robert J. Art et al., 215–17.

15. Shalikashvili, "Goldwater-Nichols"; Shelton interview; David Shilling and Christopher Lamb, author interview, May 21, 1999.

16. Bill Owens with Ed Offley, *Lifting the Fog of War* (New York: Farrar-Straus-Giroux, 2000), 207.

17. SASC, *Defense Organization,* 242.

18. Ibid., 224.

19. "About Fighting," *U.S. Naval Institute Proceedings,* 33; "The Chairman as Principal Military Adviser: An Interview with Colin L. Powell," *JFQ,* autumn 1996, 30; SASC, *Operation Desert Shield/Desert Storm,* 318.

20. Crowe, *Line of Fire,* 158; Shelton interview.

21. SASC, *Defense Organization,* 7.

22. "The Chairman," 31; Malcolm S. Forbes Jr., "Fact and Comment," *Forbes,* Mar. 18, 1991, 23–24; Katherine Boo, "How Congress Won the War in the Gulf," *Washington Monthly,* Oct., 1991, 31.

23. William J. Perry, speech honoring Sen. Sam Nunn, the Pentagon, July 12, 1996, JRL, 2.

24. Gen. John M. Shalikashvili, remarks, Association of the United States Army Land Warfare Forum Breakfast, Sept. 1, 1994, JRL; Commission on Roles and Missions of the Armed Forces, *Directions for Defense* (Washington: GPO, 1995), 2–3.

25. Shelton interview; Michael B. Donley, "It's Time for DoD to Establish a Joint Budget," unpublished paper, May 2, 2001, Donley.

26. Shelton interview.

27. Sam Nunn, "Future Trends in Defense Organization," *JFQ,* autumn, 1996, 63; Gen. John M. Shalikashvili, "A Word from the Chairman," *JFQ,* autumn–winter 1994–95, 7.

28. Col. Mackubin T. Owens Jr., "Goldwater-Nichols: A Ten-Year Retrospective," *Marine Corps Gazette,* Dec., 1996, 48–53; Paul K. Van Riper, "More on innovations and jointness," *Marine Corps Gazette,* Mar., 1998, 55–57.

29. William S. Cohen, "Message from the Secretary," *Defense Reform Initiative: The Business Strategy for Defense in the 21st Century* (Washington: Department of Defense, 1997), i.

30. John P. Kotter, *Leading Change* (Boston: Harvard Business School Press, 1996), 161.

31. Sumantra Ghoshal and Christopher A. Bartlett, "Changing the Role of Top Management: Beyond Structure to Processes," *Harvard Business Review* 73, no. 1 (Jan.–Feb., 1995): 94.

32. Office of Net Assessment, *1996 Net Assessment Summer Study: Sustaining Innovation in the U.S. Military* (Washington: Department of Defense, 1996), 2.

33. Michael Hammer, "Beyond the End of Management" in *Rethinking the Future*, ed. Rowan Gibson (London: Nicholas Brealey, 1997), 96.

34. Peter Senge, "Through the Eye of the Needle," in ibid., 125–26.

35. U.S. Commission on National Security/21st Century, *Seeking a National Strategy* (Washington: U.S. Commission on National Security/21st Century, 2000), 14; Nunn, "Future Trends," 65.

36. Perry, speech honoring Sam Nunn, 2; Owens, "'Jointness' is his Job," *Government Executive*, Apr., 1995, 61; Wickham interview.

INDEX

Photos are indicated with **bold** type.

JAMES R. LOCHER III, a graduate of West Point and Harvard Business School, began his career in Washington as an executive trainee in the Office of the Secretary of Defense. He has worked in the White House, the Pentagon, and the Senate. During the period covered by this book, he was a staff member for the Senate Committee on Armed Services. Since then, he has served as an assistant secretary of defense in the first Bush and the early Clinton administrations. Currently, he works as a consultant and lecturer on defense matters.